HANDBOOK OF ENTREPRENEURIAL DYNAMICS

HANDBOOK OF ENTREPRENEURIAL DYNAMICS
The Process of Business Creation

EDITORS

William B. Gartner
Clemson University

Kelly G. Shaver
College of William and Mary

Nancy M. Carter
University of St. Thomas

Paul D. Reynolds
Babson College & London Business School

SAGE Publications
Thousand Oaks ■ London

For information:

Sage Publications, Inc.
2455 Teller Road
Thousand Oaks, California 91320
E-mail: order@sagepub.com

Sage Publications Ltd.
1 Oliver's Yard
55 City Road
London EC1Y 1SP
United Kingdom

Sage Publications India Pvt. Ltd.
B-42, Panchsheel Enclave
Post Box 4109
New Delhi 110 017 India

Printed in the United States of America

Library of Congress Cataloging-in-Publication Data
Handbook of entrepreneurial dynamics: The process of business creation/editors, William B. Gartner . . . [et al.].
    p. cm.
Includes bibliographical references and index.
ISBN 0-7619-2758-1 (cloth)
   1. New business enterprises—Handbooks, manuals, etc.
2. Entrepreneurship—Handbooks, manuals, etc. I. Title: Process of business creation.
II. Gartner, William B.
HD62.5.H3584 2004
658.1′1—dc22   2004003253

This book is printed on acid-free paper.

04   05   06   07   10   9   8   7   6   5   4   3   2   1

Acquisitions Editor:	Al Bruckner
Editorial Assistant:	MaryAnn Vail
Production Editor:	Diane S. Foster
Copy Editor:	Robert Holm
Typesetter:	C&M Digitals (P) Ltd.
Proofreader:	Taryn L. Bigelow
Indexer:	Molly Hall
Cover Designer:	Michelle Lee

Contents

Foreword

William B. Gartner

Kelly G. Shaver

Nancy M. Carter

Paul D. Reynolds

New business creation has a significant impact on economic growth, innovation, and job creation (Reynolds, Camp, Bygrave, Autio, & Hay, 2001; Reynolds, Hay, Bygrave, Camp, & Autio, 2000). Since David Birch's 1979 study of the impact of new and small firms on creating new jobs, a considerable body of evidence has been generated that supports his conclusion that small firms are the major source of employment growth in the U.S. economy (Birch, 1979, 1987; Kirchhoff, 1994; Reynolds & White, 1997). More recent assessments, however, have indicated that the original focus was too broad. New firms, not necessarily small firms, are the dominant source of net job growth; there is a net job loss among older firms, whether small or large (Acs, Armington, & Robb, 1999). Entrepreneurial activity provides profound positive benefits across an important set of measures of social and economic well-being, much of them concentrated in new economic sectors such as information technology, when compared to service-producing or goods-producing industries (Boden, 2000).

Although entrepreneurship has been shown to provide many benefits, there has not been a systematic study of the entrepreneurial process. Although entrepreneurs contribute so much to our society, we know little about them as people. We can see the results of entrepreneurial activity in the form of new businesses and innovations, but we have limited information on how these new businesses actually came into existence. We can see the successes of entrepreneurial activity, yet we have few insights into why particular entrepreneurial efforts were successful while other efforts failed. Indeed, we have almost no information on the number and characteristics of the nascent entrepreneurs who attempt to start businesses and the likelihood that such attempts will result in the formation of new businesses.

The lack of information about this important social and economic phenomenon led to creation of the Panel Study of Entrepreneurial Dynamics (PSED), an unprecedented research program involving more than a hundred researchers from 10 countries. Central to the research program was a recognition that to develop a representative portrait of entrepreneurial activity in the United States, individuals actively involved in starting businesses were needed—individuals who could be studied in real time, rather than after the fact. Finding such individuals is no small problem. Because a very small proportion of the population of working-age adults is likely to be engaged, at any moment in time, in the process of business creation, identifying a generalizable sample of these individuals is much like the problem of "finding a needle in a haystack" (i.e., typically rates of the number of individuals, per capita, who are engaged in *new business creation* vary between 3 per 100 working-age adults in countries such as Croatia, Hong Kong, and Japan, to 20 or more per 100 working-age adults in countries such as Thailand, Uganda, and Venezuela (Reynolds, Bygrave, & Autio [and others], 2003). One has to sort through a lot of hay (people who are not attempting to start businesses) in order to find the needles that are in the process of business creation.

What distinguishes the PSED from other studies of the entrepreneurial process is that it identifies individuals in the process of creating new businesses and develops systematic, reliable, and generalizable data on important features of the new business creation process, including information on the proportion and characteristics of the adult population involved in efforts to start businesses, the activities and characteristics that constitute the nature of the business start-up process, and the proportion and characteristics of those business start-up efforts that actually become new businesses.

This handbook reports on the creation of the Entrepreneurship Research Consortium (ERC), the organizing group for the PSED; the evolution of the research program; and theories, ideas, and measures for exploring and understanding factors that encompass and influence the creation of new businesses. What makes this handbook unique, among overviews of prior theory, ideas, and research on the phenomenon of business creation, is that each chapter provides the rationale used in developing questionnaires for the PSED and specifies measures that can be used to test theory, often providing evidence from the PSED data sets on these measures' validity and reliability. In addition, inherent in each chapter is the implication that the theories about business creation can be tested using a generalizable sample of both nascent entrepreneurs and a comparison group. The handbook also describes the PSED data collection process, provides documentation of the interview schedules, codebooks, data preparation, and weighting scheme, as well as offers examples of how analyses of PSED data might be conducted. The handbook is an invitation to explore theory on the nature of business creation and to test ideas through analyses of the PSED data sets that are in the public domain.

Conceptual Model

The PSED built on earlier efforts by Paul Reynolds and colleagues to study nascent entrepreneurs in Wisconsin (Reynolds & White, 1993, 1997), as well as a small national sample of nascent entrepreneurs who were identified from a study that was "piggy-backed" onto the University of Michigan Institute for Social Research Survey of Consumer Attitudes (Curtin, 1982; Reynolds, 1997). These prior studies indicated that it was technically feasible, as well as financially feasible, to locate and survey individuals from the general population of all U.S. adults who were actively engaged in starting businesses.

Conceptually, the entrepreneurial process can be thought of as involving three stages and three transition points, all continually influenced by political, social, and economic factors. As depicted on the left side of the model (Figure F.1), the first stage of the start-up process involves the population of all individuals, some of whom might decide to start a business. These individuals come from two potential sources: all those involved in the labor force and those who are employees of existing businesses.

The first transition point in the start-up process is "conception" when individuals from these two sources elect to pursue a new business start-up. If the new business is intended to be an independent start-up, those involved are referred to as nascent entrepreneurs (NE). If the start-up effort is sponsored by an existing business, those involved are considered to be nascent intrapreneurs (NI). The primary research questions at conception are two: *What is the tendency of individuals to*

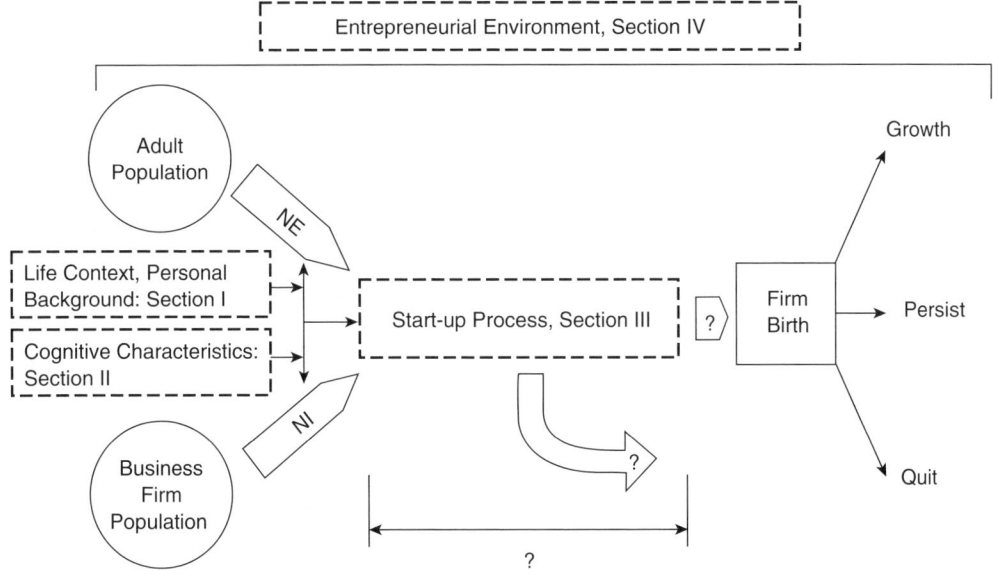

Figure F.1   The Start-up Process and Handbook Organization

begin the business start-up process? What are the features of these individuals or their situation that lead some to enter this transition? There is a great deal of speculation that entrepreneurs are very different from other individuals in the general population. An important feature of the PSED involves the identification of a comparison group of adults in the general population who are not involved with start-up activities. Because the comparison group can be weighted to mirror the characteristics of the U.S. adult population, generalizations can be made about differences between the sample of nascent entrepreneurs and the U.S. adult population as a whole.

Unlike other studies of the entrepreneurial process, the PSED provides a detailed focus on the second stage in the process of business formation: the start-up process. This stage involves factors that affect the efforts of nascent entrepreneurs to bring their businesses into existence as well as the length of time involved in their start-up efforts. The PSED describes the entrepreneurs as people, documents their activities, and summarizes the types and amounts of resources invested in the process. The primary question the PSED explores at the start-up processes stage is: *How do nascent entrepreneurs go about the process of starting firms?* An entrepreneur's start-up activities can take the form of four possible pathways: (1) The nascent entrepreneur creates an infant firm. (2) The nascent entrepreneur can be "still trying" to start the business. (3) The nascent entrepreneur can put the start-up effort "on hold" with expectations of continuing to pursue the start-up process later. And, (4) the nascent entrepreneur can "give up" and abandon the start-up effort.

If an entrepreneur's activities result in an infant firm, the second transition point in the model is "firm birth." The question at this point is *Why are some of these business start-up efforts successful in creating new firms?*

The third transition point involves the subsequent "outcomes," or activities, of the new firm; that is, once a new firm comes into existence, the firm may either grow, persist, or be discontinued. The question at this point is *Why are some new firms more likely to grow, persist, or die?*

A key insight into the PSED research process is an appreciation of the variety and diversity inherent in the phenomenon of business creation (Gartner, 1985). One can easily grasp this perspective by quickly listing the many kinds of businesses that one might encounter through a cursory scan of the Yellow Pages in the telephone book: restaurants (by type—fast food, casual, fine dining; by cuisine—ethnic, pizza, American, eclectic), services (medical, law, accounting, architecture, dry cleaning, package delivery), manufacturing (automobiles, soaps, furniture, computers, pharmaceuticals, beverages), retailing (clothing, jewelry, appliances, consumer electronics, sporting goods). How did all of these many different kinds of businesses come into existence? Indeed, how many different kinds of businesses are actually attempted? How similar (or different) is the process of starting a restaurant compared to starting a biotechnology research firm? How similar (or different) are the kinds of people who are likely to start a retail store compared to those starting a construction company? The basis for the PSED research effort is this recognition of variety of business creation efforts and the need to portray both the breadth and depth of this phenomenon.

Research Design

The research design for the PSED is presented in Figure F.2 and shows two basic features: (1) a procedure for identifying and interviewing nascent entrepreneurs and a comparison group and (2) the content of the interviews.

The first stage involves large-scale screening of households to create two samples representative of the national population of adults, those 18 years old and older. First, a sample of those involved in attempting to start a new business was identified, either nascent entrepreneurs (NE) or nascent intrapreneurs (NI). Second, a representative sample of typical adults, not involved with a business start-up, was selected to be used as the comparison group (CG). Once the screening procedures were completed, the second stage of data collection involved detailed phone interviews followed by completion of self-administered questionnaires mailed to the respondents. The third stage involved the follow-up interviews completed with nascent entrepreneurs 12 and 24 months after the first interview. Details about the research design, data collection process, the composition of the data sets, and examples of how analyses of the data might be undertaken are found in the appendixes.

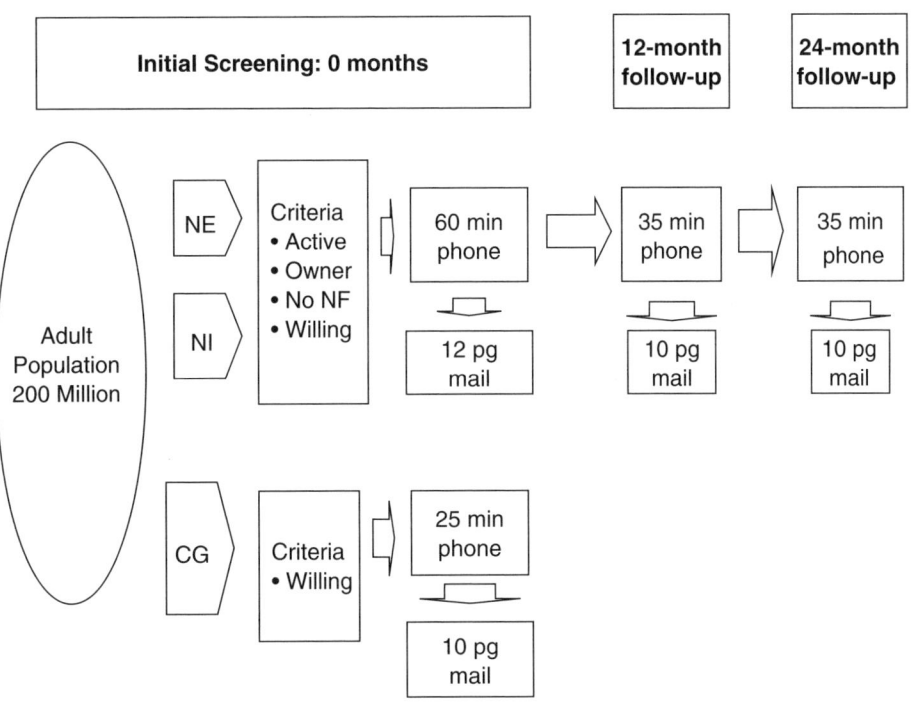

Figure F.2.   PSED Research Design Overview[a]

NOTE:

a. NE = Nascent Entrepreneurs; NI = Nascent Intrapreneurs; CG = Comparison Group; NF = New Firm

Appendix A explains the PSED research design and data collection process in detail. This appendix describes the process for contacting potential respondents, the procedure and criteria for screening respondents to identify nascent entrepreneurs, the phone and mail interview schedules used for the nascent entrepreneurs and the comparison group, and the process of data collection for the follow-up interviews. Appendix B provides information on the two primary PSED data sets: the screening data set which consists of 64,622 respondents initially contacted and the detailed data sample set of the 830 nascent entrepreneurs and 431 comparison group members. This appendix also discusses the creation of weights as a way to ensure the generalizability of the detailed data sample to accurately reflect characteristics of the population. Appendix C provides examples of how analyses of both the screening data set and the detailed data sample set might be conducted using the weights.

The Entrepreneurship Research Consortium (ERC)

To adequately capture the complex phenomenon of business creation, a social, political, and collaborative process atypical among scholars studying organizations (or anything else) was put in place. Rather than one major funding source for the PSED, there was a multitude of funding sources. Rather than one group of scholars involved in the development of the PSED, there was a multitude of groups. Rather than one particular research agenda, there was a multitude of research agendas. The fundamental value of those involved in the PSED centered on an attempt to use theory to develop questions that could depict the phenomenon of business creation in as comprehensive a manner as possible. The use of theory in the development of the PSED is therefore less an effort to create a general theory about the nature of business creation and more an effort to depict business creation in a generalizable way.

The idea to develop a consortium of individuals and institutions involved in the process of research on new business formation came about because of a collaborative effort among Paul Reynolds, Nancy Carter, and Bill Gartner in 1994 to study the new venture creation activities of a random sample of less than 100 nascent entrepreneurs (Carter, Gartner, & Reynolds, 1996). They recognized that a large sample of nascent entrepreneurs would be important for ascertaining differences and similarities among various types of nascent entrepreneurs and their businesses as well as for comparing and contrasting nascent entrepreneurs to those who were not engaged in business creation. The problem was no one particular institution was willing to fund a project that would likely cost hundreds of thousands of dollars to locate individuals in the process of business creation and then follow up on their business creation efforts over a number of years. As described in Reynolds (2000), a series of meetings and communications (letters, faxes, phone calls, and e-mails) was undertaken to generate interest in creating a large (1,000+) database of nascent entrepreneurs and a comparison group that would be created from a random-digit telephone dialing procedure.

Table F.1 lists key meetings and activities that were held to generate financial support and form teams to develop the survey instruments and questionnaires. During the early part of 1995, colleagues who we thought might be interested in

Table F.1   Key Dates in the Development of the ERC

Date	Event
January–March 1995	Colleagues contacted to gauge interest in collaborative research
April 1995	Forum at Babson Kauffman Entrepreneurship Research Conference, London, UK
May 1995	Letter campaign to the Entrepreneurship Division of the Academy of Management members ·
July–August 1995	Recruiting presentations at National Family Business Conference, Nashville, TN, and Academy of Management meeting, Vancouver, BC
November 1995	Organizing meeting of ERC, Chicago, IL
January–April,1996	Paid membership of 22 institutions designed initial questionnaires; developed administrative structure and decision processes of ERC
August 1996	Pilot study assessment and planning meeting, Cincinnati, OH
November 1996	Data analysis workshop, University of Houston, TX
January 1997	Review of initial survey results, Atlanta, GA
January 1998	Full implementation of research process
January 1998	Nat. Sci. Foundation (NSF) grant application for female oversample
February 1998–2002	Review and update meetings, University of Southern California Los Angles, CA
June 1998–2002	Review and update meetings, Babson Kauffman Entrepreneurship Research Conferences: Gent, Belgium; Columbia, SC; Babson Park, MA; Jönköping, Sweden; Boulder, CO
August 1998–2002	Review and update meetings, Academy of Management: San Diego, CA; Chicago, IL; Toronto, Canada; Seattle, WA; Washington, DC
January 1999	NSF grant application for minority oversample
2000–2003	Ewing Marion Kauffman Foundation funding for data collection
November 2001	ERC votes to transfer responsibility for the project to the Ewing Marion Kauffman Foundation
January 2002	Preferential Rights to Scholarly Analysis (PRSA) procedure abandoned
January 2003	All data shifted to the public domain on the Institute for Social Research (ISR) project Web site
December 2003	Completion of final data collection for the fourth wave of the panel study

participating in such a project were contacted. Besides making phone calls, we staged a forum at the Babson Kauffman Entrepreneurship Research Conference in London (April) to gauge interest, and we began a mail campaign that involved sending letters to all members of the Entrepreneurship Division of the Academy of Management (May). The process of organizing the ERC moved very quickly from this point on. After presentations at the National Family Business Conference in

July 1995 and the Academy of Management meeting in August 1995, there appeared to be enough interest in ERC for a meeting solely devoted to the ERC research process. This meeting was held in November at the Chicago O'Hare Hilton. More than 50 people from 6 countries attended. Design teams were formed to develop research objectives, discuss hypotheses, identify specific questionnaire items, and scholars representing their institutions made financial commitments (e.g., some scholars brought checks).

By April 1996, there were 22 institutions that had sent money to participate in the ERC, and five design teams had assembled materials for the initial household screener, and had prepared detailed phone and mail interview schedules for the nascent entrepreneurs and a comparison group, as well as a phone interview for business angels. During this time an executive committee was nominated and elected to supervise the ERC process (Candida Brush, Nancy Carter, Per Davidsson, William Gartner, Paul Reynolds, Kelly Shaver, and Mary Williams), and Babson College was selected as the host institution for the ERC. In addition, a procedure for allocating exclusive rights for analyzing data on a particular topic area was formulated (entitled: Preferential Right to Scholarly Analysis—PRSA). The PRSA process enabled scholars to submit proposals to the executive committee outlining specific research questions and hypotheses, items to be utilized, a strategy for analysis, and dissemination plans for the results. The executive committee reviewed all submitted proposals to look for overlaps. When similar topics were proposed by different groups of scholars, the executive committee asked scholars to collaborate or to narrow their research "claims" to more narrow topic issues so that other scholars could also conduct research around that topic area.

In August 1996, a "Pilot Study Assessment and Planning Meeting" was held concurrently with the national Academy of Management meeting. A "Data Analysis Workshop" of the pilot study results was held at the University of Houston in November 1996, which was followed by another meeting held in January 1997 in Atlanta. Concurrent to all of these meetings was substantial interaction among all of the scholars about their proposed PRSAs and the inclusion of questions in the questionnaires as data from the pilot studies was analyzed. By the end of 1997, two pilot studies had been conducted, all of the interview schedules were nearly complete, and a total of 34 institutions had provided funds.

As the full field data collection began to be implemented in 1998, it became apparent that the research process would require substantially more funds in order to identify the necessary number of nascent entrepreneurs, particularly women and minority nascent entrepreneurs. A proposal to supplement the nascent entrepreneur sample was submitted to the National Science Foundation (NSF) (Carter, Brush, Aldrich, Greene, & Katz, 1998) and funding was received to double the number of women nascent entrepreneurs surveyed as well as to cover the cost of a 24-month follow-up for the entire sample. In addition, a second proposal was prepared for the National Science Foundation to sponsor an oversample of Blacks and Hispanics (Greene, Carter, Reynolds, Aldrich, & Stearns, 1999). This proposal was also funded. Finally, the Kauffman Center for Entrepreneurial Leadership (now the Ewing Marion Kauffman Foundation) began to provide substantial funding for the Panel Study of Entrepreneurial Dynamics in 2000 through completion of the final and fourth wave of the data collection in 2003. The Ewing Marion Kauffman Foundation began to provide substantial funding for the PSED in 2000 through completion of the final and fourth wave of data collection in 2003. Perhaps most important, Babson College served as the host institution for the ERC, acted as the steward of the ERC funds, and allowed Paul Reynolds, the Paul T. Babson Chair of Entrepreneurship, to devote the majority of his time to service as the coordinating principal investigator for the life of the ERC and the duration of the project.

From 1998 to 2002 there were meetings and updates on the data collection process held at the Babson Kauffman Entrepreneurship Research conferences (each June), at the national Academy of Management meetings (each August), at the University of Southern California Greif Research symposiums on Emerging Organization (each February), and at a meeting at the Kauffman Center for Entrepreneurial Leadership at Kansas City, MO in July 2001. Scholars involved in the PSED had opportunities at these meetings to meet, discuss, and make decisions about this research effort.

This brief overview of some of the key events in the history of the ERC is to suggest that an emphasis on some topics in the handbook rather than others is partially a matter of who was involved in the PSED research process, as well as when they were involved and for how long they were involved. The ideas and theories used in a research program such as the PSED required scholars who were willing to champion their ideas and see them through from the inception of the ERC in 1995 through the many design meetings to formulate questions in the survey instruments, through the pilot studies, through the full field data collection, and (for longitudinal issues) through the follow-up surveys.

Development of the Handbook

The chapters included in this volume are the result of an invitation in 2001 to all scholars in the ERC who participated in the development of the PSED. A listing of the individuals is provided in Table F.2. Each scholar was asked to contribute a chapter that summarized a key theoretical perspective that was operationalized in the PSED research program and to identify variables associated with that theory. An important part of the development of the PSED questionnaires (and by implication the theory used to create the questionnaires) was a political and social process of getting agreement among scholars representing 34 sponsoring institutions. Reaching agreement on the interview schedules, particularly on specific items and groups of items on the interview schedules, was no small task. Each institution and scholar involved in the PSED had some specific interest in understanding some facet of the process of business creation. Limits on the budget, and on the time of respondents, meant that some questions about the business creation process would simply have to be omitted. The PSED reflects the spirit of compromise among differing viewpoints, as well as the persistence and tenacity of a few to see this project reach fruition. The chapters in this handbook, therefore, represent the primary theoretical viewpoints upon which the process of business creation was explored. In addition, each chapter indicates how theory about the entrepreneurial process was operationalized, and insights are offered as to the efficacy of these measures.

Table F.2   PSED Scholars

Executive Committee (as of July 11, 2002)
Paul D. Reynolds, Babson College   Project Coordinator
Candida Brush, Boston University
Nancy M. Carter, University of St. Thomas
William B. Gartner, University of Southern California
Per Davidsson, Jönköping Center for Entrepreneurial Leadership
Patricia Greene, University of Missouri–Kansas City
Kelly G. Shaver, College of William & Mary
Mary Williams, University of Pennsylvania/Widener University

Scholars (as of July 11, 2002)

Zolton	Acs	University of Baltimore
Howard E.	Aldrich	University of North Carolina at Chapel Hill
Kathleen	Allen	University of Southern California
Gry	Alsos	Bodo Graduate School of Business
Raphael	Amit	University of Pennsylvania
Erkko	Autio	Helsinki University of Technology
Ray	Babgy	Hankamer School of Business
Karen A.	Bantel	University of Michigan
Robert	Baron	Rensselaer Polytechnic Institute
Sidney L.	Barton	University of Cincinnati
Robert E.	Berney	U.S. Small Business Administration
Barbara	Bird	American University
Dieter	Bogenhold	University of Bremen
Robert	Brockhaus	Saint Louis University
David	Brophy	University of Michigan
Candida	Brush	Boston University
Lowell W.	Busenitz	University of Oklahoma
John Sibley	Butler	University of Texas at Austin
Bill	Bygrave	Babson College
Michael	Camp	Kauffman Center for Entrepreneurial Leadership
Nancy M.	Carter	University of St. Thomas
Rajeswararo	Chaganti	Temple University
Arnold	Cooper	Purdue University
Larry	Cox	Kauffman Center for Entrepreneurial Leadership
Bill	Cunningham	Xavier University
Richard	Curtin	University of Michigan
Rajiv	Dant	Boston University Marketing Department
Per	Davidsson	Jönköping University
Frederic	Delmar	Stockholm School of Economics
William	Dennis	NFIB Education Foundation
Monica	Diochon	St. Francis Xavier University

Marc	Dollinger	Indiana University
Kevin	Dooley	Arizona State University
Charles R.	Duke	Clemson University
William	Dunkelberg	Temple University
Nathaniel	Ehrlich	University of Michigan
Johathan	Emmett	University of Michigan
Cecilia	Falbe	SUNY Albany
Jim	Fiet	University of Louisville
David	Forsaith	Flinders University of S. Australia
Denis	Garand	Université Laval
William B.	Gartner	University of Southern California
Yvon	Gasse	Université Laval
Elizabeth	Gatewood	Indiana University
Murray	Gillin	Swinburne University of Technology
Patricia	Greene	University of Missouri–Kansas City
Gerald	Gustafson	Beloit College
Henrik	Hall	Jönköping University
Steven	Hanks	Utah State University
Michael	Hay	London Business School
Michael	Hennessey	Coleman Foundation
Robert	Hill	California State University, Fresno
T. L.	Hill	Temple University
Gerald E.	Hills	University of Illinois at Chicago
Sherrie	Human	Xavier University
Steven	Isberg	University of Baltimore
Svenn	Jenssen	Bodo Graduate School of Business
Jerome	Katz	Saint Louis University
Lisa	Keister	Ohio State University
Hindle	Kevin	Swinburne University of Technology
Bruce	Kirchhoff	New Jersey Institute of Technology
Matti	Koiranen	University of Jyväskylä
Lars	Kolvereid	Bodo Graduate School of Business
Bernhard	Lageman	Rheinisch-Westfälisches Institut
Rudy	Lamont	University of Maryland
Julian E.	Lange	Babson College
Rein	Lepnurm	University of Saskatchewan
Moren	Levesque	Rensselaer Polytechnic Institute
Beynamin	Lichtenstein	University of Hartford
Anders	Lundstrom	Swedish Foundation for Small Business Research
Ian	MacMillian	University of Pennsylvania
Gideon D.	Markman	University of Georgia
Colin	Mason	University of Southampton
Charles	Matthews	University of Cincinnati
Dimitris A.	Mavros	MRB Hellas S.A.
Anne	McCarthy	University of Baltimore

(Continued)

Table F.2 (Continued)

Dale	Meyer	University of Colorado, Boulder
Maria	Minniti	Babson College
Douglas D.	Moesel	University of Missouri–Columbia
James	Morgan	University of Michigan
Janet	Near	Indiana University
Lars	Nyberg	NUTEK
Thomas J.	O'Malia	University of Southern California
Hugh	O'Neill	University of North Carolina at Chapel Hill
Newman	Peery	University of the Pacific
Bruce	Phillips	U.S. Small Business Administration
Paul	Reynolds	Babson College
Alicia	Robb	U.S. Small Business Administration
Peter	Robinson	University of Calgary
Larry	Root	University of Michigan
Susan	Sanderson	Rensselaer Polytechnic Institute
Sshikhar	Sarin	Rensselaer Polytechnic Institute
Mark	Schultz	RISEbusiness
Kelly G.	Shaver	College of William & Mary
Christena	Sing	Swinburne University of Technology
Robert P.	Singh	University of the Pacific
Jacqueline	Snijders	EIM Small Business Research & Consultancy
Marc	Sommers	New Jersey Institute of Technology
Steve	Spinelli	Babson College
Caron H.	St. John	Clemson University
Tim	Stearns	California State University, Fresno
Lois A.	Stevenson	Industry Canada
Wayne H.	Stewart	Clemson University
Heleen	Stigler	EIM Small Business Research & Consultancy
Jukka	Suokas	Finnvera plc.
Edwin	van Noort	EIM Small Business Research & Consultancy
Bernhard	von Rosenbladt	Infratest Burke SozialforschungGmbH
Steve	Walsh	New Jersey Institute of Technology
Harold	Welsch	DePaul University
Friederike	Welter	Rheinisch-Westfäelisches Institut
A. R. M.	Wennekers	EIM Small Business Research & Consultancy
Page	West	Wake Forest University
David	Wilemon	Syracuse University
Mary	Williams	University of Pennsylvania
Jack	Wilson	Rensselaer Polytechnic Institute
Allan	Young	Syracuse University
Andrew	Zacharakis	Babson College
Monica A.	Zimmerman	Temple University

The relationship between the PSED research program and the organization of the handbook is included in Figure F.1. In broad terms, a number of factors are likely to influence a person's decision to engage in entrepreneurial activity and subsequently persist in efforts to start a new business. The model shows the entrepreneurial process as involving three major transitions. The first transition is the entry into the start-up process, and the second transition is the exit from the start-up process—either with a new firm birth or abandoning the effort itself. The major factors or processes that affect these transitions are indicated in the four dashed-line boxes. Two are seen as operating in parallel, perhaps with substantial interaction: the life context and personal background and individual cognitive characteristics or dispositions. These are covered in Parts I and II of the handbook. The actual nature of the start-up process itself, which can be quite complex, is covered in Part III. The environmental context in which all these processes operate is the focus of Part IV.

Part I on "life context and personal background" offers theory, measures, and some evidence on, primarily, demographic characteristics of both the individuals who indicated they were actively engaged in the business formation process (nascent entrepreneurs) and a comparison group of individuals who were selected from the survey of individuals who indicated they were not actively engaged in the business formation process. Chapters in this section cover such topics as age, gender, race and ethnicity, household structure, household income and net worth, labor force participation, residential tenure, work experience, educational background, functional expertise, family background, time use, and work participation history.

Part II covers cognitive characteristics that might be useful for exploring whether nascent entrepreneurs think in ways that are different from those individuals who have not attempted to start businesses, as well as ways these constructs can also be used to differentiate among types of nascent entrepreneurs. The topics covered in this section include career reasons, entrepreneurial expectancies, satisfaction with job and life, the adaptor/innovator style, perceived social support, entrepreneurial intensity, problem-solving style, attribution, locus of control, economic sophistication, and social skills.

Part III explores the factors that constitute the characteristics of the process of business formation itself. Chapters in this section describe the kinds of businesses undertaken (by legal form, type of economic activity, ownership structure, and location), the process of opportunity recognition, start-up activities, start-up problems, team composition, characteristics of firm founding, social networks, knowledge and use of assistance, funding, financial sophistication, and future expectations.

Part IV offers two chapters on the context of the business start-up effort, such as perceptions of entrepreneurial climate and environmental uncertainty, as well as two chapters that explore the strategic and technology orientations of the emerging new businesses.

Finally, there are three appendixes that describe the PSED data collection process, data documentation, data preparation, the use of weights, and examples of how analyses might be conducted.

An important aspect of this handbook is the multilevel, multidisciplinary perspective offered about the process of new business formation. Although each chapter focuses on a particular theory or ideas about an aspect of new business formation, the handbook, taken as a whole, suggests that new business formation is "over-determined" (Weick, 1979). Each factor specified in these chapters may account for a significant part of the variance that determines aspects of the new business formation process. New business formation is likely to be significantly affected by the kinds of individuals involved, kinds of businesses started, a variety of environments, and the ways in which these businesses are started. All of these dimensions matter—individual, firm, environment, and process—in the study of new business formation.

A Dynamic Program

It is inevitable that any book will represent current knowledge at the time its chapters were written. Because the PSED is an active ongoing research program, we recommend that scholars interested in state-of-the-art information about the data set (as well as the data set, itself) seek out the following two Web sites. The first Web site is maintained by the Institute for Social Research (ISR) at the University of Michigan at—http://projects.isr.umich.edu/PSED/. This site is likely to be maintained as long as the ISR is contracted to continue the collection of data on subsequent panels of nascent entrepreneurs. At some point, it is likely that all of the data, codebooks, and interview schedules will be transferred from this Web address to the University of Michigan Inter-University Consortium for Political and Social Research (ICPSR) data archives. Many scholars at U.S. universities have access to the ICPSR archives, as their home institutions are members of the consortium. There are, however, some institutions, particularly those outside North America, that are not participants in the ICPSR. A "parallel" Web site has been developed (www.psed.info) with the current information on the PSED data, codebooks, and interview schedules, as well as a listing of current research efforts and activities of scholars working with the PSED. This Web site is maintained through the support of one or more of the scholars and institutions involved in PSED research activities and not housed, per se, at any one specific university or research center. The www.psed.info site, therefore, should be a way to easily find information on the PSED. Finally, the editors of the handbook can be contacted to locate current information on the PSED, as well.

References

Acs, Z. J., Armington, C., & Robb, A. (1999). *Measures of job flow dynamics in the U.S. economy* (Discussion Paper). Upper Marlboro, MD: U.S. Bureau of the Census, Center for Economic Studies.

Birch, D. L. (1979). *The job generation process.* Unpublished report by the Massachusetts Institute of Technology, Program on Neighborhood and Regional Change. Washington, DC: U.S. Department of Commerce, Economic Development Administration.

Birch, D. L. (1987). *Job creation in America.* New York: Free Press.

Boden, R. (2000). *Employment establishment changes and survival, 1992–1996* (Discussion Paper). Upper Marlboro, MD. U.S. Bureau of the Census, Center for Economic Studies.

Carter, N. M., Brush, C. G., Aldrich, H. E., Greene, P., & Katz, J. A. (1998). *The influence of founder's gender in business start-ups.* Proposal to the National Science Foundation, Grant SBR-9809841.

Carter, N. M., Gartner, W. B., & Reynolds, P. D. (1996). Exploring start-up event sequences. *Journal of Business Venturing, 11*(3), 151–166.

Curtin, R. (1982). Indicators of consumer behavior: The University of Michigan Surveys of Consumers. *Public Opinion Quarterly, 46,* 340–362.

Gartner, W. B. (1985). A framework for describing and classifying the phenomenon of new venture creation. *Academy of Management Review, 10*(4), 696–706.

Greene, P. G., Carter, N. M., Reynolds, P. D., Aldrich, H. E., & Stearns, T. M. (1999). *The influence of founder's race in the start-up process.* Proposal to the National Science Foundation, Grant SBR-9905255.

Kirchhoff, B. A. (1994). *Entrepreneurship and dynamic capitalism: The economics of business firm formation and growth.* Westport, CT: Praeger.

Reynolds, P. D. (1997). Who starts new firms? Preliminary explorations of firms-in-gestation. *Small Business Economics, 9,* 449–462.

Reynolds, P. D. (2000). National study of U.S. business start-ups: Background and methodology. In J. A. Katz (Ed.), *Advances in entrepreneurship, firm emergence and growth* (Vol. 4, pp. 153–228). Stamford, CT: JAI.

Reynolds, P. D., Bygrave, W. D., & Autio, E. [and others] (2003). *Global entrepreneurship monitor: 2003 executive report.* Babson Park, MA: Babson College.

Reynolds, P. D., Camp, S. M., Bygrave, W. D., Autio, E., & Hay, M. (2001). *Global entrepreneurship monitor: 2001 executive report.* Kansas City, MO: Kauffman Center for Entrepreneurial Leadership.

Reynolds, P. D., Hay, M., Bygrave, W. D., Camp, S. M., & Autio, E. (2000). *Global entrepreneurship monitor: 2000 executive report.* Kansas City, MO: Kauffman Center for Entrepreneurial Leadership.

Reynolds, P. D., & White, S. B. (1993). *Wisconsin's entrepreneurial climate study.* Milwaukee, WI: Marquette University, Center for the Study of Entrepreneurship.

Reynolds, P. D., & White, S. B. (1997). *The entrepreneurial process: Economic growth, men, women, and minorities.* Westport, CT: Quorum Books.

Weick, K. E. (1979). *The social psychology of organizing* (2nd ed.). New York: Random House.

Acknowledgments

A s with any entrepreneurial venture, the resources to support the development and implementation of the Panel Study of Entrepreneurial Dynamics (PSED) came in stages. For seed round funding and support we gratefully acknowledge the universities and research institutions, listed in Table F.3, that funded the Entrepreneurship Research Consortium (ERC). Without their initial financial support, and perhaps more importantly the intellectual capital contributed by the membership, the panel study would not have been possible.

The research design of the PSED included a number of innovations. The first was the wide range of topics and issues covered by the data collection procedures. These reflect the substantial intellectual investment of the ERC members and the design teams that acted as a focus for the assembly of ideas and issues and their conversion into items to be included in the phone and mail questionnaires. In addition, major elements of the research methodology were developed in partnership with the University of Wisconsin Survey Research Laboratory; virtually the entire staff was involved and numerous enhancements were provided by the interviewers themselves. Associate Director Charles Palit was particularly helpful in the creation of the sampling designs that led to the current version of the screening schedule.

Victoria Ivey developed the corporate identity package for the ERC.

Having proven the venture concept, second-round funding for the research program came from several sources. The National Science Foundation provided funding for an oversample of women through Grant No. 9809841 (Nancy M. Carter, principal investigator; Howard E. Aldrich, Candida G. Brush, Patricia G. Greene, and Jerry Katz, coprincipal investigators) and an oversample of Blacks and Hispanics through Grant No. 9905255 (Patricia G. Greene, principal investigator; Howard E. Aldrich, Nancy M. Carter, Paul D. Reynolds, and Timothy M. Stearns, coprincipal investigators). These grants allowed us to double the size of the sample and to fund the 24-month follow-up surveys.

The Kauffman Center for Entrepreneurial Leadership (KCEL) (now the Ewing Marion Kauffman Foundation) began to provide substantial funding for the PSED in 2000 through 2003; the research office at the time, led by Michael Camp and Larry Cox, was a major source of strategic assistance to the program. The Kauffman Foundation sponsored the transfer of the entire data collection program and files from the University of Wisconsin Survey Research Laboratory to the University of Michigan Institute for Social Research (ISR) and has generously supported the PSED

Table F.3   Institutions Involved in Funding the Entrepreneurship Research Consortium

Funding Sponsors
Ewing Marion Kauffman Foundation
National Science Foundation

Funding Institutions
Babson College
Bodo Graduate School of Business
Boston University
Canadian Council on Small Business and Entrepreneurship
Clemson University
Coleman Foundation
EIM Small Business Research & Consultancy
Entrepreneurship Theory and Practice
Greek Entrepreneur's Club
Indiana University
Finnvera plc.
London Business School
NFIB Education Foundation
New Jersey Institute of Technology
NUTEK (Swedish Board of Industrial and Technical Development)
Rensselaer Polytechnic Institute
RISEbusiness (Research Institute for Small and Emerging Business)
RWI/Essen (Rheinisch-Westfälisches Institut für Wirtschaftsforschung)
Swinburne University of Technology
Syracuse University
Temple University
University of British Columbia
University of Cincinnati/Xavier University
University of Colorado, Boulder
University of Houston
University of Michigan
University of Missouri–Kansas City
University of North Carolina at Chapel Hill
University of Pennsylvania/Widener University
University of Southern California
University of St. Thomas
University of the Pacific
U.S. Small Business Administration: Office of Advocacy

through the third and fourth waves of data collection in 2003. The shift of all the data and research files, the reconstruction of the project, and the comprehensive documentation developed at the University of Michigan were largely due to the experience and skill of Richard Curtin, director of the Surveys of Consumers program. In addition to support for data collection, Kauffman provided support to Kelly G. Shaver for the development of programs and processes for selecting different types of nascent entrepreneurs (Shaver, Carter, Gartner, & Reynolds, 2001), to the University of Southern California for the development of an initial "user friendly" data set called "PSED LITE," and to William B. Gartner and the University of St. Thomas (to fund Nancy M. Carter) in the preparation of *The Entrepreneur Next Door,* an executive report of the initial findings of the PSED (Reynolds, Carter, Gartner, Greene, & Cox, 2002).

From the initial inception of the ERC, Babson College has served as the host institution, acting as the steward of the ERC funds in the early years of the project. In addition, Babson College provided funding that allowed Paul Reynolds, as the Paul T. Babson Chair of Entrepreneurship, to devote the majority of his time to service as the coordinating principal investigator for the life of the ERC and the duration of the PSED project.

Beginning in 1999, the Lloyd Grief Center for Entrepreneurial Studies hosted a series of all-expenses-paid workshops titled the Greif Research Symposium on Emerging Organizations to bring PSED scholars to the University of Southern California to encourage analyses of the PSED data sets and share research results. It was during the 2001 Greif symposium that the idea of a handbook on theory underlying the PSED research effort was first discussed. The 2002 Greif symposium was used to develop the outline for the book and the process for involving PSED scholars as contributors.

We are particularly indebted to Howard Aldrich, Candy Brush, and Patricia Greene for their involvement in the development of the handbook and for their willingness to provide chapters on topics that helped round out the handbook's breadth and comprehensiveness.

The publication team at Sage has significantly improved the quality of the book we submitted to them. Al Bruckner, senior acquisitions editor at Sage, immediately saw our vision for a book on the theory of the PSED and did a wonderful job of guiding us forward through the handbook's development. MaryAnn Vail has adroitly shepherded us through the publication process from author chapters to the completion of the book with expert advice and steady guidance that has made the process easy and smooth. Diane Foster evened out all of the inconsistencies in our efforts and brought forth a very coherent organizing framework and process for the book's completion. Robert Holm has done a magnificent job of melding the many different writing styles of our authors into a very readable text.

Finally, we recognize those entrepreneurs who are helping to modify and improve the economy: the 65,000 respondents who completed the PSED screening, the 1,300 respondents who provided detailed data, and the millions of future entrepreneurs who may benefit from a more complete understanding of the start-up process.

References

Reynolds, P. D., Carter, N. M., Gartner, W. B., Greene, P. G., & Cox, L. (2002). *The entrepreneur next door: Executive report of the Panel Study of Entrepreneurial Dynamics.* (Available from the Ewing Marion Kauffman Foundation, Kansas City, MO)

Shaver, K. G., Carter, N. M., Gartner, W. B., & Reynolds, P. D. (2001). Who is a nascent entrepreneur? Decision rules for identifying and selecting entrepreneurs in the Panel Study of Entrepreneurial Dynamics (PSED). In W. D. Bygrave, E. Autio, C. G. Brush, P. Davidsson, P. G. Greene, P. D. Reynolds, & H. J. Sapienza (Eds.), *Frontiers of entrepreneurship research 2001: Proceedings of the 21st Annual Babson Kauffman Entrepreneurship Research Conference* (p. 122). Babson Park, MA: Babson College.

PART I

CHAPTER 1

Overview: Life Context, Personal Background

Paul D. Reynolds

The central purpose of the Panel Study of Entrepreneurial Dynamics (PSED) is to answer the question

Where do new firms come from? or put another way,

What are the major processes that lead to the emergence of new firms?

There are a plethora of hypotheses, theories, conceptualizations, ideas, and hunches about the factors that lead to new firm creation. A large proportion of these factors or processes are reflected in the conceptual scheme and data collection processes developed for the PSED. But, as with any complex phenomenon, one cannot discuss all of it at once. The handbook has been organized to provide a systematic overview of the major topics and issues that were the basis for the data collection procedures. It also provides the actual measures developed to provide indicators of the various causal processes.

The relationship between the PSED data collection scheme and the organization of the handbook is presented in Figure 1.1. This is based on the conceptualization of the entrepreneurial process and two major transitions. The first transition is the entry into the start-up process and the second transition is the exit from the start-up process—either with a new firm birth or abandoning the effort itself. The major factors or processes that affect these transitions are indicated in the four dashed-line boxes. Two are seen as operating in parallel, perhaps with substantial interaction: the life context and personal background, and individual cognitive characteristics or dispositions. These are covered in Parts I and II of the handbook. The actual nature of the start-up process itself, which can be quite complex, is

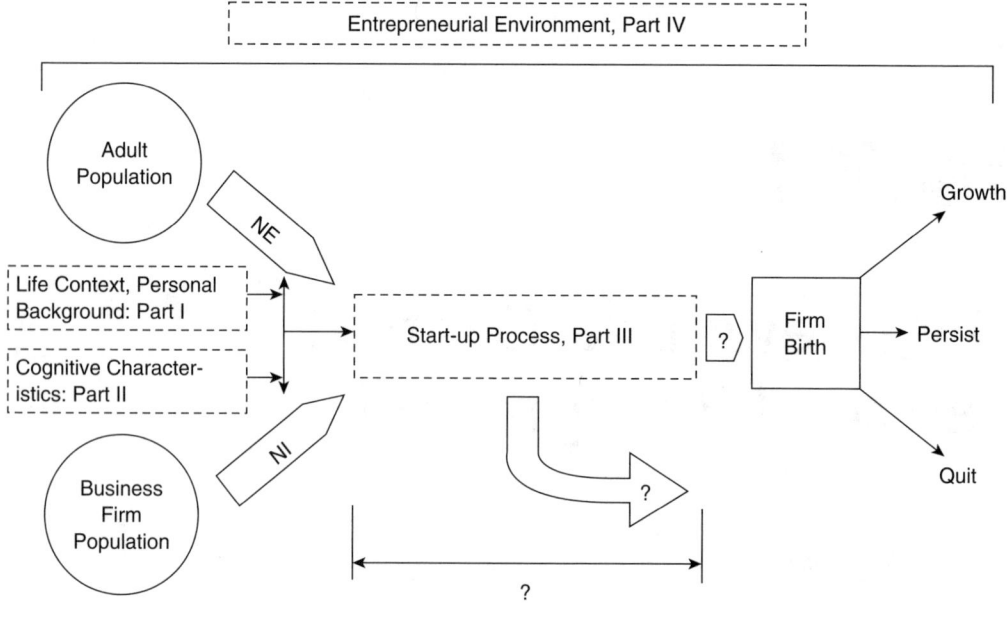

Figure 1.1   The Start-up Process and Handbook Organization

covered in Part III. The environmental context in which all these processes operate is the focus of Part IV.

Perhaps the most critical and poorly understood feature of the process is the "choice point" at which individuals elect to enter the start-up process. There is little question that their previous background, experience, and current context (Part I topics), as well as their personal cognitive capacity and dispositions (Part II topics), can influence their behavior at this juncture. The current economic, social, and political environment (Part IV) may also have an impact. Understanding the complex interactions at this choice point is a major challenge.

Focus of Part I

The chapters in Part I provide an overview of the rationale for selecting various measures and indicators of the individuals' background and current context. There are two major reasons for developing precise measures of the life context and personal background of those involved in business start-ups. The first is the most obvious: they may have a major influence on whether or not individuals choose to enter the start-up process as well as how and when they experience the transition out of the process. These are discussed in the next section of this chapter. The second major reason for assembling data on basic personal characteristics is to facilitate estimates of the amount of participation in entrepreneurial efforts in the U.S. adult population.

Capacity for Population Estimates

The capacity to develop a representative sample of U.S. adults involved in a business start-up is a critical feature of the PSED research program. It involves, among other things, gathering data in the initial screening process to provide comparisons with precise measures of the population to develop appropriate weights for each respondent. A properly weighted representative sample of U.S. adults can be used to create estimates for the entire U.S. adult population. For this reason, developing complete data on basic sociodemographic characteristics is an important feature of the initial screening procedure in which 64,000 individuals were asked about their personal participation in a new firm start-up.

The screening sample was developed by a commercial marketing research firm that provided weights for each of the 64 samples of 1,000 based on age, gender, region of residence, and household income. New sample weights were developed by the University of Michigan Institute for Social Research using the complete sample and based on age, gender, ethnic background, and educational attainment. These procedures are described in handbook Appendix B. The critical point for this discussion is that these six sociodemographic variables—age, gender, ethnic background, household income, educational attainment, and region of residence—were gathered in such a way as to facilitate comparison with descriptions in federal data sets, specifically the Current Population Survey (www.bls.census.gov/cps/cpsmain). Information for the first five variables was provided by respondents during the interview, and the last, region of residence, was based on knowing the state and county of each household based on the telephone number.

The benefit of accurate information on these sociodemographic variables is illustrated by the capacity to estimate the total activity in the U.S. population. From 10.6 to 13.2 million individuals were probably engaged in business start-ups at any given time between 1998 and 2000 (Appendix C, Table C.6). Age and gender of those in the sample were critical for this estimate. Other information gathered for the PSED suggests that from 475,000 to 669,000 new employer firms are established each year; the total annual U.S. new registrations in a comparable federal data set was 581,000 per year during this period (Chapter 23, Figure 23.1). These two measures of start-up activity outcomes are remarkably close, giving confidence that the PSED is providing an accurate measure of a national phenomenon.

Life Context, Personal Background
Factors Affecting the Entrepreneurial Process

The other major reason for collecting this information is directly related to understanding the entrepreneurial process. These life context, personal background variables may reflect processes that have a major influence on whether or not individuals chose to enter the start-up process. They may also affect how they develop and implement a business start-up as well as their success in completing the process with a new firm birth.

Increased understanding of entry into and success in the start-up process has led to a number of items reflecting the past and current lives of the participants. Some are related to the background and experience of the individual, others reflect their current personal, social, and economic context. Many may actually reflect both. For example, an individual's gender may be an indicator of prior life and work experience as well as current family, work, and social context. Current age is both a reflection of past experiences (older individuals have had more opportunity to accumulate experiences and personal wealth) and current situation (older individuals may have less energy and reduced career aspirations).

A listing of the major personal measures reviewed in Part I is presented in Table 1.1, which indicates both the chapter in which it is discussed and to what extent the measure may be considered a reflection of prior experiences or current context. In most cases, a feature is emphasized in one chapter, but several are discussed in slightly different ways in two chapters (encouragement to pursue a start-up in Chapters 4 and 8). Other aspects are treated in complementary but different ways in several chapters (labor force participation in Chapter 6, work experience in Chapter 7, and work participation history in Chapter 10). These multiple treatments—based on different aspects or different sections of the interview schedules—provide a rich description of the participants. In almost all cases, data is available on both those identified as active in starting a new firm (nascent entrepreneurs) and the comparison groups (those randomly selected to represent typical adults not involved in the entrepreneurial process).

Age. Age is so fundamental and ubiquitous that no chapter was devoted to this personal feature. Measurement of age is straightforward. Individuals are asked either their current age or the year of their birth. Those unwilling to respond (very few people do not know their age) may be asked to select an appropriate age range: 18–24 years, 25–34 years, and so forth. Age is available for 96.8% of the 64,622 individuals screened to locate nascent entrepreneurs and 96.8% of the 1,261 individuals in the detailed data file. The relationship to participation in the entrepreneurial process and business start-ups is well established—the activity peaks for those in their early 30s, is rather low for those in the late teens and early 20s, and drops off to almost nothing for those in their late 50s (Appendix C, Table C.6).

This pattern has been widely reported in every study of a representative sample of nascent entrepreneurs, including prior studies in the United States (Reynolds, 1997) and Canada (Menzies, Gasse, Diochon, & Garand, 2002), Netherlands (Wolters, 2000), Norway (Alsos & Kolvereid, 1998), and Sweden (Delmar & Davidsson, 2000), as well as an annual series of cross-national surveys that have included 38 countries sampled over 4 years (Reynolds, Hay, & Camp, 1999; Reynolds, Hay, Bygrave, Camp, & Autio, 2000; Reynolds, Camp, Bygrave, Autio, & Hay, 2001; Reynolds, Bygrave, Autio, Cox, & Hay, 2002). Although there are the occasional exceptions (Colonel Sanders was establishing the Kentucky Fried Chicken franchise when he was in his 60s), the impact of age is so powerful that it must be controlled for any assessment of any other factor—gender, ethnicity, educational attainment, household income—associated with entering the start-up process.

Table 1.1   Major Life Context, Personal Background Variables

Variable	Part I Chapter	Prior Experience	Current Context
Age		X	X
Gender	2	X	X
Ethnic Background	3	X	X
Marital Status	4		X
Household Structure: Size, Composition	4		X
Household Income	5		X
Household Net Worth	5	X	X
Labor Force Participation	6		X
Residential Tenure	6	X	X
Educational Attainment	7	X	
Work Experience	7	X	X
Functional Expertise	7		X
Family Background: Role Models	8	X	
Household, Family Encouragement	4, 8	X	X
Time Use (current activity allocation)	9		X
Work Participation History	10	X	X

Perhaps more significant, it would appear that those in their late 30s and early 40s are more successful in creating a new firm than those in their late 20s and early 30s. Both work experience and access to networks and financial assets may increase in this decade of work experience and reduce the risk of a stillborn start-up effort (Reynolds & White, 1997).

Gender. Few topics associated with entrepreneurship receive as much attention as gender, perhaps because women are a large minority of those starting new firms (4.4 of 11.8 million) but less likely to be involved than men, 4.2 per 100 compared to 7.6 per 100 (Appendix C, Table C.6). Chapter 2, by Carter and Brush, review in some detail the basis for interest in gender differences among those starting new firms. Gender differences were of such importance that supplemental funding was received from the National Science Foundation to enhance the number of women in the entrepreneur sample, and topics associated with gender were introduced throughout the data collection schedule, such as time-use diaries to track allocation of activities, reviewed in Chapter 9. Ironically, a major feature of business start-ups is that over half are team activities and this leads to different respondents on successive contacts for interviews. It was a major undertaking to establish the gender of many nascent entrepreneurs.

Ethnicity. As entrepreneurship is seen as a way for all to participate in the "American dream" of economic advancement and the good life, many are concerned that all citizens have the potential to participate, particularly those from different ethnic backgrounds. One of the unexpected findings from the original screening of 16,000 for those active as nascent entrepreneurs was the discovery of much higher rates of start-up participation among Blacks and Hispanics compared to Whites, particularly for men. This led to a second supplemental grant from the National Science Foundation for an oversample of both nascent entrepreneurs and the comparison group to enhance the number of Blacks and Hispanics. In Chapter 3, Greene and Owen review the major reasons for this interest in ethnic entrepreneurship, how ethnicity was established, and some of the major aspects affected by ethnic background.

Household Structure. Measures of three aspects of household structure are reviewed in Chapter 4 by Brush and Manolova: start-up capital, social desirability and encouragement to pursue entrepreneurial options, and household commitments (which includes marital status and the number in the household—children and adults). Much of this is a result of efforts to develop more precise information about the unique situation of women.

Household Income and Net Worth. For many, the "liquidity effect" is a major factor affecting the decision to pursue a firm start-up. It refers to an assumption in economics that only those with sufficient available financial resources are able to get involved in creating a new firm. But how should financial resources be measured; it turns out that household income and household net worth reflect two aspects of financial well-being, and they are not highly correlated. For this reason, a substantial effort was made to develop precise estimates of both household income and household net worth for all respondents; usable data is available on 90 to 95% of the respondents in the detailed samples. The interview items and procedures involved are reviewed in Chapter 5 by Kim, Aldrich, and Keister.

Labor Force Participation and Residential Tenure. Two myths pervade many discussions related to entrepreneurship—that entrepreneurs are unemployed or new immigrants or both. While the basis for these myths is hard to establish, there is no question that both of these personal characteristics are rare among those starting new firms in the United States. Chapter 6, by Reynolds, reviews how current labor force activity and both international and intranational immigrations were measured for the PSED. This analysis goes somewhat further by presenting how self-employment is determined in major U.S. federal data collection efforts—the decennial census, Current Population Survey. This makes clear that identifying the "unincorporated self-employed" is a very poor indicator of participation in new business start-ups.

Personal Background Variables. Most citizens participate in the world of work, and develop their personal "human capital" in several dimensions: through participating in educational programs, developing skills and experiences related to organizations, and becoming specialized in unique functions in work organizations. In Chapter 7, Brush and Manolova consider work experience, educational attainment, and functional expertise and the relevant indicators available in the PSED data set. The data allow the development of a multidimensional portrayal of functional skills.

Family Background. Many assume that those from entrepreneurial families, or at least small business families, are more likely to become involved in entrepreneurial activity. In Chapter 8, Matthews and Human review these perspectives and the PSED items related to the personal business experiences of the respondent's parents. They are also able to review those indicators of encouragement to start new businesses provided by family and friends.

Time Use (Activity Allocation). Many in social science have found that measures of what people say (attitudes, dispositions) are not as useful in predicting future behavior as measures of what people actually do. But it is much easier to ask individuals what they think, much harder to ask them what they are doing. Measures of time use involve reports on the allocation of all time for a 24-hour period; the most challenging feature of such efforts is not counting the minutes but keeping track of the wide diversity of activities people pursue. Time use among very busy individuals can be very revealing—as they become more careful about how they invest their time. There are, after all, only 24 hours in a day, and nascent entrepreneurs are among the busiest people in the United States. In Chapter 9, Owen and Greene review the time use section from the PSED self-completed mail questionnaire and how activity allocation varies for nascent entrepreneurs and those in the comparison group.

Work Participation History. There is much evidence of substantial variation among individuals in their work careers. Some have one or two jobs over a single 40-year work career while others may change situations several times a year. The self-administered mail questionnaire completed by nascent entrepreneurs and the comparison group allowed them to indicate their workforce behavior for the decade preceding the interview itself. In Chapter 10, Davis and Aldrich review the rationale for attending to the history of the work participation and review some issues in providing useful descriptions.

Commentary. There are many factors or processes that affect entry into and completion of a business start-up process. The PSED is the first serious effort to identify and track those U.S. adults who have elected to become involved in starting a business. A serious effort was made to capture the major aspects of their personal background and current life context. A preliminary analysis of a range of these factors has been provided in the chapters in Part I. Early indications suggest that many important life context, personal background features have been captured with reliable measures that are valid constructs. A summary of selected univariate

Table 1.2 Univariate Differences Between Nascent Entrepreneurs and the Comparison Group

Variable	Part I Chapter	Nascent Entrepreneurs vs. Comparison Group
Age		More young adults (25–44 years old)
Gender	2	More men
Ethnic Background	3	Minorities more active, especially men
Marital Status	4	More often married
Household Structure: Size, Composition	4	Slightly larger, more kids, more likely to be married or living with partner
Household Income	5	No major differences
Household Net Worth	5	No major differences
Labor Force Participation	6	More likely to be working
Residential Tenure	6	Long-term residents more active
Educational Attainment	7	Uneducated less involved, not much difference post high school
Work Experience	7	More work experience
Family Background: Role Models	8	Fathers have run larger businesses, but respondent feels less encouragement to start business from family and relatives
Household, Family Encouragement	4	Entrepreneurship more accepted as career choice
Time Use (Current Activity Allocation)	9	Spend less time on leisure, personal activities, and care of elderly, more time on child care
Work Participation History	10	Hold more work roles, especially women

(each factor taken in isolation) patterns is provided in Table 1.2. Most of these differences are both statistically significant and with modest impact.

It is clear then that more complete analysis will require careful attention to the interaction between these and other variables. A fuller understanding of the entrepreneurial process is likely to occur when the relationship between the personal background and the disposition and cognitive orientation of the individual (reviewed in Part II), and the environmental context (reviewed in Part IV), are taken into account.

There is much work to be done; all readers are invited to join in.

References

Alsos, G. A., & Kolvereid, L. (1998). The business gestation process of novice, serial and parallel business founders. *Entrepreneurship Theory and Practice, 22*(4), 101–114.

Delmar, F., & Davidsson, P. (2000). Where do they come from? Prevalence and characteristics of nascent entrepreneurs. *Entrepreneurship & Regional Development, 12*, 1–23.

Menzies, T. V., Gasse, Y., Diochon, M., & Garand, D. (2002, June). *Nascent entrepreneurs in Canada: An empirical study.* Paper presented at the 47th meeting of the ICSB World Conference, San Juan, PR.

Reynolds, P. D. (1997). Who starts new firms?—Linear additive versus interaction based models. *Small Business Economics, 9*, 449–462.

Reynolds, P. D., Bygrave, W. D., Autio, E., Cox, L., & Hay, M. (2002). *Global entrepreneurship monitor: 2002 executive report.* Kansas City, MO: Kauffman Center for Entrepreneurial Leadership.

Reynolds, P. D., Camp, S. M., Bygrave, W. D., Autio, E., & Hay, M. (2001). *Global entrepreneurship monitor: 2001 executive report.* Kansas City, MO: Kauffman Center for Entrepreneurial Leadership.

Reynolds, P. D., Hay, M., Bygrave, W. D., Camp, S. M., & Autio, E. (2000). *Global entrepreneurship monitor: 2000 executive report.* Kansas City, MO: Kauffman Center for Entrepreneurial Leadership.

Reynolds, P. D., Hay, M., & Camp, M. (1999). *Global entrepreneurship monitor: 1999 executive report.* Kansas City, MO: Kauffman Center for Entrepreneurial Leadership.

Reynolds, P. D., & White, S. (1997). *The entrepreneurial process: Economic growth, men, women, and minorities.* Westport, CT: Quorum Books.

Wolters, T. (2000). Nascent entrepreneurship in the Netherlands: A glance behind the scenes of business start-ups. In *Entrepreneurship in the Netherlands: Opportunities and threats to nascent entrepreneurs* (pp. 3–16). Zoetermeer, The Netherlands: EIM Small Business Research & Consultancy.

Gender

Nancy M. Carter

Candida G. Brush

Over the past 25 years, the number of women entering self-employment in the United States grew at an astounding rate. In 1970 it was estimated that 1.5 million women were self-employed, accounting for 5% of all firms (U.S. House of Representatives, 1988). From 1987 to 1996, the number of women-owned businesses grew 78%, well above the 48% growth posted for all U.S. businesses. Today, it is estimated that women own 10.1 million privately held businesses, generate 18.2 million jobs, and contribute more than $2.3 trillion in sales to the economy (Center for Women's Business Research, 2003). Despite this remarkable growth rate, the share of businesses owned by women remains about 30% of all firms, and the size of these firms as measured by sales and number of employees lags those of men-owned ventures (U.S. Bureau of the Census, 1996). Specifically, in 1997 the average sales of women-owned businesses was $1.8 million, and by 2000 this average reached $2.4 million, which was still lower than the national average of $12.3 million (Center for Women's Business Research, 2001).

The gap between men's and women's participation rate in self-employment is surprising. Women constitute almost 47% of the civilian workforce (Clark & Weismantle, 2003), 50% of managerial and professional specialty positions (*2002 Catalyst*, 2003), and contribute half or more of household income in the majority of households (*American Men & Women*, 2000). Why is their representation in self-employment only one third that of men's? The disparity raises questions about whether fewer women choose to be self-employed or whether they exit the start-up process before their businesses are established and consequently are under-represented in self-employment numbers.

Other chapters of this book show that little is known about the emergent process of new businesses. The paucity of information about this critical developmental phase is particularly troublesome if variation exists in the success rate of subpopulations that make it to fledgling new firm status. Women-owned businesses may represent one such group.

The Panel Study of Entrepreneurial Dynamics (PSED) offers a unique opportunity to explore why women are underrepresented in the entrepreneurial process. Do women simply choose other career paths? Or do some who choose self-employment encounter barriers during the gestation of their business, causing them to give up their efforts and disengage? Or, less extreme, do women experience difficulties that imprint their businesses in ways that constrain growth and limit future success? The PSED allows researchers the opportunity to examine these questions and test whether differences exist in entrepreneurial intentions or in the ways women and men construct their businesses that ultimately influence the outcomes of their efforts. In other words, the project's focus on who engages in entrepreneurship and how organizations actually emerge, over time, provides insight into the interactions between life course stages of individuals and life cycle stages of business development.

The Need for a Gender Perspective

The collaborative nature of the Entrepreneurship Research Consortium (ERC hereafter), the group responsible for designing the study and developing the measurement instruments, results in a data set with the potential for testing numerous theories related to entrepreneurship. Many of these theories derive from research based on male entrepreneurs or male-owned businesses. Such studies implicitly treat men as the standard against which the experiences of women are to be judged. The result is a body of literature in which men (and largely White men) are the unspoken norm. To what extent can findings from these studies generalize to the experiences of women?

Research related to social theory, including introductions of feminist ideologies, argues that gender is a socially constructed phenomenon (Eagly, 1987). Individuals born into social groups differentiated by sex, race, and class are seen as having varying power and status as a result of cultural and social structures that specify appropriate roles and behavior. Because an individual's social identity emerges from the interplay of political, economic, and social structures, the female entrepreneur is more than "other than male" (Bird & Brush, 2002). Research on how gender, occupation, and organizational structures affect female and male business owners differently must acknowledge this caveat in their design and measurement (Mirchandani, 1999).

As noted in the description of how the ERC was formed, a design team known as the Gender and Minority Variables Group (GMVG) was created with responsibility for ensuring that the procedures and instruments adopted make use of the gender and minority lens. Scholars involved in the group in 1995 when the study and instruments were designed represented multidisciplinary backgrounds and included Howard Aldrich, Candida Brush, Nancy Carter, Debbie Good, Patricia Greene, Jerry Katz, Charles Matthews, Bruce Phillips, and Mary Williams. The group's responsibilities were threefold: first, to ensure that the procedures and measures maximized participation of all respondents. For example if, as suggested by Gilligan (1982) and others, women approach things more intuitively, subjectively, and in a more personal way, procedures and measures adopted for the PSED should not be "off-putting" by being overly objective and transactional. Second, the group reviewed each of the items on the interview schedules to ensure that the language was inclusive of experiences of women and minorities and did not bias any questions such that response rates would be reduced. Third, the team reviewed categories of questionnaire items and suggested additional measures that may more uniquely capture the experiences of women and minorities. Data from these latter items are useful for theory building.

A Model of Firm Emergence

The GMVG's efforts were guided by development of a conceptual model of the causal processes underlying new firm formation that would take into account differences in the experiences of men and women. Central to the model is the assumption that organizations are dynamic phenomena, minimally requiring four properties to exist: intentionality (e.g., goal setting); resources (e.g., physical and informational); boundary (e.g., incorporation); and exchange (e.g., sales). Katz and Gartner (1988) suggest that by applying these criteria to emerging organizations researchers can compare preorganizations according to which properties are used, in which order the properties appear, and how long the properties last. The typology is useful for categorizing incubation events since each of the four properties encompasses both structural and process characteristics. This duality presents the potential for capturing the dynamic nature of organizational creation.

The model departs from the view that firm emergence is a deterministic biological process and recognizes that new firms do not just spring into being but are created by individuals who manifest varying motives and aspirations. Entrepreneurs acquire resources and find niches in opportunity structures by coordinating and directing transactions between the firm and the marketplace (Aldrich, 1999). The decision maker, or actor, scans the environment, perceives opportunity, acts on that perception, and, ultimately, passes judgment on if and when to abandon the startup. It is in the mind of the person that entrepreneurial possibilities come together (Shaver & Scott, 1991). It is during this process that nascent entrepreneurs assemble the properties that define the firm's existence.

The model proposes that the generation of firm properties is a function of three factors: (1) assets and attributes of the individual; (2) opportunities that reside in the external environment; and (3) social systems where individuals are embedded. Gender differences are likely to distinguish each of these factors (see Figure 2.1).

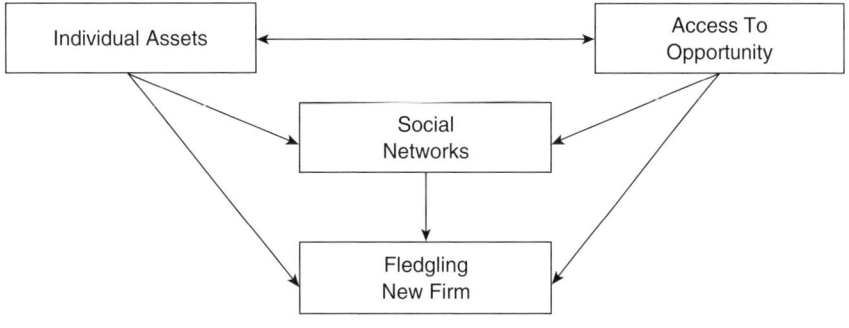

Figure 2.1   A Model of New Firm Gestation

Individual Assets

Individuals bring resources and motives with them to the entrepreneurial process that affect their probability of success. Social learning theories, social feminist theory, careers theories, and life course theories all suggest that resources and motives may change over an individual's life. Each theory specifies cumulative change in human development and offers insight about why women and men may have different interests, intentions, and accumulated resources at different stages in their life. These differences are likely to impact women's selection into self-employment and the choices they make in constructing their businesses. These theories were useful in identifying categories of assets and attributes possessed by men and women that affect, differentially, their experiences in new firm emergence: (1) human and financial capital; (2) intentions; (3) risk propensity; and (4) family business background.

Human and Financial Capital: Women's stock of resources that influence intentions for their firms and choices regarding organizational boundaries tends to be lower than that of men. For example, usefulness of educational background (formal and occupational training) varies. Although the historical gap in the level of formal education between men and women has closed in recent years, women's education in areas that would be most beneficial to self-employment still lags. Overall, women account for 56% of the nation's undergraduates (U.S. Department of Labor, 1999), but only 30% of MBA enrollment compared to 44% at top-tier law and medical schools (University of Michigan, 2000). Furthermore, women are less likely to track into technical disciplines like engineering and computer science, which would give them needed skills for launching successful businesses in manufacturing or high-tech sectors. Businesses in these traditionally male-dominated sectors, such as telecommunications or pharmaceuticals, are typically larger and have greater growth potential. In 1999, only about 20% of engineering students were women, and only half that number (10.6%) were employed engineers (Society of Women Engineers, 2001).

Women also are less likely than men to have meaningful business experiences gained from managing other people that would enhance their chances for launching and growing new ventures. The University of Michigan (2000) reports that 45% of all male MBA graduates from top business schools hold line jobs while only 37% of women MBA graduates do. Less than 8% of the topmost positions in Fortune 500 companies are held by women, and just over 5% of top earners in these companies are women (*2002 Catalyst,* 2003). In addition to education and work experience disparities, women are more likely to have careers frequently interrupted (Hakim, 1996) or work only part-time (Drobnic, Blossfeld, & Rohwer, 1999). These labor force interruptions can disadvantage an individual as they miss opportunities to gain new job skills or incur erosion in previously attained skills.

The financial resources women invest in their ventures at start-up are also lower than those reported for men. In part, this stems from two causes: the wage gap and lower levels of business loans. While the wage gap between men and women has improved with professional women earning approximately 75% of what their male counterparts are paid (Harris, 2000), their lower wages influences the amount available for starting a venture. Similarly, while women business owners have nearly achieved parity with men in being approved for loans, they still face disparities in collateral requirements, interest rates, and loan guarantees, which can limit available start-up capital (Coleman, 2000).

Intentions: Women's intentions for launching and managing new firms also may differ from men's. Self-efficacy, attribution, work values, decision making, and motivation theories (including independency, need for control, and risk-taking propensity) all hold promise for explaining why men and women make differential self-employment choices and informed our vetting of questionnaire items for the PSED.

Research shows that men stress the desire to be their own boss in starting a new business, women stress the desire to be personally challenged or to create employment in which they can balance work and family (Scott, 1986). Women tend to deal with career or manage a business and family simultaneously, often with mixed success (Longstreth, Stafford, & Mauldin, 1987; Fagan, 2001). One way women have handled these multiple responsibilities is to work part-time or to create small businesses with environments that support interpersonal culture and provide the freedom to deal with family needs. Family can be a significant source of emotional and social support for the entrepreneur, but it can also be detrimental. Women have found less support from their spouses for their entrepreneurial activities and experience work-home conflict (Stoner, Hartman, & Arora, 1990). Research also shows that the self-efficacy with which women entrepreneurs approach ventures varies depending on whether or not the industry is traditional or nontraditional (Anna, Chandler, Janse, & Mero, 2000).

Brush (1992) argues that differences between women's and men's motives signal a divergence in the basic definition of a business. Instead of an economic entity designed to achieve profit through competitive advantage, women perceive their businesses as "cooperative networks of relationships" in which business relationships are integrated rather than separated from family, societal, and personal relationships. Research is mixed in examining this premise, one study showing women are more likely to be primary manager and household manager (Miller, Winter, Fitzgerald, & Paul, 2000), whereas another showed no gender differences (Baker, Aldag, & Blair, 2003).

Risk Propensity: Women are often seen as being more risk averse than men and this orientation influences choices they make for where and how they start and manage business. The research on the subject, however, is equivocal. In a study of stock market investments, men adopted more risky positions than women, allocating a great proportion of their assets to stocks (Jianakoplos & Bernasek, 1998); but among comparisons of entrepreneurs and managers, some studies find no difference in risk-taking propensity of males and females (Masters & Meier, 1988). One recent study shows that men are more likely to pursue opportunities known to carry higher levels of risk (Baker et al., 2003). Other studies show female entrepreneurs as more likely to take risks than their female counterparts (Bellu, 1993).

Family Background: Family background also may affect women's propensity to start their own businesses. Studies based upon social learning theory propose that parental examples of career choices and daily living situations affect the likelihood of a child selecting self-employment. Several studies suggest that characteristics of mothers such as education level, work status, and self-employed status are positively related to likelihood of the daughter's being self-employed (Holmquist & Sundin, 1988). Additionally, family background informs us as to sources of social capital that emerge from the norms, networks, and relationships of a family's social structure.

Ultimately, industry selection and founding strategic choice are likely outcomes of self-efficacy, career expectations, and individual context. The high probability of gender differences among an individual's assets and attributes requires specificity in measures so that the actions and experiences of the female entrepreneur can be adequately captured.

Access to Opportunity

Despite the importance of individual assets to the success of establishing a fledgling firm, individuals obviously do not embody all requisite resources. Organizational theorists have embraced this tenet in their quest to establish dimensions of environment influential in the evolutionary process. Economists refer to the environment as opportunity structures where entrepreneurs incur risk in choosing niches favorable for maximizing returns. Inherent in the environmental perspective is the assumption that not all opportunity structures, or niches, are equal (Shane & Venkataraman, 2000). Indeed, they are diverse and uncertain. The environmental niche contains external resources available to the entrepreneur at start-up.

Gender differences occur not in the composition of opportunity structures but in access to those structures. Two groups of theories guided GMVG's review of constructs and measures useful for explaining why women might have less access to resource opportunities in the environment: discrimination theories and systemic barriers (Fischer, Reuber, & Dyke, 1993). Discrimination theories postulate bias on the part of the dominant group as the cause of differential treatment. Two forms of denial have been posed: (1) women may face gender discrimination on the part of resource lenders; and (2) believing they will be discriminated against, women may decide not to pursue the formal lending process. Research findings regarding discrimination have been mixed, with some studies offering support and others finding few differences between men and women in terms of access to financial resources, specifically where business age, firm size, and growth rate have been controlled (Haines, Orser, & Riding, 1999; Haynes & Haynes, 1999). Women, however, pay higher interest rates on their business loans than do men and have higher collateral requirements (Coleman, 2000).

In addition to discrimination, systemic barriers may come into play. These barriers arise from social, cultural, and work structures and may cause the intentions of women and men to differ. These barriers explain why women may adjust the nature of their businesses to conform to normative expectations. For example, they may choose to locate in industries where fewer external resources are necessary for success, adopt lower growth expectations since their access to financial resources to support start-up would be limited, and structure their firms to rely less on others (Anna et al., 2000).

Arguments about barriers to accessing opportunity structures and conformance to normative expectations suggest that women will have fewer external resources during the gestation of their new businesses and that women have different intentions for their new businesses than men. Both may contribute to the erosion rate of women's representation in the entrepreneurial start-up process. Finally, recent evidence suggests women evaluate opportunities differently. A recent study shows women evaluate market growth of an opportunity more positively, but they assess financial risk associated with opportunities more negatively (Baker et al., 2003).

Social Networks

The model also reflects our supposition that nascent entrepreneurs are embedded in social systems influenced by significant others. Social networks are the mechanisms through which information and resources flow and link opportunity structures and the conditions that spur individuals to perceive and act on opportunities. In other words, social networks are used to link the individual's assets and the opportunity structures that contain resources to be exploited. They represent the instrument whereby properties of emerging organizations are assembled during the gestation process.

Social network, social learning, and institutional theories from sociology were used to guide a review of questionnaire items that could assess whether gender affects the way social networks are constructed and used to acquire organizational properties during the firm gestation process.

Research shows that men's and women's personal networks differ in composition, with women's more focused on family and men's on non-kin (Moore, 1990).

Women entrepreneurs appear to rely more heavily upon male colleagues as their prime contact in their social networks but reverted to their own sex in secondary contacts (Cromie & Birley, 1991). Some have questioned whether women become channeled into contacts with resource people in the network that have inferior quality and may provide less assistance in establishing a team (Reese, 1992). Others have found that after women had established their businesses, they used network resources in ways similar to men (Aldrich, Elam, & Reese, 1997).

Entrepreneurs' personal resources likely influence how they establish and use social networks; and, concomitantly, their personal resources evolve from social relations in the network (Bird, 1989). In gestation, this linkage is seen as the conduit for intentionality and boundary properties of emerging organizations. The goals, or intentions, nascent entrepreneurs have for the new firm reflect their personal attributes and social relations. Examples of these goals include growth intentions shaped by individual desires and normative expectations, as well as the type of ownership structure chosen. Similarly, social networks, as presented in the model, serve as the mechanism of interchange between nascent entrepreneurs and opportunity structures. This linkage is seen as the channel for resource and exchange properties of emerging organizations. The linkage signifies the way entrepreneurs use their social networks to perceive and interface with the environment and as the context of their network. Having access to the right resources can influence survival and future success of a new enterprise.

The relationship in the model proposes that nascent entrepreneurs will use their personal support network (strong ties) and the resource provider network (weak ties and strangers) to accumulate social capital over the life course that facilitates the start-up process. If women have fewer individual assets, less access to opportunity structures, and less useful social networks, they are more likely to discontinue start-up efforts.

An Oversample of Women

Pilot studies to test various survey instruments and procedures for the PSED revealed that locating nascent entrepreneurs was more costly than anticipated. Consequently, to generate a large enough representative sample to have confidence regarding generalizations of the findings, members of the ERC were faced with the prospect of reallocating funds from conducting lengthy interviews with nascent entrepreneurs to emphasizing locating these individuals and collecting core information about their start-up activities. The prospect of this change was problematic for two reasons: (1) The change would require that the mail survey that contained many of the scales most likely to provide insight about female entrepreneurship be abandoned; and (2) the pilot studies and prior research on nascent entrepreneurs (Carter, 1997) showed that women were likely to constitute only one third of a random sample of nascent entrepreneurs, a number too small to make meaningful subgroup comparisons.

The possibility of this change led a subset of GMVG members to write a grant proposal to the National Science Foundation (NSF) for funding an oversample of women. The promise of the PSED was the opportunity to explore, for the first time, whether the process and outcomes of women differ from those of men. To do this would require a sample large enough to follow both men and women over a long enough period of time to detect whether there is an interaction between their life cycle stage and the problems/opportunities they encounter in the gestation/founding process. More funds and data were needed.

In 1998, NSF awarded a grant to Nancy Carter (principal investigator) and Howard Aldrich, Candida Brush, Patricia Greene, and Jerry Katz (coprincipal investigators) that would double the number of nascent entrepreneurs in the sample and cover the cost of a 24-month follow-up for the entire sample (the oversample of women and the ERC-funded sample). All procedures for the female oversample were identical to the ERC's in terms of data collection, and all data from the female oversample were combined with all other PSED data.

Gender Representation and Questionnaire Items Proposed by GMVG

Question number 201 on the phone interview instructed the interviewer to code whether the respondent was male or female and to ask, if necessary. In some cases, the start-up was being created by a team of individuals, and the details about the respondent's gender was collected as part of the team information (Q217). Because the respondent was not necessarily listed as the first team member, a gender variable, ITRWSEX, was computed to ensure that sex information on the respondent was appropriately captured. Valid values for Q201 were assigned to the new variable. If values were missing for Q201, values from Q217, which asked about each team member's gender, and Q210, which asked whether the team member was the respondent, were used to assign valid values for ITRWSEX. Males were coded 1; females, 2. To further verify the coding of the gender values of ITRWSEX, Nancy Carter performed a detailed evaluation of the gender data from the screening process done by Market Facts, comparing it to that collected by the University of Wisconsin Survey Research Laboratory. Forty-two discrepancies were identified. Using variables that reported on first name of respondent, expected ownership, relationship among team members, and interviewers' notes made at the conclusion of the interview, the sex values for ITRWSEX were verified as appropriate except in seven cases. The remaining discrepancies required recoding of the sex variable. A new variable, NCGENDER, was created that reflected these changes and should be used in all analyses that include gender.

In addition to reviewing all items on the phone and mail questionnaires with the "gender lens and making adjustments where needed," the GMVG suggested several additional sets of variables that were needed to adequately test the proposed model. These additional variables are discussed fully in subsequent chapters on household structure, personal backgrounds, time-use diaries, work participation, career reasons, start-up problems, organizing activities, and financial management/sophistication.

Findings

Table 2.1 displays the number of men and women in each of the three datasets by the nature of their involvement in the entrepreneurial process (Shaver, Carter, Gartner, & Reynolds, 2001).

Table 2.1   Gender Across Nature of Involvement in the Entrepreneurial Process

Data Source		Nature of Involvement			
Nascents		NE[a]	NI[b]	Both[c]	Total
ERC					
	Female	148	8	15	171
	Male	222	18	35	275
NSF-Women					
	Female	154	7	10	171
	Male	45	4	3	52
NSF-Minority					
	Female	49	2	10	61
	Male	78	6	16	100
Subtotals		696	45	89	830
Comparison Adults					
ERC					
	Female	No count			119
	Male	No count			104
NSF-Minority					
	Female	10	2	2	120
	Male	11	2	1	88
Subtotals		21	4	3	431
Total					1,261

NOTES:

a. NE = Nascent Entrepreneur. A "yes" response to: Are you, alone or with others, now trying to start a new business?

b. NI = Nascent Intrapreneur. A "yes" response to: Are you, alone or with others, now starting a new business or new venture for your employer? An effort that is part of your job assignment?

c. Both. Answered "yes" to both of the NE and NI questions.

Table 2.2   Prevalence Rate[a] of Entrepreneurial Activity by Gender and Age

Variable	18–24 Years	25–34 Years	35–44 Years	45–54 Years	55–64 Years	66 Up Years
Women	4.1	6.8	6.4	5.7	2.3	0.3
Men	9.1	11.3	10	8.6	5.1	1.2

NOTE: Prevalence rate is per 100 individuals.

Consistent with their proportionate representation of existing new firms in the United States, men are almost twice as likely as women to be starting new business in the United States. The screening data show the prevalence rate for men 18 years and older is 8.1 per 100 compared to 4.5 per 100 for women.

Age and gender significantly predict new start-up efforts. As shown in Table 2.2, 3 of every 1,000 women (0.3%) over the age of 65 are involved as compared to a high of 11.3 of every 100 men (11.3%) in the 25 to 34 age category. The highest prevalence rate for both men and women is among those 25 to 54 years old.

Analyses of data from questions on financing intentions, risk aversion, and household income support prior speculation that female founders are more risk averse and less likely to expect debt financing to capitalize their new businesses. Even after controlling for risk propensity, risk orientation, and nonfinancial resources, female nascent entrepreneurs in the PSED still expect less debt financing from all sources for their businesses (Carter, 2002).

Results relative to other relationships between gender and aspects of the start-up process of interest to GMVG are reported in subsequent chapters.

Implications

The participation of women in the entrepreneurial process is important for economies worldwide. Although the contributions of women-led ventures in terms of jobs, innovations, and wealth are undeniable, their representation, growth, and size lag that of men. The PSED provides a unique data set for examining questions about gender similarities and differences because it captures entrepreneurs in the midst of the nascent process. It permits the opportunity to explore factors motivating or discouraging women in the venture start-up process, as well as facilitators and barriers to growth and performance. Because a gender lens was applied to the development of the questionnaire and measures, the data should avoid the limitations inherent in other surveys and questionnaires that were developed primarily on samples of male entrepreneurs. Furthermore, the approaches used to insure adequate sampling of women will provide researchers with ample opportunity to compare male and female entrepreneurs, filling an important gap in research about entrepreneurs that often is not comparative. Finally, the opportunity to study women entrepreneurs in the start-up process using multiple theoretical perspectives should yield new insights into their entrepreneurial actions and strategies.

The literature reviewed in this chapter and the theoretical arguments outlined make a strong argument for gender being included in almost all analyses using the PSED. For too long, we have generalized from studies primarily of male business owners. The PSED offers an opportunity to see whether those generalizations were prudent.

References

Aldrich, H. E. (1999). *Organizations evolving.* Thousand Oaks, CA: Sage.

Aldrich, H. E., Elam, A. B., & Reese, P. R. (1997). Strong ties, weak ties, and strangers: Do women business owners differ from men in their use of networking to obtain assistance? In S. Birley & I. MacMillan (Eds.), *Entrepreneurship in a global context* (pp. 1–25). London: Routledge.

American men & women: Demographics of the sexes. (2000). Ithaca, NY: New Strategies.

Anna, A. L., Chandler, G. N., Jansen, E., & Mero, N. P. (2000). Women business owners in traditional and non-traditional industries. *Journal of Business Venturing, 15*(3), 279–303.

Baker, T., Aldag, R., & Blair, E. (2003, June). *Gender and entrepreneurial opportunity evaluation.* Paper presented at the 23rd Annual Babson Kauffman Entrepreneurship Research Conference, Babson College, Wellesley, MA.

Bellu, R. R. (1993). Task role motivation and attributional style as predictors of entrepreneurial performance: Female sample findings. *Entrepreneurship & Regional Development, 5,* 331–344.

Bird, B. J. (1989). *Entrepreneurial behavior.* Glenview, IL: Scott, Foresman.

Bird, B. J., & Brush, C. G. (2002). A gendered perspective on organizational creation. *Entrepreneurship Theory and Practice, 26*(3), 41–65.

Brush, C. (1992). Research on women business owners: Past trends, a new perspective and future directions. *Entrepreneurship Theory and Practice, 16*(4), 5–30.

Carter, N. M. (1997). Entrepreneurial processes and outcomes: The influence of gender. In P. D. Reynolds & S. B. White, *The entrepreneurial process: Economic growth, men, women, and minorities* (pp. 163–178). Westport, CT: Quorum Books.

Carter, N. M. (2002, June). *The role of risk orientation on financing expectations in new venture creation: Does sex matter?* Paper presented at the 22nd annual Babson Kauffman Entrepreneurship Research Conference, Boulder, CO.

Center for Women's Business Research. (2001). *Removing the boundaries, 2001.* Chevy Chase, MD: Author.

Center for Women's Business Research. (2003). *Completing the picture: Equally-owned firms in 2002.* Washington, DC: Author.

Clark, S. L., & Weismantle, M. (2003). *Employment status 2000: Census 2000 brief.* Retrieved January 2004 from www.census.gov/prod/2003pubs/c2kbr-18.pdf.

Coleman, S. (2000). Access to capital and terms of credit: A comparison of men- and women-owned small businesses. *Journal of Small Business Management, 38*(3), 37–52.

Cromie, S., & Birley, S. (1991). Networking by female business owners in Northern Ireland. *Journal of Business Venturing, 7,* 237–251.

Drobnic, S., Blossfeld, H., & Rohwer, G. (1999). Dynamics of women's employment patterns over the family life course: A comparison of the United States and Germany. *Journal of Marriage and the Family, 61,* 133–146.

Eagly, A. (1987). *Sex differences in social behavior: A social-role interpretation.* Hillsdale, NJ: Erlbaum.

Fagan, C. (2001). The temporal re-organization of employment and the household rhythm of work schedules. *American Behavioral Scientist, 44*(7), 1199–1212.

Fischer, E., Reuber, R., & Dyke, L. S. (1993). A theoretical overview and extension of research on sex, gender and entrepreneurship. *Journal of Business Venturing, 8*(2), 151–168.

Gilligan, C. (1982). *In a different voice.* Cambridge, MA: Harvard Press.

Haines, G. H., Jr., Orser, J. B., & Riding, A. L. (1999). Myths and realities: An empirical study of banks and the gender of small business clients. *Canadian Journal of Administrative Sciences, 16*(4), 291–307.

Hakim, C. (1996). Labour mobility and employment stability: Rhetoric and reality on the sex differential in labour-market behaviour. *European Sociological Review, 12,* 1–31.

Harris, S. (2000). *Women making history today: Taking aim at the male/female wage gap.* Retrieved 31 January 2000, from csmonitor.com

Haynes, G. W., & Haynes, D. C. (1999). The debt structure of small businesses owned by women in 1987 and 1993. *Journal of Small Business Management, 37*(2), 1–19.

Holmquist, C., & Sundin, E. (1988). Women as entrepreneurs in Sweden. In B. A. Kirchoff, W. A. Long, W. E. McMullan, K. Vesper, & W. E. Wetzel, Jr. (Eds.), *Frontiers of Entrepreneurship Research 1988: Proceedings of the Eighth Annual Babson College Entrepreneurship Research Conference* (pp. 625–637). Wellesley, MA: Babson College.

Jianakoplos, N. A., & Bernasek, A. (1998). Are women more risk averse? *Economic Inquiry, 26*(4), 620–630.

Katz, J., & Gartner, W. (1988). Properties of emerging organizations. *Academy of Management Review, 13,* 429–441.

Longstreth, M., Stafford, K., & Mauldin, T. (1987). Self-employed women and their families: Time use and socio-economic characteristics. *Journal of Small Business Management, 25*(3), 30–37.

Masters, R., & Meier, R. (1988). Sex differences and risk-taking propensity of entrepreneurs. *Journal of Small Business Management, 26*(1), 31–35.

Miller, N. J., Winter, M. A., Fitzgerald, M. A., & Paul, J. (2000). Family micro-enterprises: Strategies for coping with overlapping family and business demands. *Journal of Developmental Entrepreneurship, 5*(2), 87–113.

Mirchandani, K. (1999). Feminist insight on gendered work: New directions in research on women and entrepreneurship. *Gender, Work, and Organization, 6*(4), 224–235.

Moore, G. (1990). Structural determinants of men's and women's personal networks. *American Sociological Review, 55,* 726–735.

New economic realities: The rise of women entrepreneurs. (1988, June 28). A report of the Committee on Small Business, House of Representatives, Second Session. Washington, DC: Government Printing Office.

Reese, P. (1992). *Resource acquisition: Does gender make a difference?* Paper presented at the Second Annual Global Entrepreneurship Research Conference, London.

Scott, C. E. (1986). Why more women are becoming entrepreneurs. *Journal of Small Business Management, 24*(4), 37–44.

Shane, S., & Venkataraman, S. (2000). The promise of entrepreneurship as a field of study. *Academy of Management Review, 25*(1), 217–226.

Shaver, K. G., Carter, N. M., Gartner, W. B., & Reynolds, P. D. (2001). Who is a nascent entrepreneur? Decision rules for identifying and selecting entrepreneurs in the Panel Study of Entrepreneurial Dynamics (PSED). In W. D. Bygrave, E. Autio, C. G. Brush, P. Davidsson, P. G. Greene, P. D. Reynolds, & H. J. Sapienza (Eds.), *Frontiers of entrepreneurship research 2001: Proceedings of the 21st Annual Babson Kauffman Entrepreneurship Research Conference* (p. 122). Babson Park, MA: Babson College.

Society of Women Engineers. (2001). Retrieved July 2003 from www.swe.org/SWE/ProgDev/stat/stathome.html

Stoner, C. R., Hartman, R. I., & Arora, R. (1990). Work-home role conflict in female owner of small businesses: An exploratory study. *Journal of Small Business Management, 29*(1), 30–38.

2002 Catalyst census of women corporate officers and top earners. (2003). New York: Catalyst.

University of Michigan. (2000). *Women and men MBA graduates satisfied with value of MBA degrees and with careers overall.* Retrieved 18 July 2003, from www.umich.edu/~cew/mba2.html

U.S. Bureau of the Census. (1996). *1992 economic census, women-owned businesses.* Washington, DC: Government Printing Office. Retrieved January 2004 from www.census.gov/prod/1/bus/wb92-1/wb92-1.pdf

U.S. Department of Labor. (1999). Retrieved July 2003 from www.ed.gov/PDFDocs/collegeweek.pdf

CHAPTER 3

Race and Ethnicity

Patricia G. Greene

Margaret M. Owen

The U.S. government reports on minority business ownership as part of the regular economic census performed every 5 years in years ending in 2 or 7. For the purposes of this census, minority-owned businesses are all those not owned by nonminority (Caucasian) business owners. By this definition, minority-owned businesses make up approximately 15% of all U.S. firms. Between 1992 and 1997, minority firms grew at a rate that far outstripped the growth rate of non-minority firms; minority-owned firms grew at 30% while nonminority firms grew at 4% (U.S. Small Business Administration [SBA], 1997). According to the U.S. Small Business Administration, there are currently about 3 million minority-owned firms in the United States that generate approximately $495 billion in revenues and employ almost 4 million workers (SBA, 2002).

What the general numbers mask is the diversity of the phenomena of minority business ownership. During that same 5-year time frame, the number of Hispanic-owned and Asian-owned businesses each grew by 30%. The number of Black-owned businesses grew by 26% while, notably, the number of businesses owned by Native Americans grew by 84% (Greene & Chaganti, 2003). This type of variation in self-employment levels across racial and ethnic groups has been observed (Fairlie & Meyer, 1996; Reynolds & White, 1997) and yet frameworks to explain these differences and advance our understanding of ethnic economic activity remain limited. This chapter begins with a conceptual consideration of the topic of minority entrepreneurship and examines the theoretical frameworks as each relates to business creation and development. We next discuss the background of the minority ownership variables in the Panel Study of Entrepreneurical

Dynamics (PSED) and present basic descriptive statistics of the relevant variables. We conclude the chapter with suggestions for further research.

Literature Review

Sociology, anthropology, business, and labor economics literature have each contributed to the development of theoretical frameworks addressing the effect of ethnicity and race on entrepreneurship. Research into ethnicity and entrepreneurship can be traced back to classic works such as those of Weber (1930), Sombart (1914), and Simmel (1950). These scholars' concepts of the stranger as trader, combined with the social structure of societies and pervasive religious canons, have influenced subsequent literature about and study of ethnic entrepreneurship (Butler & Greene, 1997). Enclave theory and middleman theory, two of the primary explanatory frameworks, each evolved from these early frameworks.

However, there are two fundamental traps that underlie many discussions of minority entrepreneurship. First, the term *minority* itself lends itself to studies in which the aggregate nature of the data combines racial and ethnic groups that have no basis for such an aggregation other than that of being Caucasian and non-Hispanic. The assumption seems to be that these groups share some commonality at the individual, business, or community level that allows knowledge to be generated while exploring what might be quite dissimilar populations.

Second, the conceptual discussion in both academic and trade journals often uses terms such as ethnic, immigrant, and minority as interchangeable descriptors for entrepreneurial activities or behaviors by nonmajority individuals (Greene, 1997). Each of these terms has a specific definition and attachment to a set of theoretical frameworks.

Ethnic entrepreneurship is "a set of connections and regular patterns of interaction among people sharing common national background or migration experiences" (Waldinger, Aldrich, & Ward, 1990, p. 3). Given that the emphasis or grounding assumption for theoretical explanations of this phenomenon is based upon those patterns of interaction, the focus of the majority of studies in this area is the ethnic community. Examples abound in sociology where researchers have explored diverse ethnic communities in the United States, including Japanese (Bonacich & Modell, 1980; Light, 1972), Chinese (Zhou, 1992), Pakistani (Greene & Butler, 1996), and both Cuban and Mexican (Portes & Bach, 1985). A variety of studies on such communities have also been conducted in many other countries, including Israel (Lerner, 1994) and the Netherlands (Van Delft, Gorter, & Nijkamp, 1999).

Middleman minority theory is the primary theoretical explanation for ethnic entrepreneurship. It provides the explanation that a minority group arrives in a geographic location where they are a recognizable minority and as such are denied jobs in the primary labor market. In order to survive, they turn to basic types of entrepreneurial activities. Two of the fundamental characteristics of such a community are (1) bounded solidarity and (2) enforceable trust, and these interact to allow the community to survive economically and socially. The most traditional middleman minority perspectives also assume that the original minority arrivals enter as sojourners, but this assumption is often less explored in later applications. However, the sojourner element is an important one in that it provides the explanation for the types of businesses generally started as being highly liquid so the business owner can "cash out" easily and quickly when the decision is made to return home (Bonacich & Modell, 1980).

Enclave theory is an extension of middleman theory that adds the element of geographic concentration. Not all ethnic entrepreneurs live or own their businesses in physical proximity to co-ethnics. However, when they do exist, ethnic enclaves present strong cultural and economic linkages as well as physical concentrations. Enclave theory also focuses on internal labor market development as well as business enterprise formation (Portes & Bach, 1985).

Ethnic networks and social capital are also studied in an effort to understand the role they play in explaining the differences among ethnic groups' participation in the entrepreneurial process (Aldrich & Zimmer, 1986; Light & Bonacich, 1988; Portes & Bach, 1985; Waldinger et al., 1990). Ethnic entrepreneurs require social networks to support the establishment of their business start-ups (Light, 1972). The literature therefore focuses on those with strong ethnic group affiliations and those groups exhibiting high entrepreneurial participation rates to use as a basis for explaining entrepreneurial outcomes. Light and Bonacich (1988) claim that class and ethnic resources explain entrepreneurship, and these resources include not only material property and wealth but also knowledge, information, and skills. Although the community dimension and the contribution of community resources to the individual's business creation process is highly relevant (Butler & Greene, 1997), the community dimension cannot be automatically assumed for an ethnic entrepreneur (Chaganti & Greene, 2002).

Immigrant entrepreneurship is another term found in academic work in this area as well as in trade publications. However, this term has less of an identifiable theoretical foundation. Given that racial and ethnic groups have strikingly different propensities toward entrepreneurship, there is little basis for the assumption that the state of being an immigrant in itself can be correlated with specific entrepreneurial activities, behaviors, or outcomes.

Minority entrepreneurship is the final term and is often used as a catch-all expression. A variety of studies have been published that use race or ethnicity to test for differences in the demographics of entrepreneurs. For instance, comparisons have been made in characteristics of minority business owners (DeCarlo & Lyons, 1979; Hisrich & Brush, 1986; Gomolka, 1997), values (Enz, Dollinger, & Daily, 1990), and pathways to ownership (Feldman, Koberg, & Dean, 1991).

More specifically, Black business ownership has also been studied both from a theoretical and from an ad hoc perspective. Truncated middleman minority theory presents an adaptation of the middleman minority theory used to explain ethnic entrepreneurship. The truncated theoretical model for Black business owners and communities emphasizes the historical impact of racially based laws that served to restrict markets and therefore negatively impact Black-owned businesses (Butler, 1991). This work served to launch research connecting Black entrepreneurship and economic development (Boston, 1994). And finally, other and more separate studies examined issues related to owner characteristics (Auster, 1988) and the financing of the businesses (Bates, 1993; Bates & Bradford, 1979). Overall, with the exception of the middleman and enclave theories and the truncated explanation, there is little evidence of an emerging agreement on theoretical frameworks for this discussion.

Minority Entrepreneurship in the PSED

Minority entrepreneurship was a point of interest in the PSED from the early days of developing the original design of the Entrepreneurship Research Consortium (ERC) project and was approached as part of the Gender and Minority Variables Group (GMVG). As described in the previous chapter, this group included scholars from multiple disciplines who were responsible for bringing a lens sensitive to gender and minority issues to the study. The approach included issues related to procedures and measures, inclusivity of multiple types of experiences, and the generation of specific items and measures attuned to the populations under study (Carter & Brush, chap. 2).

One of the most unexpected and interesting findings that emerged from early exploratory analysis of the ERC screening data was that Black and Hispanic respondents reported working on starting a business at significantly higher rates than White respondents. These findings were particularly interesting when juxtaposed with business ownership statistics.

- African Americans are considerably less likely than the population at large to be self-employed (SBA, 1996, p. 95).
- Hispanic Americans, like African Americans, are less likely to be self-employed than non-Hispanic Whites (SBA, 1996, p. 100).

The numbers were so intriguing that following the precedent set by the members of a subset of the GMVG group, a proposal was sent to the National Science Foundation (NSF) for a second grant that would fund both an oversampling of Black and Hispanic nascent entrepreneurs as well as a follow-up control group. The group proposed the following:

ERC's preliminary analysis of screening a representative sample of US adults indicates that contextual and life course factors affecting the decision to initiate a new firm are quite different for Whites, African-Americans, and Hispanics; and that these results do not support previous research findings in the academic literature. For example, African-Americans are

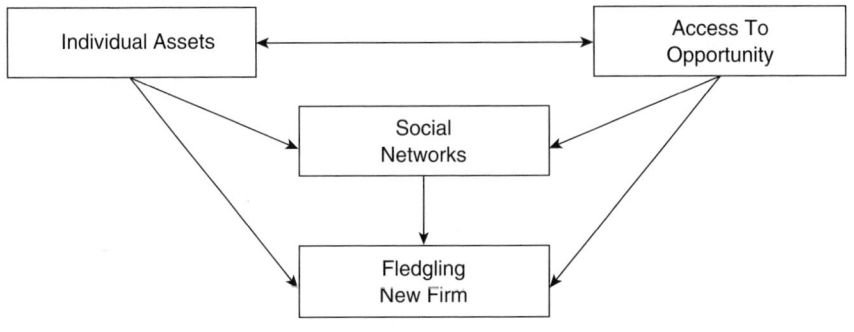

Figure 3.1   A Model of New Firm Gestation

57% more likely to report participation in a start-up than Whites; Hispanics are 20% more likely than Whites. Age, gender, and geographic context have different impacts on the sub-populations with regards to participation in start-ups. . . . This will provide an opportunity to test a theoretical model that posits differences between ethnic groups. (Greene, Carter, Reynolds, Aldrich, & Stearns, 1999, p. 1)

The theoretical model proposed for testing was the same one supporting the discussion for the overall PSED as well as the gender effort. The important relationships were posited between individual assets and attributes, access to opportunity, social networks, and the fledgling new firm (See Figure 3.1). Although pieces of this model were evident in previous research on ethnic entrepreneurs as well as research categorized as studies in minority entrepreneurship, there was not a unified approach toward testing the model and advancing the theoretical explanation.

The theoretical model guiding the PSED lends itself well to the investigation of the topic, recognizing the importance of considering the phenomenon from a "pre-organizational" perspective (Katz & Gartner, 1988). The factors most relevant are the assets of the individual, the opportunities located in the external environment, and the social systems of the individuals (Greene et al., 1999).

Individual Assets

Assets include both resources and motives related to entrepreneurship, including human capital aspects of education, experiences, and career transitions. At the time of the study, self-employed African Americans were found to have lower levels of education than self-employed Whites (SBA, 1996). Career differences were also seen in both preparatory education and actual practice. African American business owners were less likely to have a technical concentration in their education and less likely to have more than 2 years' work experience. It was also less likely that work experiences were in managerial areas (U.S. Bureau of the Census, 1992). The level of education and number of years of work experience were lower for Hispanic business owners than for African American or nonminority males (U.S. Bureau of the Census, 1992).

Access to Opportunity

The environment is the source of external resources with potential value for the business start-up process. However, opportunities are diverse and uncertain. Differential access to opportunity has been offered as a fundamental explanation for varied propensity rates for entrepreneurial behaviors between groups and genders. For African American business ownership, differential access to opportunities is explained through grounding in slavery, racism, and segregation (Bates, 1997; Butler, 1991; Greene et al., 1999; Walker, 1998). Thus environmental structural issues contribute to the explanation of rates, process, and outcomes. The results of such barriers include the types of businesses started and financial constraints (Bates, 1997; Blalock, 1967; Bonacich & Modell, 1980; Butler, 1991).

Opportunity structures have been noted to have different types of impact for Hispanic nascent entrepreneurs. The Cuban refugee enclave in Miami, Florida, is an exemplar of the ethnic entrepreneurial enclave in which an internal opportunity structure was created (Portes & Bach, 1985). However, in various studies of Mexican immigrants, the process and outcomes were quite different and reflected a greater challenge in facing structural barriers to access to resources and opportunities (Light, Bhachu, & Karageorgis, 1993; Portes & Bach, 1985).

Social Networks

Social networks are the pathway for all types of resources and connect other factors of the model. They allow the resources needed to create the businesses to connect other resource types and opportunities. Social networks of ethnic entrepreneurs have primarily been studied at the community level (Aldrich & Waldinger, 1990; Light, 1972; Greene & Butler, 1996). Each of these studies recognizes the substantial differences in communities as to the types of resources that flow through the networks and the process of acquiring the resources (Biggart, Castanias, & Davis, 1994; Bonacich & Modell, 1980; Tenenbaum, 1993). Research on the social networks of African American entrepreneurs is more limited and the findings are mixed, often reporting less active business creating networks (Bates, 1994; Light, 1972). However, studies of the history of Black businesses find a strong relationship between business emergence and Black churches and benevolent associations (Butler, 1991; Pierce, 1947; Walker, 1998).

Findings of the social networks of Hispanic business owners are similar to those relating to opportunity structures. Again, while Cuban entrepreneurs in communities such as Miami report strong social networks and resource flow, immigrant Mexican communities report quite different situations (Portes & Bach, 1985).

Measures

The categorization of measures capturing race and ethnicity is becoming increasingly more complex due to a growing sensitivity to the many types of backgrounds. At the time of the PSED original data collection, the United States defined *race* with just four categories: White, Black, American Indian or Alaskan Native, and Asian-Pacific Islander. An open-ended "Other" category was for those who felt they did not fit into any of these categories. Ethnicity was captured with a separate question as to Hispanic or non-Hispanic. The government categories were the source of the categories used in the PSED screener instrument. Ethnicity was asked first: "Are you Hispanic, Latino, or of Spanish origin?" Race was then asked, using only the categories of White, Black, Asian, or Other. These questions were asked of both the nascent entrepreneurs and the control group respondents. In an effort to create a single variable representing respondent ethnicity, those who answered White or Other to the first item and Yes to the Hispanic question were categorized as Hispanic. This classification scheme resulted in some overlapping for each ethnic category in the first question. Three percent of those who identified themselves as Black in the first question also identified themselves as Hispanic in the second question. Similarly, 8% of those respondents who identified themselves as Asian in the first question also answered Yes to the Hispanic item. Therefore, there are some identification inconsistencies in the ethnicity variable in the screening data.

In the detailed interview PSED sample, each respondent answered a single ethnic identification item as White, Black, Hispanic, Native American, or Asian. Some switching in respondents' ethnic identification between the detailed interviews and the screening interviews was observed. For example, of those who identified themselves as White in the screening interviews, 92% were classified as White in the detailed interviews. Given that these data items were captured at two different phases of the collection process, it is possible that other members of the team including spouses may have responded differently resulting in some inconsistencies in respondent reporting.

Based upon the awareness of the danger of aggregating members of disparate minority groups, the members of the GMVG added a series of questions designed to elicit more detail on race and ethnicity. These questions focused upon identifying the countries of birth of the respondents and their parents. The exact wordings for the resulting items representing race and ethnicity are listed in Table 3.1.

Several variables were subsequently created in order to identify respondents by race or ethnicity as accurately as possible. First, the variables USETHNIC and USHISP from the Market Facts screening data were used to create USRACE, which assigned one race or ethnicity category to each respondent. Second, ITRWRACE was created to include a race/ethnicity categorization for respondents who were starting a business on a team but who were not the first team member. ITRWRACE had 52 cases with missing data as to race or ethnicity. Each of the 52 cases was further evaluated by Patricia Greene for race designation using USRACE plus the other

Table 3.1   Race and Ethnicity Items in the PSED

Item Number Code	Question
USHISP	Are you Hispanic, Latino, or of Spanish origin?
USETHNIC	Which of the following best describes your race: White, Black, Asian, Other?
Q203	What would you consider to be your race or ethnic origin: White, Black or African American, Hispanic, American Indian, Southeast Asian, Other Asian or Pacific Islander, or something else?
Q357a_MT	How long have you lived in the United States? (months)
Q358	Were you born in the United States?
Q358a	What is your birth country?
Q358b	Are you a citizen of the United States?
Q358c	Where country respondent's ancestors came from?
Q358c_2	What country do you feel closest to?
Q360	Was your father born in the United States?
Q360a	In what country was your father born?
Q361	Was your mother born in the United States?
Q361a	In what country was your mother born?

variables on the questionnaires related to race/ethnicity, including length of time living in the United States, country of birth, and parents' race or ethnicity. Of the 52 cases with missing data, 39 were identified by matching with USRACE, 9 were identified using related questions, and 6 were unable to be identified and remained coded as missing. Question 203 also asked the race/ethnicity of the respondent; however, the variable had a significant number of missing answers and therefore was used only to validate other categorizations. A final review of the race/ethnicity variables found 10 cases in which the ITRWRACE value was not the most appropriate, and the cases were recoded. All changes on the race/ethnicity variables reflecting recoded missing values and misclassified data are captured in the variable PGRACE. The summary of the variables and the distribution of the cases are presented in Table 3.2 for the nascent entrepreneurs and Table 3.3 for the comparison group.

The descriptive statistics for the variables used to verify respondents' race and ethnicity in both the nascent entrepreneur and comparison groups are presented in Table 3.4.

Table 3.2   Frequency Distributions: Race and Ethnicity Variables for Nascent Entrepreneurs

Variable[a]	USETHNIC	USHISP	USRACE	Q203	ITRWRACE	PGRACE
White	586		541	252	538	564
Black	147		147	76	140	145
Hispanic		106	101	31	70	81
Asian	10		10	6	14	14
American Indian				8	9	9
Other	76	719 (Not Hispanic)	20			8
Something Else				6	8	10
Subtotal[b]	819	825	819	379	778	824
Missing	11	5	11	451	52	6
Total	830	830	830	830	830	830

NOTES:

a. Weighted Variables (WtW1).
b. Figures in the subtotal row may not be exact sums due to rounding off.

Table 3.3   Frequency Distributions: Race and Ethnicity Variables of Comparison Group

Variable[a]	USETHNIC	USHISP	USRACE	Q203	ITRWRACE	PGRACE
White	303		272	311	311	310
Black	64		64	47	47	49
Hispanic		77	70	27	26	31
Asian	12		12	8	10	10
American Indian				10	8	8
Other	49	351 (Not Hispanic)	10			
Something Else				23	24	22
Subtotal[b]	427	427	428	427	426	429
Missing	4	4	3	4	5	2
Total	431	431	431	431	431	431

NOTES:

a. Data weighted.
b. Figures in the subtotal row may not be exact sums due to rounding off.

Table 3.4   Descriptive Statistics: Related Variables

Item Number	Comparison Group					Nascent Entrepreneurs				
Variable	n (%)	Min	Max	Mean	SD	n (%)	Min	Max	Mean	SD
Q357_MT	426	30	1116	484.92	178.92	785	0.37	888	443.17	151.78
Q358 Yes No	147 122(28.2) 25(5.8)	1	2	1.17	0.38	308 250(30.1) 8(7.0)	1	2	1.19	0.39
Q358a	25					58				
Q358b Yes No	25 20(4.6) 5(1.2)	1	2	1.20	0.41	58 39(4.7) 19(2.2)	1	2	1.32	0.47
Q358c	82					103				
Q358c_2	8					0				
Q360 Yes No	427 369(85.6) 58(13.4)	1	2	1.14	0.34	815 709(85.4) 107(12.8)	1	2	1.13	0.34
Q360a	56					107				
Q361 Yes No	431 378(87.7) 53(12.3)	1	2	1.13	0.39	830 728(87.7) 90(10.8)	1	2	1.22	1.00
Q361a	53					90				

NOTE: Data weighted.

Conclusion and Future Research

Early uses of the PSESD data set for Black and Hispanic entrepreneurship resulted in a proposal to extend theory relating to organizational emergence through a consideration of teleological and dialectical motors as useful for integrating the individual and group levels of analysis that are so relevant to studies of minority entrepreneurship (Greene, Carter, & Reynolds, 2003). Building on such studies, the PSED data set has significant potential to expand our understanding of the entre-preneurial behaviors of Black and Hispanic nascent entrepreneurs.

The early findings that prompted the NSF proposal showed that Blacks and Hispanics were undertaking efforts to start businesses at a rate that far exceeded that of Whites but that more operating businesses were owned by Whites. The assumption is that Black and Hispanic nascent entrepreneurs must be falling out of the process somewhere before the business is actually opened. The longitudinal nature of the PSED data set provides the opportunity to identify such "falling out" points. The knowledge that may emerge from the theoretical frameworks and empirical analyses also has great potential to aid practitioners. Understanding when and why people chose to end their entrepreneurial activities prior to even starting a business can inform educational and training curriculums in order to more closely target the actual points of pain. This identification can lead to a business emergence process with a more successful outcome.

The theoretical frameworks described in this chapter offer guidance in investigating differences in entrepreneurial behaviors between the racial and ethnic groups but perhaps more important in focusing upon different paths and outcomes of the business creation process.

References

Aldrich, H. E., & Waldinger R. (1990). Ethnicity and entrepreneurship. *Annual Review of Sociology, 16,* 111–135.

Aldrich, H. E., & Zimmer, C. (1986). Entrepreneurship through social networks. In D. L. Sexton & R. W. Smilor (Eds.), *The art and science of entrepreneurship* (pp. 3–20). Chicago: Upstart.

Auster, E. R. (1988). The impact of owner and organizational characteristics of Black and White-owned businesses on firm profitability and survival. *American Journal of Economics and Sociology, 47*(3), 331–344.

Bates, T. (1993). *Banking on black business.* Washington, DC: Joint Center for Political and Economic Studies.

Bates, T. (1994). An analysis of Korean-immigrant-owned small-business start-ups with comparisons to African-American and nonminority-owned firms. *Urban Affairs Quarterly, 30*(23), 227–248.

Bates, T. (1997). *Race, self-employment, and upward mobility: An illusive American dream.* Baltimore: Johns Hopkins University Press.

Bates, T., & Bradford, W. (1979). *Financing black economic development.* New York: Academic Press.

Biggart, N. W., Castanias, R. P., II, & Davis, P. R. (1994). *Institutional foundations of rotating savings and credit associations.* Paper presented at the annual meeting of the American Sociological Association, Los Angeles, CA.

Blalock, H. M., Jr. (1967). *Toward a theory of minority group relations.* New York: John Wiley.

Bonacich, E., & Modell, J. (1980). *The economic basis of ethnic solidarity: Small business in the Japanese-American community.* Berkeley: University of California Press.

Boston, T. D. (1994). *Black entrepreneurship and economic development: A case study of Atlanta.* Paper presented at the meeting of the Association for the Study of Afro-American Life and History. Atlanta: Georgia Institute of Technology, Department of Economics.

Butler, J. S. (1991). *Entrepreneurship and self-help among Black Americans: A reconsideration of race and economics.* Albany, NY: SUNY Press.

Butler, J. S., & Greene, P. G. (1997). Ethnic entrepreneurship: The continuous rebirth of American enterprise. In D. L. Sexton & R. W. Smilor (Eds.), *Entrepreneurship 2000* (pp. 267–289). Chicago, IL: Upstart.

Chaganti, R., & Greene, P. G. (2002). Who are ethnic entrepreneurs? A study of entrepreneur's ethnic involvement and business characteristics. *Journal of Small Business Management, 40*(2), 126–143.

DeCarlo, J. F., & Lyons, P. R. (1979). A comparison of selected personal characteristics of minority and nonminority female entrepreneurs. *Journal of Small Business Management, 17,* 222–229.

Enz, C., Dollinger, M., & Daily, C. (1990). The value orientations of minority and non-minority small business owners. *Entrepreneurship Theory and Practice, 15,* 23–35.

Fairlie, R. W., & Meyer, B. D. (1996). Ethnic and racial self-employment differences and possible explanations. *Journal of Human Resources, 4,* 757–793.

Feldman, H. D., Koberg, C. S., & Dean, T. J. (1991). Minority small business owners and their paths to ownership. *Journal of Small Business Management, 29,* 12–27.

Gomolka, E. (1997). Characteristics of minority entrepreneurs and small business enterprises. *American Journal of Small Business, 2*(1), 12–21.

Greene, P. G. (1997). A call for conceptual clarity. Comments on Bates: Why are firms owned by Asian immigrants lagging behind black-owned businesses? *National Journal of Sociology, 10*(2), 49–55.

Greene, P. G., & Butler, J. S. (1996). The minority community as a natural business incubator. *Journal of Business Research, 36,* 51–58.

Greene, P. G., Carter, N. M., & Reynolds, P. D. (2003). Minority entrepreneurship: Trends and explanations. In C. Steyaert & D. Hjorth (Eds.), *New movements in entrepreneurship.* London: Edward Elgar.

Greene, P. G., Carter, N. M., Reynolds, P. D., Aldrich, H., & Stearns, T. (1999). *The influence of founder's race in the start-up process.* Proposal to the National Science Foundation Grant SBR-9905255.

Greene, P. G., & Chaganti, R. (2003). Levels of resources for ethnic entrepreneurs. In C. H. Stiles (Ed.), *Structure and process* (International Research in the Business Discipline, Vol. 4, pp. 59–74). New York: Elsevier Science.

Hisrich, R. D., & Brush, C. (1986). Characteristics of the minority entrepreneur. *Journal of Small Business Management, 24,* 1–8.

Katz, J., & Gartner, W. (1988). Properties of emerging organizations. *Academy of Management Review 13,* 429–441.

Lerner, M. (1994, June). *Immigrant entrepreneurial enclaves: The case of Russian immigrants in Israel.* Paper presented at the 14th annual meeting of the Babson Entrepreneurship Research Conference [Wellesley, MA].

Light, I. H. (1972). *Ethnic enterprise in America: Business welfare among Chinese, Japanese and Blacks.* Berkeley: University of California Press.

Light, I. H., Bhachu, P., & Karageorgis, S. (1993). Migration networks and immigrant entrepreneurship. In G. DeJong & R. W. Gardner (Eds.), *Immigration and entrepreneurship: Culture, capital, and ethnic networks.* New Brunswick, NJ: Transaction.

Light, I., & Bonacich, E. (1988). *Immigrant entrepreneurs: Koreans in Los Angeles.* Los Angeles: University of California Press.

Pierce, J. A. [Original work published 1947] (1996). *Negro business and business education.* NY: Plenum.

Portes, A., & Bach, R. (1985). *Latin journey: Cuban and Mexican immigrants in the United States.* Berkeley and Los Angeles: University of California Press.

Reynolds, P. D., & White, S. B. (1997). Entrepreneurial processes and outcomes: The influence of ethnicity. In P. D. Reynolds & S. B. White (Eds.), *The entrepreneurial process: Economic growth, men, women, and minorities.* (pp. 179–204). Westport, CT: Quorum Books.

Simmel, G. (1950). The stranger. In K. Wolf (Ed.), *The sociology of Georg Simmel.* Glencoe, IL: Free Press.

Sombart, W. (1914). *The Jews and modern capitalism.* New Brunswick, NJ: Transaction.

Tenenbaum, S. (1993). *A credit to their community.* Detroit, MI: Wayne State University Press.

U.S. Bureau of the Census. (1992). *Characteristics of business owners.* Washington, DC: Government Printing Office.

U.S. Small Business Administration, Office of Advocacy. (1996). *The state of small business: A report of the President.* Washington, DC: Government Printing Office.

U.S. Small Business Administration, Office of Advocacy. (1997). *Economic census. Survey of minority-owned business enterprises.* Washington, DC: Government Printing Office.

U.S. Small Business Administration, Office of Advocacy. (2002). *Minorities in business, 2001.* Washington, DC: Government Printing Office.

Van Delft, H., Gorter, C., & Nijkamp, P. (1999). *In search of ethnic entrepreneurship opportunities in the city.* (Working Paper 99-059/3). Rotterdam, The Netherlands: Tinbergen Institute.

Waldinger, R., Aldrich, H., Ward, R., & Associates. (1990). *Ethnic entrepreneurs.* Newbury Park, CA: Sage.

Walker, J. E. K. (Ed.). (1998). *Encyclopedia of African American business history.* Westport, CT: Greenwood.

Weber, M. (1930). *The Protestant ethic and the spirit of capitalism.* New York: Scribner.

Zhou, M. (1992). *Chinatown: The socioeconomic potential of an urban enclave.* Philadelphia: Temple University Press.

CHAPTER 4

Household Structure

Candida G. Brush

Tatiana S. Manolova

Household structure is a broader unit of analysis than family structure. Members living in a household may or may not be family members but typically are part of a nuclear or extended family. Household structure has an impact on venture creation because it is a direct determinant of the starting resource base for the entrepreneur. Every entrepreneur begins with an idea and personal resource endowment (e.g., education, experience, contacts, capital) that is the building block for launching the venture (Brush, Greene, & Hart, 2001). During the nascent stages of organizational formation, personal resources are transformed into the venture's resources. In this process, the initial resource endowments coming from the entrepreneur's family and household structure can influence the venture's resource base.

Household structure involves three main concepts: potential start-up capital (Bhide, 2000), social desirability and encouragement of entrepreneurial endeavors (Shapero & Sokol, 1982), and household commitments (Nieva, 1985). Each of these will be discussed briefly below.

Literature Review

Start-up Capital

Income and earnings accrued by a household are frequently a source of start-up capital for a new entrepreneurial venture. Research shows that one of the most common sources of start-up capital is the family (Wetzel, 1982). There is wide variation across households in their potential to provide funding, depending on the demographics of the household members (age, education, employment) and the gender of the household head, as well as race and ethnicity. Although the vast majority of founders do not have significant personal means (wealthy families and/or friends), hundreds of thousands of businesses are launched every year on minimal capital (Bhide, 2000; *The State of Small Business*, 1995). It is estimated that 30% of the more than 800,000 companies started each year are founded with less than $5,000, and only one third had more than $50,000 (Bhide, 2000). In many cases, the funds used for launching the venture are borrowed from family and friends (Van Osnabrugge & Robinson, 2000).

Composition of the household in terms of children, retirees, and ages of household members also affects the potential for family start-up capital. For instance, recent data from the Current Population Survey shows that in households without children, retirement (i.e., pension, social security, or survivor's benefits) was the source, following earnings, that provided the highest average percentage of income for the household (Swanson, 1995). On the other hand, patterns of asset accumulation and investment in businesses vary by social strata where wealthy individuals tend to maintain and pass their wealth on to their children, and the middle class tends to have more limited savings and higher consumption (Sherraden, 1991; Bhide, 2000).

Potential sources of start-up capital may vary depending on race/ethnicity of the household. For instance, dependent adult children were more common in Asian households than in those of other race/ethnicity groups. Among Asian households, the same percentage (22%) had dependent adult children as had contributing adult children. All other groups were more likely to have contributing than dependent adult children in the household (Swanson, 1995). Similarly, ethnic and cultural values can affect propensity to accumulate money either for intergenerational transfer of wealth, investment in assets, or potential new ventures (Sherraden, 1991). The vast majority of ethnic and immigrant entrepreneurs utilize personal savings and money from family members (Butler & Greene, 1997).

Gender of the head of household may influence the start-up capital potential of a household. According to the March 1993 Current Population Survey sample, 35% of female-headed family households had 1992 income below their poverty threshold, compared to 6% of married-couple family households. Seventeen percent of these female-headed families had income that fell below 50% of the poverty threshold, compared to 2% of married-couple families (Swanson, 1995). A recent report by the U.S. Small Business Administration notes that 52% of female-headed households earned less than $25,000 per year compared with only 27% of male-headed households (*Women in Business*, 2001). Research shows that pursuit of personal income or an aim of additional resources to improve family living standards can be motivations for women's entrepreneurship (Ducheneaut, 1997; Hisrich & Brush, 1986).

Social Desirability and Encouragement

Family members' perceptions of desirability and credibility of the venture may serve to encourage or discourage an entrepreneur in his/her venture creation process (Shapero & Sokol, 1982). The family, particularly the mother or father, plays a powerful role in influencing perceptions of desirability of entrepreneurial action for individuals. If someone close to the entrepreneur perceives a venture as unfeasible, or undesirable, this may influence the entrepreneur's propensity to start a business, cause doubts, or slow the process down. Encouragement or desirability may be reflected in various forms of support from household or family members such as information, emotional support, or labor (Butler & Greene, 1997; Shapero & Sokol, 1982). Research shows that family members provide emotional support and often business guidance (Renzulli, Aldrich, & Moody, 2000).

On the other hand, family dynamics can affect social learning and resultant attitudes toward independence and achievement, which are associated with entrepreneurial behavior (Kets de Vries, 1977). For instance, psychoanalytical models propose that entrepreneurship may result from fear, insecurity, need for control, or guilt having childhood origins from positive or negative influences of parents (Bird, 1989).

Types of encouragement and social desirability for founders and their business choices may vary depending on ethnic groups; for instance, Greek, Portuguese, or Asian immigrants typically employ family or household members in their new restaurants or food businesses to help them learn the family trade (Shapero & Sokol, 1982). Ethnic entrepreneurs as a group may experience different barriers to capitalizing on market opportunities, and, as a result, they may be able to mobilize resources more readily because of the support from their household members (Reynolds, 1991).

The extent to which women may be encouraged to start ventures is strongly influenced by cultural context. Assumptions about masculinity and femininity in work responsibilities have been widely studied cross-nationally (Hofstede, 1991). In feminine societies, women have less resistance to overcome in order to reach positions of responsibility (e.g., top decision maker, successful entrepreneur); whereas while in masculine societies both men and women may learn to be more competitive (Ducheneaut, 1997).

Expectations about the appropriateness of certain jobs or sectors of involvement for women can be influenced by perceptions of household members. For instance, some industries are perceived as traditionally male (e.g., mining, manufacturing) and therefore may not be supported as entrepreneurial choices for women (Aldrich, 1989). If these perceptions are strongly held, this can impact the self-efficacy of the woman entrepreneur (Anna, Chandler, Jansen, & Mero, 2000).

A related concept is that of role models. Social learning theory has linked parental role models and a preference for entrepreneurship (Bandura, 1977). Social learning can occur through observation of the behavior of others, often referred to as role models. An individual's socialization process usually occurs in family or household settings, and through this process, norms, aspirations, or career preferences may be modeled (Bandura, 1977). A number of studies show that entrepreneurs have a high percentage of parents (father or mother) who also were entrepreneurs (Brockhaus, 1982; Cooper & Gimeno-Gascon, 1992; Hisrich & Brush, 1986). This suggests that family members who have role models within their households who are entrepreneurs might perceive entrepreneurship as a more feasible career. Yet, empirical work is inconclusive, one study showing no significant relationship between parental background and venture survival (Cooper, Dunkleberg, & Woo, 1988) and another showing that entrepreneurial parents were associated with greater sales (Duchesneau & Gartner, 1988).

Within family and household structures, the influence of role models on women may vary. Studies from France and Great Britain show that women entrepreneurs in 66% and 40% of the cases, respectively, had at least one close family member (parent, sibling, relative) running his/her own business (Ducheneaut, 1997). On the other hand, women may be limited by role stereotypes within families in which their mothers are expected to fulfill traditional homemaker and nurturing roles (Nieva, 1985). In these cases, entrepreneurship as a career option may be less attractive to women.

Household Commitments

Within each household, there are commitments for which members are responsible. These may involve child or elder care, household maintenance, cleaning, meal preparation, or a variety of other tasks. For a single head of household, the burden of household commitments may be significant if there are many people in the household, potentially affecting the amount of time an entrepreneur may devote to his/her business. Historically, women's tasks involved being a homemaker and caretaker, but over the past three decades, significant political, social, and economic changes have created opportunities and given women greater acceptance as entrepreneurs (Brush, 1997). Yet, research shows that even though married couples share decisions about major purchases and child rearing, the physical care of children of women entrepreneurs continues to be their responsibility (Nieva, 1985; Brush, 1997). Research also shows that women do twice as much housework and that husbands are likely to do housework only when the woman is unavailable (White, Cox, & Cooper, 1992). The result is that women often combine entrepreneurial endeavors with household activities and mothering, which can sometimes lengthen start-up processes or influence business performance, create role conflict or overload, and affect personal career satisfaction (Brush, 1997; White et al., 1992). Alternatively, the combined demands of work and mothering may affect the type of business started, industrial sector choice, business location, or the work/family balance involved in entrepreneurship (Ducheneaut, 1997). Further, role stereotypes and sex segregation may negatively affect women's chances of starting businesses because women are sometimes expected to adapt to their husband's career needs (Aldrich, 1989).

In sum, the structure of the entrepreneur's household will directly influence the starting endowments and resource-building process of the new venture. Household structure is comprised of four major elements: potential start-up capital (Bhide, 2000), social desirability and encouragement of entrepreneurial endeavors (Shapero & Sokol, 1982), and household commitments (Nieva, 1985).

The Household Structure Variables

Seven items from the phone survey (items 380–384a and item 385 in the PSED data set) represent the household structure and marital status items. These items include the marital status; age of household members and gender, which reflects aspects of household commitment; and household earnings, which reflects potential start-up capital. These six items are intended to be used as single items and appear on pp. 297–298 of the PSED Codebook. In addition, items 379a and 379c from the PSED data set represent the social encouragement items. These items are intended to be used as single items as they appear on pp. 296–297 of the PSED Codebook.

The six items representing household structure (items 380–384a) were asked in the following manner: for both groups of respondents (nascent entrepreneurs and control group), the items were preceded by the following stem: "Now I have some questions about the people you live with." The response categories were self-reported. In addition, Question 385 asked the respondents how they could best describe their marital status. The interviewer asked them to choose among the following categories: never married, living with a partner, married, separated, divorced, widowed, or other.

For both groups of respondents (nascent entrepreneurs and control group), the two items representing social encouragement were preceded by the following question: "Have your family, relatives, or other close friends been encouraging you to, or discouraging you from, starting a business of your own?" In case of encouragement, the interviewer proceeded to Question 379a, asking the respondent to describem the degree of encouragement. Both groups responded on a 5-point Likert-type scale: 1 = very weak, 2 = weak, 3 = neither weak/strong, 4 = strong, 5 = very strong. In case of *discouragement,* the interviewer proceeded to Question 379c, asking the respondent to describe the degree of discouragement. Both groups responded on a 5-point Likert-type scale: 1 = very weak, 2 = weak, 3 = neither weak/strong, 4 = strong, 5 = very strong.

The exact wordings for the seven items representing household structure and marital status, as well as the two items representing social encouragement, are listed in Table 4.1.

An Analysis of the Household Structure Variables

As mentioned earlier, the items in this section of the PSED were developed on the basis of prior research. The analyses were performed on the reduced PSED data set, which includes 446 nascent entrepreneurs from the original sample, 223 nascent entrepreneur women from a National Science Foundation oversample, and 223 respondents from a comparison group. As the data on the minority oversample were not made available at the time of performing this analysis, the only oversampling included in the present data set is the oversampling for women. The usable sample was reduced by the requirement that respondent gender be consistently recorded across all stages of data collection. Following the classification scheme developed by Shaver, Carter, Gartner, and Reynolds (2001), we included in the

Table 4.1   The Seven Household Structure Items and the Two Social Encouragement Items in the PSED

Item Number	Question
Household Structure Items	
Q380	Now I have some questions about the people you live with. How many people live in your household, including yourself, all children, and all adults?
Q381	How many of these are less than 6 years old?
Q382	How many of these are 6 to 12 years old?
Q383	How many of these are 13 to 17 years old?
Q384	How many are 18 or older?
Q384a	How many of those 18 or older, including yourself, earned any money in the last year from salaries or wages?
Marital Status Items	
Q385	How would you best describe your current marital status or living arrangement–never married, living with a partner but not married, married, separated, divorced, widowed, or something else?
Social Encouragement Items	
Q379a	How would you describe the encouragement you received from family, relatives, or close friends, would you consider it very weak, weak, neither weak nor strong, strong, or very strong?
Q379c	How would you describe the discouragement you received from family, relatives, or close friends, would you consider it very weak, weak, neither weak nor strong, strong, or very strong?

sample used for the present study 574 fully autonomous nascent entrepreneurs who have not received a positive cash flow from their new businesses and 223 respondents in a control group, to a usable sample size of $N = 797$. Descriptive statistics for the household structure items are presented in Table 4.2. Descriptive statistics for the social encouragement items are presented in Table 4.3.

We next ran a series of t tests to reveal differences in respondent profiles, comparing nascent entrepreneur profile to the control group. The results are presented in Table 4.4.

Table 4.4 reveals some interesting parallels between the profiles of nascent entrepreneurs and the control group. While there appear to be no significant differences in the household structure of the two groups, there are significant differences in their marital status. Nascent entrepreneurs enjoyed both a significantly higher degree of social encouragement and a significantly lower degree of social discouragement. This supports early theoretical work suggesting that perceptions of desirability by family plays a powerful role in motivating action for an individual

Table 4.2   Descriptive Statistics: Household Structure and Marital Status Items

Variable	n	Min	Max	Mean	SD
Household Structure					
Total number of people in household, all ages	789	1.00	5.00	3.13	1.64
Total number of people less than 6 years old	672	0.00	7.00	0.40	0.80
Total number of people 6–12 years old	672	0.00	5.00	0.51	0.84
Total number of people 13–17 years old	672	0.00	5.00	0.37	0.67
Total number of people over 18 years old	672	1.00	8.00	2.22	0.79
Total number of people who earned income	789	0.00	8.00	1.70	0.90

Marital Status	Frequency	Percentage
Never married	127	15.9
Living with a partner but not married	73	9.2
Married	447	56.1
Separated	29	3.6
Divorced	93	11.7
Widowed	15	1.9
Other	6	.8

Table 4.3   Descriptive Statistics: Social Encouragement Items

Variable	n	Min	Max	Mean	SD
How much encouragement	557	1.00	5.00	3.97	0.82
How much discouragement	100	1.00	5.00	3.22	0.95

entrepreneur (Shapero & Sokol, 1982) and that a supportive home environment can be a crucial factor for an entrepreneur managing the stress and challenges of a start-up venture (Bird, 1989).

Findings to Date

Analysis of variance in respondent profiles by gender revealed several differences. Female respondents reported a significantly higher degree of social encouragement, as well as a lower degree of social discouragement (though the difference

Table 4.4   Descriptive Statistics: Household Structure and Social Encouragement by Nascent Entrepreneur Status (N = 797)

Variable	Nascent Entrepreneur				Comparison Control Group				t-test	df	p value
	n	Mean	SD	%	n	Mean	SD	%			
Household Structure											
Total number of people in household, all ages	566	3.18	1.71		223	2.99	1.44		1.46	787	0.144
Total number of people less than 6 years old	486	0.42	0.83		186	0.37	0.73		0.64	670	0.520
Total number of people 6–12 years old	486	0.53	0.87		186	0.46	0.76		0.97	670	0.333
Total number of people 13–17 years old	486	0.36	0.66		186	0.39	0.71		−0.38	670	0.704
Total number of people over 18 years old	486	2.24	0.82		186	2.16	0.70		1.25	670	0.211
Total number of people who earned income	567	1.75	0.91		222	1.58	0.86		2.44	787	0.150
Marital Status											
Never married	87			15.34	40			17.93			
Living with partner	57			10.05	16			7.17			
Married	332			58.55	115			51.57			
Separated	16			2.82	13			5.83			
Divorced	65			11.46	28			12.56			
Widowed	7			1.23	8			3.59			
Other	3			.52	3			1.34	$\chi^2 = 13.66$	1,6	.034
Social Encouragement											
How much encouragement	464	4.02	0.8		93	3.77	0.91		2.59	555	0.010
How much discouragement	77	3.12	0.93		23	3.57	0.95		−2.00	98	0.053

was marginally significant at $p < 0.074$). This finding is contrary to historical role expectations that women should manage the household and family, seek part-time employment, and pursue other less entrepreneurial endeavors (Smith, 2002). Female respondents also tended to represent families with a marginally larger number of household members between the ages of 13 and 17. There were marginally significant differences in the marital status between men and women in that a greater percentage of women were divorced (14% vs. 9.4%), whereas a slightly higher percentage of men were never married (18.5% vs. 13.76%).

Analysis of variance in respondent profiles by ethnicity revealed the following differences. Respondents other than Caucasian reported a significantly higher degree of social encouragement. This supports studies showing that ethnic and minority entrepreneurs gain strong social support from their family (Reynolds, 1991; Butler & Greene, 1997). These respondents also tended to come from families with a significantly higher number of family members below the age of 6. There were also significant differences in marital status by ethnic category.

Future research might consider the effects of household structure on the speed with which an entrepreneur is able to accomplish various start-up activities. The time commitment to family or household members might impact the planning or time frame within which an entrepreneur might launch a venture. Similarly, the household structure might impact the starting financial resources available to the entrepreneur. Encouragement/discouragement for entrepreneurial endeavors might similarly affect speed of start-up, or strategy and growth of the venture. Examination of the composition of household structure by gender, ethnicity, and marital status might similarly provide a better understanding of the similarities and differences across populations of entrepreneurs as they build their ventures.

References

Aldrich, H. (1989). Networking among women entrepreneurs. In O. Hagan, C. Rivchun, & D. Sexton (Eds.), *Women-owned businesses* (pp. 103–132). New York: Praeger.

Anna, A., Chandler, G., Jansen, E., & Mero, N. (2000). Women business owners in traditional and non-traditional industries. *Journal of Business Venturing, 15*(3), 279–303.

Bandura, A. (1977). *Social learning theory.* Englewood Cliffs, NJ: Prentice Hall.

Bhide, A. (2000). *The origin and evolution of new business.* New York: Oxford University Press.

Bird, B. J. (1989). *Entrepreneurial behavior.* Glenview, IL: Scott, Foresman.

Brockhaus, R. (1982). The psychology of the entrepreneur. In C. A. Kent, D. L. Sexton, & K. Vesper (Eds.), *The encyclopedia of entrepreneurship* (pp. 39–56). Englewood Cliffs, NJ: Prentice Hall.

Brush, C. G. (1997). Women-owned businesses: Obstacles and opportunities. *Journal of Developmental Entrepreneurship, 2*(1), 1–24.

Brush, C. G., Greene, P. G., & Hart, M. M. (2001). From initial idea to unique advantage: The entrepreneurial challenge of constructing a resource base. *Academy of Management Review, 15*(1), 64–78.

Butler, J., & Greene, P. G. (1997). Ethnic entrepreneurship: The continuous rebirth of American enterprise. In D. L. Sexton & R. Smilor (Eds.), *Entrepreneurship 2000* (pp. 267–289). Chicago, IL: Upstart.

Cooper, A. C., & Gimeno-Gascon, J. (1992). Processes of founding and new-firm performance. In D. L. Sexton & R. Smilor (Eds.), *Entrepreneurship 2000* (pp. 301–340). Chicago, IL: Upstart.

Cooper, A. C., Dunkleberg, W., & Woo, C. (1988). Survival and failure: A longitudinal study. In B. Kirchhoff, W. Long, W. E. McMullan, K. Vesper, & W. E. Wetzel, Jr. (Eds.), *Frontiers of entrepreneurship research* (pp. 225–237). Wellesley, MA: Babson College.

Ducheneaut, B. (1997, April). *Women entrepreneurs in SMEs.* Report prepared for the OECD Conference on Women's Entrepreneurship, Paris, France.

Duchesneau, D. A., & Gartner, W. (1988). A profile of new venture success and failure in an emerging industry. In B. Kirchhoff, W. Long, W. E. McMullan, K. Vesper, & W. E. Wetzel, Jr. (Eds.), *Frontiers of entrepreneurship research* (pp. 372–386). Wellesley, MA: Babson College.

Hisrich, R. D., & Brush, C. G. (1986). *The woman entrepreneur: Starting, managing and financing a successful new business.* Lexington, MA: Lexington Books.

Hofstede, G. (1991). *Cultures and organizations: Software of the mind.* New York: McGraw-Hill.

Kets de Vries, M. (1977). The entrepreneurial personality: A person at the crossroads. *Journal of Management Studies, 14*(2), 34–57.

Nieva, V. L. (1985). Work and family linkages. In L. Larwood, A. H. Stromberg, & B. Gutek (Eds.), *Women and work: An annual review* (pp. 162–190). Beverly Hills, CA: Sage.

Renzulli, L. A., Aldrich, H. E., & Moody, J. (2000). Family matters: Gender, networks and entrepreneurial outcomes. *Social Forces, 79*(2), 523–546.

Reynolds, P. D.· (1991). Sociology and entrepreneurship: Concepts and contributions. *Entrepreneurship Theory and Practice, 16*(2), 47–70.

Shaver, K. G., Carter, N. M., Gartner, W. B., & Reynolds, P. D. (2001, June). *Who is a nascent entrepreneur? Decision rules for identifying and selecting entrepreneurs in the Panel Study of Entrepreneurial Dynamics (PSED).* Paper presented at the 2001 Babson Kauffman Entrepreneurship Research Conference, Jönköping, Sweden.

Shapero, A., & Sokol, L. (1982). The social dimensions of entrepreneurship. In C. A. Kent, D. L. Sexton, & K. Vesper (Eds.), *The encyclopedia of entrepreneurship* (pp. 72–90). Englewood Cliffs, NJ: Prentice Hall.

Sherraden, M. (1991). *Assets and the poor.* Armonk, NY: Sharpe.

Smith, D. M. (2002). *Women at work: Leadership for the next century.* Upper Saddle River, NJ: Prentice Hall.

Swanson, L. (1995). *Family households.* Report presented at the Population Association of America. Retrieved October 1999 from www.cpc.unc.edu./pubs/paapapers/1995/ Swanson

The state of small business: A report of the President. (1995). Small Business Administration, Office of Advocacy, Washington, DC: Government Printing Office.

Van Osnabrugge, M., & Robinson, R. (2000). *Angel investing: Matching start-up funds with start-up companies.* San Francisco: Jossey Bass.

Wetzel, W. E., Jr. (1982). Risk capital research. In C. A. Kent, D. L. Sexton, & K. Vesper (Eds.), *The encyclopedia of entrepreneurship* (pp. 140–164). Englewood Cliffs, NJ: Prentice Hall.

White, B., Cox, C., & Cooper, C. (1992). *Women's career development: A study of high flyers.* Cambridge, MA: Blackwell.

Women in business. (2001). U.S. Small Business Administration, Office of Advocacy, Washington, DC: Government Printing Office.

CHAPTER 5

Household Income and Net Worth

Phillip H. Kim

Howard E. Aldrich

Lisa A. Keister

Entrepreneurship is central to the evolution of organizations, industries, and economies (Aldrich, 1999). Entrepreneurial activity encourages innovation, fosters job creation, and improves global competitiveness for firms, regions, and entire countries (Bednarzik, 2000). New business formation also shapes the nature of social and economic stratification in an economy, and it is a critical component of social mobility (Keister, 2000b). Organizations play an important role in distributing life chances and determining individuals' social standing and chances for upward mobility (Haveman & Cohen, 1994). Self-employment facilitates wealth accumulation, increases social contacts, and improves social and economic standing for entrepreneurs and their families (Bates, 1997; Fischer & Massey, 2000; Nee & Sanders, 1985). Many business owners, particularly those who create large firms, employ family members in their business ventures, and some pass on their businesses to their families, either during their lives or as part of an inheritance (Keister, 2000b). Successful entrepreneurs may also be able to expand their children's human capital, social connections, and occupational opportunities (Nee & Sanders, 1985).

Although entrepreneurship clearly has important social and economic consequences, we have few well-grounded empirical generalizations about the specific factors that lead to the creation of new businesses. One potentially important factor that has attracted little attention is household net worth. Wealth, or net worth, is the value of a household's assets less their liabilities. Like income, net worth is a measure of the financial resources available to the entrepreneur. Net worth, the total value of financial resources currently available, may be a more critical component of family finances than income, for a number of reasons. For instance, financial assets can be used directly as start-up capital or for later investment or indirectly for securing loans. In this chapter, we explain why household income and net worth variables are central to understanding entrepreneurship, and we explore briefly how the Panel Study of Entrepreneurial Dynamics (PSED) is uniquely designed to facilitate empirical study of this relationship.

The Importance of Income

Because accurate data on wages and salaries are widely available, income is perhaps the most commonly studied indicator of financial well-being. Several developments have made longitudinal data on income widely available: the advent of the income tax, increasingly comprehensive census data, and advances in survey data collection (Winnick, 1989, p. 160). Perhaps because income data has been fairly easy to obtain, entrepreneurship researchers have tended to focus on it.

In their study of survival prospects of new business ventures, Boden and Nucci (2000) described how individuals might weigh their participation in a start-up venture in terms of *opportunity costs* of their present income from employment. This opportunity cost approach clarifies the concept of utility that researchers use in their models to predict an individual's preference for pursuing self-employment (Blanchflower & Oswald, 1998). An entrepreneur makes two evaluations: prospects for additional income from a start-up relative to present income, as well as perceived future income from the current place of employment. At lower income levels, individuals may find that the opportunity cost is low enough to pursue the uncertainties of income from a new venture. For example, if a venture fails, an individual may be able to find wage employment elsewhere at a similar income level. Or, the projected minimal income stream from a new venture may be similar, in the short term, to an individual's current income stream. In such cases, an individual would pursue a new venture, given a higher projected long-term income stream.

However, in higher income brackets, individuals may find that the prospective gains from an entrepreneurial venture are outweighed by the loss of present and future income from their current place of employment. Furthermore, future employment prospects associated with their present occupation may be perceived more favorably than the uncertain outcome from an entrepreneurial venture. Individuals at higher income levels may perceive income streams from wage and salary employment to be more predictable and thus be reluctant to pursue a start-up venture.

In another argument for a potential negative association between income and the likelihood of becoming an entrepreneur, Evans and Leighton (1989) argued that low-wage workers are forced to pursue self-employment when they are excluded from the traditional wage labor market. Such "necessity entrepreneurship" can be contrasted with "opportunity based entrepreneurship," which would occur independently of someone's current income level (Reynolds, Camp, Bygrave, Autio, & Hay, 2001). To the extent that opportunity-based entrepreneurship dominates over necessity-based entrepreneurship, the association between income and becoming an entrepreneur will weaken.

The Importance of Net Worth

Using income alone to indicate the financial well-being of families would be adequate if income and wealth were highly correlated. However, the correlation between the two indicators is relatively low. Estimates from survey data suggest that the correlation between income and wealth is about 0.50 and that much of this already weak correlation is attributable to the inclusion of asset income (income generated by wealth) in the definition of total income. When asset income is removed from total income, the correlation between income and net worth drops to below 0.30 (Keister, 2000b). This suggests that using income alone captures only part of a household's financial picture.

There are several reasons why wealth and income are not more highly correlated. Many of the truly wealthy have rather low earnings because they are able to support current consumption with income derived from assets (Wolff, 1995). In addition, retired persons often have low incomes but substantial net worth because their wealth continues to accumulate after retirement even though earnings have ceased (Radner, 1989b). Racial differences in savings and asset accumulation also account for some of the weak correlation between wealth and income (Brimmer, 1988). In fact, many families, particularly non-White families, have zero or negative net worth regardless of income (Radner, 1989a; Winnick, 1989). For these reasons, many families found to be below the poverty line based solely on current income may be living quite comfortably on assets acquired during more prosperous years. Likewise, those with incomes above the poverty line may, in reality, have considerable debt and few assets, making them vulnerable if current income were to be reduced or to cease entirely. Hence, current income may be a poor indicator of true financial stability (Wolff, 1990).

Moreover, wealth has important advantages beyond those associated with income. Wealth provides current use value (as in the ownership of a home), generates more wealth when it is invested, provides a buffer during financial emergencies, and can be passed to future generations. Wealth provides its owners with political power, educational and occupational opportunities, and social advantages that accumulate within and across generations (Keister & Deeb-Sossa, 2000).

Access to assets is not evenly distributed. Between the 1960s and the 1990s, the total wealth owned by American households as homes, other real estate, stocks, and other financial assets (converted into 2000 dollars using the CPI) increased from about $7.8 trillion to more than $23.5 trillion (Keister, 2000b). Between 1989 and 1998, median household net worth increased more than 20%, and the number of billionaires in the Forbes 400 rose from 85 to 267 (Kennickell, 2000). In that period of an overall increase in wealth, the proportion of net worth owned by the top 1% of wealth owners rose from 30% to more than 34%, while the proportion of net worth owned by those in the bottom 90% declined from 33% to just over 30% (Keister & Moller, 2000). This difference might not seem particularly large, but enormous changes in wealth ownership at the household level are necessary to produce small distributional changes. When mediating factors such as race are considered, inequality in wealth ownership is even more severe (Keister, 2000a).

Net Worth and Entrepreneurship

For an entrepreneur, household net worth may be particularly critical. Assets can be used as start-up capital for entrepreneurs who want to start a business. Household assets can also provide a financial safety net during the transition to business ownership or during financial crises that occur later in the life of the business. Accumulated wealth also sends a positive signal to external parties, such as creditors, potentially enabling an entrepreneur to secure additional capital for start-up in the early stages of entrepreneurship or later expansion.

Although we might expect a strong positive relationship between household net worth and entrepreneurship, previous research on the effect of financial capital on new business formation has generated mixed results. Some researchers argued that financial capital is critical for entrepreneurship and that liquidity constraints inhibit start-ups (Bates, 1997; Dunn & Holtz-Eakin, 2000; Evans & Jovanovic, 1989). They reasoned that business start-ups often require a substantial sum of money in order to buy the necessary equipment and supplies. This perspective emphasizes that equity, particularly from family wealth holdings, allows entrepreneurs to obtain credit, and those with little personal wealth simply cannot secure necessary start-up capital. Thus, those with high net worth, high income, and home ownership are expected to be more likely than others to become self-employed (Evans & Leighton, 1989; Fischer & Massey, 2000). In support of this viewpoint, research has shown that obtaining money from an inheritance increases the likelihood of self-employment (Holtz-Eakin, Joulfaian, & Rosen, 1994).

Personal savings are often the key to funding new businesses. Financing through bank loans or investors can be difficult and disadvantageous for the small business owner for many reasons. For those with little or no wealth, financing through institutional loans can exact a high price in the long term. Because small businesses are higher-risk clients for potential financiers, lenders often compensate by increasing the financial costs associated with the loans, making this a less appealing path to gaining business capital in comparison to personal savings. In addition to the high costs of using financiers, small businesses also incur the cost of identifying potential financiers and undergoing bonding activities to ensure firm legitimacy. Furthermore, there is also evidence from research on home-based businesses, which comprise a large proportion of all new businesses, that few were eligible for bank loans (Jurik, 1998).

Researchers who disagree with the emphasis on financial capital argue that too much importance has been placed on the availability of monetary assets. These researchers contend that many entrepreneurs require little or no capital to begin forming a new business (Aldrich, 1999). Data from a 1992 survey show that the majority of business owners started their firms with less than $5,000 (U.S. Bureau of the Census, 1992). Others have shown that personal wealth is not a major factor in new business ownership (Aldrich, Renzulli, & Langton, 1998). Home-based businesses, for instance, which accounted for half of all new businesses in 1992, often require little capital up front.

Furthermore, small business owners can often find ways around capital constraints. Many small business owners use financial "boot-strapping" methods to decrease capital needs in the start-up phase (Freear, Sohl, & Wetzel, 1995). These methods include relatives working below market salary, using owners' personal credit cards for business expenses, borrowing from relatives, withholding owners' salaries, taking on freelance assignments from other businesses, and leasing equipment rather than buying it (Winberg & Landstrom, 2000). New business owners may be forced to start out by relying exclusively on their own and their relatives' resources (Aldrich & Waldinger, 1990).

Human capital, that is investments in skills and knowledge that boost earning power, has been proposed as a more important influence on business formation than income and wealth. Education, training, and workplace experience are the most common indicators of human capital used in labor force participation analyses, and these traits have been associated with the success of entrepreneurs (Bates, 1997; Evans & Leighton, 1989). Human capital clearly shapes entrepreneurial activity and success, but the degree to which human capital versus financial capital matters is still an open question.

Income and Net Worth Questions on the PSED

The PSED is uniquely designed to assess the role that household income and net worth play in entrepreneurship. PSED respondents were asked a series of questions designed to determine their household income and net worth. For both series of questions, respondents had the opportunity to provide an exact value. If the respondent refused, the interviewer asked a series of questions to narrow the range of possible values. In the following sections, we describe the nature of the survey questions, the methodology used to code the responses, response rates, and descriptive statistics for the recoded household income and wealth variables. We based our analysis on 1,225 cases, which is a subset of the full data set of 1,261 cases in Wave 1. Thirty-six cases were omitted due to various selection criteria that qualified a respondent as a nascent entrepreneur and due to missing information in other variables. Additional information on selection rules can be found in Shaver, Carter, Gartner, and Reynolds (2001).

Income Questions

Household income included all sources of income such as work, government benefits, and pension before taxes in the previous year. Because data collection took place at different times for different subsamples, these figures were relative figures rather than absolute figures for a specific year. Complete question wording is presented in Table 5.1. Respondents were first asked Q386 to obtain an exact report, and if necessary, taken through the sequence of categorical income questions. The initial question for this categorical sequence (Q386a) was "Is your household's annual

Table 5.1   Household Income Questions (Q386 to Q386m)

Item Number	Question
Exact Report	
Q386	What was your total household income from all sources and before taxes last year? Be sure to include income from work, government benefits, pensions, and all other sources.
Categorical Reports	
Q386a	Question stem: Then, would you tell me, is your household's total annual income, before taxes, over . . . $50,000 per year?
Q386b	$30,000 per year?
Q386c	$10,000 per year?
Q386d	$5,000 per year?
Q386e	$20,000 per year?
Q386f	$40,000 per year?
Q386g	$80,000 per year?
Q386h	$60,000 per year?
Q386i	$100,000 per year?
Q386j	$200,000 per year?
Q386k	$150,000 per year?
Q386m	$500,000 per year?

income, before taxes, over $50,000 per year?" Depending on the response, branching questions were then asked to channel respondents into one of two question series to determine a more precise range above or below $50,000.

To create a continuous household income measure, we took the following steps. For all respondents that did not provide an exact report, we examined their responses to the series of categorical questions (Q386a to Q386m). When a valid range could be determined (e.g., $20,000 to $40,000), we coded the value at the midpoint of the range. When respondents did not complete the sequence of categorical questions, we employed the following rules. When a range could be determined (i.e., a definite lower and upper bound), we again coded the value at the midpoint of the range. We assumed the lower bound could not be lower than zero. When an upper bound could not be determined, we coded the case to missing. Respondents who reported household income of greater than $500,000 per year were also coded to missing, since no other categorical question could be used to determine an upper bound. When no categorical information was provided, cases were coded to missing. After following these procedures, we achieved complete income data on 96% of the cases, as shown in Table 5.2.

Table 5.2   Coding Distribution: Household Income

Household Income Responses	Cases	Percentage
From single report (Q386)	1089	88.9
Code midpoint ($0–$50,000)	57	4.7
Code midpoint ($50–$80,000)	18	1.5
Code midpoint ($80–$100,000)	4	0.3
Code midpoint ($100–$200,000)	7	0.6
Missing (No Information)	40	3.3
Missing (Partial Information)	10	0.8
Total	1225	100.0

Net Worth Questions

The PSED asked respondents for details about their components of wealth (real and financial assets) to get a more accurate picture of the household's financial circumstances and to allow researchers to explore variations in the effects of the components of net worth on entrepreneurship. The PSED questions on net worth were modeled after questions on the Survey of Consumer Finances, an authoritative data source on household net worth collected by the Federal Reserve Board. In Table 5.3, we present the questions in the net worth module of the PSED.

Table 5.3   Household Net Worth Items in the PSED

Item Number	Question
Wealth Components Measures	
Q387a	What would be the current value of this home if it were sold today?
Q387b	If there are mortgages or land contracts on this home, land, apartment, or property, how much is still owed after the most recent payments were made? (Interviewer Probe: Do not include home equity loans or lines of credit.)
Q388	It would also be useful to know the total value of any tangible assets owned by the household, other than the primary residence. Please include all those things owned by the husband, wife, or household partner, or jointly. What would be the total current value of any other real estate, cars or other vehicles, such as boats or recreational vehicles, home furnishings, jewelry, and the like? Do not include savings and investments.
Q389	An estimate of all of the household's savings and investments would also be useful. What would be the current value of stocks, bonds, mutual funds, savings accounts, checking accounts, retirement accounts, non-incorporated business assets, and the like? (Interviewer Probe: Include all those owned either by the husband or wife, or jointly.)
Q390	Next, it would be useful to have an estimate of all the other debts or land contracts for the household, not including the first mortgage on the primary residence. What is the current value of all loans outstanding, such as mortgages on other property, home equity loans, automobile loans, credit card loans, education loans, and the like? Again, please include all debts for which either the husband or the wife are responsible.
Single Report	
Q391	What do you think is the current net worth of the household? This is the total value of what you have—physical property and all investments and checking accounts—minus what you owe—all mortgages, home equity loans, car loans, and the like—all those things owned or money owed separately, or jointly, by the husband and wife.
Categorical Reports	
Q391a	Would you consider the total household net worth to be more than $1,000,000? Again, include any assets or debts shared with a spouse or household partner.
Q391b	Is your total household net worth over $500,000?
Q391c	Is it over $750,000?
Q391d	Is it over $250,000?
Q391e	Is it over $100,000?
Q391f	Is your total household net worth over $5,000,000?
Q391g	Is it over $2,500,000?

Respondents were asked to provide their household net worth using three separate approaches. First, respondents responded to questions for each wealth component (Q387 to Q390). To determine the value of real (tangible) assets owned, respondents were asked whether they owned their own home (Q387), the value of the home if owned (Q387a), and the value of other tangible assets such as other real estate, cars, and home furnishings (Q388). To determine equity in these assets, respondents were asked the value of mortgages (Q387b), debts, and land contracts on these assets (Q390). To determine the value of financial assets, respondents were also asked the value of their savings and investments (Q389). By subtracting all liabilities (i.e., mortgage and other liabilities) from all assets (i.e., home value, savings and investments, and other assets), we created the *calculated wealth value*. Second, respondents supplied an estimate of the total current value of the household's net worth (Q391). We refer to this value as the *single wealth report*. Third, if respondents refused to give a single wealth report, they were asked a series of categorical questions that allowed them select a range for their total current household wealth (Q391a to Q391g). We refer to this value as the *categorical wealth report*.

Among the three approaches, we prefer the calculated wealth value over the other two approaches and recommend it to other investigators. We believe respondents would be more accurate in providing values for individual components rather than estimating the single wealth report. Respondents may not have accounted for or been aware of all components in calculating net worth when providing the single report or categorical information. Using the calculated wealth value approach allowed us to determine the magnitude of negative net worth, which was not captured in the single wealth report. For nearly three quarters of the cases, we utilized the calculated wealth value for the respondent's household wealth. Respondents in the cases provided complete information for all wealth components.

For the remaining cases with partially complete component information, we devised a set of complex decision rules to estimate the household wealth value in order to maximize the use of all available information. We assigned these cases to nine categories based on the combinations of missing component information. Our guiding principle still remained that respondents were more accurate in reporting wealth component information than the two other wealth estimation approaches. Thus, for each category, rules were developed for three different conditions where the single wealth and categorical wealth reports could supplement the calculated wealth value based on the available component information.

For the majority of the decision rules, we approached the estimation of the household wealth value using the *principle of midpoints*. We attempted to determine the lower and upper bounds of a range for the calculated wealth by making assumptions of how missing component information, if available, would change our estimated wealth value. Calculated wealth values with missing asset information could only increase, because an asset contributes positively to the total wealth value. In this case, the calculated wealth value would be a *lower bound*. Similarly, calculated wealth values with missing liability information gave us an *upper bound*, because a liability would be subtracted from the total wealth value, if it were known. If we were able to determine both lower and upper bounds using all information available, we took the midpoint as the assigned value. However, in some cases, only one bound could be established. To maximize the useful information obtained in these cases, we created two household wealth variables, based on conservative and aggressive estimations. For our conservative household wealth estimate, we coded the single-bounded cases as missing. However, for the aggressive estimation variable, we assigned cases the value of the bound that was calculated and an indicator variable to signify a lower or upper bound. For the remaining cases, where the bounds were not in dispute, the conservative and aggressive wealth variables were equal.

Two other scenarios relied on the principle of midpoints for cases using missing mortgage information. For cases missing mortgage information, we assumed that home equity was positive and the value of the missing mortgage would be no greater than the reported home value. As a result, under certain circumstances, we took one half of the value of the home as the midpoint in order to estimate home equity. For cases relying on the categorical wealth report, we determined the midpoint based on the ranges provided by the respondent. However, due to the question-sequencing pattern, the application of the principle of midpoints became more complicated for a small number of cases. The categorical sequence started with the respondent answering if household wealth was greater than $1 million. If the respondent answered this question, but then refused to provide additional information in the sequence, a range could not be determined and the rules on conservative/aggressive estimation applied. The omission of a question presented another complexity. The categorical sequence ended with a question of whether household wealth was less than $100,000. However, from this question, we do not know if household wealth was negative, and thus without any additional information, a lower bound could not be established.

In Figure 5.1, we diagram the decision steps used to apply the various principles we have described. After applying these decision rules, we assigned a wealth value for 88% of cases using the conservative approach and 96% of cases using the aggressive estimation approach. In Table 5.4, we show the distribution of cases in each calculated wealth category.

In Table 5.5, we provide descriptive statistics for the household income and wealth variables. The correlation between the raw household wealth variable and our calculated wealth variables (conservative and aggressive) ranges from approximately 0.72 to 0.80. The raw household wealth variable (HHNETW) is available for 968 cases and was constructed by the Survey Research Center at the University of Michigan. Although the two forms of the wealth variable correlate positively, using our proposed coding methodology allows researchers to utilize additional cases that would otherwise be considered missing. We thus recommend using our constructed wealth variable, rather than the variable in the data set. Detailed coding algorithms for using our rules are available from the authors.

(**A**) Complete Component Information
- Preferred methods of assigning wealth value
- 895 cases (73%)

(**B**) Missing Component Information Categories
- One or more wealth component items missing
- Incorporate other available information
- 330 cases (27%)

| I | II | III |
| Single Wealth Report | Categorical Wealth Report | Missing Both Single and Categorical Wealth Reports |

- Missing assets
- Missing liability
- Missing assets, missing liability
- Missing mortgage
- Missing mortgage, missing assets
- Missing mortgage, missing liability
- Missing mortgage, missing assets, missing liability
- Missing home equity, missing assets
- Missing home equity, missing assets, missing liability

- Different decision rules apply to each combination of missing component information category

- After applying decision rules, two approaches to dealing with missing cases

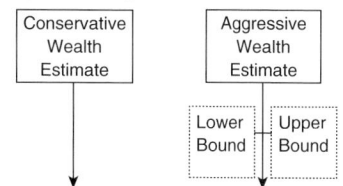

| Conservative Wealth Estimate | Aggressive Wealth Estimate |

| Lower Bound | Upper Bound |

- Principle of midpoints applies
- 148 missing cases (12% of total cases)

- When only one of the two bounds can be ascertained
- 47 missing cases (4% of total cases)

Figure 5.1 Decision Rules for Assigning Wealth Value

Table 5.4 Coding Distribution: Household Wealth

Household Wealth Responses	Cases	Percentage
Complete component information	895	73.1
Missing assets	140	11.4
Missing liability	13	1.1
Missing assets, missing liability	70	5.7
Missing mortgage	19	1.6
Missing mortgage, missing assets	20	1.6
Missing mortgage, missing liability	5	0.4
Missing mortgage, missing assets, missing liability	23	1.9
Missing home equity, missing assets	16	1.3
Missing home equity, missing assets, missing liability	24	2.0
Total	1225	100.0

Table 5.5 Descriptive Statistics: Household Income and Wealth Variables

	Mean	Median	S.D.	S.E.	Correlations with Original Wealth Variable (HHNETW)
Household Income	$54,364	$45,000	$44,450	$2,410	
Nascent Entrepreneurs	$58,062	$45,000	$70,231	$2,364	
Comparison Group	$54,131	$45,000	$42,327	$2,561	
Household Wealth					
Conservative	$208,737	$87,000	$490,177	$28,613	0.773
Nascent Entrepreneurs	$234,235	$60,000	$768,803	$31,205	0.721
Comparison Group	$207,104	$87,000	$467,111	$30,410	0.799
Aggressive	$196,780	$80,200	$470,311	$26,213	0.774
Nascent Entrepreneurs	$224,895	$60,000	$742,863	$29,043	0.716
Comparison Group	$195,016	$82,000	$448,044	$27,824	0.800

NOTE: These statistics have been calculated using survey weights—explanation on weighting methodology can be found in Appendix B of this book.

References

Aldrich, H. (1999). *Organizations evolving.* Thousand Oaks, CA: Sage.

Aldrich, H., Renzulli, L. A., & Langton, N. (1998). Passing on privilege: Resources provided by self-employed parents to their self-employed children. In K. Leicht (Ed.), *Research in stratification and mobility* (Vol. 16, pp. 291–317). Greenwich, CT: JAI.

Aldrich, H. E., & Waldinger, R. (1990). Ethnicity and entrepreneurship. *Annual Review of Sociology, 16,* 111–135.

Bates, T. M. (1997). *Race, self-employment, and upward mobility : An illusive American dream.* Baltimore, MD: Johns Hopkins University Press.

Bednarzik, R. W. (2000). The role of entrepreneurship in U.S. and European job growth. *Monthly Labor Review, 123*(7), 3–16.

Blanchflower, D. G., & Oswald, A. J. (1998). What makes an entrepreneur? *Journal of Labor Economics, 16*(1), 26–60.

Boden, R. J., & Nucci, A. R. (2000). On the survival prospects of men's and women's new business ventures. *Journal of Business Venturing, 15*(4), 347–362.

Brimmer, A. F. (1988). Income, wealth, and investment behavior in the Black community. *American Economic Review, 78,* 151–155.

Dunn, T., & Holtz-Eakin, D. (2000). Financial capital, human capital, and the transition to self-employment: Evidence from intergenerational links. *Journal of Labor Economics, 18*(2), 282–305.

Evans, D. S., & Jovanovic, B. (1989). An estimated model of entrepreneurial choice under liquidity constraints. *Journal of Political Economy, 97*(4), 808–827.

Evans, D. S., & Leighton, L. S. (1989). Some empirical aspects of entrepreneurship. *The American Economic Review, 79*(3), 519–535.

Fischer, M., & Massey, D. (2000). Residential segregation and ethnic enterprise in U.S. metropolitan areas. *Social Problems, 47*, 410–424.

Freear, J., Sohl, J. E., & Wetzel, W. E. (1995, April 9–13). *Who bankrolls software entrepreneurs?* Paper presented at the 15th Annual Babson Entrepreneurship Research Conference, London, UK.

Haveman, H. A., & Cohen, L. E. (1994). The ecological dynamics of careers: The impact of organizational founding, dissolution, and merger on job mobility. *American Journal of Sociology, 100*(1), 104–152.

Holtz-Eakin, D., Joulfaian, D., & Rosen, H. S. (1994). Sticking it out: Entrepreneurial survival and liquidity constraints. *Journal of Political Economy, 102*(1), 53–75.

Jurik, N. C. (1998). Getting away and getting by: The experiences of self-employed home-workers. *Work and Occupations, 25*, 7–35.

Keister, L. A. (2000a). Race and wealth inequality: The impact of racial differences in asset ownership on the distribution of household wealth. *Social Science Research, 29*, 477–502.

Keister, L. A. (2000b). *Wealth in America: Trends in wealth inequality.* Cambridge, UK: Cambridge University Press.

Keister, L. A., & Deeb-Sossa, N. (2000). Are baby boomers richer than their parents? Intergenerational patterns of wealth ownership in the U.S. *Journal of Marriage and the Family, 62*, 569–579.

Keister, L. A., & Moller, S. (2000). Wealth inequality in the United States. *Annual Review of Sociology, 26*, 63–81.

Kennickell, A. B. (2000). *An examination of changes in the distribution of wealth from 1989–1998: Evidence from the Survey of Consumer Finances.* Washington, DC: Federal Reserve Board.

Nee, V. G., & Sanders, J. M. (1985). The road to parity: Determinants of the socioeconomic achievements of Asian Americans. *Ethnic and Racial Studies, 8*, 75–93.

Radner, D. B. (1989a). Net worth and financial assets of age groups in 1984. *Social Security Bulletin, 52*, 2–15.

Radner, D. B. (1989b). The wealth of the aged and non-aged. In R. Lipsey & H. S. Tice (Eds.), *The measurement of saving, investment, and wealth* (pp. 645–684). Chicago: University of Chicago Press.

Reynolds, P. D., Camp, S. M., Bygrave, W. D., Autio, E., & Hay, M. (2001). *Global entrepreneurship monitor: 2001 executive report.* Kansas City, MO: Kauffman Center for Entrepreneurial Leadership.

Shaver, K. G., Carter, N. M., Gartner, W. B., & Reynolds, P. D. (2001, June). *Who is a nascent entrepreneur? Decision rules for identifying and selecting entrepreneurs in the Panel Study of Entrepreneurial Dynamics (PSED).* Paper presented at the Babson Kauffman Entrepreneurship Research Conference, Jönköping, Sweden.

U.S. Bureau of the Census, U. S. (1992). *Economic Census.* Washington, DC: Government Printing Office.

Winberg, J., & Landstrom, H. (2000). Financial bootstrapping in small businesses: Examining managers' resource acquisition behaviors. *Journal of Business Venturing, 16*, 235–254.

Winnick, A. J. (1989). *Toward two societies: The changing distributions of income and wealth in the U.S. since 1960.* New York: Praeger.

Wolff, E. N. (1990). Wealth holdings and poverty status in the U.S. *Review of Income and Wealth, 36*, 143–165.

Wolff, E. N. (1995). The rich get increasingly richer: Latest data on household wealth during the 1980s. In R. E. Ratcliff, M. L. Oliver, & T. M. Shapiro (Eds.), *Research in politics and society* (Vol. 5, pp. 33–68). Greenwich, CT: JAI.

CHAPTER 6

Labor Force Participation and Residential Tenure

Paul D. Reynolds

> *Immigrants bring innovative ideas and entrepreneurial spirit to the United States, . . .*
>
> Griswald, 2003, p. 632

> *The disadvantage theory which views entrepreneurs as misfits cast off from wage work is consistent with many of our findings.*
>
> Evans & Leighton, 1989, p. 532

Two "facts" about entrepreneurship persist with considerable tenacity:

- Most businesses are started by immigrants, and
- Most of those starting businesses are unemployed.

Much of the research related to these issues has used existing government data. But governments do not have precise data on those involved in the firm start-up process. Reliable data on the annual number of U.S. new firm births—the final transition from the start-up process—has only recently been available (Robb, 2000). Much population-based research related to these two issues—unemployment and entrepreneurship and immigrants and entrepreneurship—has been based on reports of self-employment. But self-employment is generally developed to identify those working on their own account rather than for an established business; it does not identify those in the firm start-up process.

The major technical contribution of the PSED research program has been the development of a more precise indicator of those involved in a business start-up—individuals actively involved in the entrepreneurial process. The PSED data can be used to explore these issues—the impact of labor force activity or the immigration status of individuals—only if measures of these variables are included in the PSED data collection program. For this reason such measures are included. After a review of selected issues and alternative measures of "self-employment," the PSED measures of labor force activity and immigration status will be discussed in more detail.

Unemployed and Entrepreneurship

If one starts with the assumption that starting a new business is onerous, risky, and unlikely to be rewarding, then it is reasonable to assume that only those that are desperate and unable to find a "good job" will pursue entrepreneurship. Successful, talented, and motivated individuals will seek, find, and retain employment. Since most people have jobs, locating those that are not working could be an expensive, time-consuming, and complicated process. Better to use existing data sets for which the investment in time and energy to develop a representative sample has already been made. A wide range of studies of entrepreneurship has taken this strategy. These have included time-series models (Blau, 1987), analysis of longitudinal data files (Carroll & Mosakowski, 1987; Evans & Leighton, 1989), and cross-national comparisons (Acs, Audretsch, & Evans, 1994; Blanchflower, 2000). But these analyses, as well as many others, focus on reported self-employment as the indicator of entrepreneurial activity. The value of this indicator as a reflection of new firm creation or participation in the entrepreneurial process is, at best, unclear, and at its worst, it may be misleading.

Immigrants and Entrepreneurship

All over the world, immigrants are more likely to participate in new business creation than the native born population (Light & Isralowitz, 1997; Portes, 1995; Waldinger, Aldrich, Ward, & Associates, 1990). Sociologists, in particular, have been active in the study of how new groups of immigrants adapt to a new society, often by specializing in particular industries or types of firms (Reynolds, 1991). This has included both attention to internal migration—the rural to urban migration taking place all over the world—and cross-national or international migration. New arrivals in the cities from rural areas or other countries and a strong presence of immigrants in highly visible sectors—Korean grocers in Los Angeles, immigrants from everywhere acting as self-employed taxi drivers in New York City and Washington, Indian and Pakistani convenience store operators in the U.K.—often leads to the impression that immigrants are a major source of new firm creation.

While there is little doubt that higher rates of self-employment and firm creation may occur among individual ethnic groups, particularly when they are immigrants, attempts to provide a more precise description of "immigrant entrepreneurship" often leads to analysis of large-scale national government data sets. The advantage of the scope of coverage is offset by the lack of a precise measure of entrepreneurial activity; reported self-employment is usually adopted as an indicator of entrepreneurship. An assessment based on 1980 U.S. census data considered the "ancestry" of individuals and their rates of self-employment (Fratoe, 1986); but specific data on whether or not an individual was considered part of a minority or even born outside the United States was not available. A more recent version has used a combination of U.S. Decennial Census data and Current Population Survey data for 1960 to 1990 (Camarota, 2000). Country of birth was available to determine which individuals were born in the United States. Rates of self-employment were highest among those born outside the United States through 1980 but have equaled the native born in 1990 and 2000.

The co-mingling of immigration and minority status was most prevalent in a widely cited study of Chinese- and Indian-born scientists and engineers working in the high-technology sectors of Silicon Valley (Saxenian, 1999). In this assessment, it was found that a substantial proportion, over 25%, of new high-technology firms in Silicon Valley were implemented by ethnic Chinese or Indians. (This was inferred from the presence of Chinese or Indian names as the chief operating officers of firms listed in a commercial credit rating database.) One implication is that immigrants are more likely to be "entrepreneurial." However, in personal interviews many of these immigrant founders claimed they started their firms because of a perception that promotion opportunities within their current firms were blocked— a "glass ceiling" effect. The same empirical pattern is reported elsewhere in this handbook (Appendix C) with regards to highly educated Black and Hispanic men; those with graduate training are several times more likely to be involved in new firm creation than White men with equivalent educational attainment. A similar pattern, though in reduced form, is found among highly educated White women; again, a "glass ceiling" effect is one major explanation for the difference.

This general pattern among United States minorities would suggest that minority status rather than immigration into the United States may have been a dominant factor leading highly educated Chinese and Indian employees to start new firms in Silicon Valley. Of course, the highly supportive milieu may have made this career option more attractive.

U.S. Government Measures of Self-Employment

Two examples of how the U.S. government assesses self-employment should illustrate the problems with using these measures as indicators of entrepreneurship.

U.S. Decennial Census

Every 10 years, the U.S. census is implemented to provide a complete enumeration of the entire U.S. population. The basic objective is to develop a count of the total population and where they reside. In order to gather more precise details about individuals and their lives, a special "long form" interview schedule is provided to a randomly selected 5% of the households. The items in the one-in-twenty interview form related to labor force activity are presented in Exhibit 6.1. This is the most complete and precise enumeration of labor force activity developed for the U.S. population.

There are several critical features of the interview format. For example, the instructions associated with item 27 make it clear that no citizens should attempt to report more than one work activity. If they are engaged in more than one activity, they are to select that one to which they devote the most hours. Second, if people are working on their own account, item 29 makes it clear that they should report the work in terms of whether or not the business entity is incorporated or not incorporated. Presumably those working for a partnership would report that they are working for a private, for-profit company, even if they are one of the partners owning the company.

Most critical, of course, is that there are absolutely no options that would allow people to report they are actively involved in the creation of a new business. Even if this effort took up the largest proportion of the time in each week—the most hours—there is no way to report this effort. Self-employment (incorporate or not) may be the best match, but that is not a clear or obvious response if one is working with a team to put a new firm in place. This problem will be more critical when one person in the household is reporting the work force behavior for all the others, as is the case for the U.S. Census long form. They may not be fully aware of all the work initiatives of all those in the household.

Exhibit 6.1   U.S. Census: Year 2000 Long Form Labor Force Activity Items

---

27. Industry or Employer — Describe clearly this person's chief job activity or business last week. If this person had more than one job, describe the one at which this person worked the most hours. If this person had no job or business last week, give the information for his/her last job or business since 1955.
     a. For whom did this person work?
     b. What kind of business or industry was this?
     c. Is this mainly — Manufacturing? Wholesale trade? Retail trade? Other?

28. Occupation
     a. What kind of work was this person doing?
     b. What were this person's most important activities or duties?

29. Was this person—MARK ONE BOX.
     o Employee of a PRIVATE FOR-PROFIT company or business or of an individual, for wages, salary, or commissions
     o Employee of a PRIVATE NOT-FOR-PROFIT tax-exempt, or charitable organization
     o Local GOVERNMENT employee (city, county, etc.)
     o State GOVERNMENT employee
     o Federal GOVERNMENT employee
     o SELF-EMPLOYED in own NOT INCORPORTED business, professional practice, or farm
     o SELF-EMPLOYED in own INCORPORATED business, professional practice, or farm
     o Working WITHOUT PAY in family business or farm

SOURCE: www.census.gov/dmd/www/pdf/d02p.pdf

Current Population Survey

The monthly Current Population Survey (CPS) is one of the oldest ongoing surveys of the U.S. population and is the source of the monthly estimates of U.S. unemployment. Every month, 50,000 citizens 16 years or older are interviewed during the week that includes the twelfth day of the month. The sample rotates, with a household included for 4 months, out for 8 months, and included for another 4 months. Household response rates approach 95%. The latest and most sophisticated procedures are used to draw the sample, complete the interviews, and develop weights to ensure that the sample represents the entire U.S. population. This monthly data is used as the benchmark to calibrate most of the commercial, marketing, or scientific surveys in the United States, including the screening surveys completed for the PSED respondents (Appendix B).

A critical emphasis for the CPS is the level of unemployment, so each respondent is carefully questioned about his or her participation in the labor force. A summary of the interview procedure is presented in Exhibit 6.2. The very first item is related to whether or not the "household" has a farm or business. If the answer is "No," then other questions ask about work activity. If the answer is "Yes," other questions ask about other work activities. Other items determine how many jobs a person had at the same time.

Great care is taken to determine if a person would be considered "employed."

> Employed persons are those who, during the reference week (a) did any work at all (for at least 1 hour) as paid employees; worked in their own businesses, professions, or on their own farms; or worked 15 hours or more as unpaid workers in an enterprise operated by a family member or (b) were not working, but who had a job or business from which they were temporarily absent . . .
>
> U.S. Department of Commerce, 2002, p. 5–3.

Self-employed persons are those that meet a very narrow definition:

> Self-employed persons are those who work for profit or fees in their own businesses, professions, trades, or farms. Only the unincorporated self-employed are included in the self-employed category since those whose businesses are incorporated technically are wage and salary workers because they are paid employees of a corporation.
>
> U.S. Department of Commerce, 2002, p. 5–4

Hence, a person working alone that has formally incorporated his or her business would not be considered self-employed but a worker for a corporation; the fact that the person is the sole owner of the corporation is irrelevant. It is not clear how two or more persons that have formed a legal partnership would be treated in this classification scheme.

Even more conservative is the classification of individuals pursing more than one form of self-employment.

The . . . information for individuals' second jobs is collected in order to obtain a more accurate measure of multiple jobholders . . .

. . . individuals who are self-employed unincorporated on both of their jobs are not considered multiple jobholders.

U.S. Department of Commerce, 2002, p. 5–4

So a person with one thriving business entity in which he or she is the sole employee (giving private lessons on the trumpet) that engages in a second business activity (translating German into English) is not considered a multiple job holder.

Exhibit 6.2   *Current Population Survey* Interview Procedure: Employed and Unemployed

---

1. Does anyone in this household have a business or a farm?

2. LAST WEEK, did you do ANY WORK for (either) pay (or profit)?

   [Parenthetical filled in if there is a business or farm in the household. If 1 is "yes" and 2 is "no," ask 3. If 1 is "no" and 2 is "no," ask 4.]

3. LAST WEEK, did you do any unpaid work in the family business or farm?

   [If 2 and 3 are both "no," ask 4.]

4. LAST WEEK, (in addition to the business) did you have a job, either full or part time? Include any job from which you were temporarily absent.

   [Parenthetical filled in if there is a business or farm in the household. If 4 is "no," ask 5.]

5. LAST WEEK, were you on layoff from a job?

   [If 5 is "yes," ask 6. If 5 is "no," ask 8.]

6. Has your employer given you a date to return to work?

   [If "no," ask 7.]

7. Have you been given any indication that you will be recalled to work within the next 6 months?

   [If "no," ask 8.]

8. Have you been doing anything to find work during the last 4 weeks?

   [If "yes," ask 9.]

9. What are all the things you have done to find work during the last 4 weeks?

   [Individuals are classified as <u>employed</u> if they say "yes" to questions 2, 3 (and work 15 hours or more in the reference week or receive profits from the business/farm), or 4.

   Individuals who are available to work are classified as <u>unemployed</u> if they say "yes" to 5 and either 6 or 7, or if they say "yes" to 8 and provide a job search method that could have brought them into contact with a potential employer in 9.]

SOURCE: U.S. Department of Commerce. (2002). *Current Population Survey*, (Figure 5-1, pp. 5-6).

Bureau of Labor Statistics National Longitudinal Surveys

This research program was initiated in 1966 to explore the process by which young adults manage the "transition to work" and older workers manage the "transition out of work" (www.bls.gov/nls/nlsview.htm). As the major sponsor is the U.S. Department of Labor, Bureau of Labor Statistics, the major focus is on employment experiences, not the formation of new businesses. As a consequence, the labor force activity emphasizes reported self-employment. One assessment of "entrepreneurship" utilizing the 1996 Young Men cohort (initially interviewed at ages 14–24 and then followed for 15 years) employed several adjustments to ensure that those reporting self-employment were involved in some relevant activity. This was done by checking to determine if a corporation had been formed or any self-employment income was reported for the same period (Evans & Leighton, 1989, p. 521). On the other hand, the current procedure used to determine nonjob labor force activity with these surveys is identical to that used in the Current Population Survey, discussed above. While this permits a close comparison of the results of these two federally sponsored data collection efforts, it indicates that neither effort provides much useful information about individuals creating new businesses.

Panel Study of Income Dynamics (PSID)

Implemented in 1966 as part of the research side of the War on Poverty, this project began with a representative sample of 5,000 U.S. families that were to be tracked on an annual basis to determine the temporal patterns of household economic well-being—to determine, for example, if a substantial proportion of households remained in "poverty" year after year. In order to assess household economic status, careful records were developed of all income and expenses for each household. These households were tracked annually from 1966 through 1997 (30 years) and biannually since 1999. Whereas a major methodological complexity has been tracking the composition and actual existence of households (as people are born, divorce, move out, move in, and die), the data sets now provide the capacity to track individuals over their life span (Williams & Katz, 2000; www.isr.umich.edu/src/psid).

But once again, the major focus has been on regular employment. One item included in the interview schedules for all years asks if each worker in the household is self-employed, has a job, or both. Details about these two types of work activity are then obtained, but for most years the details on self-employment are sparse. It is possible to determine that over their work career half of all U.S. men report some period of self-employment, even though the percentage in any one year is in the 10% range (Reynolds & White, 1997).

Nevertheless, the major focus is on sources of household income and there are limited details on efforts to implement a new business.

Commentary

The purpose of this assessment has been to focus on the type of individual and activity that is encompassed by the concept "self-employed"—those individuals considered "entrepreneurs" in many large-scale studies, studies exploring the relationship between labor force participation or immigration status and entrepreneurial activity. By excluding those who work for a legal entity (corporations, for sure, and perhaps partnerships), almost all of those new businesses that may be team efforts, dealing with a complex business model or requiring substantial resources (which may begin as partnerships or corporations), will not be involved.

It is hard to imagine a "work activity definition" that could be farther removed from the concept of entrepreneurship or new firm creation. It would be no surprise if the empirical patterns that emerged seemed strange or misleading. For example, it may be appropriate to consider those that are classified as "self-employed" as "misfits cast off from wage work," but it is hard to consider this a description of those engaged in creating new businesses (Evans & Leighton, 1989).

Entrepreneurial Activity: PSED Measure

The PSED definition of *nascent entrepreneur* is a person who is

- active in the start-up process,
- expects to own all or part of the firm, and
- has not had positive cash flow for over 3 months.

It is obvious that this reflects a quite different image of "business creation" than that reflected in the measures of "self-employment." Other than not working for an established business entity, there is little conceptual overlap between the two.

On the other hand, the relationships of labor force activity and immigration to entrepreneurial activity are worth serious attention. For this reason, measures of these independent variables were included in the PSED data collection effort.

Labor Force Activity: PSED Measures

Many surveys will use a question regarding labor force activity that asks a person to choose one activity from a standard list. The usual choices include full-time work, part-time work, self-employment (or own business), homemaker, student, retired, disabled, or unemployed. The research program of which the PSED is a major component has repeatedly found that a large proportion of those involved in start-ups are also engaged in other labor force activities. In fact, many individuals will simultaneously be involved in several activities—a student with a full-time job, for example, or a homemaker with a part-time job. Asking respondents to pick one "major activity" precludes assessments of the complexity of their work lives

In order to capture all the possible "labor force activities" among the PSED respondents, they were asked the question in a different form, a form that allowed them to report simultaneous activities. Table 6.1 shows the section from the

Table 6.1   Items Related to Labor Force Activity

Q331	In terms of current work activity, are you involved in any of the following? First, are you working for others for pay? NO, go to Q332
Q331a	Are you working for others more than 35 hours per week or less than 35 hours per week?
Q332	Are you a small business owner or self-employed?
Q333	Are you managing a business owned by someone else, either as the senior executive or part of the senior management team?
Q334	Are you a homemaker? NO, go to Q335 YES, go to 334b
Q334b	How many hours per week do you spend on housekeeping and child care activities?
Q335	Have you ever retired?
Q336	Are you a student? NO, go to Q336b YES, go to 336a
Q336a	Are you a student more than 35 hours per week or less than 35 hours per week?
Q337	Are you disabled and unable to work?
Q338	Are you unemployed? NO, skip to next section
Q339	Are you presently seeking full-time work, part-time work, or are you not looking for work?

interview schedule related to labor force activities. The six major labor force activities (Q331, Q332, Q333, Q334, Q335, and Q336) are *all* provided to *all* respondents. The only exception relates to items about "disabled and unable to work" or being "unemployed." Those that reported some work activity—full- or part-time work, small business owner or self-employed, or managing a business owned by another (Q331, Q332, Q333)—were not asked questions about "not working" (Q337, Q338).

A comparison of the reported labor force activity of those identified as nascent entrepreneurs and the comparison group is presented in Table 6.2. In this case, the participation in the entrepreneurial process is determined, and then respondents are asked about a range of labor force activities. The analysis compares the proportion of nascent entrepreneur and comparison group members that report each type of activity. As they could report multiple activities, the column totals exceed 100%. The statistical significance is assessed separately for each type of activity.

Table 6.2   Descriptive Statistics: Labor Force Participation by Nascent Entrepreneurs and Comparison Group

Variable	Nascent Entrepreneurs	Comparison Group	Statistical Significance
Number of cases	830	431	
Full-time work	49.1%	54.8%	0.05
Part-time work	18.6%	16.3%	0.31
Manage business owned by others	16.2%	16.9%	0.75
Small business owner or self-employed	57.1%	24.3%	0.00
Homemaker, over 20 hours per week	23.0%	29.7%	0.01
Homemaker, under 20 hours per week	14.1%	20.9%	0.00
Retired	9.5%	17.4%	0.00
Student, over 35 hours per week	2.6%	3.8%	0.21
Student, under 35 hours per week	12.5%	12.2%	0.87
Disabled	0.8%	5.7%	0.00
Unemployed, looking for work	1.2%	2.2%	0.21
Unemployed, not looking for work	2.0%	12.1%	0.00

NOTE: A person may qualify for several different activities; column totals exceed 100%.

A large percentage of nascent entrepreneurs report other work activities—50% report full-time work and 20% part-time work. Among the nascent entrepreneurs, 57% report they are a small business owner or self-employed, but some respondents may have included the current start-up activity in responding to this item. A smaller percentage of nascent entrepreneurs report they are homemakers (37% compared to 50%); the percentage that are students is equal for the two groups, and a much smaller percentage of nascent entrepreneurs report they are disabled (1% vs. 6%) or unemployed (3% vs. 14%). In fact, only 3% of the nascent entrepreneurs consider themselves unemployed compared to 14% of the comparison group. So much for "misfits cast off from wage work."

Simultaneous participation in multiple work activities is explored by counting the number of respondents reporting any of four work activities, including full-time work; part-time work; business owner or self-employed; or manager of a business owned by others. The minimum would be zero and the maximum could be four, although no one reports more than three. The results are in Table 6.3a.

As there could be some confusion about the item related to self-employment and managing a business, which may refer either to the start-up emphasized in the detailed nascent entrepreneur interview or a separate activity, the assessment is

Table 6.3a   Descriptive Statistics: Multiple Work Activity by Nascent Entrepreneurs and Comparison Group

Variable	Nascent Entrepreneurs	Comparison Group	Statistical Significance
Number of cases	830	431	
Reporting no work activity	6.3%	18.7%	
Reporting 1 work activity	54.4%	54.8%	
Reporting 2 work activities	33.3%	22.4%	
Reporting 3 work activities	6.0%	4.2%	0.00
	100.0%	100.0%	

NOTE: Activities include full-time work; part-time work; business owner or self-employed, or manager of a business owned by others.

Table 6.3b   Descriptive Statistics: Multiple Work Activity by Nascent Entrepreneurs and Comparison Group (Current Business Owner Excluded)

Variable	Nascent Entrepreneurs	Comparison Group	Statistical Significance
Number of cases	830	431	
Reporting no work activity	30.9%	27.7%	
Reporting 1 work activity	55.5%	56.8%	
Reporting 2 work activities	13.6%	15.5%	0.42
	100.0%	100.0%	

NOTE: Activities include full-time work; part-time work; or manager of a business owned by others.

provided without this item, where the range of multiple work activity could be from none to three. The results are presented in Table 6.3b.

If the current firm management or self-employment is included (Table 6.3a), there is a major difference between the nascent entrepreneurs and the comparison group; the hascent entrepreneurs are more active, with 40% reporting two or more activities, compared to 27% for those in the comparison group. In contrast, the comparison group has 19% reporting no work, compared to 6% for the nascent entrepreneurs, clearly reflecting the students, disabled, retirees, and unemployed, which are more numerous in the comparison group.

However if the ambiguous item is omitted (Q332), there is virtually no difference between the nascent entrepreneurs and the comparison group. Table 6.3b indicates that about 7 in 10 in both groups report one or two distinct work roles. The remaining difference is that *all those* in the nascent entrepreneur group are engaged in developing a new business—in addition to the reported labor force activity, they are all starting a new firm.

These patterns make clear how busy nascent entrepreneurs can be, as 70% report some other work activity and 14%—1 in 7—report *two* other work activities. These work responsibilities are in addition to organizing the plans and resources for a new business. It also makes clear they are unlikely to report "unincorporated self-employment" when asked about their primary work activity in an interview.

Immigration and Residential Tenure: PSED Measures

The two most basic issues regarding a person's residential and immigration history are where they were born and how long they have lived in an area. The relevant items from the PSED phone interview schedule are presented in Table 6.4. For the purposes of efficiency, it starts with a question about the length of time the person has lived in their county, state, and the United States, followed by questions about their country of birth and their parents' countries of birth.

This sequence is used because one common response to "How long have you lived in your county/state/the United States?" is "all my life." If a person says this, it can be assumed they lived all their life in the next higher geographical unit and were born in the United States As a result, when this happens, the computerized procedure skips immediately to questions about the parents' country of birth. Residential tenure is then computed to equal the age of the respondent at the time of the interview.

The nascent entrepreneurs and the comparison group are compared on the major variables in Table 6.5. The top part reflects a measure of immigration status based on their country of birth, their parents' country of birth, and whether or not foreign-born respondents have become U.S. citizens. There is no statistically significant difference between the nascent entrepreneurs and the comparison group in terms of immigration background. Among the nascent entrepreneurs, 93% are U.S.-born as are 94% of the comparison group.

As for residential tenure, there are some statistically significant differences, but this is mainly due to longer residential tenures associated with the comparison group. A larger proportion of the comparison group has lived "all my life" in the county, state, or the United States. Among the nascent entrepreneurs, 75% have lived in their county for 4 or more years, 85% in their state for 4 or more years; and 98% in the United States for 4 or more years. Clearly, the large majority of nascent entrepreneurs are established citizens in the region where they implement new firms. These findings are consistent with prior assessments in this research program (Reynolds & White, 1997).

To explore the relationship between immigration background and ethnicity, all the respondents in the sample—nascent entrepreneurs and comparison group—are combined for a preliminary assessment. The result is shown in Table 6.5. It

Table 6.4   Residential Tenure and Immigration Items in the PSED

Q353	What county do you live in?
Q353a	How long have you been living in the same county?
Q354	How long have you been living in the same state?
Q357	How long have you been living in the United States?
Q358	Were you born in the United States? If NO, Q358a In what country were you born? Q358b Are you a citizen of the United States?
Q360	Was your father born in the United States? If NO, Q360a In what country was your father born?
Q361	Was your mother born in the United States? If NO,
Q361a	In what country was your mother born?

Table 6.5   Descriptive Statistics: Immigration and Residential Tenure

Variable	Nascent Entrepreneurs	Comparison Group	Statistical Significance
Number of cases	818	431	
U.S.-born, both parents U.S.-born	88.2%	87.6%	
U.S.-born, one parent U.S.-born	0.8%	1.5%	
U.S.-born, neither parent U.S.-born	3.9%	5.2%	
U.S. immigrant, U.S. citizen	4.8%	4.6%	
U.S. immigrant, not a U.S. citizen	2.3%	1.2%	0.41
	100.0%	100.0%	
Lived in county up to 1 year	8.3%	6.2%	
Lived in county 1 to 4 years	17.7%	14.9%	
Lived in county 4 to 10 years	20.9%	18.4%	
Lived in county 10 to 30 years	36.8%	33.6%	
Lived in county 30 or more years	16.3%	26.8%	0.00
	100.0%	100.0%	
Lived in state up to 1 year	4.1%	1.5%	
Lived in state 1 to 4 years	9.6%	8.3%	

Lived in state 4–10 years	14.9%	12.2%	
Lived in state 10–30 years	40.0%	34.3%	
Lived in state 30 or more years	31.5%	41.7%	0.00
	100.0%	100.0%	
Lived in U.S. up to 1 year	1.1%	0.0%	
Lived in U.S. 1–4 years	0.8%	0.9%	
Lived in U.S. 4–10 years	2.5%	1.0%	
Lived in U.S. 10–30 years	39.5%	24.0%	
Lived in U.S. 30 or more years	66.1%	74.0%	0.00
	100.0%	100.0%	

NOTE: Percentages may not total exactly to 100% due to rounding to one decimal place.

should be kept in mind that half of both samples were developed from screenings to select Black and Hispanic respondents. This overall sample is not representative of the U.S. population.

Nonetheless, the results are quite striking. Among White and Black respondents, over 95% were born in the United States and 98% or more are U.S. citizens. Among Hispanics, 75% were born in the United States and 15% are naturalized citizens; a total of 91% are U.S. citizens. The "other" category includes a combination of American Indians (almost all born in the United States) and Asians from a range of countries (almost none born in the United States). The heterogeneity within the "other" group is quite striking. This assessment, however, suggests that the "immigration status" index is consistent with most expectations.

Table 6.5   Frequency Distributions: Immigration Status and Ethnic Background

Variable	White	Black	Hispanic	Other
Number of cases	870	187	111	73
U.S.-born, both parents U.S.-born	93.8%	93.4%	49.8%	63.6%
U.S.-born, one parent U.S.-born	1.3%	0.2%	1.6%	0.0%
U.S.-born, neither parent U.S.-born	1.9%	0.9%	24.1%	10.8%
U.S. immigrant, U.S. citizen	2.5%	3.8%	15.2%	18.7%
U.S. immigrant, not a U.S. citizen	0.6%	1.7%	9.3%	6.9%
	100.0%	100.0%	100.0%	100.0%

NOTE: Percentages may not total exactly to 100% due to rounding to one decimal place.

Commentary

A persuasive case can be made that much of the research that uses existing government data source records of "self-employment" as an indicator of entrepreneurial behavior is not just inappropriate but can produce misleading results. A data file with hundreds of thousands of cases is of little value if the appropriate indicators are not included.

The PSED uses an improved measure of participating in new firm creation and, in order to explore the effects of labor force status and immigration on entrepreneurial behavior, included these variables in the data from a representative sample of nascent entrepreneurs and a comparison group.

The preliminary analysis indicates that most of those involved in U.S. business start-ups are very much involved in other labor force activities (less than 1 in 30 is unemployed). Further, most starting new firms are not only U.S.-born but have lived in their county and state for a substantial time before entering the start-up process.

References

Acs, Z. J., Audretsch, D. B., & Evans, D. S. (1994). *The determinants of variation in the self-employment rates across countries and over time.* Unpublished manuscript.

Blanchflower, D. G. (2000). Self-employment in OECD countries. *Labour Economics, 7,* 471–505.

Blau, D. M. (1987). A time-series analysis of self-employment in the United States. *Journal of Political Economy, 95*(3), 445–467.

Camarota, S. A. (2000). *Reconsidering immigrant entrepreneurship: An examination of self-employment among natives and the foreign-born.* Washington, DC: Center for Immigration Studies.

Carroll, G. R., & Mosakowski, E. (1987). The career dynamics of self-employment. *Administrative Science Quarterly, 32,* 570–589.

Evans, D. S. & Leighton, L. S. (1989). Some empirical aspects of entrepreneurship. *American Economic Review, 79*(3), 519–535.

Fratoe, F. (1986). A sociological analysis of minority businesses. *Review of Black Political Economy, 15*(2), 5–30.

Griswald, D. T. (2003). Immigration. In E. H. Crane & D. Boaz (Eds.). *Cato handbook for Congress: 108th* (Chap. 63). Washington, DC: Cato Institute.

Light, I. & Isralowitz, R. E. (Eds.). (1997). *Immigrant entrepreneurs and immigrant absorption in the United States and Israel.* Aldershot, UK: Ashgate.

Portes, A. (Ed.). (1995). *The economic sociology of immigration: Essays on networks, ethnicity, and entrepreneurship.* New York: Russell Sage.

Reynolds, P. D. (1991). Sociology and entrepreneurship: Concepts and contributions. *Entrepreneurship: Theory and Practice, 16*(2), 47–70.

Reynolds, P. D. & White, S. B. (1997). *The entrepreneurial process: Economic growth, men, women, and minorities.* Westport, CT: Quorum Books.

Robb, A. (2000). New data for dynamic analysis: The longitudinal establishment and enterprise microdata (LEEM) file. In J. Katz (Ed.), *Advances in entrepreneurship, firm emergence, and growth: Vol. 4. Databases for the study of entrepreneurship* (pp. 51–144). Greenwich, CT: JAI.

Saxenian, A. L. (1999). *Silicon Valley's new immigrant entrepreneurs.* San Francisco: Public Policy Institute of California.

U.S. Department of Commerce, Economics and Statistics Administration. (2002, March). *Current population survey: Design and methodology.* Technical Paper 63RV. Available: www.bls.census.gov/cps/tp/tp63/htm

Waldinger, R., Aldrich, H., Ward, R., & Associates. (1990). *Ethnic entrepreneurs: Immigrant business in industrial societies.* Newbury Park, CA: Sage.

Williams, P., & Katz, J. (2000). Panel Study of Income Dynamics—Uses for the small business researcher. In J. Katz (Ed.), *Advances in entrepreneurship, firm emergence, and growth: Vol. 4. Databases for the study of entrepreneurship* (pp. 393–423). Greenwich, CT: JAI.

CHAPTER 7

Personal Background

Candida G. Brush

Tatiana S. Manolova

The single most important resource nascent entrepreneurs bring to an emerging venture is the composite of their personal experience, skills, and education. At emergence, the initial capabilities and expertise of the venture are embodied in the entrepreneur, providing a foundation for building the new organization. The personal background of the entrepreneur is referred to as "human capital" or the stored knowledge and skills of individuals (Becker, 1964). Human capital theory is based on the idea that people acquire individual resources to increase or enhance their productivity. These acquisitions are related to some time of education or training, as well as the amounts and types of work experiences they gain. Hence, human capital is a starting point for obtaining and developing other types of resources when a new venture is founded and directly influences its start-up process, survival, performance, and strategic direction (Vesper, 1990; Cooper, Gimeno-Gascon, & Woo, 1994; Stuart & Abetti, 1988; Brush, Greene, & Hart, 2001; Mosakowski, 1993).

Literature Review

Extensive literature examines the personal background characteristics or human capital dimensions of the entrepreneur and, in particular, achieved attributes such as experience, competencies, and education (Cooper & Gimeno-Gascon, 1992; Cooper, 1981; Chandler & Jansen, 1992; Vesper, 1990). Studies show that generally greater amounts of human capital are positively related to new venture survival and performance (Cooper & Gimeno-Gascon, 1992). Human capital variables are generally studied using three categories of variables: work experience, educational background, and functional expertise. These are discussed below.

Work Experience

Early studies examining work experience of the entrepreneur were designed to determine what characteristics distinguished entrepreneurs from those in other professions (Hornaday, 1982). Owner-founders having previous industry experience in areas similar to the industry of the new venture were more likely to have better performing ventures (Cooper & Gimeno-Gascon, 1994). Research on the background of entrepreneurs found that on average entrepreneurs had worked in slightly more than three organizations and had about 6 years of work experience (Brockhaus & Nord, 1979).

The level of decision-making experience was associated with business performance in some studies (Teach, Tarpley, & Schwartz, 1986), but others found that there was no relationship between level of previous management experience and survival (Cooper et al., 1988). Besides the type of work experience, research shows that previous entrepreneurial experience does contribute to superior business performance (Cooper, 1981). Stuart and Abetti (1988) studied founders of technical ventures finding that senior managerial experience in prior start-ups was the single greatest influence on performance.

Previous work experience has been studied as a motivator for venture start-up. In particular, dissatisfaction with previous work experience was examined as a "push" to entrepreneurial activity (Brockhaus, 1980). An extreme degree of dissatisfaction combined with unsatisfactory coworkers was more likely to push the entrepreneur to entrepreneurship, especially when it was perceived that a promotion was not likely. In contrast, Gasse (1982) notes that previous experience might have two different outcomes: first, it might provide guidelines and knowledge that is easily transferred to the new venture to increase performance; or second, it may create habits that are hard to change and act as obstacles to adaptation and better performance.

Research on career choices shows that sociopsychological rewards in employment may encourage an individual to remain in current employment rather than seek independence in self-employment. A sense of self-worth and self-esteem can be encouraged by recognition for work achievements, whereas individuals who are "misfits," unwilling to be supervised or managed, may be less often rewarded (Bird, 1989).

The influence on start-up of previous start-up experience was found to have mixed results, some studies finding a positive relationship, others finding nonsignificant results (Cooper & Gimeno-Gascon, 1992). Entrepreneurs who experience prior failure do not consider this an impediment to starting another venture (Vesper, 1990). Recent studies find owner-founder (or previous start-up) work experience positively influenced growth and survival over 6 years in high-tech firms (Westhead, 1995). Ronstadt (1984) found that entrepreneurs with prior start-up experience encountered more opportunities for other ventures, his study showing that 57% of Babson entrepreneurs were previously involved in sequential or overlapping ventures. On the other hand, other research suggests that experience in the industry may not be a precondition to venture success in fast growing ventures (Bhide, 2000).

Consequent of historical occupational segregation by industry sector, women entrepreneurs are more likely to have work experience in retail, service, and real estate sectors and less likely to have experience in finance and manufacturing (Greene, Brush, Hart, & Saparito, 2001). However, like their male counterparts, the vast majority of women entrepreneurs have experience in the area of their venture (Hisrich & Brush, 1986). Most common areas of previous work experience for women were administration, secretarial, education, and other professions (CPA, law, financial services, public relations). Women having more industry experience are more likely to have growing ventures (Brush & Hisrich, 1991), although they may grow more slowly and conservatively than male-led businesses (Cliff, 1998). However, women are less likely to have leadership and managerial decision-making experience (Greene et al., 2001).

Research on the experience of minority entrepreneurs shows they have fewer years of industry experience (Hisrich & Brush, 1986), and fewer years of current business experience. There is some evidence that minorities also perceive a ceiling to upward mobility in large organizations, which can result in job frustration and may be a catalyst for venture start-up (Bird, 1989).

Educational Background

Education is one of the most widely studied background factors in entrepreneurship research, with level of education being a popular measure (Cooper & Gimeno-Gascon, 1992). Initial studies found that on average, entrepreneurs had lower levels of education than managers, but they tended to be better educated than the general population (Collins & Moore, 1970). However, technical entrepreneurs tend to be well educated, having at least a master's degree (Cooper, 1973).

A review of 17 studies correlating education with performance found 10 studies showing positive results and 6 studies having nonsignificant results (Cooper & Gimeno-Gascon, 1992). Even though a variety of measures for performance were used, patterns did not differ significantly. Higher level of education was related to growth (Cooper et al., 1994). In contrast, some scholars have argued that formal education can be an impediment to free thinking, innovation, and entrepreneurship, instead fostering conformity and low tolerance for ambiguity (Ronstadt, 1984).

There is a general consensus that entrepreneurship skills can be taught (Vesper, 1990). Since the 1990s, recent college and university initiatives to encourage entrepreneurship education have stimulated the development of courses, entrepreneurship clubs, and other programs for undergraduate and graduate students. These courses include business basics and typically address all facets of entrepreneurial start-up from idea creation and opportunity assessment, to business plan development, to venture financing, and exit strategies (Young, 1997). In addition, there are other forms of entrepreneurial learning such as practitioner courses that are self-directed or sponsored by assistance programs, the Small Business Administration, or trade associations. The effectiveness of these programs and courses is less clear, largely because the optimal measure would be socioeconomic impact as measured in number of businesses created (McMullan & Long, 1987). However, most schools and programs assess effectiveness based on unique goals, alumni success, and other measures which are often not comparable or generalizable (Young, 1997).

Studies of women entrepreneurs find that women tend to be slightly better educated than their male counterparts, but they are more likely to have undergraduate degrees in liberal arts and humanities, instead of engineering or science (Hisrich & Brush, 1986). Women are likely to have graduate degrees, the most popular areas being business, education, or law.

Research on minority entrepreneurs shows that they are less likely than Whites to have graduated from college (Hornaday & Aboud, 1971). Another study comparing minority and nonminority entrepreneurs found minority entrepreneurs to be better educated and younger (Gomolka, 1977). Black business owners were found to have fewer years of education, while immigrant entrepreneurs were more likely than minorities to have parents with a college education (Butler & Greene, 1997). Another study of ethnic entrepreneurs finds they have fewer years of education, compared to whites (Chaganti & Greene, 2002).

Functional Expertise

The area of functional expertise has generally been measured in two ways: educational concentration or studies and work experience. Early studies found that wider variety of experience in selling, finance, and other skills were correlated with both survival and profitability, whereas experience in just selling was more often related to failure (Vesper, 1990). Studies of particular type of functional expertise (e.g., financial, marketing) and its relationship to sales produced mixed results with one study finding marketing experience led to higher sales and another cross-sectional study finding no relationship between functional experience and growth (Cooper & Gimeno-Gascon, 1992).

Type of educational background was studied relative to type of undergraduate or graduate degree. Entrepreneurs having business or engineering degrees were more likely to grow firms to greater size; however, the number of business courses was inversely related to growth for larger start-ups (Cooper & Gimeno-Gascon, 1992). Research on women entrepreneurs shows their self-assessed competence in dealing with people and idea generation/product innovation to be higher than for finance and business operations (Hisrich & Brush, 1986).

The Work and Career Variables

Twenty-six items from the phone interview (items Q340–Q352_7 in the PSED data set) represent the work and career items. These questions measure the educational background and work background that make up the career experience of nascent entrepreneurs. The items are intended to be used as single items and appear on pages 283 to 289 of the PSED Codebook. Items Q340 to Q342 are focused on the work experience of the respondents. Items Q343 to Q345 measure educational attainment.

Items Q346 to Q347 ask about the respondent's latest job experience. Items Q348 to Q352 explore career experiences. Specifically, in item Q348 the respondent is asked whether or not s/he made any suggestions for work improvements during the last year on the job. In case the respondent made any suggestions, the following questions explore the number and consequences of the suggestions at work. In case the respondent did not make any suggestions, or was the person in charge of the organization, the interviewer proceeded to items Q352_1 through Q352_7, which explore the consequences of the suggestions for the organization the respondent last worked for.

The exact wordings of the 26 items, as well as the type of scale and the variable descriptives, are presented in Table 7.1.

The Functional Expertise and Functional Experience Variables

Eighteen items from the mail survey (items QF1a1–i1 and QF1a2–i2 in the PSED data set) represent the functional expertise and functional experience items. The items appear on pages 323 to 324 of the PSED Codebook.

The nine items representing functional expertise were asked in the following manner. They were preceded by the stem: "Please write in the number of courses you have taken in the following area." The respondents then self-reported the number of courses taken in each of the following areas: sales or marketing management; accounting and financial control; production and plant management; personnel and human resource management; transportation, distribution, and inventory management; financial and capital management; technological and innovation management; mathematics; and economics, respectively.

The exact wordings for the nine items representing areas of functional expertise are listed in Table 7.2.

In addition, the mail survey included nine items representing functional work experience. These items were asked in the following manner. They were preceded by the stem: "Please write in the number of years of work experience you have in the following area." The respondents then self-reported the number of years of work experience in each of the following areas: sales or marketing management; accounting and financial control; production and plant management; personnel and human resource management; transportation, distribution, and inventory management; financial and capital management; technological and innovation management; mathematics; and economics, respectively.

The exact wordings for the nine items representing areas of functional experience are listed in Table 7.3. Descriptive statistics are presented in Table 7.4.

An Analysis of the Work, Career, and Functional Background Variables

The analyses were performed on both the phone interview and the mail survey PSED data sets, which include 446 nascent entrepreneurs from the original sample, 223 nascent entrepreneur women from a National Science Foundation oversample, and 223 respondents from a comparison group (Reynolds, 2000). As the data on the

Table 7.1   The 26 Items in the PSED and Descriptive Statistics: Work and Career Background

Item Number	Question	Response Categories	Descriptives					
			n	Min	Max	Mean	SD
Q340	How many total years of full-time, paid work experience in any field have you had?	Open-ended	568	0	60	18.21	10.88
Q341	For how many years, if any, did you have any managerial, supervisory, or administrative responsibilities?	Open-ended	558	0	53	8.82	8.40
Q342	What was the largest number of people you ever supervised?	Open-ended	490	0	2200	42.46	153.29
Q343	What is the highest level of education you have completed so far?	Ordinal Scale: 0 = no, 9 = doctorate	568	0	9	4.70	1.95
Q344	When you last attended school, what was your trade, major, or profession?	String					
Q345	In what year did you last attend school?	Open-ended	555	1943	1998		
Q346	Have you worked on a full-time basis for an established work organization anytime in the last 5 years?	Nominal	186	Yes: 109	No: 77		
Q347	What was the last year you were doing this full-time work?	Open-ended	104	1994	1998		
Q347a	And in what month did you last work?	Open-ended	109	1	16		
Q348	In the last year of your full-time work, did you make any suggestions, either formal or informal, for improving things to your supervisor, employer, or those in charge?	Nominal	488	Yes: 403	No: 69	I am the one in charge: 16	
Q349	During this 12-month period, about how many formal and informal suggestions did you make?	Open-ended	394	1	100	22.40	28.57
Q350	About how many of these suggestions were adopted—in whole or in part?	Open-ended	388	1	100	12.99	20.39
Q351*	Were you rewarded for any suggestion with a bonus, promotion, recognition, or in some other way?	Nominal	392	Yes: 182	No: 210		
Q352*	When employees at that work organization made suggestions that would improve things, did they usually get rewarded with a bonus, promotion, recognition, or in some other way?	Nominal	467	Yes: 211	No: 256		

NOTE: Items 351_1 through 351_7 and 352_1 through 352_7 ask about the specific reward/punishment that followed the suggestions at work.

Table 7.2   The Nine Functional Expertise Items in the PSED

Item Number	Question
QF1	Please write the number of courses you have taken in the following area.
QF1a1	Sales or marketing management
QF1b1	Accounting, financial control
QF1c1	Production, plant management
QF1d1	Personnel, human resource management
QF1e1	Transportation, distribution, inventory management
QF1f1	Financial and capital management
QF1g1	Technological and innovation management
QF1h1	Mathematics
QF1i1	Economics

Table 7.3   The Nine Functional Expertise Items in the PSED

Item Number	Question
QF2	Please write the number of years of work experience you have in the following area.
QF1a2	Sales or marketing management
QF1b2	Accounting, financial control
QF1c2	Production, plant management
QF1d2	Personnel, human resource management
QF1e2	Transportation, distribution, inventory management
QF1f2	Financial and capital management
QF1g2	Technological and innovation management
QF1h2	Mathematics
QF1i2	Economics

minority oversample were not made available at the time of performing this analysis, the only oversampling included in the present data set is the oversampling for women. The usable sample was reduced by the requirement that respondent gender be consistently recorded across all stages of data collection. Following the classification scheme developed by Shaver, Carter, Gartner, and Reynolds (2001), we included in the sample used for the present study fully autonomous nascent entrepreneurs who have not received a positive cash flow from their new businesses, to a usable sample size of

Table 7.4   Descriptive Statistics: Functional Experience and Functional Expertise Items

Variable	n	Min	Max	Mean	SD
Number of courses taken in:					
Sales or marketing management	495	0	36	1.37	2.98
Accounting, financial control	501	0	20	1.28	2.50
Production, plant management	503	0	25	.47	1.84
Personnel, human resource management	499	0	48	1.12	3.35
Transportation, distribution, inventory management	503	0	40	.62	2.64
Financial and capital management	503	0	48	.68	2.56
Technological and innovation management	501	0	60	1.03	4.12
Mathematics	491	0	40	3.15	4.16
Economics	499	0	20	1.20	2.00
Nymber of years of work experience in:					
Sales or marketing management	526	0	50	5.41	8.04
Accounting, financial control	526	0	38	3.93	7.25
Production, plant management	527	0	45	2.60	6.39
Personnel, human resource management	527	0	45	4.78	7.97
Transportation, distribution, inventory management	526	0	45	3.86	7.03
Financial and capital management	526	0	50	3.29	7.02
Technological and innovation management	527	0	45	2.60	6.21
Mathematics	519	0	45	4.55	8.85
Economics	523	0	45	2.79	7.37

$N = 579$ for the analyses based on the phone interview and $N = 527$ for the analyses based on the mail survey.

Findings to Date

The sample generally has significant years of paid work experience, the average being 18 years, and many have supervisory experience as well. Most respondents have at least 4 years of college (mean 4.70 and SD 95), although the most recent year when school was attended varied widely. About one fifth of the respondents had worked on a full-time basis for an established organization. The range of people supervised also varied widely (SD 153.29). With regard to the suggestions made to supervisors for improving things at work, a significant majority had made suggestions within the past year (303 of 488 responding to the question). On average, approximately 22 suggestions were made within the year, and about one third of those making suggestions were rewarded in some way.

The area of functional expertise showing the highest average for courses taken was mathematics (3.15); it also had the highest standard deviation (4.16). Most nascents had taken at least one course in sales and marketing, accounting, human resource management, technological innovation, and economics. Work experience years were highest in sales/marketing, with human resources, math, and economics also showing slightly higher averages.

Correlation analysis reveals significant positive associations across the different dimensions of functional expertise (see Table 7.5). This suggests respondents either have a broad exposure to different functional areas of management or none at all (e.g., those that have taken many classes in marketing have also taken many courses in accounting, etc., whereas those that did not take extensive classes in marketing, also did not take classes in accounting, etc.). The same was true of functional experience where highly significant positive correlations suggested those who had experience in one area of management were likely to have experience in another area (see Table 7.6).

The highly significant associations across areas of functional expertise and experience invited further analysis on profiles of expertise and experience. We tested for these profiles by conducting a principal component factor analysis (listwise deletion of missing values, varimax rotation with Kaiser normalization) of the functional expertise and functional experience items.

Functional Expertise

The factor analysis on functional expertise required five iterations to converge and resulted in the extraction of three factors with eigenvalues exceeding the threshold value of 1, which together accounted for over 55% of the variance. The rotated factor solution for functional expertise is presented in Table 7.7.

The first factor, which we named General Management, consisted of four items. These were Sales or Marketing Management[1] (factor loading 0.434), Accounting and Financial Control (factor loading 0.680), Mathematics (factor loading 0.687), and Economics (factor loading 0.829). The second factor, which we named Human and Financial Management, consisted of two items. These were Personnel and Human Resources (HR) Management (factor loading 0.875), and Financial and Capital Management (factor loading 0.884). The third factor, which we named Operations Management, consisted of three items. These were Production and Plant Management (factor loading 0.687); Transportation, Distribution, and Inventory Management (factor loading 0.708); and Technological and Innovation Management (factor loading 0.499).

None of the nine items that constituted the two scales had a cross-loading exceeding the usual rejection criterion of +/− 40%. Taken together, the high factor loadings and the low cross-loadings of the items (despite the significant correlations, as shown in Table 7.5) give us reasonable indication as to the divergent and convergent validity of the model.

We tested for reliability by calculating Cronbach's alpha for the three scales. Although it is always difficult to obtain high reliability estimates for scales consisting

Table 7.5   Correlation Matrix: Functional Expertise Items (*N* = 527)

Variable (*Number of courses taken in:*)	1	2	3	4	5	6	7	8	9
1. Sales or marketing management	—								
2. Accounting, financial control	.243**	—							
3. Production, plant management	.161**	.173**	—						
4. Personnel, HR management	.154**	.203**	.154**	—					
5. Transportation, distribution, inventory	.189**	.188**	.223**	.153**	—				
6. Financial and capital management	.136**	.330**	.132**	.649**	.157**	—			
7. Technological and innovation management	.138**	.059	.118**	.204**	.162**	.212**	—		
8. Mathematics	.131**	.222**	.093*	.032	.112*	.081	.072	—	
9. Economics	.316**	.460**	.179**	.104*	.156**	.213**	.100*	.407**	—

*p < .05; **p < .01.

87

Table 7.6   Correlation Matrix: Functional Experience Items (N = 527)

Variable (Number of years of work experience in:)	1	2	3	4	5	6	7	8	9
1. Sales or marketing management									
2. Accounting, financial control.	383**	—							
3. Production, plant management	.227**	.219**	—						
4. Personnel, HR management	.330**	.438**	.379**	—					
5. Transportation, distribution, inventory	.307**	.333**	.385**	.454**	—				
6. Financial and capital management	.408**	.614**	.309**	.504**	.465**	—			
7. Technological and innovation management	.245**	.268**	.535**	.404**	.349**	.359**	—		
8. Mathematics	.305**	.430**	.286**	.397	.401*	.455**	.384**	—	
9. Economics	.419**	.493**	.317**	.399*	.426**	.489**	.401**	.741**	—

*p < .05; **p < .01.

Table 7.7   Rotated Factor Loadings for the Functional Expertise Items: A Three-Factor Solution
(N = 527)

Variable	Item Number (Number of classes taken in:)	Factor 1: General Management	Factor 2: Human and Financial Management	Factor 3: Operations Management
QF1a1	Sales or marketing management	**.434**	6.095E-02	.378
QF1b1	Accounting, financial control	**.680**	.313	5.713E-02
QF1c1	Production, plant management	.124	1.921E-02	**.687**
QF1d1	Personnel, HR management	2.320E-02	**.875**	.152
QF1e1	Transportation, distribution, inventory	.125	3.869E-02	**.708**
QF1f1	Financial and capital management	.170	**.884**	8.268E-02
QF1g1	Technological and innovation management	−5.49E-02	.275	**.499**
QF1h1	Mathematics	**.687**	−8.32E-02	2.264E-02
QF1i1	Economics	**.829**	7.446E-02	.121
	Eigenvalue	2.578	1.394	1.053
	Percentage of variance accounted for	28.648	15.492	11.704
	Cronbach's alpha	.5647	.7705	.3224

of a small number of items, the low coefficient alphas (especially for the Operations Management scale) suggest that future researchers should utilize the scales with caution.

Functional Experience

The factor analysis on functional experience required three iterations to converge and resulted in the extraction of two factors with eigenvalues exceeding the threshold value of 1, which together accounted for over 58% of the variance. The rotated factor solution for functional experience is presented in Table 7.8.

The first factor, which we named General Management, consisted of six items. These were Sales or Marketing Management[2] (factor loading 0.643), Accounting and Financial Control (factor loading 0.796), Personnel and HR Management (factor loading 0.523), Financial and Capital Management (factor loading 0.759), Mathematics (factor loading 0.670), and Economics (factor loading 0.744). The second factor, which we named Operations Management, consisted of three items. These were Production and Plant Management (factor loading 0.856); Transportation, Distribution, and Inventory Management (factor loading 0.484); and Technology and Innovation Management (factor loading 0.806).

Table 7.8   Rotated Factor Loadings for the Functional Experience Items: A Two-Factor Solution
($N = 527$)

Item Number	Variable (Number of years of work experience in:)	Factor 1: General Management	Factor 2: Operations Management
QF1a2	Sales or marketing management	**.643**	7.551E-02
QF1b2	Accounting, financial control	**.796**	6.789E-02
QF1c2	Production, plant management	9.953E-02	**.856**
QF1d2	Personnel, HR management	**.523**	.473
QF1e2	Transportation, distribution, inventory	.474	**.484**
QF1f2	Financial and capital management	**.759**	.238
QF1g2	Technological and innovation management	.184	**.806**
QF1h2	Mathematics	**.670**	.339
QF1i2	Economics	**.744**	.313
	Eigenvalue	4.189	1.099
	Percent variance accounted for	46.542	12.207
	Cronbach alpha	.8073	.6824

Two of the nine items that constituted the two scales had cross-loadings exceeding the usual rejection criterion of +/– 40%. These were Personnel and HR Management and Transportation, Distribution, and Inventory Management (See Table 7.8). For consistency and completeness of presentation, we have assigned those two items according to the higher corresponding loading. Future researchers, however, should interpret the convergent validity of the model with caution.

We tested for reliability by calculating Cronbach's alpha for the two scales. The scales manifested very acceptable reliability, with coefficient alphas well above .65 for both scales.

Future Research Directions

The personal background items might be used to examine different aspects of human capital. Questions 340 to 342 and 346 to 348, which examine previous experience, are all open-ended questions but yield continuous numeric data and therefore can be analyzed using parametric statistics. Education items (343, 344, 345) are also open questions but yield continuous data. Items that measure functional experience and functional expertise yield continuous data and may be best used as single items or as scaled items based on the factor analyses above. Items measuring suggestions and rewards for these provide the overall number of suggestions made and number adopted, again providing continuous data.

Future analyses might examine all of the personal background items as these relate to the start-up behaviors, the nature of the venture, and survival and growth. In addition, subgroup analyses using gender or race and ethnicity are possible for deeper exploration of relationships. Comparison of work and career patterns by gender or race and ethnicity, as these may affect the start-up process, is also possible. Examination of the relationship between the suggestions made and the start-up process might provide insight into the idea/action orientation of nascent entrepreneurs (Bird, 1989). Future researchers do need to treat work and career items with care, however, because of the uneven cell counts (e.g., White entrepreneurs in the sample outnumber minority entrepreneurs by a factor of three). Including the minority oversample in the analysis would, therefore, present a more balanced point of comparison. Initial comparisons of functional expertise between men and women show that women tend to take more work-related classes and have more work experience in marketing and sales, whereas men more often have greater experience in math and take more classes in technological and innovation management.

Notes

1. Here and hereafter in the description of the functional expertise items, the items represent the number of courses taken in each functional area.
2. Here and hereafter in the description of the functional experience items, the items represent the number of years of work experience in each functional area.

References

Becker, G. (1964). *Human capital: A theoretical and empirical analysis, with special reference to education.* New York: Columbia University Press.

Bhide, A. (2000). *The origin and evolution of new business.* New York: Oxford University Press.

Bird, B. J. (1989). *Entrepreneurial behavior.* Glenview, IL: Scott, Foresman.

Brockhaus, R. (1980). The effect of job dissatisfaction on the decision to start a business. *Journal of Small Business Management, 18*(1), 35–42.

Brockhaus, R., & Nord, W. R. (1979). An exploration of factors affecting the entrepreneurial decision: Personal characteristics vs. environmental calculations. In R. Huseman (Ed.), *Proceedings of the 39th Annual Meeting of the Academy of Managment* (pp. 364–368). Briarcliff Manor, NY: Academy of Management.

Brush, C. G., Greene, P. G., & Hart, M. M. (2001). From initial idea to unique advantage: The entrepreneurial challenge of constructing a resource base. *Academy of Management Executive, 15*(1), 64–80.

Brush, C. G., & Hisrich, R. D. (1991). The impact of antecedent influences on the survival and growth of women-owned businesses. *Journal of Managerial Psychology, 5*(5), 9–16.

Butler, J., & Greene, P. G. (1997). Ethnic entrepreneurship. In D. L. Sexton & R. Smilor (Eds.), *Entrepreneurship 2000* (pp. 267–289). Chicago, IL: Upstart.

Chaganti, R., & Greene, P. (2002). Who are the ethnic entrepreneurs? A study of entrepreneurs' ethnic involvement and business characteristics. *Journal of Small Business Management, 40*(2), 126–143.

Chandler, G., & Jansen, E. (1992). Founders' self assessed competence and venture performance. *Journal of Business Venturing, 7*(3), 223–236.

Cliff, J. (1998). Does one size fit all? Exploring the relationship between attitudes towards growth, gender and business size. *Journal of Business Venturing, 13*(6), 523–542.

Collins, O. F., & Moore, D. G. (1970). *The organization makers: A behavioral study of independent entrepreneurs.* New York: Meredith.

Cooper, A. C. (1973). Technical entrepreneurship: What do we know? *Research and Development Management, 3*(2), 59–64.

Cooper, A. C. (1981). Strategic management: New ventures and small businesses. *Long Range Planning, 14*(5), 39–45.

Cooper, A. C., & Gimeno-Gascon, F. J. (1992). Entrepreneurs, processes of founding and firm performance. In D. Sexton & J. Kasarda (Eds.), *The state of the art of entrepreneurship* (pp. 301–340). Boston: PWS-Kent.

Cooper, A. C., Gimeno-Gascon, F. J., & Woo, C. (1994). Initial human and financial capital as predictors of new venture performance. *Journal of Business Venturing, 9*(5), 371–395.

Gasse, Y. (1982). Elaborations on the psychology of the entrepreneur. In D. Sexton & J. Kasarda (Eds.), *The state of the art of entrepreneurship* (pp. 57–71). Boston: PWS-Kent.

Gomolka, E. (1977). Characteristics of minority entrepreneurs and small business enterprises. *American Journal of Small Business, 2*(1), 12–21.

Greene, P. G., Brush, C. G., Hart, M., & Saparito, P. (2001). Patterns of venture capital funding: Is gender a factor? *Venture Capital, 3*(1), 62–83.

Hisrich, R. D., & Brush, C. G. (1986). Characteristics of the minority entrepreneur. *Journal of Small Business Management, 24,* 1–8.

Hornaday, J. (1982). Research about living entrepreneurs. In C. A. Kent, D. L. Sexton, & K. Vesper (Eds.), *The encyclopedia of entrepreneurship* (pp. 20–38). Englewood Cliffs, NJ: Prentice Hall.

Hornaday, J., & Aboud, J. (1971). The characteristics of successful entrepreneurs. *Personnel Psychology, 24,* 141–153.

McMullan, W. E., & Long, W. (1987). Entrepreneurship education in the 1990's. *Journal of Business Venturing, 3,* 1–10.

Mosakowski, E. (1993). A resource-based perspective on the dynamic strategy performance relationship: An empirical examination of the focus and differentiation strategies in entrepreneurial firms. *Journal of Management, 19*(4), 819–939.

Reynolds, P. D. (2000). National panel study of U.S. business startups: Background and methodology. In J. A. Katz (Ed.), *Databases for the study of entrepreneurship* (Vol. 4, pp. 153–227). New York: Elsevier Science.

Ronstadt, R. (1984). Ex-entrepreneurs and the decision to start an entrepreneurial career. In J. Hornaday, F. Tarpley, Jr., J. Timmons, & K. Vesper (Eds.), *Frontiers of Entrepreneurship Research 1984: Proceedings of the 1984 Entrepreneurship Research Conference* (pp. 112–115). Wellesley, MA: Babson College.

Shaver, K. G., Carter, N. M., Gartner, W. B., & Reynolds, P. D. (2001, June). *Who is a nascent entrepreneur? Decision rules for identifying and selecting entrepreneurs in the Panel Study of Entrepreneurial Dynamics (PSED).* Paper presented at the 2001 Babson Kauffman Conference in Entrepreneurship Research, Jönköping, Sweden.

Stuart, R., & Abetti, P. (1988). *Field of study of technical ventures—Part III: The impact of entrepreneurial management experience on early performance.* Paper presented at the eighth annual Babson College Entrepreneurship Research Conference, Calgary, Alberta, Canada.

Teach, R. D., Tarpley, F., & Schwartz, R. (1986). Software venture teams. In R. Ronstadt, J. Hornaday, R. Peterson, & K. Vesper (Eds.), *Frontiers of Entrepreneurship Research 1986: Proceedings of the Sixth Annual Babson College Entrepreneurship Research Conference* (pp. 546–562). Wellesley, MA: Babson College.

Vesper, K. (1990). *New venture strategies.* Englewood Cliffs, NJ: Prentice Hall.

Westhead, P. (1995). Survival and employment growth contrasts between types of owner-managed high-technology firms. *Entrepreneurship Theory and Practice, 20*(1), 5–28.

Young, J. (1997). Entrepreneurship education and learning for university students and practicing entrepreneurs. In D. L. Sexton, & R. Smilor (Eds.), *Entrepreneurship 2000* (pp. 215–238). Chicago, IL: Upstart.

CHAPTER 8

Family Background

Charles H. Matthews

Sherrie E. Human

For several decades scholars and practitioners have attempted to understand and predict individuals' career selection in general (e.g., Holland, 1973) and entrepreneurial career selection in particular (e.g., Baucus & Human, 1994; Scott & Twomey, 1988). In recent years, conceptual frameworks to guide empirical research regarding individuals' self-employment choices have been borrowed from the social sciences. Sociologists have documented the "transmission of parental self-employment status" (Erikson & Goldthorpe, 1992; Laferrere, 2001, p. 4). Entrepreneurship researchers have used frameworks such as Bandura's social learning theory (1977), Ajzen's theory of planned behavior (1991), and Blau and Duncan's (1967) concept of occupational inheritance to examine self-employment selection (e.g., Scherer, Adams, Carley, & Wiebe, 1989; Kolvereid, 1996a; Aldrich, Renzulli, & Langton, 1998, respectively).

In addition to frameworks building on the social sciences, entrepreneurship scholars have adopted models in the careers literature to conceptualize entrepreneurial career development, such as Dyer's (1994) theory of entrepreneurial careers and Katz's (1992) model of employment status choice. Both of these models proposed key antecedents such as role models or family business background that influence entrepreneurial career choices. Over the years, scholars have continued to develop and refine measures of respondents' family background regarding business ownership. As Chrisman and Chua (2003) note, "We need to obtain a better understanding of the conditions under which the positive forces of family involvement can be unleashed and directed toward economic, and non-economic, objectives" (p. 34).

This chapter describes the relevant literature for and development of the family background items used in the Panel Study of Entrepreneurial Dynamics (PSED). It should be noted that both the "Person" and the "Gender Ethnic and Minority" Design Teams contributed to this section of the interview items in the PSED. Chapter 16 of this volume presents the Person Team's approach to these questions. The current chapter focuses on the family background items' development and rationale from the work of the Gender Ethnic and Minority Team and presents descriptive statistics for these items from the telephone interview responses.

Literature Review on Family Background Measures

In early studies of occupational structures and inheritance, Blau and Duncan (1967) and Morgan (1972) measured family background by asking respondents whether their fathers were self-employed. Over the years, this simple measure of the presence or absence of exposure to a father's business was expanded to include whether respondents experienced the entrepreneurial process through both mothers and fathers, extended family members, friends, and persons important to the respondent (e.g., Brockhaus & Horwitz, 1986; Collins & Moore, 1970; Shapero & Sokol, 1982). For instance, Scott and Twomey's (1988) study of factors that influence entrepreneurial aspirations included parental role models as a predisposing factor for entrepreneurial career aspirations. Their results, examining 436 responses from undergraduates in the United Kingdom, the United States, and Ireland, indicated that respondents whose parents owned a small business full-time showed the highest preference for self-employment. Several studies over the years have found support for similar parental business ownership measures to identify entrepreneurial career interest or actions, including Scherer, Adams, Carley, & Wiebe (1989) and Brenner, Pringle, and Greenhaus (1991), who investigated undergraduate students, and Lentz and Leband (1990) and Young and Welsch (1993), who studied current business owners in the United States and Mexico, respectively. In addition to predicting business start-up behaviors from family background variables, researchers have also examined and found support for new venture success by whether the founder was raised by entrepreneurial parents (e.g., Duchesneau & Gartner, 1990).

Matthews and Moser (1995, 1996) built on and expanded the family background measure beyond mother and father by asking undergraduate student respondents about the business ownership experience of their extended family including brother, sister, aunt, uncle, cousin, grandfather, grandmother. In addition, these authors also asked about the size of the family members' businesses in terms of number of employees. To further specify the measure of exposure to a family business ownership background, Aldrich et al. (1998) added questions regarding the duration of family business ownership experience, such as "number of years parents owned business" and "number of years respondent worked in parents' business."

In addition to theoretical perspectives focusing on the direct relationship between the presence or absence of entrepreneurial role models and business ownership perceptions, a second theoretical perspective has examined family background and role models as indirect influences on career preference or expectations. That is, researchers using Ajzen's theory of planned behavior (1991), Shapero and Sokol's model of entrepreneurial intentions (1982), and Katz's model of employment status choice (1992) proposed that family background or role models influenced career choice indirectly by first influencing respondents' attitudes toward self-employment. That is, respondents with business ownership role models were expected to perceive a business ownership career path as more desirable than respondents not having that exposure.

Thus, according to these models, it was important that researchers not only ask respondents about the presence or absence of key role models or family business but also ask about respondents' attitudes toward and encouragement from family, role models, and other important social groups. Indeed, scholars have found support for this perspective. Krueger (1993), Kolvereid (1996b), and Tkachev and Kolvereid (1999) examined responses of U.S., Norwegian, and Russian students, respectively, regarding the presence or absence of family business ownership and whether family, close friends, and people important to the students offered encouragement regarding pursuing self-employment. Delmar and Davidsson (2000), in addition to examining the existence of role models for a sample of Norwegian nascent entrepreneurs, also examined respondents' impressions of self-employment from those role models. All of these studies suggest that positive impressions of and encouragement from family and social groups may indirectly influence entrepreneurial behaviors through their direct influence on attitudes toward those behaviors.

Davidsson, in Part II of this handbook, provides preliminary evidence from the Swedish sister project (cf. Davidsson & Honig, 2003; Delmar & Davidsson, 2000). He notes that presence of a parental role model (Q362) has a significant, but relatively weak, positive effect on the probability of becoming a nascent entrepreneur (NE).

To summarize, the research focusing on family background and role models in business as predictors of self-employment have examined the presence or absence and extent of such background, including the existence of family members and/or non-family members as role models, the duration of the role models' entrepreneurial activities, and the size and number of those activities (e.g., size and number of family businesses). In addition, scholars have examined attitudes toward and encouragement from role models. With the inclusion of this latter set of factors, researchers allowed that business exposure and role models may be more of an indirect influence on self-employment via attitudes toward this career path rather than the direct influence on entrepreneurial behaviors. As researchers on the PSED discussed which measures of family background and role models in business to include, it was agreed that including key measures of all of these perspectives would be important for building on these well-established research streams. The specific measures included in the PSED are described in the following section.

The PSED Variables Representing Family Background

Twenty items included in the initial telephone survey (Q362–379c) represent the family background variables. Table 8.1 presents the wording for these 20 items organized into the conceptual categories of "primary family role models," "extended family and other role models," and "attitudes toward and encouragement by role models."

It should be noted that responses to a number of the items in this section are dependent on the answer to previous items in this section, thus accounting for the variance in the number of responses for some items. For example, the structure of the items on family background begins with assessing whether or not the respondent's mother or father, alone or together, ever worked for themselves or ran their own business (Q362). Once this was determined, specific questions probed for more information about the number of businesses owned by the father or mother, the size of those businesses, and the respondent's work history with those businesses. Therefore, the number of respondents who had a parent in these categories would affect the number of responses in the more detailed inquiries.

Similarly, subsequent items asked for information on extended family or other role model background (Q376–377) and attitudes toward and encouragement by those role models (Q378–379c). Only those respondents who indicated in earlier items that such a relationship existed would be asked these questions, again accounting for the number of missing values and variance across the variables.

Table 8.1   Wording and Conceptual Categories: Family Background Items

Item Number	Primary Family Role Models Items
Q362	Did your parents ever work for themselves or run their own businesses, alone or together?
Q363	Was it only your father's business, only your mother's business, a joint business, two separate careers running businesses, or some other combination of activity?
Q364	How many different businesses did your father own or run on his own?
Q365	For how many years did your father own or run his own business(es)?
Q366	What was the largest number of paid employees, family and non-family, that ever worked for any of his businesses?
Q367	Did you ever work for your father's business, full- or part-time?
Q368	How many different businesses did your mother own or run on her own?
Q369	For how many years did your mother own or run her own business(es)?
Q370	What was the largest number of paid employees, family and non-family, that ever worked for any of her business(es)?
Q371	Did you ever work for your mother's business, full- or part-time?

(Continued)

Table 8.1 (Continued)

Item Number	Primary Family Role Models Items
Q372	How many different businesses did your parents jointly own or run?
Q373	For how many years did your parents own or run their own business(es) jointly?
Q374	What was the largest number of paid employees, family and non-family, that ever worked for any of your parents' jointly owned or run business(es)?
Q375	Did you ever work for your parents' jointly owned or run business(es), full- or part-time?
	Extended Family and Other Role Models Items
Q376	Among other relatives or kin, apart from your parents, did most, some, a few, or noneown their own business?
Q377	Among close friends and neighbors, did most, some, a few, or none own their own business?
	Attitudes Toward and Encouragement by Role Models Items
Q378	From observing family, kin, and close friends with their own businesses, what is your overall impression of running a business as a career—would you say very positive, positive, neutral, negative, or very negative?
Q379	Have your family, relatives, or other close friends been encouraging you to, or discouraging you from, starting a business of your own?
Q379a	How would you describe the encouragement you received from family, relatives or other close friends, would you consider it very weak, weak, neither weak nor strong, strong, or very strong?
Q379c	How would you describe the discouragement you have received from family, relatives, or other close friends? Would you say it is very weak, weak, neither weak nor strong, strong, or very strong?

A Preliminary Analysis of the Variables Representing Family Background

Tables 8.2 and 8.3 provide descriptive statistics for the 20 family background variables. Preliminary observations indicate that with the exception of Q366 (father's largest number of employees), weighting the data revealed little difference in the descriptive statistics between the unweighted and weighted samples. Furthermore, there are only small differences between the family business backgrounds of nascent entrepreneurs and the comparison group with the exception of number employed by father's business (Q366); number of years mother ran her own business (Q369); and the largest number of paid employees, family and non-family, that ever worked for any of your parents' jointly owned or run business(es) (Q374). Nascent entrepreneurs reported that "father's largest number of employees" was more than twice that reported by the comparison group (84.32 vs. 36.45). On the other hand, the

Table 8.2 Descriptive Statistics: 20 Family Background Items in the PSED From First Telephone Interview (unweighted)

Item Number	Variable	Nascent Entrepreneur						Comparison Group					
		n	Missing	Mean	Med	Min	Max	n	Missing	Mean	Med	Min	Max
Q362	Parents: Self-employed or own businesses	807	23	1.49	1.00	1	2	424	7	1.58	2.00	1	2
Q363	Mother, Father, joint ownership of business	415	415	2.23	2.00	1	5	178	253	2.08	2.00	1	5
Q364	Father: How many businesses owned or run	245	585	1.66	1.00	0	10	101	330	1.90	1.00	0	20
Q365	Father: Years owned or run businesses	224	606	21.56	20.00	1	60	96	335	21.38	20.00	1	68
Q366	Father: Largest number of employees	208	622	67.07	5.00	0	9,000	91	340	105.55	4.00	0	9,000
Q367	Respondent: Worked for father's businesses	241	589	2.31	2.00	1	3	100	331	2.42	3.00	1	3
Q368	Mother: How many businesses owned or run	118	712	1.21	1.00	0	5	39	392	1.41	1.00	0	8
Q369	Mother: Years owned or run businesses	103	727	11.91	10.00	1	47	38	393	10.45	8.50	1	55
Q370	Mother: Largest number of employees	102	728	4.38	2.00	0	100	37	394	6.05	2.00	0	75
Q371	Respondent: Worked for mother's businesses	108	722	2.53	3.00	1	3	38	393	2.66	3.00	1	3
Q372	Parents: How many businesses jointly owned or run	136	694	1.65	1.00	0	20	61	370	1.70	1.00	1	15
Q373	Parents: Years owned or run businesses	127	703	20.13	17.00	1	60	57	374	21.56	20.00	2	60
Q374	Parents: Largest number of employees	122	708	8.84	5.00	0	150	55	376	171.85	6.00	0	9,000
Q375	Respondent: Worked for parent's businesses	122	708	2.02	2.00	1	3	54	377	2.07	2.00	1	3
Q376	Other relatives own businesses	805	25	2.92	3.00	1	4	423	8	3.05	3.00	1	4
Q377	Friends and neighbors own businesses	803	27	2.88	3.00	1	4	422	9	3.08	3.00	1	4
Q378	Respondent impression of owning businesses as career	746	84	1.85	2.00	1	4	372	59	2.16	2.00	1	5
Q379	Encouragement from family and relatives to start businesses	811	19	1.50	1.00	1	4	428	3	2.46	2.00	1	4
Q379a	How much encouragement to start businesses	652	178	4.00	4.00	1	5	207	224	3.87	4.00	1	5
Q379c	How much discouragement from starting businesses	118	712	3.09	3.00	1	5	36	395	3.28	3.00	1	5

Table 8.3 Descriptive Statistics: 20 Family Background Items in the PSED From First Telephone Interview (weighted)

Item Number	Variable	Nascent Entrepreneur						Comparison Group					
		n	Missing	Mean	Med	Min	Max	n	Missing	Mean	Med	Min	Max
Q362	Parents: Self-employed or own businesses	811	19	1.48	1.00	1	2	422	9	1.51	2.00	1	2
Q363	Mother, Father, joint ownership of business	418	412	2.20	2.00	1	5	207	224	2.08	2.00	1	5
Q364	Father: How many businesses owned or run	252	578	1.75	1.00	0	10	120	311	1.93	1.00	0	20
Q365	Father: Years owned or run businesses	231	599	20.73	20.00	1	60	116	315	20.96	20.00	1	68
Q366	Father: Largest number of employees	214	616	84.32	5.00	0	9,000	107	324	36.45	3.00	0	9,000
Q367	Respondent: Worked for father's businesses	248	582	2.28	2.00	1	3	118	313	2.44	3.00	1	3
Q368	Mother: How many businesses owned or run	109	721	1.19	1.00	0	5	43	388	1.22	1.00	0	8
Q369	Mother: Years owned or run businesses	95	735	11.40	10.00	1	47	41	390	9.97	10.00	1	55
Q370	Mother: Largest number of employees	94	736	3.97	2.00	0	100	40	391	4.69	1.00	0	75
Q371	Respondent: Worked for mother's businesses	100	730	2.57	3.00	1	3	41	390	2.67	3.00	1	3
Q372	Parents: How many businesses jointly owned or run	139	691	1.59	1.00	0	20	71	360	1.63	1.00	1	15
Q373	Parents: Years owned or run businesses	130	700	18.95	15.00	1	60	69	362	22.83	20.00	2	60
Q374	Parents: Largest number of employees	125	705	9.25	1.75	0	150	68	363	56.51	5.43	0	9,000
Q375	Respondent: Worked for parent's businesses	125	705	2.00	2.00	1	3	68	363	2.04	2.00	1	3
Q376	Other relatives own businesses	809	21	2.92	3.00	1	4	422	9	2.99	3.00	1	4
Q377	Friends and neighbors own businesses	807	23	2.87	3.00	1	4	424	7	3.02	3.00	1	4
Q378	Respondent impression of owning businesses as career	750	80	1.85	2.00	1	4	389	42	2.25	2.00	1	5
Q379	Encouragement from family and relatives to start businesses	816	14	1.51	1.00	1	4	427	4	2.65	4.00	1	4
Q379a	How much encouragement to start businesses	656	174	3.98	4.00	1	5	178	253	3.79	4.00	1	5
Q379c	How much discouragement from starting businesses	119	711	3.08	3.00	1	5	43	388	3.53	3.00	1	5

comparison group reported that the "largest number of paid employees, family and non-family, that ever worked for any of your parents' jointly owned or run business(es)" was six times that reported by the nascent entrepreneurs (56.51 vs. 9.25). In addition, nascent entrepreneurs did report slightly stronger encouragement for starting a business from family, relatives, or other close friends than the comparison group (Q379).

Current Research Using Family Background Variables

Given that the economic vibrancy of most nations is focused on the role of family and privately held businesses, it is both desirable and valuable to pursue our understanding of the factors that may influence such endeavors. Indeed, considerable research has and continues to be focused on the process and impact of family and privately held firms. Of particular interest here is the role of family background on nascent entrepreneurial activity.

Using the PSED data, Crosa, Aldrich, and Keister (2002) examine "having self-employed (s-e) parents" as a predictor of being a nascent entrepreneur. Specifically, they hypothesize that

Human capital will have a positive effect on entrepreneurship, in four specific ways:

1. Higher education will increase the likelihood of being a nascent entrepreneur.

2. Age will have a curvilinear relationship to being a nascent entrepreneur, initially positive and then negative.

3. Having self-employed parents will increase the likelihood of being a nascent entrepreneur.

4. Current self-employment will be positively associated with being a nascent entrepreneur.

Interestingly, although Crosa et al (2002) initially show that those with self-employed parents are more likely to be nascent entrepreneurs than those without self-employed parents, the relationship becomes insignificant after controls are introduced. They note that the apparent effect of self-employed parents is thus actually mediated through education and current self-employment status, as well as the parents' ethnicity. Thus, their hypothesis that those with self-employed parents are more likely to become nascents than those without self-employed parents was not supported.

Although Crosa et al. (2002) study provides an insight into the potential role that family background may play in the initiation of new ventures, much work remains to be done. It is anticipated that the data of the PSED will play an important role in continuing to advance our understanding of the role that parental and family background plays in contributing to our understanding of nascent entrepreneurism.

References

Ajzen, I. (1991). The theory of planned behavior. *Organizational Behavior and Human Processes, 50,* 179–211.

Aldrich, H. E., Renzulli, L. A., & Langton, N. (1998). Passing on privilege: Resources provided by self-employed parents to their self-employed children. *Research in Social Stratification and Mobility, 16,* 291–317.

Bandura, A. (1977). *A social learning theory.* Englewood Cliffs, NJ: Prentice Hall.

Baucus, D. A., & Human, S. E. (1994). Second-career entrepreneurs: A multiple case study analysis of entrepreneurial processes and antecedent variables. *Entrepreneurship Theory and Practice, 19*(2), 41–71.

Blau, P. M., & Duncan, O. D. (1967). *The American occupational structure.* New York: Free Press.

Brenner, O. C., Pringle, C. D., & Greenhaus, J. H. (1991). Perceived fulfillment of organizational employment versus entrepreneurship: Work values and career intentions of business college graduates. *Journal of Small Business Management, 29*(3), 62–75.

Brockhaus, R. H., & Horwitz, P. S. (1986). The psychology of the entrepreneur. In D. L. Sexton & R. W. Smilor (Eds.), *The art and science of entrepreneurship* (pp. 25–48). Cambridge, MA: Ballinger.

Chrisman, J., & Chua, L. (2003). *Current trends and future directions in family business management studies: Toward a theory of the family firm* (2003 Coleman White Paper Series). United States Association for Small Business and Entrepreneurship. Retrieved from www.usasbe.org/knowledge/whitepapers/index.asp

Collins, O. F., & Moore, D. G. (1970). *The organization makers: A behavioral study of independent entrepreneurs.* New York: Meredith.

Crosa, B., Aldrich, H., & Keister, L. (2002). Is there a wealth affect? Financial and human capital as determinants of business startups. In *Frontiers of entrepreneurship research 2002: Proceedings of the 22nd Annual Babson Kauffman Entrepreneurship Research Conference* (pp. 1–13). Babson Park, MA: Babson College.

Davidsson, P., & Honig, B. (2003). The role of social and human capital among nascent entrepreneurs. *Journal of Business Venturing, 18*(3), 301–331.

Delmar, F., & Davidsson, P. (2000). Where do they come from? Prevalence and characteristics of nascent entrepreneurs. *Entrepreneurship & Regional Development, 12,* 1–23.

Duchesneau, D. A., & Gartner, W. B. (1990). A profile of new venture success and failure in an emerging industry. *Journal of Business Venturing, 5,* 297–312.

Dyer, W. G., Jr. (1994). Toward a theory of entrepreneurial careers. *Entrepreneurship Theory and Practice, 19*(2), 7–21.

Erikson, R., & Goldthorpe, J. (1992). *The constant flux: A study of class mobility in industrial societies.* Oxford, UK: Clarendon.

Holland, J. L. (1973). *Making vocational choices.* Englewood Cliffs, NJ: Prentice Hall.

Katz, J. A. (1992). A psychosocial cognitive model of employment status choice. *Entrepreneurship Theory & Practice, 17*(1), 29–37.

Kolvereid, L. (1996a). Organizational employment versus self-employment: Reasons for career choice intentions. *Entrepreneurship Theory and Practice, 20*(3), 23–31.

Kolvereid, L. (1996b). Prediction of employment status choice intentions. *Entrepreneurship Theory and Practice, 21*(1), 47–57.

Krueger, N. (1993). The impact of prior entrepreneurial exposure on perceptions of new venture feasibility and desirability. *Entrepreneurship Theory and Practice, 18*(1), 5–21.

Laferrere, A. (2001). Self-employment and intergenerational transfers. *International Journal of Sociology, 31*(1), 3–26.

Lentz, B. F., & Laband, D. N. (1990). Entrepreneurial success and occupational inheritance among proprietors. *Canadian Journal of Economics, 23*(3), 563–579.

Matthews, C. H., & Moser, S. B. (1995). Family background and gender: Implications for interest in small firm ownership. *Entrepreneurship & Regional Development, 7,* 365–377.

Matthews, C. H., & Moser, S. B. (1996). A longitudinal investigation of the impact of family background and gender on interest in small firm ownership. *Journal of Small Business Management, 34*(2), 29–44.

Morgan, J. N. (1972). *A panel study of income dynamics: Study, design, available data: 1968–1972 interviewing years* (Vols. 1 & 2). Ann Arbor, MI: Institute for Social Research, Survey Research Center.

Scherer, R. F., Adams, J. S., Carley, S. S., & Wiebe, F. A. (1989). Role model performance effects on development of entrepreneurial career preference. *Entrepreneurship Theory and Practice, 13*(3), 53–71.

Scott, M. G., & Twomey, D. F. (1988). The long-term supply of entrepreneurs: Students' career aspirations in relation to entrepreneurship. *Journal of Small Business Management, 26*(4), 5–13.

Shapero, A., & Sokol, L. (1982). The social dimensions of entrepreneurship. In C. Kent, D. Sexton, & K. Vesper (Eds.), *The encyclopedia of entrepreneurship* (pp. 72–90). Englewood Cliffs, NJ: Prentice Hall.

Tkachev, A., & Kolvereid, L. (1999). Self-employment intentions among Russian students. *Entrepreneurship & Regional Development, 11,* 269–280.

Young, E. C., & Welsch, H. P. (1993). Major elements in entrepreneurial development in central Mexico. *Journal of Small Business Management, 31*(4), 80–85.

CHAPTER 9

Time Use

Margaret M. Owen

Patricia G. Greene

T ime is one of the most crucial resources a nascent entrepreneur needs in order to start and grow a business. Previous chapters of this book implicitly address time by examining topics such as labor force participation in which one consideration is the amount of time the nascent entrepreneur spends working for someone else as opposed to working on the emerging business. The analysis of household structures might also be construed as implicitly investigating time use by asking whether there is a spouse that potentially spends time helping launch the business or whether there are dependents in the home that require time to be spent on their care. And finally, studies that explore the use of networks and business assistance services implicitly include time aspects by questioning the number of times a contact is made or a service used. For the purposes of this chapter, the explicit concern is the manner in which nascent entrepreneurs prioritize and apply their time.

Time allocation studies seek to provide substantive information on how individuals and societies use their time and how time use patterns change over specific periods of time. Time use data's comparative value lies in the undeniable fact that, unlike other resources, time is a resource allocated equally (Fleming & Spellerberg, 1999). Each person's day is comprised of 24 hours. However, patterns of time use show tremendous variation across such demographic and socioeconomic factors as gender and race as well as age, education, income, and employment status. Multinational studies indicate that national time use patterns differ as well (Szalai, 1972; Gershuny, 2000; Harvey, Fisher, Gershuny, & Akbari, 2000). Time use surveys provide a context for understanding how various paid, domestic, and leisure activities are socially constructed and integrated into different sections of the population (Fleming & Spellerberg, 1999; Gershuny, 2000). How time is organized and structured as well as the determinants of such allocations is at the core of most time use research.

Time use information has been used to measure both production and consumption activity in a given economy. Frequently, productive work is narrowly defined to include only paid work. However, focusing exclusively on paid work fails to provide a complete picture of a nation's labor resources. Moreover, it does not account for or explain constraints and opportunities related to the use of time (Pentland, Harvey, Lawton, & McColl, 1999). Including a measure of nonmarket production provides a more accurate description of a national economy by recognizing that productive work includes paid work as well as household activities such as child and elder care, time allocated to food preparation, and other household chores as well as voluntary and community work. Time also is the fundamental resource for leisure activities. The amount of time available for rest and recreation is an important aspect of personal well-being and a measure of the overall standard of living of a given population (Fleming & Spellerberg, 1999).

Among the time use studies conducted thus far, none have focused specifically on patterns of time allocation by those individuals who are establishing their own firms—nascent entrepreneurs. This chapter provides the background for using the empirical data (where no prior empirical data existed) and suggests further analysis on differences in time use by nascent entrepreneurs.

Literature Review

Time-diary research and surveys have a long history. Accounting methods used to research living conditions among working class families in England and France at the end of the nineteenth century are recognized as the precursor to today's time budget/time use research methods in which behavior is measured in terms of the use of time in hours and minutes (Fleming & Spellerberg, 1999). Prior to World War II, time use surveys emerged as a statistical tool for social research and the development of social indicators (Fleming & Spellerberg, 1999). Time use surveys were conducted only intermittently until Alexander Szalai and his team conducted the first comparative cross-sectional time-diary study (Multinational Comparative Time-Budget Research Project) in the mid-1960s (Szalai, 1972). This pioneering study had a lasting effect on the collection of time use data by providing a coding framework subsequently adopted by many national time use studies.

Moreover, the report generated by the study itself, *The Use of Time,* broadened the types of analyses that could be generated from time use data, thus serving to advance the range of data collected as well as the methods for collection in later studies. Prior to the 1980s, no national statistical offices in any of the developed countries published official estimates of unpaid or domestic work (Ironmonger, 2000a). Over the past two decades, the recognition that unpaid work in the home and community represents a large but invisible part of a country's economy has grown, and efforts have been made to develop methods for measuring the value of this work and include aspects of unpaid production in national accounting systems (Fleming & Spellerberg, 1999; Ironmonger, 2000b).

One outcome of these initiatives has been a growing awareness of the need to address gender differences and potential explanations for gender inequality. Time use surveys are recognized as the best way of measuring unpaid work and are the starting point for methodologies for estimating its value. The distribution of paid and unpaid work is biased according to gender with women contributing the larger share of the unpaid work and men involved in more of the paid work. The imbalance supports the demands for better statistics on women's lives, and the recognition of women's economic contribution to national economies requires statistics on unpaid work. Such an interest in gender gave rise to one of the few time use studies in entrepreneurship, and it is one that considers not only time use but also families and socioeconomic characteristics (Longstreth, Stafford, & Mauldin, 1987).

The use of a diary methodology has become increasingly widespread as evidenced by Australia's full-scale national surveys conducted in 1992 and 1997. Recurring national time use studies in Japan, Korea, Finland, Canada, the Netherlands, and Norway have been conducted every 5 to 10 years (Pentland et al., 1999). In the early 1990s, EUROSTAT undertook the development of a harmonized approach to time use data collection, and subsequent initiatives were launched by the United Nations Statistical Office (UNSO) to construct a uniform classification system for time use studies (Fisher, Gauthier, Gershuny, & Victorino, 2000; Pentland et al., 1999).

Time use studies provide a database to address questions on everyday life and result in information on the activities of a population. They have the advantage of integrating a broad range of related information, placing the performance of a specific activity within the context of other activities, as well as relating it to the demographic and socioeconomic position of the performer. Comparisons of such data are based on the relationship between the four broad categories of paid work, unpaid work, leisure or free time, and personal care (including sleep). The amount of time spent on each category is assessed for the population as a whole and for different groups within the population. Reports of time use survey most often present aggregate data in hours and minutes spent on a selected list of activities.

The most basic time use questions addressed by the Panel Study of Entrepreneurial Dynamics (PSED) include

- How do nascent entrepreneurs allocate their time on a workday?
- How do nascent entrepreneurs allocate their time on a nonworkday?
- How do members of the comparison group allocate their time on a workday?
- How do members of the comparison group allocate their time on a nonworkday?

The Time Use Diary Variables

Data for the time use studies were collected in the PSED mail questionnaire due to the diary nature of the data being collected. Exhibit 9.1 displays the exact wording of the five items from the mail survey that represent the time use diary variables.

Questionnaire participants were asked to complete a time diary detailing daily activities for 2 days, a workday and a day off. Because weekday activity patterns typically differ from those of weekend days, data were collected for both. Ideally, the study of working hours as well as leisure time involves observing diaries covering a week or even a year (Juster & Stafford, 1985; Harvey, 1993; Harvey, Fisher, Gershuny, & Akbari, 2000). The principal advantage includes more representative

Exhibit 9.1   Time Use Diary Items in the PSED Mail Questionnaire

Consider two of your typical days over the past several weeks. First, a typical "workday," second, a typical "day off"—a day where you had little or no work activities.

M1.   In the last week, how many days were workdays?   _____ days

M2.   What day of the week was your last typical workday?   **[CIRCLE ONE DAY ONLY]**

| Sunday | Monday | Tuesday | Wednesday | Thursday | Friday | Saturday |

M3.   In the last month, how many days were days off?   _____days

M4.   What day of the week was your last typical day off?   **[CIRCLE ONE DAY ONLY]**

| Sunday | Monday | Tuesday | Wednesday | Thursday | Friday | Saturday |

M5.   For the last typical workday and day off, please indicate how much time (within a quarter of an hour) was devoted to each daily activity. It should total to 24 hours.

DAILY ACTIVITIES	**Typical Workday [Hours]**	**Typical Day Off [Hours]**
a. Sleeping	_____	_____
b. Personal care (dressing, bathing, grooming)	_____	_____
c. Meals, eating	_____	_____
d. All work for pay, including travel	_____	_____
e. Working on a new business start-up, including travel	_____	_____
f. Household work (e.g. cooking, cleaning, laundry, yard work, repairs, etc.)	_____	_____
g. Infant and child care (feeding, bathing, dressing, etc.)	_____	_____
h. Care of older family members (chores, errands)	_____	_____
i. Personal time with spouse, others	_____	_____
j. Reading, TV, sports, recreation, hobbies, going out	_____	_____
k. Other (specify) _____	_____	_____
TOTAL	**24 hours**	**24 hours**

estimates capable of capturing rare activities or events of short duration. However, such surveys are scarce. Moreover, it has been shown that a sample of 2 days per respondent provides for greater reliability of estimated times spent on a range of activities (Kalton, 1985). Therefore, this method should minimize systematic differences in time use due to day of the week variations. This method, however, precludes an analysis of seasonal activity patterns.

Each PSED respondent's use of time during a single day was measured by employing a self-reporting technique with the help of a diary. Participants in this study were presented with a precoded list of activities and asked to recall and record the category of activity in which they were engaged at any particular point in time during the day for both a typical workday and a day off. Within the time use research community, much debate has centered on the definition of activity categories (Fisher et al., 2000). As mentioned, efforts have been made to harmonize the data collection process and the definition of activity categories to allow for cross-national comparison of time use data (Szalai, 1972). The classification list used in this study includes 11 general activity categories for both workdays and days off. The categories used are less detailed than the 20/22-category list developed by Szalai (1972) or the 40-category classification used in the Multinational Time Use Study (MTUS) initiated in the 1980s by Gershuny (2000). This is largely because the PSED was not designed exclusively as a time use study but rather as a broader data collection effort that employed a time use component.

The PSED does not make a distinction between primary or secondary activities that may be performed simultaneously such as doing household chores, talking on the phone, or working on a business plan while watching children or eating a meal while reading a business book. When analyzing results, it is therefore possible to look at primary activities only. Excluding secondary activities results in the underreporting of such activities. Noisy data can result because there is a problem of boundaries between activities and the difficulty of capturing them (blending between home and work).

Secondary activity is especially applicable to the analysis of child care (Robinson & Godbey, 1997). Most child care is reported as a secondary activity, and women do more child care. In the Robinson and Godbey study, adding secondary activity actually increased total time spent on child care by more than 50%.

An Analysis of the Time Use Diary Variables

For purposes of this chapter, analyses were performed on the data set drawing from items from the mail questionnaire (the time use diary items). The analysis is based upon the full PSED data set and does not use a reduced set to address any additional classifications of respondents (Shaver, Carter, Gartner, & Reynolds, 2001). The analysis is performed on a weighted sample in order to allow for appropriate tests of statistical significance (Reynolds, 2000). The weighting variable "WTW1" is used with the nascent entrepreneur sample and the weighting variable "WTCG" is used for the comparison group. The sample includes respondents from the original PSED sample as well as the NSF-funded women and minority oversampling efforts. Descriptive statistics for the combined comparison groups from the main study and the minority oversample are also presented.

Pattern of Nascent Entrepreneurs Time Use

Descriptive statistics for the time use items of the full sample of nascent entrepreneurs are presented in Tables 9.1 and 9.2.

Table 9.1 Descriptive Statistics: Nascent Entrepreneurs Workdays/Days Off

Item Number	Variable	Nascent Entrepreneurs						Comparison Group					
		n	Min	Max	Mean	SD	%	n	Min	Max	Mean	SD	%
QM1	No. workdays in last week	544	0	7	5.13	1.49		344	0	7	4.56	1.78	
QM3	No. days off in last month	507	0		6.91	5.12		324	0	31	8.40	6.52	
QM2	Last typical workday												
	Sunday						7						4
	Monday						8						6
	Tuesday						4						6
	Wednesday						5						5
	Thursday						11						12
	Friday						37						46
	Saturday						28						20
QM4	Last typical day off												
	Sunday						59						57
	Monday						7						9
	Tuesday						3						5
	Wednesday						3						4
	Thursday						5						5
	Friday						8						8
	Saturday						15						13

Table 9.2 Descriptive Statistics: Nascent Entrepreneurs Workday/Day Off Time Allocation

Variable	Workday						Day Off						Stat. Sign.
	Item Number	n	Min	Max	Mean	SD	Item Number	n	Min	Max	Mean	SD	
Sleeping-hours	QM5a1	546	0	16	6.67	1.35	QM5a2	532	0	24	7.88	1.88	0.00
Personal care	QM5b1	546	0	5	1.05	0.56	QM5b2	532	0	24	1.21	1.74	0.16
Meals, eating	QM5c1	546	0	15	1.56	1.19	QM5c2	532	0	24	1.78	1.57	0.01
All work for pay, including travel	QM5d1	546	0	21	6.96	4.07	QM5d2	531	0	24	0.60	1.91	0.00
Working on a new business start-up	QM5e1	546	0	15	2.03	2.70	QM5e2	532	0	24	2.07	2.67	ns
Household work	QM5f1	546	0	15.5	1.34	1.62	QMf2	532	0	24	2.67	2.21	0.00
Infant and child care	QM5g1	546	0	24	0.70	1.70	QMg2	532	0	24	1.07	2.35	0.00
Care of older family members	QM5h1	546	0	8	0.27	0.77	QMh2	532	0	24	0.55	1.66	0.00
Personal time with spouse, others	QM5i1	546	0	10	1.73	1.33	QMi2	532	0	24	3.48	2.83	0.00
Reading, TV, sports, recreation, hobbies, going out	QM5j1	546	0	9	1.50	1.37	QMj2	532	0	24	2.93	2.59	0.00
Other	QM5k1	544	0	22	0.38	1.33	QMk2	532	0	24	0.47	1.52	0.25

Table 9.1 provides the information on the number of workdays in the last week, the last typical workday, as well as information about days off for the nascent entrepreneurs and the comparison group. The results show that the mean number of days off in the last month is greater for those in the comparison group than the nascent entrepreneurs (8.40 and 6.91, respectively).

Table 9.2 provides a comparative analysis between how nascent entrepreneurs use time on days designated as workdays and days designated as days off. Sleep appears to be a dominant activity in terms of amount of time spent for both workdays and days off. Clearly there are variations. As one would expect, workdays are consumed principally with work-related activities. Paid work represents the single largest activity category during the workweek. Day off activities are oriented toward household tasks, family care, and leisure pursuits. An increase in sleep, household work, and time spent with one's spouse and leisure activities such as reading, sports, hobbies, and watching television are observed. Many of the "free time" activities take place during the week as well but with more time allocated to them on the day off. Statistical differences were found between the means in almost every category with the exception of "working on a new business startup" and the "other" category. It seems that the nascent entrepreneur works on the business start-up about the same amount of time on both workdays and nonworkdays.

Table 9.3 presents the difference in time allocation for the comparison group between workdays and days off. Again, all differences are significant with the exception of the measures for "Working on a new business start-up" and "other." It is interesting that those in the comparison group report working on a start-up, which presents the possibility that they are also nascent entrepreneurs. This may be because analyses in this chapter did not reduce the overall sample as described in the appendices (i.e., removing individuals from the comparison group who met the criteria as nascent entrepreneurs). However, the overall patterns of time use prioritization appear to be very similar to those of the nascent entrepreneurs. Sleeping is given the most amount of time on days off and the second most time on workdays. Paid work dominates time use on days designated as workdays. However, "Working on a new business start-up" is the third largest time use for nascent entrepreneurs, whereas members of the comparison group report "reading, TV, sports, recreation, hobbies, going out" as their third use. The order of the top four uses of time on days off is identical for nascent entrepreneurs and the comparison group respondents.

Conclusion and Future Research

Research in the area of time use has a rigorous history and is expanding into additional topical and geographical areas. It is a newer entry into the field of entrepreneurship and, until the PSED, has never been applied to people in the process of starting a new business. The PSED data on time use provides researchers with an opportunity to examine the role of both paid and unpaid work in the venture creation process. There are a variety of potential approaches. One line of research might focus upon demographic differences between nascent entrepreneurs and the

Table 9.3 Descriptive Statistics: Comparison Group Workday/Day Off Time Allocation

Variable	Workday						Day Off						
	Item Number	n	Min	Max	Mean	SD	Item Number	n	Min	Max	Mean	SD	Stat. Sign.
Sleeping-hours	QM5a1	336	0	10	6.73	1.39	QM5a2	337	0	24	7.71	1.70	0.00
Personal care	QM5b1	335	0	7	1.05	0.58	QM5b2	336	0	20	1.24	1.10	0.00
Meals, eating	QM5c1	336	0	5	1.44	0.76	QM5c2	336	0	20	1.88	1.12	0.00
All work for pay, including travel	QM5d1	336	0	15	7.22	3.98	QM5d2	336	0	16	0.37	1.44	0.00
Working on a new business start-up	QM5e1	335	0	10	0.44	1.46	QM5e2	336	0	16	0.52	1.68	1.54
Household work	QM5f1	336	0	12	1.59	1.66	QMf2	336	0	20	3.50	2.43	0.00
Infant and child care	QM5g1	336	0	16	0.86	2.00	QMg2	336	0	20	1.09	2.32	0.00
Care of older family members	QM5h1	334	0	16	0.41	1.41	QMh2	336	0	16	0.61	1.66	0.00
Personal time with spouse, others	QM5i1	335	0	20	1.83	1.98	QMi2	336	0	22	3.73	2.90	0.00
Reading, TV, sports, recreation, hobbies	QM5j1	335	0	12	1.91	1.46	QMj2	336	0	24	3.62	2.56	0.00
Other	QM5k1	335	0	16.5	0.70	2.17	QMk2	336	0	9.75	0.53	1.46	1.61

comparison group members, including those of gender, race and ethnicity, age, or education. Another could investigate differences by socioeconomic variables, such as household income or home ownership. A final suggestion is to consider the analysis of the use of time according to the growth aspirations of the nascent entrepreneurs to see if individuals with more expansive views of their emerging business spend their time different than those with a more lifestyle-oriented approach.

The PSED is a powerful tool for the study of time use, not only for the strength of the type of questions that can be addressed but also for its methodology. Time use data have certain properties that make analysis difficult. One challenge is to obtain accurate measures of time allocation estimates due to the limited recall ability of the respondents. For the purposes of these types of studies, a short and recent time span for recording activities is essential to data reliability (Juster & Stafford, 1985). The nature of the PSED provides the first opportunity to analyze time use data without the potential bias from retrospective data and allows researchers to capture the time use of nascent entrepreneurs and the members of the comparison group as they are actually spending their time.

References

Fisher, K., Gauthier, A. H., Gershuny, J., & Victorino, C. (2000). *Exploring new ground for using the multinational time use study.* ISER working papers from Institute for Social and Economic Research, University of Essex, Colchester, U.K.

Fleming, R., & Spellerberg, A. (1999). *Using time use data. A history of time use surveys and uses of time use data.* Wellington, New Zealand: Statistics New Zealand.

Gershuny, J. (2000). *Changing times. Work and leisure in postindustrial society.* New York: Oxford University Press.

Harvey, A. S. (1993). Guidelines for time use data collection. *Social Indicators Research, 30,* 197–228.

Harvey, A. S., Fisher, K., Gershuny, J., & Akbari, A. (2000). *Examining working time arrangements using time use survey data.* ISER working papers from Institute for Social and Economic Research, University of Essex, Colchester, U.K

Ironmonger, D. S. (2000a). *Household production and the household economy* (Research Paper No. 759). Melbourne, Australia: The University of Melbourne, Department of Economics.

Ironmonger, D. S. (2000b). *An overview of time use surveys.* International Seminar on Time Use Studies. New Delhi, India: Central Statistical Organization Ministry of Statistics and Programme Implementation, Government of India.

Juster, F. T., & Stafford, F. P. (Eds.). (1985). *Time, goods, and well-being.* Ann Arbor: University of Michigan, Institute of Social Research.

Kalton, G. (1985). Sample design issues in time diary studies. In F. T. Juster & F. P. Stafford (Eds.), *Time, goods, and well-being* (pp. 92–112). Ann Arbor: University of Michigan, Institute of Social Research.

Longstreth, M., Stafford, K., & Mauldin, T. (1987). Self-employed women and their families: Time use and socioeconomic characteristics. *Journal of Small Business Management, 25*(3), 30–37.

Pentland, W. E., Harvey, A. S., Lawton, M. P., & McColl, M. A. (1999). *Time use research in the social sciences.* New York: Kluwer Academic/Plenum.

Reynolds, P. D. (2000). National Panel Study of U.S. Business Startups: Background and methodology. In J. A. Katz (Ed.), *Advances in entrepreneurship, firm emergence, and growth: Vol. 4. Databases for the study of entrepreneurship* (pp. 153–227). Stamford, CT: JAI Press.

Robinson, J., & Godbey, G. (1997). *Time for life. The surprising ways Americans use their time.* University Park: Pennsylvania State University.

Shaver, K. G., Carter, N. M., Gartner, W. B., & Reynolds, P. D. (2001, June). Who is a nascent entrepreneur? Decision rule for identifying and selecting entrepreneurs in the *Panel Study of Entrepreneurial Dynamics (PSED)*. Paper presented at the Babson Kauffman Entrepreneurship Research Conference, Jönköping, Sweden.

Szalai, A. (Ed.). (1972). *The use of time. Daily activities of urban and suburban populations in twelve countries.* Mouton & Co, European Coordination Centre for Research Documentation in the Social Sciences. The Hague, The Netherlands: Mouton.

CHAPTER 10

Work Participation History

Amy E. Davis

Howard E. Aldrich

The work participation history section of the mail questionnaire was designed to focus on the timing of events within the life course of individuals and their families over the years prior to the interview, from 1987 forward. It focuses on transitions into and out of significant life events, such as employment, self-employment, being enrolled in an educational institution, and being unemployed. Such information allows us to understand the changing context within which individuals have entered the entrepreneurial process, as well as the role that entrepreneurship plays in people's careers. In this chapter, we first describe the rationale for collecting such information, using a life course perspective. We then discuss the design of these measures and present descriptive statistics, examining similarities and differences by gender and nascent entrepreneur status. Finally, we discuss ways in which the work history data in the Panel Study of Entrepreneurial Dynamics (PSED) can be used to illuminate important issues regarding entrepreneurship and careers.

Life Course Perspective

The life course perspective has developed across a variety of social and behavioral sciences during the past two decades and "refers to the social patterning of events and roles over the life-span, a process ever subject to the interaction of individual behavior with a changing society" (Elder & Caspi, 1990, p. 202). Life course researchers focus on movements into and out of roles and relationships, such as moving from school into employment and marriage. As an inherently dynamic approach to studying social life, the life course perspective "reflects the interweave of work, family, and community role trajectories, the interdependencies of paths among family members, and the changing circumstances and options of both families and family businesses" (Moen, 1998, p. 16).

Social scientists use a life course perspective to place people's working lives within a wider social context (Rosenfeld, 1992). In American society, work is an important context for the expression and further development of both identity and knowledge. Temporal organization is embedded in peoples' work histories, generically labeled "careers." Over three decades ago, sociologist Harold Wilensky (1961, p. 523) defined a career as "a succession of related jobs, arranged in a hierarchy of prestige, through which persons move in an ordered (more or less predictable) sequence."

Most Americans build their careers as employees, working as members of organizations. For many in the post–World War II era, lifetime employment with a single organization was typical. In the last two decades, organizational policies have increasingly emphasized "employment flexibility" in the United States and elsewhere. Through the 1980s and into the 1990s, contingent and temporary employment grew very rapidly. A study of job stability in the United States (Swinnerton & Wial, 1995) found modest but statistically significant decreases in job stability for the period of 1987–1991, compared to 1979 to 1983. This evidence suggests that the lifetime number of employers for which the average American worker will work is probably increasing.

Moreover, many people not only work for multiple organizations but also switch occupations one or more times during the life course. They may also pursue education later in life. Thus, people's careers have become more volatile over time.

The career histories experienced by Americans manifest a great deal of heterogeneity across three dimensions relevant to becoming a nascent entrepreneur: number of employers, extent of knowledge accumulation, and the role of personal identity. These three dimensions are derived from a reading of the July 1994 special issue of the *Journal of Organizational Behavior,* through the lens of the life course perspective (Baker & Aldrich, 1996). The first dimension is simply the number of employers (including spells of self-employment) included in a person's work history. The second dimension is the extent to which the knowledge and competencies employees gain are cumulative over the course of their careers. The third career dimension is the extent to which employees themselves play an instrumental role in structuring their work histories through their personal identities, as well as the extent to which work histories structure personal identities.

The three dimensions—identity, knowledge accumulation, and employers—specify outcomes of career processes that take place over the course of peoples' lives. The dimensions should be thought of as continuous variables describing a three-dimensional space within which very few points (representing individual career patterns) are impossible but in which clusters tend to occur. Career processes reflect the interactions of agency, which refers to peoples' abilities to make choices and influence their own lives, with changing structures of constraints and opportunities (Elder & O'Rand, 1995, pp. 454–455).

Workers whose skills are based on a rapidly changing state of the art and who are not learning new skills quickly enough at work might find themselves pursuing additional education throughout their entire lifetimes. Continued vocational education becomes a seemingly permanent component of employees' personal lives. For example, many software engineers continue to take night classes, year after year, to maintain the currency of their skills.

Although many jobs in the post–World War II era were characterized by 40-hour workweeks, the economy is now marked by a polarization of work hours, meaning that the number of people working greater or less than 40 hours per week has increased, whereas the number of people working around 40 hours has decreased. Specifically, work hours have increased for those at the high end of the economic distribution but decreased for those at the low end, mainly because of involuntary part-time work (Jacobs & Gerson, 2001). Work hours are correlated with characteristics like age and gender in that younger people and women tend to work fewer hours.

Changes in the hours that people devote to work have important consequences for entrepreneurship. If people use their own time to develop and maintain vocational knowledge, the incremental time burden represents a further encroachment of work into formerly personal time. Alternatively, to the extent that what it means to be competent changes over time, those who have been repeatedly exploiting old skills will end up effectively losing ground to others who have been learning new skills.

Life course concepts of control cycles, situational imperatives, and accentuation provide a framework for understanding how individuals deal with discontinuities in their working lives (Elder & O'Rand, 1995). Life course theorists have suggested,

> When social change creates a disparity between claims and resources, goals and accomplishments, the corresponding loss of control prompts efforts to regain control. The entire process resembles a control cycle—losing control is followed by efforts to restore control over life outcomes, a process featuring reactant behavior. (Elder & O'Rand, 1995, p. 468)

The idea of "losing control" can be directly interpreted, therefore, as an interruption, or breaching of identity in one's career.

Situational imperatives are changes in circumstances that result in a substantial reduction in an individual's personal control (Elder & O'Rand, 1995, p. 468). During times of transition, particularly during stressful periods, prominent individual characteristics tend to become even more pronounced. Elder and Caspi (1990) labeled this the "accentuation principle." When long established identities are threatened, people tend to rely more heavily on what has worked in the past, rather than changing their sense of self or searching for new ways of coping.

We expect work histories to shape individuals' work values and perceptions of risk. Some features of individuals' work histories may make them more or less favorable toward taking on the role identity of "nascent entrepreneur." For example, many people associate business ownership with risk, and their work histories may make them more willing to take on a risk. Others have argued that nascent entrepreneurs differ from others not because they are greater risk takers but because they feel that entrepreneurship is not really a risky endeavor, given their abilities (Simon, Houghton, & Aquino, 2000). These perceptions, and also work values and preferences, may be shaped by individuals' work histories, such as how often they have experienced career transitions or interruptions (Carr & Sheridan, 2001). Johnson (2001), for example, found that work values often change in response to work experiences.

Entrepreneurial, educational, homemaking, and labor force interruption experiences may also have important consequences for nascent entrepreneurship. Several studies found that previous experience with entrepreneurship increases the likelihood of trying it again (Dennis, 2002, p. 1; Van Auken, 1999). Education has also been shown to be an important predictor of participation in self-employment (Carr, 1996). Education has an important influence on the continuity of women's careers, decreasing the likelihood that they will leave the labor force (Blair-Loy, 1999; Drobnic, Blossfeld, & Rohwer, 1999). Time spent homemaking has been shown to have negative consequences for self-employment (Longstreth, Stafford, & Mauldin, 1987).

Time out of labor force is detrimental to employees, according to several studies, and we believe that it is detrimental to entrepreneurs, as well (Groot, Schippers, & Siegers, 1990). When people leave the labor force, they lose the financial resources they had obtained from wages, health insurance, and other benefits. The value of their education depreciates, and they lose opportunities to gain new skills through job experience. In addition, they may suffer the loss of prior networks and fail to gain new ones. These resources are consequential for entrepreneurship. However, time out of the labor force resulting from a layoff may make entrepreneurship seem less risky. For example, the probability of unemployment is positively associated with rates of self-employment (Eisenhauer, 1995).

Families and Careers

The dynamics of household formation and dissolution play a role in making entrepreneurial careers more or less likely for men and women (Aldrich & Cliff, 2003). Members of families consisting of two spouses with good jobs, each able to cover the other's insurance needs and pay the bills during spells of unemployment or reeducation, should be well positioned for becoming nascent entrepreneurs. Such households, however, constitute a minority of all American family units today. About 55% of all households in the United States consist of a married couple. In 1940, almost 70% of families were traditional, "husband employed, wife homemaker" families, but by 1990, that figure had dropped to only 20% (Ahlburg & DeVita, 1992, p. 25). Single-parent households, single-person households, and dual-career families have increased in recent years. These family changes have an influence on individuals' careers and also affect whether they enter nascent entrepreneurship.

Family characteristics have been shown to have important consequences for individuals' careers and are important to consider when interpreting work history data (Carr, 1996; Rosenfeld, 1992). For example, the ages at which persons marry or become parents affect career processes (Alon, Donahoe, & Tienda, 2001; Bielby,

1992). Marriage and parenthood also influence labor force participation rates and hours worked (Kaufman & Uhlenberg, 2000). Many have found that women some-times enter self-employment in an attempt to balance work and family demands, often with limited success (Carr, 1996; Jurik, 1998).

Family effects on individuals' careers vary by gender. Marriage and parenthood are often correlated with higher earnings for men and lower earnings for women. Women are more likely than men to enter and exit the labor force at any given period of time, but women's labor force participation has become more continu-ous over time (Hakim, 1996). In the United States, most women, even those with children under the age of 6, participate in the labor force, and the relationship between having young children and women's employment has become weaker in recent years (Bernhardt, 1993). Women who become parents are also more likely than men to work part-time (Bernhardt, 1993; Drobnic, Blossfeld, & Rohwer, 1999; Rosenfeld, 1992). Part-time work has important consequences for nascent entrepreneurship to the extent that it is associated with fewer formal and on-the-job training opportunities, managerial experiences, and fringe benefits.

In addition to individuals' careers being affected by whether they are married or are parents, individuals' careers are affected by their family members' careers. For example, women married to men with high incomes experience less mobility than do others, and having young children is associated with a transition from full-time to part-time work for women (Rosenfeld, 1992). In addition, several researchers have noted how a spouse's employment characteristics affect an individual's pay and participation in household labor (Brayfield, 1995; Pavalko & Elder, 1993).

Age, Period, and Cohort Effects

Age, period, and cohort effects influence career development as well as organizatio-nal change (Aldrich, 1999). *Age effects* refer to changes associated with individuals' chronological ages, regardless of time in history. For example, young age is associ-ated with enrollment in education, middle age is associated with employment, and older age is associated with retirement. There are age-graded roles in which particular career and family activities and statuses are normatively linked to particular age ranges, and certain stages of careers are associated with different strategies for balanc-ing work and family. Bielby (1992) found that middle age is associated with the highest job involvement, for example. Age may also affect entry into self-employment, with people more often entering self-employment after age 35 and those entering self-employment at an early age differing from those entering later in life (Carr & Sheridan, 2001, p. 203).

Given the volatility of the labor market, however, age effects are not as predictable as they once were. Traditional models of the life course projected a linear path, in which individuals first entered education, then employment, and then retirement. The greater complexity and diversity of people's careers today is captured in an emergent model of the life course proposed by Singh and Verma (2001). In their model, people may simultaneously engage in education and employment, and even retirement, and may reenter these different roles multiple times.

Period effects refer to influences of historical events on individuals, regardless of their age. For example, legislation regarding women's rights enhanced opportunities for women during the 1970s (Blair-Loy, 1999). During the period in which the PSED data was collected, several events relevant to entrepreneurship occurred: expansion of businesses related to technology and the Internet, low unemployment, and high stock market values. The 1990s was also a period of continuing decline in the manufacturing sector and expansion of the service and information sector, as well as nonstandard employment relationships and nonstandard hours. When analyzing the PSED, these historical events should be considered because some patterns observed may be unique to the time period when the data were collected.

Cohort effects are influences of historical events that affect people differently, depending on their ages. For example, researchers often examine how historical events that occurred during a cohort's childhood and adolescence affect later developments in its life course. Individuals who grew up during the Depression had a different transition to adulthood than did individuals growing up during the post–World War II era, for example (Shanahan, Miech, & Elder, 1998). Blair-Loy (1999) found that young women in her sample were unaware of the importance of legislation in the 1970s in providing opportunities for them. She found that the young women less often experienced sex discrimination, also a cohort effect. Researchers studying life course events longitudinally often confine their research to a single cohort.

Because of the design of the PSED, researchers cannot disentangle age and cohort effects. The PSED has multiple birth cohorts, with respondent ages ranging from 18 to 92. Although the data is panel in nature, the time between follow-ups is too short to determine age effects. When researchers find differences between younger and older people in the PSED, they should exercise caution before making claims as to whether these effects are age- or cohort-related.

Typical human capital measures such as years of experience (such as full-time, managerial, occupational, industrial, or organizational) and level of education are important to the study of entrepreneurship, but the work history measures provide information other measures fail to illuminate. With the work history measures, we can examine the degree of continuity in a person's recent career history and better understand what recent career history characteristics lead to nascent entrepreneurship. Studies that find an effect of education or experience are useful, but the work history measures better measure the complexity characteristic of so many people's careers.

Description of Work History Data from Mail Questionnaire

The work history portion of the PSED can be found on page 6 of the mail questionnaire, item 01. It has been reproduced in Figure 10.1. On the mail questionnaire, respondents were asked to fill out a chart describing their work history from 1987 to 1998. They were asked, "For each of the last twelve years, please indicate your major activities. Put an 'x' in each box that applies. For example, if you were a

01. For each of the last eleven years, please indicate your major activities. Put an "x" in each
    box that applies. For example, if you were a student part-time and employed part-time in
    1990, you would put an "x" in two rows for the 1990 column.

Major Activities	87	88	89	90	91	92	93	94	95	96	97	98
a. Employed full-time												
b. Employed part-time												
c. Self-employed full-time												
d. Self-employed part-time												
e. Student full-time												
f. Student part-time												
g. Unemployed seeking work												
h. Unemployed not seeking work												
i. Unpaid volunteer worker												
j. Homemaker												
k. Disabled, unable to work												
l. Retired												

Figure 10.1   Work History Items in the PSED Mail Questionnaire

student part-time and employed part-time in 1990, you would put an 'x' in two
rows for the 1990 column." The major activities are employed full-time; employed
part-time; self-employed full-time; self-employed part-time; student full-time;
student part-time; unemployed seeking work; unemployed not seeking work;
unpaid volunteer worker; homemaker; disabled, unable to work; and retired.
Respondents were allowed to select as many activities as they felt were appropriate
for each year. Thus, the raw data have 144 variables for the work history section.
There are many ways to generate summary measures for these variables, and we
have selected a few for discussion. We believe these variables capture some of the
complexity in people's work histories.

Some characteristics of the life course are not available in the PSED. These
include respondents' dates or ages of marriage, dates of birth/adoption or age of
any children, and dates of divorce/remarriage. We also do not have information
regarding spouses' ages or work participation histories. These factors may exert
important influences on individuals' work histories as well as their participation in
nascent entrepreneurship, but we cannot explore them. Some of these questions
have been added to Wave 4 of the PSED and thus will be available for analysis in the
future.

Researchers have not resolved how to deal with the complexity of information
available through work history or life history tables. Some solutions include a
person-centered approach (Singer, Ryff, Carr, & Magee, 1998) or sequence analysis
(Blair-Loy, 1999). Researchers also often construct pathway types (Moen & Han,
2001). Examples of pathway types include stable employment, homemaker career,

and intermittent employment (Hakim, 1996). Another typology is delayed-entry career, orderly career, high-geared career, steady part-time career, and intermittent career (Moen & Han, 2001).

If we had asked respondents to select one and only one activity for each year, or to rank the activities within each year in order of importance, we could have constructed measures such as number of disruptions. However, given that respondents were not restricted in the number of activities they could list, we constructed other measures. Asking respondents to select only one activity would probably be inappropriate because many people take on multiple roles and have complex career lives, sometimes participating in homemaking, employment, self-employment, and education simultaneously.

Measures

Trying to summarize a person's work history into a single variable or typology is an oversimplification. Therefore, we examine several characteristics of individuals' work histories. We examine years as student, employee, and self-employed and consider both total (full-time and part-time) participation and full-time participation. These variables, along with the "homemaker" variable, do not indicate if this is the only or primary role that respondents held during these years but simply that they recorded it as a significant activity. We expect that employment will be more common among the comparison group and self-employment will be more common among the nascent entrepreneurs. We expect that the homemaker role will be more common among women than men. We distinguish total from full-time because part-time work and full-time work may have different implications for entrepreneurial or employee careers.

We created two measures to examine the extent to which people were *not* engaged in either education or employment. If respondents said that they were neither a full-time nor part-time employee, student, or self-employed, they were given a 1 for that year. For the years *not in full-time employment or education*, respondents were given a 1 if they said they were not engaged in full-time employment, self-employment, or were students. We look at these two measures of disengagement from labor force activity because we believe that they will vary by gender and have consequences for nascent entrepreneurship. We believe that women are more likely than men to have time out of employment or education, especially after the birth of a child. We also believe that "time out" may impede participation in entrepreneurship because these people have lost skills and networks during this time out.[1] Means and standard deviations for these variables are in years. The *percentage yes* for these measures indicate whether respondents were *ever* engaged in this role during any of the 12 years.

Number of roles ever held is a measure of the extent to which a person has a boundaryless career, in which he or she may transition from being a full-time employee to a part-time student, to self-employed over the course of the 12 years. This variable could range between 1 and 12. Our measures do not examine employees' mobility within organizations (such as a promotion to management), nor do they measure movement from employer to employer if the employment status stays the same. In other words, if a person quit one organization as a full-time employee one day and started work at another organization as a full-time employee the next, our measures would not detect this type of mobility. Our measure does not detect changes in occupations either. Therefore, it is a conservative measure of the volatility of people's work histories. We expect that women and nascent entrepreneurs will have higher values for this variable than will men and the comparison group.

Average number of roles held per year is a measure of the extent to which people engage in multiple activities either simultaneously or within the course of 1 year. This variable potentially ranges from 1 to 12. For example, some respondents report that they are simultaneously self-employed full-time and a part-time student for a given year, or they report simultaneously being a homemaker, self-employed part-time, and an unpaid volunteer. We expect that the average number of roles per year will vary by gender and by nascent entrepreneur status. Because women are more likely to report being a homemaker and their labor force participation rate is quite high, even for those with young children, we expect that more women than men will report being both a homemaker and an employee. We expect that nascent entrepreneurs will score higher on this measure than the comparison group because they may be more likely to pursue part-time education later in life or work as employees while starting businesses.

Descriptive Statistics

Initially, 871 respondents answered the mail questionnaire. Nine observations were deleted as a result of data cleaning. Women, minorities, and nascent entrepreneurs were oversampled in the PSED. For example, nascent entrepreneurs represent only 6% of the population but more than half of the original sample. Weights are applied to the raw data so that they better represent the characteristics of the population and inferences can be made beyond the data. Thus, observations from members of groups that were oversampled (such as nascent entrepreneurs) are downweighted and observations from members of groups that were undersampled (such as nonentrepreneurs) are given more weight. When weights are applied, nascent entrepreneurs only make up 45 of the 862 respondents in the mail questionnaire.

Weighted descriptive statistics of our measures are presented in Table 10.1, by sex and nascent entrepreneur status. The vast majority of respondents have engaged in employment as an employee (89.57% as full-time and 94.49% as full- or part-time). Men and women are equally likely to have reported being an employee, but men nascent entrepreneurs report significantly more years than women nascent entrepreneurs (7.43 years vs. 6.33 years). The nascent group is significantly more likely to report self-employment activities compared to the comparison group, but there are not gender differences within the comparison group. In the nascent group, men are more likely to report full-time self-employment than are women.

About half of the respondents have engaged in either part-time or full-time educational activities in the last 12 years. In the nascent group, women are significantly

Table 10.1　Descriptive Statistics: Work History Measures, by Gender and Nascent Entrepreneur Status and Gender (weighted and unweighted)

| Variable | Unit of Analysis | N Entire Sample | Comparison Group | | | Nascent Entrepreneurs | | | CGI/ NE |
			Men	Women	Stat. Sign.	Men	Women	Stat. Sign.	Stat. Sign.
Total employee activity	% yes	94.49	93.82	95.44		93.03	93.35		
	mean yrs	8.72	9.12	8.36		8.88	8.54		
	SD	4.05	3.93	4.13		4.12	4.01		
Full-time employee activity	% yes	89.59	87.72	89.79		86.57	86.62	**	
	mean yrs	7.37	7.98	6.85		7.43	6.33		
	SD	4.48	4.43	4.48		4.51	4.28		
Total self-employment activity	% yes	30.66	32.50	25.89		60.90	61.34		***
	mean yrs	1.69	2.07	1.21		3.09	2.72		***
	SD	3.39	3.77	2.89		4.00	3.49		
Full-time self-employment activity	% yes	14.49	17.44	9.57		39.1	26.16	**	***
	mean yrs	0.63	0.85	0.36		1.59	0.97	**	***
	SD	2.14	2.55	1.55		2.97	2.31		
Total educational activity	% yes	44.32	40.06	47.51		45.87	57.97	**	
	mean yrs	2.52	2.61	2.52		2.58	2.66		
	SD	3.67	3.75	3.62		3.72	3.33		
Full-time educational activity	% yes	29.27	25.86	31.64		32.66	41.36	*	
	mean yrs	1.67	1.42	1.88		1.73	1.78		
	SD	3.23	3.00	3.41		3.26	2.95		
Homemaker	% yes	29.57	3.86	53.88	***	6.61	48.06	***	*
	mean yrs	2.43	0.24	4.48	***	0.32	3.90	***	*
	SD	4.44	1.44	5.25		1.70	5.15		
Not engaged in employment or education	% yes	30.15	23.08	37.29	*	15.26	33.83	***	*
	mean yrs	1.68	1.34	2.04		0.75	1.47		**
	SD	3.24	3.06	3.42		2.37	2.85		
Not engaged in full-time employment or education	% yes	52.89	47.37	57.85		46.74	62.55	***	
	mean yrs	2.96	2.48	3.43		1.87	3.47	***	
	SD	4.00	3.78	4.17		3.20	3.99		
Average number of roles held per year	mean	1.58	1.44	1.71	***	1.41	1.71	***	
	SD	0.66	0.59	0.69		0.57	0.71		
Number of roles ever held	mean	3.32	2.94	3.63	**	3.34	4.09	***	*
	SD	1.78	1.63	1.83		1.85	1.82		
n, weighted		862	387	430		27	18		
n, unweighted		862	142	173		264	283		

NOTE: Variable values range from 0 to 12. *t* tests used for significance tests of means; chi-square tests used for significance tests of percentages.

* = $p < .05$; ** = $p < .01$; *** = $p < .001$

more likely than men to have engaged in education and full-time education. Women in both the comparison group and nascent sample are more likely to report homemaking activities. In addition, the nascent group reports overall more home-making than the comparison group. Women are more likely than men to report not being engaged in education or employment within both groups. The comparison group is more likely than the nascent group to report not being in education or employment, probably because some people in the comparison group are retired.

For full-time employment or education activity, there are gender differences only among nascents. Women within each group hold more roles than men per year. Women also report more roles over the 12 years in each group, and nascents report more roles than does the comparison group. Note that in many cases, there are no significant differences between men and women or between nascent entre-preneurs and the comparison group. Possible differences between them may be suppressed because these variables are strongly influenced by age and family, which should be considered in any multivariate analysis.

Implications

The work history data available in the PSED can be used to explore a variety of issues related to family, careers, and entrepreneurship. We first discuss some possible future inquiries and then mention caveats researchers should note when designing research projects using the PSED.

Researchers can examine how respondents' household situations at the time of the interview have influenced their work histories. For example, Davis (2004) will address how gender and family characteristics have influenced work participation histories in her dissertation. Although retrospective data on family life such as date of marriage and date of birth are unavailable, information about people's current household situation can be used to determine how it has affected their work history in the form of participation in education, homemaking, or labor force interrup-tions. Multivariate analysis can be used to help determine what household factors influence work history and whether these vary by characteristics like age and ethnicity.

Researchers may want to examine how characteristics other than current house-hold situation affect work histories. For example, the PSED contains a great deal of information regarding how respondents' family of origin, and information about parents' occupation or entrepreneurship experience or family size influence work histories. Family of origin has been shown to have important effects on labor force participation and attitudes regarding entrepreneurship, work, and family (e.g., Rozier & Thompson, 1998). Researchers may also want to examine ethnic differences to determine how ethnicity affects work history.

For those interested in entrepreneurship, more pertinent lines of inquiry may include examining how work history affects participation in nascent entrepreneur-ship and how the start-up process unfolds. For example, researchers can examine how time out of the labor force or participation in education influences the decision to become a nascent entrepreneur. Researchers may wish to create work history typologies to explore different pathways to nascent entrepreneurship. Alternatively, examining only nascent entrepreneurs, researchers can examine how work history influences later events in the start-up process such as quitting a current job to pursue start-up full-time, start-up status in subsequent waves (operating business, active start-up, inactive start-up, quit venture), or devoting fewer hours to housework to devote more time to the start-up.

Caveats

As mentioned previously, age and cohort effects cannot be distinguished, given that the data were collected in a relatively narrow window of time. This period is unique, characterized by the Internet boom of the late 1990s and later the bust. Some phenomena observed in the PSED data may be strongly influenced by these period effects. In addition, we do not have detailed information about family life history such as when children were born/adopted or when marital unions were formed or dissolved. Researchers are therefore limited in the extent to which they can examine family and career dynamics over the life course. Also, the work history is not complete because it only includes 12 years of retrospective data. Therefore, this information will be less complete for older people than for younger people.

Notes

1. We do not present results for number of years unemployed seeking work, unemployed not seeking work, volunteer, disabled, or retired. Researchers whose questions require inquiry into such issues may construct these measures.

References

Ahlburg, D. A., & DeVita, C. J. (1992). New realities of the American family. *Population Bulletin, 47*(2), 1–35.

Aldrich, H. E. (1999). *Organizations evolving.* London: Sage.

Aldrich, H. E., & Cliff, J. E. (2003). The pervasive effects of family on entrepreneurship: Toward a family embeddedness perspective. *Journal of Business Venturing, 18*(5), 573–596.

Alon, S., Donahoe, D., & Tienda, M. (2001). The effects of early work experience on young women's labor force attachment. *Social Forces, 79*(3), 1005–1034.

Baker, T. & Aldrich, H. E. (1996). Prometheus stretches: Identity, knowledge cumulation, and multi-employer careers. In M. Arthur & D. Rousseau (Eds.), *The boundaryless career: A new employment principle for a new organizational era* (pp. 132–149). New York: Oxford University Press.

Bernhardt, E. M. (1993). Fertility and employment. *European Sociological Review, 9*(1), 25–42.

Bielby, D. D. (1992). Commitment to work and family. *Annual Review of Sociology, 18*, 281–302.

Blair-Loy, M. (1999). Career patterns of executive women in finance: An optimal matching analysis. *American Journal of Sociology, 104*(5), 1346–1397.

Brayfield, A. (1995). Juggling jobs and kids: The impact of employment schedules on fathers' caring for children. *Journal of Marriage and the Family, 57*(May), 321–332.

Carr, D. (1996). Two paths to self-employment? Women's and men's self-employment in the United States, 1980. *Work and Occupations, 23*(1), 26–53.

Carr, D., & Sheridan, J. (2001). Family turning-points and career transitions at midlife. In V. W. Marshall, W. R. Heinz, H. Krüger, & A. Verna (Eds.), *Restructuring work and the life course* (pp. 201–227). Toronto, Canada: University of Toronto.

Davis, A. E. (2004). *Going it alone? The effects of gender, family, and membership in startup teams on entrepreneurship.* Dissertation proposal, University of North Carolina at Chapel Hill, Department of Sociology.

Dennis, W. J., Jr. (Series Ed.). (2002). *Pre-owner experience* (National Small Business Poll, Issue 8). Washington, DC: NFIB Research Foundation.

Drobnic, S., Blossfeld, H., & Rohwer, G. (1999). Dynamics of women's employment patterns over the family life course: A comparison of the United States and Germany. *Journal of Marriage and the Family, 61*(1), 133–146.

Eisenhauer, J. G. (1995). The entrepreneurial decision: Economic theory and empirical evidence. *Entrepreneurship: Theory and Practice, 19* (summer), 67–79.

Elder, G. H., Jr., & Caspi, A. (1990). Studying lives in a changing society: Sociological and personological explorations. In A. I. Rabin, R. A. Zucker, R. A. Emmons, & S. Frank (Eds.), *Studying persons and lives* (Henry A. Murray Lecture Series, pp. 201–247). New York: Springer.

Elder, G. H., & O'Rand, A. M. (1995). Adult lives in a changing society. In K. S. Cook, G. A. Fine, & J. S. House (Eds.), *Sociological perspectives on social psychology* (pp. 452–475). Boston: Allyn & Bacon.

Groot, L. F. M., Schippers, J. J., & Siegers, J. J. (1990). The effect of unemployment, temporary withdrawals and part-time work on workers' wage rates. *European Sociological Review, 6*(2), 257–273.

Hakim, C. (1996). Labour mobility and employment stability: Rhetoric and reality on the sex differential in labour-market behaviour. *European Sociological Review, 12*(1), 1–31.

Jacobs, J. A., & Gerson, K. (2001). Overworked individuals or overworked families? Explaining trends in work, leisure, and family time. *Work and Occupations, 28*(1), 40–63.

Johnson, M. K. (2001). Change in job values during the transition to adulthood. *Work and Occupations, 28*(3), 315–345.

Jurik, N. (1998). Getting away and getting by: The negotiation of paid work and family responsibilities in home businesses. *Work and Occupations, 25*, 7–35.

Kaufman, G., & Uhlenberg, P. (2000). The influence of parenthood on work effort of married men and women. *Social Forces, 78*, 931–947.

Longstreth, M., Stafford, K., & Mauldin, T. (1987). Self-employed women and their families: Time use and socioeconomic characteristics. *Journal of Small Business Management, 25*(3), 30–37.

Moen, P., & Han, S. (2001). Reframing careers: Work, family, and gender. In V. W. Marshall, W. R. Heinz, H. Krüger, & A. Verna (Eds.), *Restructuring work and the life course* (pp. 424–445). Toronto: University of Toronto.

Moen, P. (1998). A life course approach to the entrepreneurial family In R. Heck (Ed.), *The entrepreneurial family* (pp. 16–29). Needham, MA, Family Business Resources.

Pavalko, E. K., & Elder, G. H., Jr. (1993). Women behind the men: Variations in wives' support of husbands' careers. *Gender and Society, 7*(4), 548–567.

Rosenfeld, R. A. (1992). Job mobility and career processes. *Annual Review of Sociology, 18,* 39–61.

Rozier, C. K., & Thompson, M. (1998). Female entrepreneurs in a female-dominated health profession: An exploratory study. *Journal of Developmental Entrepreneurship 3,* 149–163.

Shanahan, M. J., Miech, R. A., & Elder, G. H., Jr. (1998). Changing pathways to attainment in men's lives: Historical patterns of school, work, and social class. *Social Forces, 77,* 231–256.

Simon, M., Houghton, S. M., & Aquino, K. (2000). Cognitive biases, risk perception, and venture formation: How individuals decide to start companies. *Journal of Business Venturing, 15,* 113–134.

Singer, B., Ryff, C. D., Carr, D., & Magee, W. J. (1998). Linking life histories and mental health: A person-centered approach. *Sociological Methodology, 28,* 1–51.

Singh, G., & A. Verma. (2001). Is there life after career employment? Labour-market experience of early "retirees." In V. W. Marshall, W. R. Heinz, H. Krüger, & A. Verma (Eds.), *Restructuring work and the life course* (pp. 288–302). Toronto, Canada: University of Toronto.

Swinnerton, K., & H. Wial. (1995). Is job stability declining in the United States economy? *Industrial and Labor Relations Review, 48*(2), 293–304.

Van Auken, H. E. (1999). Obstacles to business launch. *Journal of Developmental Entrepreneurship, 4,* 175–187.

Wilensky, H. L. (1961). Orderly careers and social participation: The impact of work history on social integration in the middle mass. *American Sociological Review, 26,* 521–539.

PART II

CHAPTER 11

Overview: The Cognitive Characteristics of the Entrepreneur

Kelly G. Shaver

Ever since McClelland's (1961) work on the relationship between independence training, achievement motivation, and industrial output, scholars have been interested in psychological factors that might be involved in entrepreneurial behavior. In some ways the professional literature has paralleled the popular wisdom, with substantial research attention devoted to the study of such things as risk preferences, desire for autonomy, creativity, and search for financial gain. A few authors (e.g., Miner, 1996) have even claimed that there is a distinct set of traits that together compose an entrepreneurial personality. Critiques of the early work by Gartner (1989) and by Shaver and Scott (1991), however, have led most investigators interested in person variables to believe that it is more fruitful to investigate particular *dimensions*—on which all people (including entrepreneurs) can be compared—than to look for the human equivalent of the round peg that would fit into the round hole of the "entrepreneurial personality."

This search for particular dimensions on which entrepreneurs could be compared to others is reflected in the spirit, processes, and outcomes of the Person Variables Design Team for the Panel Study of Entrepreneurial Dynamics (PSED). Participants in this team contributed theoretical rationales for including particular dimensions and provided specific operationalizations of the constructs inherent in the dimensions. Throughout, we expected that nascent entrepreneurs would be different from nonentrepreneurs in *degree* (relative placement on various dimensions) but not necessarily different in *kind* (possessing psychological features simply not shared by nonentrepreneurs).

As noted in the more complete description of how the Entrepreneurship Research Consortium (ERC) was organized, a series of research development meetings was held beginning in 1995. At the Chicago meeting in October 1995, the initial plan to have as many as two dozen design teams was changed to reduce the number of teams to *three:* the external environment, the organization and firm, and the individual entrepreneur. This latter team, which then became known as the Person Variables Group (PVG), was to encompass psychological variables and sociodemographic characteristics (e.g., gender, ethnicity) attached to the individual entrepreneur. At that point in the process, the scholars involved included Ray Bagby, Nancy Carter, Per Davidsson, Marc Dollinger, Bill Gartner, Yvon Gasse, Betsy Gatewood, Deborah Good, Patti Greene, Gerry Hills, Chuck Matthews, James Morgan, Dennis Organ, Kelly Shaver, and Harold Welsch.

Not all of these people were able to attend the October meeting, but those in attendance agreed on an overarching question, "What are the behaviors and psychological characteristics that together account for most of the person-based variability in the emergence of new businesses?" Perhaps more important, those in attendance also agreed on three fundamental assumptions that would guide the work of the group:

- Study of psychological variables must be theory-driven, not theory-building.
- No complete psychological scales can be used, because of space limitations.
- The study would extend beyond the currently planned 18-month period.

The next large group meeting was held in mid-November of 1995. At that meeting, based in part on suggestions from members of the PVG, Shaver brought along a list of references and possible candidates for theory, the latter including achievement, attribution, creativity, equity, expectancy, locus of control, planned behavior, risk perception, self-efficacy, and social comparison. Other topics presented in the meeting included entrepreneurial commitment, opportunity recognition, minority/ethnic issues, job satisfaction, the role of knowledge and skill, and gender differences. After discussion, the group consensus choice for topics to be included in the person variables portion of the research instrument became

- Attributions for success and failure
- Creativity of the entrepreneur
- Ethnic and minority entrepreneurship
- Expectancies and risk predictions
- Knowledge, skill, and experience
- Opportunity recognition processes
- Planning activities
- Personal commitment to entrepreneurship
- Reasons for starting, including intentions and goals

Finally, the group agreed on its operating procedures. Within-group correspondence was to be by e-mail (a technology side note: in 1995, this was still an issue that needed discussion!), with the list of topics to be circulated within a few days following the meeting. Group members would then have a week to volunteer to be *topic champions* responsible for a review of theoretical and empirical research in the topic area and for suggesting, at minimum, variables to be included and, at maximum, specific item wordings. Any topics listed for which no champion volunteered would then be announced again and if not picked up, would simply be dropped. This particular operational feature captured the overall spirit of the ERC: topics were tied completely to the interests of scholars whose institutions supported the organization. So, after the data collection has been completed, it is worth remembering that the answer to "Why didn't you include _____ (insert your favorite topic here)?" is simply that no early participant in the ERC was interested in the topic.

At the beginning of 1996, the PVG exchanged ideas about the topics and questions, discussed scoring procedures, and considered whether particular items should be covered in the planned phone interview or in the planned mail questionnaire to be sent following the phone interview. By March 1996, literature reviews had been provided for the topics shown in Table 11.1, which also shows the location in the present volume of the relevant material. Between that time and the time of the initial pretesting later in the year, two additional design teams came into being, and new members joined the ERC. In conjunction with these changes in the overall organization of the ERC, some topics originally considered as part of the PVG migrated to other teams, and new person variables were added. Specifically, there were four "departures." The first to go was the material on start-up behaviors

Table 11.1   Person Variables Design Team as of March 1996: Scholars and Topics

Researcher	Institutional Team	Person Variables Topic	Location in Present Handbook
Marc Dollinger	Indiana Univ.	Creativity	15
Bill Gartner and Nancy Carter	Univ. of Southern California and Marquette Univ.	Start-up behaviors	26
Betsy Gatewood	Univ. of Houston	Expectancy theory	13
Patti Greene	Univ. of Missouri, Kansas City	Minority entrepreneurship	3
Gerry Hills	Coleman Chairs	Opportunity recognition	24
Chuck Matthews	Univ. of Cincinnati	Planning activities	26
Jim Morgan	Univ. of Michigan	Economic insight and achievement	20
Janet Near	Indiana Univ.	Job satisfaction	14
Kelly Shaver	Univ. of Houston	Attributions	19
Harold Welsch	Coleman Foundation	Personal commitment	17
Mary Williams	Widener Univ.	Risk perception	none

(Gartner and Carter, now Chapter 26) now set apart from any particular team, as these behaviors were going to serve as primary variables of value to anyone in the ERC. Second, the topic of minority entrepreneurship (Greene, Chapter 3) was more appropriately joined to a newly created Gender Team (Carter directed this team, and the "reasons" questions accompanied her). Third, the topic of planning activities (Q111 to Q115, now part of the discussion on start-up activity in Chapter 26) also joined the Gender Team. Finally, risk perception (Williams) was not included, as Williams moved to a newly created Strategy and Finance Design Team. There were three major additions to the summary developed in March. The first was material on perceived social support among important role models (Davidsson, Chapter 16) that had been considered in earlier PVG discussions. Next was material on individual problem-solving style (Ford & Matthews, current Chapter 18). The third was the topic of an entrepreneur's social skills (Baron, current Chapter 21), added by Gideon Markman after the first pretest of the overall instrument.

Item Development

With most of the PVG team members having contributed theoretically-based arguments for their items, the production of the actual items required very little in the way of development-on-the-spot at successive meetings of the ERC. Pilot testing of the overall instrument occurred during the late spring and early summer of 1996. Data were available in the late fall; and in January of 1997, a meeting was held in Atlanta for the purpose of pruning the interview schedule and questionnaire. At this meeting, the PVG considered a total of 117 items, 89 of which had originally been contributed by the PVG and another 28 of which had not been the subject of discussion by the PVG. There was substantial pressure to reduce the overall size of the phone and mail interview schedules, and the PVG responded to this pressure by agreeing to drop some of its items. This was done by implementing three major principles within the group: (a) concentration on the core mission of the ERC—start-ups in process, (b) elimination of all nonproductive items (e.g., extremely small response rates), and (c) insistence on a theoretical or empirical justification for every retained item. Additionally, the PVG proposed to the full ERC the institutionalization of incentives for parsimony through a "scarcity-based" decision scheme of one sort or another and through identification of the particular *researcher* responsible for putting in every item in the phone and mail question sets. Although the PVG followed this latter principle itself, no other design team did so. Also on the basis of pretesting, the PVG recommended wording change for several of its items. A summary of these revisions is shown as Appendix 11.1 (for historical accuracy, it should be noted that decisions made outside the discussions of the PVG resulted in the continued inclusion of quite a number of items the group had recommended for deletion). There was a second pilot test, discussed in a general membership design meeting held in Chicago in November of 1997. After what the diplomats might call a "frank exchange of views," the group eventually voted to proceed with a combined phone and mail study, and all of the PVG items present in the February 1997 listing were included essentially as is.

People Creating Organizations: Why and How

In broadest outline, the PSED describes both the people involved in creating organizations and the processes they go through to do so. Part I of the present volume contains chapters that present the social "roots" of the entrepreneurs. Thus, it addresses questions about the sociodemographic characteristics of nascents, their family background and current household structure, and enabling factors such as their net worth and work history. In terms used in the psychological literature, these are all *inter*personal factors. By contrast, Part II concentrates on *intra*personal factors—the motivations, cognitive processes, and personal skills of the entrepreneur.

One of the first questions anyone asks about people starting businesses is "Why do they want to do it?" This section of the handbook begins with three chapters that directly address that question. "Career Reasons," Chapter 12, by Carter, Gartner, and Shaver, describes the reasons people have offered for their career choices, including the choice of starting an organization on one's own. The 18 PSED items discussed in this chapter represent six major motive categories—financial success, innovation, independence, recognition, roles that have been defined for the person, and self-realization. These six motive categories originated with the SARIE (Society of Associated Researchers of International Entrepreneurship) studies in the late 1980s and have been the basis for numerous cross-national comparisons (e.g., Scheinberg & MacMillan, 1988). Here they permit comparisons between the reasons nascent entrepreneurs offer for their start-up choice and those offered by nonentrepreneurs for their own career choices. Where the career reasons chapter has its origins in a long-standing empirical tradition, Chapter 13, "Entrepreneurial Expectancies," by Gatewood takes its cues from prior conceptual work on the relationship between expectancies and performance outcomes in an organizational setting. In any of these expectancy-value models (e.g., Porter & Lawler, 1968), people's work motivation is thought to be a product of the subjective likelihood that a successful performance will lead to valued outcomes. Within the context of the PSED, expectancy questions were also asked of both nascents and members of the comparison group. The last entry in the "why" section is Chapter 14, "Job and Life Satisfaction," by Johnson, Rode, Arthaud-Day, and Near. Popular wisdom holds that some entrepreneurs create businesses because they have been "pulled" into it by irresistible opportunities; others do so because they have been "pushed" out of participation in the corporate workforce, sometimes by conditions they have found personally intolerable. If this is true then, compared to nonentrepreneurs, entrepreneurs in the PSED ought to have lower levels of satisfaction with their last organizational employment. Together, these three chapters offer readers insights into the motivational processes of people engaged in starting their own businesses.

Even among people who believe they understand *why* someone would start a business organization, there is often wonder about "How can anyone do this?" Starting a business requires choices about how to organize the operation and how to make best use of family background and personal experience. Persistence in the process requires intense commitment, a problem-solving style that allows dealing with adversity, and the cognitive capacity to start all over again following failure. Finally, succeeding by succeeding (rather than by not failing) calls on a person's understanding of basic economic principles and on the social skills necessary to convince others to join in the fledgling enterprise. In turn, these are the *how* questions addressed by the remaining chapters in the section.

Chapter 15, "Decision-Making (Innovator/Adaptor) Style," by Johnson, Danis, and Dollinger, compares those who would seek to adapt existing forms to new areas to those who would prefer to innovate. The chapter describes Kirton's (1976) work on "Adaptors" and "Innovators," and captures the fundamental difference by asking whether people would prefer to do things better, or do things differently. As with the reasons, expectancy, and job satisfaction items, the PSED has obtained information from both the nascent entrepreneurs and the comparison group concerning their adaptor-innovator preferences. Whether the new organization is to be based on doing things better or on doing them differently, few nascent entrepreneurs start their companies completely on their own. At the very least, they are part of a family constellation that may have provided social support for, or experience in, entrepreneurial endeavors. These are the aspects of "Role Models and Perceived Social Support" described in Chapter 16 by Davidsson. Will a nascent entrepreneur whose prior experience includes participation in a parent's business have a better chance at eventual success than a nascent entrepreneur without this storehouse of experiential knowledge?

Regardless of the personal and family resources available to a nascent entrepreneur, success may require a single-minded, all consuming focus like that described in "Entrepreneurial Intensity," Chapter 17, by Liao and Welsch. Some speakers on the entrepreneurship lecture circuit talk about a fictitious entrepreneur approached by the devil, who promised the entrepreneur unimaginable financial rewards in exchange for the entrepreneur's spouse and children. The joke is in the tag line, when the entrepreneur asks the devil, "What's the catch?" But, as often happens, there's some truth in the story: "I don't really know what I want to do" is an acceptable statement coming from a college undergraduate in the process of deciding on a major. But it isn't part of the road to success for an entrepreneur. Inevitably, there will be bumps in that road. What happens when they are encountered may be influenced by the entrepreneur's problem-solving preferences described in Chapter 18, "Individual Problem Solving," by Ford and Matthews. Do entrepreneurs hang back, preferring to gather more information before proceeding, or do they plunge ahead hoping for the best? In the PSED, the problem-solving preferences were assessed only among the nascent entrepreneurs, but they will still provide important insights into the relationship between problem-solving style and success in organizing and maintaining the business. Sometimes, no matter what an entrepreneur does (or, sometimes, *because* of what the entrepreneur does) failure just happens. "Attribution and Locus of Control," Chapter 19, by Shaver, uses entrepreneurs' open-ended responses to "Why do you want to start this business," as a window into the possible explanations that might be offered for setbacks so important that most people would consider them failures. Because the question is specific to those starting businesses, this PSED string variable was collected only from nascent entrepreneurs. The psychological literature is replete with explanations of why people continue to do what they are good at. But many entrepreneurs dust themselves off and start again, even after having "failed." Does it matter whether the explanation of events is internal to the person or in the external environment? These chapters indicate the range of cognitive variables included in the PSED, from those requiring detailed content analysis to those involving closed-ended scales. As a set, they can help us understand the elusive entrepreneurial mind-set.

For the moment, let's assume that most entrepreneurs are on the road to (eventual) success. But the domain is success *in business,* not success in one's personal life. And success in business requires at least some understanding of fundamental economic realities. This is the topic addressed in "On Economic Sophistication," Chapter 20, by Morgan. Plenty of entrepreneurs with excellent ideas eventually fail because of an inability to manage business details like cash flow. Others are unable to separate their personal desires from economic realities such as, "Should I put more money into this project?" Because the notion of "sunk costs" is one that ought to be understood whether one is starting a business or not, in the PSED, the economic understanding variables were asked of both nascent entrepreneurs and the comparison group. Finally, without regard to their sophistication in matters economic, entrepreneurs are, fundamentally, in the people-organizing business. Chapter 21, "Social Skills," by Baron, describes the social awareness and communication skills that are likely to set successful entrepreneurs apart from those who merely plod along. Drawing on an extensive literature in social psychology, this chapter describes the PSED items dealing with social perception, impression management, and one aspect of emotional intelligence (expressiveness), which enable entrepreneurs to convince others to participate in a venture that has no track record. In the case of both economic understanding and social skills, what you don't know *can* hurt you—which is why the PSED includes these variables, as well as the others described in Part II.

Appendix 11.1

Person Variables List
First Pretest
Modification of Items
February 11, 1997

The Person Variables Group considered a total of 117 items, some of which are "common resources," at its design team meeting in Atlanta. This total included 89 items originally contributed by the Person Variables Group and 28 items originally contributed by some other design team. We dropped a total of 43 items, 30 of which were originally contributed by our design team. The modified list was distributed to the Person Variables Group by e-mail on Friday, January 24, with a request for modifications of items still awaiting revision. ERC members with questions about any item to be revised were encouraged to contact directly the person responsible for the revision. Revisions were received by 12:00 noon on February 11 from Betsy Gatewood (expectancy) and Per Davidsson (background). On any remaining subscales targeted for cuts by the group in Atlanta, I have simply made the cuts based on the frequency (actually, the lack of frequency) at which items were answered. The list of all Person Variables is shown below, and a list of specific wording changes for items to be revised is also attached.

Variable		Nascent Source	Control Source	Action	Person Responsible
Achievement Motivation (no items dropped)					
1	ACHIEVE1 Why you might quit a job	N1	N1		
2	ACHIEVE2 Which type of job you prefer	N2	N2		
3	ACHIEVE3 Which is truer, friends or better	N3	N3		
4	ACHIEVE4 Which is truer, friends or pay to say	N4	N4		
5	ACHIEVE5 Which monetary outcome you prefer	N5	N5		
6	ACHIEVE6 How react to praise of work	N6	N6		
7	ACHIEVE7 Can do anything set mind on	P1	P1		
8	ACHIEVE8 Do job as thoroughly as possible	P2	P2		
9	ACHIEVE9 Spend time making unit work better	P3	P3		
Attribution Questions (no items dropped)					
10	ATTRIB1	Q109a			
11	ATTRIB2	Q109aX			
12	ATTRIB3	Q109aS			
Background Items (These are a "common resource." Yet, 10 items to be dropped.)					
13	BACK1	Q175	Q875		
14	BACK2	Q175a	Q875a		
15	BACK3	Q175b	Q875b		
16	background 3a	Q175c	Q875c		
17	background 3b	Q175d	Q875d		
18	background 3c	Q175e	Q175e	For items	Revisions
19	background 3d	Q175f	Q175f	13 to 28	of these items
20	BACK4	Q178	Q878	the total	done by
21	BACK5	Q178a	Q878a	will be reduced	Per Davidsson.
22	BACK6	Q178b	Q878b	by half.	
23	background 6a	Q178c	Q878c	Total of	
24	background 6b	Q178d	Q878d	8 or 9 items	
25	background 6c	Q178e	Q878e	will remain.	
26	background 6d	Q178f	Q878f		
27	background 6e	Q178g	Q178		
28	background 6f	Q179a	Q879a		
29	BACK7 Impression of business from relatives	Q181	Q881	Revise	Davidsson
30	BACK8 Encouragement from relatives	Q182	Q882	DROP	
31	BACK9 How much encouragement	Q182a	Q882a		
32	BACK10	Q182c	Q882c	DROP	
Personal Commitment (one item dropped, two others dropped from control only)					
33	COMMIT1 Own business instead of career	P4		DROP	
34	COMMIT2 No limit to effort	P5		DROP	

| 35 | COMMIT3 | Do whatever it takes #1 | P6 | P6 | |
| 36 | COMMIT4 | Do whatever it takes #2 | P7 | P7 | DROP |

Locus of Control (no items dropped)

37	LOCUS1	No trouble making and keeping friends	P8	P8
38	LOCUS2	Make my plans work	P9	P9
39	LOCUS3	Worked hard to get whatever received	P10	P10

Creativity Measures (two items dropped)

40	CREATE1	Doing things better or differently	Q164a	Q864a	
41	CREATE2	Time to answer Create 1	Q164d	Q864d	
42	CREATE3	Confidence in answer to Create 1	Q164e	Q864e	DROP
43	CREATE4	Match of self to firm (higher = LESS)	Q165	Q865	
44	CREATE5	Associates share better or differently	Q166	Q866	
45	CREATE6	Confidence in answer to Create 5	Q167	Q867	DROP

Economic Understanding (no items dropped)

| 46 | ECONUND1 | Buy another ticket | P11 | P11 |
| 47 | ECONUND2 | Consider investment value | P12 | P12 |

Expectancy Items (two items dropped from nascents, six added to controls)

48	EXPECT1	Local business environment favorable	QM1	QM1	DROP	
49	EXPECT2	With hard work can successfully start	QM2	QM2	Write	Revisions
50	EXPECT3	Starting more desirable than other	QM3	QM3	version	of these
51	EXPECT4	Business help achieve other goals	QM4	QM4	for	items
52	EXPECT5	My skills and abilities are valuable	QM5	QM5	control	done by
53	EXPECT6	My past experience valuable	QM6	QM6	subjects.	Betsy
54	EXPECT7	A lot of my own effort required	QM7	QM7	DROP	Gatewood
55	EXPECT8	I'm confident I can put in the effort	QM8	QM8	revise	

Opportunity Recognition (12 items dropped)

56	OPPREC1		A1		
57	OPPREC2		A2		
58	OPPREC3		A3	DROP	
59	OPPREC4		A4		
60	OPPREC5		A4a	DROP	
61	OPPREC6		A5a	For items	
62	OPPREC7		A5b	61 to 78,	Revisions
63	OPPREC8		A5c	the total will	done by
64	OPPREC9		A5d	be reduced	Gerry Hills

65	OPPREC10	A5E			by half.
66	OPPREC11	A5F			Remainder
67	OPPREC12	A5G			become "check
68	OPPREC13	A5H			all that apply"
69	OPPREC14	A5I			as clarification
70	OPPREC15	A5J			for item 56.
71	OPPREC16	A5K			
72	OPPREC17	A5L			
73	OPPREC18	A5M			
74	OPPREC19	A5N			
75	OPPREC20	A5O			
76	OPPREC21	A5P			
77	OPPREC22	A5Q			
78	OPPREC23	A5R			
		OTHER			
79	OPPREC24	QM9			
80	OPPREC25	QM10			
81	OPPREC26	QM11			
82	OPPREC27	QM12			
83	OPPREC28	QM13			
84	OPPREC29	QM14			

Satisfaction Questions (three items dropped)

85	SATISFY1	Times quit with job lined up	O1a	O1a	DROP
86	SATISFY2	Times quit with no job lined up	O1b	O1b	DROP
87	SATISFY3	Satisfaction with last job	O3	O3	DROP
88	SATISFY4	Happy with my life overall	P13	P13	
89	SATISFY5	Choose same career path again	P16	P16	

Other Items Not Originally Contributed by Person Group (13 items dropped)

90	Q104	DROP	For items
91	Q105		90 to 97,
92	Q106	DROP	several were
93	Q107		dropped
94	Q108		because of
95	Q109		conflict with
96	Q110	DROP	comparable
97	Q117		items we
98	Q118	DROP	contributed.
99	Q119	DROP	The remaining
100	Q120	DROP	items in this
101	Q121	DROP	set should
102	Q122	DROP	be reordered
103	Q123	DROP	as follows:
104	P14	DROP	91, 97, 95,
105	P15	DROP	93, and 94.

106		P17		DROP
107		P18		DROP
108	Hours devoted to start-up last week (HRSLSTWK)	Q129b		We
109	Total hours devoted to start-up (TOTALHRS)	Q129c		consider
110	Total cash put into the start-up (TOTCASH)	Q129d		these items
111	Expected firm income year 1 (EXINYR1)	Q155		to be
112	Expected firm income year 5 (EXINYR2)	Q155b		a common
113	Expected firm income year 10 (EXINYR10)	Q155c		resource
114	GENDER	Q129j	Q429j	needed
115	AGE	Q129k	Q429k	by all
116	Ethnic Identification (ETHNICID)	Q129l	Q429l	design
117	Educational Attainment (EDUCATT)	Q130	Q430	teams.

References

Gartner, W. B. (1989). Some suggestions for research on entrepreneurial traits and characteristics. *Entrepreneurship Theory and Practice, 14*(1), 27–38.

Kirton, M. J. (1976). Adaptors and innovators: A description and measure. *Journal of Applied Psychology, 61,* 622–629.

McClelland, D. C. (1961). *The achieving society.* New York: Free Press.

Miner, J. B. (1996). Evidence for the existence of a set of personality types, defined by psychological tests, that predict entrepreneurial success. In P. Reynolds, S. Birley, J. E. Butler, W. D. Bygrave, P. Davidsson, W. B. Gartner, & P. P. McDougall (Eds.), *Frontiers of entrepreneurship research 1996* (pp. 62–76). Babson Park, MA: Babson College.

Porter, L. W., & Lawler, E. E. (1968). *Managerial attitudes and performance.* Homewood, IL: Irwin.

Scheinberg, S., & MacMillan, I. C. (1988). An 11-country study of motivations to start a business. In B. A. Kirchoff, W. A. Long, W. E. McMullan, K. H. Vesper, and W. E. Wetzel, Jr. (Eds.), *Frontiers of entrepreneurship research 1988* (pp. 669–687). Wellesley, MA: Babson College.

Shaver, K. G., & Scott, L. R. (1991). Person, process, choice: The psychology of new venture creation. *Entrepreneurship Theory and Practice, 16*(2), 23–45.

CHAPTER 12

Career Reasons

Nancy M. Carter

William B. Gartner

Kelly G. Shaver

A s outlined in Kolvereid (1996b), the reasons that potential entrepreneurs offer for getting into business should have a significant influence on whether they actually engage in entrepreneurial activity (Krueger & Brazeal, 1994). New businesses are not created by accident. There is enough impeding the process involved in business startup to suggest that entrepreneurial actions are clearly intentional. Reasons for getting into business (or not), therefore, matter because reasons are traditionally considered to be the basis of intentions (Shaver, 1985). More than a few studies of the new venture creation process describe individuals persisting at a variety of activities over a period of months, or years, in order to achieve the creation of a new firm (Carter, Gartner, & Reynolds, 1996; Gatewood, Shaver, & Gartner, 1995). When obstacles arise in connection with any of these activities, entrepreneurs must find ways to overcome them in order to ensure what Heider (1958) called "equifinality" of the outcome. Therefore, in theoretical terms, new venture creation is an intentional act that involves repeated attempts to exercise control over the process in order to achieve the desired outcome.

AUTHORS' NOTE: Paper prepared for the 2nd Annual Greif Research Symposium on Emerging Organizations, Los Angeles, CA: November 2000.

Literature Review

Research about entrepreneurship career choice has paralleled the human development field's exploration for careers, but with few cross-citations. The primary difference is that the careers literature spanned all work options whereas the entrepreneurship research focused on choices among different kinds of entrepreneurial activities or between self-employment and any other career option.

A hallmark of research on career choice in the human development area was the creation of the Work Importance Study (WIS), an international research consortium involving researchers from 11 countries (Super, Sverko, & Super, 1995). Parallel to the WIS development, researchers interested in reasons that entrepreneurs offer for explaining their intentions for self-employment also were developing a cross-national program. Labeled the SARIE (Society of Associated Researchers of International Entrepreneurship) research (Birley & Westhead, 1994; Blais & Toulouse, 1990; Dubini, 1988; Scheinberg & MacMillan, 1988; Shane, Kolvereid, & Westhead, 1991), these scholars began by generating a list of reasons for the entrepreneurial career choice. Initially, the theoretical justification for their list of reasons was based on the following ideas: need for independence, need for material incentives, desire to escape or avoid a negative situation, need for social approval, and a drive to fulfill personal values or norms. It was hypothesized that entrepreneurs, irrespective of country of origin, would rate these needs and desires higher than nonentrepreneurs. A list of 38 statements (reasons) was generated and used in a survey of over 1,400 independent business owners/founders in 11 countries. Subsequent research on data from their survey has sought to develop empirically driven classifications of these reasons.

Scheinberg and MacMillan (1988) conducted a factor analysis of the 38 items and eliminated 17 items that either had unacceptable cross-loadings or were single-item factors. In their analysis of the remaining 21 items, Scheinberg and MacMillan found six broad factors of reasons for business creation that they called need for approval, perceived instrumentality of wealth, communitarianism, need for personal development, need for independence, and need for escape. In comparing entrepreneurs by country, they found that the reasons for business creation varied. For example, U.S. and Denmark entrepreneurs scored highest on the "need for independence" factor, whereas entrepreneurs from China and Portugal scored highest on "need for approval." Scandinavian countries, such as Sweden, Norway, and Denmark, had entrepreneurs who offered low scores on the instrumentality of wealth factor.

In a follow-up study, Shane et al. (1991) factor analyzed 23 items (Scheinberg and MacMillan's 21 plus 2 more on tax policy) from a survey of 597 owner-managers in 3 of the 11 countries, Great Britain, New Zealand, and Norway, and identified four broad factors that explained an entrepreneur's reasons for business creation. They called these four factors recognition, independence, learning, and roles and identified a number of nationality and gender differences but no overall main effect for any specific item.

Based on these two previous explorations, Birley and Westhead (1994) developed a questionnaire of 23 reasons for starting businesses that was administered to

405 owner-managers of independent businesses in the United Kingdom. A factor analysis of the 23 reasons produced 7 factors that the authors labeled need for approval, need for independence, need for personal development, welfare (in terms of contributing to a sense of community) considerations, perceived instrumentality of wealth, tax reduction, and following role models. Each of these studies involved surveys of individuals who had already started firms.

Other academic efforts directed toward exploring the reasons entrepreneurs offer for starting new businesses have used, or identified, reasons different from those used in the prior three studies. In another retrospective study, Kolvereid (1996a) explored the reasons given for self-employment versus organizational employment using a group of 372 Norwegian business school graduates. He designed a classification scheme that posited 11 types of reasons for choosing between self-employment and organizational employment: security, economic opportunity, authority, autonomy, social environment, work load, challenge, self-realization, participate in the whole process, avoid responsibility, and career. He found that only four constructs contained at least 15 responses: security, authority, workload, and challenge. Results for these four are highly significant; security and workload were offered as reasons for organizational employment, with authority and challenge as reasons for preferring self-employment. Like the preceding three studies, this research surveyed these people years after their occupational choices had already been made.

In one of the few prospective studies, Gatewood et al. (1995) asked 142 pre-venture clients from a small business development center (SBDC) their reasons for wanting to start a business. Responses to this question were open-ended. Most respondents provided no more than two distinct answers to the question. Although there were obviously differences in individual wording, six kinds of answers accounted for 93% of the first two reasons offered. These reasons were identification of a market need (29% of the total), autonomy and independence (an additional 18%), a desire to make more money (18%), a desire to use knowledge and experience (16%), the enjoyment of self-employment (7%), and a desire to show that it could be done (5%).

When taken together, the research generated from the SARIE studies (i.e., Birley & Westhead, 1994; Scheinberg & MacMillan, 1988; Shane et al., 1991) and the Gatewood et al. (1995) prospective study reveal five categories of reasons individuals give for starting businesses. The first category labeled, Innovation, involves reasons that describe an individual's intention to accomplish something new. The category contains items Shane et al. (1991) considered as "learning" and Birley and Westhead (1994) and Sheinberg and MacMillan (1988) considered "need for personal development." The second category, Independence, describes an individual's desire for freedom, control, and flexibility in the use of one's time (Schein, 1978). Items in this category have been consistently identified in three of the SARIE-based studies. The third category, which we labeled External Validation, combines two categories of items from the previous research: recognition and need for approval. Items in this category describe an individual's intention to have status, approval, and recognition from one's family, friends, and from those in the community (Bonjean, 1966). The fourth category, Roles, contains items from Shane et al. (1991) that describe an individual's desire to follow family traditions or emulate the example of others. The last category, Financial Success, involves reasons that describe an individual's intention to earn more money and achieve financial security. Although Shane et al. (1991) did not find a financial success factor, the other two studies (Birley & Westhead, 1994; Scheinberg & MacMillan, 1988) did (which they labeled as "perceived instrumentality of wealth").

In addition to the five categories identified from the SARIE-based studies, evidence in previous research on gender in entrepreneurship (e.g., Brush, 1992; Carter, 1997; Fischer, Reuber, & Dyke, 1993) led us to believe a sixth factor, Self-Realization, should be added to the classification scheme. There is evidence that men are more likely to seek to create financial wealth, whereas women are more likely to pursue goals of interest to them.

Gender Differences in Career Choice

Research on the gender differences in career choices shows important discrepancies. For example, the theoretical models that describe the career paths of men are less suited to the experiences of women or persons of color (Farmer, 1997). Women are seen as experiencing more complexity in making career choices because of their need to balance employment, child care, and housing. Fulfilling multiple roles requires women to strategize time and space constraints as they make economic and social decisions in concert (Gilbert, 1997).

One explanation for gender differences in career development is that differing societal expectations for men and women lead to divergent motivations or work preferences (Harriman, 1985). It is claimed that sex-role socialization experiences teach young girls what roles are appropriate or not. These experiences are seen as constricting career choices, compromising career potential (Gottfredson, 1981), and influencing women's beliefs, attitudes, and self-conceptions, which ultimately affects their work motivation and choices (Farmer, 1997). Several studies of choices involving the start-up of a business support this perspective whereas others provide evidence that the entrepreneurial career choice is gender-blind.

Some studies of job preferences have revealed that women want work that is intellectually stimulating and provides opportunities for personal and professional growth (Bigoness, 1998). Brush (1992) found women business owners tend to balance economic goals with other kinds of goals, such as personal enjoyment and helping others. Sexton and Bowman-Upton (1990) found that female business owners score lower on energy level and risk taking and higher on autonomy and change than male business owners. Fischer et al. (1993) found that on three motivational factors (financial, lifestyle, and social/recognition) women scored higher than men on financial motivation, a result they found "somewhat unexpected" (p. 162). Buttner and Moore (1997) found that "pull factor" motivations, such as self-determination and seeking challenge were more important to women than to men.

Conversely, Fagenson (1993) in a comparison of the values of entrepreneurs and managers found more similarities among women and men than differences. Women were found to value equality more than men, and men tended to value family security more than women, but the greater differences were found between entrepreneurs and managers. Entrepreneurs were found to value self-respect, freedom, a sense of accomplishment, and an exciting life more than managers.

Although the findings are mixed, there appear to be significant differences in the motivations that impel women and men to pursue entrepreneurial careers, especially if more weight is given to the results of prospective studies like those of Gatewood et al. (1995) and Carter (1997). In their study of pre-venture clients, Gatewood et al. found that nascent women entrepreneurs who offered internal reasons (e.g., "I always wanted to be my own boss") and nascent men entrepreneurs who offered external accounts (e.g., "There was a market need") were more likely to start businesses than would-be entrepreneurs who gave other types of reasons. In a study of 92 nascent entrepreneurs, Carter (1997) used a similar list of reasons and generated a set of four factors describing work interests or values: autonomy or independence, task interest, wealth or income, and a desire to stay in the community. She found that nascent men entrepreneurs rated wealth and prestige higher than nascent women entrepreneurs. Both men and women rated the autonomy factor higher than the other factors. Women appeared to place a higher value on staying in the community, relative to their ranking on wealth.

The Reasons Variables

Table 12.1 displays the wording of the 18 items from the mail survey (items QG1a–r in the PSED data set) that represent the reasons variables. Twelve of these items were adopted from the SARIE survey, with 10 of these being a subset of the 14 items Shane et al. (1991, p. 445) found significant in their factor analysis comparing the motivations of entrepreneurs in Britain, New Zealand, and Norway. From their findings, we selected and adapted items with loadings greater than .50 from each of their four factor constructs. Table 12.2 maps the PSED items to the SARIE theoretical constructs identified in the literature.

Alphabetic designations are listed in Tables 12.1 and 12.2: Three items represent Innovation (m = to develop an idea for a product; c = to be innovative and in the forefront of new technology; h = to continue to grow and learn as a person). Two items represent Independence (b = to have greater flexibility for my personal and family life; f = to have considerable freedom to adapt my own approach to work). Three items represent External Validation (a = to achieve a higher position for myself in society, e = to be respected by my friends; l = to achieve something and get recognition for it). And two items represent Roles (d = to continue a family tradition, i = to follow the example of a person I admire). We also adapted two items from other SARIE studies (Birley & Westhead, 1994; Scheinberg & MacMillan, 1988) having to do with financial success (g = to give myself, my spouse, and children financial security; k = to earn a larger personal income). In addition to these two items, we added two items to the financial success category (n = to have a chance to build great wealth or a very high income, j = to build a business my

Table 12.1   The 18 Reasons Items in the PSED

Nascent Entrepreneurs: To what extent are the following reasons important to you in establishing this new business?
Comparison Group: To what extent are the following important to you in your decisions about your work and career choices?

Item Number	Wording
QG1a	To achieve a higher position for myself in society
QG1b	To have greater flexibility for my personal and family life
QG1c	To be innovative and in the forefront of new technology
QG1d	To continue a family tradition
QG1e	To be respected by my friends
QG1f	To have considerable freedom to adapt my own approach to work
QG1g	To give myself, my spouse, and children financial security
QG1h	To continue to grow and learn as a person
QG1i	To follow the example of a person I admire
QG1j	To build a business my children can inherit
QG1k	To earn a larger personal income
QG1l	To achieve something and get recognition for it
QG1m	To develop an idea for a product
QG1n	To have a chance to build great wealth or a very high income
QG1o	To fulfill a personal vision
QG1p	To lead and motivate others
QG1q	To have the power to greatly influence an organization
QG1r	To challenge myself

children can inherit). Finally, four items (items o, p, q, r in Table 12.1) were added to represent the pursuit of Self-Realization that can motivate individuals to become entrepreneurs (o = to fulfill a personal vision; p = to lead and motivate others; q = to have the power to greatly influence an organization; r = to challenge myself).

The 18 items were asked in the following manner: For the nascent entrepreneurs, the items were preceded by this stem: "To what extent are the following reasons important to you in establishing this new business?" For the comparison group, the items were preceded by this stem: "To what extent are the following important to you in your decisions about your work and career choices?" Both groups responded to each item on a 1 to 5 scale: 1 = to no extent, 2 = to a little extent, 3 = to some extent, 4 = to a great extent, 5 = to a very great extent.

Table 12.2   Categories of Entrepreneurship Reasons

Researchers	Innovation	Independence	External Validation	Roles	Financial Success
Scheinberg & MacMillan (1988)	**Need for Personal Development** m. To develop idea for product/business h. To keep learning c. To be innovative and in the forefront of new technology * To make a direct contribution to success of company	**Need for Independence** *. To control my own time b. To have greater flexibility for private life f. To have freedom to adapt my own approach to work	**Need for Approval** e. To be respected by friends l. To achieve something and get recognition a. To achieve higher position in society * To increase status of family * To have more influence in community		**Perceived Instrumentality of Wealth** k. Desire to have high earnings * Needed more money to survive g. To give self and family security * Access to indirect benefits
Shane et al. (1991)	**Learning** m. To develop an idea for a product c. To be innovative and in the forefront of new technology h. To continue learning	**Independence** *. To control my own time b. To have greater flexibility for my personal and family life f. To have considerable freedom to adapt my own approach to work	**Recognition** a. To achieve a higher position for myself in society * To have more influence in my community e. To be respected by friends l. To achieve something and get recognition for it * To increase the status and prestige of my family	**Roles** d. To continue a family tradition * To have more influence in my community i. To follow the example of a person I admire	
Birley & Westhead (1994)	**Need for Personal Development** h. To continue learning c. To be innovative and be in the forefront of technological development m. To develop an idea for a product	**Need for Independence** f. To have considerable freedom to adapt my own approach to my work *. To control my own time b. To have greater flexibility for my personal and family life	**Need for Approval** l. To achieve a higher position for myself in society * To increase the status and prestige of my family e. To be respected by friends k. Desire to have high earnings * To have more influence in my community		**Perceived Instrumentality of Wealth** g. To give myself, my spouse, and children security * To contribute to the welfare of my relatives

NOTE: * Item not used in subsequent analyses for this research.

An Analysis of the Reasons Variables

As noted, the 18 PSED items relating to career choice were developed on the basis of prior research to reflect six categories of reasons: Innovation, Independence, Recognition, Roles, Financial Success, and Self-Realization. We tested the internal consistency of the model by subjecting the data (459 nascent entrepreneurs; 302 comparison group members) to a principal components factor analysis. Rather than accept the default eigenvalue criterion for termination of iteration, we specified that the analysis should identify six factors. The resulting factor structure was subjected to a varimax rotation. Because missing data reduced the number of participants, the weights applied to the reasons questions were adjusted to total 459 in the nascent entrepreneur category and 302 in the comparison group. The factor analysis of these weighted items accounted for a total 68% of the variance. Rotation converged in nine iterations. Only two items failed to load on the theoretical dimensions expected (h = grow and learn as a person; and q = power to influence the organization). As displayed in Table 12.3, four of the factors (Financial Success, Roles, Recognition, Independence) identically matched their conceptual counterparts (Cronbach's alpha reliabilities were, respectively, .77, .58, .75, and .63). The reliability coefficients for Roles and Independence were low but were based on only two items each (which makes it difficult to obtain high Cronbach's alpha levels). Because the scales matched their conceptual counterparts, we considered the reliabilities acceptable. The remaining two factors, Self-Realization and Innovation, varied slightly from their theoretical dimensions. Item h, conceptually related to Innovation, loaded on the Self-Realization factor, whereas item q, conceptually aligned with Self-Realization, loaded on the Innovation factor. Because we judged item h to have face validity with Self-Realization and its factor loading was comparable to others in that scale, we considered item h as part of the Self-Realization scale rather than the Innovation scale (Cronbach's alpha = .76). Similarly, as the loading on Innovation for item q exceeded an absolute value of .40, we included it in that scale (Cronbach's alpha = .70). Additionally, item e cross-loaded on Recognition and Roles. Because its conceptual alignment was on Recognition and its factor loading was over .60, we retained it on this scale. Eliminating it would have dropped the reliability coefficient from .75 to .65.

These results make it clear that the conceptual explanations of career choice provided by prior research have been incorporated successfully into the 18 "reasons" items in the PSED. We are especially heartened by the fact that for the first time, such items have been asked *in advance of* the creation of a new business. We are also heartened by the fact that comparable questions dealing with career choice have been asked of a representative sample of nonentrepreneurs.

Findings to Date

Hypotheses tests comparing the reasons that nascent entrepreneurs offered for their work and career choices and those given by a group of nonentrepreneurs found that the factor scores of nascent entrepreneurs and nonentrepreneurs were not significantly different on Self-Realization, Financial Success, Innovation, and

Table 12.3   Factor Analysis of Reasons for Career Choice Items: Six-Factor Solution (*N* = 761)

	1	2	4	5	3	6
Factor:	Self-Realization	Financial Success	Recognition	Roles	Innovation	Independence
Sum of squared rotated loadings	2.61	2.41	1.96	1.91	1.84	1.53
Percentage variance accounted for	14.49	13.41	10.88	10.62	10.23	8.50
QG1# Cronbach's alpha	.75[a]	.77	.75	.60	.69[b]	.63
Self Realization						
r To challenge myself	.75					
o To fulfill a personal vision	.70					
p To lead and motivate others	.65					
q Power to influence an organization					.40	
Financial Success						
k To earn a larger personal income		.82				
g Financial security		.77				
n Build great wealth, high income		.70				
j Build business children can inherit		.58				
Recognition						
l Achieve something, get recognition			.77			
e To be respected by my friends			.64			
a Gain a higher position for myself			.60			
Roles						
d To continue a family tradition				.77		
i Follow example of person I admire				.73		
Innovation						
c Innovative, forefront of technology					.76	
m To develop an idea for a product					.73	
H Grow and learn as a person	.66					
Independence						
b Greater flexibility for personal life						.79
f Free to adapt my approach to work						.72

NOTES:

a. Cronbach's alpha reported for this factor is with item q removed and item h added.

b. Cronbach's alpha reported for this factor is with item h removed and item q added.

Independence. Nascent entrepreneurs, however, rated reasons concerning Roles and Recognition significantly lower than nonentrepreneurs. Gender differences in reasons also emerged; male nascent entrepreneurs and nonentrepreneurs rated Financial Success and Innovation higher than did females, regardless of their group of origin (Carter, Gartner, Shaver, & Gatewood, 2003). Differences also have been found among racial groups. Comparisons of the reasons of Blacks, Whites, and Hispanics reveal that minority (Black and Hispanic) nascent entrepreneurs offer significantly different from the reasons for starting new businesses from the reasons expressed by White nascent entrepreneurs and the career choice reasons offered by the comparison group (Carter, Gartner, & Greene, 2002).

References

Bigoness, W. (1988). Sex differences in job attribute preferences. *Journal of Organizational Behavior, 9,* 139–147.

Birley, S., & Westhead, P. (1994). A taxonomy of business start-up reasons and their impact on firm growth and size. *Journal of Business Venturing, 9,* 7–31.

Blais, R. A., & Toulouse, J. M. (1990). National, regional or world patterns of entrepreneurial motivation? An empirical study of 2,278 entrepreneurs and 1,733 non-entrepreneurs in fourteen countries on four continents. *Journal of Small Business and Entrepreneurship, 7,* 3–20.

Bonjean, C. M. (1966). Mass, class and the industrial community: A comparative analysis of managers, businessmen, and workers. *American Journal of Sociology, 72*(2), 149–162.

Brush, C. G. (1992). Research on women business owners: Past trends, a new perspective and future directions. *Entrepreneurship Theory and Practice, 2*(1), 1–24.

Buttner, E. H., & Moore, D. P. (1997). Women's organizational exodus to entrepreneurship: Self-reported motivations and correlates with success. *Journal of Small Business Management, 35,* 34–46.

Carter, N. M. (1997). Entrepreneurial processes and outcomes: The influence of gender. In P. D. Reynolds & S. B. White (Eds.), *The entrepreneurial process: Economic growth, men, women, and minorities* (pp. 163–178). Westport, CT: Quorum Books.

Carter, N. M., Gartner, W. G., & Greene, P. G. (2002, August). Already there? The career reasons of minority nascent entrepreneurs. In D. H. Nago (Ed.), *Academy of management best papers proceedings: 2002* (pp. ENT D1–D6). Academy of Management National Meeting, Denver, CO.

Carter, N. M., Gartner, W. B., & Reynolds, P. D. (1996). Exploring start-up event sequences. *Journal of Business Venturing, 11*(3), 151–166.

Carter, N. M., Gartner, W. B., Shaver, K. G., & Gatewood, E. J. (2003). The career reasons of nascent entrepreneurs. *Journal of Business Venturing, 18,* 13–39.

Dubini, P. (1988). The influence of motivations and environment on business start-ups: Some hints for public policies. *Journal of Business Venturing, 4,* 11–26.

Fagenson, E. A. (1993). Personal value systems of men and women entrepreneurs versus managers. *Journal of Business Venturing, 8,* 409–430.

Farmer, H. S. (1997). Gender differences in career development. In H. S. Farmer & Associates (Eds.), *Diversity & women's career development* (pp. 127–160). Thousand Oaks, CA: Sage.

Fischer, E. M., Reuber, A. R., & Dyke, L. S. (1993). A theoretical overview and extension of research on sex, gender, and entrepreneurship. *Journal of Business Venturing, 8,* 151–168.

Gatewood, E. J., Shaver, K. G., & Gartner, W. B. (1995). A longitudinal study of cognitive factors influencing start-up behaviors and success at venture creation. *Journal of Business Venturing, 10,* 371–391.

Gilbert, M. R. (1997). Identity, space and politics: A critique of the poverty debates. In J. P. Jones, III, H. J. Nast, & S. M. Roberts (Eds.), *Thresholds in feminist geography: Difference, methodology, representation* (pp. 29–45). Oxford, UK: Rowman & Littlefield.

Gottfredson, L. (1981). Circumscription and compromise: A developmental theory of occupational aspirations. *Journal of Counseling Psychology, 28,* 545–579.

Harriman, A. (1985). *Women/men/management.* New York: Praeger.

Heider, F. (1958). *The psychology of interpersonal relations.* New York: Wiley.

Kolvereid, L. (1996a). Organizational employment versus self-employment: Reasons for career choice intentions. *Entrepreneurship Theory and Practice, 20*(3), 23–31.

Kolvereid, L. (1996b). Prediction of employment status choice intentions. *Entrepreneurship Theory and Practice, 21*(1), 47–58.

Krueger, N. F., Jr., & Brazeal, D. V. (1994). Entrerpeneurship potential and potential entrepreneurs. *Entrepreneurship Theory and Practice, 19*(3), 91–104.

Schein, E. H. (1978). *Career dynamics: Matching individual and organizational needs.* Reading, MA: Addison-Wesley.

Scheinberg, S., & MacMillan, I. C. (1988). An 11 country study of motivations to start a business. In B. A. Kirchoff, W. A. Long, W. E. McMullan, K. H. Vesper, & W. E. Wetzel, Jr. (Eds.), *Frontiers of entrepreneurship research* (pp. 669–687). Wellesley, MA: Babson College.

Shane, S., Kolvereid, L., & Westhead, P. (1991). An exploratory examination of the reasons leading to new firm formation across country and gender. *Journal of Business Venturing, 6,* 431–446.

Shaver, K. G. (1985). *The attribution of blame: Causality, responsibility, and blameworthiness.* New York: Springer-Verlag.

Sexton, D. L., & Bowman-Upton, N. (1990). Female and male entrepreneurs: Psychological characteristics and their role in gender related discrimination. *Journal of Business Venturing, 5,* 29–36.

Super, D. E., Sverko, B., & Super, C. M. (1995). *Life roles, values and careers: International findings of the Work Importance Study.* San Francisco: Jossey-Bass.

CHAPTER 13

Entrepreneurial Expectancies

Elizabeth J. Gatewood

Recent theoretical and empirical research in entrepreneurship posits that individual-level differences are likely to be the primary explanation for why some individuals undertake new venture creation activities but others do not (Baron, 1998; Douglas & Shepherd, 2000; Krueger, Reilly, & Carsrud, 2000; Shane & Venkataraman, 2000). Despite a continuing debate about the value of trait-based comparisons between entrepreneurs and others, there is a growing recognition that cognitive and social psychological processes might lead to a keener understanding of factors that influence entrepreneurial behavior. Because every major cognitive motivational theory gives expectancy some role in determining action (Ambrose & Kulik, 1999), expectancy theory could be the basis of a framework for explaining why some individuals choose to create organizations.

Literature Review

Expectancy has been a dominant theoretical framework for explaining human motivation in work environments (Ambrose & Kulik, 1999; Katzell & Thompson, 1990; Wanous, Keon, & Latack, 1983). It has been used to account for everything from occupational preferences to job satisfaction to volunteer attendance decisions. The theory's fundamental premise is that behavior is a function of an individual's expectancy that a response will bring reinforcement, together with the perceived value of that reinforcement (Rotter, 1954). Specifically, Vroom (1964) proposed that individuals understand the possible consequences of their actions and make choices among alternatives based on a combination of the perceived value of outcomes and the probability that those outcomes will be achieved. Although expectancy theory has been used frequently to study the effort that individuals put forth in jobs, it has been argued that the expectancy approach is more appropriate for explaining occupational or organizational choice than for level of work effort. Occupational choice presents fewer situational constraints than on-the-job behavior; the alternative choices are inherently discrete and distinct, therefore, are more reliably measured; and the choices are made under less time pressure than daily working decisions (Wanous et al., 1983). If this is true, then expectancy seems a logical choice for the study of entrepreneurship because a person who elects to create a new venture is clearly making an occupational choice among alternatives (Davidsson, 1991).

Expectancy theory, sometimes referred to as "VIE" theory, has three variables of interest: valence, instrumentality, and expectancy (Mitchell & Mickel, 1999). *Valence* refers to the individual's preference for a particular outcome—the attractiveness, value, or worth of the outcome. Because the same outcome can have different valences for different people, it is the perceived value of the outcome, not its objective value that is of interest to the theory. Some outcomes may be ends in themselves (otherwise known as *first-level outcomes*); others may have value only because they are instrumental in achieving other desired objectives (known as *second-level outcomes*). *Instrumentality*, therefore, is the perceived relationship between first-level and second-level outcomes. *Expectancy* is generally defined as a belief concerning the likelihood that a particular act will be followed by a particular outcome. Expectancies are influenced by individual factors (abilities, effort, past experiences) and by situational constraints.

The theory assumes that behavior will be undertaken when the individual believes that he or she is able to perform at the required level, that successful performance will lead to certain outcomes, and that these outcomes have direct positive value or will lead to other valued outcomes. Expectancy evaluation, however, is not a static process. For example, individuals can reassess their expectancy beliefs (Klein, 1989). If such changes do not substantially diminish the expected likelihood of achieving the outcome, motivated behavior should continue. On the other hand, if the reassessment substantially diminishes the expected success, withdrawal from the situation should result. As another example, change can also occur in valence and instrumentality. If a goal becomes significantly less attractive, or if a first-level outcome is seen as less likely to lead to a valued secondary goal, persistence may diminish or alternative choices may be made.

Both individual factors (what Katzell and Thompson, 1990, call "endogenous factors") and situational variables ("exogenous factors") will enter into the person's expectancy judgments, instrumentality judgments, and assessments of values. Expectancy judgments may be affected by perceptions of one's own skills and abilities, generalizations from past experiences (especially other entrepreneurial experiences), the perceived difficulty of the task, or the amount of effort required. Instrumentality judgments may be affected by perceptions of the environmental and situational constraints, such as the availability of capital, network contacts, and potential market demand for the product or service.

Entrepreneurship Motivational Research

In their review of over 200 papers on work motivation, Ambrose and Kulik (1999) considered expectancy theory to be one of our "old friends." What gives expectancy the status of an interesting old friend is its more recent combination with other views of work motivation, such as arousal theories, equity theory, goal-setting theory, and subjective expected utility theory (Harder, 1991; Henry & Strickland, 1994; Klein, 1991; Sawyer, 1990; Yancey, Humphrey, & Neal, 1992).

Ambrose and Kulik (1999) argued that there was little to be gained by "research that merely examines applications of expectancy theory" (p. 241). On the other hand, Ambrose and Kulik also suggested that some of the most promising recent expectancy research attempted to combine expectancy principles with individual decision making and corporate strategic decision processes (Chen & Miller, 1994). Decisions, evaluation of risk, and choices among strategic alternatives are at the heart of entrepreneurial activity, so expectancy principles may still have quite valuable things to say about the choice to become an entrepreneur.

Indeed, entrepreneurship researchers have offered expectancy and subjective expected utility "like" models to describe the factors that influence an individual's choice to pursue an entrepreneurial career. Two articles provide good examples of how expectancy ideas have been incorporated (but not directly referenced) into models describing the cognitive mechanisms influencing the choice to start a business. Douglas and Shepherd (2000) offer a model of entrepreneurial intentions that is grounded in ideas in economics. In their model, the choice to pursue entrepreneurship is based on a person's utility function, which reflects perceptions about the income anticipated, the amount of work effort anticipated to achieve this income, the risk involved, plus other factors such as the person's attitudes for independence and perceptions of the anticipated work environment. In a mathematical model of these variables, they suggest that individuals will seek to maximize their utility from their work choices. When external conditions (such as funding) and the presence of opportunities are also favorable, individuals choosing entrepreneurship are more likely to have high abilities for entrepreneurship and, therefore, expend more effort toward success at entrepreneurship.

The Douglas and Shepherd (2000) utility framework has obvious similarities to an expectancy approach, though they do not specifically say so. They implicitly suggest that perceived utility is a function of an individual's perception of the likelihood that personal abilities and efforts in entrepreneurial activity will be successful (expectancy) and that the outcomes will be of value (instrumentality and valence).

In a second study, Krueger et al. (2000) compared predictions from two models of factors that influence entrepreneurial intentions, one based on Ajzen's theory of planned behavior (Ajzen, 1987) and the other based on Shapero's model of the "entrepreneurial event" (Shapero, 1982). Both models suggest that an individual's expected values will influence the perceived desirability of the intention to pursue entrepreneurship. In an empirical comparison of both models, using a survey of 97 senior university business students, Krueger et al. (2000) found that measures of perceived desirability and expected utility were significantly correlated with intentions for entrepreneurship. Their conclusion was that in the direct comparison,

Shapero's model was preferable to the theory of planned behavior for explaining occupational intentions. For our purposes, however, it is worth noting that both models contain terms—feasibility, desirability, anticipated effort—that are also at home in expectancy theory.

Expectancy and Occupational Choice

Vroom's (1964) expectancy model of motivation had been found to predict career preferences and choice (see reviews by Van Eerde & Thierry, 1996; Wanous et al. 1983). Vroom distinguished between occupational preference and occupational choice. The preferred occupation would be the one the individual perceives as having the greatest attractiveness. The occupational choice is the one the individual perceives as both attractive and attainable. When applying expectancy theory to organizational or occupational choice, therefore, the variables of interest are (a) the attractiveness of the organization or occupation to the individual, which is a function of the valence of the occupation and the perceived instrumentality of the occupation; and (b) the expectancy of success in the occupation (Brooks & Betz, 1990). For example, an individual may feel positive to entrepreneurship because of a belief that starting a company would be a highly valued event that would lead to other valued outcomes, such as monetary rewards and independence. That individual might not choose that occupation, however, because of low expectations about being successful. Another individual might have high expectations for success but perceive the occupation negatively, for example, as requiring long hours and with low social status. That individual is also unlikely to choose the occupation. It is the individual who both perceives starting a business as a desired outcome, leading to other desired outcomes, and expects to be successful who will choose to engage in entrepreneurial activity.

According to Olson, Roese, and Zanna (1996), "Expectancies represent the mechanism through which past experiences and knowledge are used to predict the future" (p. 211). Much of our knowledge is based on our direct personal experiences. Indirect experiences and other beliefs—for example, causal attributions—also influence our expectancies (e.g., see Shaver, Chapter 19, in the present volume). Expectations that reflect past behavior strengthen the expectancy-outcome link. Past behavior affects future behavior through multiple channels (Oulette & Wood, 1998). Previous research on expectancy theory has suggested that perceptions of skills and ability will influence expectancy perceptions (Rasch & Tosi, 1992).

Because most expectancy studies have involved correlation analysis, the relationship between effort and valence and expectancy could be in the opposite direction than typically envisioned; that is, effort may cause valence and instrumentality rather than the reverse (Behling & Starke, 1973). Mitchell (1974) examined the literature for longitudinal research that could test this hypothesis, but he found little support for the argument that effort caused expectancies. Yet Mitchell concluded that limitations on the individual's ability to carry out intentions will lower expectancy beliefs. Rasch and Tosi (1992) found that the effort software developers intended to exert was related to their expected performance. And finally, Olson et al. (1996) note that although expectancies influence attributions, attributions also influence expectancies. If an individual perceives that success is a function of effort, then the intention to exert effort should lead to heightened expectancy; therefore, a variable of interest is the individual's intention to exert effort.

One of the important advantages of using expectancy principles to produce questions for the PSED is that doing so avoids, to a significant extent, a version of the correlation/causality problem pointed out by Mitchell (1974). Specifically, when one asks about "expectancy for success" at the same time one asks about "effort expended," the respondent's answers are quite apt to be influenced by the level of success the person has already achieved in the work setting under consideration. This problem is avoided by studies of intentions (e.g., Krueger et al. 2000), but such studies then create their own particular limitation: subsequent follow-up is essential to determine which of the various intentions has been put into action. By asking expectancy questions at the beginning of the entrepreneurial process, we have effectively eliminated any influence on the answers that might have come from "success" in the endeavor (any respondent whose business was already in operation was excluded from the sample). And by asking the questions in the context of a study with built-in follow-up, it should be possible to examine whether initial expectancies are indeed related to the actual behavior they presumably described.

Gender Differences in Expectancies

Previous research suggests that males and females in general, and male and female entrepreneurs in particular, may have different expectancies, effort, and performance beliefs. An early review of sex differences (Maccoby & Jacklin, 1974) showed very few differences between males and females. One of the few differences noted was achievement-related self-confidence. *Self-confidence,* defined as performance expectancies and self-evaluations of performance, was lower for women than men, although these differences may be affected by situational characteristics. Lenney (1977) found that lower self-confidence for females was related to the nature of the task, performance feedback, and the presence of social comparison or evaluation. For example, Giles & Larmour (2000) found women who did not intend to apply for a promotion were significantly more likely than women who had application intentions to believe that out-of-work responsibilities, their lack of aggressiveness, and their gender would disadvantage them. Men, on the other hand, attributed more importance to ability and qualifications.

Hackett and Betz (1981) showed that the expectations of personal efficacy influence career decisions. They found that women held lower expectancies for personal efficacy (the ability to perform a task or behavior) for nontraditional female occupations than for traditional occupations. The personal efficacy beliefs of women may affect their entrepreneurial career intentions. Kourilsky and Walstad (1998) found that females were significantly less interested in starting businesses, less confident in their abilities, and less tolerant of market dynamics than males.

Males and females have been found to differ in their reliance on ability and effort in making performance self-predictions. Whitley, McHugh, and Frieze (1986) reported that males relied more on ability self-assessments and females in how much effort they intended to expend. Finally, Henry and Strickland (1994) found that self-assessed ability and effort were predictive of task performance for males but not for females.

Prior research in entrepreneurship has indicated differences between men and women for the reasons they start businesses. For example, Brush (1992) discovered that women business owners seek to balance economic goals with other kinds of goals, such as personal enjoyment and helping others. Scott (1986) found that male entrepreneurs stressed wanting to be their own boss whereas female entrepreneurs placed more emphasis on personal challenge and satisfaction. Buttner and Moore (1997) also found that "pull factor" motivations, such as seeking challenge and self-determination, were more highly valued by women than men. Gatewood, Shaver, and Gartner (1995) found that nascent women entrepreneurs who offered internal attributions (e.g., "I always wanted to be my own boss") and nascent men entrepreneurs who offered external attributions (e.g., "I had identified a market need") were more likely to start businesses than entrepreneurs who gave other types of reasons. Carter (1997) in a study of nascent entrepreneurs found that men rated wealth and prestige higher than women. She also found that both men and women rated autonomy higher than other factors, and women appeared to place a higher value on community, relative to their ranking on wealth. However, Fagenson (1993) found that sex had little influence on value systems when comparing men and women entrepreneurs and managers. The two differences reported were that women valued equality more than men, and men valued family security more than women. In contrast, entrepreneurs and managers had very different value systems. Although sex differences findings are not universal, there is substantial literature that shows some differences for male and female entrepreneurs; therefore, people using the PSED expectancy variables should be careful to split their samples by respondent sex.

The Expectancy Variables

As described in Reynolds (2000), the development of the questionnaires (phone and mail) for the PSED survey of the nascent entrepreneurs and the control group involved dozens of scholars. Given the wide variety of research interests, the limited budget for the survey process, and the limited time an individual might allocate to responding to a survey, not all questions that each scholar would ideally want to include in the PSED questionnaires were asked. In developing questions, the Person Variables Group aimed for parsimony and format consistency. There were eight expectancy questions that were asked in the pretest PSED mail survey to test the variables of interest. After a first pilot study, there was substantial pressure to reduce the number of items in the questionnaire (although there turned out to be differences in individual responses to this pressure). As a result, when our assessment of the reliability of the expectancy scale revealed that two items could be dropped

Exhibit 13.1   Expectancy Questions in the PSED mail Questionnarie

For Nascent Entrepreneurs: Your reactions to this specific business start-up would also be very useful. How would you respond to the following descriptions of the firm and its situation?

For the Control Group: How would you respond to each of the following statements about starting your own business?

(Circle one number in each row: 1 = completely disagree, 2 = generally disagree, 3 = neutral, 4 = generally agree, 5 = completely agree)

K1a   If I work hard, I can successfully start a business. (expectancy)

K1b   Starting a business is much more desirable than other career opportunities I have. (valence)

K1c   If I start a business, it will help me achieve other important goals in my life. (instrumentality)

K1d   Overall, my skills and abilities will help me start a business. (endogenous influence)

K1e   My past experience will be very valuable in starting a business. (endogenous influence)

K1f   I am confident I can put in the effort needed to start a business. (effort intention)

without changing the overall reliability, the two items (The local business environment in my area is very favorable to new business start-ups; A lot of my own effort would be required to start a business.) were eliminated. The six remaining questions (designated K1a–K1f), in the order they appeared in the questionnaire, are shown in Exhibit 13.1 along with their expectancy theory designations.

Preliminary Analysis of the Expectancy Variables

The "time zero" wave of the PSED was conducted during 1998 to 2000 (the time lag resulted from the fact that funds for an oversample of minorities were not received until nearly a year after the initial screening had begun). The six expectancy items (K1a–K1f) were included in the mail questionnaire, and 871 responses were received. Of course, not all respondents answered all six expectancy questions, so the effective number of responses ranged from a low of 855 to a high of 864. The Pearson correlations (pairwise deletion of missing responses) among items are shown in Table 13.1, for unweighted data. Although the corrected mail weights (postsampling stratification weights based on demographic variables, corrected for mail response rate by respondent sex and nascency) should be used for any comparisons across respondent groups, they are unnecessary for correlational analysis. Nevertheless, just to be safe, we also conducted the correlational analysis

Table 13.1 Correlations Among Expectancy Items (unweighted)

	2	3	4	5	6
1. Work hard, start a business	0.41	0.37	0.37	0.27	0.41
n	862	863	864	859	858
2. Starting business more desirable		0.62	0.47	0.37	0.50
n		862	863	859	857
3. Will help me achieve other goals			0.47	0.36	0.48
n			864	859	859
4. Skills and abilities will help				0.64	0.56
n				860	859
5. Past experience very valuable					0.52
n					855
6. Confident I can put in effort					

on properly weighted data. The pattern of results is essentially the same as that shown in Table 13.1, with only 1 of the 15 correlations changing by as much as 3 hundredths of a point.

All the correlations were statistically significant at $p < .01$ or less; and a scale created from all items had a Cronbach's alpha of $\alpha = .83$ (on a total N of 853). Despite this good internal consistency, it is worth noting that the correlations themselves ranged from a low of .27 (work hard vs. value of experience) to a high of .64 (skills and abilities vs. value of experience). This combination of consistency and variability suggests that, depending on one's conceptual purposes, the six items might either be grouped together as a scale or analyzed individually.

Findings to Date

The results of Shaver, Gatewood, and Gartner (2001) indicate that the scores on the overall scale measure of expectancies are higher for nascent entrepreneurs than for the respondents in the comparison group.

References

Ajzen, I. (1987). Attitudes, traits, and actions: Dispositional prediction of behavior in social psychology. *Advances in Experimental Social Psychology, 20,* 1–63.

Ambrose, M. L., & Kulik, C. T. (1999). Old friends, new faces: Motivation research in the 1990s. *Journal of Management, 25,* 231–292.

Baron, R. A. (1998). Cognitive mechanisms in entrepreneurship: Why and when entrepreneurs think differently than other people. *Journal of Business Venturing, 13,* 275–294.

Behling, O. C., & Starke, F. A. (1973). The postulates of expectancy theory. *Academy of Management Journal, 16,* 373–398.

Brooks, L., & Betz, N. E. (1990). Utility of expectancy theory in predicting occupational choices in college students. *Journal of Consulting Psychology, 37*(1), 57–64.

Brush, C. G. (1992). Research on women business owners: Past trends, a new perspective and future directions. *Entrepreneurship Theory and Practice, 2*(1), 1–24.

Buttner, E. H., & Moore, D. P. (1997). Women's organizational exodus to entrepreneurship: Self-reported motivations and correlates with success. *Journal of Small Business Management, 35*(1), 34–46.

Carter, N. M. (1997). Entrepreneurial processes and outcomes: The influence of gender. In P. D. Reynolds & S. B. White (Eds.), *The entrepreneurial process: Economic growth, men, women, and minorities* (pp. 163–177). Westport, CT: Quorum Books.

Chen, M., & Miller, D. (1994). Competitive attack, retaliation and performance: An expectancy-valence framework. *Strategic Management Journal, 15,* 85–102.

Davidsson, P. (1991). Continued entrepreneurship: Ability, need, opportunity as determinants of small firm growth. *Journal of Business Venturing, 6,* 405–429.

Douglas, E. J., & Shepherd, D. A. (2000). Entrepreneurship as a utility maximizing response. *Journal of Business Venturing, 15,* 231–251.

Fagenson, E. A. (1993). Personal value systems of men and women entrepreneurs versus managers. *Journal of Business Venturing, 8,* 409–430.

Gatewood, E. J., Shaver, K. G., & Gartner, W. B. (1995). A longitudinal study of cognitive factors influencing start-up behaviors and success at venture creation. *Journal of Business Venturing, 10,* 371–391.

Giles, M., & Larmour, S. (2000). The theory of planned behavior: A conceptual framework to view the career development of women. *Journal of Applied Social Psychology, 30,* 2137–2157.

Hackett, G., & Betz, N. E. (1981). A Self-efficacy approach to the career development of women. *Journal of Vocational Behavior, 18,* 326–339.

Harder, J. W. (1991). Equity theory versus expectancy theory: The case of major league baseball free agents. *Journal of Applied Psychology, 76,* 458–464.

Henry, R. A., & Strickland, O. J. (1994). Performance self-predictions: The impact of expectancy strength and incentives. *Journal of Applied Social Psychology, 24,* 1056–1069.

Katzell, R. A., & Thompson, D. E. (1990). Work motivation: Theory and practice. *American Psychologist, 45,* 144–153.

Klein, H. J. (1989). An integrated control theory model of work motivation. *Academy of Management Review, 14,* 150–172.

Kourilsky, M. L., & Walstad, W. B. (1998). Entrepreneurship and female youth: Knowledge, attitudes, gender differences, and educational practices. *Journal of Business Venturing, 13,* 77–88.

Krueger, N. F., Reilly, M. D., & Carsrud, A. L. (2000). Competing models of entrepreneurial intentions. *Journal of Business Venturing, 15,* 411–432.

Lenney, E. (1977). Women's self-confidence in achievement settings. *Psychological Bulletin, 84,* 1–14.

Maccoby, E. E., & Jacklin, C. N. (1974). *The psychology of sex differences.* Stanford, CA: Stanford University Press.

Mitchell, T. R. (1974). Expectancy models of job satisfaction, occupational preference and effort: A theoretical, methodological, and empirical appraisal. *Psychological Bulletin, 81,* 1053–1077.

Mitchell, T. R., & Mickel, A. E. (1999). The meaning of money: An individual difference perspective. *Academy of Management Journal, 24,* 568–578.

Olson, J. M., Roese, N. J., & Zanna, M. P. (1996). Expectancies. In E. T. Higgins & A. W. Kuglanski (Eds.), *Social psychology: Handbook of basic principles* (pp. 211–238). New York: Guilford.

Oulette, J. A., & Wood, W. (1998). Habit and intention in everyday life: The multiple processes by which past behavior predicts future behavior. *Psychological Bulletin, 124,* 54–74.

Rasch, R. H., & Tosi, H. L. (1992). Factors affecting software developers' performance: An integrated approach. *MIS Quarterly, 16,* 395–413.

Reynolds, P. D. (2000). National panel Study of U.S. Business startups: Background and methodology. In J. A. Katz (Ed.), *Advances in entrepreneurship, firm emergence, and growth* (Vol. 4, pp. 153–227). Westport, CT: JAI.

Rotter, J. B. (1954). Social learning and clinical psychology. Englewood Cliffs, NJ: Prentice Hall.

Sawyer, J. E. (1990). Effects of risk and ambiguity on judgments of contingency relations and behavioral resource allocation decisions. *Organizational Behavior and Human Decision Processes, 45,* 85–110.

Scott, C. E. (1986). Why more women are becoming entrepreneurs. *Journal of Small Business Management, 24*(4), 37–44.

Shane, S., & Venkataraman, S. (2000). The promise of entrepreneurship as a field of research. *Academy of Management Review, 25,* 217–226.

Shapero, A. (1982). Social dimensions of entrepreneurship. In C. Kent, D. Sexton, & K. Vesper (Eds.), *The encyclopedia of entrepreneurship* (pp. 72–90). Englewood Cliffs, NJ: Prentice Hall.

Shaver, K. G., Gatewood, E. J., & Gartner, W. B. (2001, August). *Differing expectations: Comparing nascent entrepreneurs and non-entrepreneurs.* Paper presented at the meeting of the Academy of Management, Washington, DC.

Van Eerde, W., & Thierry, H. (1996). Vroom's expectancy models and work-related criteria: A meta-analysis. *Journal of Applied Psychology, 75,* 68–76.

Vroom, V. H. (1964). *Work and motivation.* New York: Wiley.

Wanous, J. P., Keon, T. L., & Latack, J. C. (1983). Expectancy theory and occupational/organizational choices: A review and test. *Organizational Behavior and Human Performance, 32,* 66–86.

Whitley, B. E., Jr., McHugh, M. C., & Frieze, I. H. (1986). Assessing the theoretical models for sex differences in causal attributions of success and failure. In J. S. Hyde & C. C. Linn (Eds.), *The psychology of gender: Advances through meta-analyses* (pp. 102–135). Baltimore, MD: Johns Hopkins University Press.

Yancey, G. B., Humphrey, E., & Neal, K. (1992). How perceived incentive, task confidence, and arousal influence performance. *Perceptual & Motor Skills, 74,* 279–285.

CHAPTER 14

Job and Life Satisfaction

Kevin L. Johnson

Marne L. Arthaud-Day

Joseph C. Rode

Janet P. Near

Job satisfaction has always been relatively high among American workers; since the late 1940s, about 80% have said they were "quite satisfied" or "very satisfied" with their jobs or used similar response scales to assess their satisfaction. Likewise, relative to other cultures (e.g., Japan: see Near, 1984), life satisfaction among Americans has been quite high and comparable to life satisfaction among Westerners in general (Near & Rechner, 1993). Given that Americans spend more hours at work than workers in other cultures, it is perhaps surprising that job satisfaction explains only small to moderate amounts of variance in life satisfaction. Some authors have used the metaphor that overall life satisfaction or happiness can be viewed as a pie, with slices of the pie represented by satisfaction with specific domains of life, such as family satisfaction or leisure satisfaction (Andrews & Withey, 1976). The slice of the pie represented by job satisfaction is only about 10% (Rain, Lane, & Steiner, 1991) or 16% when the correlation between job and life satisfaction is corrected for attenuation (Tait, Padgett, & Baldwin, 1989). However,

AUTHORS' NOTE: We would like to thank Indiana University Kelley School of Business for funding and to acknowledge the support of the Entrepreneurship Research Consortium (ERC) and the Ewing Marion Kauffman Foundation for the development of the Panel Study of Entrepreneurial Dynamics (PSED) data.

the size of the job satisfaction slice falls to about 5%, when the effects of other domain satisfactions are controlled through multivariate multiple regression (Rice, Near, & Hunt, 1980). In longitudinal analyses, it is clear that job satisfaction and life satisfaction are circular, each explaining variance in the other; however, over a 5-year period, Near (1984) found that job satisfaction explained more variance in life satisfaction than life satisfaction explained in job satisfaction, consistent with Andrews and Withey's (1976) basic model.

Even if job satisfaction is not a strong predictor of life satisfaction for the average American worker, the question arises whether job satisfaction is a stronger predictor of life satisfaction for employees in certain kinds of occupations (Kabanoff & O'Brien, 1980). Job satisfaction was a stronger predictor of life satisfaction for executives (e.g., Judge, Boudreau, & Bretz, 1993), for university faculty (Olsen & Near, 1994; Sorcinelli & Near, 1989) and for entrepreneurs (e.g., Daily & Near, 2000). Arguably, each of these occupational groups is one in which we would expect that job satisfaction would be a big part of the life satisfaction "pie."

Our purpose in studying job and life satisfaction among nascent entrepreneurs is to examine how the relationship varies over time. We expect that some organizationally employed individuals start businesses because of two motivations: they are people with low job satisfaction in their current jobs, and they are people whose job satisfaction is a stronger predictor of life satisfaction than it is for the typical American worker. Clearly, other variables also influence the decision to start a business, but we are interested in examining the "push" motivation produced by low job satisfaction, when job satisfaction is something that is highly valued by the individual because it affects overall life satisfaction for that particular individual.

In the next sections, we will provide an overview of the job and life satisfaction items based on extant research and conclude with the descriptive statistics.

Development of Job Satisfaction Measures

Job satisfaction is one of the most widely studied constructs within the organizational behavior literature. Although many job satisfaction definitions have been proposed, one of the most widespread working definitions was proposed by Locke (1976) who defined *job satisfaction* as "a pleasurable or positive emotional state resulting from the appraisal of one's job or job experiences" (p. 1300). Another commonly used definition is "an affective (that is, emotional) reaction to a job, that results from the incumbent's comparison of actual outcomes with those that are desired" (Cranny, Smith, & Stone, 1992, p. 1). Despite some differences in definitional wordings, researchers generally agree that job satisfaction, like other attitudes, encompasses two components, one affective and the other cognitive (e.g., Crites, Fabrigar, & Petty, 1994).

There are two types of job satisfaction measures: "facet" measures, which include measures of satisfaction with specific job elements such as pay and coworkers, and "facet-free" or "overall" measures. Two popular facet measurement instruments include the Job Descriptive Index (JDI) (Smith, Kendall, & Hulin, 1969) and the Minnesota Satisfaction Questionnaire (MSQ) (Weiss, Dawis, England, & Lofquist, 1967). The JDI taps satisfaction with coworkers, pay promotion opportunities, supervision, and the work itself, whereas the MSQ assesses satisfaction with 20 aspects of the work environment that correspond to the 20 psychological needs identified in Dawis, Lofquist, and Weiss's (1968) theory of work adjustment. Widely used measures of overall job satisfaction include the 5-item measure used by Quinn and Staines (1979) in the Quality of Employment Survey conducted by the Institute of Social Research at the University of Michigan and single-item measures that are commonly included in large-scale surveys such as the General Social Survey (Davis, 1999) and Longitudinal Surveys of Youth (Olsen, 1999).

Although facet-specific and facet-free job satisfaction measures both provide assessments of one's feelings about one's job, research indicates that summing across facet scores is not equivalent to measuring overall job satisfaction (Brief, 1998). For example, Quinn and Staines (1979) reported a correlation of only 0.46 between the facet-specific and facet-free job satisfaction scales used in the 1969 Quality of Employment Survey. Similarly, Scarpello and Campbell (1983) found the correlations between the sum of the MSQ facets and a single-item measure of overall job satisfaction to be only 0.32. These findings have led some to argue that overall job satisfaction is more complex than the sum of the presently measured parts (Wanous, Reichers, & Hudy, 1997) or at the very least that individuals vary in the relative emphasis that they place on specific job elements when making overall job satisfaction evaluations (Brief, 1998). Thus, the choice of which type of job satisfaction measure to use, facet-specific or facet-free, should be driven by the study's purpose and research objectives.

In this survey, job satisfaction was measured with a single, facet-free, self-report item ("How satisfied were you with this job?") using a 5-point Likert-type scale ranging from 1 (completely dissatisfied) to 5 ("completely satisfied"). Although traditionally attitudes are measured with multiple item scales, research indicates that single-item job satisfaction measures such as this one are both reliable and valid. For example, Wanous et al. (1997) reported mean corrected correlations between single- and multi-item measures of general job satisfaction across eight samples of 0.72. Further, on the basis of multiple analyses, Wanous et al. concluded, "a minimum estimated reliability for the single-item measure close [to] .70 is reasonable" (p. 250). Thus, the job satisfaction measure used in this survey represents a reasonably valid and reliable measure of general job satisfaction and should be useful when analyzing phenomena that relate to the cognitive and affective reactions to those job elements deemed most important to the individual in question.

Development of Life Satisfaction Measures

Overall life satisfaction was measured with a single self-report item ("I am very happy with my LIFE overall") using a 5-point Likert-type scale ranging from 1 (completely untrue) to 5 (completely true). The use of single-item measures for life satisfaction or well-being is well established in the literature, with the more prominent examples being the Gurin, Veroff, and Feld (1960) satisfaction item, Andrews and Withey's (1976) delighted–terrible scale, and Fordyce's (1988) Happiness Measure (Larsen, Diener, & Emmons, 1985). The item used in this particular survey most closely resembles one of the five items from Diener's (Diener, Emmons, Larsen, & Griffin, 1985) satisfaction-with-life scale ("I am satisfied with my life."), although the Andrews and Withey item stem ("How do you feel about your life as a whole?") and the Gurin et al. item stem ("Taking all things together, how satisfied are you with things these days?") also provide close parallels.

Self-report measures such as the one used in this survey are generally considered the most direct method of assessing respondents' feelings about their lives (Andrews & Crandall, 1976; Pavot & Diener, 1993). Overall, they have demonstrated good temporal reliability and psychometric properties (Larsen et al., 1985; Pavot & Diener, 1993; Pavot, Diener, Colvin, & Sandvik, 1991). Well-being (a construct closely identified with happiness and/or life satisfaction) appears to remain relatively stable over the long term, with test-retest reliabilities in the 0.5 to 0.6 range over a 6-year period (Heady & Wearing, 1989) and predictable relationships with personality dimensions such as extraversion and neuroticism (e.g., Costa & McCrae, 1980). At the same time, well-being measures are appropriately responsive to changes in life circumstances (Atkinson, 1982).

Some of the advantages of single-item, self-report measures are their ease of administration and prevalence of use in large-scale, national surveys. For example, the Gurin et al. (1960) satisfaction item has regularly appeared in surveys sponsored by the National Opinion Research Center, providing a valuable source of normative satisfaction data for the U.S. population. On the other hand, use of single-item measures has been criticized on the basis that they are more sensitive to item placement, cognitive context, survey wording, transient mood, and response bias than their multi-item counterparts (Larsen et al., 1985; Pavot & Diener, 1993). Some evidence has been provided for the greater susceptibility of single-item measures to contextual effects and item placement, but importantly, such artifacts do not result in a statistically significant difference in validity from multi-item scales (Pavot & Diener). Single-item reliabilities (test-retest) also tend to be slightly lower but still in the acceptable range, provided the item has an adequate response range (i.e., > 3-point scale) and clearly labeled anchors (Larsen et al.). Moreover, in omnibus tests of validity, all global satisfaction/ well-being measures have converged significantly with one another (Larsen et al., 1985) and with peer reports (Pavot & Diener, 1993; Pavot et al., 1991). Overall, therefore, research has indicated that single-item measures of satisfaction have satisfactory validity and reliability and may be used with confidence when time and/or space constraints prevent the use of longer measures.

Controls for social desirability are not considered necessary as social desirability appears to be a personality characteristic that enhances well-being, as opposed to a source of error variance (Diener, Sandvik, Pavot, & Gallagher, 1991).

Job and Life Satisfaction Variables

Clearly, the nature of the relationship between job satisfaction and life satisfaction remains a subject of continual interest and debate among scholars. Some even contend that the relationship is reciprocal (Schmitt & Badeian, 1982; Schmitt &

Mellon, 1980). Regardless, we believe satisfaction is an important motivator and one of particular interest for aspiring entrepreneurs. Thus, it is a worthwhile endeavor to understand the nature and relevant boundaries of the relationship.

Indeed, in the entrepreneurial literature it has been shown that entrepreneurs tend to be overly confident in their own abilities and expect to succeed where others have already failed (Cooper, Woo, & Dunkelberg, 1988). Therefore, it suggests that entrepreneurs hold themselves in high regard or have high levels of esteem for themselves and their abilities. Given that "self-esteem is widely recognized as a central aspect of psychological functioning . . . and is strongly related to many other variables, including general satisfaction with one's life" (Crocker & Major, 1989, p. 609), we believe that studies that seek to explore motivation should also consider the impact of satisfaction. Consequently, we included two satisfaction (one job satisfaction, one life satisfaction) items in the mail survey.

After questions concerning one's prior employment (e.g., role, tenure, size of organization, type of organization), the respondent was asked to respond to the job satisfaction item (QI8): "How satisfied were you with this job?" 1 = very dissatisfied, 2 = somewhat dissatisfied, 3 = neither satisfied nor dissatisfied, 4 = somewhat satisfied, and 5 = very satisfied.

There were over 30 items following the job satisfaction item before the life satisfaction item was asked. The life satisfaction item (QL1m) was one of 25 items (QL1a–QL1y) that had the following stem: "The following statements can be used to describe most people. How accurately would they describe you? (Circle one number in each row.)" Item: I am very happy with my life overall. 1) Completely untrue, 2) Mostly untrue, 3) It depends, 4) Mostly true, and 5) Completely true.

There were a total of 891 valid respondents. This included a group of more than 300 respondents who, though not pursuing a new business start-up, were also asked about their levels of satisfaction. Our interests focus on the nascent entrepreneurs group; however, we have also included some basic, preliminary information regarding both groups in Table 14.1.

The indifference point for each satisfaction item was 3 (Neither satisfied nor dissatisfied, or It depends). A comparison of the means test in Table 14.1 indicates that all responses were significantly different from the indifference point. The comparisons were conducted based on both gender and classification as an entrepreneur or as a nonentrepreneur. The gender breakdown shows 49% male in the data set. The mean job satisfaction for males was 3.08 with a standard deviation of 1.38. The mean job satisfaction for females was 3.03 with a standard deviation of 1.37. The mean life satisfaction was higher for both males and females at 3.91 and 3.99, respectively, with lower standard deviations (0.88 and 0.89, respectively). For the 554 nascent entrepreneurs in the data set, job satisfaction had a mean of 3.57 and standard deviation of 1.23. Life satisfaction had a mean of 3.96 and standard deviation of 0.87.

Although these are only two items, previous research does support the validity and reliability of single-item measures of satisfaction. Therefore, it is our hope that the inclusion of these items will allow more complete research regarding entrepreneurs' motivations and the nature of job and life satisfaction. Combined with the rather wide-ranging nature of the data set, these variables should afford future scholars some valuable insights into this research arena.

Table 14.1   One-Sample *t* Test Comparing Mean Group Satisfaction Levels to Indifference Levels Indicating Clear Responses From Each Group

Gender	Variable	Indifference Test Value = 3					
		t	*df*	Stat. Sign. (2-tailed)	Mean Difference	95% Confidence Interval	
						Lower	Upper
		Nascent Entrepreneurs					
Male	I am very happy with my life overall.	17.190	268	.000	.92	.82	1.03
	How satisfied were you with this job?	8.181	269	.000	.61	.46	.75
Female	I am very happy with my life overall.	19.684	284	.000	.99	.89	1.09
	How satisfied were you with this job?	7.213	283	.000	.53	.39	.68
		Nonentrepreneurs					
Male	I am very happy with my life overall.	12.769	157	.000	.89	.75	1.03
	How satisfied were you with this job?	−8.935	156	.000	−.83	−1.01	−.64
Female	I am very happy with my life overall.	14.113	180	.000	.99	.85	1.13
	How satisfied were you with this job?	−8.666	179	.000	−.77	−.94	−.59

References

Andrews, F. M., & Crandall, R. (1976). The validity of measures of self-reported well-being. *Social Indicators Research, 3,* 1–19.

Andrews, F. M., & Withey, S. B. (1976). *Social indicators of well-being: Americans' perceptions of life quality.* New York: Plenum.

Atkinson, T. (1982). The stability and validity of quality of life measures. *Social Indicators Research, 10,* 113–132.

Brief, A. P. (1998). *Attitudes in and around organizations.* Thousand Oaks, CA: Sage.

Cooper, A., Woo, C., & Dunkelberg, W. (1988). Entrepreneurs' perceived chances for success. *Journal of Business Venturing, 3,* 97–108.

Costa, P. T., & McCrae, R. R. (1980). Influence of extraversion and neuroticism on subjective well-being: Happy and unhappy people. *Journal of Personality and Social Psychology, 38,* 668–678.

Cranny, C. J., Smith, P. C., & Stone, E. F. (1992). *Job satisfaction: How people feel about their jobs and how it affects their performance.* New York: Lexington.

Crites, S. L., Fabrigar, L. R., & Petty, R. E. (1994). Measuring the affective and cognitive properties of attitudes: Conceptual and methodological issues. *Personality and Social Psychology Bulletin, 58,* 60–67.

Crocker, J., & Major, B. (1989). Social stigma and self-esteem: The self-protective properties of stigma. *Psychological Review, 96*(4), 608–630.

Daily, C. M., & Near, J. P. (2000). CEO satisfaction and firm performance in family firms: Divergence between theory and practice. *Social Indicators Research, 51,* 125–170.

Davis, J. A. (1999). *Cumulative General Social Survey 1972–1998.* Ann Arbor, MI: Inter-University Consortium for Political Research.

Dawis, R. V., Lofquist, L. H., & Weiss, D. J. (1968). *A theory of work adjustment* (Rev. ed.) (Minnesota Studies in Vocational Rehabilitation, No. 23). Minneapolis: University of Minnesota.

Diener, E., Emmons, R. A., Larsen, R. J., & Griffin, S. (1985). The satisfaction with life scale. *Journal of Personality Assessment, 49(1),* 71–75.

Diener, E., Sandvik, E., Pavot, W., & Gallagher, D. (1991). Response artifacts in the measurement of subjective well-being. *Social Indictors Research, 24,* 35–56.

Fordyce, M. W. (1988). A review of research on the happiness measures: A sixty second index of happiness and mental health. *Social Indicators Research, 20,* 355–381.

Gurin, G., Veroff, J., & Feld, S. (1960). *American's view of their mental health.* New York, Basic.

Heady, B., & Wearing, A. (1989). Personality, life events, and subjective well-being: Toward a dynamic equilibrium model. *Journal of Personality and Social Psychology, 57,* 731–739.

Judge, T. A., Boudreau, J. W., & Bretz, R. D. (1993). Job and life attitudes of executives. *Journal of Applied Psychology, 79,* 767–782.

Kabanoff, B., & O'Brien, G. E. (1980). Work and nonwork: A review of models, methods and findings. *Psychological Bulletin, 88,* 66–70.

Larsen, R. J., Diener, E., & Emmons, R. A. (1985). An evaluation of subjective well-being measures. *Social Indicators Research, 17,* 1–17.

Locke, E. A. (1976). The nature and causes of job satisfaction. In M. D. Dunnette (Ed.), *Handbook of industrial and organizational psychology* (pp.1297–1349). Chicago: Rand McNally.

Near, J. P. (1984). Relationships between job satisfaction and life satisfaction: Test of a causal model. *Social Indicators Research, 15,* 351–367.

Near, J. P., & Rechner, P. L. (1993). Cross-national variations in predictors of life satisfaction: Differences among West European countries. *Social Indicators Research, 29,* 109–121.

Olsen, R. (1999). *The National Longitudinal Surveys NLSY79 user's guide.* Prepared for the U.S. Department of Labor by the Center for Human Resource Research. Columbus, OH: Ohio State University.

Olsen, D., & Near, J. P. (1994). Predictors of life satisfaction: Work and nonwork satisfaction and interrole conflict. *Review of Higher Education, 17,* 179–195.

Pavot, W., & Diener, E. (1993). The affective and cognitive context of self-reported measures of subjective well-being. *Social Indicators Research, 28,* 1–20.

Pavot, W., Diener, E., Colvin, C. R., & Sandvik, E. (1991). Further validation of the satisfaction with life scale: Evidence for cross-method convergence of well-being measures. *Journal of Personality Assessment, 57*(1), 149–161.

Quinn, R. P. & Staines, G. L. (1979). *The 1977 Quality of Employment Survey.* Ann Arbor, MI: University of Michigan, Institute for Social Research at the Survey Research Center.

Rain, J. S., Lane, I. M., & Steiner, D. D. (1991). A current look at the job satisfaction/life satisfaction relationship: Review and future considerations. *Human Relations, 44,* 287–307.

Rice, R. W., Near, J. P., & Hunt, R. G. (1980). The job satisfaction-life satisfaction relationship: A review of empirical research. *Basic and Applied Social Psychology, 1,* 37–64.

Scarpello, V., & Campbell, J. P. (1983). Job satisfaction: Are all the parts there? *Personnel Psychology, 36,* 577–600.

Schmitt, N., & Badeian, A. G. (1982). A comparison of LISREL and two-stage least squares analysis of a hypothesized life-job satisfaction reciprocal relationship. *Journal of Applied Psychology, 67,* 806–817.

Schmitt, N., & Mellon, P. M. (1980). Life and job satisfaction: Is the job central? *Journal of Vocational Behavior, 16,* 51–58.

Smith, P. C., Kendall, L. M., & Hulin, C. L. (1969). *The measurement of satisfaction in work and retirement: A strategy for the study of attitudes.* Chicago: Rand McNally.

Sorcinelli, M. D., & Near, J. P. (1989). The relation between work and life away from work among university faculty. *Journal of Higher Education, 60,* 61–80.

Tait, M., Padgett, M. Y., & Baldwin, T. T. (1989). Job and life satisfaction: A reexamination of the strength of the relationship and gender effects as a function of the date of the study. *Journal of Applied Psychology, 74,* 502–507.

Wanous, J. P., Reichers, A. E., & Hudy, M. J. (1997). Overall job satisfaction: How good are single-item measures? *Journal of Applied Psychology, 82,* 247–252.

Weiss, D. J., Dawis, R. V., England, G. W., & Lofquist, L. H. (1967). *Manual for the Minnesota Satisfaction Questionnaire.* Minneapolis: University of Minnesota Press.

CHAPTER 15

Decision-Making (Innovator/Adaptor) Style

Kevin L. Johnson

Wade M. Danis

Marc J. Dollinger

C ognitive style refers to "consistent individual differences in preferred ways of organizing and processing information and experience" (Messick, 1976, p. 5). In addition to individual differences in perceptions, thinking, learning, and problem solving, cognitive style includes how we relate to others (Witkin, Moore, Goodenough, & Cox, 1977). Differences in cognitive style may then also influence the nature of our relationships, which is particularly important given the tendency to think of the entrepreneur as an individual. After all, we speak of management teams, boards of directors, but only the sole entrepreneur. However, rarely does an entrepreneur initiate a new venture entirely alone without interaction. Businesses do not exist in isolation, nor does the entrepreneur, who may engage a close business associate or even an entire team in the new venture process. Studies have shown how mental models by top management teams are related to new venture performance and how groups with different perspectives on issues arrived at consensus (Ensley & Pearce, 2001; Mohammed & Ringseis, 2001).

AUTHORS' NOTE: We thank the Indiana University Kelley School of Business for funding and acknowledge the support of the Entrepreneurship Research Consortium (ERC) and the Ewing Marion Kauffman Foundation for the development of the Panel Study of Entrepreneurial Dynamics (PSED) data.

But how do cognitive processes influence and drive decisions and outcomes for the entrepreneur? What cognitive distinctions might we find and/or explore of those who pursue entrepreneurial activities or careers?

The overall purpose of this chapter is to introduce the cognitive style variables available in the Panel Study of Entrepreneurial Dynamics (PSED) data set that we believe will further research efforts in entrepreneurship. We begin with an introduction of the theoretical background of cognitive approaches with emphasis on the two styles presented in the Kirton Adaption-Innovation (KAI) theory of cognitive style. The applicability of the KAI styles to entrepreneurial research is then discussed followed by a general discussion of the actual variables.

As indicated, the basic premise behind our cognitive approach is based on the KAI theory of cognitive styles in which cognitive style is said to develop early in life and remain a stable component of the cognitive process that fundamentally influences an individual's decisions (Kirton, 1976). Indeed, the KAI cognitive style theory has a tenacious aspect. For people to alter their cognitive style requires increased effort as well as increased discomfort. Consequently, when under stress, one will tend to utilize that which is most familiar, and most comfortable, perhaps even at the expense of efficacy.

The KAI model of cognitive style describes two familiar styles—the Innovator and the Adaptor—that have become well-known and widely used (Dollinger & Danis, 1998). However, these are by no means the only cognitive styles. There are numerous measures, classification schemes, and/or dimensions of cognitive styles, a partial list of which includes the Allinson Hayes Cognitive Style Index, the Gregorc Style Delineator, Kolb's Learning Style Inventory, the Christensen's Lifescripts, the Social Style Profile, the popular Myers-Briggs Type Indicator (developed from Jung's Psychological Types), and the Kirton Adaption-Innovation Inventory, which is the focus of our study (Gregorc, 1982; Kolb, 1976; Merrill & Reid, 1981; Myers & McCaulley, 1985).

Measures such as the Myers-Briggs Type Indicator (MBTI), the Cognitive Style Index (CSI), and the Christensen Lifescripts are particularly popular in business related studies. For example, the MBTI is utilized in industrial environments for organizational climate as well as decision-making studies. Lifescripts is one of several measures designed for management consulting purposes, reflecting the way people utilize information; and the CSI has been used in large-scale organizational studies on both management and nonmanagement personnel to determine whether one is more analytical or more intuitive. Table 15.1 lists the dimensions of these and other popular cognitive style measures. These cognitive style measures are, in fact, related to one another with at least one common link, which is the KAI Inventory (Bokoros & Goldstein, 1992).

Because the KAI Inventory measures differences in cognitive style along the Innovator-Adaptor dimensions, it is well suited for entrepreneurial studies, especially given the underlying creative aspects of the domain and the uncertain and challenging nature of decision making in new ventures. Additionally, the KAI model has been validated in several languages and has high construct validity (i.e., the relationship between the measure and the underlying construct), content validity (i.e., the adequacy with which the measure assesses the domain of interest), and criterion validity (i.e., the

Table 15.1   Dimensions of Some Common Cognitive Style Measures

Measure	Dimensions and/or Styles
Jung's Psychological Types (Later the Myers-Briggs Type Indicator [MBTI]	Sensing-Intuition Thinking-Feeling Extraverted-Introverted Judging-Perceiving (Dimension added by Myers and Briggs)
Gregorc Style Delineator	Sequential-Random processing Concrete-Abstract data (Styles: Abstract sequential, abstract random, concrete sequential, and concrete random)
Allinson Hayes Cognitive Style Index (CSI)	Intuition-Analysis (Higher score = more analytical, less intuitive)
Cognitive Styles Analysis (CSA)	Wholist-Analytic Verbalizer-Imager (Styles: Wholist imager, analytic verbalizer, wholist verbalizer, and analytic imager)
Rowe's Decision Style Inventory (DSI)	Cognitive complexity Environmental complexity (Styles: Directive, analytic, conceptual, and behavioral)
Kolb's Learning Style Inventory (LSI)	Abstract conceptualization-Concrete experience Active experimentation-Reflective observation (Styles: Convergers, divergers, accommodators, and assimilators)
Chirstensen's Lifescripts	Styles: Analyzer, controller, supporter, and promoter

relationship between the measure and another independent measure) (Bobic, Davis, & Cunningham, 1999). Further, Bobic et al. found that KAI scores were stable over time and not affected by training.

The KAI particular measure posits that some individuals are more conventional in their approach to solving problems. They tend to rely upon proven, traditional methods for making decisions. Their creativity is perhaps less recognized due to their conforming behavior; yet, they may still be creative in certain contexts. For example, some individuals may be better suited for the more tedious tasks that require attention to detail. Additionally, they may tend to develop solutions that are techniques, which are not necessarily different but somehow utilize existing knowledge to do the same things better. This distinction might be comparable to someone who thinks up an entirely different communications system (e.g., Alexander Bell) versus someone who improves upon or makes an existing communications system better (e.g., replacing runners with horses, then stagecoaches, and then cars). Such "better" oriented individuals are classified as Adaptors.

In contrast to Adaptors, Innovators are less conventional in their approach to solving problems. They rely on unique approaches to problems and are not constrained, as Adaptors are, in their decision making to existing solutions or technologies.

Innovators make decisions in unorthodox manners and display what we might call traditional creative behavior—or even eccentricity.

Each cognitive style has its relative strengths and weaknesses depending upon the specific situation. Thus, in general, neither KAI style is deemed superior to the other in either creativeness or effectiveness. Clearly, there are situations in which someone is preferred who is better able to attend to the intricate details of a problem (the Adaptor), and there are situations in which someone is preferred whose primary focus is on a bigger picture and relishes opportunities to inspire different, even unproven possibilities (the Innovator). In fact, Kirton advocates a balance between Adaptors and Innovators and a test of the strength of this balance has also been supported in a recent study (Bobic et al., 1999). Still, given the focus of this work, it should be noted that much of the previous KAI research did not specifically focus on entrepreneurs.

These two intriguing styles may afford considerable insight into the realm of entrepreneurship and thus inspired the inclusion of a variable in the PSED study to identify the preferred styles. Although the data set also identifies the style of those identified as nonentrepreneurs, we were specifically interested in those identified as nascent entrepreneurs. Lastly, space and financial constraints of the study were such that we were unable to include the original 32-item scale, so we developed a single-item proxy on the basis of pilot tests for inclusion in the PSED survey. We suggest that the proxy may serve best as an exploratory measure, due to the well-known shortcomings associated with single-item indicators. Indeed, efforts to incorporate the full 32-item instrument (or a reduced version) in a follow-up study would be worthwhile once the phenomenon of interest has been clearly identified or defined using the proxy.

Cognition and Entrepreneurial Research

For purposes of the PSED study, we focused on the cognitive style of the individual nascent entrepreneur and his or her associate(s), accordingly. Entrepreneurship can be defined as the creation of value, typically via the development of a new organization designed to exploit a perceived opportunity. This definition indicates that a product or service, which did not previously exist, is brought into existence to either establish or fulfill a need (creation of value), and thus require the development of an organization that is able to capitalize on an opportunity that others are unable to either recognize or exploit. Implicitly, this definition acknowledges the innovative characteristic of such an endeavor and leaves open the application of entrepreneurship to individuals as well as corporate entities. In his book, *Entrepreneurship: Strategies and Resources,* Dollinger defines entrepreneurship as "the creation of an innovative economic organization (or network of organizations) for the purpose of gain or growth under conditions of risk and uncertainty" (1995, p. 7). He also reminds us that many have provided definitions of entrepreneurship, including Knight (circa 1921), Schumpeter (circa 1934), Hoselitz (circa 1952), Cole (circa 1959), McClelland (circa 1961), Casson (circa 1982), Gartner (circa 1985), and Stevenson, Roberts, and Grousbeck (circa 1989). However, the common threads appear to be creativity and innovation, risk and uncertainty, and economic organizations as captured in Dollinger's definition.

It has been found that individuals who engage in entrepreneurial endeavors tend to be overly optimistic about their ability to successfully start a new venture (Cooper, Woo, & Dunkelberg, 1988). Although optimism may be common to a range of individuals, it appears to be quite pronounced in entrepreneurs. Entrepreneurs are adamant about their ability to succeed where others have failed under similar if not identical situations. They believe that their successes are their own and their failures are due to unlucky circumstances. This illusion is a "self-serving bias" that allows the entrepreneur to continue to pursue risky adventures (Bradley, 1978). Thus, entrepreneurs' cognitive views of their abilities reflect the "above average effect" commonly mentioned in the psychological literature (Dunning, Meyerowitz, & Holzberg, 1989). Consequently, we reasoned that entrepreneurs could differ from the general population in their cognitive processes, thus possessing a distinction that could contribute to their ability to successfully identify and exploit opportunities where others failed. In other words, if scholars contend that entrepreneurially minded individuals are indeed more creative than nonentrepreneurially minded individuals, then their self-perception may be accurate, even more so if creativity is a decisive factor in entrepreneurial success. But, if the comparison is relative to other "would-be" entrepreneurs—who perhaps pursue new businesses but are initially unsuccessful—then our nascent entrepreneurs erroneously believe themselves to be better suited for the task, thereby creating a truly self-serving condition the benefit of which may only be in the form of enhanced confidence and determination.

Although not causally linked, a recent trait study by Baum, Locke, and Smith (2001) demonstrated that individual differences have an indirect association with venture growth and significant direct effects on general and specific competencies, motivation, and competitive strategies (Baum et al., 2001). Obviously, this further supports the importance of the self in entrepreneurship. Generally, earlier studies sought to identify the individual differences of the successful entrepreneur (McClelland, 1987), but the trait approach became increasingly recognized as a futile avenue for investigating entrepreneurship, perhaps prematurely so given that the creation of a new venture still requires a person "in whose mind all of the possibilities come together, who believes the innovation is possible, and who has the motivation to persist until the job is done" (Shaver & Scott, 1991, p. 39). Still, we believe some of the greatest potential in entrepreneur studies lies in the cognitive approach.

Do entrepreneurs simply think differently—maybe there is an entrepreneur aptitude test? Since the late 1980s, numerous studies have recognized the importance of a cognitive approach to understanding entrepreneurs in the context of new venture creation. In fact, Forbes reviews numerous journals in search of studies that have sought to take a cognitive approach to understanding entrepreneurship and provides an overview of them (Forbes, 1999).

Cognitive Style Variables

As a proxy for the complete KAI Inventory, four cognition variables (items Q327–Q330 of the PSED data set) were developed based on the following common stem: Some people can be characterized as being precise, reliable, efficient, and well-disciplined—the kind of person that prefers "doing things better." Others can be described as more non-conforming, questioning, and challenging of authority. Such people, comfortable with unstructured situations, prefer "doing things differently."

This passage was read to every interviewee (entrepreneur or nonentrepreneur), each of whom was then asked to reply to the following question (item Q327): "If someone asked you which kind of person you are, would you say that you preferred 'doing things better' or 'doing things differently?'"

This was followed by item Q328, which was as follows: "How well does your preferred style of problem solving match the types of problems encountered in starting a new business? Would you say your style is often a good match, sometimes a good match, sometimes a poor match, or often a poor match?"

Entrepreneurs do not pursue opportunities in isolation but often work with business associates or even teams. This associate may be a confidant, adviser, or a more active partner in the venture. Support has been found for a balance of styles on a team (Bobic et al., 1999), and item Q329 was designed to get at this issue: "Consider your closest associate helping you start this business. Would you consider this a person who prefers to do things better, or to do things differently?"

Likewise, we wanted to ascertain the interviewee's perception of the appropriateness of his or her closest business associate's style to the problems encountered. Thus, item Q330 was as follows: "How well does the problem-solving style of your closest associate match the types of problems encountered in starting a new business? Would you say this person's style is often a good match, sometimes a good match, sometimes a poor match, or often a poor match?"

Due to the constraints of this study, single-item proxies of Innovators versus Adaptors were developed that were inspired by an original multiple-item measure. Each item, due to this constraint, also had a corresponding time variable that measured the time it took for the interviewee to respond. This was initially done in order to determine and quantify any potential ambiguity in the interviewee's understanding of the item as well as to determine if a substantially different response time existed with the item between the entrepreneurs and the nonentrepreneurs. Response times averaged between 12 and 13 seconds with no significant difference between groups. We believe that this indicates sufficient understanding by the groups. Basic count data regarding the style are provided in Table 15.2, including gender counts for those interested in possibly testing for gender distinctions.

Lastly, with the inclusion of oversampling for women and minorities, we have a total sample of 1,261 individuals. Of these, 856 clearly classified themselves as Adaptors and 342 as Innovators. Thus, 95% of the interviewees were successfully classified according to the KAI Inventory. The balance either responded as both or said they didn't know or weren't sure. Preliminary analysis suggests that a cognitive distinction may indeed exist between entrepreneurs and nonentrepreneurs (Johnson, Danis, & Dollinger, 2001). Further study and controls for gender, race, business, and other factors will be necessary as we continue to explore the phenomenon.

Table 15.2   Frequency Distribution: Cognitive Variable (Q327) in the PSED Data Set

		KAI Classification		
Adaptor	*Innovator*	*Refused/Missing*	*Both*	*Total*
856	342	21	42	1,261
		Sample Breakdown by Gender		
		Total With Oversampling		
	Males	597		
	Females	664		
	Total	1,261		

References

Baum, J. R., Locke, E. A., & Smith, K. G. (2001). A multidimensional model of venture growth. *Academy of Management Journal, 44*(2), 292–303.

Bobic, M., Davis, E., & Cunningham, R. (1999). The Kirton Adaption-Innovation Inventory: Validity issues, practical questions. *Review of Public Personnel Administration, 19*(2), 18–30.

Bokoros, M. A., & Goldstein, M. B. (1992). Common factors in five measures of cognitive style. *Current Psychology, 11*(2), 99–109.

Bradley, G. (1978). Self-serving biases in the attribution process: A reexamination of the fact or fiction question. *Journal of Personality and Social Psychology, 36,* 56–71.

Cooper, A., Woo, C., & Dunkelberg, W. (1988). Entrepreneurs' perceived chances for success. *Journal of Business Venturing, 3,* 97–108.

Dollinger, M. J. (1995). *Entrepreneurship: Strategies and resources.* Homewood, IL: Irwin.

Dollinger, M. J., & Danis, W. M. (1998). Preferred decision-making styles: A cross-cultural comparison. *Psychological Reports, 82,* 755–761.

Dunning, D., Meyerowitz, J. A., & Holzberg, A. D. (1989). Ambiguity and self-evaluation: The role of idiosyncratic definitions in self-serving assessments of ability. *Journal of Personality and Social Psychology, 57*(6), 1082–1090.

Ensley, M. D., & Pearce, C. L. (2001). Shared cognition in top management teams: Implications for new venture performance. *Journal of Organizational Behavior, 22,* 145–160.

Forbes, D. P. (1999). Cognitive approaches to new venture creation. *International Journal of Management Reviews, 1*(4), 415–439.

Gregorc, A. F. (1982). *Gregorc Style Delineator: Development, technical and administrative manuals.* Columbia, CT: Gregorc.

Johnson, K. L., Danis, W. M., & Dollinger, M. J. (2001, August). *The impact of cognitive styles of decision-making in new venture creation on the expectations and perceptions of the nascent entrepreneur.* Paper presented at the annual meeting of the Academy of Management, Washington, DC.

Kirton, M. J. (1976). Adaptors and innovators: A description and measure. *Journal of Applied Psychology, 61*(5), 622–629.

Kolb, D. A. (1976). *Learning Style Inventory: Technical manual.* Boston: McBer.

McClelland, D. (1987). Characteristics of successful entrepreneurs. *Journal of Creative Behavior, 21,* 219–233.

Merrill, D. W., & Reid, R. H. (1981). *Personal styles and effective performance.* Radnor, PA: Chilton.

Messick, S. (1976). Personality consistencies in cognition and creativity. In S. Messick (Ed.), *Individuality in learning* (pp. 4–22). San Francisco: Jossey-Bass.

Mohammed, S., & Ringseis, E. (2001). Cognitive diversity and consensus in group decision making: The role of inputs, processes, and outcomes. *Organizational Behavior and Human Decision Processes, 85*(2), 310–335.

Myers, I. B., & McCaulley, M. H. (1985). *Manual: A guide to the development and use of the Myers-Briggs Type Indicator.* Palo Alto, CA: Consulting Psychologists Press.

Shaver, K. G., & Scott, L. R. (1991). Person, process, choice: The psychology of new venture creation. *Entrepreneurship: Theory and Practice, (16)*2, 23–45.

Witkin, H. A., Moore, C. A., Goodenough, D. R., & Cox, P. W. (1977). Field-dependent and field-independent cognitive styles and their educational implications. *Review of Educational Research, 47,* 1–64.

CHAPTER 16

Role Models and Perceived Social Support

Per Davidsson

Theory and Previous Research

This chapter deals primarily with questions Q362 to Q379c of the initial phone interview. This package of questions investigates whether the interviewees have self-employed parents or other close role models, as well as the extent and characteristics of their parents' business endeavors and the interviewees' involvement in it. Questions also go into how the interviewees perceive such role models and whether they have received encouragement or discouragement from family and friends with respect to starting their own firms. It should be noted that both the Person and the Gender Design Teams contributed to this section of the interview. Chapter 8 of this volume, Family Background, presents the Gender Team's approach to these questions, as well as response frequencies for all items in this section of the interview. The following presentation of the items' background and rationale originates from the work in the Person Team.

It is well known that early entrepreneurship research put much emphasis on identifying the psychological characteristics of entrepreneurs—with meager results (Gartner, 1988; Kilby, 1971). Somewhat ironically, many of those early studies actually came up with very strong results on some person characteristics that were sociological rather than psychological in nature (Stanworth, Blythe, Granger, & Stanworth, 1989), but as these characteristics were treated as "control variables," they were for a long time largely ignored.

Apart from the overrepresentation of males—which is only indirectly a topic for this chapter—one of the most consistent results in research on business founders and owner-managers is the marked overrepresentation, among those who founded their own businesses, of individuals with close role models. Three large-scale (400–1,500 respondents) studies conducted by this author in Sweden in the 1980s and early 1990s suggest about 40% of small business owner-managers had a self-employed parent, compared with about 15% of other vocational groups (see Davidsson, 1989, 1995a, 1995b for descriptions of the respective studies, although this particular result is not highlighted). In a survey of more than 600 respondents in the United Kingdom, between 30% and 47% of individuals either considering, about to start, or already in business had a father who had also been in business compared with some 20% of employees generally (Stanworth et al., 1989; Storey, 1994). Similar results have been reported in a multitude of other studies, very convincingly so by, for example, de Wit and van Winden (1989), who used longitudinal sociological data on a very large sample of founders and nonfounders in the Netherlands.

For a long time, researchers exhibited relatively little theoretical interest in this recurring finding. Eventually, however, it was highlighted in contributions that take a social learning perspective on entrepreneurship (Boyd & Vozikis, 1994; Krueger, 1994; Krueger & Brazael, 1994; Scherer, Adams, Carley, & Wiebe, 1989; Scherer, Brodzinsky, & Wiebe, 1991). This has led to an interest not only in the presence of role models but also in what kind of experience and impressions this has brought. Scherer et al. (1989) found that mere presence of a role model, and the role model's perceived performance, had separate and additive positive effects on "entrepreneurial preparedness" and "entrepreneurial career expectancy." Krueger (1993) found a positive relationship between perceived "positiveness" of the role model experience and perceived desirability of founding a firm. In my own research on entrepreneurial intentions, in a random sample of more than 1,000 Swedish adults who were currently not running their own business, the perception of the role model on a "very negative" to "very positive" scale was a very strong predictor of the intention score (Davidsson, 1995b). Converted to frequencies, it turned out that among those respondents who had received a very negative role model impression, none stated that it was likely, very likely or dead certain that they would run their own firm within 5 years. This proportion then increased in an almost perfectly linear fashion by 10% per scale step so that the corresponding percentage was 39% for those with a very positive role model perception (Davidsson, 1995b).

According to social learning theory (Bandura, 1982, 1986), what is being transferred from parent to child through "vicarious learning" is an amalgam of knowledge, skills, and attitudes. From other theoretical perspectives, it may be of interest to sort out more precisely what type of inspiration and/or resources underlie the overrepresentation of children of business owner-managers among business founders. Aldrich, Renzulli, and Langton (1998) seems to be the only study to date that has explicitly addressed this issue. The "role model" effect could be mainly a matter of "human capital" (Becker, 1964; Mincer, 1974; Schultz, 1959), that is, transfer of practical business knowledge and skills, and possibly attitudes as well. It may also be a matter of "social capital"—getting access to important network contacts, encouragement, and possibly also free riding on the parent's good reputation (Lin, Ensel, & Vaughn, 1981; Portes, 1998). Alternatively, it is simply a matter of "financial capital" through inheritance or the parents serving as business angels with direct infusion of money or providing collateral for bank loans.

Whatever the exact mechanism, the relative closeness of the role model also appears to be important. In my own research on entrepreneurial intentions (Davidsson, 1995b), those with a self-employed father had higher intention scores than those who only had a relative or friend who was self-employed, and this middle group in turn had higher intention scores than those who had no self-employed role model whatsoever. There was no indication in that particular research that the role model should be of the same sex as the respondent in order to have an influence. The notion that *any* role model, related or not—personally acquainted or portrayed in the media—would have a potential influence on individuals' propensities to go into business for themselves is also in line with Cialdini's (1988) reasoning on "social proof." Cialdini holds that social proof—"others do it, hence it is appropriate"—is one of the major principles of social influence, and he supports his argument with compelling empirical evidence from various areas of human endeavor.

The Items

The main PSED items related to role models and perceived social support are the following:

Q362. Did your parents ever work for themselves or run their own business, alone or together? (yes/no → go to Q376/don't know → go to Q376)

Q363. Was it only your father's business, only your mother's business, a joint business, two separate businesses, or some other combination of activity? (only father/only mother/joint business/each parent separately/some other combination)

Depending on the answer to Q363, the respondent was taken to one or more versions of the following package. The displayed version is the "joint" version. Q364 to Q367 and Q368 to Q370 are the corresponding "father only/separately" and "mother only/separately" versions, respectively. All items can be found in Chapter 8 of this volume, as well as on-line in the University of Michigan Codebook (at http://projects.isr.umich.edu/psed).

Q372. How many different businesses did your parents jointly own or run? (open; years)

Q373. For how many years did your parents own or run their own business jointly? (open; years)

Q374. What was the largest number of paid employees, family or nonfamily, who ever worked for any of your parents' jointly owned business(es)? (open; number)

Q375. Did you ever work for your parent's jointly owned business, full- or part-time? (yes, full/yes, part/no/don't know)

The interview then moves on to the presence of other role models and to the kind of impression or encouragement/discouragement family and friends have provided:

Q376. Among other relatives and kin, apart from your parents, did most, some, a few, or none own their own business? (most/some/a few/none/don't know)

Q377. Among close friends and neighbors, did most, some, a few or none own their own business? (most/some/a few/none/don't know)

Q378. From observing family, kin, and close relatives, what is your overall impression of running a business as a career—would you say very positive, positive, neutral, negative, or very negative? (5-point scale plus don't know)

Q379. Have your family, relatives, or other close friends been encouraging you to, or discouraging you from, starting a business of your own? (encouraging/discouraging → go to Q379c/both or mixed/do not care → go to Q380/don't know → go to Q380)

Q379a. How would you describe the encouragement you received from your family, relatives, or other close friends; would you consider it very weak, weak, neither weak nor strong, strong, or very strong? (5-point scale plus don't know)

Q379c. How would you describe the discouragement you received from your family, relatives or other close friends; would you consider it very weak, weak, neither weak nor strong, strong, or very strong? (5-point scale plus don't know. Of course, scores on this item should be reversed)

It may be noted that items Q362, Q363, Q376, and Q377 concern whether any role models have been present, who they were, and how many there were. Q364 and Q375 add information that gives some ground for exploring the specific mechanism of the role model effect. For example, does it matter whether and how much respondents have worked for their parents' firms? They also provide an opportunity for testing hypotheses of the kind "like father, like son"—that habitual entrepreneurs would breed habitual entrepreneurs; growth-oriented entrepreneurs breed growth-oriented entrepreneurs, and the like.

As noted above, the quality of the role model experience appears to have separate and possibly stronger effects on followers than has mere presence. Q378 is identical (albeit translated) to the question I used and found strong effect for in Davidsson (1995b). Similar items were used by Krueger and Scherer and their respective collaborators (Krueger, 1994; Krueger & Brazael, 1994; Scherer et al. 1989; Scherer et al. 1991). The questions Q379 to Q379c ask more precisely about encouragement/discouragement and were developed specifically for the PSED study. These items certainly add to the possibility of understanding the nature of the role model effect.

Of course, the items in this section should not necessarily be used in isolation. Analysts employing a human capital or social capital perspective would no doubt regard the above as indicators among others, and those who employ other theoretical perspectives may also find useful items in other sections of the questionnaires, which they would like to use alongside the above. With respect to perceived social support, it deserves mention that section B1 in the mail questionnaire includes items that reflect perceptions of a supportive environment (or the converse) beyond the circles of family and friends.

Preliminary Results and
Some Additional Research Ideas

As mentioned already, frequencies for all variables in the Q362 to Q379c range are reported in Chapter 8 of this handbook. The Swedish sister project arrived at the following results (cf. Davidsson & Honig, 2003; Delmar & Davidsson, 2000). Presence of a parental role model (Q362) has a significant but relatively weak positive effect on the probability of becoming a nascent entrepreneur (NE). The same is true for positive impression of a parental role model (Q378). Once in the process, we found no significant effect of parental role model presence. Unexpectedly, having friends or neighbors in business (Q377) was ascribed a stronger effect on entering the process than were parents, and the former variable was also ascribed some significant effect on making progress in the start-up process and eventually achieving first sales. Equally strong effects on NE status and progress in the process (accumulation of gestation activities over time) were found for the encouragement variable (Q379a–c). The other items have as yet not been tested in the Swedish study or were dropped for reasons of multicollinearity.

Preliminary, unpublished analyses of an early version of the American PSED data set suggested there is no effect whatsoever of the mere presence of a parental role model for U.S. males (Davidsson, 2000). For females, there appears to be a weak effect of (same sex) parental role model presence on NE status, especially for those who have worked in their parent's firm. For both sexes, there was a strong overrepresentation among NEs of positive role model impressions as well as encouragement, relative to the comparison group.

The absence of any parental role model effect among U.S. males—if it holds up (which seems to be the case; cf. Chapter 8 in this volume)—is a very interesting result in itself. Contrast this with the following statement from an era and country where individual entrepreneurial initiative was regarded as anything but heroic, namely Great Britain in 1971:

> It is our impression that the general climate is now so antipathetic to business and particularly small business that except for those whose father is in business on his own account . . . the tendency is for young people not to adopt independent business as a career. (Bolton, 1971)

The quote is in line with the notion that in the cultural climate in Europe—and to a certain extent in the United States—from the late 1960s until a turning point that started to become evident perhaps some time in the early 1980s, one almost had to have it in the family in order to come up with the idea of going into business for oneself. What a stark contrast to today's United States—and Sweden, too, for that matter! This interpretation accords with results showing strong overrepresentation of parental role models in studies dating back to the 1970s and early 1980s, weaker although not completely nonexisting effects in more recent Scandinavian studies (Davidsson & Honig, 2003; Kolvereid, 1996; Reitan, 1998), and zero effect among American males in the PSED. When entrepreneurship is highly valued in the culture and everywhere present in the media and in education, it does not take parental role models in order to get the inspiration and knowledge needed for going into business for oneself. However, encouragement from the closer environment seems to be of importance for this decision and possibly also for being successful at completing the process.

To recapitulate, earlier studies have demonstrated effects of varying strength of the presence of close role models on the propensity for becoming a business founder. They have also demonstrated that the image of business ownership-management conveyed by such role models has a separate and probably stronger effect than mere role model presence. The items included in PSED hold promise of leading to a deeper theoretical understanding of these relationships as they allow to some extent the formal testing of alternative theoretical interpretations. Just to mention one example, the direct effect of encouragement (or discouragement) will certainly be better captured by the PSED compared to earlier studies. The possible link between "cultural climate" and importance of close role models suggests that differences by sex, ethnic group, and geographic location should be carefully examined—assuming that the perceived appropriateness of such a career choice varies across such subgroups. Finally, the longitudinal nature of the PSED data allows analyses of the impact of role models and perceived social support on process and subsequent outcomes and thus allows the opportunity to ask and answer questions that no earlier studies have been able to address. The opportunities lie wide open!

References

Aldrich, H., Renzulli, L., & Langton, N. (1998). Passing on the privilege: Resources provided by self-employed parents to their self-employed children. In K. Liecht (Ed.), *Research in social stratification and mobility*. Greenwich, CT: JAI.

Bandura, A. (1982). Self-efficacy mechanism in human agency. *American Psychologist, 37*, 122–147.

Bandura, A. (1986). *Social foundations of thought and action: A social cognitive theory*. Englewood Cliffs, NJ: Prentice Hall.

Becker, G. S. (1964). *Human capital*. Chicago: University of Chicago Press.

Bolton, J. E. (1971). *Small firms. Report of the Committee of Inquiry on small firms*. London: Her Majesty's Stationery Office.

Boyd, N. G., & Vozikis, G. S. (1994). The influence of self-efficacy on the development of entrepreneurial intentions and actions. *Entrepreneurship Theory and Practice, 18*(4), 63–77.

Cialdini, R. B. (1988). *Influence: Science & practice*. New York: HarperCollins.

Davidsson, P. (1989). *Continued entrepreneurship and small firm growth*. Unpublished doctoral dissertation, Stockholm School of Economics, Stockholm, Sweden.

Davidsson, P. (1995a). Culture, structure and regional levels of entrepreneurship. *Entrepreneurship & Regional Development, 7*, 41–62.

Davidsson, P. (1995b). *Determinants of entrepreneurial intentions* (Working Paper 1995:1). Jönköping, Sweden: Jönköping International Business School.

Davidsson, P. (2000, November). *The changing role of role models.* PowerPoint presentation at the second annual Grief Research Symposium on Emerging Organizations, Los Angeles, CA.

Davidsson, P., & Honig, B. (2003). The role of social and human capital among nascent entrepreneurs. *Journal of Business Venturing, 18*(3), 301–331.

Delmar, F., & Davidsson, P. (2000). Where do they come from? Prevalence and characteristics of nascent entrepreneurs. *Entrepreneurship & Regional Development, 12,* 1–23.

De Wit, G., & Van Winden, F. A. A. M. (1989). An empirical analysis of self-employment in the Netherlands. *Small Business Economics, 1*(4), 263–272.

Gartner, W. B. (1988). "Who is an entrepreneur" is the wrong question. *American Small Business Journal, 12*(3), 11–31.

Kilby, P. (1971). Hunting the heffalump. In P. Kilby (Ed.), *Entrepreneurship and economic development* (pp. 1–40). New York: Free Press.

Kolvereid, L. (1996). Organizational employment versus self-employment: Reasons for career choice intentions. *Entrepreneurship Theory and Practice, 20*(3, Spring), 23–31.

Krueger, N. (1993). The impact of prior entrepreneurial exposure on perceptions of new venture feasibility and desirability. *Entrepreneurship Theory and Practice, 18*(1), 5–21.

Krueger, N. (1994, August). *Strategic optimism: Antecedents of perceived probabilities of new venture success.* Paper presented at the annual meeting of the Dallas, Texas, Academy of Management.

Krueger, N., & Brazael, D. V. (1994). Entrepreneurial potential and potential entrepreneurs. *Entrepreneurship Theory and Practice, 18*(3), 91–104.

Lin, N., Ensel, W., & Vaughn, J. (1981). Social resources and strength of ties: Structural factors in occupational status attainment. *American Sociological Review 46*(4), 393–405.

Mincer, J. (1974). *Schooling, experience and earnings.* New York: Columbia University Press.

Portes, A. (1998). Social capital. *Annual Review of Sociology, 23,* 1–24.

Reitan, B. (1998). *Perspectives on new venture creation: The stimulation of entrepreneurial potential and new venture attempts among young people.* Unpublished doctoral dissertation, Norwegian Technological University, Trondheim, Norway.

Scherer, R. F., Adams, J. S., Carley, S. S., & Wiebe, F. A. (1989). Role model performance effects on development of entrepreneurial career preference. *Entrepreneurship Theory and Practice, 13*(3), 53–71.

Scherer, R. F., Brodzinsky, J. D., & Wiebe, F. A. (1991). Examining the relationship between personality and entrepreneurial career preference, *Entrepreneurship & Regional Development, 3,* 195–206.

Schultz, T. (1959). Investment in man: An economist's view. *The Social Service Review, 33*(2), 69–75.

Stanworth, J., Blythe, S., Granger, B., & Stanworth, C. (1989). Who becomes an entrepreneur? *International Small Business Journal, 8,* 11–22.

Storey, D. J. (1994). *Understanding the small business sector.* London: Routledge.

CHAPTER 17

Entrepreneurial Intensity

Jianwen Liao

Harold Welsch

Literature Review and Theory

Traditionally, entrepreneurship research as a field is concerned with the question of "Who is an entrepreneur?" There has been considerable interest in the ability to identifying the components of these characteristics and the personal traits that would determine how entrepreneurs differ from other individuals (Shaver & Scott, 1991). Many traits have been offered, including ambition, need for achievement, risk taking, and locus of control (Brockhaus, 1982; Casson, 1982). However, findings from this direction of research are fragmented and inconclusive. There is no clear evidence that these attributes will differentiate entrepreneurs from other individuals. Gartner's (1985) seminal research goes even further and suggests that focusing on the individual entrepreneur is the wrong question.

In a study involving members of the National Federation of Independent Business (NFIB), Cooper and Dunkelberg (1986) observed that there are several paths by which one might become a small business owner, including founding the business, purchasing the business, inheriting the business, and being promoted or brought in by other owners. They hypothesized that significant differences in the "degree of entrepreneurship" or "entrepreneurship intensity" could be expected. However, they never developed an empirical/operational measure of entrepreneurial intensity. They suggested that it may not be directly measurable or observable but may be inferred through its reflection in a set of characteristics that they identified from previous research (Keats & Bracker, 1988). These included background, attitudes, and "a complex set of factors associated with previous careers, incubator organizations and the processes of starting" (p. 62). According to Cooper and Dunkelberg, these characteristics collectively reflected the conceptual variable "degree of entrepreneurship." Until now, no actual measure of entrepreneurship intensity has been developed. This conception of entrepreneurial intensity focused more on the paths or origins of entrepreneurial endeavors. The approach taken in this paper is more individually based, not contextually.

Entrepreneurial intensity has its foundation in the Protestant work ethic (Weber, 1905) and the achievement motive (McClelland, 1961). It has a secondary base in commitment, internal locus of control, diligence, and determination.

Despite religious pluralism in U.S. society, the strains of Protestantism have exerted a powerful influence on people's thoughts and actions since the early history of the country. The main core asserts that spiritual salvation was to be attained through striving. More recently, the Protestant work ethic has evolved outside of its religious context to a point where spiritual values are set aside. In its non-religious role, it assumes hard work is performed for the material benefits and personal recognition it affords. It has evolved into a form of a type A behavior.

Type A behavior in its early characterization was identified by excessive and competitive drive and an enhanced set of time urgency. Later, additional components were identified, such as intense sustained desire to achieve, an eagerness to compete, persistent drive for recognition, a continuous involvement in deadline activities, a habitual propensity to accelerate mental and physical functions, and consistent alertness. Price (1982) has suggested that this behavior pattern is learned in open, competitive economies where upward mobility is possible. Success was thought to be a function of individual effort and that progress is best defined in terms of material or tangible achievements.

The visualization of a successful enterprise, combined with parental and spousal support, in addition to the right circumstances, such as life stage, education, and a nutrient-rich environment, can cause an individual to generate a great "fire in the belly," termed high "entrepreneurial intensity (EI)." This level of commitment to the entrepreneurial endeavor can be characterized as the passion required for entrepreneurial success (Selz, 1992). It is further characterized by a single-minded focus to start a business and work toward its survival and growth, often at the expense of other worthy and important goals. The theoretical base and rationale actually arose from an argument generated from central/eastern Europe regarding entrepreneurial intentions and behaviors. The first argument contends that eastern Europeans "unlearned" the work ethic by being provided for "cradle to grave" and having secure jobs and social benefits from their socialistic governments. Therefore, entrepreneurial intensity should be weak or nonexistent. The counterargument posits that the Protestant work ethic (Weber, 1905) originated in Europe and is inherent and permeates the central/eastern European culture. The individuals are hard workers, exhibiting sacrifice, determination, and diligence, with a focused commitment to entrepreneurship, and it was only temporarily suppressed by the Socialist/Communist regimes. Therefore, entrepreneurial intensity should be high. Thus, it is a question of what caused entrepreneurial intensity. Was it the environment or was it inherent in individuals? While comparative analysis across countries has not yet been completed, preliminary results show EI to be related to entrepreneurial motivations, willingness to make sacrifice and incur opportunity costs, intentions to grow the business, and various demographic variables. The EI variable holds promise to show how culture and history have affected on this distinguishing factor.

The variable EI has been created to measure how focused or committed the entrepreneur is to his or her (potential) start-up endeavor. Commitment to the entrepreneurial endeavor can be described as passion required for firm gestation and characterized as a single-minded focus to work toward the health of the venture. It has two interrelated aspects. First is focus, which refers to the extent to which an entrepreneur is willing to give up other pursuits to create and own a business. Second is commitment, which refers to the extent to which an entrepreneur is willing to spend time and resources on venture creation and development. Both focus and entrepreneurial commitment combined are hypothesized to be a (the) critical variable measuring the strength of entrepreneurial initiative. For example, individuals have multiple commitments, such as the dichotomy between professional and organizational commitment. There are other possible commitments, such as to unions or associations as well as work groups, jobs, and tasks. The person may also be committed to him- or herself and social groups outside of the workplace, such as recreational groups or the family. People may be committed to other people and the values and goals of these people. The EI concept is based on the contention that entrepreneurs will place the highest value on their efforts leading to the success of their enterprise.

The Differences Between Entrepreneurial Intensity and Entrepreneurial Orientation

Entrepreneurship orientation (EO) is defined as the processes, practices, and decision-making activities that lead to the creation of a new venture (Lumpkin & Dess, 1996). The key dimensions that characterize entrepreneurial orientation include autonomy, innovativeness, risk taking, proactiveness, and competitive aggressiveness. Each of these dimensions is useful in predicting the successful creation of a venture, venture survival, and venture performance (Wiklund, 1999).

It is evident that entrepreneurial orientation is mainly related to the directionality or the propensity for someone to lead a new entry. By contrast, the construct of *entrepreneurial intensity* (EI) captures the degree of entrepreneurship—the level of commitment and focus of an entrepreneur in leading a new entry. These two concepts are complementary but clearly differentiate each other. The existing research has placed great emphasis on entrepreneurial orientation and its relationship to venture creation and performance. However, the question of how the degree of entrepreneurship, or entrepreneurial intensity, affects the venture creation process and venture performance and how it interplays with contextual and other individual variables receive scant, if any, attention. By clarifying and validating such an important construct, we may be able shed new light on many contentious and inconclusive findings in entrepreneurship research.

Measurement of Entrepreneurial Intensity

Cooper and Dunkelberg (1986) suggested that EI may not be directly observable but may be inferred through its reflection in a complex set of factors associated with professional career and processes of start-up. We developed a new operationalized variable composed of 12 original items that have been pretested in 10 different countries with considerable success (Welsch, 1998; Gundry & Welsch, 2001). The entrepreneurial intensity scale has been administered in the United States, Mexico, Russia, Poland, Romania, Hungary, and several Baltic countries with significant success. Entrepreneurs in various stages of development and various industries in these countries have responded to the items on a 5-point scale. Preliminary alphas of scale reliability range in the high 70s to low 80s.

   As indicated in Table 17.1, the initial pilot testing on data of the Entrepreneurial Profile Questionnaire (EPQ) suggests 4 of the 10 items (a, c, d, h) capture the domain of entrepreneurial intensity and achieve reasonable reliability (Welsch, 1998).

Table 17.1   Scales of Entrepreneurial Intensity

EPQ Items	Items Included in the PSED Questionnaires
a) My personal philosophy is to do "whatever it takes" to establish my own business	QL1f
b) I plan to eventually sell my business	
c) I would rather own my own business than earn a higher salary employed by someone else	QL1d
d) Owning my own business is more important than spending more time with my family	QL1g
e) I would rather own my own business than pursue another promising career	
f) My business is the most important activity in my life	
g) I will do whatever it takes to make my business a success	
h) There is no limit as to how long I would give a maximum effort to establish my business	QL1e
i) I would be willing to make significant personal sacrifices in order to stay in business	
j) I would go to work somewhere else only long enough to make another attempt to establish my own firm.	

1. Owning my own business is more important than spending time with my family.

2. There is no limit to how long I would give a maximum effort to establish my business.

3. I would rather own my own business than pursue another promising career.

4. My personal philosophy is to do "whatever it takes" to establish my own business.

The four items were included in the survey along with other items related to locus of control, self-efficacy, and sociability. They were asked in the following manner. For both nascent entrepreneurs and the comparison group, the items were preceded by this stem: "The following statement can be used to describe most people. How accurately would they describe you?" Both groups responded to each item on a 5-point Likert-type scale: 1 = completely untrue; 2 = mostly untrue; 3 = it depends; 4 = mostly true; and 5 = completely true.

Measurement Validation

Sample. The analysis was conducted using the data from the Panel Study of Entrepreneurial Dynamics (PSED), which includes 751 combined observations of nascent entrepreneurs and a comparison group. Details about the data collection procedures and screening procedures are provided in Reynolds (2000). The list deletion approach was used in the analysis. The final sample consists of 563 observations.

Multivariate Normality. Most of the estimation techniques used in structural equation modeling (SEM) assume multivariate normality. Multivariate normality is the assumption that each variable and all linear combinations of the variables are normally distributed. Using PRELIS, we screened the four measured items for both univariate and multivariate normality. In both cases, we found that all four measures are significantly skewed and kurtotic. However, we decided not to transfer the data to restore normality. In a large sample like ours, a variable with statistically significant skewness often doesn't deviate enough from normality to make a substantive difference in the analysis. The impact of departure from zero kurtosis also diminishes (Tabachnick & Fidell, 1996).

Confirmatory Factor Analysis. Using LISREL 8 (Jöreskog & Sörbom, 1993), as indicated in Figure 17.1, we estimated the tested validity and reliability of our measurement.

The results of LISREL were examined for offending estimates. These are estimated coefficients in the structural model that exceed acceptable limits. In our model, no offending estimates were found based on the following criteria: (1) negative error variance for any constructs and observed variables; (2) standardized coefficients exceeding or very close to 1; and (3) very large standard errors associated with any estimated coefficients.

Multiple measures were used to assess the overall model fit to the observed pattern of correlation in the data (Hair, Anderson, Tatham, & Black, 1995). The

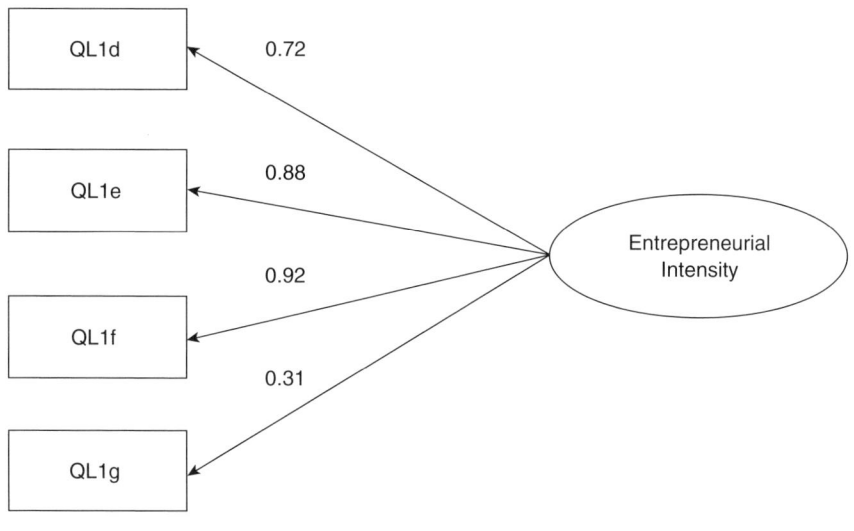

Figure 17.1   Confirmatory Factor Analysis: Entrepreneurial Intensity

chi-square statistic is 3.08 ($df = 2$, $p = 0.214$), demonstrating that the differences of the model and the observed data are not significant. The goodness-of-fit index (GFI) assesses the correspondence of the observed covariance matrix with that predicted from the proposed model. Our LISREL results show that GFI for the model is .99, which exceeds the generally acceptable value of 0.90. It therefore lends additional support to a good fit between the proposed theoretical model and observed data. Another measure of overall model of fit is the adjusted goodness-of-fit index (AGFI), assessing the parsimony of the model by evaluating the fit of the model versus the number of estimated coefficients needed to achieve the level of fit. The AGFI for our model is .98, greater than the recommended level of 0.90. The root mean square residual (RMSR) is the square root of the mean of the squared residuals—an average of the residuals between observed and estimated input covariance matrix. For our model, the RMSR is 0.031, below the recommended value of 0.06. In general, various model fit indices suggest that our model is truly representative of the observed data.

We evaluated our measurement model by construct convergent validity. Convergent validity can be tested by examining the significance of the path coefficient on its posited latent variables. As indicated in Figure 17.1, all the path coefficients included in the measurement models are statistically significant ($p < 0.05$), suggesting convergent validity was achieved.

We used the following formula (Equation 17.1) to calculate the composite reliability of entrepreneurial intensity (Hair et al., 1995):

$$\text{Construct reliability} = \frac{(\Sigma \text{std, loading})^2}{(\Sigma \text{std, loading})^2 + \Sigma \varepsilon_j}$$

where the standardized loadings are obtained directly from the program output and ε_j is the measurement error for each indicator. The construct reliability for our model is 0.769, which exceeds the recommended value of 0.5 (which roughly corresponds to a standardized loading of 0.7).

Entrepreneurial Intensity as a Differentiating Factor

Previous research related to traits and personal attributes fails to yield factors that were able to differentiate nascent entrepreneurs and the general public. A high degree of risk-taking behavior does not make a person an entrepreneur. In a similar vein, a person who is not an entrepreneur may well exhibit a high degree of risk-taking behavior. To test the extent to which entrepreneurial intensity differentiates entrepreneurs from the comparison group, we followed these steps. First, two groups were created, with 392 nascent entrepreneurs and 175 from the comparison group (general public). Second, we conducted ANOVA to test the differences between groups across the four items related to entrepreneurial intensity. The results are reported in Table 17.2.

As indicated in Table 17.2, we found that nascent entrepreneurs and the general public are statistically different across the four items of entrepreneurial intensity. This demonstrates that EI or "the degree of entrepreneurship" is probably a more

Table 17.2   ANOVA: Nascent Entrepreneurs and Comparison Group

Item Number	Variable	Means		ANOVA F Test
		Nascent Entrepreneurs	Comparison Group	
QL1d	I would rather own my own business than earn a higher salary employed by someone else	4.05	3.27	69.712***
QL1e	There is no limit as to how long I would give a maximum effort to establish my business	3.90	3.36	30.219***
QL1f	My personal philosophy is to do "whatever it takes" to establish my own business	3.77	2.91	77.662***
QL1g	Owning my own business is more important than spending more time with my family	1.77	1.65	6.068***

*** $p < 0.01$

important factor in differentiating nascent entrepreneurs from others. Clearly, there may also be substantial differences in the degree of entrepreneurial intensity between entrepreneurs and others in the population as well as smaller differences among (nascent) entrepreneurs.

Entrepreneurial Intensity: Future Research Directions

An entrepreneurial intensity (EI) model may be conceived as the central or most important component of the entrepreneurial process. As such, it needs to be explored in terms of its antecedents and outcomes (Figure 17.2).

Entrepreneurial intensity may be related to several antecedents in the environment as well as personal/demographic characteristics. Consequences of high entrepreneurial intensity are expected to manifest themselves in behaviors that lead to entrepreneurial success, such as start-up, loans, and increases in sales, profitability, survivability, and growth. This suggests that the level of entrepreneurial intensity will affect the level of task motivation, the degree to which an individual perceives that he/she has the ability to control the success of the business. A second major research question: Is entrepreneurial intensity stable over time or does it dissipate or increase along stages of development of the business life cycle?

The question arises about the precursors to EI and whether one is born with these (inherent) or they are absorbed or learned throughout the life process. This issue is similar to the question of whether entrepreneurs are born or made. An argument can be made that we are born unequally with certain dispositions, such as aggressiveness, impulsiveness, tendency for action, or extroversion. This would

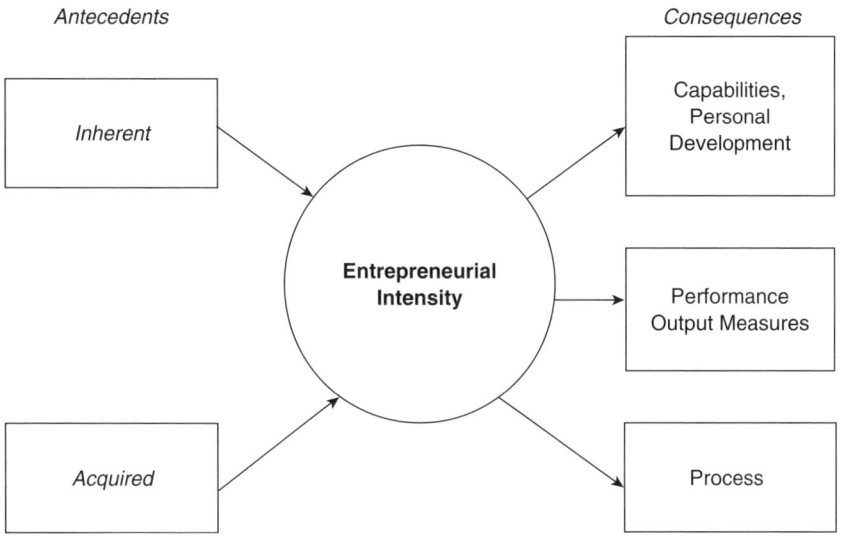

Figure 17.2   Entrepreneurial Intensity: Its Antecedents and Consequences

imply that entrepreneurs come into this world with certain predispositions that result in intensely focused/committed behaviors.

On the other hand, certain learned or acquired behaviors, such as watching parents, uncles, aunts, mentors, and role models perform successful entrepreneurial behaviors, may also lead to EI. This latter approach would imply that EI could range in scope from lower to higher levels of intensity depending on the effectiveness of the absorption/learning process.

In any case, the individual is chosen as the unit of analysis since he or she is often the main determinant of organizational success. The primacy of the individual in entrepreneurial research is competently discussed in Shaver and Scott (1991). Man, Lau, and Chan (2002) later contended that "being persistent and committed to the task will enhance performance of the firm in the long term" (p. 137). They also reinforce the idea that the basic role played by the owner-manager is one of the major factors of small and medium enterprises (SME) competitiveness because of the concentration of decision-making power of the entrepreneur in an SME environment, thereby affecting the firm's overall strategy. Other students (Slevin & Covin, 1997) suggest that the influential role of the entrepreneur is a critical factor in determining the performance of the firm, especially when it remains small.

The concept of EI can be effectively utilized to predict a series of important outcomes that can be categorized into three major groupings identified as capabilities, performance, and process. A person with high EI can be sharply contrasted to a dilettante who dabbles in everything lightly for short periods of time. Such a person is not someone who is casually and nonprofessionally involved in an activity, such as an amateur, dabbler, or patzer. Rather, it would be a person who has a long-term orientation, longer attention span, and would not be constrained by immediate gratification.

Other capabilities that could be predicted to result from EI are the ability to start a business, engage in more extensive learning behavior, have more sets of experiences, acquire more valuable skills, engage in more varied activities, develop more entrepreneurial competencies, engage in more personal growth and development, and possess a higher entrepreneurial orientation. Such a person would more likely have a vision, a higher clarity of vision, and a greater probability of implementing that vision. Such an entrepreneur would also be more serious, be more attuned to the environment, be more likely to act on changes, follow a more proactive approach, and achieve personal financial success.

Performance outcomes are predicted to include external financing, the ability to increase market share, and the ability to achieve higher firm performance—including short-term success factors such as growth and successfully taking the company public, as well as long-term factors such as acquiring other companies, staying with the firm through many cycles, and merging with other companies.

Process outcomes would include engaging in a series of nascent behaviors, engaging in more information absorption and adaptiveness, having a wider network with more significant relationships, becoming more competitive, enhancing the firm's innovative capability, adopting more innovations and innovative activity, making more concrete company goals and plans, having a greater likelihood of goal accomplishment, and having a greater ability to acquire capital (financial, human, informational).

Additional EI models would explore whether EI remains high or low across various stages of growth and identify variations across different contexts, such as cultural, ethnic, structural, and economic conditions.

References

Brockhaus, A. L. (1982). The psychology of the entrepreneur. In C. A. Kent, D. L. Sexton, & K. H. Vesper (Eds.), *Encyclopedia of entrepreneurship* (pp. 39-57). Englewood Cliffs, NJ: Prentice Hall.

Casson, M. (1982). *The entrepreneur: An economic theory.* Tatowa, NJ: Barnes and Noble Books.

Cooper, A., & Dunkelberg, W. (1986). Ownership structure and entrepreneurship. *Strategic Management Journal, 7,* 503–522.

Gartner, W. B. (1985). A conceptual framework for describing the phenomenon of new venture capital. *Academy of Management Review, 10*(4), 696–706.

Gundry, L., & Welsch, H. (2001). The ambitious entrepreneur: High growth strategies of women based enterprises. *Journal of Business Venturing, 16*(5), 453–470.

Hair, J., Anderson, R., Tatham, R., & Black, W. (1995). *Multivariate data analysis* (5th ed.). Englewood Cliffs, NJ: Prentice Hall.

Jöreskog, K., & Sörbom, D. (1993). *LISREL user's guide.* Uppsala, Sweden: University of Uppsala.

Keats, B. & Bracker, J. (1988). Toward a theory of small firm performance: A conceptual model. *American Journal of Small Business, 12*(4), 41–58.

Lumpkin, G. T., & Dess, G. G. (1996). Clarifying the entrepreneurial orientation construct and linking it to performance. *Academy of Management Review, 21*(1), 135–172.

Man, T. W. Y., Lau, T., & Chan, K. F. (2002). The competitiveness of small and medium enterprises: A conceptualization with focus on entrepreneurial competencies. *Journal of Business Venturing, 17*(2), 123–143.

McClelland, D. (1961). *The achieving society.* New York: Free Press.

Price, V. (1982). *Type A behavior pattern: A model for research and practice.* London: Academic Press.

Reynolds, P. (2000). National Panel Study of U.S. Business Startups: Background and methodology. In J. A. Katz (Ed.), *Advances in entrepreneurship, firm emergence, and growth* (pp. 153–227). Stamford, CT: JAI.

Selz, M. (1992, April 6). Young America still fosters entrepreneurial ambitions. *Wall Street Journal,* p. B2.

Shaver, K. G., & Scott, L. R. (1991). Person, process, choice: The psychology of new venture creation. *Entrepreneurship Theory and Practice, 16*(2), 23–45.

Slevin, D. P., & Covin, J. G. (1997). Strategy formation patterns, performance, and the significance of context. *Journal of Management, 23*(2), 189–209.

Tabachnick, B., & Fidell, L. (1996). *Using multivariate statistics.* (3rd ed.). New York: HarperCollins.

Weber, M. (1905). *The Protestant ethic and the spirit of capitalism.* New York: Knopf.

Welsch, H. (1998). North American entrepreneurs. In A. Morrison (Ed.), *Entrepreneurship: An international perspective* (pp. 115–136). Oxford, UK: Butterworth-Heinemann.

Wiklund, J. (1999). The sustainability of the entrepreneurial orientation-performance relationship. *Entrepreneurship Theory and Practice, 24*(1), 37–48.

CHAPTER 18

Individual Problem Solving

Matthew W. Ford

Charles H. Matthews

Individual Problem Solving

Problems are often viewed as deviations from standards of performance (e.g., Kepner & Tregoe, 1965). Solving the classic problem requires that a standard has been set, that the deviation from standard can be recognized, and that some means or method can be applied to close the gap between actual and desired performance. However, many problems are ill-structured. Ill-structured problems are characterized by a deficiency of information about the problem and about the relationship between present and desired states of affairs, as well as by a lack of methodology for solving the problem (Simon, 1960). Addressing ill-structured problems often requires considerable creativity (Evans, 1992).

Nearly every decision made by an entrepreneur is a consequence of solving a problem. In small operational businesses, entrepreneurial managers constantly solve problems related to selling output, hiring talent, accessing capital, and managing growth (Dodge, Fullerton, & Robbins, 1994; Franklin & Goodwin, 1983; Huang & Brown, 1999). In the preoperational environment of the nascent firm, the frequency and degree of difficulty associated with problem solving is magnified. After all, the nascent firm context does not provide the organizational frames of reference and performance feedback that facilitate problem solving in operational firms (e.g., Mullins, 1996). Indeed, it can be argued that the unstructured context of new venture creation constitutes one of the most ill-structured managerial problem-solving situations imaginable.

The Panel Study of Entrepreneurial Dynamics (PSED) project includes an early effort to gather empirical data about problem solving in the context of the nascent entrepreneur. Elsewhere in this volume, PSED items that focus specifically on cognitive aspects of entrepreneurial decision making are addressed. The purpose of this chapter is to introduce and discuss additional PSED questions related to individual problem solving. Sourced from various locations in the mail questionnaire, these items help define the problem-solving environment and preferences of the nascent entrepreneur. As such, the questions aggregate information that should be useful for studies of problem solving in a firm's early stages.

Problem Identification Versus Solution Development

Managerial problem-solving processes commonly progress through a sequence that includes phases of problem identification and solution development (e.g., Archer 1980; Merrifield, Guilford, Christensen, & Frick, 1962; Simon, 1960). Problem identification has been proposed to be particularly important when there is uncertainty about strategic direction (Weber, 1984). However, problem identification is a difficult process that is often rushed or taken for granted (Volkema, 1997). Recognizing that a problem exists often requires individuals to compare an observed discrepancy to an accumulated set of experiences (Cowan, 1986). Nascent entrepreneurs may have difficulty with problem identification because founders sometimes lack personal or organizational bases for comparison in order to assess whether a discrepancy constitutes a problem. The firm's nascent context reduces frames of reference available to entrepreneurs for problem identification.

Developing solutions to problems may also pose a challenge to the nascent entrepreneur. Specifically, nascent entrepreneurs often lack access to groups that can assist in solution development and testing. Evidence suggests that managers commonly rely on others in their organization to help them with problem solving (Stevenson & Gilly, 1991) and that groups tend to outperform individuals in problem solving (Cooke & Kernaghan, 1987). Expertise also tends to facilitate effective problem solving (e.g., Hershey, Walsh, Read, & Chulef, 1990). These resources are commonly limited in the nascent firm.

QI9 of the mail questionnaire seeks to assess whether nascent founders perceive more difficulty in identifying problems or in developing solutions for problems once they are identified. The question asks,

In dealing with problems on the job or in business or in organizational settings, which of the following has been the most difficult?

1. Identifying the important problems that require attention

2. Developing solutions for the problems, once they are identified

3. Neither

Results from the PSED survey indicate that respondents tend to find developing solutions to problems as more difficult than identifying the problems that require attention (Exhibit 18.1).

Exhibit 18.1   Problem-Solving Items in the PSED Mail Questionnaire and Frequency Distribution of Responses

QI9 In dealing with problems on the job or in business or in organizational settings, which of the following has been the most difficult?

317	Identifying the important problems that require attention
563	Developing solutions for the problems, once they are identified
3	Neither
22	NA

QJ1 When making important decisions about business, work, or other aspects of your life, which of these would you consider your problem solving to be?

170	Most of the time it is calculating and analytical
144	Most of the time it is intuitive, relying on my gut feelings
583	It tends to vary, depending on the situation
8	NA

QJ2a In your work, how often does the following happen? I face new, complex, or unpredictable situations:

195	Very often
246	Often
298	Sometimes
124	Rarely
25	Never
17	NA

QJ2b In your work, how often does the following happen? I feel overloaded, pushed to my physical or mental limits

77	Very often
146	Often
332	Sometimes
242	Rarely
83	Never
25	NA

QL1r When confronted with a difficult problem, I tend to delay a decision so I can collect more information

17	Completely untrue
51	Mostly untrue
255	It depends
434	Mostly true
140	Completely true
8	NA

QC1 How accurately would the following statements describe the start-up problems with your new business?

Being taken seriously	Support from family	Health insurance	Balance in life	Lack of mentors	Response
79	126	99	34	73	Completely untrue
91	94	66	55	110	Mostly untrue
183	83	166	127	144	It depends
131	141	94	191	150	Mostly true
72	110	117	148	78	Completely true
6	8	20	7	7	NA

Systematic Nature of Problem Solving Process

Simon (1960) differentiated between programmed and nonprogrammed decisions. Programmed decisions result from problems that are repetitive and routine, and a procedure has been defined for handling them. Nonprogrammed decisions are novel and based on an unstructured problem. Processes for solving unstructured problems lack definition due to the unique characteristics of each challenge. Individuals often make nonprogrammed decisions by employing creative, intuitive problem-solving methods (Brookfield, 1987). Research suggests that entrepreneurs who prefer more intuitive problem-solving methods are prone to start ventures, whereas entrepreneurs who prefer rational, systematic problem-solving approaches tend to operate one business over the long run, as well as engage in more administrative activities (Buttner & Gryskiewicz, 1993).

QJ1 of the mail questionnaire seeks to identify the systematic nature of the problem-solving process used by the individual. The question asks,

When making important decisions, about business, work, or other aspects of your life, which of these would you consider your problem solving to be

1. Most of the time it is calculating and analytical.

2. Most of the time it is intuitive, relying on my gut feelings.

3. It tends to vary, depending on the situation.

The results presented in Exhibit 18.1 suggest no particular bias towards analytical or intuitive problem-solving styles. Most respondents view themselves as alternating between analytical and intuitive problem-solving and decision-making styles depending on the situation.

Situational Complexity/Uncertainty and Personal Capacity Overload

Problem-solving contexts that push decision makers to their cognitive limits constrain effective solutions (March & Simon, 1958). Characteristics of challenging problem-solving contexts include poor visibility of salient problem variables, complex relationships among those variables, competing goals of possible solutions, and time delays that limit evaluation of solution efficacy (Funke, 1991). Complex, uncertain environments are commonly associated with ill-structured problems (Fernandes & Simon, 1999).

Factors that influence personal stress levels, such as time pressures or competing priorities, can also influence individual problem-solving capacity. The relationship between stress and problem solving is not necessarily negative (Hammond, 2000), although it is thought that extremely stressful work situations overload the individual and impair effective functioning (Gaines & Jermier, 1983). Research suggests that entrepreneurs experience lower levels of stress than managers, perhaps due to a stronger internal locus of control that allows entrepreneurs to effectively deal with stress (Rahim, 1996).

QJ2 of the mail questionnaire includes two items that provide some information about the degree to which individuals perceive complexity and stressful overload in their situations. The question asks the respondent to indicate the frequency (1 = very often, 2 = often, 3 = sometimes, 4 = rarely, 5 = never) of the following two items during the respondent's work:

a. *I face new, complex, or unpredictable situations.*

b. *I feel overloaded, pushed to my physical or mental limits.*

The findings presented in Exhibit 18.1 suggest that about half of the respondents find themselves in a complex situation on a routine basis. Less than half of those surveyed seem to feel that they are routinely overloaded to their physical or mental limits.

Preference for Information Search

Information search is a fundamental component of problem solving, particularly when defining a problem or developing solutions (Simon, 1960). Some individuals prefer to gather more information than others during the problem-solving process. Decision makers who prefer complete sets of information to characterize problems and their potential solutions might ignore alternatives that are only partially characterized (Schwenk, 1985). Personality variables, such as self-esteem, appear to influence the extent of information search (e.g., Weiss & Knight, 1980).

Research suggests that entrepreneurs generally differ from managers in their information preferences and routines. Compared to their executive counterparts, entrepreneurs use more nonverbal scanning approaches, spend significantly more time searching for information in off hours, and tap different information sources (Kaish & Benjamin, 1991). Entrepreneurs often gather relatively few observations during the decision-making process—a characteristic that causes entrepreneurs to overgeneralize (Busenitz & Barney, 1997).

QL1r of the mail questionnaire seeks information to identify the degree to which individuals postpone problem solving in favor of obtaining additional information. The question asks the respondent to indicate the degree of truth (1 = completely untrue, 2 = mostly untrue, 3 = it depends, 4 = mostly true, 5 = completely true) in the following statement:

When confronted with a difficult problem, I tend to delay a decision so I can collect more information.

The findings reported in Exhibit 18.1 suggest that the majority of respondents tend to delay problem solving in order to obtain more information.

Types of Problems That Founders Face

Problems faced by small business managers are often operational in nature, addressing such issues as finding new customers, obtaining financing, recruiting employees, and managing growth (Alpander, Carter, & Forsgren, 1990; Said & Hughley, 1977). Nascent entrepreneurs likely face challenges other than, or in addition to, the problems encountered by managers of operating firms. For example, problems with establishing credibility may hinder a founder's ability to procure capital and other resources necessary to move the venture to the operational phase. The relationship between a nascent entrepreneur and family may be strained during the start-up period because of the extraordinary time requirements commonly associated with a new venture. A nascent entrepreneur might also struggle to find mentors or others who could provide valuable advice and support.

QC1 of the mail questionnaire assessed the extent to which individuals perceived such issues as problems. The question asks:

How accurately would the following statements describe the start-up problems with your new business? Respondents used a 5-point scale (1 = completely untrue; 5 = completely true) to the following issues:

a. *Being taken seriously as a business person*

b. *Receiving support from spouse, family, and friends*

c. *Getting suitable health insurance for self and family members*

d. *Balancing time between business, personal, and family life*

e. *Lack of mentors or others who can provide advice and support*

Results reported in Exhibit 18.1 suggest that some of the major problems facing the respondents relate to obtaining support from family and finding balance between work and personal life.

Summary, Limitations, and Future Research

Data from the PSED questions reviewed in this chapter provide insight into a variety of individual problem-solving issues in the nascent firm context. These insights enrich, or in some cases conflict with, previous thought. Although often regarded as intuitive problem solvers, many nascent entrepreneurs seem to lack general allegiance to this spontaneous style, alternating instead between structured and intuitive problem-solving processes as a function of the problem. Moreover, the PSED data suggest that nascent entrepreneurs tend not to make "snap" decisions and often delay the problem-solving process in order to gather pertinent information. The data also suggest that, although many entrepreneurs routinely find themselves in complex problem-solving environments, the majority do not feel overloaded to the point of impairment. Such findings are consistent with the notion that stressful environments do not necessarily weaken problem solving and may in some cases facilitate the process (e.g., Hammond, 2000). These findings are also consistent with previous research suggesting that entrepreneurs generally do not endure excessive stress—at least when compared to their managerial counterparts in larger firms (Rahim, 1996). Finally, many nascent entrepreneurs appear to perceive problems of personal nature to be significant. Obtaining family support and maintaining acceptable balance were cited by large percentages of respondents as being problematic to the start-up of their firms.

The items reviewed in this chapter possess some limitations. Readers have most likely noted that, unlike the measures presented elsewhere this volume, the items covered here do not constitute a single set of measures designed to test a unified theory or to reflect a specific factor of individual problem solving. Rather, the items reflect a rather loosely grouped set of factors relating to process, context, and outcomes of entrepreneurial problem solving. Some of these factors have been dimensionalized to a greater degree in other studies. For example, various measures of stress have been developed and employed in entrepreneurship research (e.g., Rahim, 1996). The single item nature of the concepts discussed in this chapter also limits their usefulness in certain analytical approaches such as factor analysis and structural equation modeling.

That said, we see a number of opportunities in these data. The items can be employed to compare problem-solving characteristics of various groups surveyed in the PSED project. A comparison of nascent entrepreneurs to the control group used in the survey constitutes a fundamental study. Potentially more interesting investigations lie in comparing subgroups of entrepreneurs. For instance, do problem-solving characteristics of founders of lifestyle firms differ from those of high-growth ventures? Research could also investigate relationships between the individual problem-solving items reviewed here. For instance, does preference for a particular problem-solving style (i.e., rational vs. intuitive) relate to a nascent entrepreneur's difficulty in finding solutions to a problem? To what extent might complex problem-solving situations relate to a founder's perception of stress and overload? Do nascent entrepreneurs who postpone problem solving to gather more information find the generation of potential solutions more or less difficult?

The individual problem-solving items discussed here could be incorporated into other active research streams as well. For example, our interest in factors that influence nascent firm planning (e.g., Matthews, Ford, & Human, 2002) prompts us to consider how a founder's problem-solving characteristics, such as information gathering tendency and intuitive problem-solving preference, influence propensity to plan. Because perceptions of environmental uncertainty significantly and negatively relate to planning formality (Matthews & Scott, 1995), we also want to investigate how problem-solving characteristics influence perceptions of uncertainty and the explanatory power of the uncertainty/planning relationship.

We are hopeful that research stemming from the PSED initiative will inspire comparisons of nascent entrepreneurs to individuals in operating firms. A number of studies have compared problem-solving characteristics of managers to entrepreneurs (e.g., Kaish & Benjamin, 1991; Rahim, 1996). However, the entrepreneurs used in most extant investigations were obtained from firms that were already operational. Data presented here reinforce the notion that the world of the nascent entrepreneur differs from that of the operational venture—particularly in the context of problem solving. For example, the PSED data suggest that founders encounter more difficulty in crafting solutions to problems rather than in identifying the problems themselves. However, entrepreneurs in operational firms appear to distribute their energies among the various problem-solving phases relatively evenly (Olson, 1986). Just as previous research has compared entrepreneurs to their managerial counterparts in larger firms, we suspect future work will focus on distinguishing between pre- and postoperational start-ups. Such work will extend our understanding of how firms begin and evolve through their early stages.

References

Alpander, G. G., Carter, K. D., & Forsgren, R. A. (1990). Managerial issues and problem-solving in the formative years. *Journal of Small Business Management, 28*(2), 9–19.

Archer, E. A. (1980). How to make a business decision: An analysis of theory and practice. *Management Review,* (February), 54–61.

Brookfield, S. D. (1987). *Developing critical thinkers: Challenging adults to explore alternative ways of thinking.* San Francisco: Jossey-Bass.

Busenitz, L. W., & Barney, J. B. (1997). Differences between entrepreneurs and managers in large organizations: Biases and heuristics in strategic decision-making. *Journal of Business Venturing, 12*(1), 9–30.

Buttner, E. H., & Gryskiewicz, N. (1993). Entrepreneurs' problem-solving styles: An empirical study using the Kirton adaption/innovation theory. *Journal of Small Business Management, 31*(3), 22–31.

Cooke, R. A., & Kernaghan, J. A. (1987). Estimating the difference between group versus individual performance on problem-solving tasks. *Group & Organization Studies, 12*(3), 319–342.

Cowan, D. A. (1986). Developing a process model of problem recognition. *Academy of Management Review, 11*(4), 763–776.

Dodge, H. R., Fullerton, S., & Robbins, J. E. (1994). Stage of the organizational life cycle and competition as mediators of problem perception and for small businesses. *Strategic Management Journal, 15,* 121–134.

Evans, J. R. (1992). Creativity in MS/OR: Improving problem solving through creative thinking. *Interfaces, 22*(2), 87–91.

Fernandes, R., & Simon, H. A. (1999). A study of how individuals solve complex and ill-structured problems. *Policy Sciences, 32,* 225–245.

Franklin, S. G., & Goodwin, J. S. (1983). Problems of small business and sources of assistance: A survey. *Journal of Small Business Management, 21*(2), 8–12.

Funke, J. (1991). Solving complex problems: Exploration and control of complex systems. In R. Sternberg & P. Frensch (Eds.), *Complex problem solving: Principles and mechanisms* (pp. 185–222). Hillsdale, NJ: Lawrence Erlbaum.

Gaines, J., & Jermier, J. M. (1983). Emotional exhaustion in a high stress organization. *Academy of Management Journal, 26,* 567–586.

Hammond, K. (2000). *Judgments under stress.* New York: Oxford University Press.

Hershey, D. A., Walsh, D. A., Read, S. J., & Chulef, A. S. (1990). The effects of expertise on financial problem solving: Evidence for goal-directed, problem-solving scripts. *Organizational Behavior and Human Decision Processes, 46*(1), 77–91.

Huang, X., & Brown, A. (1999). An analysis and classification of problems in small business. *International Small Business Journal, 18*(1), 73–85.

Kaish, S., & Benjamin, G. (1991). Characteristics of opportunities search of entrepreneurs vs. executives: Sources, interests, general alertness. *Journal of Business Venturing, 6*(1), 17–61.

Kepner, C. H., & Tregoe, B. B. (1965). *The rational manager.* New York: McGraw-Hill.

March, J. G., & Simon, H. A. (1958). *Organizations.* New York: John Wiley.

Matthews, C. H., Ford, M. W., & Human, S.E. (2002). From credit cards to venture capital: Financing complexity and planning sophistication in nascent ventures. Paper presented at the 22nd annual Babson Kauffman Entrepreneurship Research Conference, Denver, Co.

Matthews, C., & Scott, S. G. (1995). Uncertainty and planning in small and entrepreneurial firms: An empirical assessment. *Journal of Small Business Management, 33*(4), 34–52.

Merrifield, P. R., Guilford, J. P., Christensen, P. R., & Frick, J. W. (1962). The role of intellectual factors in problem solving. *Psychological Monographs, 76*(10), 1–21.

Mullins, J. W. (1996). Early growth decisions of entrepreneurs: The influence of competency and prior performance under changing market conditions. *Journal of Business Venturing, 11*(2), 89–105.

Olson, P. D. (1986). Entrepreneurs: Opportunistic decision makers. *Journal of Small Business Management, 24*(3), 29–35.

Rahim, A. (1996). Stress, strain, and their moderators: An empirical comparison of entrepreneurs and managers. *Journal of Small Business Management, 34*(1), 46–58.

Said, K. E., & Hughley, J. K. (1977). Managerial problems of the small firm. *Journal of Small Business Management, 15*(1), 37–47.

Schwenk, C. R. (1985). Management illusions and biases: Their impact on strategic decisions. *Long Range Planning, 18*(5), 74–80.

Simon, H. A. (1960). *The new science of management.* New York: Harper & Row.

Stevenson, W. B., & Gilly, M. C. (1991). Information processing and problem solving: The migration of problems through formal positions and networks of ties. *Academy of Management Journal, 34*(4), 918–928.

Volkema, R. J. (1997). Managing the problem-solving process: Guidelines for team leaders and facilitator. *Human Systems Management, 16*(1), 27–34.

Weber, C. E. (1984). Strategic thinking—Dealing with uncertainty. *Long Range Planning, 17*(5), 60–70.

Weiss, H. M., & Knight, P. A. (1980). The utility of humility: Self-esteem, information search, and problem-solving efficiency. *Organizational Behavior and Human Performance, 25*(2), 216–226.

CHAPTER 19

Attribution and Locus of Control

Kelly G. Shaver

Attribution theory sets for itself the task of describing how ordinary individuals account for events, their own behavior, and the behavior of others (Shaver, 1975). This subfield within social psychology was founded by Heider (1958) and formalized by Jones, Kelley, and their associates (e.g., Jones & Davis, 1965; Jones, Kanouse, Kelley, Nisbett, Valins, & Weiner, 1972; Kelley, 1967; Kelley, 1973). Heider initially described attribution as the process engaged in by a "naïve psychologist" (his term for an untrained observer) searching for underlying regularities to explain events and behavior. Whereas attributions are often event-specific, locus of control is a well-known individual difference measure of the extent to which people believe that they can influence the rewards they receive from the external world (Rotter, 1966; Strickland, 1989).

Attribution Theory

An early distinction built into attribution theory is, not surprisingly, the difference between the person and the external environment, with behavior jointly determined by both (Heider, 1958). So sometimes the regularities sought by the naïve perceiver are enduring characteristics or properties of the person; other times they are stable features of the surrounding environment. Not all "regularities" are invariant over time, so perceivers also consider more transient aspects of either person or situation.

As an example, consider a kayaker attempting to run the rapids in a river swollen by the spring rains. We stand on the shore, hear and feel the power of the river, and watch transfixed as the kayaker begins the run, maneuvers around the boulders, paddles strenuously to stay upright and on course, and then safely enters a calm stretch below the white water. Anyone who is not also an expert will wonder just how the kayaker did it—even "made it look easy."

In attribution language, we are looking for the cause of this impressive performance. A thorough search for an explanation leads us first to the *opportunity* provided by the much higher than usual water flow. We have seen the same river during a drought, when the water level was so low that small children could safely hop from one rock to the next without getting their feet wet. Thus, the river's present near-flood level is a variable cause in the environment without which no kayaker could even make the attempt. And even though it might look easy, we can see that a lot of *effort* (an internal variable cause) has been required. We also know that to prevent drowning during periods of heavy flow, the municipal authorities require skill-based licenses of anyone who plans to use this section of the river for recreation during flood stage. If we believe that people abide by the rules, then we can assume that the kayaker possesses a high degree of *skill,* a stable cause internal to the person. In the case of many successful performances, one can assume that the actor's skill had to have exceeded the task *difficulty* (a stable characteristic within the environment). When the "task" is running rapids, however, there is probably also some good *luck* (another variable external characteristic) involved.

To summarize this example in abstract terms, causes of events can be either internal to the person or in the external environment. This dimension represents what Weiner (1974) called the *locus of causality* (to be distinguished from locus of control, to be described in a moment). Within these groupings, they can be either stable or variable, what Weiner called the *stability* of the cause. The two dichotomized dimensions thus create four cells—internal stable (ability), internal variable (effort or motivation), external stable (difficulty), and external variable (examples being opportunity and luck).

These four cells together encompass most of the variability in people's explanations for task success when the behavior being described is considered intentional. Other dimensions have been suggested, such as "globality"—the number of different domains across which a judgment is made (Abramson, Seligman, & Teasdale, 1978)—and "controllability" (Anderson, 1991). But these two are not likely to contribute added value to our understanding of entrepreneurship. In theoretical terms, new venture creation is an intentional act that involves repeated attempts to exercise control over the process in a specific domain, in order to achieve the desired outcome. This is exactly the sort of activity that Malle (1999) has argued ought to be described as "reason-based," not "cause-based" (for a discussion of the reasons behind entrepreneurial action, see the Carter, Gartner, and Shaver chapter 12 in the present volume). Whether true control *can* be exerted is not the issue. Indeed, it is entirely possible that for some activities, the environment's contribution to success may exceed that of the person. But this particular empirical fact would not change the conceptual point: in principle, the act of business creation is a domain-specific intentional action (see Krueger, Reilly, & Carsrud, 2000) that requires control.

It is important to note that intentional control over a process does not guarantee that the outcome will always be positive. For example, Hornaday and Tieken (1983) studied 21 inductees admitted by Babson College to its Academy of Distinguished Entrepreneurs. These individuals are honored for their dynamic entrepreneurial performance and for their potential as role models and mentors for the Babson students who aspire to become entrepreneurs. Of the 21 inductees, 9 had been in ventures prior to their current one, and 5 of those 9 had been failures. Indeed, one of the inductees had experienced several failures. This kind of experience is not unusual. As Ronstadt notes "a strong majority of all seasoned entrepreneurs (6.5 years experience as entrepreneurs) do create multiple ventures, sometimes finding a 'dry hole,' sometimes encountering limited success, and occasionally striking a 'gusher.'" (as cited in Kopsco, Ronstadt, & Rybolt, 1987, p. 261).

The psychological literature is filled with explanations for why people continue in pursuits in which they have enjoyed success. Indeed, achievement motivation (see Chapter 11, the Overview for this section) and expectancy theory (Chapter 13, by Gatewood) both describe motives behind a desire to follow one success with another. There are, however, very few psychological theories that deal with persistence after setbacks or failures. Attribution theory is one of these few. Specifically, if an entrepreneur whose newly organized business fails attributes the cause of the failure to *external* factors (lack of a market, entry by numerous competitors, or a technological innovation that failed to live up to its potential), there is no reason to avoid trying again. Indeed, the lessons learned from one venture may be a source of strength for the next. Only if he or she believes that the source of failure was *internal* would an entrepreneur have reason to wonder whether another venture should be attempted. Even then, if the presumed internal cause is a *variable* one, such as insufficient effort, a past failure need not imply that a new venture will also fail. Thus an internal *stable* attribution ("I must not have what it takes . . .") might be the only rationale for rejoining the corporate workforce.

It is clear that the attribution approach can account for entrepreneurial events after the fact. Moreover, it is plausible to argue that an entrepreneur's attributions for prior success or failure could influence future choices to repeat (or cease) entrepreneurial activity. For nearly half of the solo start-ups in the Panel Study of Entrepreneurial Dynamics (PSED), however, the venture being described is their first (Q200). How can attributions that explain past events help us understand *current* organizing activity when there is no "past" involved? The answer is that there are reliable individual differences in attributional style (see an expanded version of the Attributional Style Questionnaire, or ASQ, in Peterson & Villanova, 1988). True, some events have clear internal causes, others have clear external causes. But most actions of any social importance have more than one potential cause. In these cases in which there are what Kelley (1973) called "multiple sufficient causes," reasonable people can disagree about what might be *the* cause. In such a case, people whose predilections lead them to look for causes internal to people (perceivers who might score on the "internal" end of the ASQ, or whom Dweck, Chiu, & Hong, 1995, would call "entity theorists") may concentrate on the enduring characteristics of the actor. Alternatively, people whose predilections lead them to look for changeable external causes (who would be on the external end of the ASQ, whom Dweck et al. would call "incremental theorists") are more likely to concentrate on factors outside the person.

The fact that there are individual differences in attributional style, when coupled with the idea that attributions may be related to entrepreneurial persistence, leads to the expectation that attributional analysis of an entrepreneur's reasons for entering business might be related to later success in organizing the venture. This line of reasoning was first tested by Gatewood, Shaver, and Gartner (1995). These investigators interviewed 142 preventure clients of a Small Business Development Center, asking each person to describe the planned business, and then asking "Why would you start this business?" Respondents' open-ended answers were separated into discrete elements (more about that in a moment), and each element was coded as representing one of the four attributional cells (internal/external by stable/variable). A year later, 85 of the respondents indicated which of 29 business-organizing activities they had performed, how much time they had devoted to each one, and whether they had made a sale. With having made a sale as the operationalization of "success in business organizing," the results showed differences between females and males. For women, sales were related to having given internal stable reasons for wanting to start (e.g., "I have always wanted to be my own boss"). For men, sales were related to having given external stable reasons for wanting to go into business (e.g., "I had identified a market need").

That initial reasons for wanting to start are related to later organizing success, and the fact that there were sex differences in the patterns, makes it reasonable to assume that attributions should be assessed in the same fashion within the PSED. Moreover, the longitudinal nature of the PSED and the effort to be expended in maintaining contact even with the "quits" allows us to observe what attributional patterns will be associated with *failure* as well as with *success*. Consequently, the PSED respondents were asked (the PSED item numbers from the Codebook are in parentheses):

- Why do you want to start this business? (Q104)
- Why do you expect the new business to be successful? (Q106)
- What major problems have you had in starting this business? (Q107)
- What other major problems do you expect in the future? (Q107a)

Locus of Control

People repeat behaviors that have brought them rewards in the past. This is the fundamental thrust of the principle of *reinforcement,* one of the most thoroughly tested and widely confirmed ideas in modern psychology. But even this revered principle does not apply with equal force to everyone. People who believe that they are largely responsible for their own fates will seek opportunities to gather rewards. Alternatively, people who believe that rewards will come (or not) regardless of anything they do will coast passively through life, just hoping for the best. The former individuals have what Rotter (1966) first identified as an *internal locus of control* of reinforcement; the latter have an *external locus of control.*

As it was originally designed, the internal-external locus of control scale (or I-E scale) consisted of 23 item pairs, with respondents forced to choose which member of each pair best described them (Rotter, 1966). To measure *generalized* expectancies for internal versus external control, the original scale (a) contained item pairs from many different domains of action and (b) assumed that the result was unidimensional. An early factor analysis of the scale (Collins, 1974) based on separating the 23 pairs into 46 separate Likert-type-scaled items revealed *four* factors, not one. As a consequence, most subsequent research has used one of the factor-analyzed versions (the one by Levenson, 1981, is especially popular) or one of the other "control" scales specifically designed to cover multiple domains (e.g., Paulhus, 1983). Important reviews of the locus of control concept have been provided by Strickland (1989) and more recently by Judge, Erez, Bono, and Thoresen (2002).

Although some prior research in entrepreneurship has claimed to find differences between entrepreneurs and nonentrepreneurs in locus of control, such studies have seldom used one of the multidimensional measures. This means that it is impossible to know whether the differences obtained are in some domain that might be relevant to business creation (personal efficacy, for example) or in another domain with far less relevance to the task at hand (such as beliefs in powerful others; see Shaver & Scott, 1991, for a more detailed critique).

In a massive data collection effort like the PSED, there are so many different topic areas to be covered that one must necessarily "hit the highlights." Nowhere is this truer than in the assessment of many psychological characteristics. When taken on their own, recognized psychological scales typically contain large numbers of items. Even the relatively efficient "Big-Five" NEO-PI is 60 items (Costa & McCrae, 1992). But taken together, all of the personal characteristics designed in the Person Variables Design Team for the PSED constituted a grand total of 77 items. So clearly it was not possible to include an entire scale to assess locus of control.

Prior research with entrepreneurial samples (Calver & Shaver, 1998; Shaver, Gartner, Gatewood, & Vos, 1996) had used a measure of locus of control based on Paulhus's view that the self exists as the center of three concentric "spheres of control." The innermost sphere has the most to do with individual achievement, and what matters here is *personal efficacy.* Next, when the person interacts with others, *interpersonal control* is important. Finally, because people exist as part of a larger social system, *sociopolitical control* can also be involved. In his validity studies, Paulhus (1983) created a separate subscale for each kind of control, with 10 items per subscale. But in the context of entrepreneurship research, either conducted as part of a business counseling session (Shaver et al., 1996) or as part of the PSED, even 30 items is too many. So Shaver et al. (1996) selected from the Paulhus (1983) scale only the four highest-loading items on each of the three factors of control. For the PSED, the 12-item set was reduced to 3, shown below in the order they appeared in the mail questionnaire (item numbers from the Codebook are shown in parentheses):

- I have no trouble making and keeping friends. (QL1h)
- When I make plans, I am almost certain to make them work. (QL1i)
- When I get what I want, it is usually because I worked hard for it. (QL1j)

The first listed item, making friends, is the positively worded highest-loading item from the Paulhus (1983) interpersonal control subscale. The second and third listed items are the two highest-loading items on the Paulhus (1983) personal efficacy scale. To minimize the number of items in the PSED, no items from Paulhus's sociopolitical subscale were included.

Scoring of Attribution and Locus of Control Items

The attribution questions were asked near the beginning of the telephone interview, right after the respondent had been asked whether the start-up effort was being done "on your own, as part of your current job for an employer, or as a mixture of both?" The first of them is the conceptual equivalent of the "Why?" question asked by Gatewood et al. (1995); the others expand the universe of activities that can be addressed with attributional coding.

Each question was posed by the telephone interviewer, who then attempted to type the respondent's answer, staying as close to the verbatim answer as possible. Not surprisingly, as there were different interviewers and as the interviews took place over a period of time, the "verbatim" responses contained different personal abbreviations (e.g., some people spell out a term like "because," whereas others use an abbreviation like "b/c" or simply "bc"). There are also what appear to be words that do not make any sense alone (e.g., "resailing") and need to be evaluated in terms of the context to determine whether they have one referent (such as "retailing") or another completely different referent (such as "reselling"). As a consequence, the "mechanical" application of a computerized content analysis program would produce results of questionable quality (even if all synonyms could be specified in advance). On the other hand, the items can be coded successfully using the attributional dimensions of locus of causality and stability of influence. But this is true only if the coding procedures are specified in detail, and if coders are given sample items already precoded on which to train until they reach an acceptable criterion of matching (i.e., at least 90% accuracy with the sample set). A full description of the coding procedures, including a "training set" and a "testing set" of responses, is provided by Shaver, Gartner, Crosby, Bakalarova, and Gatewood (2001).

Whereas the attribution items were string variables that must be content analyzed in order to be scored, the three locus of control items were 5-point Likert-type scales preceded by the stem, "The following statements can be used to describe most people. How accurately would they describe you?" Response options were "completely untrue" (scored as 1), "mostly untrue," "it depends," "mostly true," and "completely true" (scored as 5). Beginning with the cleaned data set ($N = 1,216$), there were 871 people who completed parts of the mail questionnaire that contained the locus of control items. Of these 871, only 855 answered all three items. The postsampling stratification weights (WTW1 for nascent entrepreneurs and WTCG for people in the comparison group) built into the data set at the telephone interview stage were first renormalized to reflect the losses of respondents from telephone interview to mail survey. This renormalization was accomplished separately for the six groups of respondents created by the combination of respondent sex (NCGENDER) and the respondent grouping variable that separates people into fully autonomous, partially autonomous, and comparison group (AUTONSU3).

Table 19.1   Descriptive Statistics: Locus of Control Items (renormalized weights)

Item Number	Question	Nascent Entrepreneurs (Fully Autonomous Only)			
		Females n = 241		Males n = 232	
		Mean	SD	Mean	SD
QL1h	No trouble making and keeping friends	3.97	.90	3.95	.95
QL1i	Almost certain to make plans work	3.95	.67	3.82	.77
QL1j	When I get what I want . . .	4.21	.77	4.19	.75

The resulting mail weights were then renormalized (separately for the six groups) for the 855 people who answered all three locus of control questions. Mean scores for these items, shown separately for female and male nascent entrepreneurs (fully autonomous only), are presented in Table 19.1.

Progress to Date

The coding of open-ended answers to the "Why" questions requires a significant investment of time beyond that required for analysis of closed-ended responses. Moreover, for purposes of comparison to past attribution research, it is best to wait (at least until Wave 2, or possibly Wave 3) to determine which nascent entrepreneurs have been successful in organizing their enterprises. For this reason, as of early summer 2003, data based on the attribution classifications for the full data set have not yet been presented or submitted for publication. The detailed coding system for attributions, however, has been described in an article by Shaver et al. (2001). That article was based on the "mixed gender" and "women oversample" groups (the minority oversample was not available at the time). One of the initial concerns was that the amount of space available for recording verbatim answers (a total of 255 characters) might not be sufficient to capture the full response. Fortunately, data for the first two samples showed, among other things, that 94% of the responses to Q104 were captured well within the space limits. In addition to its application to the "why start" questions, the attributional coding approach has also been used to characterize the opportunities (QA1) and problems (Q107) identified by respondents. Nascent entrepreneurs showed a "self-serving" bias, describing opportunities as internal and stable, while describing problems as external and variable (Gartner & Shaver, 2002).

The locus of control items have, to our knowledge, been used primarily as control items, sometimes as covariates and sometimes as separate indexes of the possible motivations of the nascent entrepreneurs versus respondents in the comparison group. In this latter use, Schjoedt and Shaver (2002) found essentially no differences between the two major groups in terms of overall beliefs in locus of control.

References

Abramson, L. Y., Seligman, M. E. P., & Teasdale, J. D. (1978). Learned helplessness in humans: Critique and reformulation. *Journal of Abnormal Psychology, 87*, 49–74.

Anderson, C. A. (1991). How people think about causes: Examination of the typical phenomenal organization of attributions for success and failure. *Social Cognition, 9*, 295–329.

Calver, J. R. O., & Shaver, K. G. (1998, June). *Who is on the Fast Trac™? Person variables and venture growth following entrepreneurship education.* Paper presented at the 18th annual Babson Kauffman Entrepreneurship Research Conference, Ghent, Belgium.

Collins, B. E. (1974). Four components of the Rotter Internal-External scale: Belief in a difficult world, a just world, a predictable world, and a politically responsive world. *Journal of Personality and Social Psychology, 29*, 381–391.

Costa, P. T., & McCrae, R. R. (1992). *NEO-PI/FFI manual supplement.* Odessa, FL: Psychological Assessment Resources.

Dweck, C. S., Chiu, C., & Hong, Y. (1995). Implicit theories and their role in judgments and reactions: A world from two perspectives. *Psychological Inquiry, 6*, 267–285.

Gartner, W. B., & Shaver, K. G. (2002, June). *The attributional characteristics of opportunities and problems described by nascent entrepreneurs in the PSED.* Paper presented at the 22nd annual Babson Kauffman Entrepreneurship Research Conference, Boulder, CO.

Gatewood, E. J., Shaver, K. G., & Gartner, W. B. (1995). A longitudinal study of cognitive factors influencing start-up behaviors and success at venture creation. *Journal of Business Venturing, 10*, 371–391.

Heider, F. (1958). *The psychology of interpersonal relations.* New York: Wiley.

Hornaday, J. A., & Tieken, N. B. (1983). Capturing twenty-one heffalumps. In J. A. Hornaday, J. A. Timmons, & K. H. Vesper (Eds.), *Frontiers of entrepreneurship research* (pp. 23–50). Wellesley, MA: Babson College.

Jones, E. E., & Davis, K. E. (1965). From acts to dispositions: The attribution process in person perception. In L. Berkowitz (Ed.), *Advances in experimental social psychology* (Vol. 2, pp. 219–266). New York: Academic Press.

Jones, E. E., Kanouse, D. E., Kelley, H. H., Nisbett, R. E., Valins, S., & Weiner, B. (Eds.). (1972). *Attribution: Perceiving the causes of behavior* (pp. 1–26). Morristown, NJ: General Learning Press.

Judge, T. A., Erez, A., Bono, J. E., & Thoresen, C. J. (2002). Are measures of self-esteem, neuroticism, locus of control, and generalized self-efficacy indicators of a common core construct? *Journal of Personality and Social Psychology, 83*, 693–710.

Kelley, H. H. (1967). Attribution processes in social psychology. In D. Levine (Ed.), *Nebraska symposium on motivation, 1967* (pp. 192–238). Lincoln: University of Nebraska Press.

Kelley, H. H. (1973). The processes of causal attribution. *American Psychologist, 28*, 107–128.

Kopsco, D., Ronstadt, R., & Rybolt, W. (1987). The corridor principle: Independent entrepreneurs versus corporate entrepreneurs. In N. Churchill, J. A. Hornaday, B. Kirchhoff, O. Krasner, & K. H. Vesper (Eds.), *Frontiers of entrepreneurship research* (pp. 259–274). Wellesley, MA: Babson College.

Krueger, N. F., Jr., Reilly, M. D., & Carsrud, A. L. (2000). Competing models of entrepreneurial intentions. *Journal of Business Venturing, 15*, 411–432.

Levenson, H. (1981). Differentiating between internality, powerful others, and chance. In H. M. Lefcourt (Ed.), *Research with the locus of control construct* (Vol. 1, pp. 15–63). New York: Academic Press.

Malle, B. F. (1999). How people explain behavior: A new theoretical framework. *Personality and Social Psychology Review, 3*, 23–48.

Paulhus, D. (1983). Sphere-specific measures of perceived control. *Journal of Personality and Social Psychology, 44,* 1253–1265.

Peterson, C., & Villanova, P. (1988). An expanded attributional style questionnaire. *Journal of Abnormal Psychology, 97,* 87–89.

Rotter, J. B. (1966). Generalized expectancies for internal versus external locus of control of reinforcement. *Psychological Monographs, 80,* 1–28.

Schjoedt, L., & Shaver, K. G. (2002). *The lure, not the salvation: Push and pull in entrepreneurial motivation.* Unpublished manuscript. Williamsburg, VA: College of William & Mary.

Shaver, K. G. (1975). *An introduction to attribution processes.* Cambridge, MA: Winthrop.

Shaver, K. G., Gartner, W. B., Crosby, E., Bakalarova, K., & Gatewood, E. J. (2001). Attributions about entrepreneurship: A framework and process for analyzing reasons for starting a business. *Entrepreneurship Theory and Practice, 26*(2), 5–32.

Shaver, K. G., Gartner, W. B., Gatewood, E. J., & Vos, L. H. (1996). Psychological factors in success at getting into business. In P. D. Reynolds, S. Birley, J. E. Butler, W. D. Bygrave, P. Davidsson, W. B. Gartner, & P. P. McDougall (Eds.), *Frontiers of entrepreneurship research* (pp. 77–90). Babson Park, MA: Babson College.

Shaver, K. G., & Scott, L. R. (1991). Person, process, choice: The psychology of new venture creation. *Entrepreneurship Theory and Practice, 16*(2), 23–45.

Strickland, B. R. (1989). Internal-external control expectancies: From contingency to creativity. *American Psychologist, 44,* 1–12.

Weiner, B. (1974). *Achievement motivation and attribution theory.* Morristown, NJ: General Learning Press.

CHAPTER 20

On Economic Sophistication

James N. Morgan

Decisions by entrepreneurs should benefit from normative theories of economics about optimal choices. There is some literature on decision problems, starting with Martin's (1975) book on Bayesian decision problems and Markov chains. More recently, the focus has been on errors and mistakes, as in Russo and Schoemaker's (1989) book on decision traps, and in the guise of Sherlock Holmes stories by Bruce (2001). And there is a growing body of experiments showing how common are departures from optimal choices (Frederick, Loewenstein, & Donoghue, 2002; Kahneman & Riede, 1998; Kahneman & Tversky, 2000; Rabin & Thaler, 2001; Thaler, 2000). For a recent summary, see Connolly, Arkes, and Hammond (2000), or Kahneman (2003). Most of this work focuses on dealing with risk and with intertemporal discounting, or with game strategies. Do people interpret risky choices by multiplying the reward times the probability of getting it? Do they reduce the value of future gains or costs by an interest rate reflecting interest foregone or earned by waiting? Because there is so much obvious departure from theoretical optimality revealed in these studies, there is clearly room for those who are more sophisticated to do better in the real world. Hence, there is reason to believe that if the theories of optimal decision are correct, then those who follow them should succeed better as entrepreneurs. They might follow them without understanding them, but we cannot investigate their decision processes, only their understanding (i.e., their level of economic sophistication). They might make better selections of projects, convince funders that they know what they are doing, but the ultimate test is a successful business, or perhaps the wisdom to ignore sunk costs and get out.

There are a few of these basic economic principles (insights) that should be crucial to an entrepreneur's decision making. A subset of them was assessed in the first wave questionnaire of the Panel of Entrepreneurial Dynamics (PSED), and perhaps analysis of subsequent success or failure can be related to the level of economic sophistication. What are these insights?

Crucial to all is the notion that sunk costs are sunk. The past is irrelevant except as it helps us predict or influence the future. Past costs will not be recovered, nor past gains lost, so only the future matters. Of course, large gains or losses can alter one's net worth and affect future decisions that way, though probably not about the particular source of the gain or loss. There are times when one should abandon ship. It may or may not be wise to throw good money after bad. Second, the future must be converted to present values so they are comparable, and as much as possible in present dollars. So future benefits and costs must be translated into present, discounted, real, expected, after tax, money amounts. Nonmoney amounts can be monetized using opportunity cost, as in the foregone interest on funds tied up or the market depreciation on assets. Uncertain amounts can be converted to expected values by multiplying by the probability. Before-tax amounts can be reduced by the marginal tax rate. And all can be "discounted" to the present at 3% because any market interest rates above that reflect expected inflation. Then, one can introduce immeasurable considerations—psychological costs or benefits that cannot be measured in dollars, like the prestige of a fancy new car or the glory of being a businessman. Unfortunately, we were unable to formulate and include items to test respondents' awareness of all these principles.

These same principles apply to many consumer decisions (Morgan, 2002). Aside from the experience of those teaching courses in consumer economics, there is very little evidence on the difficulty of conveying these few basic insights so that they can be used (Larrick, Nisbett, & Morgan, 1993; Nisbett, Morgan, & Larrick, 1990). One clever experiment by Nisbett taught sunk cost ideas to half a sample of basketball ticket holders, then after a very one-sided game found that those exposed to the idea left early to save half an hour getting out of the parking lot. (Of course, some might stay out of loyalty or social pressure.) In an earlier study of the affluent, we asked people what fraction of the added income from working more would be taken in income taxes (marginal tax rate), then asked whether that had any effect on how much they worked (Morgan, Barlow, & Brazer, 1966). Having already told us they worked 60 to 80 hours a week, they mostly said "No." (Because they were salaried, the payoff to extra work was in profits or advancement, of course.) They were also not giving appreciated assets to charity, even though there were tax advantages in doing so rather than giving cash, perhaps because some were vague about their own marginal tax rate.

So if people are ignoring basic economic insights, but can learn and use them, the level of economic sophistication by nascent entrepreneurs should account for some of their later success or failure. In the PSED, there were questions attempting to measure achievement motivation, and attitudes toward risk (at identical expected values), and sense of personal efficacy. We are not dealing with the issue of motivation here. Actually, the risk question can be used as a measure of achievement motivation. The argument is that the lower the probability of success, the higher the achievement is valued, but the lower the "expected value" (Atkinson, 1958). Hence, the product of the two reaches its maximum at 50/50, just as the sampling error of a percentage, the square root of pq/n, does. And we know something about respondents' education (Q343). But only two questions were at their level of economic sophistication, both getting at the same principle: sunk costs, which in a rational model should not affect decisions about the future unless they help predict future things.

Item QL1k. If I am about to leave home for a game or concert and discover I lost the ticket, I will buy another and go anyway (responses in five categories from completely true to completely untrue).

Interpretation: Sophisticated respondents should say yes. The loss will not go away, so if the game or concert was worth it, it should still be worth it. The naïve notion that one shouldn't spend $100 fails to realize that the second decision is only whether, after having suffered a $50 loss, one still thinks it worth $50 to get to the concert or game. In the short-run entrepreneurial world, ignoring sunk costs might lead to earlier abandonment, but it might also lead to other decisions that improved success.

Item QL1l. When I decide whether to keep or sell an investment, I consider the investment's current value rather than what I paid for it (five categories of replies from completely true to completely untrue).

Interpretation: Sophisticated respondents should say yes. Past gains or losses are also "sunk," that is, will be there regardless of future decisions, so one should ignore original costs and pay attention to present values. However, some may have been so sophisticated as to think of the tax implications of realizing capital gains or losses.

Although analysis of this hypothesis must wait until we have measures of much later subsequent success or failure by entrepreneurs with different levels of economic sophistication, we can look at the second wave follow-up. The two tables include all who were trying to start a business at the first wave.

This table can, of course, be showing what leads to nonresponse as well as business success or failure, but a lot of that nonresponse could be because the endeavor had ceased. (An analysis using only the 370 replies to the third wave shows similar small results.) At any rate, Table 20.1 shows no statistically significant effects of sophistication about sunk costs on the business outcomes. Perhaps we need more time to assess outcomes. The question might well have revealed a desire to show that the respondent considered everything, rather than any sophisticated choice strategy, because nearly half of those who said it was completely untrue that they would buy another ticket were operating a business.

Table 20.2 tests the notion that sophistication in considering only current value, not original (sunk) cost, might carry over into business success. But reporting that one would also consider original cost in deciding whether to sell an investment might indicate sophistication about capital gains taxation. In any case, the table shows a statistically insignificant tendency for those who would consider only present value to be somewhat more likely (36%) to be in business or still trying, in line with our theory.

Table 20.1   Follow-up State of Business, by Whether Would Ignore Sunk Costs, Nascent
Entrepreneurs Only (*N* = 830)

Response	*n*	Operating Business	Active Start-up	Inactive Start-up	No Longer Worked On	Non-Response
				Status of Start-up at Wave 2 (S502)		
Completely untrue	57	45%	21%	5%	10%	19%
Mostly untrue	90	18%	17%	13%	15%	37%
It depends	250	27%	13%	10%	20%	30%
Mostly true	100	25%	11%	11%	13%	40%
Completely true	58	30%	9%	8%	18%	35%
No reply	275	15%	8%	9%	11%	57%

NOTE: Using weights WTW1.

Table 20.2   Follow-up State of Business, by Whether Would Ignore Original Cost When Selling an
Investment, Nascent Entrepreneurs Only (*N* = 830)

Response	*n*	Operating Business	Active Start-up	Inactive Start-up	No Longer Worked On	Non-Response
				Status of Start-up at Wave 2 (S502)		
Completely untrue	22	18%	17%	4%	17%	44%
Mostly untrue	54	17%	20%	10%	13%	40%
It depends	195	28%	10%	9%	18%	35%
Mostly true	196	27%	14%	12%	15%	32%
Completely true	85	36%	16%	7%	16%	25%
No reply	278	16%	8%	9%	11%	56%

NOTE: Using weights WTW1.

Actually, we ran a SEARCH program sweeping across 28 potential explanatory
variables searching for the best chi-square, and the most important was education,
with the very highly educated more likely to be running a business. As for the other
basic economic insights, it is not easy to create simple questions to measure how

well people understand the need for present-value benefit-cost calculations, know to use a low real interest rate for discounting but try to earn market rates, and monetize non-cash costs like depreciation and foregone interest. Historians claim that the reason American railroads went bankrupt was that they ignored obsolescence, assuming that if one merely replaced worn out track and trains, that was good enough; but depreciation has to include obsolescence, too. Many a small-scale entrepreneur fails to take account of depreciation, foregone interest, or the opportunity cost of his/her and the family's time. Cash flow can be deceptive. Perhaps we could have asked whether respondents calculated profits after deducting these items and what interest rate they used in costing funds tied up. An interesting possibility would be to introduce some questions in a follow-up interview that would assess the respondents' economic sophistication, perhaps in the context of their actual business operations. Asking whether there was a "business plan" does not explicitly refer to a benefit-cost analysis, much less to an even more sophisticated attempt to estimate an "internal rate of return" (i.e., the discount rate that makes the present value of an investment zero). We could ask whether future costs and returns are discounted to present values and at what interest rate. We could ask about which expenditures to treat as investment and which as current costs. How about allowances for depreciation on the investments. Do they take account of foregone interest and of taxes? Do they know about legal limits on depreciation and about double declining balance depreciation on real estate? If some have learned a lot of economics in the course of their activities, there should be differences in the success of those who did and those who did not. We might also ask about whether bailing out was considered, and the circumstances. That would get more directly at their treatment of sunk costs. A more sophisticated approach would be to seek for rules of thumb that approximate optimality, such as "satisficing" (Simon, 1982), by asking whether an investment would "pay for itself in X years." I am not aware of any empirical studies on these strategies.

References

Atkinson, J. W. (1958). Toward experimental analysis of human motivation in terms of motives, expectancies, and incentives. In J. W. Atkinson (Ed.), *Motives in fantasy, action, and society* (pp. 288–305). Princeton, NJ: Van Nostrand.

Bruce, C. (2001). *Conned again, Watson!: Cautionary tales of logic, math, and probability.* Cambridge, MA: Perseus.

Connolly, T., Arkes, H. R., & Hammond, K. R. (Eds.). (2000). *Judgment and decision making: An interdisciplinary reader.* New York: Cambridge University Press.

Frederick, S., Loewenstein, G., & Donoghue, T. O. (2002). Time discounting and time preference: A critical review. *Journal of Economic Literature, 40,* 351–401.

Kahneman, D. (2003). A psychological perspective on economics. *American Economic Review, 93,* 162–168.

Kahneman, D., & Riede, M. (1998). Aspects of investor psychology. *Journal of Portfolio Management, 24,* 52–65.

Kahneman, D., & Tversky, A. (2000). *Choices, values, frames.* New York: Russell Sage.

Larrick, R., Nisbett, R., & Morgan, J. (1993). Who uses the cost-benefit rules of choice? Implications for the normative status of microeconomic theory. *Organizational Behavior and Human Decision Processes, 56,* 331–347.

Martin, J. J. (1975*). Bayesian decision problems and Markov chains.* Melbourne, FL: Krieger.

Morgan, J. (1995). Justifying the use of economics in ordinary decisions. *Financial Planning and Counseling, 6,* 45–52.

Morgan, J. (2002, April). *First and foremost, consumers need basic economic insights.* Paper presented at the annual conference of the American Council on Consumer Interest, Universal City, CA.

Morgan, J., Barlow, R., & Brazer, H. (1966). *Economic behavior of the affluent.* Washington, DC: Brookings Institute.

Nisbett, R., Morgan, J., & Larrick, R. (1990). Teaching the use of cost-benefit reasoning in everyday life. *Psychological Science, 1,* 362–370.

Rabin, M., & Thaler, R. (2001). Anomalies: Risk aversion. *Journal of Economic Perspectives, 15,* 219–232.

Russo, J., & Schoemaker, P. (1989). *Decision traps: Ten barriers to brilliant decision making and how to overcome them.* New York: Doubleday.

Simon, H. (1982). *Models of bounded rationality.* Cambridge: MIT Press.

Thaler, R. (2000). From homo economicus to homo sapiens. *Journal of Economic Perspectives, 14,* 133–141.

CHAPTER 21

Social Skills

Robert A. Baron

Why are some entrepreneurs more successful than others in converting opportunities they have recognized into viable new ventures? This has long been a central issue in the field of entrepreneurship (e.g., Venkataraman, 1997), but as yet, no unified or compelling answer has emerged. In the past, efforts to grapple with this complex issue generally proceeded from two distinct perspectives which, in the terminology of organizational behavior, can be described as basically *micro* or *macro* in nature.

Research conducted within the micro perspective focused primarily on the characteristics of individual entrepreneurs. Initially, such investigations sought to identify the traits that distinguish entrepreneurs from other persons, or successful entrepreneurs from ones who are less successful (see, e.g., Shaver & Scott, 1991). In general, this research yielded mixed and inconclusive results, although more recent investigations employing valid and reliable measures of personality and more sophisticated research designs (e.g., Ciavarella, Buchholtz, Riordan, R. D. Gatewood, & Stokes, in press) indicate that successful entrepreneurs may indeed differ from unsuccessful ones in some respects. Additional evidence indicates, however, that entrepreneurs and nonentrepreneurs do not diverge greatly with respect to their career goals (Carter, Gartner, Shaver, & E. J. Gatewood, 2003).

More recent work conducted from a micro perspective has focused, instead, on *cognitive processes* that may influence entrepreneurs' success (e.g., Baron, 1998; Busenitz & Barney, 1997; Mitchell et al., in press) and on their skills, abilities, talents, and motives (e.g., Sternberg, 2004). This research has yielded many valuable insights into the factors that influence individuals' decisions to become entrepreneurs and their relative success in this role (e.g., Baron, 2004).

In contrast, research conducted from the macro perspective has focused mainly on factors in the external environment that shape the fate of new ventures. Such factors include features of the economic, technological, and societal context in which new ventures operate (e.g., economic and market conditions, government policy, etc.). Research conducted from this macro perspective has identified a wide range of environmental factors that significantly influence the founding, success, and mortality of new ventures (e.g., market size and growth, industry life cycle; e.g., Shane, 2001).

Together, the micro and macro perspectives have provided important insights into the question of why only some entrepreneurs succeed in launching new ventures. However, neither approach considers an additional set of factors that may also play a role in this respect. These factors operate at what, in the field of organizational behavior, is termed the *group* or *interpersonal* level—a level of analysis intermediate in scope between those described above. Included at this level of analysis are all aspects of relationships between entrepreneurs and other persons with whom they interact (e.g., venture capitalists, potential or actual partners, employees, customers) and all aspects of entrepreneurs' behavior when dealing with such persons (e.g., efforts to influence or persuade them in various ways; providing them with feedback and other forms of communication; working with them to make decisions or perform specific tasks, etc.). Several forms of evidence suggest that such interpersonal factors may play an important role in entrepreneurs' success.

First, support for this perspective is provided by a growing body of research on the nature and effects of social capital (e.g., Eisenhardt & Schoonhoven, 1990). As defined by Nahapiet and Ghoshal (1998), *social capital* is the sum of the actual and potential resources individuals obtain from their relationships with others. Social capital, in other words, reflects the broad range of benefits individuals gain from having effective interpersonal relationships with others both inside and outside their organization. Recent findings indicate that included among such benefits are increased efficiency in obtaining information, enhanced levels of cooperation and trust (e.g., Putnam, 1993), and reduced intergroup conflict (Labianca, Brass, & Gray, 1998). That social capital is also beneficial to entrepreneurs is suggested by recent findings indicating that entrepreneurs possessing high social capital (as based on networks, status, personal ties, and referrals) are more likely to receive funds from venture capitalists than entrepreneurs who are lower on this dimension (Shane & Cable, 2002). In short, a high level of social capital may well assist entrepreneurs in their efforts to launch new ventures.

A second and related source of evidence for the suggestion that interpersonal (group-level) factors may play a key role in the successful launch of new ventures is provided by an extensive body of research on the nature and impact of *social skills*—competencies that assist individuals to interact effectively with others (e.g., Segrin & Kinney, 1995). This large body of literature suggests that social skills strongly determine the outcomes individuals experience in a wide range of contexts, including job interviews, yearly performance reviews (Wayne, Liden, Graf, & Ferris, 1997), court proceedings (e.g., Riggio & Throckmorton, 1988; Robbins & DeNisi, 1994), and negotiations (Lewicki, Saunders, & Minton, 1997). In general, then, social skills appear to be an important "plus" in many business contexts.

Although social capital and social skills refer to similar constructs, they differ in at least one basic respect: social capital refers primarily to the benefits obtained from effective relationships with others. In contrast, social skills refer to the specific proficiencies or behaviors that play a role in establishing such relationships. Thus, specific social skills may provide an important foundation for the development of social capital. For this reason, as well as several others, items designed to assess them were included in the Panel Study of Entrepreneurial Dynamics (PSED).

How can a high level of social competence (i.e., a high level of several complementary social skills) contribute to entrepreneurs' success in launching new ventures? Central to the reasoning proposed here is the following suggestion: *social skills are relevant to many tasks entrepreneurs must perform—and perform well—if they are to succeed.* Such tasks include (1) raising needed capital, (2) generating enthusiasm and commitment among others, (3) communicating effectively with people from a wide range of backgrounds, (4) choosing excellent partners and/or key employees and then developing effective long-term relationships with these persons, and (5) negotiating with others over a vast array of issues (see, e.g., Cable & Shane, 1997; Carter, Gartner, & Reynolds, 1996). All of these tasks involve interacting with other persons; thus, it seems possible that the greater entrepreneurs' social skills, the more effective they will be in performing these tasks and, hence, in launching new ventures.

This reasoning is also consistent with several findings and proposals in the entrepreneurship literature. For example, in a study of the factors influencing the success of new ventures, Duchesneau and Gartner (1990) found that entrepreneurs whose companies are successful engage in more communication with others and are more effective in this activity than entrepreneurs whose companies fail. Similarly, in a discussion of cooperation between entrepreneurs and venture capitalists, Cable and Shane (1997) note that such cooperation may increase when the entrepreneur and venture capitalist share a positive social or business relationship. Finally, the suggestion that social skills play a role in entrepreneurs' success appears to be consistent with suggestions by Gartner, Bird, and Starr (1992) that one of the key activities performed by entrepreneurs in starting new ventures is convincing others to share their beliefs about what the emerging organization can and will become. It seems reasonable to suggest that entrepreneurs may be aided in their efforts to accomplish these tasks by proficiency with respect to several social skills (e.g., effectiveness in persuasion).

One additional point should be noted. While social skills are useful in many different contexts, it seems possible that they might be especially valuable to entrepreneurs who, during the process of new venture creation, must form new relationships with many different persons (e.g., customers, suppliers, new employees). Further, entrepreneurs must form such relationships in environments that are uncertain and unstructured (see, e.g., Carter, Gartner, & Reynolds, 1996; Gartner, 1990). It is precisely in such contexts—ones in which individuals cannot fall back upon established relationships or the clearly prescribed norms present in many existing organizations—that social competence might prove most useful.

In sum, research findings from several diverse literatures provide a basis for predicting that entrepreneurs who are skilled at interacting with others may have an important edge in starting new ventures and turning them into profitable companies. The basic thesis of this chapter, then, is this: *All other factors being equal, the greater entrepreneurs' level of social skills, the greater their success in establishing new ventures.*

But which specific social skills are most useful to entrepreneurs? It is on this question that the remaining two sections of this chapter focus.

Specific Social Skills: Their Nature and Relevance to Entrepreneurs' Success

When asked to comment on the nature of success, Albert Einstein replied by means of the following equation: "If A is a success in life, then $A = x + y + z$, where $x = $ work, $y = $ play, and $z = $ keeping your mouth shut" (Einstein, 1950). By "keeping your mouth shut," Einstein went on to explain, he meant knowing how to get along with others—what has been described here by the term *social skills*. As noted above, it is suggested that possession of such skills may influence entrepreneurs' success in founding new ventures. Previous research on social skills has identified a number of different proficiencies useful in interacting with others. For the present purposes, however, this extensive body of literature was carefully reviewed on the basis of two primary criteria: (1) relevance to outcomes in business settings—only social skills that have been shown to have strong effects in such contexts should be considered, and (2) relevance to tasks performed by entrepreneurs—only social skills with effects relevant to the tasks and situations faced by entrepreneurs should be considered. On the basis of these two criteria, four specific social skills were selected:

- *social perception*—Accuracy in perceiving others, including accurate perceptions of their traits, motives, and intentions
- *impression management*—Proficiency in the use of a wide range of techniques for inducing positive reactions in others
- *persuasion and social influence*—Skill at using various techniques for changing others' attitudes or behavior in desired directions
- *emotional intelligence*—Proficiency with respect to a cluster of skills relating to the emotional side of life (e.g., being able to regulate one's own emotions in various situations and being able to influence others' emotional reactions)

The nature of each of these skills and its potential relevance to entrepreneurs' success will now be reviewed.

Social Perception: Accuracy in Understanding Others

While we spend our lives surrounded by other persons and interact with them on an almost continuous basis, they often remain something of a mystery. They say and do things we do not expect, have motives we do not understand, and often see the world very differently than we do. Yet, because other persons play such a crucial role in our lives, this is one mystery we cannot afford to leave unsolved. As a result, we often engage in social perception—efforts to obtain accurate information about others. The goal of social perception is straightforward: obtaining accurate knowledge of others' traits, motives, intentions, and emotions. The benefits of having such knowledge are obvious: often it is essential for interacting effectively with them. To mention just two examples, salespersons who can accurately gauge the reactions of potential customers have an important edge over ones who cannot. Similarly, negotiators who can accurately judge the truthfulness of statements made by their opponents often have an important advantage over ones who are less skilled at this task. Is accuracy in social perception potentially relevant to entrepreneurs' success in starting new ventures? Several factors suggest that it is.

Consider, first, the task of obtaining financing. Not only must entrepreneurs prepare an excellent business plan, they must usually also meet with venture capitalists or representatives of other potential sources of funding and make verbal presentations to them. In this context, skill at social perception can be very useful. The ability to "read" one's audience—to determine how they are reacting to various aspects of a presentation—has been found to be an important contributor to success in such situations (Larkin, 1987). Thus, it seems reasonable to suggest that entrepreneurs who are proficient at social perception stand a better chance of obtaining funding than those who are not.

Another context in which being skilled at social perception can be extremely beneficial to entrepreneurs is negotiation. Entrepreneurs engage in this activity frequently, especially during the early days of their new ventures' existence, (e.g., Carter, Gartner, & Reynolds, 1996). They must negotiate with partners, prospective employees, venture capitalists, suppliers, customers, and many others. Research findings suggest that individuals who are skilled at social perception often find it easier to determine when their opponents are being honest and when these persons are bending the truth to their own advantage. Because knowledge of an opponent's actual break-even point plays an important role in successful negotiations (Lewicki et al., 1997), it seems possible that proficiency in social perception may contribute significantly to entrepreneurs' success.

On the basis of such considerations, it was predicted that the greater entrepreneurs' proficiency with respect to social perception (i.e., the ability to form accurate perceptions of others), the greater their success in establishing new ventures. Two items in the PSED were designed to measure skill at social perception: "I am a good judge of other people," and "I usually know what is appropriate in any situation."

Impression Management: The Fine Art of Looking Good

It is a basic fact of life that most people wish to make a favorable impression on others when meeting them for the first time. In order to accomplish this goal, they often engage in active attempts at impression management—tactics designed to induce positive reactions on the part of others (Wayne & Liden, 1995). Individuals use a wide range of tactics to produce favorable impressions on others, including efforts to improve their own appearance through flattery, agreeing with the target persons, doing small favors for them, or expressing attitudes and preferences that are currently in vogue.

A substantial body of evidence suggests that such tactics often succeed; they help individuals make favorable impressions on others and so gain many desirable outcomes (e.g., Wayne & Liden, 1995). It seems reasonable to suggest that skill at impression management might be useful to entrepreneurs because it is relevant to key tasks they must perform that can strongly influence their success.

First, consider again the task of raising capital. In describing the process through which they make the decision to support or not support a particular project, venture capitalists generally report that how entrepreneurs present themselves during face-to-face meetings and presentations is one of the factors they consider with care. Although recent findings suggest that venture capitalists may overemphasize the amount of attention they actually direct to such factors (e.g., Shepherd & Zacharakis, 2002), it still seems likely that venture capitalists' decisions are influenced to a significant degree by their reactions to the entrepreneur (e.g., Cable & Shane, 1997). Indeed, findings reported by Zacharakis and Meyer (1995) suggest that venture capitalists' often focus on factors such as whether they believe they can work well with the entrepreneur and weight these factors heavily in reaching their decisions. It seems possible, then, that the greater entrepreneurs' skill in inducing positive reactions and impressions in others, the greater their likelihood of obtaining necessary financial resources.

A second context in which skill at impression management might be extremely useful to entrepreneurs is that of attracting key personnel. Talented people usually have many opportunities; yet, it is precisely these people entrepreneurs wish to recruit and retain. How can they do so? Partly through the offer of economic benefits: shares in the company, stock options, and the like. But often these have no immediate economic value; they are promises of "things to come," which can't be converted at present into hard cash. In view of this fact, how can entrepreneurs get talented people to accept the risks and sign on? Partly through their ability to make a good first impression on these people, so that they conclude that working with the entrepreneur will be exciting, fun, and potentially profitable (e.g., Gartner, Bird, & Starr, 1992). On the basis of these considerations, it was predicted that the greater entrepreneurs' skill with respect to impression management, the greater their success in establishing new ventures. Three items on the PSED assessed this skill: "I am concerned about what others think of me," "I can talk to anybody about anything," and "I am a loner."

Persuasion and Influence: Changing Others' Attitudes and Behavior

Much as we would like it to be otherwise, other people do not always share our views; further, they often behave in ways other than those we would prefer. Because of these facts, most of us are both the recipients and users each day of many acts of social influence—efforts to change others' attitudes, beliefs, or behavior (Cialdini, 1994). As readers already know from their own experience, efforts to exert social influence take many different forms. However, these have often been classified into two major groups of procedures: techniques relating to *persuasion* and techniques for gaining *compliance.*

Persuasion often focuses on efforts to change attitudes (and so, perhaps, behavior), through what seem to be logical arguments. In reality, persuasive appeals are often far from logical; they often lean more heavily on the induction of strong emotions such as fear or anger than on well-reasoned arguments. However, even in such cases, the form of logical argument is often retained.

Efforts to gain compliance, in contrast, focus on the task of getting others to say "yes" to various requests (Cialdini, 1994). These range from the *foot-in-the-door,* in which requesters begin with a small request and then, after this is accepted, escalate to a larger one (DeJong & Musilli, 1982) through the *door-in-the-face* technique, in which they start with a large request and when this is rejected, back down to a smaller one—the one they wanted all along (Cialdini et al., 1975). Other techniques include the *low-ball,* which involves changing an arrangement after it has been made (a common practice among auto dealers), the *deadline technique,* in which it is suggested that a special price or deal will no longer be available after a particular date, thus putting pressure on target persons to comply, and putting others in a good mood before making requests.

Research on social influence suggests that individuals vary greatly in terms of their proficiency with respect to both persuasion and tactics for gaining compliance (Cialdini, 1994). Not surprisingly, such differences are also related to success in a wide range of occupations—sales, law, and medicine, to name just a few. There appear to be grounds for suggesting that skill in persuasion and social influence may also play a role in entrepreneurs' success—again, primarily because the ability to influence others is related to key tasks performed by entrepreneurs (e.g., Carter et al., 1996). Tasks for which skill at exerting social influence may be relevant include recruiting and hiring key employees, negotiating the purchase or lease of facilities or equipment, persuading customers or suppliers to become associated with the new venture, and so on. All of these activities require face-to-face contact between entrepreneurs and other persons, and it is in such contexts that skills at persuasion and gaining compliance might prove highly beneficial to entrepreneurs. On the basis of this reasoning, it was predicted that the greater entrepreneurs' proficiency with respect to persuasion and other techniques for exerting social influence, the greater their success in establishing new ventures. Unfortunately, length limitations made it impossible to include items relevant to this skill in the PSED.

Emotional Intelligence and Entrepreneurial Success

In a widely read book, Goleman (1995) suggests that *emotional intelligence*—a cluster of skills relating to the emotional side of life—is an important ingredient in personal success. Included in the concept of emotional intelligence (which is quite distinct from the kind of intelligence measured by standard IQ tests) are the following skills: (1) the ability to recognize and manage one's own emotions (e.g., to conceal one's emotions; to refrain from "emotional outbursts" such as losing one's temper), (2) the capacity to motivate oneself and restrain impulses, (3) the ability to recognize and influence others' emotions, and (4) the ability to develop effective interpersonal relationships.

Although there is considerable controversy over whether emotional intelligence is a unitary construct and whether current measures of it possess adequate reliability and validity (e.g., Davies, Stankov, & Roberts, 1998), all of these skills appear to be related to activities performed by entrepreneurs and so may play a role in their success. Because the ability to recognize others' emotions has already been considered under the heading of social perception, this discussion will focus on two other aspects of emotional intelligence: the ability to regulate one's own emotions and the ability to influence others' emotions.

Because they operate in rapidly changing and highly unpredictable environments, entrepreneurs may often be pushed to the limits of their information processing capacity (cf., Baron, 1998). Similarly, because they often work extremely long hours and have many demands on their time, entrepreneurs may also often find themselves at or near the limits of their physical resources. It is precisely under such conditions that individuals become vulnerable to "emotional explosions"— instances in which even relatively trivial events evoke powerful emotional outbursts, especially ones relating to anger or hostility. Because such outbursts can prove very costly (e.g., they can disrupt established working relationships), it seems especially important for entrepreneurs to develop proficiency in controlling their own emotions, or at least the overt expression of them.

Turning to the ability to influence others' emotions, one crucial activity performed by entrepreneurs is that of generating excitement and enthusiasm. As one venture capitalist put it in comments directed to the present author: "Why should I get excited about a project unless the person presenting it is excited?" Enthusiasm, in short, is not only contagious—it also sells. When it is present, it can be one factor helping to tip decisions by venture capitalists, potential customers, and others in favor of the entrepreneur. For this reason, it seems possible that entrepreneurs who are high in *expressiveness*—the ability to express their own emotions clearly and vigorously—may often have an important edge over those who are more reserved (Friedman, Riggio, & Cassella, 1988). And indeed, research findings suggest that persons high in this ability are more successful than those who are not in occupations ranging from sales to medicine (Friedman et al., 1988). On the basis of these and related findings, it was predicted that the greater entrepreneurs' proficiency with respect to various aspects of emotional intelligence (e.g., the ability to regulate their own emotions; the ability to influence others' emotions; the capacity for self-motivation), the greater their success in establishing new ventures. Two items on the PSED were specifically designed to assess expressiveness: "Emotion I feel on the inside shows on the outside," and "I rarely show my feelings."

Table 21.1 presents an overview of the various social skills discussed and their potential relationships to both tasks performed by entrepreneurs and their success in starting new ventures; Table 21.2 presents the means, standard deviations, and intercorrelations of the seven items designed to measure social skills included in the PSED.

Table 21.1   Overview of Specific Social Skills Potentially Relevant to Entrepreneurial Success

Social Skill	Description	Potential Relevance to Tasks Performed by Entrepreneurs	Specific Predictions
Accuracy in Social Perception	Ability to perceive accurately the emotions, traits, motives, and intentions of others	Beneficial in making presentations (e.g., during efforts to obtain financing), in attracting, selecting partners and employees, during negotiations	The greater entrepreneurs' proficiency with respect to social perception (i.e., the ability to form accurate perceptions of others), the greater their success in establishing new ventures.
Effectiveness in Impression Management	Tactics designed to induce liking and a favorable first impression on the part of others	Useful in obtaining financing, attracting key employees, customers, suppliers	The greater entrepreneurs' proficiency with respect to impression management (i.e. the ability to induce positive impressions in others), the greater their success in establishing new ventures.
Skill in Persuasion and Social Influence	Ability to change others' attitudes and/or their behavior in desired directions	Useful in obtaining financing, recruiting key employees, during negotiations, dealing with customers, suppliers, etc.	The greater entrepreneurs' proficiency with respect to persuasion and other techniques for exerting social influence, the greater their success in establishing new ventures.
Emotional Intelligence	A cluster of skills relating to emotional side of life—e.g., the abilities to regulate one's own emotions, to influence the emotional reactions of others, and to motivate oneself	Beneficial during negotiations, in generating enthusiasm and commitment on the part of others, and in maintaining high levels of effort over long periods of time, even in the face of initial setbacks	The greater entrepreneurs' proficiency with respect to various aspects of emotional intelligence (e.g, the ability to regulate their own emotions; the ability to influence others' emotions; the capacity for self-motivation), the greater their success in establishing new ventures.

Table 21.2   Descriptive Statistics: Social Skill–Related Items in the PSED

Item; Social Skill Assessed [a]	Mean	SD	1	2	3	4	5	6	7
							Intercorrelations		
1. I rarely show my feelings (QL1s)	3.19	1.28	—	-.03	.53*	-.36	-.42*	-.20	.15
2. I usually know what is appropriate (QL1t) in any situation	4.16	.77		—	-.11	-.03	-.05	-.03	.12
3. I consider myself a loner (QL1u)	2.50	1.39			—	-.09	.01	.08	-.01
4. Emotion I feel on the inside shows (QL1v) on the outside	2.31	.89				—	-.01	.19	-.14
5. I am often concerned about what (QL1w) others think of me	3.09	1.30					—	.10	.05
6. I am a good judge of other people (QL1x)	3.91	.70						—	.13
7. I can talk to anybody about anything (QL1y)	3.90	1.27							—

NOTE: a. Item numbers on the PSED are shown in parentheses. Data are from the mail questionnaire, Wave 1, nascent entrepreneurs only.

* = $p < .05$, two-tailed.

The Role of Social Skills in New Venture Creation: Empirical Evidence

Previous sections of this chapter point to the conclusion that specific social skills may play a role in entrepreneurs' success in starting new ventures. Is this actually so? Surprisingly, only one investigation known to the present author has directly assessed this possibility (Baron & Markman, 2003). In two related studies, entrepreneurs in different industries (cosmetics, high tech) completed a questionnaire designed to assess their standing on all of the social skills considered above. All seven items designed to measure social skills on the PSED were incorporated into this scale. A factor analysis on the items included in this questionnaire, plus a follow-up parallel analysis (to determine how many factors to retain), indicated that the scale assessed four distinct social skills: (1) social perception (5 items; e.g., "I can usually read others well—tell how they are feeling in a given situation."); (2) social adaptability (5 items; e.g., "I can adjust to any social situation"); (3) expressiveness (4 items; e.g., "What I feel inside shows outside"); (4) impression management (2 items; "I am good at flattery and can use it to my advantage" and "I can appear to like someone even when I do not"). Confirmatory factor analysis offered support for the validity of this four-factor model. Contrary to initial expectations, the items included did not yield reliable measures of either emotional intelligence or persuasion but instead yielded a reliable factor relating to *social adaptability*—the ability to adapt to a wide range of social situations and get along with people from many different backgrounds (e.g., "I can easily adjust to being in just about any social situation"). Interestingly, one item included on the PSED originally designed to assess skill at impression management loaded highly on the social adaptability factor: "I can talk to anybody about anything."

The social skills identified above were then included as predictor variables in hierarchical regression analyses (separate analyses for the data from the two groups of entrepreneurs); the dependent variable was a measure of entrepreneurs' financial success (average income entrepreneurs obtained by entrepreneurs from their businesses during a 3-year period). Items measuring impression management were not included in these analyses because the measure of this factor failed to attain acceptable levels of reliability.

Results indicated that for both samples of entrepreneurs, skill at social perception was significantly related to entrepreneurs' financial success. In addition, social adaptability, a second social skill, was significantly related to financial success for the first sample of entrepreneurs (cosmetics industry). Finally, expressiveness was significantly related to another financial measure for the second sample of entrepreneurs: revenues from sales.

These findings are subject to many limitations; for instance, they provide no direct evidence on precisely how social skills affect entrepreneurs' financial success, and they cannot address the question of whether social skills contribute to financial success or, alternatively, success leads to more effective social skills. However, overall, these results suggest that social competence may indeed be one factor contributing to their success in launching new ventures. In other words, these finding suggest that in order to obtain a comprehensive answer to the question "Why are some entrepreneurs more successful than others in starting a new venture?" it may be useful to examine interpersonal or group-level variables as well as micro-level and macro-level variables.

Since several items included in the research conducted by Baron and Markman (2003) were also used in the PSED, it will be possible to determine—as relevant longitudinal data become available—whether these items (and the variables they reflect) are related to the success actually attained by nascent entrepreneurs. On the basis of previous findings (e.g., Baron & Markman, 2003), it is tentatively predicted that specific social skills (e.g., social perception, social adaptability) may indeed be related to such success. Of course, the smaller number of social skill items on the PSED may make it difficult to observe such relationships. Nevertheless, the possibility that they exist is worthy of careful attention in future research for the following reason: in contrast to personal traits, social skills are readily open to modification. Indeed, several programs for enhancing individuals' social skills exist and have been used with considerable success (e.g., Bandura, 1998; Segrin & Kinney, 1995). If such programs can be modified for use with entrepreneurs, the training they provide might well assist entrepreneurs to avoid the costly social errors that can result in failure even when their ideas are sound and their motivation, talent, and experience are high. Given the importance of entrepreneurs in creating wealth for their societies as well as themselves (Venkataraman, 1997), this would appear to be a highly desirable outcome and one with important social benefits.

References

Bandura, A. (Ed.). (1998). *Self-efficacy in changing societies.* New York: Cambridge University Press.

Baron, R. A. (1998). Cognitive mechanisms in entrepreneurship: Why and when entrepreneurs think differently than other people. *Journal of Business Venturing, 12,* 275–294.

Baron, R. A. (2004). The cognitive perspective: A valuable tool for answering entrepreneurship's basic "why?" questions. *Journal of Business Venturing, 19,* 221–240.

Baron, R. A., & Markman, G. D. (2003). Beyond social capital: The role of entrepreneurs' social competence in their financial success. *Journal of Business Venturing, 18,* 41–60.

Busenitz, L. W., & Barney, J. B. (1997). Biases and heuristics in strategic decision making: Differences between entrepreneurs and managers in large organizations. *Journal of Business Venturing, 20,* 25–39.

Cable, D. M., & Shane, S. (1997). A prisoner's dilemma approach to entrepreneur-venture capitalist relationships. *Academy of Management Review, 32,* 142–176.

Carter, N. M., Gartner, W. B., & Reynolds, P. D. (1996). Exploring start-up event sequences. *Journal of Business Venturing, 11,* 151–166.

Carter, N. M., Gartner, W. B., Shaver, K. G., & Gatewood, E. J. (2003). The career reasons of nascent entrepreneurs. *Journal of Business Venturing, 18,* 13–39.

Cialdini, R. B. (1994). Interpersonal influence. In N. S. Shavitt & T. C. Brock (Eds.), *Persuasion* (pp. 195–281). Boston: Allyn & Bacon.

Cialdini, R. B., Vincent, J. E., Lewis, S. K., Catalan, J., Wheeler, D., & Darby, B. L. (1975). Reciprocal concessions procedure for inducing compliance: The door-in-the-face technique. *Journal of Personality and Social Psychology, 31,* 206–215.

Ciavarella, M. A., Buchholtz, A. K., Riordan, C. M., Gatewood, R. D., & Stokes, G. S. (in press). The big five and venture survival: Is there a link? *Journal of Business Venturing.*

Davies, M., Stankov, L., & Roberts, R. D. (1998). Emotional intelligence: In search of an elusive construct. *Journal of Personality and Social Psychology, 7,* 989–1015.

DeJong, W., & Musilli, L. (1982). External pressures to comply: Handicapped versus non-handicapped requesters and the foot-in-the-door phenomenon. *Personality and Social Psychology Bulletin, 8,* 522–527.

Duchesneau, D. A., & Gartner, W. B. (1990). A profile of new venture success and failure in an emerging industry. *Journal of Business Venturing, 5,* 297–312.

Einstein, A. (1950). Quoted in *Observer,* January 15, 1950.

Eisenhardt, K. M., & Schoonhoven, C. B. (1990). Organizational growth: Linking founding team, strategy, environment and growth among U.S. semi-conductor ventures (1978–1988). *Administrative Science Quarterly, 28,* 274–291.

Friedman, H. S., Riggio, R. E., & Casella, D. F. (1988). Nonverbal skill, personal charisma, and initial attraction. *Personality and Social Psychology Bulletin, 14,* 203–211.

Gartner, W. (1990). What are we talking about when we talk about entrepreneurship? *Journal of Business Venturing, 5,* 15–29.

Gartner, W. B., Bird, B. J., & Starr, J. A. (1992). Acting as if: Differentiating entrepreneurial from organizational behavior. *Entrepreneurship Theory and Practice, 16,* 13–32.

Goleman, D. (1995). *Emotional intelligence.* New York: Bantam.

Labianca, G., Brass, D. J., & Gray, B. (1998). Social networks and perceptions of intergroup conflict: The role of negative relationships and third parties. *Academy of Management Journal, 41,* 55–67.

Larkin, J. E. (1987). Are good teachers perceived as high self-monitors? *Personality and Social Psychology Bulletin, 23,* 64–72.

Lewicki, R. J., Saunders, D. M., & Minton, J. W. (1997). *Essentials of negotiation.* Homewood, IL: Irwin.

Mitchell, R. K., Busenitz, L., Lant, T., McDougall, P. P., Morse, E. A., & Smith, J. B. (in press). Toward a theory of entrepreneurial cognition. *Entrepreneurship Theory and Practice.*

Nahapiet, J., & Ghoshal, S. (1998) Social capital, intellectual capital, and the organizational advantage. *Academy of Management Review, 23,* 242–266.

Putnam, R. D. (1993). The prosperous community: Social capital and public life. *American Prospect, 13,* 35–42.

Riggio, R. E., & Throckmorton, B. (1988). The relative effects of verbal and nonverbal behavior, appearance, and social skills on valuations made in hiring interviews. *Journal of Applied Social Psychology, 18,* 331–348.

Robbins, T. L., & DeNisi, A. S. (1994). A closer look at interpersonal affect as a distinct influence on cognitive processing in performance evaluations. *Journal of Applied Psychology, 79,* 341–353.

Segrin, C., & Kinney, T. (1995). Social skills deficits among the socially anxious: Rejection from others and loneliness. *Motivation and Emotion, 19,* 1–24.

Shane, S. (2001). Technology regimes and new firm formation. *Management Science, 47*(9), 1173–1181.

Shane, S., & Cable, D. (2002). Network ties, reputation, and the financing of new ventures. *Management Science, 48*(3), 364–381.

Shaver, K. G., & Scott, L. R. (1991). Person, process, choice: The psychology of new venture creation. *Entrepreneurship Theory and Practice 16,* 23–42.

Shepherd, D. A., & Zacharakis, A. L. (2002). Venture capitalists' expertise: A call for research into decision aids and cognitive feedback. *Journal of Business Venturing, 17,* 1–20.

Sternberg, R. (2004). Successful intelligence as a basis for entrepreneurship. *Journal of Business Venturing, 19,* 189–202.

Venkataraman, S. (1997). The distinctive domain of entrepreneurship research. In J. Katz (Ed.), *Advances in entrepreneurship, firm emergence, and growth* (Vol. 3, pp. 119–138). Greenwich, CT: JAI.

Wayne, S. J., & Liden, R. C. (1995). Effects of impression management on performance ratings: A longitudinal study. *Academy of Management Journal, 38,* 232–260.

Wayne, S. J., Liden, R. C., Graf, I. K., & Ferris, G. R. (1997). The role of upward influence tactics in human resource decisions. *Personnel Psychology, 40,* 979–1006.

Zacharakis, A. L., & Meyer, G. D. (1995). The venture capitalist decision: Understanding process versus outcome. In J. Hornaday, F. Tarpley, J. Timmons, & K. Vesper (Eds.)., *Frontiers of entrepreneurship research.* Wellesley, MA: Babson College.

PART III

CHAPTER 22

Overview: The Start-up Process

William B. Gartner

Nancy M. Carter

The chapters in this Part III focus, primarily, on *how* nascent entrepreneurs engage in the creation and development of new business ventures. Where as entrepreneurs may possess various demographic and cognitive characteristics that increase the likelihood they may successfully create a new business venture, the successful creation of a new business requires action. Entrepreneurs cannot think a business into existence, nor does one's age, income, skills, or abilities provide a "free pass" entitling one to new business ownership. Entrepreneurs must do something, and their actions must involve creating a specific kind of business that fits with the specific social, economic, and environmental context. Accounting for the details of how and what occur in the business formation process is, therefore, the subject of chapters in this section.

A reader might want to surmise that the chapters in Part III are arranged, somewhat sequentially, from the process of recognizing an opportunity through the characteristics of the new firm and the founder's expectations for growth and development. We would hope that the reader will hold in check any assumptions about the process of business creation until all of the chapters are read. We see these chapters as a "gestalt" of issues that influence the creation of a new business. A primary goal of the Panel Study of Entrepreneurial Dynamics (PSED) research effort is to understand how the process of organization formation works. The chapters that are presented in this section provide theory and ideas about all of the factors that influence the process of business formation, as well as characterize the business formation process. As research on the PSED is undertaken, a clearer picture of the various ways that new businesses are created will emerge. The remainder of this chapter provides a brief overview of each of the chapters and some concluding comments about how one might make sense of Part III, overall.

A primary concern in the creation of the PSED has been to develop a sample of nascent entrepreneurs who reflect the population of all individuals currently engaged in business creation. Ideally, any findings generated from the PSED sample would be generalizable for an understanding of entrepreneurship in the United States, as a whole. Paul Reynolds has provided a wealth of evidence in other chapters in this book (Chapter 1 and Appendixes A and B) demonstrating that the nascent entrepreneurs who are participants in the PSED sample are an accurate reflection of all nascent entrepreneurs in the United States. The focus of his chapter on the nature of business startups (Chapter 23) is to explore whether the number and distribution of the kinds of businesses that nascent entrepreneurs are intending to create reflect the number and distribution of the kinds of businesses found in other descriptions of the population of U.S. businesses. His analyses indicate that the kinds of businesses nascent entrepreneurs were intending to start, as characterized by NAICS (North American Industry Classification System), are "broadly representative of the U.S. entrepreneurial process in 1998–1999." Differences in the distribution of businesses by economic sector between the PSED sample and Small Business Association (SBA) (reflecting businesses with employees) and IRS (reflecting individual filings of Schedule C returns) population distributions are likely to reflect attempts at business formation into industries with low perceived barriers to entry and high liabilities of newness. For example, 24% of the nascent entrepreneurs in the PSED sample intend to start firms in the retail trade category, although there are only 12.5% of the IRS population of individuals filing schedule C business activity forms indicating retail businesses. The PSED sample reflects attempts to start a business whereas the SBA and IRS distributions reflect established businesses. Reynolds also explores characteristics of the legal form of organization (i.e., sole proprietorship, partnership, corporation), organizational form (i.e., independent start-up, takeover, franchise, business-sponsored), and ownership structure (i.e., percentage ownership by natural persons and/or business entities). He ends his chapter with a comparison of estimates of the number of PSED firms that filed FICA payments with the federal government with actual counts of the population of all new firms filing FICA payments, on average, from 1998 to 2000. He concludes the PSED sample of nascent entrepreneurs provides "a credible prediction of the annual number of new employer firms in the United States." By as many metrics as could be utilized, the PSED sample appears to be a very robust reflection of all entrepreneurial activity in the United States at the end of the millennium.

In Chapter 24, Hills and Singh explore the importance of recognizing opportunity in the context of business creation. After Shane and Venkataraman (2000) suggested that opportunity recognition was the quintessential characteristic of entrepreneurship, a flood of scholars have sought to maneuver this concept into their models of the entrepreneurial process. Hills and Singh provide historical overview of theory and research on opportunity recognition construct and offer evidence from the PSED. The evidence they present suggests that there is no one particular way in which opportunities are recognized by nascent entrepreneurs. Some individuals engage in a lengthy search for opportunities; others consider only one. Some individuals decide to start businesses before they have identified an opportunity; others seize their opportunity first. In addition, once these nascent entrepreneurs identify an opportunity, there is wide variation in whether they perceive that the opportunity changed (or not) during their attempts at the organization formation process. Given the variety of questions asked about the opportunity recognition in the PSED, coupled with data on factors that are likely to influence this construct (e.g., type of business, background, and skills of the nascent entrepreneur) Hills and Singh invite researchers to explore a rich and complicated view of how and why the opportunity recognition process unfolds in new business creation.

As was mentioned in the Foreword to the handbook, there are often a variety of ways that different ideas about aspects of the business formation process are measured. The topic of "start-up problems" is one issue about which PSED researchers asked both open-ended (e.g., Q107—"What major problems have you had in starting this business?") and fixed-response questions to better understand how nascent entrepreneurs perceived their situations. In Chapter 25, Brush and Manolova offer a number of theories (e.g., life cycle, evolutionary, resource-based, resource dependence, and behavioral psychology) that can be used to identify the kinds of problems that entrepreneurs face. They use these theories as a springboard to develop a measure that identifies two factors of start-up problems that nascent entrepreneurs face: personal challenges and social challenges. Some preliminary analyses of these factors are offered comparing nascent entrepreneurs by gender and ethnicity. The findings suggest that women and minorities are more concerned about personal and social challenges involved in business start-up than are White men.

The specific activities that characterize the process of business formation in the PSED are the subject of Chapter 26 by Gartner, Carter, and Reynolds. They provide a history of prior research efforts to identify and measure, in a quantifiable way, the various actions and events that nascent entrepreneurs undertake (alone and with others on their team) to create new businesses. These items can be used to identify what activities nascent entrepreneurs initiated/completed, when these activities were initiated/completed, and the sequence in which these activities were initiated/completed—and whether these activities resulted in the completion of a new business. Theory to explain why certain activities and sequences of activities might lead to business formation is offered in Gartner and Carter (2003). In this handbook chapter, they report some preliminary findings that indicate that the sample of nascent entrepreneurs in the PSED represents the "stock" of all individuals attempting to get into business during the period 1998 to 2000. It is suggested that researchers interested in comparing nascent entrepreneurs at the same "starting point" in the process of business formation develop a rationale for selecting cases to study. They conclude with their view that the process of organization formation involves "variation" and that scholars should pay attention to the many ways that nascent entrepreneurs engage in different activities and sequences of activities to successfully start a new business.

A majority of nascent entrepreneurs do not begin the process of business formation alone—they form teams. In Chapter 27, Aldrich, Carter, and Ruef provide the theoretical rationale for why nascent entrepreneurs would be likely to join with other individuals as equity owners in the business formation process. They also offer a logic for how teams are likely to be formed and suggest that three uncertainty-reducing mechanisms (homophily, familiarity, and reputation) might guide team member choice. The PSED reflects two of these mechanisms: homophily, which measures similarity among people, and familiarity, which measures the association (such as kinship and work relations) among people. After describing the questions that characterize aspects of homophily and familiarity in the PSED, they offer some information about team composition. The majority of start-up teams involve two people, and, in those instances, the majority of these teams consisted of spouses. Their chapter ends with some insights into the implications of their recent findings on teams about homophily with respect to gender, ethnicity, and occupation (Ruef, Aldrich, & Carter, 2003). Teams appear to be composed, primarily, of strong ties that are based more on trust and familiarity, rather than on skills and competence. Findings such as this pose interesting questions about the value of trust, functional skills, and knowledge among team members as they may influence both the likelihood of success at firm founding and subsequent survival and growth.

One of the primary outcomes of the process of creating a new venture would obviously be, a new venture. In Chapter 28, Carter, Gartner, and Reynolds point out many of the theoretical and empirical difficulties with identifying when the creation of a new business ends and the new business begins. Their review of previous research and theory on identifying new firms offers a variety of ideas and measures for specifying the existence of a new business. New businesses make themselves known through such indicators as sales to customers, a business license, payment of sales taxes, incorporation, a business phone listing, hiring of employees, payment of payroll taxes, and the founder's belief that a new business exists. Using data from the PSED, they suggest that nascent entrepreneurs consider a number of new business indicators as correlates to their decision of whether their efforts are a new business or they are still trying to start a new business. In addition, nascent entrepreneurs do not use the same new firm indicators when making this judgment. Based on the insight that some of the "still trying" nascent entrepreneurs have achieved many of the new firm indicators, yet believe they are not in business, Carter, Gartner, and Reynolds suggest that the achievement of a multitude of new firm indicators may predict a greater degree of hardiness and sustainability of a new business over time. A single measure, such as the use of first sales to indicate the existence of a new business, is likely to have many limitations. Scholars are cautioned of the need to provide theoretical justifications for their indicators of new firm existence, as these indicators are often the bases for measures of the dependent variables in PSED studies.

Nascent entrepreneurs are likely to rely on the help of others (beyond members of their founding team) in order to create a new business. In Chapter 29, Aldrich and Carter provide a theoretical rationale for the value of an individual's social network for establishing a new business. The relations that an individual has can be characterized by their diversity and their affective or emotional strength. Ideas are offered that individuals with networks of relationships that are diverse (e.g., sex, age, occupation, ethnicity) are more likely to have access to the kinds of resources necessary (e.g., ideas, sources of capital, investors, customers) for new venture creation. Relationships with affective or emotional strength are often referred to as "strong ties." Strong ties provide nascent entrepreneurs with trust, predictability, and voice so that they can assume that these individuals will not act opportunistically (betray them), can be counted on, and will often tell them the truth about situations rather than sneaking away. Weak ties are those relationships where there is often little contact or emotional investment. Relationships with customers or clients, or people who would "take my phone call," would be examples of weak ties. Both strong and weak ties have various benefits for nascent entrepreneurs. Strong ties can provide the kind of emotional support needed for nascent entrepreneurs to weather the uncertainties of business formation, whereas weak ties might provide connections to the resources necessary to create the business. Aldrich and Carter link the theory on social networks to the development of measures in the PSED for ascertaining both the characteristics of an individual's social network and the benefits received from each of these network ties. Information on social networks was collected for the nascent entrepreneurs as well as for individuals in the comparison group (as it pertained to how these individuals were helpful in their career). The comparisons they make between these two groups provide some surprising insights. Individuals in the comparison group appeared to have significantly more helpers in their networks than did the nascent entrepreneurs. And, individuals in the comparison group were more likely to have business associates in their networks compared to nascent entrepreneurs. Nascent entrepreneurs were more likely to have nonspouse family members as helpers in their social network (38%) compared to the comparison group (26%). Aldrich and Carter end their chapter by suggesting that the theory and emerging evidence on social networks will lead to important insights into how and why nascent entrepreneurs involve and depend on other people for the development of their businesses. Although it appears that nascent entrepreneurs depend on their strong ties to a greater degree than others, the use of weak ties to connect to capital and other resources may be a significant determinant for successful business creation.

A variety of business assistance programs at the federal, state, and local levels exist to help nascent entrepreneurs in their efforts to start and grow their businesses. After summarizing prior theory, policy, and evidence on the value of such programs, Dennis and Reynolds, in Chapter 30, pose a number of questions about business assistance: Are nascent entrepreneurs aware of business assistance programs? Do they use them? When in the start-up process does such assistance occur? What kinds of assistance are offered? Is this assistance perceived as valuable? Does assistance appear to lead to the successful start-up of new businesses? Dennis and Reynolds provide some preliminary analyses that indicate that over two thirds of all U.S. adults (nascent entrepreneurs and those not starting businesses) have some knowledge of business assistance programs and that there is little difference both in contact with and knowledge of business assistance programs between the two groups (nascent entrepreneurs and the comparison group). Nascent entrepreneurs are likely to know about more types of business assistance programs and to contact more business assistance programs than those not engaged in start-ups. As would be expected, nascent entrepreneurs spend more time than others in business assistance programs. Both groups (nascent entrepreneurs and the comparison group) appear to use equal percentages of business assistance involving getting help about general training and more knowledge of the start-up process. Nascent entrepreneurs are more likely to use specific types of assistance, such as new production technology training. And, finally, those nascent entrepreneurs who use business assistance programs are more likely to start a new business than those who do not.

All efforts at starting a new business will involve financial resources, of some kind, and in varying amounts. In Chapter 31, Stouder and Kirchhoff offer prior theoretical and empirical information on the kinds and amounts of financial resources that individuals are likely to use in the development of their businesses. Prior research has been primarily focused on larger and established firms and little theoretical effort has been devoted toward providing insights into the resource acquisition issues involved with nascent entrepreneurs seeking to fund their prospective businesses. Empirical evidence suggests that nascent entrepreneurs depend on more than their own financial resources and that many entrepreneurs are likely to use institutional debt (such as bank loans, credit cards) that was personally guaranteed. The list of questions in the PSED that are asked about the kinds of financing used by nascent entrepreneurs is substantial. Stouder and Kirchhoff present findings on a select number of the finance questions for those nascent entrepreneurs who indicated they had a business in operation when they were contacted for the first follow-up interview. Nearly all of the nascent entrepreneurs (93%) invest in their own businesses through an equity investment, and the median amount of equity was $10,000. Nearly all equity comes from the nascent entrepreneurs and their team. Only 5.4% of the new businesses used equity from family, friends, or relatives. A majority of nascent entrepreneurs used some form of debt to finance their businesses. For those who used debt (35% did not), the median debt use was $15,000. Approximately 25% of nascent entrepreneurs were likely to use bank or finance company debt, and nearly 50% of nascent entrepreneurs made personal loans to the business. The overall median total start-up financing for nascent entrepreneurs who indicated they had a new business in operation was $20,000. Stouder and Kirchhoff conclude by suggesting that the population of new business start-ups, overall, is primarily dependent on financing raised by the founders and the founding team through personal assets and credit cards. While it might be expected that institutional financing by banks would not play a minimal role in new venture creation, the lack of funding participation by family and friends suggests that the risk of new venture creation is primarily borne by those directly involved (the founders).

While all nascent entrepreneurs will need financial resources in the new business development process, it is likely that many of these individuals will not have the financial sophistication to use these financial resources in an efficient and effective manner. In Chapter 32, Katz and Cabezuelo posit a new concept, called "financial sophistication," that measures a nascent entrepreneur's understanding of the financial elements of a business and how these financial elements work. Based on prior theory and evidence from the financial activities of individuals in the general population,

Katz and Cabezuelo indicate that many individuals do not use any formal record keeping to track their financial status, and they suggest that it is very likely that nascent entrepreneurs will not use such methods, as well. The financial sophistication measure ascertains three issues: presence of formal records, presence of a business checking account, and the use of cash or accrual method of accounting. Their analyses of nascent entrepreneurs in the PSED suggest that the financial sophistication measure does correlate with efforts to use other kinds of financial methods in their business, and they surmise that the financial sophistication measure may be of use in predicting whether nascent entrepreneurs can successfully start a business, or not.

The final chapter in this Part III explores the future expectations that nascent entrepreneurs have for the growth of their prospective new ventures. In Chapter 33, Human and Matthews review the entrepreneurship literature on growth expectations and suggest that the growth expectation construct has been hypothesized to be an important way to differentiate between entrepreneurs and small business owners, and between ventures that are likely to become high-growth ventures, and those that are not. Human and Matthews identify 10 items based on prior theory that are used to represent future expectations of the new business. Preliminary analyses of some of these items indicate a very large variation in future expectations. For example, expected income in the firm's first year of operations ranges from less than $25,000 to over $45 million, with a median value of approximately $30,000; expected income in the firm's fifth year of operations ranges from $0 to $80 million, with a median value of $100,000. Most nascent entrepreneurs intend to grow and keep business growth within the range of their own skills and abilities to manage this growth.

As we indicated at the beginning of this overview, the process of business formation involves an appreciation of the activities involved as well as recognition of the kinds of businesses started and the context in which this start-up process occurs. The chapters in this Part III offer an intellectual foundation for seeing many of the characteristics of the phenomenon of the business start-up process. Making connections among these characteristics is likely to be a fruitful path for future scholarly activity.

References

Gartner, W. B., & Carter, N. M. (2003). Entrepreneurial behavior and firm organizing processes. In Z. J. Acs, & D. B. Audretsch (Eds.), *Handbook of entrepreneurship research* (pp. 195–221). Boston: Kluwer.

Ruef, M., Aldrich, H. E., & Carter, N. M. (2003). The structure of founding teams: Homophily, strong ties, and isolation among U.S. entrepreneurs. *American Sociological Review, 68*(April), 195–222.

Shane, S., & Venkataraman, S. (2000). The promise of entrepreneurship as a field of research. *Academy of Management Review, 25,* 217–226.

CHAPTER 23

Nature of
Business Start-ups

Paul D. Reynolds

The basic focus of the Panel Study of Entrepreneurial Dynamics (PSED) research program is the origin of new U.S. businesses. The United States already has, of course, a great many business entities—over 5 million with employees and another 20 million in the form of full- or part-time self-employment. Much effort is devoted to describing the existing population of U.S. businesses. These descriptions use a number of business attributes to facilitate their descriptions, including

- Type of economic activity
- Legal form
- Nature of the ownership structure
- Type of location

A description of the PSED start-up cohort on such features helps provide a more detailed understanding of new and emerging firms.

There are two major reasons for developing descriptions of new start-ups. First, these features of the new firm may have a direct bearing on the speed and success of completing the start-up process and creating a successful new firm. For example, it may be easier to launch a new firm in some sectors than others; the legal form may affect the ability to secure financial support. Second, as the sample is designed to represent all start-up activity in the United States, it would be helpful to be able to make comparisons with other descriptions of the population of U.S. businesses.

There are, of course, a variety of sources that provide information on the population of U.S. businesses: the Internal Revenue Service; the Bureau of Labor Statistics; the Census Bureau within the Department of Commerce; a variety of phone directory and business listing services; and credit-rating services, of which Dun & Bradstreet is among the best known. If the measures of business activity from the PSED sample are comparable to those collected from other data sources, it increases confidence that the PSED sample represents entrepreneurial activity in the United States. Such a comparison is provided in the final section of this chapter—the match is very good. This will increase confidence in the general application of information derived from the PSED that is *not* available from any other source to the entire United States.

Type of Business Activity: Economic Sector

There are several issues involved in developing a scheme for describing business activity. Perhaps most important is the choice of classification schemes. Business activity is so fundamental to all analysis of economic activity—for scholarly, government, as well as business objectives—that it receives a great deal of attention. This need has been so fundamental that most countries of the world have had economic sector classification schemes in place for some time, centuries for the more developed countries. The lack of harmonization across national schemes is, however, one of the complicating factors. Further, the actual classification schemes tend to change over time, as the scope and nature of economic activity shifts.

The initial coding scheme used for PSED business activity was the 1987 version of the U.S. Standard Industrial Classification (SIC 1987), a classification scheme based on the nature of the production activity carried out by a business establishment.[1] During the 2 years data collection was underway for the PSED, a newer version was implemented in the United States. The North American Industry Classification System: 1997 (NAICS 1997) was harmonized for and adopted by the three North American Free Trade Association partners: Canada, Mexico, and the United States. This is now being replaced by the NAICS 2002 version, and a NAICS 2007 revision is in development (updates and details can be found at www.census.gov/epcd/www/ naics.html. The major change, however, was between the SIC 1987 (the last version of the previous system initiated in 1939) and the major reorganization represented by the NAICS system. The 10 major categories of SIC 1987 were reorganized into the 20 major categories of the NAICS system. These 20 new categories provide a more precise overview of the national economic system; "information" and "accommodations and food service" are now treated as separate major categories. The new system is intended to have a correspondence with the International Standard Industrial Classification (ISIC) adopted by the United Nations Statistical Office (United Nations, 1990; http://esa.un.org/unsd/ cr/registry/regist2.asp).

But how does one determine the nature of business activity for either a new or existing firm. For the PSED the primary measure was a single question (Q183), "What will be the major product or service of this new business?" For many start-ups, the answer to this item is relatively easy to code. But if the answer is too brief or too succinct, there can be confusion in assigning the business activity to the right category. For example, if the response was "carpets!" the firm may be coded in one of several categories, which are radically different. For example, the business may make carpeting (SIC 2273; NAICS 3144), sell it wholesale (SIC 5023; NAICS 44121), sell it retail (SIC 5713; NAICS 44221), or install carpeting (SIC 1752; NAICS 23522). Not only are these different sectors at the four- or six-digit level of detail, they are different sectors in the 10 (SIC 1987) or 20 (NAICS 1997) general categories: manufacturing, wholesale trade, retail trade, and construction.

In order to provide for a basic allocation of all economic activity into the most general levels, the initial question about the major product or service is followed by a series of questions designed to ensure that the general level of activity can be determined. These are asked as a series of questions, such that when one sector is identified, the interview skips to the next section. The procedure is illustrated in Exhibit 23.1. Note that the more prevalent sectors are asked in the earlier items, so that individuals with more popular business activities will quickly move to the next section of the interview.

The result of this effort is a portrayal of the economic activities represented by the PSED cohort as shown in the first column of Table 23.1. The original classification of activities using the SIC 1987 classification scheme (variable SUSECTOR) has been converted to the NAICS 1997 categories, relying on the cross-reference

Exhibit 23.1   Classifying Business Activity Items in the PSED

Q184a   Would consider this new business to be in retail; a restaurant, tavern, bar, or nightclub; customer or consumer services, such as a repair shop, motel, or rental agency; health, education, or social services; or something else?
   1) Retail [SKIP TO NEXT SECTION]
   2) Restaurant, tavern, bar, or nightclub [SKIP TO NEXT SECTION]
   3) Customer or consumer services [SKIP TO NEXT SECTION]
   4) Health, education, or social services [SKIP TO NEXT SECTION]
   5) Something else [GO TO Q185]
   8) Don't know [GO TO Q185]

Q185   Would consider this new business to be in manufacturing, construction, agriculture, mining, or something else?
   1) Manufacturing [SKIP TO Q185a]
   2) Construction [SKIP TO NEXT SECTION]
   3) Agriculture [SKIP TO NEXT SECTION]
   4) Mining [SKIP TO NEXT SECTION]
   5) Something else [GO TO Q186]
   8) Don't know [GO TO Q186]

Q185a   Would you say it is making a product that is durable—designed to last over 3 years, or nondurable—designed to last less than 3 years?
   1) Durable [SKIP TO NEXT SECTION]
   2) Nondurable [SKIP TO NEXT SECTION]
   8) Don't know [GO TO NEXT SECTION]

Q186   Would consider this new business to be in wholesale distribution, transportation, utilities, communications, or something else?
1) Wholesale distribution [SKIP TO NEXT SECTION]
2) Transportation [SKIP TO NEXT SECTION]
3) Utilities [SKIP TO NEXT SECTION]
4) Communications [SKIP TO NEXT SECTION]
5) Something else [GO TO NEXT ITEM]
8) Don't know [GO TO Q187]

Q187   Would consider this new business to be in finance, insurance, real estate, or some type of business consulting or service, or something else?
1) Finance [SKIP TO NEXT SECTION]
2) Insurance (including brokers) [SKIP TO NEXT SECTION]
3) Real estate [SKIP TO NEXT SECTION]
4) Business consulting or service [SKIP TO Q187a]
5) Something else [GO TO Q188]
8) Don't know [GO TO Q188]

Q187a   What would best describe the type of business service or consulting—will this be a law firm or accounting practice; a computer or World Wide Web programming firm; provide business consulting; provide business services, such as bookkeeping, credit bureaus, temporary help agencies, or copy services; or something else?
1) Law or accounting practice [SKIP TO NEXT SECTION]
2) Computer/World Wide Web programming [SKIP TO NEXT SECTION]
3) Business consulting [SKIP TO NEXT SECTION]
4) Business services [SKIP TO NEXT SECTION]
5) Something else [GO TO Q188]
8) Don't know [GO TO Q188]

Q188   Your business does not seem to fit into any of these categories, how would you describe it?

table provided on the NAICS website. Of the 830 start-ups in the PSED sample, a determination could be made for 812, of which 809 are private sector business activities—3 were forms of public administration.

For comparison, two other descriptions of the U.S. business population are provided. One is based on all firms with employees, developed by the Census Bureau of the Department of Commerce from the files maintained by the U.S. Social Security Administration. The Social Security Administration has records of all payments on behalf of employees provided to the federal social security programs and hence, data on all firms with employees. In 1998, they had information on 5,579,200 firms or legal entities that represented 6,941,800 establishments (some firms control and manage more than one establishment). The distribution of these firms across the NAICS 1997 categories is presented in the middle data column in Table 23.1.

Table 23.1   U.S. Business Economic Activity: Population and PSED Sample Compared

Economic Sector (NAICS 1997)	PSED Sample[a]: (1997–1999)	Firms with Employees[b]: (SBA: 1998)	Businesses Tax Filings[c]: (IRS: 1999)
Total Entities	809	5,579,200	24,449,000
Agricultural, forestry, hunting, and fishing	2.4%	0.5%	2.3%
Mining	0.0%	0.4%	0.7%
Utilities	0.1%	0.1%	0.1%
Construction	7.0%	12.3%	12.4%
Manufacturing	4.7%	5.7%	2.9%
Wholesale trade	3.1%	6.5%	3.1%
Retail trade	24.0%	13.2%	12.5%
Transportation, warehousing	1.2%	2.8%	4.0%
Information	7.9%	1.4%	1.5%
Finance, insurance	2.7%	4.0%	4.2%
Real estate, property rental, leasing	3.6%	4.3%	9.2%
Professional, scientific, technical services	11.2%	11.5%	13.4%
Management of companies, enterprises	0.1%	0.5%	0.2%
Administrative, and support, waste Management and remedial services	8.5%	5.4%	7.0%
Educational services	1.8%	1.0%	1.5%
Health care, and social assistance	4.4%	9.4%	7.7%
Arts, entertainment, and recreation	4.6%	1.7%	4.8%
Accommodation, and food services	0.4%	7.5%	2.6%
Other services (except public administration)	12.1%	11.8%	9.8%
Total	100.0%	100.0%	100.0%
Auxiliaries, public administration	3	5,300	
Unclassified	18	56,800	292,000

NOTES:

a. Weighted sample based on conversion of SIC 1987 to NAICS 1997 at the leading two-digit level.

b. From Table A.6, from Department of Advocacy, U.S. Small Business Administration, *The State of Small Business: 1999-2000.* Washington, DC, U.S. Government Printing Office, 2001.

c. From Table 701, *Statistical Abstract of the United States: 2002.* Note that this total, 24.4 million, is somewhat less that the number of Business Master File accounts, which is 39 million in the year 2000 (Internal Revenue Service Data Book 2000, Table 5).

Another source of businesses by sector is the annual counts of business tax returns assembled by the Internal Revenue Service. In 1999, they received 24,449,000 returns, excluding farm sole proprietorships, which are a small proportion of the overall number. The distribution of these firms across the NAICS 1997 categories is presented in the right data column in Table 23.1.

There is a general correspondence between the three sources. In most cases the sector percentage in the PSED sample is within the range between the employee firms and income tax return data. This is most appropriate, as the PSED sample includes a substantial number of sole proprietorships as well as firms that will have employees. The major exceptions are the high proportions in the PSED cohort in the retail trade and information sectors and lower proportions for finance and insurance, health care and social assistance, and accommodations and food services sectors. Because the PSED sample represents those in the start-up process and these other descriptions reflect operating businesses, a precise match is unlikely. For example, individuals with few resources or qualifications may be active in the retail sector in the start-up phase but may fail to convert this initiative into a new going concern. This could lead to a higher proportion of retail start-ups in the PSED sample.

The current match of emphasis in Table 23.1 suggests that the PSED sample is based on the same population as employee firms providing FICA payments or business entities filing annual federal income tax returns. This provides confidence that the PSED sample is broadly representative of the U.S. entrepreneurial process in 1998 through 1999.

Legal Form

Other than what a business actually does, nothing is more important than the legal form. The legal form can affect a number of features of a business, such as the nature of the administrative structure and decision-making processes, the amount and form of financial support available to the firm, and the way financial risk and liability may be shared among the owners. The three basic legal forms in the United States are corporations, partnerships, and sole proprietorships.

The PSED respondents are asked to identify (Q189) the expected initial legal form of the new business—at the time of the interview. The respondents are given six choices—sole proprietorship, two types of partnership (general and limited), and three types of corporations (c-corporations, Subchapter S, and limited liability companies). For ease of comparison, they are consolidated into three basic types in Table 23.2, where they are presented in the second and third columns.

The U.S. Internal Revenue Service (IRS) provides a count of the three legal forms based on annual tax returns. Nonfarm sole proprietorships are inferred from the inclusion of Schedule C or CZ forms—Profit or Loss from a Business, Net Profit from a Business—with individual tax returns. They are filed in the millions—17.5 million in 1999. The proportions reported by the IRS for 1999 are presented in the right column of Table 23.2.

Table 23.2   U.S. Businesses Legal Form: Population and PSED Sample Compared

Legal Form		PSED Sample[a]: (1997–1999)	Businesses Tax Filings[b]: (IRS: 1999)
Total entities		830	24,449,000
Sole proprietorship		52.7%	71.9%
Partnerships		28.2%	7.9%
General partnerships	20.9%		
Limited partnerships	7.3%		
Corporations		18.9%	20.2%
C-corporations	8.9%		
Subchapter S	6.5%		
Limited liability companies	3.5%		
Total		100.0%	100.0%
Unclassified (not included in proportions)		66	

NOTES: Percentages may not total exactly to 100% due to rounding to one decimal point.

a. Weighted sample from PSED data file.

b. From Table 701, *Statistical Abstract of the United States: 2002*. The primary source of data on nonfarm proprietorships are the Schedule C and CZ forms filed with individual tax returns. Only nonfarm proprietorships are included.

The PSED sample appears to have fewer sole proprietorships and more partnerships than reported by the Internal Revenue Service. But this may reflect the early stages of the business life course in the PSED sample. Many of these new firms will modify their legal form as they gain experience and adapt to new circumstances. Of particular note is the high proportion of PSED nascent entrepreneurs that report a partnership. This is four times the proportion from the IRS data for the entire country. Perhaps partnerships are not as viable in the long term as the other legal forms.

Nature of Start-up Structure

The type of situation in which a start-up emerges can be quite complex. A major distinction is between those that are implemented by one or more individuals (natural persons) and those initiated by an existing business or organization. When an existing business implements a new firm, it can either be as simple as one restaurant opening on another site or as complex as a new subsidiary created as a separate legal entity. Table 23.3 reflects the responses from 809 of the nascent entrepreneurs, where

Table 23.3   Frequency Distribution: Nature of Start-up Structure in the PSED Cohort

Form		PSED Sample: (1997–1999)
Total entities		830
Independent Start-up		85.9%
Takeover of an existing business		2.5%
Nonfamily business	1.5%	
Family business takeover	0.5%	
Business inherited	0.4%	
Other takeover	0.1%	
Franchise, multilevel marketing		6.1%
Franchise	0.7%	
Multilevel marketing	4.7%	
Other franchise, multilevel marketing	0.7%	
Business sponsored		5.2%
Branch	2.6%	
New legal entity	2.6%	
Total		100.0%
Unclassified (not included in proportions)		21

NOTES: Percentages may not total exactly to 100% due to rounding to one decimal point.

it appears that 86% of the sample reflects the individual efforts of one or more persons.

That 14% in other categories includes 2.5% that involve the takeover of an existing business—which may reflect the purchase of an existing business or a transfer of ownership within a family group. Franchise and multilevel marketing represent another 6.1% in which the new firm will be part of a larger, preexisting business operation. Multilevel marketing (like Amway or Mary Kay Cosmetics) is of particular interest, for in this case each sales agent is legally treated as an independent contractor, although the degree of independence is subject to some discussion. Finally, there are new branches or subsidiaries established by existing firms that involve another 5.2% of the nascent entrepreneurs.

The ownership structure of the new firm is of considerable significance, and a major aspect of the interview schedule helped define this feature. The respondent was asked to identify—by first name—all potential owners of the new firm and the percentage of the firm each would own. This provides a precise

Table 23.4 Frequency Distribution: Ownership Structure Based on Team Allocations in the PSED Cohort

Reported Ownership Structure	PSED Sample (1997–1999)
Total entities	830
Natural persons will own 100% of the new firm	87.0%
Natural persons own over 50%, independent start-up	0.8%
Natural persons own over 50%, franchise or multilevel marketing	6.1%
Natural persons own over 50%, business sponsored	5.2%
Natural persons own less than 50%	0.8%
Total	100.0%

NOTE: Percentages may not total exactly to 100% due to rounding to one decimal point.

Table 23.5 Frequency Distribution: Organizational Form and Ownership Structure in the PSED Cohort

Owned by Natural Persons	100%	50% or More	50% or More	50% or More	Less Than 50%
External Ownership		Prior Business Owners	Franchise, MLM	Business Sponsors	Business
Organizational Form					
Independent start-up	98%	1%			*%
Takeover of an existing business					
Nonfamily business	100%				
Family business takeover	100%				
Business inherited	100%				
Other takeover	100%				
Franchise, multilevel marketing					
Franchise			100%		
Multilevel marketing	2%		98%		
Other franchise, multilevel marketing			100%		
Business sponsored					
Branch				93%	7%
New legal entity				80%	20%
Total	87%	1%	6%	5%	1%

NOTES: *less than 1%.

description of the ownership structure, as presented in Table 23.4. One or more natural persons were expected to own 87% of the new firms, and a variety of other arrangements were identified for the other 13%. However, for 12% in which there was shared ownership, natural persons were expected to have over 50% of the ownership of the new firm. In less than 1% of the cases, natural persons are to own less than 51%, including 4 cases where no natural persons would own any of the new firm. The pattern indicates that some complications in the screening process may have occurred; "nonowners" were to have been excluded from the PSED sample. There may have been, however, a change in the expected ownership structure between the screening interview and the initial detailed phone interview.

The relationship between these two aspects of the new firms is presented in Table 23.5. It reflects a high level of consistency between these two aspects of the new firms in their start-up phase. It makes clear that most new businesses, almost nine in ten, are implemented by one or more natural person, and that there is a small set of situations in which other existing business entities have a major role in implementing a new start-up.

The results are less clear when the reported legal form is considered in terms of the organizational form, as shown in Table 23.6. The reports on the expected ownership of the new firm are not always consistent with the proposed legal form. For example, for 12% of the sole proprietorships, the respondent reported that other businesses would own part of the new firm—which is not consistent with the sole proprietorship legal form. This may reflect confusion among some respondents about the precise definition of a sole proprietorship.

Table 23.6 Frequency Distribution: Organizational Form and Ownership Structure in the PSED Cohort

Owned by Natural Persons	100%	50% or More	50% or More	50% or More	Less Than 50%
External Ownership		Prior Business Owners	Franchise, MLM	Business Sponsors	Businesses, Other Institutions
Legal Form					
Sole proprietorship	88%	*%	5%	6%	*%
General partnership	90%	1%	6%	3%	1%
Limited partnership	88%	3%	7%	2%	
C-corporation	79%	2%	5%	9%	4%
Subchapter S corporation	93%	3%	3%	1%	
Limited liability company	62%	4%	3%	22%	9%
Total	87%	1%	5%	6%	1%

NOTE: *less than 1%.

Effects on Transitions to an Operating Business

One of the purposes of determining the characteristics—or expected characteristics—of a new start-up business is to determine if it is related to the outcome of the start-up process itself. For this preliminary assessment, three outcomes are considered, reported at the first follow-up interview following the initial interview: reports of a going business, reports of continued work on the start-up, and lack of an ongoing effort to develop the start-up into a going business. This latter category includes both those that report they have quit the effort entirely and those that report they are planning to return to work on the start-up when conditions change. For the entire sample, about 30% report a going business is in place, about 32% report they are still working on the start-up, and about 38% are not actively involved at the time of the second interview. (More details are to be found in Appendix C.)

The relationship of economic sector, legal form, and organizational form to these outcomes is presented in Table 23.7.

The economic sectors have been aggregated into five broad categories to increase the number of cases and improve statistical stability. Whereas there are some small differences in the proportion reporting a going business—from 23% in transformative to 34% in distribution, the overall differences are not statistically significant. About the same percentage in all sectors report no active work on the start-up at the time of the first follow-up interview.

Legal forms have been consolidated into the three major categories, and the differences are statistically significant. Those planning a partnership are less likely to report a going business and most likely to report no current activity on the project. Those planning a corporate form appear to be more likely to have a going concern in place.

The organizational type shows the strongest differences, with over 50% of firm takeovers and business-sponsored start-ups reporting operating businesses in the follow-up. This is clearly statistically significant. However, the number of cases in these two categories is small, and the patterns for the 88% that are independent start-ups are—not surprisingly—typical of the whole sample.

Correspondence With Other National Data Sets

One technique for determining if a new data collection procedure is providing accurate information is to compare the results with other efforts designed to describe the same phenomena. As there have not been any other initiatives to estimate the number of nascent entrepreneurs—those in the start-up process—no direct comparisons are possible. There are, however, several efforts to provide annual counts of the number of new businesses implemented in the United States. These other projects would capture start-up efforts that manage to become, by some criteria, operational and included in a national registry. If the PSED data can be utilized to estimate the number of new businesses identified in other data sets, it would suggest that the PSED procedures are capturing the same population of activity as reflected in the other data gathering program.

For example, the U.S. census has a program that uses the federal social security payments to determine the number of U.S. business establishments and firms. Part

Table 23.7   PSED Sample: Selected Characteristics and First Follow-up Outcomes

	Operating Business	Active Start-up	Inactive Start-up or Quit	Row Total
Total Sample	30%	32%	38%	100%
Economic Sector				
Extractive (agriculture, mining)	30%	36%	34%	100%
Transformative (construction, manufacturing)	23%	43%	34%	100%
Distribution (utilities, wholesale, transportation, information)	34%	30%	36%	100%
Business services (finance, insurance, real estate, professional services, management services, administrative, and support)	31%	28%	41%	100%
Consumer oriented (retail, educational services, health care & social assistance, arts, entertainment & recreation; accommodation & food services, other services)	30%	32%	38%	100%
(chi-square stat. sign. = 0.65)				
Legal Form				
Sole proprietorship	32%	31%	37%	100%
Partnership	25%	31%	44%	100%
Corporation	38%	34%	28%	100%
(chi-square stat. sign. = 0.05)				
Organizational Form				
Independent start-up	28%	34%	38%	100%
Franchise, multi level marketing	29%	27%	44%	100%
Takeover of existing firm (family and non-family)	55%	16%	29%	100%
Business sponsored	53%	13%	34%	100%
(chi-square stat. sign. = 0.01)				

of this effort tracks new firms that enter the registry for the first time. The procedure has located 589,982 new employer firms in the United States in 1998; 579,609 in 1999; and 574,300 in the year 2000 (SBA, 2003, Table 3; http://www.sba.gov/advo). This would be an average of 581,297 for the 3 years covered by the PSED screening.

It is possible to estimate the number of new employer firms from the PSED data, but a number of adjustments are required. Because the PSED data is based on representative samples, it is appropriate to consider the confidence associated with the estimates. The basic steps that are required are as follows:

1. An estimate of the total number of U.S. adults involved in entrepreneurial activity is computed (Appendix C, Table C.1). It is estimated that 11,871,000 adults are involved in a given year, with a 95% confidence interval from 10,627,000 to 13,120,000.

2. But the typical start-up initiative has about 2 potential owners (mean is 1.77, 95% confidence interval is 1.70 to 1.83). The 95% confidence interval on the range of new start-up initiatives is then from 5,805,000 to 7,765,000 with a mean of 6,722,000.

3. The PSED data asks those in the start-up process if a FICA payment has been filed with the federal government and, if so, the year it was first filed. It is possible to locate those start-ups where this filing occurred in the same year as the initial screening interview. Presumably this was the year the firm would have been identified by the Census program to track new employer firms. For the start-ups in the PSED sample, the 95% confidence interval on this behavior was from 6.82% to 7.18%, with a mean of 7.00%. This results in a 95% confidence interval of new employer firms of 396,000 to 557,000, with a mean of 470,000.

4. As reported in Appendix A, the screening of adults to locate those that may be starting new firms involved an initial call and two additional attempts to complete an interview at this phone number. There is credible evidence to suggest (Appendix A, Table A.8) that if more effort was devoted to trying to complete these interviews—perhaps up to 10 callbacks—the actual proportion of nascent entrepreneurs would have increased by 20%. If this adjustment is made to the estimates above, the 95% confidence interval is 475,000 to 669,000, with a mean of 565,000.

This final confidence interval encompasses the average new employer firm counts from the SBA data for the 3 years of 581,000.

These four estimates and relationship to the employer firm count for the United States are presented in Figure 23.1. A log scale is used to represent the total counts so all four estimates can be presented in the same figure. It starts with the estimate of individuals involved in start-ups to the left, and the adjustments are reflected in revised estimates as one moves to the right and stops with the new employer firm counts from the U.S. Census.

It seems reasonable to conclude that the PSED, despite its small sample of 830 nascent entrepreneurs, provides a credible prediction of the annual number of new employer firms emerging in the United States. Hence, the scope of activity that is the basis for the PSED data sets is probably very similar to that activity creating the new employer firms identified by the U.S. Census based on the new FICA payments.

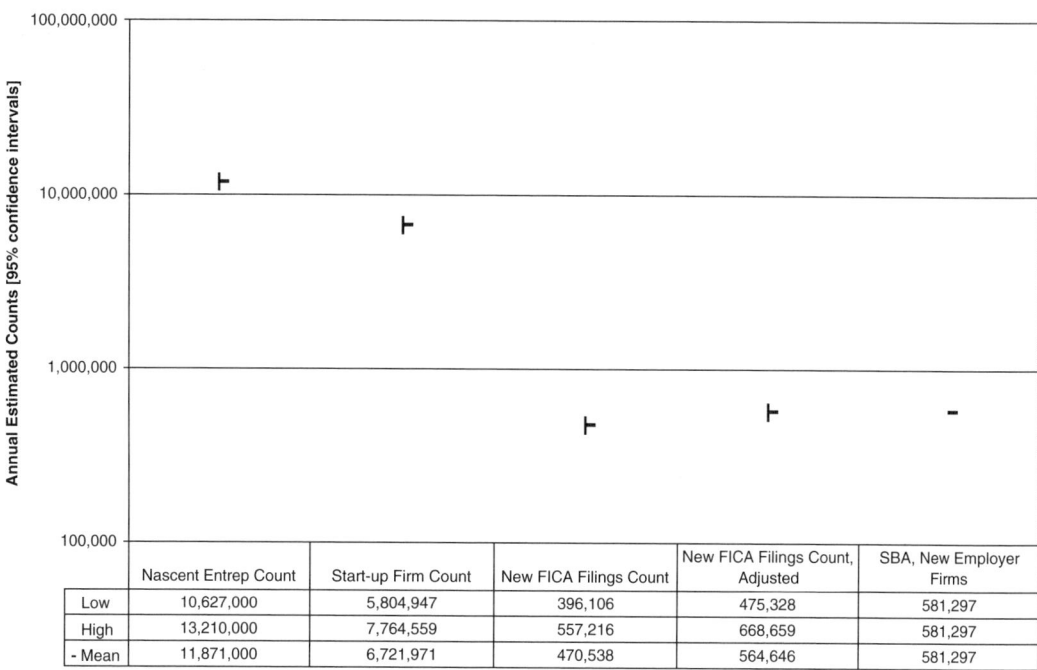

Figure 23.1   Annual New Employer Firms 1998–2000: U.S. Census Counts and PSED Estimates Compared

Commentary

There are a number of ways to describe businesses in the United States: nature of the economic activity, legal form of the business, and the annual number of new firms that emerge to join the population of existing firms. Data collected and included in the PSED data set provide the capacity for matching the PSED sample with established descriptions of U.S. businesses. On all three measures, the PSED sample appears to be similar to, but not always identical with, patterns in the other descriptions on entire censuses of U.S. businesses.

These characteristics can also be considered in terms of the impact on the outcome of the start-up. A preliminary analysis suggests no systematic association with economic sector but a systematic relationship to legal form and the organizational form of the start-up. But the substantive impact is not large, and it is clear that these are just two indicators for a more complex set of factors associated with the entrepreneurial process.

The results of the PSED research design—where careful random samples of those in the start-up process were developed and detailed interviews used to assembled data to permit comparisons with existing federal registries of new firms—indicate a rather close match, given the sample sizes and the loose correspondence in the time frames. The purpose of the PSED project was to capture the start-up process in the early stages and track the major events, including the actions that would lead the nascent business to be incorporated into existing business registries. It appears to have been successful in this regard. Analysts can proceed with confidence and assume that the PSED sample represents all U.S. business start-ups in this period.

Note

1. A market-based, rather than a production-based, classification scheme—the North American Product Classification System (NAPCS)—is under development (U.S. Office of Management and Budget, 2002, p. 102; http://www.census.gov/naics).

References

United Nations, Department of Social and Economic Affairs, Statistical Office. (1990). *International standard classification of all economic activities* (ISIC), Revision 3. New York: United Nations.

U.S. Bureau of the Census. (2002). *Statistical abstract of the United States: 2002* (122nd ed.). Washington, DC.

U.S. Office of Management and Budget, Executive Office of the President. (2002). *North American industry classification system: 2002*. Springfield, VA: National Technical Information Service.

U.S. Small Business Administration, Office of Advocacy. (2003). *Small business economic indicators for 2002*. Washington, DC: Author.

CHAPTER 24

Opportunity Recognition

Gerald E. Hills

Robert P. Singh

D rawing on theories and frameworks from other disciplines is one valuable way to contribute to a conceptual understanding of entrepreneurship. But reasonably clear boundaries and/or unique definitional variables are necessary for entrepreneurship to develop into a *separate* field or discipline (Shane & Venkataraman, 2000). Shane and Venkataraman make a compelling argument that entrepreneurial opportunity recognition and exploitation are constructs that fall within the *unique* domain of entrepreneurship and should be the central focus of research in the field.

The fundamental activity of entrepreneurship is new venture creation (Gartner, 1990), and new venture creation is a process (e.g., Bygrave & Hofer, 1991; Lumpkin & Dess, 1996). Opportunity recognition is at the beginning of the entrepreneurship process (Christensen, Madsen, & Peterson, 1994), as well as a recurring step in the business life cycle. Bygrave (1989) called the founding of an organization to pursue an entrepreneurial opportunity the "Entrepreneurial Event." It is arguably more of a process than an event, and Stevenson and Jarillo-Mossi (1986) view entrepreneurship as the process of creating value by combining resources to exploit an opportunity. Bygrave and Hofer (1991) propose a definition of the entrepreneur as "someone who perceives an opportunity and creates an organization to pursue it." Clearly, more and more scholars today are underscoring the critical definitional importance of *opportunity* to entrepreneurship. Although scholars have not fully agreed on a definition of *entrepreneur* or *entrepreneurship*, the level and quality of debate has created important progress (e.g., Gartner, 1990; Shane & Venkataraman, 2000; Stearns & Hills, 1996).

Based on the definition offered by Christensen and Peterson (1990), we define opportunity recognition as perceiving a possibility for new profit potential through (a) the founding and formation of a new venture or (b) the significant improvement of an existing venture. From this definition, opportunity recognition can be conceived as an activity that can occur both prior to firm founding and after firm founding throughout the life of the firm.

Systematic or Informal

Entrepreneurs are often conceived of as unique and innovative in their approach to business and the market (e.g., Schumpeter, 1934). Opportunity recognition may be the result of systematic search (Vesper, 1996) and/or careful strategic planning (Timmons, 1990, 1994). However, Hills (1996) found that formal customer surveys and market analyses were not considered as important as "gut feel" to entrepreneurs when it came to evaluating opportunities. This belief in informally obtained market knowledge may also exist when it comes to identifying opportunities; formal search for ideas is not the method of choice for all entrepreneurs.

In a study of software firms, Teach, Schwartz, and Tarpley (1989) found different styles of opportunity recognition among the entrepreneurs studied. Only about half favored systematic approaches to searching for opportunities. In addition, Teach and his colleagues (1989) also reported that firms founded on venture ideas that were "accidentally" discovered, which had not been subjected to formal screening, achieved break-even sales faster than those firms that had undergone more formal search and planning techniques. It should be noted that the importance of formal search and planning to subsequent survival and performance is likely to be moderated by such variables as industry maturity and barriers to entry. In mature industries with significant barriers to entry, careful planning and formal evaluation of opportunities may be critical to success; but in high-growth industries without barriers to entry, it may be better to quickly enter the market to exploit opportunities because the carrying capacity of the industry is high and there is no need to become a specialist. The software companies analyzed by Teach et al. (1989) represented firms in a growing industry, often with limited downside risk, so the results could have been different if firms in a more mature industry had been studied.

Timmons (1990, 1994) takes a strategic approach to opportunity recognition, describing it as a screening and evaluation activity that reviews business ideas and selects the better opportunities. Some authors such as Long and McMullan (1984) and Vesper (1996) present discovery questions to assist potential entrepreneurs to systematically identify opportunities. Yet, there are many entrepreneurs who do not undergo a formal search for opportunities but instead recognize a need and then create a venture (Bhave, 1994). Also, strategic search and planning may not yield a better opportunity (Teach et al., 1989). Drucker (1985) provides examples of failed products that were extensively researched prior to market introduction.

Opportunity Recognition as a Process

Some researchers have developed conceptual models of the opportunity recognition process (e.g., Bhave, 1994; Christensen et al., 1994; Gaglio & Taub, 1992; Long & McMullan, 1984; Lumpkin, Hills, & Shrader, 2004; Singh, 2000). As Gaglio and Taub (1992) point out, the typical process is portrayed as having four major steps: (1) the Pre-recognition Stew, (2) the Eureka! Experience, (3) Further Development of the Idea, and (4) the Decision to Proceed.

Hills (1996) compared the responses of a group of highly successful entrepreneurs ($n = 53$) to a representative sample of entrepreneurs ($n = 187$) on a variety of opportunity recognition items. More than 85% of both groups indicated that identifying opportunities was "several learning steps over time" rather than a one-time occurrence. Additionally, more than 80% of both groups reported that the consideration of one opportunity led to other opportunities. This would seem to indicate that opportunity recognition is usually a process with intermediate steps rather than a one-time cognitive breakthrough resulting from an enlightenment experience.

Christensen and his colleagues (1994) discuss feasibility and desirability as important factors for determining opportunity whereas Long and McMullan (1984) describe the opportunity recognition process as being at least partially under the control of the entrepreneur. They argue that in order for an opportunity to become realizable, a significant amount of preparation is required. And it is this preparation that "personalizes" the opportunity making it inaccessible to most other people. The Long and McMullan (1984) model parallels the Gaglio and Taub (1992) summary model and the Christensen et al. (1994) model. A confluence of factors, including both uncontrolled factors (cultural, social, economic and job forces, and personality) and controlled factors (alertness, job selection, study, moonlight venturing, and lifestyle), affect the ability of a potential entrepreneur to recognize the opportunity, and the evaluation and elaboration phase (strategic planning) occurs after the recognition of the opportunity. Based on the controlled and uncontrolled factors, an individual can have what Long and McMullan (1984) call an "aha" experience when the opportunity is recognized. Afterwards, the opportunity is elaborated and evaluated before a decision about whether to proceed is made. During the elaboration stage, the opportunity may be honed and modified to maximize the profit potential.

First: Business Idea or Start a Business?

Bhave (1994) also proposed a process model of venture creation with opportunity recognition being the key early stage in the sequence of events leading to the creation of the venture. Perhaps his most important contribution to the literature was his identification of two types of opportunity recognition based on Cyert and March's earlier typology, which divided the concept into two categories: externally stimulated and internally stimulated opportunity recognition.

Externally stimulated opportunities are those where the decision to start a business precedes opportunity recognition. Entrepreneurs who recognize the opportunities for their ventures using this process presumably engage in an ongoing search for opportunities, which they filter, massage, and elaborate before founding their firms. Internally stimulated opportunity recognition happens when entrepreneurs have a business idea first, discovering problems to solve or needs to fulfill, and only later decide to create ventures. Bhave's (1994) opportunity recognition model highlights the likelihood that opportunities can result from different sequential processes.

In addition to the distinction between internally and externally stimulated opportunities, an important contribution by Bhave (1994) is the filtration and the refinement that can take place before the business concept is identified. He defines the business concept as a fully refined opportunity. The model indicates that opportunity recognition does not occur through a discrete linear process. Rather, a "simmering" effect takes place as a variety of opportunities are examined before one is selected as the final business concept to launch. Numerous business ideas may be considered, at least briefly. The development of ideas into entrepreneurial opportunities may require modifications and go through several revisions. For some entrepreneurs, the recognition of the idea and opportunity may be simultaneous, but for others it may take weeks, months, and even years before recognizing an opportunity from new venture ideas.

Industry Experience and the "Corridor Principle"

Entrepreneurship is a market-driven phenomenon (Hills, 1994) and market demand is one antecedent to opportunity recognition. Yet, one cannot rely solely on market demand to predict opportunity recognition because in many cases the demand for a product is not readily evident, particularly in the case of innovative new products that are unknown to customers. However, having experience and knowledge within an industry facilitates entrepreneurs recognizing market gaps and assessing the market potential of a new venture (Singh, 2000).

Prior research has shown that experience in an industry helps to provide many entrepreneurs with their venture ideas (Vesper, 1996). In addition, it is possible that discussions with industry contacts and business associates may lead to opportunities (Burt, 1992; Johannisson, 1990; Singh, 2000). Once the business is founded, entrepreneurs may discover ideas through their day-to-day business operations. According to Ronstadt's (1988) "corridor principle," once entrepreneurs found their firms they begin a journey down a corridor, and as they proceed through the corridor, windows of opportunity open up around them. The key point is that entrepreneurs would not see these opportunities if they had not entered the corridor (i.e., founded their firm and entered the marketplace). Hills (1996) found support for the corridor principle, noting that entrepreneurs reported that "immersion" in an industry was needed to identify opportunities and that the consideration of one opportunity often led to other opportunities.

Christensen and Peterson (1990) concluded that not only specific problems and social encounters are often a source of venture ideas but also that profound market or technological knowledge is a prerequisite for venture ideas. Industry experience can be seen as a primary means of developing market knowledge.

Further, being in the marketplace and seeing the needs of customers first hand can help an entrepreneur recognize potential opportunities.

Cognitive Factors for Opportunity Recognition

Do successful entrepreneurs have a "sixth sense" that allows them to recognize opportunities? We know that in some cases the opportunity for a business, product, or service may have been waiting to be discovered for a long time before it was introduced to the market. It is possible that entrepreneurs have what Kirzner (1979) describes as entrepreneurial "alertness" (Gaglio & Katz, 2001). Research has shown that entrepreneurs often perceive themselves to be alert to opportunities (Hills, 1996; Hills, Lumpkin, & Singh, 1997). Based on Kirzner's work, Kaish and Gilad (1991) searched for differences between entrepreneurs and managers in terms of entrepreneurial alertness.

Also, Gaglio and Taub (1992) examined whether the concept of entrepreneurial alertness is a unique cognitive skill of entrepreneurs. Although their results were supportive of the alertness construct, Gaglio and Taub's study was exploratory. As Busenitz (1996) pointed out, Kaish and Gilad's (1991) study had several methodological limitations, so he argued for the development and refinement of measures of entrepreneurial alertness. Despite the potential importance of the alertness concept to opportunity recognition, it was deemed too complex for inclusion in the opportunity recognition section of the Panel Study of Entrepreneurial Dynamics (PSED).

Social Networks and Opportunity Recognition

Social encounters are a source of venture ideas (Christensen & Peterson, 1990) and thus can lead to opportunity recognition. However, there is little research on this important subject. Theories about the importance of weak ties (Granovetter, 1973) and structural holes (Burt, 1992) may shed light on the importance of social networks to opportunity recognition and differences in the types of opportunities identified.

Koller (1988) studied the sources of new venture ideas and the PSED questionnaire item is based on Koller's. He surveyed 65 entrepreneurs in several industries and found that half reported their ideas had come through networking contacts. The other half had recognized their business ideas on their own. Further, he found significant differences in the types of opportunities identified between the two groups. Those who came up with the ideas themselves were more likely to obtain them from prior experience and be motivated out of a "desire for entrepreneurship" than those who got their ideas from their social network. In addition, fewer than 25% of his respondents had no experience in their firm's industry prior to founding. Industry experience can be an important way for an entrepreneur to expand his/her business network and thus have access to information.

In an exploratory paper on the importance of social networks to opportunity recognition, Hills, Lumpkin, and Singh (1997) found significant differences between "solo entrepreneurs" (those who identified their business idea alone) and "network entrepreneurs" (those who did not develop their business idea alone) on a number of different issues. They found that network entrepreneurs identified significantly more opportunities than solo entrepreneurs but were less likely to describe themselves as being opportunistic, as having special alertness or sensitivity to opportunities, or as being creative. Solo entrepreneurs were significantly more likely to set aside time to be creative and were more likely to go through a formal search. They also agreed that prior employment and "immersion" in an industry are needed to identify opportunities. Network entrepreneurs, on the other hand, believed they were more likely to see real opportunities after entering a market. These findings suggest important differences between the two types of entrepreneurs. Network entrepreneurs learned of more opportunities than solo entrepreneurs and took advantage of more opportunities in which they had no direct experience. They were more likely to take advantage of opportunities in industries in which they were not "immersed" (or had personal experience) than were solo entrepreneurs. It was hypothesized that network entrepreneurs used their network contacts to provide feasible opportunities and could defer to the expertise and experience of their contact(s) to reduce uncertainty. It is possible that network entrepreneurs do not have to be as engaged in search activities or be as creative as solo entrepreneurs because they have access to a wider range of information and creativity through network ties.

Questionnaire Items

The PSED opportunity recognition questionnaire items were developed by Professor Gerald Hills at the University of Illinois at Chicago with suggestions from Professors Kelly Shaver and Paul Reynolds. In the following section, the exact wording of the items can be found along with descriptive statistics. These items have been used in several studies (Hills, 1996; Hills et al., 1997; Singh, 2000) and Hills (1996) pointed out that a number of the items were replicated and modified from earlier questionnaires developed by Teach et al. (1989), Christensen and Peterson (1990), and Kaish and Gilad (1991) and that they were all pretested on a convenience sample of entrepreneurs.

It was a challenging experience, even before the subject of opportunity recognition was proposed as the theoretical core of the entrepreneurship field, to decide which few questionnaire items to include in the PSED. One objective was quite simply to ask important questions, questions which would yield valuable descriptive results, from a generalizable sample. Based on a thorough understanding of the limited opportunity recognition literature at the time, it was concluded that the existing work had not yielded generalizable knowledge pertaining to several of the more fundamental issues. Is the nature of opportunity recognition processes different for different groupings of nascent entrepreneurs? Which comes first, the opportunity or the desire to start a business? How many ideas are considered before selecting one, and do ideas undergo modification? Are deliberate search activities commonly engaged in by some nascent entrepreneurs but not others? What are the underlying sources of ideas and opportunities? Although there were clearly many equally important questions that could have been asked, the questions selected seemed, and still seem, to be exceptionally important. Second, the questions were based on prior literature (as shown above) and were variables consistent with the conceptual frameworks at the time, particularly from Long and McMullan (1984) and Bhave (1984). Third, all of the variables are potentially important predictor variables, in combination with numerous other variables in the PSED. Variables such as the "number of ideas considered" could also be used as dependent variables. Fourth, certain of the measurement items could also be combined to measure concepts such as formal/informal search and limited/extensive search. Four variables may be used to support this two-by-two classification, and nascent entrepreneurs may be analyzed accordingly. Finally, all of the items are best asked of *nascent* entrepreneurs, before any memory loss occurs. And most of the items lend themselves to longitudinal analysis. Other forms of analysis are now discussed, partly in reference to specific questionnaire items.

Opportunity Recognition Questions and Preliminary Findings

In this section, we present the wording of the opportunity recognition questions, and provide descriptive statistics based on the results gained through 476 respondents to the PSED mail questionnaire. They were not part of the phone survey. The PSED includes six opportunity recognition questions, several of which required respondents to complete multi-item responses. The comparison group samples are not used in this analysis. There are several other items in the database that pertain to "opportunity," particularly those developed by Professor Jim Fiet.

The first question is "Briefly, how did the idea for starting a business develop?" The question is open-ended, which allows researchers to utilize potentially rich data for content analyses. One published paper to date illustrates the value of these unstructured responses (Gartner, Carter, & Hills, 2003).

Table 24.1 presents the wording for the second question and the descriptive statistics for responses. Respondents were required to select the single best response. The question is based on Bhave's (1994) proposition that some entrepreneurs first decide they want to start a business and then identify an opportunity whereas others first recognize an opportunity and then subsequently decide to found a new venture. The question can be used to distinguish the two different entrepreneurship processes and examine related differences, including those with externally versus internally stimulated opportunities.

Based on the preliminary results, it is striking that 42% of respondent entrepreneurs made a decision to found a venture and then recognized an opportunity to pursue whereas 37% first recognized an opportunity and then founded a business. Both paths are clearly utilized. The remaining 21% reported that the ideal opportunity and the decision to start a business were simultaneous. Among other

Table 24.1   Opportunity Recognition Question 2

Which came first for you, the business idea or your decision to start some kind of business?

Response	Percentage (n)
Business idea or opportunity came first	36.9 (174)
Desire to start a business came first	42.1 (199)
Idea or opportunity and desire to have a business came at the same time	21.0 (99)

NOTE: Total $N = 472$ (4 not ascertained).

potential studies, these three types of processes (or entrepreneurs) may produce different types of firms (e.g., high-growth versus lifestyle ventures), may utilize different types of social networks, and may offer different survival and growth prospects. Future in-depth studies may reveal significant differences between these three types of processes or entrepreneurs, which could yield profound implications for both entrepreneurship education and practice. A dissertation study in progress at the University of Illinois at Chicago will be among the first to explore this finding (Murphy, 2003).

Question 3 asks respondents to identify the number of ideas that were considered before the idea for the current business was selected (see Table 24.2). Twenty-eight percent of the nascent entrepreneurs reported that they only examined one opportunity, 38% considered two or three, and 25% reported that they considered five or more. We now know for the first time the large variance of ideas considered by different entrepreneurs. Once again, different types of processes and/or entrepreneurs can be identified—those who focus on one opportunity versus those who examine and consider several or many opportunities before selecting one. A fundamental research question to be answered based on these findings: "Is multiopportunity recognition better than a solo opportunity focus?" For example, committing significant time and energy to one ideal opportunity may keep entrepreneurs focused, which could improve the chances of success. On the other hand, considering several opportunities before selecting one may allow an entrepreneur to "filter" opportunities and then select a more lucrative venture. These are empirical questions that we can now answer using longitudinal data.

The purpose of Question 4 is to ascertain the amount of change that is made to the original venture ideas or opportunities over time. Table 24.3 summarizes the finding that half of the respondents made no change to the original concept whereas 50% made "little" to a "great deal" of change. In fact, one of every eight entrepreneurs, even very early stage nascent entrepreneurs, changed the idea a "great deal." Understanding how and why some entrepreneurs modify their

Table 24.2   Opportunity Recognition Question 3

If you were looking for an appropriate idea for a business, about how many were considered before selecting this idea?

Number of Opportunities	Percentage (n)
1	27.8 (125)
2	18.4 (83)
3	19.1 (86)
4	10.0 (45)
5	7.1 (32)
6–9	10.7 (48)
10–19	4.4 (20)
20–39	0.7 (3)
40+	1.8 (8)

NOTE: Total $N = 450$ (26 not ascertained). Mean $= 3.14$. $SD = 2.04$.

business concepts while others do not is important to understanding the process of opportunity recognition. It is also possible that the PSED data may help to measure and better explain the level of importance of business plan development and research before founding a new venture. Preliminary analysis indicates that there is a significant positive correlation between measures of business plan activities and the amount of change to the idea/opportunity. Business plan development could result in nascent entrepreneurs modifying concepts as research on the intended opportunity is conducted. Given the conflicting empirical evidence that writing a business plan improves the chances for success of a new venture, there may be a relationship between changes in the original business concept and success, perhaps moderated by business plan development. An even more probable finding is that entry into the market and customer feedback will fuel changes to the business concept. In any event, how change, or no change, to the original venture concept impacts survival and success is an important question that can now be empirically studied.

The major sources that led the respondents to identify the business idea can be obtained from Question 5 (summarized in Table 24.4). Respondents could check all items that applied to the identification of their business idea, but what clearly emerged was that industry or market experience was the most important source of new venture ideas that led to the founding of firms (56%). These findings reinforce previous research but with a high level of generalizability due to the quality of the PSED sample (Singh, 2000; Vesper, 1996). It is notable that social and professional network contacts were clearly important to idea identification. After prior experience,

Table 24.3   Opportunity Recognition Question 4

Has the business idea or opportunity changed very much since the beginning or is it pretty much the original concept?

Response	Percentage (n)
Idea/opportunity has changed a great deal	13.2 (62)
Idea/opportunity has changed a little	36.4 (171)
Idea/opportunity is about the same	50.4 (237)

NOTE: Total $N = 470$ (6 not ascertained).

Table 24.4   Opportunity Recognition Question 5

Which of the following led to your business idea?

Response	Percentage Respondents Who Said Yes (n)
It developed from another idea I was considering	23.1 (472)
My experience in a particular industry or market	55.9 (472)
Thinking about solving a particular problem	29.9 (472)
Discussions with my friends and family	42.4 (472)
Discussions with potential or existing customers	30.9 (472)
Discussions with existing suppliers or distributors	15.9 (472)
Discussions with potential or existing investors/lenders	8.1 (472)
Knowledge or expertise with technology	28.6 (472)
Other (please specify)	8.9 (472)

a large percentage of entrepreneurs identified friends and family (42%), customers (31%), suppliers (16%), and potential investors (8%) as the source of the ideas for their business.

A closer analysis of the social network sources found that 62% indicated that they had obtained the idea for their business from business associates, friends, or family. This percentage is consistent with other empirical studies of social network information sources for new venture ideas (Hills et al., 1997; Koller, 1988; Singh, 2000). It seems reasonable to expect that working in an industry provides access to social contacts that can help an entrepreneur identify new venture ideas within that industry. Of the entrepreneurs who indicated that social contacts were important idea sources, 56% also indicated prior experience was one of their idea sources. Are different sources more important than others? And how important is some experience industry and/or social network contacts to opportunity recognition and new firm performance? These are just some of the questions that can be answered from the PSED data.

Consistent with other research findings (Hills, 1996; Hills et al., 1997; Singh, 2000), most entrepreneurs agree that entrepreneurship is a multistep process (see Table 24.5). Just over 70% of respondents reported that "identifying business opportunities has involved several learning steps over time, rather than a one-time thing." At the same time, 30% agreed that "the best business ideas just come, without a need to search for them." And 40% said they engaged in some level of "deliberate, systematic search." This may indicate that there are two types of entrepreneurs—those who have opportunities that emerge versus those who seek out opportunities. Once again, this supports Bhave's (1994) model. Further research is needed to determine what, if any, differences emerge as a result of the two different processes. The descriptive findings by themselves (Table 24.5) provide important new knowledge. Yet there is a great opportunity to extend the analysis to answer "Why?" given the breadth of the PSED database.

Table 24.5   Opportunity Recognition Question 6

Your reactions to this specific business start-up would also be very useful. How would you respond to the following descriptions of the firm and its situation?

1 = COMPLETELY DISAGREE
2 = GENERALLY DISAGREE
3 = NEUTRAL
4 = GENERALLY AGREE
5 = COMPLETELY AGREE

Question	1	2	3	4	5	Mean	N
I have engaged in a deliberate, systematic search for an idea for a new business	24.7% (117)	14.8% (70)	27.3% (129)	23.5% (111)	9.7% (46)	2.79	473
The best business ideas just come, without a need to search for them	16.3% (77)	24.3% (115)	29.2% (138)	20.5% (97)	9.7% (46)	2.83	473
For me, identifying business opportunities has involved several learning steps over time, rather than a one-time thing	5.9% (28)	7.2% (34)	16.1% (76)	45.9% (216)	24.8% (117)	3.76	471

Discussion and Future Research

The preliminary findings reported in this chapter suggest that opportunity recognition does have distinctive characteristics that can be identified and tested. The opportunity recognition variables contained within the PSED questionnaire, in combination with other variables, produce a rich set of data that can be utilized by researchers to examine a wide range of issues. Other questionnaire items discussed in this book measure such variables as investment capital, social network relationships, cognitive factors, personal characteristics, and many others that potentially yield significant findings and new knowledge about entrepreneurial processes.

A major benefit of the PSED data is that it is longitudinal. For firms that fail during the study period, analyses may be conducted to measure the effects of different opportunity recognition processes on performance. Further, it is possible that certain opportunity recognition behaviors and actions help reduce the liability of newness (Stinchcombe, 1965) and improve the chances for success. The performance implications of the opportunity recognition process are largely unexplored in the opportunity recognition literature. Does having more ideas, or changing the ideas/opportunity definitions over time, impact performance? Or is there some link between performance and internally versus externally stimulated opportunities? To answer such questions, more extensive studies involving finer grain analysis of the longitudinal PSED data would enrich our understanding of the opportunity recognition–firm performance relationship.

The discussion of the PSED opportunity recognition question items in the prior section presented several potential research questions, but many other research questions exist. First, breaking out the respondents into various industry groups may yield important results. There may be differences in the importance of social networks to opportunity recognition across industries.

In addition, PSED research should also examine the role of social networks in the opportunity recognition processes of women and minority entrepreneurs. The PSED sample allows for such analyses. Research has shown that women and minorities develop different types of networks than their White male counterparts.

Conclusion

The process of identifying venture ideas and then developing them into bona fide business opportunities is a key element of the new venture creation process. This chapter has explored several aspects of this important entrepreneurial activity. Overall, the preliminary findings show support for the proposition that opportunity recognition is a process that occurs in different ways, over time, for different entrepreneurs. There is still relatively little empirical study of the antecedents to, and processes of, entrepreneurial opportunity recognition. Researchers will have the opportunity to segment entrepreneurs based on the different processes they used to identify opportunities. The data holds the promise of providing numerous important implications for both practitioners and researchers far beyond the preliminary, yet important, findings in this chapter.

References

Bhave, M. P. (1994). A process model of entrepreneurial venture creation. *Journal of Business Venturing, 9,* 223–242.

Burt, R. S. (1992). *Structural holes: The social structure of competition.* Cambridge, MA: Harvard University Press.

Busenitz, L. (1996). Research on entrepreneurial alertness. *Journal of Small Business Management, 34*(4), 35–44.

Bygrave, W. (1989). The entrepreneurship paradigm (I): A philosophical look at its research methodologies. *Entrepreneurship Theory and Practice, 14*(1), 7–26.

Bygrave, W., & Hofer, C. (1991). Theorizing about entrepreneurship. *Entrepreneurship Theory and Practice, 15,* 7–25.

Christensen, P. S., Madsen, O. O., & Peterson, R. (1994). Conceptualizing entrepreneurial opportunity recognition. In G. E. Hills (Ed.), *Marketing and entrepreneurship: Research ideas and opportunities* (pp. 61–75*).* Westport, CT: Quorum Books.

Christensen, P. S., & Peterson, R. (1990, April). *Opportunity identification: Mapping the sources of new venture ideas.* Paper presented at the *10th annual Babson College Entrepreneurship Research Conference,* Aarhus, Denmark.

Drucker, P. F. (1985). *Innovation and entrepreneurship: Practice and principles.* New York: Harper & Row.

Gaglio, C. M., & Katz, J. (2001). The psychological basis of opportunity identification: Entrepreneurial alertness. *Journal of Small Business Economics, 16,* 95–111.

Gaglio, C. M., & Taub, R. P. (1992). Entrepreneurs and opportunity recognition. In N. C. Churchill, S. Birley, W. D. Bygrave, D. E. Muzyka, C. Wahlbin, & W. E. Wetzel, Jr. (Eds.), *Frontiers of Entrepreneurship Research* (pp. 136–147) Wellesley, MA: Babson College.

Gartner, W. B. (1990). What are we talking about when we talk about entrepreneurship? *Journal of Business Venturing, 5,* 15–28.

Gartner, W. B., Carter, N. M., & Hills, G. E. (2003). The language of opportunity. In C. Steyaert & D. Hjorth (Eds.), *New movements in entrepreneurship* (pp. 103–124). London: Edward Elgar.

Granovetter, M. (1973). The strength of weak ties. *American Journal of Sociology, 78*(6), 1360–1380.

Hills, G. E. (Ed.). (1994). *Marketing and entrepreneurship: Research ideas and opportunities.* Westport, CT: Quorum Books.

Hills, G. E. (1996). *Opportunity recognition: Perceptions and behaviors of entrepreneurs.* Research report submitted to the Ewing Marion Kauffman Foundation, Kansas City, MO.

Hills, G. E., Lumpkin, G. T., & Singh, R. (1997). Opportunity recognition: Perceptions and behaviors of entrepreneurs. *Frontiers of entrepreneurship research* (pp. 168–182). Wellesley, MA: Babson College.

Johannisson, B. (1990). Economics of overview—Guiding the external growth of small firms. *International Small Business Journal, 9,* 32–44.

Kaish, S., & Gilad, B. (1991). Characteristics of opportunity search for entrepreneurs versus executives: Sources, interests, general alertness. *Journal of Business Venturing, 6*(1), 45–61.

Kirzner, I. M. (1979). *Perception, opportunity, and profit: Studies in the theory of entrepreneurship.* Chicago: University of Chicago Press.

Koller, R. H. (1988). On the source of entrepreneurial ideas. In B. A. Kirchhoff, W. A. Long, W. E. McMullan, K. H. Vesper, & W. E. Wetzel, Jr. (Eds.), *Frontiers of entrepreneurship research* (pp. 194–207). Wellesley, MA: Babson College.

Long, W., & McMullan, W. E. (1984). Mapping the new venture opportunity identification process. In J. A. Hornaday, F. A. Tarpley, Jr., J. A. Timmons, & K. H. Vesper (Eds.), *Frontiers of entrepreneurship research* (pp. 567–590). Wellesley, MA: Babson College.

Lumpkin, G. T., & Dess, G. G. (1996). Clarifying the entrepreneurial orientation construct and linking it to performance. *Academy of Management Review, 21,* 135–172.

Lumpkin, G. T., Hills, G. E., & Shrader, R. C. (2004). Opportunity recognition. In H. Welsch (Ed.), *Entrepreneurship: The road ahead, 2004.* London: Routledge.

Murphy, P. (2003). *A logic for entrepreneurial discovery.* Unpublished doctoral dissertation, University of Illinois at Chicago.

Ronstadt, R. (1988). The corridor principle. *Journal of Business Venturing, 3,* 31–40.

Schumpeter, J. (1934). *The theory of economic development.* Cambridge, MA: Harvard University Press.

Shane, S., & Venkataraman, S. (2000). The promise of entrepreneurship as a field of research. *Academy of Management Review, 25,* 217–226.

Singh, R. P. (2000). *Entrepreneurial opportunity recognition through social networks.* New York: Garland.

Stearns, T., & Hills, G. E. (1996). Entrepreneurship and new firm development: A definitional introduction. *Journal of Business Research, 36,* 1–4.

Stevenson, H. H., & Jarillo-Mossi, J. C. (1986). Preserving entrepreneurship as companies grow. *Journal of Business Strategy, 7,* 10–23.

Stinchcombe, A. L. (1965). Social structure in organizations. In J. G. March (Ed.), *Handbook of organizations* (pp. 142–193). Chicago: Rand McNally.

Teach, R. D., Schwartz, R. G., & Tarpley, F. A., Jr. (1989). The recognition and exploitation of opportunity in the software industry: A study of surviving firms. In R. H. Brockhaus, Jr., N. C. Churchill, J. A. Katz, B. A. Kirchhoff, K. H. Vesper, & W. E. Wetzel, Jr. (Eds.), *Frontiers of entrepreneurship research* (pp. 383–397). Wellesley, MA: Babson College.

Timmons, J. A. (1990). *New business opportunities: Getting to the right place at the right time.* Acton, MA: Brick House.

Timmons, J. A. (1994). *New venture creation: Entrepreneurship for the 21st century* (4th ed.). Burr Ridge, IL: Irwin.

Vesper, K. (1996). *New venture experience* (Rev. ed.). Seattle, WA: Vector Books.

CHAPTER 25

Start-up Problems

Candida G. Brush

Tatiana S. Manolova

The process of creating a new entrepreneurial organization is fraught with a variety of challenges and problems. Creating a new venture is not a singular occurrence; rather it is a sequence of events that may vary in timing, order, and type, depending on the entrepreneur and the venture (Cooper, 1982; Gartner, 1985; Vesper, 1990; Carter, Gartner, & Reynolds, 1996; Gartner, 2001). Significant literature on organizational life cycles identifies phases of organizational development and associated obstacles, crises, and challenges (Grenier, 1972; Lippitt & Schmidt, 1967; Churchill & Lewis, 1983; Cooper, 1982). In preorganization or gestation, the challenges are quite different from those encountered at later stages (Katz & Gartner, 1988; Vesper, 1990; Reynolds & Miller, 1992). Because there is no formal organization, no sales, or employees, the entrepreneur's role is to organize and coordinate the tasks of creation so that the enterprise may develop effective procedures, attract resources, and gain commitment of participants (Becker & Gordon, 1966; Penrose, 1959; Aldrich, 1999). Identification of the types of problems encountered varies depending on the theoretical perspective adopted. For the preventure and organizing phases, theory anchors for perspectives on start-up problems include life cycle, evolutionary, resource-based competencies, resource dependence, and behavioral psychology, which are reviewed below (See Table 25.1).

Table 25.1   Literature Review: Theories, Start-up Problems, and Associated Authors

Theory	Problems	Associated Authors

Life cycle	Know-how
	Opportunity identification
	Product/service idea
	   development
	Resource acquisition
	Developing systems/
	   structures
		Bird, 1989;
		Churchill & Lewis, 1983;
		Grenier, 1972;
		Hanks et al., 1993
		Lippitt & Schmidt, 1967;
		Vesper, 1990;

Evolutionary	Legitimacy
	Constructing social
	   networks
	Acquiring learning &
	   knowledge
	Assembling resources
		Aldrich, 1999
		Van de Ven, et al., 1989;

Resource-based competencies	Building resource base	Greene & Brown,1997 Greene, Brush, & Hart, 2001; Lichtenstein & Brush, 2001;

Resource dependence	Controlling external
	   contingencies
	Identifying and attracting
	   resources
		Bruno & Tyebjee, 1982

Behavioral psychology	Expectations and perceived risks Intentions	Bird, 1989 Shaver & Scott, 1991;

Literature Review

Life Cycle Perspective

Several authors identify a variety of stages or phases of new venture development, but there is no agreement on the number of stages from emergence to decline (Grenier, 1972; Lippitt & Schmidt, 1967; Churchill & Lewis, 1983; Cooper, 1982). The criteria for determining stages varies by context across dimensions, including age, size, growth rate, task, dominant problems, and managerial priority (Hanks, Watson, Jansen, & Chandler, 1993). The start-up phase is referred to in various ways: preorganization (Katz & Gartner, 1988), launch (Lippitt & Schmidt, 1967), gestation (Reynolds & Miller, 1992), start-up (Vesper, 1990), and survival (Churchill & Lewis, 1983). For the emergence or start-up stage, problems are most often described in the form of management challenges, or tasks that the entrepreneur must overcome to move to the next phase of development. These can be grouped into categories of know-how, opportunity identification, product-service idea development, resource acquisition, and developing systems and structures.

A beginning challenge is identifying the venture opportunity. This may involve varying degrees of planning, or it may be an unplanned sequence of events, but the entrepreneur is faced with examining the possible market for a product or service, the formulation of the service, and the method of delivery (Cooper, 1982; Vesper, 1990). Following through on an identified opportunity requires action orientation and risk assessment, as well as identification of proper resources to support the new venture (Stevenson & Gumpert, 1985; Bird, 1989). Moving forward on the opportunity by developing the product or service can present a challenge to nascent entrepreneurs.

Another challenge in venture development is acquisition of resources. Studies show that seeking information through networks and making contacts in financial networks are central to greater success in survival (Cooper, Dunkelberg, & Woo, 1988). In early stages, formalization and structure of the organization is centralized and informal in terms of decision making, systems, and procedures (Churchill & Lewis, 1983). For the organization to move forward to the next phase, emerging systems must be formalized and functions specialized (Vesper, 1990).

For women entrepreneurs, acquisition of financial resources can be a greater challenge than for their male counterparts (Carter, Williams, & Reynolds, 1997). Research shows that bankers perceive men to be rated higher on characteristics associated with successful entrepreneurship than women (Buttner & Rosen, 1988). Studies of women's backgrounds and experience show a smaller percentage of women have work experience and educational backgrounds in certain industries (e.g., manufacturing and technology) and functional areas (e.g., finance) suggesting they may have less "know-how" at the outset (Brush, 1997).

Evolutionary Theory

The evolution of a new venture results from the operation of four generic processes: variation, selection, retention, and diffusion (Campbell, 1965). The transition from fledgling firm to new firm involves a selection process in which failure results from the firm's liability of newness. Certain types of variations permit resource acquisition and legitimation, which occur through the operation of market forces, competitive pressures, and internal organizational structuring (Aldrich, 1999). New organizations are constructed through a disorderly process, and the nascent entrepreneur faces challenges in acquiring information permitting the transition from gestation to fledgling firm (Reynolds, 1992). Social networks structure the context within which nascent entrepreneurs start their firms. Nascent entrepreneur's personal networks play a significant role in this process because they facilitate the entrepreneur's ability to gain social, emotional, and material support. For women entrepreneurs, underrepresentation in male networks, particularly financial networks, can be a significant obstacle (Carter, 1994; Aldrich, 1989). Similarly, not all demographic groups have the same network opportunities because of their favorable or unfavorable location, structural positions, or ethnic background; minority populations may face systematic barriers to ownership through residential segregation (Aldrich, 1999).

Research shows nascent entrepreneurs are subject to information overload, time pressures, and emotional involvement (Baron, 1998). Nascent entrepreneurs are more successful if they develop knowledge structures that encourage other people's belief in their competence and credibility so they may gain access to resources (Aldrich, 1999). Making sense out of the uncertainty of a new venture so that others can buy into it is a particular challenge because of the complexity and uncertainty of the start-up process (Van de Ven, Angle, & Poole, 1989).

Resource-Based Perspective

At venture start-up, entrepreneurs make judgments about resources that they believe can be combined and developed into unique capabilities (Penrose, 1959). In the earliest phase, identification and acquisition of resources is a crucial challenge because the organization has no administrative history, systems, or structures within which to organize resources (Brush, Greene, & Hart, 2001; Katz & Gartner, 1988). Building a resource base from scratch involves sorting resources into different types (e.g., social, financial, technical, physical, human, and organizational) and determining how they may be effectively applied to the productive process (Penrose, 1959). Start-up problems revolve around the decision choices in assembling, attracting, combining, and transforming personal resources into organizational resources (Brush et al., 2001). Emerging ventures are faced with developing an optimal resource base, a process that includes acquiring, recombining, and even spinning off resources that are not salient or critical to the productive process (Lichtenstein & Brush, 2001). Research shows that human, organizational, and social capital are important to the acquisition of other resources, particularly financial and physical capital, and that patterns of resource acquisition have performance implications (Lichtenstein & Brush, 2001).

Research about ethnic entrepreneurs shows that they may suffer a disadvantage because they are outside the mainstream of society, often being immigrants to a particular area. While ethnic groups often have advantages in working together to provide financial resources and support systems for community members, in early stages of business formation they may be disadvantaged in gaining access to traditional sources of capital (e.g., bank funding) (Butler & Greene, 1997).

Studies of women entrepreneurs suggest that the burden of child and dependent care may diminish the initial time and funding a woman may be able to devote to creating a solid resource base (Brush, 1997). Other research shows women start their ventures with less capital and are outside the financial network, which may limit their ability to expand and grow their venture quickly (Hisrich & Brush, 1986; Carter et al., 1997).

Resource Dependence Theory

This perspective views organizations as resource-dependent on their external environment (Pfeffer & Salancik, 1978). The focus of this approach is on the strategic actions of the new organization taken to manage interdependencies with other organizations and the environment (Aldrich, 1999). The environment is composed of three dimensions: concentration, munificence, and interconnectedness; the patterns and linkages between the environment and organizations are characterized by two dimensions: conflict and interdependence; and the degree to which the future can be predicted is summarized in a global construct: uncertainty (Bruno & Tyebjee, 1982). A premise of this perspective is that the munificence of the environment might provide greater access to resources for the new firm, conditioned on existing competitors. The small size and informal structure of a new firm may create significant obstacles to survival because size increases stability; interdependence (e.g., vertical integration) ensures a firm's supply and distribution environment (Bruno & Tyebjee, 1982).

Unemployment rates, wealth, local government policies, interest rates, and other resources are factors contributing to the munificence of an environment (Kirchhoff & Acs, 1997). New ventures that start small and enter highly competitive environments or industries may face greater or lesser obstacles in their interfirm power relations or in gaining control of resources (Cooper et al., 1988). Barriers to entry and industry profitability can increase the challenges for small and new ventures (Reynolds, 1992).

Behavioral Psychology Theory

Variations in entrepreneurial activity are primarily a function of the social cognition of the entrepreneur (Shaver & Scott, 1991). Cognitive processes guide the ways entrepreneurs perceive the environment and guide their resource- and information-gathering processes. From this perspective, there are two major challenges: expectations about certain events and perceived risk. Expectancy of being able to make something happen is an important entrepreneurial competency (Bird, 1989). This is also referred to as self-efficacy, self-confidence, or a "can do" attitude. This expectancy of being able to make something happen is important and related to perceived control (Shaver & Scott, 1991). Entrepreneurs who are less certain about their ability to make a difference, to control the venture creation process, will face greater difficulties in the start-up process and influencing others to participate (Bird, 1989). Further, expectations for the entrepreneur's success or failure also can influence the start-up process and eventual success (Shapero & Sokol, 1982). Relatedly, studies show that women may have lower self-efficacy than their male counterparts, which may lengthen the start-up process or influence the industry choice (Anna, Chandler, Jansen, & Mero, 2000).

Entrepreneurs face uncertainty and loss in many areas: financial, social, familial, emotional, physical, career, and organizational (Bird, 1989). The entrepreneur's risk orientation will influence start-up behaviors. The extent to which an entrepreneur is more or less comfortable with various risks or uncertainties, and the steps taken to manage these risks through personal interactions, information gathering, or other techniques, can be a start-up obstacle (Cooper & Gimeno-Gascon, 1992; Bird, 1989; Baron, 1998).

The Start-up Problem Variables

Although many different start-up problems and challenges following aforementioned theories were considered in the process of developing the survey, it was not possible to include all of these due to space limitations. We considered including questions about difficulties in acquiring capital and developing products and services, but many aspects of these start-up activities were captured in other parts of the questionnaire. We decided on five items, which were included the mail survey (items QC1a-e in the PSED data set) and represent the start-up problem items. The items appear on pages 314 to 315 of the PSED Codebook. The five items representing start-up problems were asked in the following manner: they were preceded by the stem: "How accurately would the following statements describe the start-up problems with your new business?" The respondents replied on a 5-point Likert-type scale: 1 = completely untrue; 2 = mostly untrue; 3 = it depends; 4 = mostly true; 5 = completely true. The five items included were anchored in different theories. Resource-based theory considers the starting resources of the nascent entrepreneur and the challenges in building a resource base for the venture (Brush et al. 2000), and one item measured balance of "time." Behavioral psychology is concerned with expectations and perceptions of the entrepreneur, and one item measured extent to which the nascent entrepreneur was taken seriously (Shapero & Sokol, 1982; Bird, 1989). Evolutionary theory considers the networks and social support of the entrepreneur in starting a new organization (Aldrich, 1999) and one item measured support of family, friends, and spouse. A second item measured mentors and others who can provide support and advice. Organizational life cycle literature considers the ways that ventures set up systems and processes (Churchill & Lewis, 1983), and one item measured the health insurance for family and the nascent entrepreneur.

The exact wordings for the five items representing start-up problems are listed in Exhibit 25.1.

Exhibit 25.1   The Five Start-up Problem Items in the PSED

QC1. How accurately would the following statements describe the start-up problems with your new business **[CIRCLE ONE NUMBER IN EACH ROW].**

1 = Completely untrue	**3 = It depends**			**4 = Mostly true**	
2 = Mostly untrue				**5 = Completely true**	
a. Being taken seriously as a business person	1	2	3	4	5
b. Receiving support from those close to me (spouse, family, and friends)	1	2	3	4	5
c. Getting suitable health insurance for myself and family members	1	2	3	4	5
d. Balancing time between business, personal, and family life	1	2	3	4	5
e. Lack of mentors or others who can provide advice and support	1	2	3	4	5

An Analysis of the Start-Up Problem Variables

As mentioned earlier, the five items in this section of the PSED were developed on the basis of prior research. The analyses were performed on the mail survey PSED data set, which includes 482 nascent entrepreneurs and 176 in a comparison group (Reynolds, 2000). As the data on the minority oversample were not made available at the time of performing this analysis, the only oversampling included in the present data set is that for women. The usable sample was reduced by the requirement that respondent gender be consistently recorded across all stages of data collection. Following the classification scheme developed by Shaver, Carter, Gartner, and Reynolds (2001), we included in the sample used for the present study fully autonomous nascent entrepreneurs who have not received a positive cash flow from their new businesses to a usable sample size of $n = 402$. Descriptive statistics are presented in Table 25.2. The correlation matrix is presented in Table 25.3.

Table 25.2   Descriptive Statistics: Business Start-up Problem Items

Variable	n	Min	Max	Mean	SD
Being taken seriously	402	1	5	3.03	1.23
Receiving support	400	1	5	2.99	1.47
Getting health insurance	392	1	5	3.13	1.39
Balancing time	401	1	5	3.66	1.16
Lack of mentors	401	1	5	3.05	1.21

Table 25.3   Correlation Matrix: Business Start-up Problem Items

Variable	1	2	3	4	5
1. Being taken seriously	—				
2. Receiving support	.374**	—			
3. Getting health insurance	.125*	.044	—		
4. Balancing time	.168**	.020	.204**	—	
5. Lack of mentors	.167**	.107*	.161**	.227*	—

*$p < .05$; **$p < .01$ (two-tailed).

We tested the predictive validity of the model by subjecting the data to a principal component factor analysis (listwise deletion of missing values, varimax rotation with Kaiser normalization). This analysis required three iterations to converge and resulted in the extraction of two factors with eigenvalues exceeding the threshold value of 1, which together accounted for over 55% of the variance. The rotated factor solution is presented in Table 25.4.

Table 25.4 Rotated Factor Loadings for the Start-up Problem Items: A Two-Factor Solution ($N = 402$)

Item Number	Variable	Factor 1: Personal Challenges	Factor 2: Social Challenges
C1a	Being taken seriously	0.202	**0.789**
C1b	Receiving support	−4.57E-02	**0.854**
C1c	Getting health insurance	**0.659**	2.32E-03
C1d	Balancing time	**0.735**	1.221E-02
C1e	Lack of mentors	**0.617**	0.187
	Eigenvalue	1.638	1.146
	Percentage variance accounted for	32.76	22.91
	Cronbach's alpha	0.54	0.42

The first factor, which we named "personal challenges," consisted of three items. These were getting suitable health insurance (factor loading 0.659), balancing time (factor loading 0.735), and lack of mentors (factor loading 0.617). The second factor, which we named "social challenges," consisted of two items. These were being taken seriously (factor loading 0.789) and receiving support (factor loading 0.854).

None of the five items that constituted the two scales had a cross-loading exceeding the usual rejection criterion of +/− 40%. Taken together, the high factor loadings and the low cross-loadings of the items (despite the significant correlations, as shown in Table 25.3) give us reasonable indication as to the divergent and convergent validity of the model.

We tested for reliability by calculating Cronbach's alpha for the two scales. Although it is always difficult to obtain high reliability estimates for scales consisting of a small number of items (two and three items, respectively, in this case), the low coefficient alphas suggest that future researchers should utilize the scales with caution.

In addition, we compared the start-up problems by gender and ethnicity. *T* tests are presented in Tables 25.5 and 25.6, respectively. As the results suggest, compared to their male counterparts, women are significantly more worried about receiving the support of those close to them, as well as about balancing their business and personal agendas, a concern shared by minority entrepreneurs as well. On the other hand, White entrepreneurs are significantly more concerned about the lack of mentors relative to entrepreneurs with other ethnic backgrounds.

Future Research Directions

Further analysis of start-up problems might include relationships between the personal background variables (e.g., type of work experience, years of education,

Table 25.5 Descriptive Statistics: Start-up Problems by Gender (*N* = 402)

Variable	Male			Female			*t* test	*df*	*p* value
	n	*Mean*	*SD*	*n*	*Mean*	*SD*			
Social Problems									
Being taken seriously	220	3.07	1.30	182	2.98	1.15	.730	400	.466
Receiving support	219	2.86	1.47	181	3.16	1.45	−2.054	398	**.041**
Personal Problems									
Getting health insurance	214	3.07	1.45	178	3.20	1.31	−.865	390	.388
Balancing time	220	3.59	1.20	181	3.74	1.12	−1.319	399	**.188**[t]
Lack of mentors	220	3.07	1.25	181	3.04	1.17	.242	399	.809

Table 25.6 Descriptive Statistics: Start-up Problems by Ethnicity ($N = 402$)

Variable	White			Other			t test	df	p value
	n	Mean	SD	n	Mean	SD			
Social Problems									
Being taken seriously	304	3.03	1.23	93	2.98	1.23	.352	395	.725
Receiving support	302	3.00	1.45	93	2.96	1.52	.247	393	.805
Personal Problems									
Getting health insurance	297	3.17	1.37	90	2.98	1.45	1.158	385	.248
Balancing time	303	3.59	1.16	93	3.81	1.15	−1.566	394	**.118**[†]
Lack of mentors	303	3.00	1.22	93	3.23	1.17	1.553	394	**.121**[†]

functional experience, and functional expertise). Relationships between start-up problems and nature of the start-up (e.g., business type, sector, location) would also be of interest. Start-up problems might be analyzed relative to the speed of start-up, start-up activities, and the use of outside assistance.

References

Aldrich, H. (1989). Networking among women entrepreneurs. In O. Hagan, C. Rivchun, & D. Sexton (Eds.), *Women-owned businesses* (pp. 103–132). New York: Praeger.

Aldrich, H. (1999). *Organizations evolving.* Thousand Oaks, CA: Sage.

Anna, A., Chandler, G., Jansen, E., & Mero, N. (2000). Women business owners in traditional and non-traditional industries. *Journal of Business Venturing, 15*(3), 279–303.

Baron, R. (1998). Cognitive mechanisms in entrepreneurship: Why and when entrepreneurs think differently than other people. *Journal of Business Venturing, 13*(4), 275–294.

Becker, S. W., & Gordon, G. (1966). An entrepreneurial theory of formal organizations, Part I: Patterns of formal organizations. *Administrative Science Quarterly,* (Dec), 315–344.

Bird, B. J. (1989). *Entrepreneurial behavior.* Glenview, IL: Scott, Foresman.

Bruno, A., & Tyebjee, T. (1982). The environment for entrepreneurship. In C. A. Kent, D. Sexton, & K. Vesper (Eds.), *The encyclopedia of entrepreneurship* (pp. 288–315). Englewood Cliffs, NJ: Prentice Hall.

Brush, C. G. (1997). Women-owned businesses: Obstacles and opportunities. *Journal of Developmental Entrepreneurship, 2*(1), 1–24.

Brush, C. G., Greene, P. G., & Hart, M. (2001). From initial idea to unique advantage: The entrepreneurial challenge of constructing a resource base. *Academy of Management Executive, 15*(1), 64–78.

Butler, J. & Greene, P. G. (1997). Ethnic entrepreneurship: The continuous rebirth of American enterprise. In D. L. Sexton & R. Smilor (Eds.), *Entrepreneurship 2000* (pp. 267–289). Chicago, IL: Upstart.

Buttner, E. H., & Rosen, B. (1988). Bank loan officer's perceptions of characteristics of men, women and successful entrepreneurs. *Journal of Business Venturing, 3*(3), 249–258.

Campbell, D. T. (1965). Variation and selective retention in socio-cultural evolution. In H. R. Barringer, G. I. Blanksten, & R. W. Mack (Eds.), *Social change in developing areas: A reinterpretation of evolutionary theory* (pp. 19–48). Cambridge, MA: Schenkman.

Carter, N. M. (1994). *Reducing barriers between genders: Differences in new firm start-ups.* Unpublished paper presented at the meeting of the Academy of Management, Dallas, TX.

Carter, N. M., Gartner, W. B., & Reynolds, P. D. (1996). Exploring start-up event sequences, *Journal of Business Venturing, 11,* 151–166.

Carter, N. M., Williams, M., & Reynolds, P. D. (1997). Discontinuance among new firms in retail: The influence of initial resources, strategy and gender. *Journal of Business Venturing, 11*(3), 249–258.

Churchill, N. C., & Lewis, V. (1983). Five stages of business growth. *Harvard Business Review, 61*(3) 30–50.

Cooper, A. C. (1982). The entrepreneurship-small business interface. In C. A. Kent, D. L. Sexton, & K. Vesper (Eds.), *The encyclopedia of entrepreneurship* (pp. 193–206). Englewood Cliffs, NJ: Prentice Hall.

Cooper, A. C., Dunkelberg, W., & Woo, C. (1988). Survival and failure: A longitudinal study. In B. Kirchoff, W. Long, W. E. McMullan, K. Vesper, & W. E. Wetzel, Jr. (Eds.), *Frontiers of entrepreneurship research* (pp. 225–237). Wellesley, MA: Babson College.

Cooper, A. C., & Gimeno-Gascon, J. (1992). Entrepreneurs, processes of founding and new firm performance. In D. L. Sexton & J. Kasarda (Eds.), *The encyclopedia of entrepreneurship* (pp. 301–340). Boston: PWS-Kent.

Gartner, W. B. (1985). A conceptual framework for describing the phenomenon of new venture creation. *Academy of Management Review, 10*(4), 696–706.

Gartner, W. B. (2001). Is there an elephant in entrepreneurship? Blind assumptions in theory. *Entrepreneurship Theory and Practice, 25*(4), 27–40.

Greene, P. G., & Brown, T. (1997). Resource needs and the dynamic capitalism typology. *Journal of Business Venturing, 12*(3), 8–17.

Grenier, L. E. (1972). Evolution and revolution as organizations grow. *Harvard Business Review, 50*(4), 37-46.

Hanks, S., Watson, C., Jansen, E., & Chandler, G. (1993). Tightening the life-cycle construct: A taxonomic study of growth stage configurations in high technology organizations. *Entrepreneurship Theory and Practice, 18*(2), 5–31.

Hisrich, R. D., & Brush, C. G. (1986). *The woman entrepreneur: Starting, managing and financing a successful new business.* Lexington, MA: Lexington Books.

Katz, J., & Gartner, W. B. (1988). Properties of emerging organizations. *Academy of Management Review, 13*(3), 429–442.

Kirchhoff, B., & Acs, Z. (1997). Births and deaths of new firms. In D. L. Sexton & R. Smilor (Eds.), *Entrepreneurship 2000* (pp. 167–192). Chicago, IL: Upstart.

Lichtenstein, B., & Brush, C. G. (2001). How do "resource bundles" develop and change in new ventures? A dynamic model and longitudinal exploration. *Entrepreneurship Theory and Practice, 25*(3), 37–58.

Lippitt, G. L., & Schmidt, W. H. (1967). Crises in developing organizations. *Harvard Business Review, 45*(6), 102–112.

Penrose, E. (1959). *Theory of the growth of the firm.* New York: John Wiley.

Pfeffer, J., & Salancik, G. (1978). *The external control of organizations: A resource dependence perspective.* New York: Harper & Row.

Reynolds, P. D. (1992). Predicting new-firm births. In D. L. Sexton & J. Kasarda (Eds.), *The state of the art of entrepreneurship* (pp. 268–300). Boston: PWS-Kent.

Reynolds, P. D. (2000). National Panel Study of U.S. Business Startups: Background and methodology. In J. A. Katz (Ed.), *Databases for the study of entrepreneurship: Vol. 4. Advances in entrepreneurship, firm emergence, and growth* (pp. 153–227). New York: Elsevier Science.

Reynolds, P. D., & Miller, B. (1992). New firm gestation: conception, birth and implications for research. *Journal of Business Venturing, 7*(5), 405–417.

Shapero, A., & Sokol, L. (1982). The social dimensions of entrepreneurship. In C.A. Kent, D. L. Sexton, & K. Vesper (Eds.), *The encyclopedia of entrepreneurship* (pp. 72–90). Englewood Cliffs, NJ: Prentice Hall.

Shaver, K. G., Carter, N. M., Gartner, W. B., & Reynolds, P. D. (2001). *Who is a nascent entrepreneur? Decision rules for identifying and selecting entrepreneurs in the Panel Study of Entrepreneurial Dynamics (PSED).* Paper presented at the 2001 Babson Kauffman Entrepreneurship Research Conference, Jönköping, Sweden.

Shaver, K., & Scott, L. (1991). Person, process, choice: The psychology of new venture creation. *Entrepreneurship Theory and Practice, 15*(2), 23–47.

Stevenson, H., & Gumpert, D. (1985). The heart of entrepreneurship. *Harvard Business Review,* Apr-May, 895–904.

Van de Ven, A., Angle, H. L., & Poole, M. S. (1989). *Research on the management of innovation.* New York: Harper & Row.

Vesper, K. H. (1990). *New venture strategies.* Englewood Cliffs, NJ: Prentice Hall.

CHAPTER 26

Business Start-up Activities

William B. Gartner

Nancy M. Carter

Paul D. Reynolds

B usiness start-up activities are events, behaviors, and the accomplishments of individuals that lead to the emergence of new businesses. The value of studying business start-up activities is based on a number of assumptions. First, without the organization creation activities of individuals, there are no organizations. So, while organization formation occurs within a particular context (Gartner, 1985; Schoonhoven & Romanelli, 2001)—environmental, economic, social, community, political—organizations are not created by their context. Entrepreneurs are necessary for entrepreneurial behavior, and it is through the actions of entrepreneurs that organizations come into existence. It should be noted that it would be the behaviors of *all* individuals involved in the formation of a firm that would constitute business start-up activities, since a significant percentage of firm formation activities involve teams of individuals (Ruef, Aldrich, & Carter, 2003).

Second, creation of a business is a process that typically involves undertaking a number of start-up activities that occur over a period of time.

Third, the creation of an organization is the principal outcome of business start-up activities, so the primary dependent variable for research on business start-up activities will involve determining whether an organization comes into existence, or not (see Chapter 28, Firm Founding). Although a number of other outcomes of entrepreneurial activity might occur in the organization formation process (e.g., the creation of new products; the identification of new markets, new customers, and groups of customers; the acquisition of new skills and knowledge) the fundamental outcome of business start-up activities is the organization itself.

Finally, we note that the activities involved in start-up of a business are a multilevel phenomenon, so it is often difficult to separate what constitutes an independent variable (an entrepreneurial activity) from a dependent variable (a characteristic of a new organization, itself). For example, the activity of making sales is both an important individual-level entrepreneurial behavior and an important characteristic that indicates that an organization exists. An individual is actually involved in creating a sales transaction, yet, making sales is a critical signifier of an important organizational characteristic (Katz & Gartner, 1988; Reynolds & Miller, 1992). Demarcating when this transition between a business start-up activity and a new business occurs is surprisingly difficult to do (Reynolds & Miller, 1992).

Prior Research on Business Start-up Activities

A number of scholars have suggested a variety of activities that are necessary for organization creation, as well as an explicit, or sometimes implied, sequence of how these activities will occur. For example, Gartner and Starr (1993) identified 24 different lists of entrepreneurial activities taken from various scholarly books and articles when they attempted to generate a comprehensive list of entrepreneurial behaviors and sequences of entrepreneurial behaviors. It should be noted that most of these lists of activities were based on anecdotal evidence rather than on systematic research studies. Gartner and Starr (1993) indicated that the predominant way in which entrepreneurial activity was construed involved viewing the process of organization creation in a mechanistic way (Morgan, 1996), that is, seeing entrepreneurial activity as a set of behaviors involved with assembling various resources that can ultimately be combined into an organization. Van de Ven, Angle, and Poole (1989) describe this process of assembly as an accumulation or epigenetic model of change: "Over time, these entrepreneurs accumulate the external resources and technology necessary to transform their ideas into a concrete reality by constructing a new business unit" (p. 225). For example, Vesper (1990, p. 109) specifies that the process of organization creation involves the acquisition of five key ingredients: (1) *technical know how* to generate the company's product or service, (2) the *product or service idea,* which provides direction for the organization's efforts, (3) *personal contacts,* "because ventures are not started in isolation," (4) *physical resources,* and (5) *customer orders.* He then presents anecdotal evidence to indicate that these five key ingredients can be combined in a variety of different sequences (e.g., 1–2–3–4–5, 4–1–5–2–3, 5–3–1–4–2, etc.). Vesper's suggestion that the sequence of start-up activities may not follow a logical progression (e.g., 1–2–3–4–5) seems to have systematic empirical support (Reynolds & Miller, 1992). Yet, most lists of entrepreneurial activities do suggest a particular sequence of activities, such as Birley (1984), who assumes that the venture creation process will occur in the following order: (1) decision to start a business, (2) quit job, (3) incorporate, (4) establish bank account, (5) acquire premises and equipment, (6) receive first order, (7) pay first tax, (8) hire full-time employees.

Since the Gartner and Starr (1993) overview of entrepreneurial behavior research, there have been few systematic empirical studies of how entrepreneurial activities might lead to the formation of an organization. The empirical studies that have explored a comprehensive view of the constellation of activities that might result in organization formation can be identified as those involved with in-depth event histories of a few organizations created while studying the innovation process (e.g., Van de Ven et al., 1989) or studies that have explored whether a specified list of entrepreneurial activities is involved in creating a broad range of different types of firms (e.g., Carter, Gartner, & Reynolds, 1996; Gatewood, Shaver, & Gartner, 1995). Since Van de Ven and his colleagues have primarily focused on the nature of innovation within established organizations as a way to understand entrepreneurial behavior, and since their line of research has been discussed in detail elsewhere (Poole, Van de Ven, Dooley, & Holmes, 2000), we will summarize their efforts by suggesting that their findings indicate a multitude of different entrepreneurial activities and a variety of sequences of these activities can result in the formation of a new business. Indeed, Cheng and Van de Ven (1996) indicate that the initial stages of a venture's development can be understood as following a chaotic pattern. Overall, the findings from these innovation studies indicate that the pattern of activities that might lead to organization formation does not appear to follow the same sequential process.

Of the two examples of studies that have looked at a broad range of individuals involved in the process of business start-up, Gatewood et al. (1995) studied 147 nascent entrepreneurs who had contact with a Small Business Development Center (SBDC) between October 1990 and February 1991 and explored whether certain cognitive factors as well as certain entrepreneurial activities led to the formation of a business (measured by whether sales had occurred) 1 year later (by February 1992). After a review of previous literature to identify specific entrepreneurial activities and the use of a focus group of SBDC counselors to enlarge and revise this list, 29 separate entrepreneurial activities were generated that were grouped into five categories of behavior: gathering market information, estimating potential profits, finishing the groundwork for the business, developing the structure of the company, and setting up business operations. This list of 29 entrepreneurial activities was mailed to the nascent entrepreneurs in the follow-up survey. Nascent entrepreneurs were asked to indicate whether any of the 29 activities were undertaken, and, for those activities, to estimate the number of hours they had devoted to them. When an analysis of these responses was undertaken, Gatewood et al. (1995) found that activities involved with setting up business operations (e.g., purchasing raw materials and supplies; hiring and training employees; producing, distributing, and marketing a product or service) were significantly correlated to the creation of a new firm (as measured by sales). The other categories of activities were not significantly correlated to the subsequent establishment of a firm. It should be noted that this study did not attempt to explore whether any particular sequence of these activities might result in a new firm since specific dates for each activity were not ascertained on the survey.

Carter et al. (1996), using data from a random sample of 683 adult residents in Wisconsin and 1,016 adults across the United States, identified 71 nascent entrepreneurs who had provided information on their start-up activities. These nascent entrepreneurs were initially surveyed about their start-up activities between 1992 and 1993 and were reinterviewed 6 to 18 months later. This study explored three broad questions: What activities do nascent entrepreneurs initiate when attempting to start a business? How many activities do they initiate? When are particular activities initiated? Approximately one half of the respondents had initiated a business by the time of the follow-up interview, over 30% were still engaged in activities to start a business, and 20% had given up on their efforts at business formation. In general, those nascent entrepreneurs who were able to establish a business were more likely to engage in more business formation activities, and engage in these business formation activities earlier, than the other two groups. For the first year of the startup process, the activity levels of those nascent entrepreneurs who "gave up" were very similar to the activity levels of those nascent entrepreneurs who established businesses. In subsequent periods, the nascent entrepreneurs who gave up engaged in fewer activities than those who successfully established firms. Those nascent entrepreneurs who were in the "still trying" stage were likely to engage in fewer activities compared to the other two groups. Similar to the findings of Gatewood et al. (1995), it appeared that the nascent entrepreneurs who were able to successfully start a new business engaged in activities that made their businesses more tangible to others: they looked for facilities and equipment, they sought and got financial support, formed a legal entity, bought facilities and equipment, and were more likely to devote full-time to the business. Both of these studies suggest that individuals involved in business start-up activities do not consistently follow the same sequence of activities (e.g., Birley, 1984). The process of organization formation appears to allow for many different ways that conception of the formation of a new business could occur, as well as many different pathways (sets of activities and sequences of activities) from which a new business could emerge. Finally, it should be noted that what we know about the start-up activities of individuals involved in the process of organization formation is based on relatively small sample sizes (71 and 147).

Developing the Business
Start-up Activities in the PSED

The origins of the business start-up activities that were asked of the nascent entrepreneurs in the Panel Study of Entrepreneurial Dynamics (PSED) are listed in Table 26.1. This list of activities was generated primarily from combining lists of activities from Reynolds & Miller (1992), Carter et al. (1996), and Gatewood et al. (1995) and then making a case to all of the members of the Entrepreneurship Research Consortium (ERC) for having questions about all these activities asked in the phone interview portion of the survey of nascent entrepreneurs. After input from all of the ERC membership, this list was pared down and additional activities were added. For example, the behavior, "arranged child care . . ." was added by the gender group because there was prior theory and evidence to suggest that this activity might predict the likelihood that female nascent entrepreneurs would have the time to successfully start new businesses (Carter, 1997). As we noted earlier, activities that might be considered as markers of the existence of an organization are also listed as start-up behaviors. We added four other start-up marker activities: bank account opened; business has own phone listing; business has own phone line; and paid managers or employees who are not owners a salary. These particular activities were added after reviewing the literature on identifying organizations

Table 26.1   Sources of Business Start-up Activities in the PSED

		Reynolds & Miller, 1992	Gatewood, Shaver, & Gartner, 1995	Carter, Gartner, & Reynolds, 1996
Activities:				
Personal Commitment			Devoted 35+ hours/ week on business	Devoted 35+ hours/week on business
				Arranged child care
Financial Support		Saved money to invest	Saved money to invest	Saved money to invest
		Asked for funding	Asked for funding	Asked for funding
		Established credit with suppliers	Got financial support	Established credit with suppliers
			Invested own money	Invested own money
Hiring		Hired employees or managers	Hired employees	Hired employees/managers
		Organized team	Organized team	Organized team
		Prepared business plan	Prepared business plan	Prepared business plan
		Developed prototype	Developed prototype	Developed model or procedures of product/service
		Applied for copyright, patent, trademark	Applied for license, patent, or permits	Applied for copyright, patent, trademark
		Purchased, rented, or leased major equipment	Purchased facilities, equipment, or property	Purchased, rented, or leased major equipment
			Rented or leased facilities/equipment/ property	
		Defined market opportunity		Defined market opportunity
		Developed financials		Developed financials
		Started marketing, promotion		Started marketing, promotion
		Purchased raw materials, supplies		Purchased raw materials, supplies
		Took a class or workshop on starting business		Took a class on starting a business
			Formed legal entity	
				Opened business bank account

(Continued)

Table 26.1 (Continued)

	Reynolds & Miller, 1992	Gatewood, Shaver, & Gartner, 1995	Carter, Gartner, & Reynolds, 1996
Indicators			
Sales	Received money, income, or fees	Received money, income, or fees	Received money, income, or fees
		Positive cash flow	Positive cash flow
			Paid managers and employees who are not owners a salary
		Filed federal taxes	Filed federal taxes
		Paid FICA	Paid FICA
		Unemployment insurance	Unemployment insurance
		D&B listing	D&B listing
			Business phone listing
			Business phone line

(Birley, 1984; Kalleberg, Marsden, Aldrich, & Cassell, 1990; Busenitz & Murphy, 1996). It is our contention that these markers might also be important behaviors in the organization formation process as well. Such an activity as "business has own phone listing," is not only a signifier for determining that an organization might exist, it is a way for a nascent entrepreneur to demonstrate to others (potential customers, investors, employees, suppliers) that the emerging organization should merit their involvement (Gartner, Bird, & Starr, 1992).

The specific start-up activities questions that were asked of the nascent entrepreneurs are listed in Exhibit 26.1. All of the business start-up activity questions were asked in the initial interview (Q questions) and for those behaviors that were not completed at the time of the initial interview, asked again in the follow-up interviews (R questions for Wave 2, and S questions for Wave 3). It should be noted that all of the questions asked for an indication of a specific time when an activity was completed (month and year or season and year). In the Gatewood et al. (1995) study, nascent entrepreneurs were asked to indicate whether an activity was initiated and to estimate the number of hours spent on that particular activity. In Carter et al. (1996), nascent entrepreneurs were also asked to indicate whether a start-up activity had been initiated and if so, to provide a year and month when this activity was undertaken. In the PSED, questions and responses for each start-up activity were similar to Carter et al. (1996) since we thought that the designation of a time when certain start-up activities occurred would be very useful for conducting event history analyses. We did not request an estimation of the number of hours devoted to each start-up activity because we were concerned about the ability of nascent entrepreneurs to (1) accurately recall the number of hours devoted to a particular

Exhibit 26.1   Business Start-up Activity Items in the PSED

The wording of questions is taken from the initial interview.

Q109   First, did you spend a lot of time thinking about starting the new business, or did the idea suddenly occur? (1 = spent a lot of time thinking; 2 = idea suddenly occurred; 3 = both; 0 = other)[a]

Q110   And in what year? (did you start to think about this new business)? (four-digit year; 9999 = don't know or not applicable)[b]

Q110a   And in what month? (actual month 1 – 12; 13 = winter; 14 = spring; 15 = summer; 16 = fall; 99 = don't know; not applicable)

Q111   A business plan usually outlines the markets to be served, the products or services to be provided, the resources required, including money, and the expected growth and profit for the new business. Has a business plan been prepared for this start-up? (1 = yes; 2 = no)

Q112   Has it (preparing a business plan) not yet been done or is it not relevant to this business? (1 = not yet done; 2 = not relevant to this business)

Q113   Is the business plan in process or completed? (1 = in process; 2 = completed)

Q114   What is the current form of your business plan — unwritten or in your head, informally written, formally prepared, or something else? (1 = unwritten/in head; 2 = informally written; 3 = formally prepared; 4 = both 1 and 2; 0 = something else)

Q116   Has a start-up team been organized? (A start-up team is more than one person that helps to put the firm in place, expecting to share ownership. If both married partners own and operate a business, that is a start-up team.) (1 = yes; 2 = no)

Q117   Will a start-up team be organized, or is it not relevant to this business? (1 = team will be organized; 2 = not relevant to this business)

Q118   Is organizing a start-up team in process or completed? (1 = in process; 2 = completed)

Q120   At what stage of development is the product or service this start-up will be selling? (1 = completed and ready for sale or delivery; 2 = prototype/procedure tested with customers; 3 = model/procedure is being developed; 4 = still in idea stage; 0 = no work has been done on a product or service)

Q122   Have marketing or promotional efforts been started for the product or service this start-up will be selling? (1 = yes; 2 = no)

Q124   Has an application for patent, copyright, or trademark relevant to this new business been submitted? (1 = yes; 2 = no)

Q125   Will a patent, copyright, or trademark application related to this business be submitted, or is it not relevant? (1 = will be submitted; 2 = not relevant)

Q126   Has the patent, copyright, or trademark been granted or is it in the process? (1 = granted; 2 = in process)

Q128   Have any raw materials, inventory, supplies, or components for the new start-up been purchased? (1 = yes; 2 = no)

Q129   Will any raw materials, inventory, suppliers or components be purchased or is this not relevant? (1 = intend to purchase; 2 = not relevant)

Q131   Have any major items like equipment, facilities, or property been purchased, leased, or rented for the new start-up? (Major is defined as any item with a retail or sale value of more than $1,000. And this could be physical space or internet space, like a Website.) (1 = yes; 2 = no)

Q132   Will there be a purchase, lease, or rent of any major items like equipment, facilities, or property, or is this not relevant? (1 = will be a purchase, lease, or rent; 2 = not relevant)

Q134   Has an effort been made to define the market opportunity by talking with potential customers or getting information about the competition? (1 = yes; 2 = no)

(Continued)

Exhibit 26.1 (Continued)

Q135	Will an effort be made to define the market opportunities, or is this not relevant? (1 = effort will be made; 2 = not relevant)
Q137	Have projected financial statements, such as income and cash flow statements or break-even analysis, been developed? (1 = yes; 2 = no)
Q139	Are you now saving money to invest in this business? (1 = yes; 2 = no)
Q140	Have you finished saving money to invest in the new firm, or is that still in process? (1 = finished saving money; 2 = still in process)
Q141	Do you intend to start saving money to invest in the firm, have you finished saving money to invest, or do you consider it not relevant in this case? (1 = intend to start saving; 2 = finished saving; 3 = not relevant in this case)
Q143	Have you invested any of your own money in this business? (1 = yes; 2 = no)
Q145	Have financial institutions or other people been asked for funds? (1 = yes; 2 = no)
Q146	Is asking others or institution for funds completed or still in process? (1 = completed; 2 = in process)
Q147	Will others or financial institutions be asked for funds, or is this not relevant for this start-up? (1 = others will be asked; 2 = not relevant)
Q149	Has credit with a supplier been established? (1 = yes; 2 = no; 3 = not relevant)
Q150	Have you arranged child care or household help to allow yourself time to work on the business, either formally or informally with friends and relatives? (1 = yes; 2 = no)
Q153	Have you begun to devote full-time to the business, that is, 35 or more hours per week? (1 = yes; 2 = no)
Q155	Have any employees or managers been hired for pay—workers that would NOT share ownership? (1 = yes; 2 = no)
Q156	Will any employees or managers be hired for pay, or are they not relevant for this business (1 = will be hired; 2 = not relevant)
Q160	Has a bank account been opened exclusively for this new business? (1 = yes; 2 = no; 3 = using an existing commercial account)
Q162	Has the new business received any money, income, or fees from the sale of goods or services? (1 = yes; 2 = no)
Q163	Does the monthly revenue now exceed the monthly expenses? (1 = yes; 2 = no)
Q165	Are salaries for the managers who are also owners included in the computation of monthly expenses? (1 = yes; 2 = no)
Q167	Have you taken any classes or workshops on starting a business? (1 = yes; 2 = no)
Q171	Does the new business have its own listing in the phone book? (Enter "yes" if no phone listing because it is only an Internet business.) (1 = yes; 2 = no; 3 = sharing existing business listing)
Q175	Has the new business paid any state unemployment insurance taxes? (1 = yes; 2 = no)
Q177	Has the new business paid any federal social security taxes, sometimes called FICA payments? (1 = yes; 2 = no)
Q179	Has the new business filed a federal income tax return? (1 = yes; 2 = no)
Q181	To your knowledge, is the new business listed with Dun & Bradstreet, the credit-rating firm? (1 = yes; 2 = no)

NOTES:

a. For all questions that are not date and time related: 8 = don't know; 9 = not applicable.

b. Every behavior question has a year and month question as to when the activity was completed or undertaken.

start-up activity and (2) accurately recall the amount of time for a particular effort vis-à-vis their other efforts. In addition, we were concerned about the relevance of comparisons between the amount of time some nascent entrepreneurs devoted to particular start-up efforts vis-à-vis other nascent entrepreneurs given that there is significant variation in the timing and sequencing of start-up activities. Previous research indicates substantial variation in the duration between start-up events and the sequence of each start-up activity in relationship to other start-up activities. Even if computational techniques can solve some of the concerns about whether hourly estimations can reasonably reflect the effort of nascent entrepreneurs across the start-up behaviors, time limitations of the phone survey precluded our asking for estimations of the hours devoted to each start-up behavior. It should also be noted that many efforts at starting new businesses involve team efforts (Ruef et al., 2003), so that attempting to ascertain the effort undertaken (estimating the number of hours worked) on various start-up activities of the various team members of the start-up would have been difficult if not impossible to achieve in the PSED survey. Asking whether an activity had been attempted (and accomplished) in the firm formation process by any of the members of the venture team seemed to be a question that any member of a venture team could reasonably answer.

Business Start-up Activities

The descriptive statistics that are reported here focus on two major issues in the study of the business formation process. The first issue involves the identification of the kinds of activities that would signify the moment of business start-up "conception." Recognizing the point that business formation first began for each nascent entrepreneur gets to the heart of the fundamental nature of the start-up process. The second issue involves recognizing characteristics of the "sampling frame" of business start-up activities that make up the PSED sample. This might be labeled as the issue of differentiating between the "rate" of nascent entrepreneurs beginning to engage in the process of business formation and the "stock" of all nascent entrepreneurs who are activity engaged in the process of business formation.

By asking individuals the question, "Have you, alone or with others, been actively engaged in starting a business in the past 12 months?" a number of people would be prompted to consider whether their prior behaviors would constitute the process of business start-up. In Table 26.2, we report the frequencies for the first activity that nascent entrepreneurs reported they engaged in. Although it is not surprising that a majority of respondents (52%) reported that their first activity was "spent a lot of time thinking about the business," there were a number of cases in the sample in which nascent entrepreneurs were first engaged in activities that would be considered as signifiers of the *completion* of business start-up (e.g., received money for sales, hired employees, paid taxes) (see Chapter 28 for further discussion of this issue). The "conception" of the business, that is, the initial activity that would signify to these nascent entrepreneurs that the process of business formation has begun, is not always "thought." Indeed, some nascent entrepreneurs identify their first activity as an event that should come last. This may reflect some aspect of the process of enactment

Table 26.2   Frequency Distribution: First Business Start-up Activity (weighted)

Activity	n^a	$\%^b$
Spent a lot of time thinking about starting business	428	52
Took classes or workshops on starting business	148	18
Saving money to invest in business	134	16
Invested own money in business	108	13
Developed model or procedures for product/service	92	11
Defined market opportunities	61	7
Raw materials, inventory, supplies purchased	57	7
Business plan prepared	55	7
Start-up team organized	49	6
Major items like equipment, facilities, or property purchased, leased	26	3
Marketing or promotional activities started	25	3
Arranged child care or household help to allow time for business	20	2
Credit from supplier established	19	2
Files federal income tax return	18	2
Devoted full time to business	16	2
Applied for patent, copyright, or trademark	13	2
Projected financial statements developed	12	1
Bank account opened exclusively for this business	11	1
Received money, income, or fees from sale of goods or services	8	1
Asked financial institutions or people for funds	6	<1
Hired employees or managers	4	<1
Paid federal social security taxes (FICA)	3	<1
Monthly revenues exceeded monthly expenses	2	<1
Business had own phone listing	3	<1
Business had own phone line	2	<1
Paid state unemployment insurance	1	<1
Business listed with D&B	1	<1

NOTES:

a. Total does not sum to number of eligible nascent entrepreneurs (822) since some respondents indicated simultaneous first behaviors.

b. Percentage of 822 eligible nascent entrepreneurs who reported item as one of first behaviors.

(Weick, 1979), wherein action precedes thought and individuals engage in making sense of what has occurred. Out of the activities and events that are occurring in their lives, they identify a particular event that signifies to them this realization that they are engaged in starting a business. The conception of a business, therefore, is the recognition that other activities (besides thinking about starting a business) might have been the critical initial impetus that began the start-up process. Conception in the business start-up process begins with individuals realizing that their activities represent the process of business formation, rather than something else. As Reynolds (2000) has pointed out, the PSED survey process itself may act in the manner of the Hiezenberg principle: the act of surveying individuals about their business formation activities prompts those surveyed to realize they are engaged in business formation activities. Be that as it may, the recognition that a number of nascent entrepreneurs identify "nonthought" activities as their first business start-up activities might presage future research that shows a variety of business start-up activity sequences that result in new businesses.

Figure 26.1 presents the number of cases in the PSED by the number of years between the identification of first activity and the time of the first PSED phone survey. For example, of the 822 total cases presented in Figure 26.1, there were 38% of the nascent entrepreneurs who had initiated their first behavior 5 years *before* they were initially contacted for the PSED survey. What Figure 26.1 shows is the distribution of the "stock" of all nascent entrepreneurs who were "Alone or with others, actively engaged in starting a business in the past 12 months." The 14% of individuals who initiated their first business start-up activity within the prior 12 months of the survey would be considered the yearly "rate" of nascent entrepreneurs entering the start-up process. The sample of nascent entrepreneurs in the PSED is, therefore, not just individuals who initially began the process of business formation in the 12 months prior to the survey, but also individuals who have been "still trying" to start a business over a period of many years. The implication of Figure 26.1 is that the entire sample of nascent entrepreneurs in the PSED does not reflect a cohort of individuals who have initiated the start-up of a business at the same time. Our analogy for the sample of nascent entrepreneurs in the PSED is that of a racetrack, where we have a sample of all individuals who are trying to run to the "started a new business" finish line. Some of these nascent entrepreneurs have been on the racetrack for years, and some of these nascent entrepreneurs have just begun the race. What scholars using the PSED sample must realize is that the nascent entrepreneurs who have engaged in business start-up many years before they were surveyed may not, in some significant ways, be similar to the group of individuals who are first engaged in start-up activities in the 12 months prior to the survey (Gartner, Carter, Lichtenstein, & Dooley, 2003). What would be missing from the group of nascent entrepreneurs in the PSED who engaged in trying to start a business 5 years earlier are all those nascent entrepreneurs who began at the same time but over the past 5 years gave up or successfully started a business. The racetrack is, therefore, missing all of those entrepreneurs who, over the years, are no longer in the race because they have already finished the race, or they dropped out. The sample of nascent entrepreneurs in the PSED, therefore, represents the stock of all nascent entrepreneurs who are "still trying" to start a business at the time of the PSED survey.

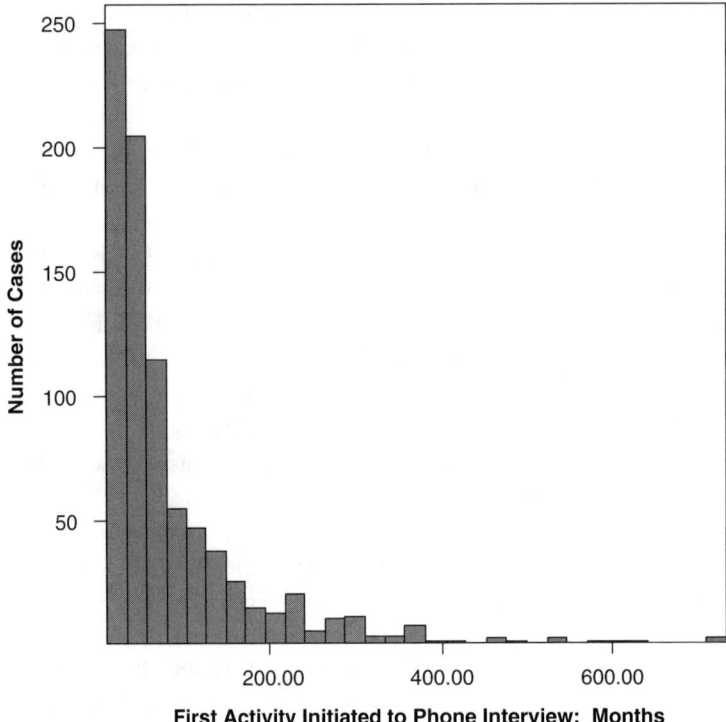

Figure 26.1   First Business Start-up Activity to Initial Phone Interview (Months)

NOTES:

Unweighted analyses

N = 822 (removes 6 new businesses and 2 cases without data on "activities" from the sample of 830 nascent entrepreneurs)

Mean = 76.97 months

Median = 43.07 months

Standard deviation = 94.26 months (distribution of time is highly skewed rendering the median a more appropriate indicator than the mean value)

Minimum = 1.25 months

Maximum = 735.49 months

14% of cases initiated an activity 1 year (12 months) prior to first phone interview

30% within 2 years (cumulative) (24 months)

45% within 3 years (cumulative) (36 months)

54% within 4 years (cumulative) (48 months)

62% within 5 years (cumulative) (60 months)

The implication of this insight is far from simple or obvious. It behooves scholars using the PSED sample to seriously consider the theoretical and empirical value of using the entire stock of nascent entrepreneurs in the PSED sample compared to the selection of a narrower subset of individuals who might reasonably reflect a similar cohort of individuals initiating their business start-up at the same time. For studies that seek to compare the efficacy of various start-up activities or sequences of start-up activities, a selection of nascent entrepreneurs with first start-up activities close to the time of the survey is likely to be the most methodologically conservative and theoretically justifiable strategy for exploring this phenomenon.

While a substantial amount of descriptive information on the activities of individuals in the process of starting businesses is likely to be generated from the PSED, scholars are likely to want to understand *why* certain entrepreneurial behaviors and sequences of behaviors might affect the likelihood of successful organization creation. In Gartner and Carter (2003), we offer a variety of theories and explanations that may be appropriate.

If our experiences in studying the process of organization formation have shown us anything, it is that there is substantial variation in the kinds of organizations that are started by nascent entrepreneurs; substantial variation in the characteristics that would signal to researchers that these organizations do, indeed, exist; and substantial variation in when these characteristics that signal the existence of these new organizations occur. There is no escaping this fact—entrepreneurial behavior is fundamentally an activity involved with generating "variation" as an organizational phenomenon (Aldrich, 1999; Katz & Gartner, 1988; Weick, 1979). There is no one particular way in which organizations emerge because there is no one particular kind of organization that results as an outcome of the start-up process. Research is needed and required that can both recognize variation in the phenomenon of organization creation while also offering insights into how these diverse activities might lead to patterns of successful formation of organizations.

References

Aldrich, H. E. (1999). *Organizations evolving.* London: Sage.

Birley, S. (1984). Finding the new firm. *Proceedings of the annual meeting of the Academy of Management, 47,* 64–68.

Busenitz, L. W. & Murphy, G. B. 1996. New evidence in the pursuit of locating new businesses. *Journal of Business Venturing, 11*(3), 221–231.

Carter, N. M. (1997). Entrepreneurial processes and outcomes: The influence of gender. In P. D. Reynolds & S. B. White (Eds.), *The entrepreneurial process* (pp. 163–178). Westport, CT: Quorum Books.

Carter, N. M., Gartner, W. B., & Reynolds, P. D. (1996). Exploring start-up event sequences. *Journal of Business Venturing, 11*(3), 151–166.

Cheng, Y., & Van de Ven, A. H. (1996). Learning the innovation journey: Order out of chaos? *Organization Science, 7*(6), 593–614.

Gartner, W. B. (1985). A conceptual framework for describing the phenomenon of new venture creation. *Academy of Management Review, 10,* 696–706.

Gartner, W. B., Bird, B. J., & Starr, J. (1992). Acting as if: Differentiating entrepreneurial from organizational behavior. *Entrepreneurship Theory and Practice, 16*(3), 13–32.

Gartner, W. B., & Carter, N. M. (2003). Entrepreneurial behavior and firm organizing processes. In Z. J. Acs & D. B. Audretsch (Eds.), *Handbook of entrepreneurship research* (pp. 195–221). Boston: Kluwer.

Gartner, W. B., Carter, N. M., Lichtenstein, B. M. B., & Dooley, K. (2003, August). *When are new firms founded?* Paper presented at the annual meeting of National Academy of Management, Seattle, WA.

Gartner, W. B., & Starr, J. (1993). The nature of entrepreneurial work. In S. Birley & I. C. MacMillan (Eds.), *Entrepreneurship research: Global perspectives* (pp. 35–67). Amsterdam, The Netherlands: North-Holland.

Gatewood, E. J., Shaver, K. G., & Gartner, W. B. (1995). A longitudinal study of cognitive factors influencing start-up behaviors and success at venture creation. *Journal of Business Venturing, 10*(5), 371–391.

Kalleberg, A. L., Marsden, P. V., Aldrich, H. E., & Cassell, J. W. (1990). Comparing organizational sampling frames. *Administrative Science Quarterly, 35*(4), 658–688.

Katz, J. A., & Gartner, W. B. (1988). Properties of emerging organizations. *Academy of Management Review, 13*(3), 429–441.

Morgan, G. (1996). *Images of organization* (2nd ed.). Thousand Oaks, CA: Sage.

Poole, M. S., Van de Ven, A. H., Dooley, K., & Holmes, M. E. (2000). *Organizational change and innovation processes: Theory and methods for research.* Oxford, UK: Oxford University Press.

Reynolds, P. D. (2000). National Panel Study of U.S. Business Startups. In J. A. Katz (Ed.), *Databases for the study of entrepreneurship: Vol. 4. Advances in entrepreneurship, firm emergence, and growth* (pp. 153–227). Stanford, CT: JAI.

Reynolds, P. D., & Miller, B. (1992). New firm gestation: Conception, birth, and implications for research. *Journal of Business Venturing, 7*(5), 405–418.

Ruef, M., Aldrich, H. E., & Carter, N. M. (2003). The structure of organizational founding teams: Homophily, strong ties, and isolation among U.S. entrepreneurs. *American Sociological Review, 68*(2), 195–222.

Schoonhoven, C. B., & Romanelli, E. (2001). *The entrepreneurship dynamic.* Palo Alto, CA: Stanford University Press.

Van de Ven, A. H., Angle, H. L., & Poole, M. S. (1989). *Research on the management of innovation.* New York: Harper & Row.

Vesper, K. H. (1990). *New venture strategies* (2nd ed.). Englewood Cliffs, NJ: Prentice Hall.

Weick, K. E. (1979). *The social psychology of organizing* (2nd ed.). New York: Random House.

CHAPTER 27

Teams

Howard E. Aldrich

Nancy M. Carter

Martin Ruef

Founding a new organization is difficult and demanding work. Many people begin entirely on their own although they may turn to others for help with various aspects of the founding. Others begin with a team, making the enterprise a collective effort from the start. Why do some founders decide to go it alone rather than join with others? If the start-up is not a solo venture, then on what basis do founders choose members? Despite its obvious importance to entrepreneurship research, little systematic research exists on the actual process by which start-up teams are formed (Cooper & Daily, 1997, p. 131). The PSED data provide an opportunity to test several theoretical perspectives on why and how entrepreneurial teams are formed.

Items about the ownership team on the Panel Study of Entrepreneurial Dynamics (PSED) conform to the perspective of Kamm, Shuman, Seeger, and Nurick (1990, p. 7) who defined an entrepreneurial team as "two or more individuals who jointly establish a business in which they have an equity (financial) interest. These individuals are present during the pre-start-up phase of the firm, before it actually begins making its goods or services available to the market." By this definition, a person has to be involved from the beginning and also must have an equity stake in the venture to be considered a member of the team.

Subsequent researchers have added elements to this definition, such as including founders who joined the team within the first 2 years of its beginning (Francis & Sandberg, 2000). Cooper and Daily (1997) noted several other possible dimensions to a team, such as the extent to which people perceive themselves as a team, whether people are involved full-time, and the extent to which they actually collaborate. These elaborations are reflected in PSED data collection for the second, third, and fourth waves, which asked questions about changes in the ownership team.

Why Choose to Have a Team?

Two interconnected themes about start-up teams run through the literature: (1) new ventures derive many instrumental benefits from teams and (2) many of the benefits are social psychological in nature. First, much of the literature on start-up teams is based on the assumption that they represent a deliberate choice by a lead entrepreneur or set of founders. Implicit in discussions of why teams are formed is the assumption that they are normally planned rather than emergent. However, authors also recognize that other factors play a role in team formation, such as the existence of previous relations between founders.

Previous authors have identified many purported instrumental benefits that result from using teams rather than going it alone. Lechler (2001) reviewed a dozen empirical studies of team formation and functioning, many of which compared the success of teams to that of single founders. In almost every case, regardless of the outcome measured, teams did better. Seven of the studies were from Germany and one from Canada, with the most recent U.S. study from 1989. By the time of their 1993 review article, Kamm and Nurik (1993) seemed to take for granted the superiority of teams over solo founders.

What are the potential instrumental benefits from an entrepreneurial team? Vesper (1990, p. 47) presented a comprehensive list of benefits that has not been superseded by subsequent research. He noted that teams can draw from a larger pool of labor and may have a richer set of skills and other resources than is possessed by a single founder. Gartner (1985, p. 703), for example, argued that "high technology industries might require more skills than an individual would be likely to have, necessitating that individuals combine their abilities in teams in order to start an organization successfully." With a team, as opposed to an individual founder, a single individual's departure is not necessarily disastrous. Assuming that the team contains a rich skill set, the new venture will not need to recruit management talent as early in the growth process as will a solo founder. Finally, Vesper noted two external benefits from a team founding: outsiders may treat a team's ability to recruit other people to the venture as a sign of its managerial capabilities, and potential investors may see the willingness of others to join that team as a sign of the venture's commercial viability.

Not every author sees the instrumental benefits of entrepreneurial teams as more beneficial, on every dimension, than solo ventures. In her article on corporate entrepreneurship, Mosakowski (1998) argued that in teams the entrepreneurial resources of creativity, foresight, intuition, and alertness are spread across a large number of individuals. Similarly, the team functions of initiating decisions, ratifying them, and monitoring outcomes will be spread across multiple individuals. To ensure venture success, teams must deal with the potential problems of shirking, monitoring, and distributing incentives. The monitoring role is most likely to be played by a small number of individuals at the top of the organization. She argues that the team dynamics involved in these processes will create limits to growth that individual entrepreneurs do not face.

In addition to claimed instrumental benefits, a number of authors have pointed to the social psychological benefits derived from relationships between team members (Bird, 1989). Unlike a solo entrepreneur, who must bear the burden of making decisions and facing their consequences with no one else to blame, entrepreneurial teams spread the responsibility across individuals. Having to defend decisions to other individuals also having an equity stake in the venture can make team members more confident in their decisions. Francis and Sandberg (2000, p. 6) noted that friendships "may hold teams together and stimulate heroic efforts during difficult times."

Team members, then, can provide anything from material and cognitive resources to emotional support. Although most previous research has emphasized the instrumental contributions that team members make, we believe that team members also make important social psychological contributions. In addition to providing introductions to important people, team members can supply personal services, such as household help or child care, to help with the start-up.

How Teams Are Formed

Knowing that teams may carry advantages not available to solo founders tells us about why someone might choose to have a team but little about how a team of founders actually came together. Indeed, even framing the question as one of "how teams are formed" presumes that an active agent was involved in their creation. As with the question of why people use teams rather than going it alone, most researchers on entrepreneurial teams have written as if they were intentionally planned. However, there's a growing recognition in the literature that we cannot take for granted the process by which teams form.

Team formation is inextricably linked with who becomes involved as a founder. Do founders recruit team members for who they are, whom they know, and what they can contribute, or perhaps for all these reasons? If a team is formed because it provides benefits beyond going it alone, then it follows that people would be recruited for instrumental reasons. This view suggests that founders engage in an open search, using the fundamental criterion of what a potential team member can add to the venture (Mosakowski, 1998). According to this view, the lead entrepreneur or the team's core members will not merely consider people whom they know but also entertain the possibility of bringing strangers into the team.

Hinds, Carley, Krackhardt, and Wholey (2000, p. 227) noted that individuals attempt to reduce uncertainty when putting together a team. In their study of how students at Carnegie Mellon University chose work-group members, they found that participants felt they could reduce uncertainty if they could exercise control over who participates in the group: "Thus, in putting together project teams and work groups, individuals will, when given the chance, construct the group that they feel is most likely to succeed." They argued that three uncertainty-reducing mechanisms guided people's choices of team members: (1) homophily, (2) familiarity, and (3) reputation for competence. Two of these mechanisms are reflected in PSED measures.

Homophily

In the sociological and social-psychological literatures, homophily is typically invoked as a primary explanation for who is included in groups. The "birds of a feather" hypothesis represents one of the oldest contributions of the sociological literature on differential association (Lazarsfeld & Merton, 1954). The homophily principle asserts that contact occurs more frequently between people with similar characteristics than between people with dissimilar characteristics.

Homophily matters because positive relations between group members can have a positive effect (Hinds et al., 2000, pp. 228–229). Homophily makes it more likely that people share a common language and knowledge base, and perhaps also work with shared models of their tasks and context. Homophily also facilitates greater trust and reciprocity between group members. Consequently, homophily should lead to more frequent communication among members and greater predictability of one another's behaviors. This tendency toward homophily might be especially likely in organizational founding teams, which require sizable investments of time and resources (Bird, 1989).

Familiarity

As a complementary principle to homophily, the principle of familiarity asserts that people who associate with one another, under certain conditions, become more likely to continue the association subsequently in other circumstances. Kinship and work relations have been identified as factors producing interpersonal familiarity.

Previous studies have suggested that the quality of preexisting relations among potential team members may play a more important role than instrumental considerations. Kamm and Nurik (1993, p. 18) noted that personal relationships among team members may "take top priority in the beginning, at least." Chandler and Hanks (1998, p. 323), in their study of 12 new venture teams, found that most team members "knew each other as co-workers or as family members."

The quality of interpersonal relations between potential team members figured prominently in Bird's (1989) discussion of team formation. She noted several characteristics of prior relationships between individuals that might affect their likelihood of joining the same team. First, some people are simply more likable than others, perhaps because of their physical attractiveness or aura of confidence. Second, people in close proximity to one another, either geographically or via direct communication lines, are more likely to get to know one another. Third, given the opportunity to interact, people might discover that they find something rewarding in the other person, such as possessing similar attitudes or interests.

Finally, Bird implied that working together is easier if people possess complementary characteristics, rather than overlapping ones. Some research in social psychology suggests that men and women may weight these principles of attraction differently (Nevid, 1984).

In the spirit of Bird's (1989) argument, Francis and Sandberg (2000) developed a comprehensive argument concerning the role of friendship within entrepreneurial teams. Although mainly devoted to propositions concerning team functioning, they noted that friendships "may serve as the basis for forming new teams" (p. 6). Friendship may lead people to become involved in ventures which are not attractive, from a strict business point of view, but which do give them a chance to associate with others whom they know. They may be willing to invest more resources than they would in a venture founded by strangers and also to offer their services at reduced prices. The perceived advantages of cooperation and trust gained from working with friends can lead to more emphasis on implicit agreements and less on black-letter contracts.

The PSED offers a unique opportunity to examine the emergence of start-up teams in new business ventures. The first wave of PSED data can be used to examine principles underlying initial team formation while the second, third, and fourth waves provide information on changes to the team composition. This allows examination of the question, "How do teams emerge," rather than making the assumption that they are intentionally planned.

Rationale for Team Questions in the PSED

Although the items included in the PSED that are intended to measure team formation and emergence processes can be used to test a number of theoretical perspectives, they were chosen to reflect sociological principles about choice: choice on the basis of homophily, purposive choice, and choice constrained by context or opportunity structure. Homophily refers to the tendency of people to associate with others similar to themselves, such as choosing others on the basis of gender or ethnicity. Purposive choice reflects people's tendencies to choose others who possess valuable skills, such as education or experience. Finally, opportunity structures set a context within which the first two principles operate. Founders cannot choose someone whom they have not met or have no way to reach, such as a person who works in another organization or lives in another city.

Questions regarding a respondent's intentions to have a start-up team and characteristics of the team are in phone interview schedule items Q206 to Q233d. Exhibit 27.1 shows the questions asked. As with the questions asked about "helpers," (Q241–Q262) questions about team members were designed to tap three facets of a team member's relation to the planned venture and to other members of the team. First, how similar are the team members to one another? Second, how did team members know one another before the start-up effort began? Third, in what ways have team members contributed to the start-up effort and on what terms?

Exhibit 27.1 Questionnaire Items for Assessing Start-up Team

Q206	You have said that you and (from Q195) expect to own part of this new business. We would like to make a list of all those who will own part of the business. Please give me only their first names, so we can talk about them without revealing their full identity. Include any businesses or financial institutions that will own part of the new business. I will also ask what percentage of the new firm each is expected to own. If there are more than five, please select the five who will have the highest level of ownership in the new firm.

Questions asked about each (name) of five most important team members.

Q210e	Is (name) a person or not a person?
Q211	How many total hours, including the past week, has (name) devoted to this new business start-up?
Q212	About how much money, in total dollars, has (name) contributed to the new business, either to purchase ownership or as a loan to the new business?
Q213	How many years of work experience has (name) had in this industry—the one where the new business will compete?
Q214	How many other businesses has (name) helped to start as an owner or part owner
Q217	Sex—Is (name) male or female?
Q218	Age—How old is (name)?
Q219	Race/Ethnicity—Would you say (name) is
	White
	Black/African American
	Hispanic/Latino
	American Indian
	Southeast Asian
	Other Asian/Pacific Islander
	Or something else?
Q220	What is, or was, (name's) primary occupation?
	In addition to time and personal investments of money, in what other ways has (name) helped with the start-up? For example, has (name) provided:
Q221	Introductions to other people?
Q222	Information or advice?
Q223	Training in business-related tasks or skills?
Q224	Access to financial resources (equity, loans, or loan guarantees)?
Q225	Physical resources (use of land, space, buildings, or equipment)?
Q226	Business services (legal, accounting, clerical assistance)?
Q227	Personal services (household help)?
Q227c	Morale or emotional support?
Q227f	Labor?
Q227i	Ideas or creativity?
Q228	Any other type of service or assistance?
Q229	Which of these forms of assistance has been MOST IMPORTANT for the new business start-up?
Q230	Was the assistance provided free, at a discounted price, at the normal market price, as part of a barter or exchange relationship, or for some other reason?

Q233	Are you and (name) spouses, or partners; relatives; business associates or work colleagues; friends or acquaintances; strangers before joining the start-up team; (you/they) have some other type of relationship; or is either or both not a person, like a business or financial institution? (Relationships between each team member were recorded.)
Q233a	Are you and (name) spouses, or "partners sharing a household? (Spousal relationships between any team members were recorded.)
Q233b	Are you and (name) relatives or family members living in the same or different households? (Family relationships between all team members were recorded.)
Q233c	Are you and (name) business associates or work colleagues from the same company or work organizations or are you from different work settings? (Work relationships between all team members were recorded.)
Q233d	How did you and (name) first meet? Did you meet when the start-up team was organized, did you meet through a common friend, or did you meet in some other way? (Acquaintance relationships between all team members were recorded.)

The first question, Q206, was designed to identify social entities, including persons and nonpersons, who were expected to own part of the new business. If more than five people or nonpersons were named, only the five with the most ownership in the new business were asked about in subsequent questions. Nonpersons could be organizations or institutions that sponsored or funded the new business. Some of the team questions are relevant to nonpersons as well as persons, but many are not. Questions 210e, 211, and 212 tap into how much time and money the team member—person or nonperson—contributed to the new business.

Questions 213 through 220 provide information about work and business experience, sex, age, race and ethnicity, and occupation of the team members. These questions are asked in the same way as those concerning the helpers who were not expected to take ownership in the new business. Thus, comparisons can be made between the diversity within the founding team and within the set of helpers.

We also asked how the respondent would describe his or her relationship to the team member, presenting a list of role relationships from which respondents could choose. This question can be taken to indicate diversity in the kinds of role relationships respondents have with team members, and it can also be used to assess tie strength. In Question 233 and follow-ups, respondents were questioned not only about their relationship with the team member but also about relations between all of the team members who were listed. Thus, a composite picture can be drawn of how the team members knew one another before the start-up process began.

Questions 221 through 228 asked in what ways a team member had helped with the start-up. Altogether, 10 different kinds of help were specifically asked about, and an eleventh category was included for respondents who wished to tell us about a resource that was not included in the choices they were given. Preliminary analysis of the first wave data for the mixed gender and female samples indicated that three categories could be added to the list of how team members helped with the start-up. A review of the "other kinds of assistance" option revealed that providing moral or emotional support, labor, or creativity or ideas was a frequent response. Since collection of the minority oversample data was lagged by a year, these categories could be added to the questionnaire before those individuals were interviewed. As such, responses to Q256_C, Q256F, and Q256I reflect only responses by individuals in the minority oversample. Similarly, Q258, which asked about which form of assistance was most important, was amended to include these three categories to the list of types of assistance.

Because of time constraints, we could not ask respondents to indicate the significance of each resource, and so instead in Question 229 we asked them which form of assistance had been the most important for the new business start-up. Asking this question allowed us to come back to it in subsequent waves and ask the respondent if the helper had, in fact, delivered on the kind of assistance that was promised and also to rate how important it actually had been in the start-up effort.

Earlier studies have shown that much of what a nascent entrepreneur needs is obtained free, at a discounted price, or as part of a barter or exchange relationship. Accordingly, Question 230 asked respondents to indicate the terms on which the resource was made available to the start-up. In addition to the above choices, we also asked whether it was obtained at a market price. Answers to this question not only indicate the kind of resources that a nascent entrepreneur obtained from helpers but also might be taken as an indirect indication of the strength of the tie between the respondent and the helper.

There were several questions regarding construction of a start-up team included in the "activities" portion of the interview. These items were included to examine the activities that individuals pursue during the start-up process (Q116, Q117, Q118, Q119, Q119a). The questions do not specify ownership as a criterion for team member inclusion and consequently are more likely to reflect efforts to assemble a management team rather than an ownership team as specified in the team items described above.

Descriptive Statistics

Table 27.1 displays descriptive statistics for questions about the start-up team.

After weighting the data to compensate for the two oversamples, the 816 nascent entrepreneurs interviewed reported 395 solo efforts and 421 entrepreneurial teams. Persons were classified as team members if they owned some equity in the start-up. Including the solo efforts and the teams, a total of 1,423 individuals were identified as involved in these start-ups. Of this total, 62% were men and 38% were women. Men and women were not distributed proportionately, however, across solo and team efforts. Forty-four percent of the 395 solo efforts were undertaken by women.

As shown in Table 27.1, the great majority of the 421 team efforts involved only two people, constituting 38% of all start-ups and 74% of the team efforts. About 13% involved three people, 7% involved four people, and about 5% involved five or more people.

About 36% of all teams are single sex: 7% composed only of women and 29% are composed only of men. The majority of teams, therefore, are of mixed sex. Teams of two are the most likely to be mixed, as about two thirds of them contain a man and woman. Teams with more than three members are slightly less likely to be mixed, as about 52% contain people of both sexes.

Table 27.1   Descriptive Statistics: Organizational Founding for Individuals and Teams

Variable	Number of Cases	Unit of Analysis	Proportion (weighted)
Size (Individual) (Team)	816	One member	395
		Two members	312
		Three members	55
		Four members	31
		Five + Members	23
Gender composition (Individual)	1,423	Male	0.62
		Female	0.38
Gender composition (Multimember Team)	421	All Male	0.29
		All Female	0.07
		Mixed gender	0.64
Ethnicity composition (Individual)	1,347[a]	White	0.72
		Black	0.17
		Hispanic	0.09
		Asian	0.02
Ethnicity composition (Team)	399[b]	Single ethnicity	0.86
		Multiple ethnicities	0.14
Industry (Team)	421	Primary / manufacturing	0.21
		Personal service	0.18
		Retail / wholesale	0.28
		Business / professional Service	0.33
Relational composition (Multimember team)	421	With spouses / partners	0.53
		With nonspouse family member	0.18
		With business associates	0.15

NOTES:

a. Excludes multimember teams involving other ethnicities or with missing information.

b. Excludes multimember teams with any missing information on occupational composition.

Before concluding that entrepreneurial teams exhibit much sex diversity, it is necessary to further explore the causes of the diversity. Many businesses are started by heterosexual married or cohabiting couples, thus introducing sex diversity into the team population by default. If pairs of spouses or partners constitute a high percentage of team members, then the extent of sex homophily may be understated. Among the 421 teams, 223 had a spouse or partner pair.

In addition to spouse and partner ties, ties to relatives and family members also appear to reduce the level of sex homophily. Seventy-six (18%) of the teams included a nonspouse family member or relative. Business colleagues and work associates are another important source of team members, and 63 (15%) contained members linked by business or work relations.

The majority of the individuals in the start-up process are White (72%). Only 17% classify themselves as Black, 9% as Hispanic, and only 2% as Asian. Only 14% of the teams represent differing race/ethnicity among the team members. The vast majority of teams are composed of a single ethnicity (86%).

Previous research speculates that teams are more common in "upstream industries," those closer to the source of raw materials. Results displayed in Table 27.1 indicate that over a third (36%) of the teams report starting the business in the business/professional service sector. Twenty-eight percent are starting in retail/wholesale.

Conclusion

With the PSED data, researchers can explore several principles by which entrepreneurial teams are formed. In a field that often treats strategic purposive choice as an implicit guiding principle for entrepreneurial behavior, the PSED data provides an opportunity to challenge the strategic view. For example, in our analysis of entrepreneurial teams, we used the first wave of the PSED data to test for the operation of five mechanisms affecting the composition of entrepreneurial teams (Ruef, Aldrich, & Carter, 2003). We found strong support for one mechanism that influences group composition: homophily with respect to gender, ethnicity, and occupation. We found mixed support for two other mechanisms—constraints based on degree of prior familiarity and ecological constraint, based on a group's relative size in the population of nascent entrepreneurs. The constraint imposed by "strong" ties, such as romantic relationships and family ties, was quite pronounced, but "weak" ties, measured by business acquaintances, imposed no significant network constraint. We suggested that ecological constraint contributes to the disproportionate isolation of numerical minorities—such as women and blue-collar workers—in the population of entrepreneurs. We found little empirical support for two other mechanisms of group composition: functional diversification of achieved characteristics and differential homophily based on status expectations.

We note three interesting research implications that could be pursued with the PSED data. First, sociological theories of entrepreneurial team formation pose a challenge to strategic theories of how entrepreneurial teams are formed. Strategic theories of team formation assume that economic rationality will prevail and lead to team member choices based upon the functional diversification of member characteristics. However, our research so far has found that team composition is driven by similarity, not difference. Organizational founders appear more concerned with trust and familiarity than with functional competence. Indeed, they almost seem to be discounting competency in favor of rewarding trust. To investigate this issue further, researchers could look more closely at the specific contributions made by team members and the terms on which they are made. At the level of specialized contributions, perhaps we will find distinctive functional competencies are relevant, even within fairly homogeneous teams.

Second, because the PSED is a longitudinal data set, it can be used to assess the long-term consequences of building entrepreneurial teams based on homophily rather than difference. Do the benefits of recruiting trustworthy others as team members outweigh the possible cost of excluding strangers? We found that the number of distinctive occupational categories in teams involving strangers was significantly higher than the number found in teams without strangers. These results showed that avoiding the inclusion of strangers could decrease functional diversity and thus potentially damage the success of the new venture. If emerging businesses benefit from strong, in-group-based ties among their members, then homophily should have a positive effect on survival. If, however, such ties reduce a team's ability to respond to unforeseen or radically changing circumstances, then homophily may be a handicap for teams.

Third, organizations are a significant sorting point along many dimensions of membership, especially gender and occupations. New organizations can both reproduce and challenge the existing social order, either perpetuating or disrupting tendencies already present in the culture. Within the United States, the composition of founding teams reflects the tendency toward gender, ethnic, and occupational homophily. If our preliminary results hold up over the multiple waves of the PSED, they suggest that new organizations will exacerbate the already strong tendencies toward homophily in social relationships. However, we may find that homogeneous organizations ultimately do not do as well as heterogeneous ones. Founders might then be encouraged to search more widely for team members rather than fall back on the familiar and the trustworthy. Research results on entrepreneurial teams thus might have important public policy consequences as well as practical economic significance.

References

Bird, B. J. (1989). *Entrepreneurial behavior.* Glenview, IL: Scott, Foresman.

Chandler, G. N., & Hanks, S. H. (1998). An investigation of new venture teams in emerging businesses. In P. D. Reynolds, W. Bygrave, & N. M. Carter, (Eds.), *Frontiers of entrepreneurship research* (pp. 318–330). Wellesley, MA: Babson College.

Cooper, A. C., & Daily, C. M. (1997). Entrepreneurial teams. In D. L. Sexton & R. W. Smilor (Eds.), *Entrepreneurship 2000* (pp. 127–150). Chicago, IL: Upstart.

Francis, D. H., & Sandberg, W. R. (2000). Friendship within entrepreneurial teams and its association with team and venture performance. *Entrepreneurship Theory and Practice, 25*(2), 5–25.

Gartner, W. B. (1985). A conceptual framework for describing the phenomenon of new venture creation. *Academy of Management Review, 10*(4), 696–706.

Hinds, P. J., Carley, K. M., Krackhardt, D., & Wholey, D. (2000). Choosing work group members: Balancing similarity, competence, and familiarity. *Organizational Behavior and Human Decision Processes, 81*(2), 226–251.

Kamm, J. B., & Nurick, A. J. (1993). The stages of team venture formation: A decision-making model. *Entrepreneurship Theory and Practice, 17*(2), 17–27.

Kamm, J. B., Shuman, J. C., Seeger, J. A., & Nurick, A. J. (1990). Entrepreneurial teams in new venture creation: A research agenda. *Entrepreneurship Theory and Practice, 14*(4), 7–17.

Lazarsfeld, P., & Merton, R. K. (1954). Friendship as a social process: A substantive and methodological analysis. In M. Berger, T. Abel, & C. Page (Eds.), *Freedom and control in modern society* (pp. 18–66). New York: Octagon Books.

Lechler, T. (2001). Social interaction: A determinant of entrepreneurial team venture success. *Small Business Economics, 16*(4), 263–278.

Mosakowski, E. (1998). Entrepreneurial resources, organizational choices, and competitive outcomes. *Organization Science, 9*(6), 625–643.

Nevid, J. F. (1984). Sex differences in factors of romantic attraction. *Sex Roles, 11,* 401–411.

Ruef, M., Aldrich, H. E., & Carter, N. M. (2003). The structure of founding teams: Homophily, strong ties, and isolation among U.S. entrepreneurs. *American Sociological Review, 68* (April), 195–222.

Vesper, K. H. (1990). *New venture strategies.* Englewood Cliffs, NJ: Prentice Hall.

CHAPTER 28

Firm Founding

Nancy M. Carter

William B. Gartner

Paul D. Reynolds

The theoretical model of the start-up process presented in the Foreword of this handbook specifies three major transitions in the start-up process: (1) entry into the start-up process by people in the general population, and (2) exit from the start-up process—either as a new firm birth, or (3) an abandoning of the effort. The subsequent chapters demonstrate that what happens between the point of entry and that of exit is quite complex, including even pinpointing when the beginning commences. We show in this chapter that designating the point at which the start-up process transitions from gestation to firm founding can be equally difficult to specify. At some point in the creation of a new business, the entrepreneur and others should be able to perceive the existence of a new firm, or not. But when this tipping point occurs and what are appropriate indicators to discern whether a new firm "exists" remains nebulous.

Identifying appropriate measures that signify the existence of a new firm is important because it can help firm founders and others (publicpolicy makers and those individuals involved in supporting firm creation) recognize whether certain kinds of firm creation efforts might lead to viable new firms or whether these efforts should be abandoned. There are economic, social, and psychological costs and benefits associated with start-up, and knowing when initiating efforts pass over the "finish line" of gestation to firm birth has implications for the entrepreneurs, their families, their communities, and other stakeholders in the micro and macro environment.

Scholars also would find useful the identification of markers that designate firm formation "success." Prior studies on identifying appropriate samples for studying "new" firms have found that measures used to select businesses for inclusion in the samples are not well correlated (Aldrich, Kalleberg, Marsden, & Cassell, 1989; Birley, 1984; 1986; Kalleberg, Marsden, Aldrich, & Cassell, 1990; Busenitz & Murphy, 1996; Murphy, 2002). The lack of correlation suggests that each firm marker potentially identifies a different group of firms, or firms at different stages in their life course. For example, ecological research often designates *new* as an operating business. A major criticism of this definition is that by focusing on operating start-ups, only outcomes of successful founding attempts are studied. Unsuccessful attempts that would have discontinued prior to achieving operating status are not included in the samples, understating the organizational diversity that exists in the population (Amburgey & Rao, 1996).

What then is the point of demarcation that differentiates emerging organizations from those few operational start-ups? What might be used to determine whether a successful launch of a new business has occurred or not? The choice is made difficult because many markers can be considered both firm formation activities as well as start-up indicators as discussed in the chapter on organizing activities. Demarcating when this transition actually occurs is surprisingly difficult to do (Reynolds & Miller, 1992).

What Constitutes "Founded"?

There are few studies that have examined new firms still in the gestation process. Insight about which indicators are appropriate for designating a firm founding comes instead from the growing body of research that focused on identifying samples of new ventures. These research efforts attempted to determine the impact of using different sample sources by examining the overlap between firms listed in state unemployment insurance (ES202) files , Dun & Bradstreet's Market Indicator (DMI) files, local telephone white page listings, state sales tax records, chamber of commerce membership lists, physically canvassing an area, and association membership directories (Birley, 1984; Aldrich et al., 1989; Kalleberg et al., 1990; Busenitz & Murphy, 1996; Murphy, 2002). The purpose of the comparisons was to determine which sampling source offered the greatest viability, efficiency, and effectiveness for identifying firms early in the start-up process. The presumption was that some sources are better than others for identifying entities at the very early stage of their emergence.

An unintended outcome of these comparisons is the wide variety of definitions of what constitutes an organization. Each of the sampling sources imposed different criteria for whether a venture was included in the sample and implicitly defined the tipping point at which an effort transitioned from gestation to new-firm status. For example, Aldrich et al. (1989) found that physically canvassing an area to identify businesses was the best way to find new firms. This method depended on physical location, or "visibility," as the criterion for an organization's emergence. Alternatively, Busenitz & Murphy (1996) found sales tax records to be a better source arguing that even ventures yet to gain physical visibility, those operating out of homes, can be up and operating, shipping product, and paying sales tax before becoming visible to canvassers. They found that fully 58% of their sample was "invisible," yet were already included in sales tax records.

Variability in the start-up indicators across the various sample sources represents different theoretical perspectives about organization emergence. Economists focus on entrance and exit of an entity into and out of a competitive market, conceptualizing each of the transitions as an event. A distinction is sometimes made between types of organizational births, start-ups and entries. Budros (1993), for example, demonstrated that opening a new organization in the life insurance market has different consequences and outcomes than when an ongoing organization entity enters into a new market.

Organizational researchers expanded Budros's (1993) distinction further by differentiating (1) sponsored entities from the lateral entries of established organizations (Carroll, Bigelow, Seidel, & Tsai, 1996) and (2) takeovers and changes in legal form from de novo start-ups (Aldrich et al., 1989). The date of incorporation is often used in these theoretical perspectives as the indicator representing when an entity is considered "founded."

Sociologists tend to define new organizations in terms of boundary criteria. This perspective views organizations based on institutional arguments that organizations are socially construed (Hannan, 1986) and their validation (existence) comes from external legitimizing factors (Aldrich, 1999; Aldrich & Fiol, 1994). The development of boundaries provides signals to external constituents that an organization exists. For example, getting a phone listing for the business not only signifies that an organization might exist, it is a way for a nascent entrepreneur to demonstrate to others (potential customers, investors, employees, suppliers) that the emerging organization should merit their involvement (Gartner, Bird, & Starr, 1992). Most of the boundary measures that have been used by organizational ecologists denote legal establishment (Baum & Oliver, 1992; Ranger-Moore, Banaszak-Holl, & Hannan, 1991; Budros, 1993), or operational start-up (Schoonhoven, Eisenhardt, & Lyman, 1990; Hannan & Carroll, 1992, 1995; Ingram & Inman, 1996).

Other organization theory proposes a life cycle progression for firm founding, specifying distinct phases and order for the organization's emergence. For example, Birley (1984) proposed a sequence of eight events ranging from intention, to start, to hiring full-time employees that characterize organization emergence. She noted that founding can be arbitrarily designated at any of the eight points but that the choice would have consequences for researchers seeking a representative sample of new ventures. Life cycle models assume that emergence will occur linearly and that there will be little iteration among the life cycle phases.

Emergence as a Process

Early theoretical perspectives and definitions viewed organization founding as a discrete event. More recent positions recognize that emergence is a process made up of multiple stages, including, for example, announcement, incorporation, and operational start-up (Hannan & Freeman, 1989, p. 148). If only boundary indicators such as legal establishment and operational start-up are used as indicators of founding, the phenomenon will not be captured until late in the emergence process. To characterize the very earliest stages of emergence, multiple indicators are needed that reflect the complexity of the process. Katz and Gartner (1988) proposed a model that has the potential for assessing the complexity of this very earliest stage. Extending McKelvey's (1980) definition of an organization, Katz and Gartner proposed that there are four "properties" that identify emergence: *intention* (characteristics that demonstrate purpose and goals), *resources* (physical components, such as human and financial capital), *boundary* (barrier conditions that distinguish the organization as such—incorporation, phone listing, a tax identification number), and *exchange* (transactions between the emerging organization and others, such as sales, loans, or investment). They indicated that an emerging organization would "reveal" itself in different ways and that a focus on any one of these four properties would result in an observer noticing, at different times, aspects of an organization coming into existence.

Reynolds and Miller (1992) tested the emergence model using samples derived from DMI files in Minnesota and Pennsylvania. Firm founders were interviewed about the occurrence (month and year) of four "gestation markers" in the creation of their businesses: *personal commitment* (when members of the start-up team first made an investment of personal time and resources), *financial support* (when first outside financial support was obtained), *sales* (when first sales income was received), and *hiring* (when firm first hired anyone, full- or part-time). In the Katz and Gartner (1988) framework, these variables would be categorized as personal commitment—*intention,* sales and financial support—*exchange,* and hiring—*resources.* Reynolds and Miller (1992, p. 408) found that

> None of these features of gestation in living systems are shared by new firms. Not all events occur. Every possible sequence of events was present. There is substantial variation in length of the gestation period.

In other words, firms do not "signal" their existence in the same way. About one half of all of the firms in their sample did not report all four events. Half of the firms indicated that their last event was hiring employees or receiving sales income, 40% indicated receiving financial support as their last event, and 25% indicated personal commitment came last. After a number of analyses to explore various sequences of start-up events, Reynolds and Miller (1992, p. 416) concluded that

> The most important implication is the importance of separating the founding process into two parts. The gestation period, from conception to birth, should be treated separately from the post-birth period.

How Many Properties Are Enough?

The framework proposed by Katz and Gartner (1988) and its empirical test ushered in a greater recognition of different theoretical perspectives for identifying organizations and a greater awareness that preorganization is composed of numerous stages or subprocesses. Whereas researchers previously had viewed the start-up process in terms of "big chunk," discrete stages, recognition was evolving that greater diversity in the form and the dynamics of subprocesses better characterized start-up. The notion that organizational emergence could be conceptualized as "moving from an amorphous stage of potentiality, through growing coherence, to a stage where they are fully formed" (Aldrich et al., 1989, p. 369), provoked calls for greater specificity. Questions were posed requiring answers: What happens in the amorphous stage of potentiality? What indicators distinguish the transition from growing coherence fully formed? Or what is minimally required to be "fully formed?" Katz and Gartner (1988) presumed that all four of the properties specified in their framework would need to be manifest in order for the emerging organization to be "an organization" but specified no minimal number of activities required to consider a particular property complete. Similarly, Carter et al. (1996) found that while nascent entrepreneurs who perceived that they had succeeded in getting a business operating had performed more activities than those who reported the start-up effort as still in gestation, or who had discontinued and given up, they did not determine the precise number of activities that tipped the effort from gestation to start-up. Using 14 organizing activities and 6 start-up indicators they examined the rate and pattern of nascent entrepreneurs who were in the process of starting businesses. They found that buying facilities or equipment (a "visible" boundary indicator) and getting outside financial support (an exchange indicator) discriminated nascent entrepreneurs who started a business from those who had quit or were still trying. Because their sample was small ($N = 71$), Carter et al., recommended that additional research examine not only the pattern and timing of the organizing activities, and start-up indicators, but contingencies that might affect the processes including perceptions about success, level of access to scarce resources, level of commitment, industry characteristics, and firm strategy.

The recommendation that future research must consider how contextual factors moderate the sequencing of subprocesses during emergence, and perhaps the number minimally needed to represent organizational founding, echoed previous research. Halliday, Powell, & Granfors (1987) contended that the context of the environment (i.e., competitiveness) and flexibility of the organization's structure distinguish minimalist organizations from other organizations. "Minimalist" organizations were seen as differing from nonminimalist organizations along four core dimensions: fewer resources required to be established (lower initial costs); fewer resources required to maintain existence (lower maintenance costs); having reserve infrastructures; and being more adaptable. The distinction between the two types of organizations was not that between profit and nonprofit organizations since minimalist organizations are found in highly competitive market-organized environments (e.g., software development, investment advisors, and other professional enterprises, as well as firms in cottage industries). Instead, the context of the environment (i.e., competitiveness) and the flexibility of the organization's structure were seen as the differentiating characteristics. The presumption is that the sequencing and number of start-up indicators needed to qualify a minimalist firm as founded varies from that required of nonminimalist organizations to reach the designation.

Busenitz and Murphy (1996) implicitly provided further support that context moderates the dynamics among the subprocesses of emergence through their finding that start-up indicators of founding differ across entry mode, industry sections, and location of the businesses. They found that of the 152 "new" businesses in their sample, 80% were operated by the founder, 14% had been purchased, 1% were franchisees, and 4% were "other" (e.g., joint ventures). Similarly, Aldrich and Kenworthy (1999, p. 31) supported the notion of context determining appropriateness of start-up indicators in their contention that emergence depends on fitness of the entity and that fitness is "the interactive product of what nascent entrepreneurs offer to particular local environments."

More recently, Ruef (2001) proposed five subprocesses indicative of firm founding, the emerging dynamics of which are subject to contingencies: *initiation, resource mobilization, legal establishment, social organization,* and *operational start-up.* He saw all five as required before an organization is fully formed but expected that the pattern or sequence of the subprocesses would vary by the social context (structural, strategic, and environmental contingencies). Among the 591 business professionals he surveyed, he found that social context has a fairly pervasive impact on the occurrence and sequence of founding process with the exception of the timing of legal establishment.

Using the PSED to Test Firm Founding

The literature review makes clear that choosing indicators to signify firm founding is a thorny issue and ultimately must be driven by theory. The PSED offers the potential for testing a number of theoretical perspectives regarding firm founding. The phone questionnaire used for the first-round interview (Wave 1) contained 26 items that assess various organizing activities and start-up indicators (Q109 to Q181). Most of the items asked the respondent whether they had yet engaged in the activity (1 = yes; 2 = no) and if the response was yes, in which month and year the activity had occurred. A few of the items had other categorical responses. For example, Q120 asked, "At what stage of development is the product or service this start-up will be selling: (1) Completed and ready for sale or delivery; (2) A prototype or procedure has been tested with customers; (3) A model or procedure is being developed; or (4) Still in the idea stage"? Several of the dichotomous (yes-no) items also contain contingent questions asking for greater specificity regarding the status of the activity. For example, Q145 asked respondents whether financial institutions or other people had been asked for funds. If they responded "yes," they were asked whether asking others, or institutions, for funds was completed or still in process? If they said they had not asked for outside funds, they were asked whether others, or financial institutions, would be asked or whether outside funding was not relevant for the start-up. In the follow-up phone interview (Wave 2) conducted approximately 12 months after the first phone interview, respondents were asked about activities and start-up indicators that they had not reported completed during the first phone interview. Additionally, during the follow-up interview (Wave 2), they were asked to describe the current status of their start-up efforts (R502 for the mixed gender and female oversamples; S502 for the minority oversample): Is it an operating business (coded 1), still in active start-up phase (coded 2), still a start-up but currently inactive (coded 3), or no longer being worked on by anyone (coded 4)?

Recognizing that some items might be classified both as organization activities and start-up indicators, we selected for this chapter items that are most likely to represent firm founding. We display these in Table 28.1, according to how they align with the Katz and Gartner (1988) framework to illustrate one theoretical approach that can be tested with the data. Other items could be selected to test alternative theoretical frameworks.

Table 28.1   Firm Founding Items in the PSED

Q109. I will read a list of things people sometimes do when starting a business. Please tell me if YOU have done any of the following.

Dimension	Item Number	Question
Intention	R502	How would you describe the current status of this start-up effort? Is it now an operating business, still in an active start-up phase, still a start-up but currently inactive, no longer being worked on by anyone, or something else?
Resource	Q153	Have you begun to devote full-time to the business—35 or more hours per week?
	Q155	Have any employees or managers been hired for pay—workers that would NOT share ownership?
	Q120	At what stage of development is the product or service this start-up will be selling? (Considered a start-up indicator if response was: completed and ready for sale or delivery)
Exchange	Q149	Has credit with a supplier been established?
	Q162	Has the new business received any money, income, or fees from the sale of goods or services?
	Q163	Does the monthly revenue now exceed the monthly expenses?
Boundary	Q160	Has a bank account been opened exclusively for this new business?
	Q171	Does the new business have its own listing in the phone book?
	Q131	Have any major items like equipment, facilities, or property been purchased, leased, or rented for the new start-up?
	Q181	To your knowledge, is the new business listed with Dun & Bradstreet, the credit-rating firm?
	Q175	Has the new business paid any state unemployment insurance taxes?
	Q177	Has the new business paid any federal social security taxes (FICA payments)?
	Q179	Has the new business filed a federal income tax return?

Descriptive Statistics

To report descriptive statistics about the firm founding indicators, we considered data from the 830 nascent entrepreneurs in the PSED. We eliminated from consideration six respondents who reported already having 90 days of positive cash flow at the time of the initial phone interview (considering them as new businesses) and two who provided no data for the firm organizing/founding activities except thinking about starting a new business. Because we were interested in firm founding indicators, we further reduced the sample for analysis to those 609 who responded to the first follow-up interview. Analyses were weighted by adjusting WTW2 to reflect the attrition in the sample size.

Questionnaire items R502 and S502 (Wave 2) asked respondents at the time of the first follow-up phone interview to describe the current status of their start-up effort. Nearly equal numbers reported an operating business ($n = 184$; 30%), or that they were still in an active start-up phase ($n = 190$; 31%). Twenty percent ($n = 120$) reported they still considered their effort a start-up but that they were currently inactive; and 19% ($n = 116$) reported that the initiative was no longer being worked on by anyone. Those reporting an operating business and those who were still in an active start-up phase were given a detailed interview including questions asking about the status of each of the organizing and firm founding activities. Budget constraints precluded asking these questions of those in the inactive category or of those who gave up. Thus, it is the 374 operating and active start-ups that we are interested in here.

Table 28.2 reports the percentage of respondents who had completed each of the founding indicators at the time of the first follow-up interview. The findings indicate that almost 80% had purchased, leased, or rented equipment, facilities, or property for the business and that three fourths (75%) had received income from the sales of goods or services. Conversely, less than 10% reported being listed with Dun & Bradstreet and only 25% reported having paid unemployment insurance taxes. Not surprisingly, those who reported operating businesses were substantially more likely to have reported completing the founding indicators than those still in active start-up.

When firm founding activities occur is key to understanding the transition, or tipping point, at which an emerging firm becomes one that is fully operational. Previous research has reported that there is considerable variation in the sequencing of founding indicators (Reynolds & Miller, 1992). Because PSED data contain information on whether each of the activities occurs, and if it did, when, sequencing among the indicators can be examined. Table 28.3 displays the distribution of the first founding indicators by those with operating businesses and those with active start-up efforts. The results indicate that overall one third (33%) reported that purchasing, leasing, or renting equipment, facilities, or property was their first founding indicator, followed by establishing credit with a supplier and receiving money from sales. The implication of the findings displayed in the table is that not only are there differences between those who report an operating business and those still in active start-up, but there also appear to be considerable variations among the sequencing of the founding indicators. No one indicator can be designated as the first founding indicator to occur.

Table 28.2   Percentage of Founding Indicators Completed at First Follow-up Interview

Founding Indicator	% Still Active n = 184	% Operating n = 190	% Total n = 374
Major items like equipment, facilities, or property have been purchased, leased, or rented for the new start-up?	74	85	79
New business has received money, income, or fees from the sale of goods or services?	61	89	75
Bank account been opened exclusively for this new business?	46	75	60
Credit with a supplier been established?	52	65	58
Product or service is completed and ready for sale or delivery.	37	78	57
Begun to devote full time to the business—35 or more hours per week?	44	59	51
Monthly revenue now exceeds the monthly expenses?	25	65	45
New business has filed a federal income tax return?	31	55	43
Employees or managers have been hired for pay?	27	39	33
New business has its own listing in the phone book?	18	49	33
New business has paid any federal social security taxes (FICA payments)?	19	40	29
New business has paid any state unemployment insurance taxes?	12	25	18
New business is listed with Dun & Bradstreet, the credit-rating firm?	5	13	9

NOTE: Weighted by WTW2 adjusted for sample attrition.

Additional insight about the sequencing of firm emergence can be gained by examining the time that elapses between the first organizing activity a nascent entrepreneur undertakes and each of the founding indicators. An understanding of this gestation window may have implications for the costliness and success of firm emergence. Table 28.4 reports a preliminary step in developing the continuum for plotting the sequencing of activities. The results represent the median number of months between the first organizing activity undertaken and each of the founding indicators across the two types of firm status. The timing variable is highly skewed given the long time period some of the nascent entrepreneurs have been in the start-up process as discussed in Chapter 26. Consequently, we report the median value here for illustrative purposes. The findings indicate that 50% of the nascent entrepreneurs who filed a federal income tax return did so within the first 18 months

Table 28.3   Frequency Distribution: First Founding Indicator

Founding Indicator [a,b]	% Still Trying	% Operating	Total N	% Total[c]
Major items like equipment, facilities, or property purchased, leased	38	28	120	33
Credit from supplier established	18	21	71	20
Received money, income, or fees from sale of goods or services	18	17	64	18
Files federal income tax return	13	20	60	17
Bank account opened exclusively for this business	11	17	52	14
Devoted full-time to business	13	11	43	12
Perceived operating business	—[d]	15	29	8
Monthly revenues exceeded monthly expenses	4	5	17	5
Business has own phone listing	2	6	14	4
Hired employees or managers	2	5	13	4
Paid federal social security taxes (FICA)	3	3	10	3
Paid state unemployment insurance	2	2	7	2
Business listed with Dun & Bradstreet	0	1	2	<1

NOTES:

a. Weighted by WTW2 adjusted for sample attrition.

b. Date information associated with the stage of product development asked about when it first started, not when the product/service was complete and ready to ship to customer as it was used in the analyses reported in Table 28.2. Consequently, it is not included in analyses involving the time of the founding indicators.

c. Total does not sum to number of eligible nascent entrepreneurs (374) since some respondents indicated simultaneous first behaviors.

d. Nascent entrepreneurs who reported still trying to get the business established at the time of the first follow-up interview were not asked this question.

of their start-up efforts. Similarly, 50% who opened a bank account; established credit; purchased, leased, or rented equipment or property; received sales; or paid federal social security tax did so within the first 2 years. It is noteworthy that 50% of those who reported being listed with Dun & Bradstreet or who reported attaining profitability indicate that more than 3 years elapsed since their first organizing activity and these founding activities.

Respondents who reported having an operating business at the first follow-up were asked to indicate in what year and in what month the firm became an operating business (R563 for the mixed gender and female oversamples; S563 for the

Table 28.4   Median Months From First Activity to Firm Founding Indicator[a]

Founding Indicator	% Still Trying	% Operating	% Total	% Total N
New business has filed a federal income tax return?	19.83	16.99	17.63	162
Bank account been opened exclusively for this new business?	23.01	24.01	23.03	227
Major items like equipment, facilities, or property have been purchased, leased, or rented for the new start-up?	24.01	23.45	24.01	297
Credit with a supplier been established?	25.95	22.01	24.01	216
New business has received money, income, or fees from the sale of goods or services?	31.35	20.82	25.03	279
New business has paid any federal social security taxes (FICA payments)?	28.71	23.66	25.99	109
New business has paid any state unemployment insurance taxes?	25.99	29.89	26.43	69
Begun to devote full-time to the business—35 or more hours per week?	31.97	25.03	27.04	192
Perception of having operating business?	—[b]	29.22	29.22	164
New business has its own listing in the phone book?	32.99	26.76	31.05	99
Employees or managers have been hired for pay?	55.29	25.79	32.99	123
New business is listed with Dun & Bradstreet, the credit-rating firm?	28.47	37.19	33.71	30
Monthly revenue now exceeds the monthly expenses?	45.07	37.02	37.92	166

NOTES:

a. Weighted by WTW2 adjusted for sample attrition.

b. Nascent entrepreneurs who reported still trying to get the business established at the time of the first follow-up interview were not asked this question.

minority oversample). Interestingly, a number of respondents gave a date that preceded the initial interview, and Table 28.4 shows that the perception is not the last of the founding indicators to occur. Indeed, 50% of those who report a date when the effort became an operating effort indicate that the perception occurred nearly 2.5 years (29 months) after the initial organizing effort. Further analyses of the data are needed to better understand the significance of this finding.

Our findings appear to support the exploratory efforts of Carter et al. (1996) and Reynolds and Miller (1992) who suggest that a constellation of founding indicators need to be accomplished before nascent entrepreneurs believe they have an operating business. Indeed, nascent entrepreneurs do not, as a whole, use the same firm founding indicators as a means of supporting their perception of success at new firm founding. While no effort has been made in this chapter to explore how the order and timing of founding indicators corresponds with the emergence of different types of businesses or how different contextual situations might affect the process, it is likely that certain clusters of founding markers may signal the founding of different types of new businesses.

Implications

We believe that the findings presented in this chapter offer evidence that firm founding, as a phenomenon, is multidimensional in nature and that using only one measure of success at founding (such as Q162—Has the new business received any money, income, or fees from the sale of goods and services?) should only be attempted when a strong theoretical rationale for the use of one measure is provided. We urge all scholars who are considering *sales* as the dependent measure of success at firm founding to provide a theoretical logic for this choice. It should also be noted that a founder's perception of success at creating an operating business does not ensure that others would necessarily be able to observe success as well. Ways that others would identify a new business (e.g., tax returns, unemployment insurance, Dan & Bradstreet) would not necessarily correlate with the founder's perception that a new business is operating. It will likely be of interest to public policymakers to know the length of time that these emerging businesses take to show up on the tax rolls.

Finally, while firm founding itself may appear, to some, to be an arbitrary marker on the path from organization conception to subsequent firm growth (or failure), it is entirely possible that the identification of the markers of firm formation success might significantly predict the "hardiness" and viability of these new firms to survive and prosper. Although some firm founders may perceive an operating business exists, such a perception might not help sustain these individuals' efforts to undertake the necessary steps to actually build a sustainable business. As was noted earlier, there are many nascent entrepreneurs who have achieved many of the firm founding indicators who perceive that they are still trying to achieve a new business. These "still trying" efforts may, over time, become the more viable and high-growth businesses in the sample.

References

Aldrich, H. E. (1999). *Organizations evolving*. London: Sage.

Aldrich, H. E., & Fiol, M. (1994). Fools rush in? The institutional context of industry creation. *Academy of Management Review, 19*(4), 645–670.

Aldrich, H., Kalleberg, A., Marsden, P., & Cassell, J. (1989). In pursuit of evidence: Sampling procedures for locating new businesses. *Journal of Business Venturing, 4*(6), 367–386.

Aldrich, H. E., & Kenworthy, A. L. (1999). The accidental entrepreneurs: Campbellian antinomies and organization foundings. In J. A. C. Baum & B. McKelvey (Eds.), *Variations in organization science: Essays in honor of Donald T. Campbell* (pp. 19–33). Thousand Oaks, CA: Sage.

Amburgey, T. L., & Rao, H. (1996). Organizational ecology: Past, present and future directions. *Academy of Management Journal, 39*(5), 1265–1286.

Baum, J. A. C., & Oliver, C. (1992). Institutional embeddedness and the dynamics of organizational populations. *American Sociological Review, 57*, 540–549.

Birley, S. (1984). Finding the new firm. *Academy of Management Proceedings, 47*, 64–68.

Budros, A. (1993). An analysis of organizational birth types: Organizational start-up and entry in the nineteenth-century life insurance industry. *Social Forces, 72*(1), 199–221.

Busenitz, L. W., & Murphy, G. B. (1996). New evidence in the pursuit of locating new businesses. *Journal of Business Venturing, 11*(3), 221–231.

Carroll, G., Bigelow, L., Seidel, M. D., & Tsai, L. (1996). The fates of de novo and de alio producers in the American automobile industry, 1885–1982. *Strategic Management Journal, 17*, 117–137.

Carter, N. M., Gartner, W. B., & Reynolds, P. D. (1996). Exploring start-up event sequences. *Journal of Business Venturing, 11*(3), 151–166.

Gartner, W. B., Bird, B. J., & Starr, J. (1992). Acting as if: Differentiating entrepreneurial from organizational behavior. *Entrepreneurship Theory and Practice, 16*(3), 13–32.

Halliday, T. C., Powell, M. J., & Granfors, M. W. (1987). Minimalist organizations: Vital events in state bar associations, 1870–1930. *American Sociological Review 52*(August), 456–471.

Hannan, M. T. (1986). *Competitive and institutional process in organizational ecology* (Tech. Rep. No. 86-13). Ithaca, NY: Cornell University, Department of Sociology.

Hannan, M. T., & Carroll, G. R. (1992). *Dynamics of organizational populations.* New York: Oxford University Press.

Hannan, M. T., & Carroll, G. R. (1995). Theory building and cheap talk about legitimation: Reply to Baum and Powell. *American Sociological Review, 60*, 539–544.

Hannan, M. T., & Freeman, J. H. (1989). *Organizational ecology.* Cambridge, MA: Harvard University Press.

Ingram, P., & Inman, C. (1996). Institutions, intergroup competition, and the evolution of hotel populations around Niagara Falls. *Administrative Science Quarterly, 41*, 629–658.

Kalleberg, A. L., Marsden, P. V., Aldrich, H. E., & Cassell, J. W. (1990). Comparing organizational sampling frames. *Administrative Science Quarterly, 35*(4), 658–688.

Katz, J. A., & Gartner, W. B. (1988). Properties of emerging organizations. *Academy of Management Review, 13*(3), 429–441.

McKelvey, B. (1980). *Organizational systematics.* Berkeley: University of California Press.

Murphy, G. B. (2002). The effects of organizational sampling frame selection. *Journal of Business Venturing, 17*(3), 237–252.

Ranger-Moore, J., Banaszak-Holl, J., & Hannan, M. (1991). Density dependent dynamics in regulated industries: Founding rates of banks and life insurance companies. *Administrative Science Quarterly, 36*, 36–65.

Reynolds, P. D., & Miller, B. (1992). New firm gestation: Conception, birth, and implications for research. *Journal of Business Venturing, 7*(5), 405–418.

Ruef, M. (2001). *Origins of organization: The entrepreneurial process.* (Working Paper). Palo Alto, CA: Stanford University.

Schoonhoven, C. B., Eisenhardt, K. M., & Lyman, K. (1990). Speeding products to market: Waiting time to first product introduction in new firms. *Administrative Science Quarterly, 35*(1), 177–207.

CHAPTER 29

Social Networks

Howard E. Aldrich

Nancy M. Carter

Social networks play a significant role in many facets of organizational emergence. Indeed, the larger network structure in which entrepreneurs are embedded constitutes a significant portion of their opportunity structure (Aldrich & Whetten, 1981). Nascent entrepreneurs' *personal networks*—the set of persons to whom they are directly linked—affect their access to social, emotional, and material support. All nascent entrepreneurs draw upon their existing social networks and construct new ones in the process of obtaining knowledge and resources for their organizations.

The Panel Study of Entrepreneurial Dynamics (PSED) collected data on respondents' social network ties in three different sets of questions. First, for the nascent entrepreneur (NE) sample, questions were asked about ties between members of the founding team. That portion of the study is described in Chapter 27. Second, NE respondents were asked about their relationships to people who were not owners but who were being helpful in the start-up process. We call such persons the "helpers." Third, the comparison group (CG) respondents were asked a set of questions about people who were helpful to them in their working career that followed the same format as the NE helper questions. Thus, researchers can compare the kinds of social relationships respondents turn to for help with a business start-up and with their occupational careers. In this chapter, we focus on the parallel questions asked of nascent entrepreneurs and typical adults in the comparison group.

Basic Network Concepts

Network analysts distinguish between two complementary dimensions of someone's social relations: (1) their diversity or heterogeneity and (2) their affective or emotional strength. The usefulness of any relation is context-dependent. In the context of entrepreneurial networks, people need access to information and other resources. Thus, multiple diverse contacts are important, regardless of their strength. We first explain why diversity in social relations conveys advantages to nascent entrepreneurs and then consider the contribution of relational strength to entrepreneurial action.

Diversity or Heterogeneity

Diversity in network ties is crucial for nascent entrepreneurs, as diversity increases access to a wider circle of information about potential markets, new business locations, innovations, sources of capital, and potential investors. By *diversity,* we mean ties to persons of differing social locations and characteristics along a variety of dimensions, such as sex, age, occupation, and ethnicity. Diversity depends on the range of sectors through which a nascent entrepreneur moves.

A network made up of homogeneous ties may have limited value to a nascent entrepreneur, depending upon the context (Granovetter, 1974). In homogeneous networks, information known to one person is rapidly diffused to others and interpreted in similar ways. Two forces promote homogeneity in personal networks. First, people tend to associate with others who have similar values and interests (Burt, 1982, pp. 55–60; Fischer, 1982; Kandel, 1978; Marsden, 1987; McPherson & Smith-Lovin, 1987). Second, people tend toward emotional and personal balance across their social relations (Cartwright & Harary, 1956; Davis, 1963; Holland & Leinhardt, 1972; Ridgeway & Walker, 1994). For example, a nascent entrepreneur's strong friendship with someone increases the likelihood of that person becoming friendly with other persons strongly linked to the entrepreneur.

As ties to the same kinds of people accumulate, the marginal value of succeeding ties drops. Ties to more than one person with similar characteristics or in similar social locations are *redundant* and thus of questionable value in providing new information. An entrepreneur gains little new information from talking to more than one person, if all of them are in nearly identical social locations or share many characteristics in common. For this reason, Burt (1992) argued that when it comes to the flow of information, the strength of ties is less important than whether they are nonredundant with other ties. We turn now to the contribution of strong and weak ties to entrepreneurial action.

Affective or Emotional Strength

The types of relationships that make up a person's total set of relations can be classified according to the *strength of the relationship:* strong, weak, and ties to strangers. A network's level of diversity depends, in part, upon the mix of strong and weak ties. Models of entrepreneurship and business life cycles emphasize the context-dependent nature of the three types of relations. For nascent entrepreneurs, strong and weak ties may be more important than contacts with strangers for the mobilization of resources in the early stages of business development. Later, when a newly founded organization has achieved some stability, arm's length transactions and contacts with strangers assume more importance.

The most reliable relationships in a personal network are *strong ties*, which are usually of long duration. People rely on strong ties for advice, assistance, and support in all areas of their lives, such as asking for help in dealing with an ethical dilemma at work or asking someone to watch their children on short notice. They are long-term, two-way relationships, not governed by short-term calculations of self-interest. Many contain an implicit principle of reciprocal obligations. Consequently, strong ties are typically more reliable than other ties and involve a strong degree of trust and emotional closeness (Granovetter, 1993; Marsden & Campbell, 1984). Individuals tend to make heavy investments in this type of relationship, requiring fairly frequent contact with the other person.

Because of the effort involved in creating and sustaining a strong tie, most people have on the order of 5 to 20 strong ties in their personal networks (Fischer, 1982). Researchers have found that the exact number of strong ties reported is very sensitive to how people are asked to think about their relations. Research on entrepreneurial networks has found that most business owners report 3 to 10 strong ties (Aldrich, Reese, & Dubini, 1989). Attempting to manage large numbers of ties may produce role strain. Nonetheless, gains from extensive ties with others may outweigh the costs (Aldrich, 1979, pp. 259–263; Marks, 1977; Sieber, 1974). A business owner's strong-tie network usually consists of a majority of business associates, a few close friends, and one or two family members (Aldrich, Elam, & Reese, 1996).

Strong ties provide a sheltered sector within which entrepreneurs can avoid the opportunism and uncertainty otherwise possible in market-mediated transactions. In social situations in which people expect to deal with each other over an extended period, strong ties yield three benefits: trust, predictability, and voice. *Trust* tells founders whom they can count on in difficult situations, and it substantially enhances predictability in relations. *Predictability* refers to how the other party will behave if situations change. And, finally, using *voice* in a relation means the persons involved will make their complaints known and negotiate over them, rather than silently sneaking away (Hirschman, 1982). Long-term relationships enhance these benefits, increasing the likelihood of further interaction. Increased frequency of contact, in turn, carries many benefits. Through frequent contacts, strong bonds develop, tacit knowledge is transferred, and each party develops more informal control over the other (Jones, Herterly, & Borgatti, 1997, p. 922).

Whereas strong ties are based on trust, *weak ties* are superficial or casual and normally involve little emotional investment. Weak-tie relationships are typically of shorter duration and involve lower frequency of contact. They are also less reliable and more uncertain than strong ties and often fade into dormancy, although they can be revived when assistance is required. They can be thought of as arm's length relations, involving persons from whom we seek resources but whose full support we cannot count on. Individuals have many more weak ties than strong ties. Examples of weak ties include relationships with customers or clients who are known on a first-name basis but with whom interactions do not go beyond business related interactions.

Rationale for Questions Asked in the PSED

Researchers interested in the entire role set of a respondent typically use the General Social Survey format, called a name generator. They ask people to list up to five people with whom they discuss important matters and then ask further questions about each person named. Given the way this question is asked, it usually results in the naming of strong ties. An alternative format, the position generator, gives respondents a set of occupations, statuses, or other positions and then asks whom they know in each position, followed by additional questions. Given the way this question is asked, strong or weak ties may be elicited.

Given time constraints, we used *neither* a name *nor* a position generator to ask about helpers in the PSED. Instead, we asked only about those persons who had been helpful to the respondent, either with the start-up process or work career. Thus, we expected the ties identified to be mostly strong rather than weak ones. Our network questions were designed to capture three aspects of respondents' relationships with helpers who were not on the start-up team. First, how similar are the helpers to the respondent and to other helpers and to the team members? Second, how strong is the tie between the respondent and the helpers? Third, in what ways has the helper contributed to the start-up effort and on what terms? Exhibit 29.1 shows the questions that were asked, and we turn now to an explanation of how these questions fit into our three-part objectives.

Diversity

Question 241 asked respondents to indicate which people were not on the start-up team but who nonetheless have been particularly helpful in getting the business started, and a follow-up question asked how many there were. Respondents in the comparison group were asked to identify people who have been helpful in their work career. Regardless of the number named, we were only able to ask about the first five helpers identified. In practice, few people named more than three helpers, and so this restriction is not problematic. We asked questions about the sex, age, race and ethnicity, and occupation of the helper. We also asked how the respondent would describe his or her relationship to the helper, presenting a list of role relationships from which respondents chose. This question can be taken to indicate diversity in the kinds of role relationships a respondent has with helpers, but it can also be used to assess tie strength. A final question that might be used to characterize the extent of diversity among helpers is question 261 asked if the helper has ever been involved in starting a business. These questions and their response categories exactly parallel those we asked concerning team members.

Tie Strength

Beginning with Question 248, we asked a series of questions designed to assess the strength of the tie between the respondent and the helper. Question 248 asked the

Exhibit 29.1   Social Network Ties in the Phone Interview Schedule, Items Q241–Q262

Q241	*Nascent:* Are there other people, those that would NOT be on the start-up team, who have been particularly helpful to you in getting the business started?
	Comparison: Are there people who have been particularly helpful to you in your work career?
Q242	How many are there?

Questions asked about each (name) of five most important "helpers"

Q245	Sex—Is (name) male or female?
Q246	Age—How old is (name)?
Q246	Race/Ethnicity—Would you say (name) is
	White
	Black/African American
	Hispanic/Latino
	American Indian
	Southeast Asian
	Other Asian/Pacific Islander
	Or something else?
Q248	How long have you known (name)?
Q249	How many times have you talked with (name) about business matters in the last month?
	How has (Name) helped with start-up?
Q250	Introductions to other people
Q251	Information or advice
Q252	Training in business-related tasks or skills
Q253	Access to financial resources (equity, loans, or loan guarantees)
Q254	Physical resources (use of land, space, buildings, or equipment)
Q255	Business services (legal, accounting, clerical assistance)
Q256	Personal services (household help)
Q257	Other kinds of assistance
Q256c	Moral or emotional support
Q256f	Labor
Q256i	Creativity or ideas
Q258	Which of these forms of assistance has been MOST IMPORTANT for the new business start-up?
Q259	Was the assistance provided free, at a discounted price, at the normal market price, as part of a barter or exchange relationship, or for some other reason?
Q260	What (is/was) (name's) occupation?
Q261	(Has/did) (name), alone or with others, ever start a business?
Q262	How would you describe your relationship to (name)? (spouse/partner, family member or relative, a business associate or work colleague, a friend or acquaintance, a teacher or counselor, or do you have some other type of relationship with (name)?

---

respondent how long he/she has known the helper because a number of previous studies have argued that ties of long duration almost always reflect a strong commitment and most likely reciprocal relations between two people. Question 249 asked how many times the respondent had talked with the helper about business matters in the past month. Although we have no measure of the *content* of these conversations, we assume that more frequent contact indicates a stronger relationship.

A third question that can also be used to assess the strength of a tie concerns how the respondent describes his or her relationship to the helper. Using Question 262, we can separate kin from nonkin relationships, and also business ties from friendship ties. Because of time limitations, we were not able to ask a question concerning the multiplexity of the relationship. Respondents were asked to pick only one of the kinds of relationships offered, and thus they were forced to consider which one type of relation took priority. Unlike with team members, we were not able to ask how helpers related to each other, only how they related to the respondent.

Type of Contribution

Based on our pretesting, we identified a set of resources that nascent entrepreneurs often obtained from others. In the first wave of interviewing, we discovered that several other kinds of resources were frequently mentioned, and so they were added as response possibilities in subsequent waves (Q256c, moral or emotional support; Q256f, labor; Q256i, creativity or ideas). Altogether, 10 different kinds of help were specifically asked about, and an eleventh category was included for respondents who wished to tell us about a resource that was not included in the choices they were given (Q257). Because of time constraints, we could not ask respondents to indicate the significance of each resource, and so instead we asked them which form of assistance had been the most important for the new business start-up. Asking this question allowed us to come back to it in subsequent waves and ask the respondent if the helper had, in fact, delivered on the kind of assistance that was promised and also to rate how important it actually had been in the start-up effort.

Earlier studies have shown that much of what a nascent entrepreneur needs is obtained free, at a discounted price, or as part of a barter or exchange relationship. Accordingly, we asked respondents to indicate the terms on which the resource was made available to the start-up. In addition to the above choices, we also asked whether it was obtained at a market price. Answers to this question not only indicate the kind of resources that a nascent entrepreneur obtained from helpers but also might be taken as an indirect indication of the strength of the tie between the respondent and the helper.

Descriptive Statistics

In Table 29.1, we show descriptive statistics for selected questions about the helpers.

The findings reflect removal of several cases from the full sample of 1,261. Cases were deleted if (1) "nonpersons" expected to own more than 50% of the venture, (2) infant businesses reported 90 days of positive cash flow, (3) respondent failed to provide sociodemographic information needed to classify the respondent's gender or race/ethnicity (one), and (4) individuals in the comparison group qualified for a nascent entrepreneur interview. After removing these cases and weighting the data to compensate for the two oversamples, 1,225 cases remained for consideration. Of this total, 804 were nascent entrepreneurs and 413 were from the comparison

Table 29.1 Descriptive Statistics: Social Network "Helper" Groups for Individuals and Teams

Variable	No. of Cases	Unit of Analysis	Weighted Count[a] Proportion	
			Nascent Entrepreneurs	Comparison Group
Use helpers	1215	Yes	63%	74%
Size (individual)	204	One member	30%	17%
(Group)	201	Two members	29%	18%
	163	Three members	19%	23%
	66	Four members	8%	8%
	170	Five + members	14%	34%
Total	804			
Gender composition	1401	Male	62%	66%
(Individual)	806	Female	38%	34%
Gender composition team	332	All male	42%	40%
(Multimember)	148	All female	20%	16%
	324	Mixed gender	38%	44%
Ethnicity composition (Total Individual)	2132	White	76%	83%
Nascent	1191	Black	16%	10%
Comparison	945	Hispanic	6%	5%
		Asian	2%	2%
Ethnicity same as respondent team	541[b]	Single ethnicity	73%	70%
(Multimember)	208	Multiple ethnicities	27%	30%
Relational composition	104	With spouses / partners	14%	12%
(Multimember team)	268	With nonspouse family member	38%	26%
	378	With business associates	34%	69%
	417	With friend	56%	45%
	68	With teacher	6%	12%
Age of helpers	783	Years	42.6	49.6
Average time known	794	Years	11.8	16.4
Times talked with in past month	792	Median	3	6

Variable	Cases	Unit of Analysis	Weighted Count[a] Proportion	
			Nascent Entrepreneurs	Comparison Group
Most Important Form of Assistance	776	Introductions to other people	27%	26%
		Information or advice	47%	59%
		Training in business-related tasks or skills	29%	48%
		Access to financial resources (equity, loans, or loan guarantees)	12%	7%
		Physical resources (use of land, space, buildings, or equipment)	10%	3%
		Business services (legal, accounting, clerical assistance)	12%	7%
		Personal services (household help)	9%	11%
		Other kinds of assistance	21%	16%

NOTES:

a. Each variable independently weighted to reflect cases lost because of missing information.

b. Includes respondent and multimember teams that have data for both sex and ethnicity. Excludes multimember teams involving other ethnicities or with missing information.

group. The weights for each analyses reported in Table 29.1 are adjusted independently for the number of missing cases on that particular variable.

The number of respondents indicating they relied on helpers differed across the two groups. Seventy-four percent of the comparison group respondents indicated there were people helpful to them in their work career, but only 63% of the nascent entrepreneurs indicated there were people, beyond the start-up team, who had been particularly helpful in getting their business started (Question 241).

As shown in Table 29.1, typical adults in the comparison group report having sub-stantially more helpers than do the nascent entrepreneurs. The majority of the nascent entrepreneurs report having only one (30%) or two helpers (29%), whereas over one third of the typical adults (34%) report having five helpers in their social network.

The distribution of male and female helpers was similar across groups. Sixty-two percent of the nascent entrepreneurs' and 66% of the typical adults' helpers were male. About 40% of both groups reported having helper groups comprised only of men (42% nascent entrepreneurs vs. 40% typical adults). Slightly more of the typical adults' social networks were composed of both men and women (44%) than were those of the nascent entrepreneurs (38%). Only 20% of the nascent entrepreneurs and 16% of the typical adults reported relying exclusively on female helpers for advice.

Family played a more significant role in the social network of nascent entrepreneurs than for typical adults. Thirty-eight percent of nascent entrepreneurs named non-spouse family members as part of their "helper" network, and 14% identified spouse or partner. The impact is probably even greater than reflected by these percentages because over half (53%) of the nascent entrepreneurs had already reported their spouse or partner as part of the start-up team. Recall that helpers were others beyond the start-up team who were relied on for advice. In contrast, the typical adults rely less on the strong ties of family and more on weak ties. Only 12% reported their spouse or partner as part of their social network, and only about one fourth (26%) named other family members. Instead, nearly 70% named businesses associates (69%), twice that of the nascent entrepreneurs (34%). Nascent entrepreneurs were slightly more likely to name a friend as particularly helpful although both groups saw such individuals as an important part of their social network (56% nascent entrepreneurs vs. 45% typical adults).

The majority of the helpers in the social networks are White; over three fourths of the nascent entrepreneurs' helpers (76%) were identified as White versus 83% for the typical adults. Nascent entrepreneurs were more likely than adults in the comparison group to name Blacks as part of their social network (16% vs. 10%). Only about 5% of the helpers were identified as Hispanic; 6% of nascent entrepreneurs' social network, and 5% of the comparison groups. Two percent of the helpers named by both groups were identified as Asian.

Helpers in the social network of the typical adults were slightly older, on average, than those of nascent entrepreneurs (49.6 years vs. 42.6 years), and the respondents had known them longer. The typical adults reported knowing their helpers an average of 16 years (16.4 years), whereas nascent entrepreneurs reported knowing their helpers for about 12 years (11.8 years). Furthermore, contact between the typical adults and helpers in their social network was more active. Typical adults reported talking to their helpers about business matters twice as often in a particular month (six times) as did the nascent entrepreneurs (three times).

An individual's social network can provide a variety of resources helpful for building careers or businesses. Respondents were asked which of several resources was most important or helpful. Fifty-nine percent of the typical adults reported that at least one of their helpers provided access to information or advice—the resource they saw as most important—and nearly 48% reported at least one person provided training in business-related tasks or skills. In contrast, while nascent entrepreneurs also saw information or advice and training as important, they also viewed introductions to other people and other kinds of assistance as important resources their social network was providing.

Implications

Using PSED questions on the involvement of non-start-up-team members (helpers) in the start-up process, investigators can address a number of interesting questions from the entrepreneurship literature. First, studies have repeatedly shown that women turn mainly to men in their business discussion networks, and men also depend almost entirely upon other men. As discussed in Chapter 27, the composition of entrepreneurial start-up teams in this data set shows that after removing spouses and partners from consideration, a very high degree of gender homophily exists, with same-sex teams much more likely than mixed-sex teams, compared to the expected level if teams were randomly mixed. Thus, the composition of teams and the composition of business networks reported in previous research shows that they differ in a fundamental way, with much lower gender asymmetry in discussion networks than in team composition. In particular, women in teams depend much more heavily on other women than women who are reporting on their business discussion networks. Using the PSED, we can investigate the extent to which resource-seeking behavior by women follows gendered lines or is gender blind.

Some previous studies have shown that when it comes to the actual use of their relationships for instrumental purposes, women act in about the same way as men. For example, a study in the Research Triangle Park in North Carolina (Aldrich et al., 1996) showed that women were just as aggressive as men in the number of persons they contacted for resources and were no less likely than men to contact strangers. They also rated the assistance they received at about the same level as men. In the PSED data, we have more details on the kinds of assistance sought and the terms on which it is available and will be able to see if men and women pursue the same strategy with regard to relations with helpers.

Second, our research on team composition in the PSED has found that teams are extremely homogeneous when it comes to race and ethnicity. White entrepreneurs mostly team up with other Whites, and minority entrepreneurs with other members of their same minority group. As long as resources are equally distributed across ethnic groups, such homophily should not pose problems for a start-up. However, to the extent that resources are unequally available, through different ethnic groups, a non-diverse set of helpers could be a disadvantage for nascent entrepreneurs.

In preliminary analyses of ethnic differences in start-up success, it appears that a team's ethnic composition makes a difference in the extent to which it succeeded in creating an operating business by the following interview. If helpers who are not on the start-up team do, in fact, make an important contribution to the start-up efforts, a diverse group of helpers might compensate for a team being composed of homogeneous nascent entrepreneurs.

Third, with regard to tie strength, investigators still have no clear evidence that weak ties play the kind of role that social network theory claims for them. That is, weak ties are proposed as ways to allow nascent entrepreneurs to escape from otherwise embedded networks of strong ties. However, regarding business start-ups, it could be that the trust engendered by strong ties enables nascent entrepreneurs to obtain help that would be difficult to garner from outsiders. Conversely, seeking help through weak ties could lead to unexpected windfalls of resources that were unknown to a nascent entrepreneur because of the precarious nature of the weak tie. We might thus expect that strong ties that seem to characterize the process of team formation itself might be complemented by helpers who are linked by weak ties to the start-up.

A closer examination of the terms on which resources have been made available might shed some light on the importance of strong versus weak ties. We might find that strong ties, such as to family and friends of long duration, provide only a limited range of resources. Conversely, we might find that weak ties, such as to business associates or others, make available a wider range of resources to the start-up.

Fourth, the section on the helpers who are not members of the start-up team was included because we hypothesized that homophily within the team could compromise its ability to obtain diverse resources. We thus need to examine the extent to which the resources provided by helpers are, in fact, different from those already available through team members. We can also examine the extent to which team size is related to the kinds of resources that helpers provide.

References

Aldrich, H. E. (1979). *Organizations and environments.* Englewood Cliffs, NJ: Prentice Hall.

Aldrich, H. E., Elam, A. B., & Reese, P. R. (1996). Strong ties, weak ties, and strangers: Do women business owners differ from men in their use of networking to obtain assistance? In S. Birley & I. MacMillan (Eds.), *Entrepreneurship in a global context* (pp. 1–25). London: Routledge.

Aldrich, H. E., Reese, P. R., & Dubini, P. (1989). Women on the verge of a breakthrough?: Networking among entrepreneurs in the United States and Italy. *Journal of Entrepreneurship & Regional Development, 1*(4), 339–356.

Aldrich, H. E., & Whetten, D. (1981). Making the most of simplicity: Organization sets, action sets, and networks. In P. Nystrom & W. H. Starbuck (Eds.), *Handbook of organizational design* (pp. 385–408). New York: Oxford University Press.

Burt, R. S. (1982). *Toward a structural theory of action.* New York: Academic Press.

Burt, R. S. (1992). *Structural holes: The social structure of competition.* Cambridge, MA: Harvard University Press.

Cartwright, D., & Harary, F. (1956). Structural balance: A generalization of Heider's theory. *Psychological Review, 63,* 277–293.

Davis, J. A. (1963). Structural balance, mechanical solidarity, and interpersonal relations. *American Journal of Sociology, 68*(4), 444–462.

Fischer, C. S. (1982). *To dwell among friends.* Chicago: University of Chicago Press.

Granovetter, M. (1974). *Getting a job: A study of contacts and careers.* Cambridge, MA: Harvard University Press.

Granovetter, M. (1993). The nature of economic relationships. In R. Swedberg (Ed.), *Explorations in economic sociology* (pp. 3–41). New York: Russell Sage.

Hirschman, A. O. (1982). *Exit, voice and loyalty.* Cambridge, MA: Harvard University Press.

Holland, P. W., & Leinhardt, S. (1972). Some evidence on the transitivity of positive interpersonal sentiment. *American Journal of Sociology, 72*(6), 1205.

Jones, C., Herterly, W. S., & Borgatti, S. P. (1997). A general theory of network governance: Exchange conditions and social mechanisms. *Academy of Management Review, 22*(4), 911–945.

Kandel, D. B. (1978). Homophily, selection, and socialization in adolescent friendships. *American Journal of Sociology, 84*(2), 427–436.

Marks, S. R. (1977). Multiple roles and role strain: Some notes of human energy, time and commitment. *American Sociological Review, 42*(6), 921–936.

Marsden, P. V. (1987). Core discussion networks of Americans. *American Sociological Review,* *52*(1), 122–131.

Marsden, P. V., & Campbell, K. (1984). Measuring tie strength. *Social Forces, 6*(2), 482–501.

McPherson, J. M., & Smith-Lovin, L. (1987). Homophily in voluntary associations: Status distance and the composition of face-to-face groups. *American Sociological Review, 52*(3), 370–379.

Ridgeway, C. L., & Walker, H. A. (1994). Status structures. In K. Cook, G. A. Fine, & J. S. House (Eds.), *Sociological perspectives on social psychology* (pp. 281–310). Boston: Allyn & Bacon.

Sieber, S. (1974). Toward a theory of role accumulation. *American Sociological Review, 39*(4), 567–578.

CHAPTER 30

Knowledge and Use of Assistance

William J. Dennis, Jr.

Paul D. Reynolds

New businesses have long been considered an important contribution to the U.S. economy as well as an egalitarian career opportunity—one that should be available to all. A wide range of programs to provide help and assistance has therefore been initiated by federal, state, regional, and local governments as well as a host of foundations, associations, and various professional groups intending to facilitate new business creation. In turn, the use and impact of such programs has become a focus of substantial research on the facilitation of new business creation.

Given that the Panel of Entrepreneurial Dynamics (PSED) research program was based on a representative sample of those creating new firms, it provided an opportunity to determine the extent to which business assistance programs were utilized in the start-up process, what assistance they provided, and if this assistance had positive impacts on the outcome.

Background

Nascent entrepreneurs and those who have just started their businesses consistently identify start-up problems that potentially could be minimized or resolved through publicly subsidized assistance (Reynolds & Miller, 1988; Cooper, Dunkelberg, Woo, & Dennis, 1990; Reynolds & White, 1993, 1997; Dennis, 1999; Kouriloff, 2000). Yet, small business programs traditionally have targeted operating enterprises. Over the last two decades that focus has been slowly shifting in recognition of the crucial role of new firms in job growth and the potential of business ownership for alleviating certain social problems.

The federal government has provided public programs to directly support small business at least since the 1930s. The lead agency for this assistance is now the U.S. Small Business Administration (SBA). But a host of other federal agencies have also developed finance and management/technical assistance programs targeting small businesses in selected geographic locations, industries, owned by ethnic minorities and disadvantaged persons, and performing particularly desirable functions such as research and development. Federal small business support still targets operating firms. But evidence of the shift toward greater inclusion of business formation can be seen in SBA's strategic plan, a plan that pointedly includes an objective to assist formation of 16,000 new businesses annually (U.S. Small Business Administration [SBA] 2001).

State and local governments supplement federal efforts with programs of their own (SBA, 1993; Kayne, 1999). Many of these fall under the broad heading of "economic development." Although initially an exercise in smokestack chasing—or attracting expansion plants in basic industries—economic development became notably more focused on homegrown new business and entrepreneurship in the 1980s (Bradshaw & Blakely, 1999). It evolved in the 1990s to assume a greater role in the coordination of resources such as public/private partnerships. Yet state and local initiatives to foster new enterprises flourish, at least in numbers of programs.

Private nonprofit organizations, particularly trade, professional, and business associations, also provide assistance. There are over 4,000 such national organizations and a much greater number of regional, state, local, and neighborhood groups (Maurer & Sheets, 1998). Almost all offer some type of educational programs for their members, and a large majority also offer public information, conduct industry research, or develop statistical materials. They also often have a unique advantage over other providers by possessing vast amounts of industry-specific knowledge. But differing from public resources, many association services are available to members only, or the owners of existing operating firms.

The potential sources of help are rounded out by education institutions offering subsidized assistance in the form of traditional classroom activity and extension-type outreach; for-profit vendors, periodically organizing training sessions or demonstrations on items such as computer or telephone systems; and a vast industry of for-profit service providers that are the primary source of assistance for virtually all operating businesses.

Previous Research

Program evaluation is the favored way to assess the viability of public initiatives. But evaluation of program effectiveness, in this instance, programs designed to assist individuals forming enterprises, is very difficult to conduct properly under the best of circumstances (Storey, 2000). Issues such as the displacement of private by public resources and opportunity costs are particularly difficult to assess (Bartik, 1996). The PSED presents additional issues in this regard. Its relatively small sample and the plethora of available support programs—in the thousands—make it impossible to evaluate individual programs. More important, the immediate focus is the nascent entrepreneur, not the programs. Traditional program evaluation is therefore inappropriate.

Most of what we know about the use and value of public assistance programs to encourage the formation of new enterprises, at least from the program beneficiary's perspective, comes from owners of operating firms. These owners report somewhat greater use of advisory services than financial programs but infrequent use of either in formation or operation of their firms (Bureau of the Census, 1992, 1997; Cooper et al., 1990; *Minolta/Gallup*, 1987; Dennis, 2002, 2003). Reflections on the entry process are likely biased, even when entry is of recent origin (e.g., Cooper et al., 1990). Further, such assessments only offer a perspective of those who have successfully completed the process to create an operating new firm.

Reports from service providers, particularly from advisory service providers (SBA, 2003), vary substantially from those of owners. In surveys, providers claim much greater use than do owner. Reynolds and White (1997), using a population of nascent entrepreneurs, found a reasonable resolution of those conflicting perspectives when they discovered substantial use by those entering and those in the entry process. SBA officials corroborate their results when reporting that most advisory service clients are not owners of functioning firms (author conversations with officials).

The same data conflict does not appear with respect to finance programs. Both owners and providers agree that only a tiny percentage use government finance programs to start or operate a business (Bureau of the Census, 1992, 1997; Cooper et al., 1990; Bitler, Robb, & Wolken, 2001; Dennis, 2003). However, proportionately more use SBA-guaranteed loans to start firms than use conventional loans to start theirs (Price Waterhouse, 1992; Government Accounting Office [GAO], 1996).

Ethnic and racial minorities are more likely to use public resources than White males, sometimes by a ratio of 4 or 5 to 1 in cases where the minority are African Americans (Bureau of the Census, 1992, 1997; GAO, 1996). It is not clear, however, that those who are resource-constrained are also those most likely to use public resources. Use can reflect awareness of options that, in turn, may be lower among those with resource constraints.

Nascent or new entrepreneurs must be aware of resources, public or private, before they can use them. Operating business owners are often not aware of the potential public resources available to them (Dennis & Douglas, 1984; Reynolds & White, 1997; White & Reynolds, 1994; Masten, Hartmann, & Safari, 1995; Moini, 1998). Owners of younger firms seem less aware of macroenvironmental factors than owners of older firms (Mohan-Neil, 1995) and are less apt to contact government (Dennis, 2003). Logically, nascent and aspiring entrepreneurs should be even less aware than their operating counterparts though White and Reynolds (1994) find the awareness level of nascent and new entrepreneurs similar.

The lack of awareness of public resources is likely to be related to the lack of awareness of private resources. The absence of prior knowledge tends to limit rather than stimulate search among fledgling entrepreneurs (Woo, Folta, & Cooper, 1992; Pineda, Lerner, Miller, & Phillips, 1998). Those with smaller social networks are less aware of resources, public or private (Hjalmarsson & Johansson, 2003). As a result, the lack of awareness of public resources may be symptomatic of a broader lack of awareness though it could also suggest ample resource availability in the private sector with little or no need to investigate public resource availability.

Awareness affects the overall demand for public resources for obvious reasons but also because those who use a particular program once are inclined to use it again (Reynolds & White, 1997; Masten et al. 1995).

Policy Issues

Transparent political considerations aside (Bean, 1996; Buss, 1999; Corder, 1998; Saiz, 2001), the provision of public assistance programs targeted to support new and small businesses (and their owners) effectively assumes some type of market failure (Bartik, 1990). However, for present purposes we start with the proposition that numerous new and growing businesses are important and good. The greater inclusion among business owner ranks of resource-constrained individuals and minority group members is also important and good. We are not presently concerned with direct cost, displacement, or similar issues that constitute a full program evaluation. Rather, the pertinent policy questions focus on the effectiveness of public assistance in moving individuals through the start-up and growth process. Those questions involve issues of program awareness, use, and outcomes. The following constitutes a modest list of specific questions:

1. Do public resources help individuals move through the various stages in the entrepreneurial process?
    a. Is the use of public assistance—all factors equal— associated with movement of individuals from nascent entrepreneurs to new business owners?
    b. Is the use of public assistance—all factors equal—associated with the survival of new businesses?
    c. Is the use of public assistance—all factors equal—associated with the growth of new businesses?

2. Who is aware of and who uses public resources?
    a. Are public resources more likely to be known by and/or used by those who are more resource-constrained or less resource-constrained?
    b. Are public resources more likely to be known by and/or used by disadvantaged or minority groups than by others?
    c. Are public resources more likely to be known by and/or used by those who also make extensive use of private resources (public resources are just another resource) or by those who can locate no other resources (public resources are unique)?

3. Do the financial or advisory forms of public resources produce differing results to the questions above? Similarly, do the intensity of use and/or the breadth of use produce differing results to these questions?
    a. What is the perceived value of public resources? Is the perceived value of public resources associated with more positive outcomes?
    b. Does the perceived per unit value diminish (increase) with use?

Objectives for Business Assistance Data Collection

The major objectives in the design of the PSED business assistance section reflected the policy issues developed above. While all could not be approached with this single study, the interview schedules were designed to provide information on the following:

What was the level of awareness of business assistance programs?

How many of the start-ups actually utilized any business assistance programs?

When did this occur in the start-up process?

What transpired in the assistance-providing event?

How did the clients react to the assistance provided?

Was there any relationship between receiving assistance and the outcome of the start-up process?

The answers to these issues would be based on a nationally representative sample of business start-ups, which would provide strong confidence in the overall results. Unfortunately, the number of responses in any given geographic area or for specific programs would preclude information that could be used to adjust or modify any single program.

Section Design

The section related to assistance for business start-ups was asked of all respondents, both nascent entrepreneurs and those in the comparison group. The 21 items (22 in the follow-up interviews) were relatively straightforward. Their location and role in the skip pattern is presented in Exhibit 30.1. The variable labels for the initial interview as well as the first and second follow-up are provided in the first three columns. The skip patterns are provided for the initial interview. The entire section was placed after a discussion of the detailed characteristics of the start-up team and before a discussion of sales expected for the new firm.

Those who had made no contact with assistance programs (Q303) were immediately transferred to the penultimate question (Q315) for the section. This question asked if they could have made contact with an assistance program. If they said yes, they were asked about the number of programs they could have contacted (Q316).

If they reported contact with an assistance program (Q303), they were asked when the first contact was made (Q304, Q304a) and how many assistance agencies were contacted (Q305). In the follow-up interviews, respondents still active in the start-up process were asked about new contacts since the last interview (R758, S758).

For details about one program, the focus of the interview shifted to the most recent contact for assistance. This avoids memory loss and confusion about programs when more than one had been contacted by the respondent. The questions focused on the type of helping program (Q306, Q306a, Q306b Q306c, and Q306d), name of the program (Q307), and city and state of location (Q308,

Q308a). A description of the interaction was related to questions about hours spent with the program staff (Q309), why the effort was expended (Q309a), what the program did for the start-up (Q310), and an estimate of the fair market value of the services provided (Q311). Three items allowed the respondent to evaluate the program for others (Q312), including scales on positive (Q313) and negative assessments (Q314) of this "most recent program visited."

Exhibit 30.1 Business Assistance Section: Item Overview

Item Number	1st Follow-up	2nd Follow-up		Other Choices	Yes/ One or More	No/ None	Don't Know/ Refused
Q303	R755	S755	Contact with business assistance programs?		Q304	Q315	Q315
Q304	R756	S756	Year of first contact				Q305
Q304a	R756a	S756a	Month of first contact				
Q305	R757	S757	How many contacted?				
	R758	S758	Since last interview, how many new contacts with business assistance programs have been made?			S769a	
Q306	R759	S759	Major type of helping program?	Q306a to Q306d			Q307
Q306a	R759a	S759a	Type of government agency	Q307			
Q306b	R759b	S759b	Type of educational institution	Q307			
Q306c	R759c	S759c	Type of business association	Q307			
Q306d	R759d	S759d	Type of not-for-profit	Q307			
Q307	R760	S760	Name of program				
Q308	R761	S761	City where located				
Q308a	R761a	S761a	State where located				
Q309	R762	S762	Hours spent with program getting help?				
Q309a	R762a	S762a	Why spend the effort to get help				
Q310	R763	S763	What did the program do for start-up?				
Q311	R764	S764	Fair market value of services provided				
Q312	R765	S765	Recommend to others starting businesses?		Q313	Q314	OUT
Q313	R766	S766	How valuable the help provided		OUT	OUT	OUT
Q314	R767	S767	How bad the help provided?		OUT	OUT	OUT
Q315	R768	S768	Could you have made any contact with business assistance programs?		Q316	OUT	OUT
Q316	R769	S769	How many could you have contacted?				
OUT			NEXT SECTION				

Preliminary Results

Some of the issues associated with business start-ups can be approached individually and initial assessments are provided below. Others are interrelated with complex features of the start-up process and require a more complex assessment. For example, the initial contact with business assistance initiatives as part of the start-up sequence requires a careful development of the start-up sequence itself. This goes beyond the scope of this section. Nonetheless, some assessment of the knowledge and contact with business assistance, types of programs contacted, nature of the exchange between the assistance source and the clients, as well as an assessment of the value of the service, is possible. The final discussion considered the association between contact for assistance and the outcome of the start-up process.

Knowledge, Contact With Business Assistance Programs

In terms of involvement with business assistance services, respondents could be classified in three groups: made contact with a program, knowledge of but no contact with a program, and no knowledge of any businesses assistance program. Table 30.1 shows the distribution for nascent entrepreneurs and the comparison group. The nascent entrepreneurs had two chances to report contact with or knowledge of assistance programs—the initial detailed interview and the first follow-up interview.

The patterns for the two groups are almost identical and there is no statistically significant difference between them. About 20% of nascent entrepreneurs make contact with a helping program, almost half know of programs they do not contact, and about one third do not know of any programs to contact. About two thirds of U.S. adults—whether or not they are engaged in a business start-up—appear to know of programs that are available to help those creating new firms. This knowledge is so widespread, it is unlikely to have a major effect on encouraging individuals to enter the entrepreneurial process.

Table 30.1   Knowledge of and Contact with Business Assistance Programs

Variable	Nascent Entrepreneurs	Comparison Group
Number of cases	830	431
Made contact with a business assistance program	19.7%	15.4%
Knew of programs, but no contact made	45.8%	46.8%
No knowledge of programs, no contact	34.5%	37.8%
Total	100.0%	100.0%

NOTE: Pearson likelihood chi-square tests significant at 0.15 level.

The number of programs people know about and contact is, however, highly associated with the participation in the start-up process. As shown in Table 30.2, nascent entrepreneurs contact significantly more programs than typical adults; 27% contact four or more compared to 9%. Table 30.3 indicates that nascent entrepreneurs who do not contact helping programs also know about a much greater number of programs than typical adults; 53% know about four or more compared to 37%. This may reflect greater awareness of the promotional material regarding assistance programs or more extensive search efforts to locate assistance programs.

Table 30.2   Number of Business Assistance Programs Contacted

Variable	Nascent Entrepreneurs	Comparison Group
Number of cases	160	64
One	36.2%	60.4%
Two or three	36.6%	30.3%
Four to nine	14.8%	6.8%
Ten or more	12.4%	2.5%
Total	100.0%	100.0%

NOTE: Pearson likelihood chi-square tests significant at 0.003 level.

Table 30.3   Number of Business Assistance Programs Known About

Variable	Nascent Entrepreneurs	Comparison Group
Number of cases	361	171
One	11.4%	10.9 %
Two or three	35.6%	52.4%
Four to nine	35.9%	21.0%
Ten or more	17.2%	15.8%
Total	100.0%	100.0%

NOTE: Pearson likelihood chi-square tests significant at 0.001 level.

Types of Business Assistance Programs

The types of assistance programs contacted by the nascent entrepreneurs and comparison group members are presented in Table 30.4. Government sponsored programs are by far the most frequently cited, mentioned as the last contact by 46% of the nascent entrepreneurs and 52% of the comparison group. Educational institutions are another major source, mentioned by 21% of the nascent entrepreneurs and 16% of the comparison group. Equally significant are those provided by business or professional associations or service groups, mentioned by 25% of both the nascent entrepreneurs and the comparison group. For-profit assistance programs are mentioned by a smaller percentage of nascent entrepreneurs, 7%, and the comparison group, 4%.

Table 30.4   Types of Business Assistance Programs Contacted

	Nascent Entrepreneurs	Comparison Group
Number of cases	122	59
Government: Federal	24.5%	35.4%
Government: State	10.1%	11.7%
Government: Local	6.9%	4.6%
Government: Other	4.3%	
Educational: Public (Secondary) School	1.1%	
Educational: Vocational-technical center	2.3%	
Educational: Two-year college	0.6%	2.6%
Educational: Four-year college	1.2%	3.1%
Educational: University	12.8%	8.2%
Educational: Other	2.9%	2.6%
Business Assoc/Service Group: Business association	10.2%	13.3%
Business Assoc/Service Group: Service group	2.6%	0.6%
Business Assoc/Service Group: Professional association	6.2%	5.0%
Business Assoc/Service Group: Other	5.9%	5.7%
For profit: No fee		0.5%
For profit: Small or token fee	1.0%	0.5%
For profit: Full fee charged	5.3%	2.5%
For profit: Other	0.6%	
Not elsewhere classified, unknown	1.6%	3.7%
Total	100.0%	100.0%

NOTE: Pearson likelihood chi-square tests not statistically significant.

Time Devoted to the Assistance Program

The amount of time devoted to working with the assistance program varies dramatically from less than an hour to over 2,000 hours—a full year of contact—for one case. The range of involvement for nascent entrepreneurs and those in the comparison group is presented in Table 30.5; those from both samples report low and extremely high levels of involvement. The typical amount of commitment is somewhat higher among nascent entrepreneurs—largely because one third of the comparison group spent less than an hour with the service provider—and the difference is statistically significant.

Table 30.5   Business Assistance: Time Spent by Client

Variable	Nascent Entrepreneurs	Comparison Group
Number of cases	116	59
Up to 1 hour	13.4%	33.7%
From 2 to 5 hours	41.1%	23.8%
From 6 to 10 hours	14.7%	13.2%
From 11 to 25 hours	13.0%	9.3%
From 26 to 100 hours	9.6%	9.6%
From 101 to 500 hours	6.9%	4.4%
Over 500 hours	1.2%	6.1%
Total	100.0%	100.0%

NOTES: Pearson likelihood chi-square tests significant at 0.02 level.

Percentages may not total exactly to 100% due to rounding to one decimal place.

A preliminary assessment of the kind of help provided for both nascent entrepreneurs as well as those in the comparison group is presented in Table 30.6. The types of assistance received are quite similar, with about two thirds as one of three types: general training and information on business start-ups; specific training in creating a new business or managing a business, including preparing detailed business plans; and help, guidance, or the actual provision of funds for a new business start-up. Nascent entrepreneurs are more likely to report more specific types of training and assistance, such as learning a new production technology or training with a new product or service. This accounts for the statistically significant difference between the two groups.

Table 30.6   Business Assistance: Type of Help Provided

Variable	Nascent Entrepreneurs	Comparison Group
Number of cases	167	64
General training and or information	29.1%	22.7%
Learn how to start-up, manage a new business	25.2%	24.9%
Information, application assistance on financing, or funds received	10.6%	15.2%
Learn technological or management techniques	3.8%	14.2%
Networking or referral assistance for support or clients	6.6%	3.8%
Help with legal, administrative, or political issues	6.3%	4.5%
Learn new production skills or product details	7.5%	
Emotional support or counseling	2.1%	5.2%
Learn new technology	1.8%	
Helpful, no specific details	0.4%	
Not helpful	6.7%	9.5%
Total	100.0%	100.0%

NOTES: Pearson likelihood chi-square tests significant at 0.05 level.

Percentages may not total exactly to 100% due to rounding to one decimal place.

Assessment of the Assistance Provided

The clients' assessment of the assistance was obtained in two ways: (1) an estimate of the market value of the services received and (2) judgments about the help received from the assistance program.

While some clients considered the assistance to have no monetary value, Table 30.7 clearly indicates that this was less than 1 in 10. The majority of both nascent entrepreneurs and those in the comparison group considered the help to be of significant value. The median value was between $500 and $1,000, and almost 20% considered the value to be worth over $2,000. This would suggest that some of the assistance was considered to be a serious professional contribution to the creation of the new firm.

Perhaps more striking are the client judgments regarding the value of the service itself, as shown in Table 30.8. About 80% of all clients considered the assistance to be either very or extremely valuable and over 90% to have some value. Less than 4%—1 in 25—were extremely negative about the help they received.

Table 30.7   Business Assistance: Client Estimate of Market Value of Service

Variable	Nascent Entrepreneurs	Comparison Group
Number of cases	114	62
No cash value	9.6%	11.3%
Up to $49	3.8%	10.6%
From $50 to $99	7.1%	13.7%
From $100 to $499	29.3%	28.9%
From $500 to $999	16.0%	11.1%
From $1,000 to $1,999	15.2%	9.8%
From $2,000 to $4,999	8.4%	10.0%
From $5,000 and up	10.7%	4.6%
Total	100.0%	100.0%

NOTES: Pearson likelihood chi-square tests not statistically significant.

Percentages may not total exactly to 100% due to rounding to one decimal place.

Table 30.8   Client Assessments of Business Assistance Provided

Variable	Nascent Entrepreneurs	Comparison Group
Number of cases	114	62
Extremely valuable	52.7%	36.5%
Very valuable	29.5%	35.7%
Somewhat valuable	14.7%	21.0%
Neutral		2.6%
Waste of time		0.5%
Slightly misleading	1.9%	0.6%
Dangerously misleading	1.3%	3.1%
Total	100.0%	100.0%

NOTES: Pearson likelihood chi-square tests not statistically significant.

Percentages may not total exactly to 100% due to rounding to one decimal place.

Assistance and Start-up Outcomes

A preliminary assessment of the association between receiving assistance and the outcome of the first follow-up interviews was possible for 615 of the nascent

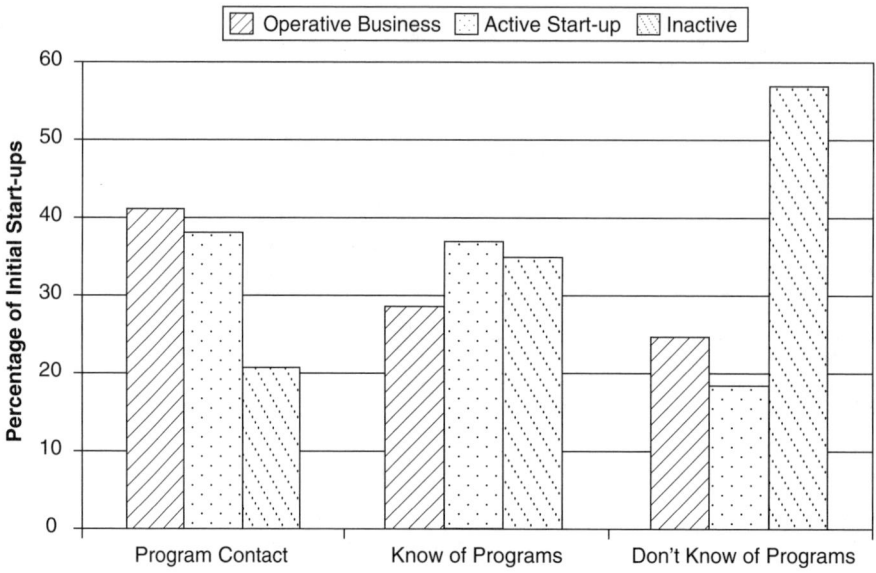

Figure 30.1   Knowledge, Contact With Business Assistance Programs and First Follow-up Outcomes

entrepreneurs. The results are presented in Figure 30.1. The nascent entrepreneurs are considered in terms of active engagement with a business assistance program, knowledge of programs but no contact, and no knowledge of business assistance programs.

There is a clear, unequivocal, and highly significant pattern. Over half of those who report no knowledge or contact with an assistance program are no longer actively involved with the business start-up. But 80% of those who report involvement with business assistance programs report either a going business or active efforts to implement the new firm. Those with knowledge of programs but no contact are intermediate between these extremes.

The preliminary assessment of the empirical patterns with the PSED representative sample of U.S. business startups is quite straightforward and consistent with previous research (Reynolds & White, 1997):

- About one third of those starting new businesses do not know of any assistance programs.
- About 20% (1 in 5) of those starting new businesses are actively engaged with business assistance programs.
- Program assistance is provided in a wide range of programs from government, educational institutions, and business, professional, and service associations.
- The evaluation of the assistance is extremely positive; strong negative reactions are very rare.
- Business start-ups that get involved with business assistance programs are more likely to develop a going business.

The causal mechanism associated with the last issue, the association between receiving assistance and success in creating a business, is complicated. While business assistance programs may help start-ups become more successful, those entrepreneurs who are careful and deliberate in assembling resources for a start-up may contact assistance programs as part of their start-up planning. Receiving business assistance may be a good indicator of a high quality start-up team, one that is able to implement a new firm.

Conclusions

Many if not most of the public resources in small business support programs appear to be consumed by individuals who have not yet formed their businesses. This is particularly true of advisory services. Although the intent of these programs traditionally has been to help operating firms survive and grow, the screening and birthing functions they have assumed appear to be the dominant form of assistance provided. This changing customer base implies the presence of a subtle and likely unintended shift in focus from a small business to an entrepreneurship policy orientation (Lundström & Stevenson, 2001). The question is why. The answer could be tied to the type of information sought, its specificity, its immediate availability, or provider expertise. For example, over half of sample nascents reported receiving very general types of information, topics of doubtful use to a more mature population. But the important point is that it appears nascent and new business owners are gravitating to publicly supported assistance while more established owners remain with the private sector.

There is a clear relationship between the propensity to initiate operations and use of public programs. While further investigation is necessary to determine if the relationship is a function of public program use, multiple resource use, or some other factor, the tie between positive outcomes and program use suggests value in the services received. The perceived dollar value of those services reinforces the point. The follow-up question is whether a relationship between public program use survival and growth will also appear.

The lack of awareness of public resource availability and the failure to contact a public program is related to terminating start-up efforts. An immediate reaction might be that the lack of awareness is a lack of marketing, or effective marketing, by program sponsors. However, the issue is likely to be more complex. Two of three potential users are aware of available public support. The operating hypothesis, therefore, is that the lack of awareness of public programs is tied to an overall awareness problem. An overall awareness problem raises questions about the individual's capacity to successfully operate an enterprise in a competitive and changing environment. Additional marketing of public assistance will not resolve the larger problem.

References

Bartik, T. J. (1990). The market failure approach to regional economic development policy. *Economic Development Quarterly, 4*(4), 361–370.

Bartik, T. J. (1996). Eight issues for policy toward economic development incentives. *The Region, 10*(2), 43–46.

Bean, J. J. (1996). *Beyond the broker state: Federal policies toward small business, 1936–1961.* Chapel Hill: University of North Carolina Press.

Bitler, M. P., Robb, A. M., & Wolken, J. D. (2001). Financial services used by small businesses: Evidence from the 1998 survey of small business finances. *Federal Reserve Bulletin, 87,* 183–205.

Bradshaw, T. K., & Blakely, E. J. (1999). What are "Third-Wave" state economic efforts? From incentives to industrial policy. *Economic Development Quarterly, 13*(3), 229–244.

Bureau of the Census. (1992). *1987 economic census, characteristics of business owners* (CBO87–1). U.S. Department of Commerce: Washington, DC.

Bureau of the Census. (1997). *1992 Economic census, characteristics of business owners* (CBO92–1). U.S. Department of Commerce: Washington, DC.

Buss, T. F. (1999). The case against targeted industry strategies. *Economic Development Quarterly, 13*(4), 339–356.

Cooper, A. C., Dunkelberg, W. C., Woo, C. Y., & Dennis, W. J., Jr. (1990). *New business in America: The firms & their owners.* NFIB Research Foundation: Washington, DC.

Corder, J. K. (1998). The politics of federal credit subsidy: Small Business Administration 7(a) loan guarantees. *American Review of Public Administration, 28*(2), 166–186.

Dennis, W. J., Jr. (1999). *Wells Fargo/NFIB series on business starts and stops.* Washington, DC: NFIB Education Foundation.

Dennis, W. J., Jr. (Ed.). (2002). *National small business poll: Workplace safety* (Vol. 2, No. 1). Washington, DC: NFIB Research Foundation.

Dennis, W. J., Jr. (Ed.). (2003). *National small business poll: Contacting government* (Vol. 3, No. 1). Washington, DC: NFIB Research Foundation.

Dennis, W. J., Jr., & Douglas, S. L. (1984). *Small business evaluates SBA.* Washington, DC: National Federation of Independent Business.

General Accounting Office (GAO). (1996). *A comparison of SBA's 7(a) loans and borrowers with other loans and borrowers.* Report to the Small Business Committee, United States Senate, (GAO/RCED–96–222). Washington, DC: Author.

Hjalmarsson, D., & Johansson, A. W. (2003). Public advisory services. *Entrepreneurship & Regional Development, 15*(1), 83–98.

Kayne, J. (1999). *State entrepreneurship policies and programs.* Kansas City, MO: Ewing Marion Kauffman Foundation.

Kouriloff, M. (2000). Exploring perceptions of *a priori* barriers to entrepreneurship: A multidisciplinary approach. *Entrepreneurship Theory and Practice, 25*(2), 59–79.

Lundström, A., & Stevenson, L. (2001). *Entrepreneurship policy for the future.* Örebro, Sweden: Swedish Foundation for Small Business Research.

Masten, J., Hartmann, G. B., & Safari, A. (1995). The use of publicly supported technology assistance agencies. *Journal of Small Business Management, 33*(3) 26–37.

Maurer, C., & Sheets, T. E. (Eds.). (1998). *Encyclopedia of associations, Vol. 1* (33rd ed.). Detroit, MI: Gale.

Minolta/Gallup small business survey. (1987). Princeton, NJ: Gallup.

Mohan-Neill, S. I. (1995). The influence of firm's age and size on its environmental scanning activities. *Journal of Small Business Management, 33*(4), 10–21.

Moini, A. H. (1998). Small firms exporting: How effective are government export assistance programs? *Journal of Small Business Management, 36*(1), 1–15.

Pineda, R. C., Lerner, L. D., Miller, M. C., & Phillips, S. J. (1998). An investigation of factors affecting the information-search activities of small business managers. *Journal of Small Business Management, 36*(1), 60–71.

Price Waterhouse (1992). *Evaluation of the Small Business Administration's 7(a) guaranteed business loan program.* Prepared for the U.S. Small Business Administration (Contract No. SBA–5033–FAD–90).

Reynolds, P. & Miller, B. (1988). *1987 Minnesota new firms study: An exploration of new firms and their economic contributions.* Minneapolis: University of Minnesota, Center for Urban and Regional Affairs.

Reynolds, P. D., & White, S. B. (1993). *Wisconsin's entrepreneurial climate study.* Madison: Wisconsin Innovation Network and Wisconsin Housing and Economic Development Authority.

Reynolds, P. D., & White, S. B. (1997). *The entrepreneurial process: Economic growth, men, women, and minorities.* Westport, CT: Quorum Books.

Saiz, M. (2001). Politics and economic development: Why governments adopt different strategies to induce economic growth. *Policy Studies Journal, 29*(2), 203–214.

Storey, D. (2000). Six steps to heaven: Evaluating the impact of public policies to support small businesses in developed economies. In D. L. Sexton & H. Landström (Eds.), *The Blackwell handbook of entrepreneurship* (pp. 176–193). Oxford, UK: Blackwell.

U.S. Small Business Administration (SBA). (1993). *The states and small business: A directory of programs and activities.* Washington, DC: Government Printing Office.

U.S. Small Business Administration (SBA). (2001). *SBA FY2001–FY 2006 strategic plan.* Retrieved July 2003 from www.sba.gov/strategic/2001startegicplan.pdf

U.S. Small Business Administration (SBA). (2003). *SBA budget request and performance plan: FY 2003 congressional submission.* Retrieved July 2003 from www.sba.gov/aboutsba/2003/fy2003budget.pdf

White, S. B., & Reynolds, P. D. (1994). What can the public sector do to increase new business starts? In W. D. Bygrave, S. Birley, N. C. Churchill, E. Gatewood, F. Hoy, R. H. Keeley, & W. E. Wetzel, Jr. (Eds.), *Frontiers of entrepreneurship research,* (pp. 1–15). Wellesley, MA: Babson College.

White, S. B., & Reynolds, P. D. (1996). Government programs and high growth new firms. In P. D. Reynolds, S. Birley, J. E. Butler, P. Davidsson, W. B. Gartner, & P. P. McDougall (Eds.), *Frontiers of entrepreneurship research* (pp. 621–635). Wellesley, MA: Babson College.

Woo, C. Y., Folta, T., & Cooper, A. C. (1992). Entrepreneurial search: Alternative theories of behavior. In N. C. Churchill, S. Birley, W. D. Bygrave, D. F. Muzyka, C. Wahlbin, & W. E. Wetzel, Jr. (Eds.), *Frontiers of entrepreneurship research* (pp. 31–41). Wellesley, MA: Babson College.

CHAPTER 31

Funding the First Year of Business

Michael Stouder

Bruce Kirchhoff

One main critical task facing entrepreneurs is to acquire and manage the resources needed to start the firm (Greene & Brown, 1997), especially financial capital resources. Indeed, inadequate initial capitalization is often mentioned as a reason for business failure.

Based on the literature, we are persuaded that small firm capital markets are markedly different from those utilized by large publicly traded firms. Small firm capital markets do not approach the "economic efficiency" of the public capital markets utilized by large public firms. And small firms do not have access to public markets because of their small size capital needs and the high transaction costs of entering these markets. There is evidence that in many cases, small firm capital markets are not markets in the usual sense but are randomly distributed individualistic organizations that function separately and behave uniquely. Furthermore, it appears that transactions between small firms and their funding sources are plagued by a variety of costly information problems. These are likely to be driven by the unique characteristics of small firm capital markets, as well as by the unique characteristics of small firms and their owners. Overall, the picture that emerges points to an economically inefficient and nonequilibrium market situation, consistent with Schumpeterian and evolutionary capitalism models of entrepreneurship (Kirchhoff, 1994).

This view supports several widely held beliefs regarding the financing behaviors of nascent entrepreneurs. Foremost is the extent to which nascent entrepreneurs will avoid external funding sources and instead utilize internal sources. In cases in which internal sources are insufficient, rational nascent entrepreneurs will utilize financial capital from sources (or markets) that are responsive to their unique situation. In the main, these will consist of professional lenders such as banks and finance companies, team member sources, family and friends, and rarely, professional venture capital teams. Knowing the extent of use of financial resources and their sources is important to both the suppliers and seekers of financial capital. The PSED seeks to provide such information.

This chapter provides a literature review that describes the extant literature which constituted the theory base for the development of the finance items in the PSED questionnaire. This is followed by a section describing the results of prior research found in the literature. This is followed by a complete listing of all finance items in the questionnaire. Following this, is a section describing the results of analysis relevant to the theory base developed in the literature review.

Literature Review and Theory

Theory development in the area of start-up funding is scant. The literature review suggests that there is no well-developed comprehensive theory of small business finance available to explain start-up or capital structure. Also, there is a shortage of empirical research on the capital structure decisions of firms in the start-up stage. None-the-less, there are numerous insights in the literature as well as a small but growing body of empirical explorations that are suggestive of an initial explanatory framework.

To some extent, the PSED was designed to obtain information about phenomena that had been previously unexamined. For the Finance Team, a key research area was how start-ups obtain funding, especially in nascency. Early research consisted of normative, anecdotal, and experience-based accounts, such as offered by Levin and Travis (1987). In addition, there are a few nontheoretical empirical investigations, such as Van Auken and Carter (1989). Also, while not specifically dealing with nascent ventures, Barton & Matthews (1989) note that the literature has attempted to explain small firm financing using primarily modern financial theory and agency theory. They suggest a theoretical basis, especially as it pertains to financial decision making, may be better approached from a strategic management perspective.

A major question is whether or not it is possible to draw on mainstream financial theory to explain entrepreneur financial strategies. Modern finance theory is based on theory that seems to adequately explain the behavior of large, publicly traded firms, operating in a context of well-developed, efficient, and sophisticated capital markets. Financial managers traditionally have paid attention to the relative level of debt and equity in firms (capital structure) because they believe that these relative levels have financial implications for the success of these firms as measured by overall market value of the firm.

It is outside the scope of this chapter to delineate these complex financial theory arguments, but two points are important. First, little is known empirically about capital structure decisions in firms (Myers, 1984). Second, most research on capital structure typically assumes a large publicly traded firm context in which capital markets are assumed to be efficient.

On the other hand, small firms and especially new ventures are the most likely to encounter imperfect capital markets (Ang, 1991, 1992; Levin & Travis, 1987; Berger & Udell, 1998). For this reason alone small firms are different from large public firms. It is therefore reasonable to be cautious and selective in the use of mainstream finance theories in theoretical accounts of financial structures of small firms and start-ups.

In general, small firms will certainly face some of the same capital structure issues as large firms (Ang, 1991). For instance, both types of firms will have to satisfy information requirements of potential lenders and investors. In this case, large firm theories may help to inform the small firm case. However, it is also likely that small firms will face unique capital structure issues, especially the availability of equity versus debt capital, thereby necessitating the use of an alternative small firm financial theory.

On the other hand, it is possible to draw specifically on the small firm finance literature that explicitly or implicitly assumes that small firms are distinctive and operate in an environment of inefficient and/or constrained financial markets. Bear in mind that small operational firms are very different from start-up firms.

Small firms and new ventures have other peculiarities that must be accommodated by researchers, such as determining the distinction between debt and equity. Traditionally, a firm's capital structure is defined as the mixture of debt and equity used to fund the assets of the firm. In large firms, debt and equity may be discerned from an examination of the firm's publicly available financial statements and documentation. Admittedly, some forms of equity/debt are designed to obscure this simplified division, but let us ignore such instruments (e.g., convertible bonds, preferred stock, etc.) and accept the simplifying assumptions.

The case among small firms is much worse. The distinction between debt and equity is almost always ambiguous (Ang, 1991). Levin and Travis (1987) argue that in small firms equity and debt are often blended in strategic ways for personal reasons. For example, in order to safeguard personal investments and avoid taxes owner-managers will make loans to their firms rather than equity investments. And, start-up small firms are rarely able to acquire debt without pledging personal assets as collateral. Such loans guaranteed by the personal finance of the owner(s) are certainly far from the definition of firm debt.

Inasmuch as it may be problematic to use the traditional large firm definition of capital structure (mixture of debt and equity), it is possible to utilize other classification schemes. For example, Chandler and Hanks (1998) simply differentiate between internal and external sources of funding. Thus, capital structure is the "internal capital provided by the founder or founding team and outside capital provided by investors or lending institutions" (p. 355). More generally, they define it as "the relative mix of capital provided by the founder(s) versus that obtained from external sources" (p. 355). Chandler and Hanks note that this definition has some precedent in the literature.

Similarly, Berger and Udell (1998) define internal sources as "funds provided by the start-up team, family and friends prior to and at the time of the firm's inception" (p. 622) a definition which additionally evokes a stage theory of small firm finance (e.g., Churchill & Lewis, 1983).

Definitional issues aside, a key area of concern is the relative ease or difficulty nascent entrepreneurs face in order to obtain funding. Anecdotal and conventional wisdom suggest that small firms and especially early stage firms suffer from a notable lack of access to financial capital. But conventional notions may obscure many of the subtleties of small firm capital markets. While small firms do not have access to the types of capital markets available to large publicly traded firms, they can access more specialized small firm funding sources (Berger & Udell, 1998). At the same time, these diverse sources are somewhat disorganized and comparatively inefficient (Levin & Travis, 1987), especially with regard to the availability of information about sources, uses, and the quality of the firms involved as compared to public markets (Ang, 1991; Wetzel, 1987).

The main theoretical causes of this situation appear to be information problems on both the demand and supply side of the market (Ang, 1991; Berger & Udell, 1998). Those sources that provide funds must determine risk profiles on small firms that publish nothing about themselves except in confidential reports that cause one to be suspicious of the content. And small firm owners must sort through an arcane, fragmented, often idiosyncratic pool of capital suppliers, if they can even find them. Novice or naïve entrepreneurs are likely to be especially baffled and threatened by this market, especially when they face some of the stringent equity or guarantee requirements of these sources.

Small firms typically do not obtain funding by issuing equity or debt securities in public markets. "Informational opacity" and high issue costs usually put public finance out of the reach of small firms (Berger & Udell, 1998, p. 628). Instead, small firms primarily utilize "private" capital sources when seeking external funding.

One important characteristic of private capital suppliers is the variety of specialized functions they may perform. For example, venture capitalists and commercial banks render intermediation functions between buyers (borrowers) and sellers (lenders). In this case, intermediaries pool the financial resources of a number of sellers and then manage the downstream transactions with individual buyers (Berger & Udell, 1998).

The foregoing literature review is focused primarily on definitional issues and funding sources for nascent entrepreneurs for the purposes of this book chapter. For a more comprehensive review of these and other theoretical issues surrounding new venture funding, see Stouder (2002).

Prior Empirical Research on Debt Versus Equity and Small Firm Capital Access

Van Auken and Carter (1989) surveyed a representative sample ($N = 96$) of Iowa small businesses regarding their initial and subsequent financing. New venture financing was composed of 45% equity and 55% debt. Furthermore, 31% of the surveyed firms financed with equity only, and 30% were financed entirely with debt.

Ou (1999) analyzed financing data from the Federal Reserve's 1993 National Survey of Small Businesses (of varying age) and found relatively few sources used by small firms. Credit borrowing in varying amounts was widely observed (75%) and banks were a main source (37%). Other borrowing sources included credit cards, lines of credit, vehicle loans, and loans by the owners to the firm. Use of bank loans appeared to increase with the size of the firm.

Berger and Udell (1998, p. 620) analyzed this same data and reported that the main sources of finance (82%) for small firms during their first 2 years of operation are commercial banks, trade credit, individuals, friends and family, and other team members. Interestingly, and in spite of conventional wisdom, the authors note that in young firms internal finance does not exceed external finance (p. 625). Additionally, they cite a study by Fluck, Holtz-Eakin, and Rosen (1997) that shows a higher proportion of external sources of finance even among startups, which is consistent with Van Auken and Carter (1989) data.

The high proportion of external institutional debt is surprising, based on the level of information problems of early stage firms. But Berger and Udell (1998) point out that institutional loans to very early stage firms typically are not provided without a personal financial pledge or guarantee; the limited liability provisions so often touted as advantages of corporations over sole proprietorships are ineffective. Thus "external" sources in this case are ambiguous since it is probable that these are not completely separate from the debts of the owners (p. 626).

Winborg and Landström (1997) surveyed a sample ($N = 262$) of small Swedish firms and found substantial evidence supporting a variety of informal "bootstrapping" funding measures as defined by Bhide. Bhide (1992) also found that in rapid growth firms ($N = 100$), 80% were financed primarily through a few internal sources, such as personal savings, credit cards, and second mortgages. The median initial capital amount was around $10,000. Growth in the early stages was funded through debt and retained earnings. Bhide refers to this conservative style of funding as "bootstrapping."

A small number of researchers have contributed to the empirical understanding of small firms' capital access. Van Auken and Carter (1989) in their survey of small businesses in Iowa ($N = 96$) found that relatively few sources of capital were used to initially fund the sample firms.

On the other hand, perhaps entrepreneurs have a more diverse set of funding options than generally believed even if they do not actually exercise those options. Thorne (1989) enumerated a variety of nontraditional sources he believes entrepreneurs routinely turn to when financing their firms.[1] Winborg and Landström (1997) found evidence for the use of nontraditional sources, suggesting that such sources are an effective source of financial strength.

Finance Variables in the PSED

Without any doubt, acquisition of financial resources is a major subject for every entrepreneur. To address this important subject, the Finance Team followed a procedure similar to other subject areas incorporated into the ERC/PSED questionnaire. The finance variables were selected based upon the need for reliable, representative, descriptive information about nascent entrepreneurial activity, in general, and entrepreneurial finance acquisition activity, in particular. As discussed in the literature review, a well developed theoretical basis for inclusion of specific financial variables for nascent, small, entrepreneurial, and family business ventures is not well established. Nonetheless, the ERC/PSED Finance Team was both inclusive and rigorous in its approach to seeking meaningful and valuable variables for inclusion in this historic research. Indeed, when the Finance Team first met, there was little discussion of theory, but an eagerness born of experience to discover exactly how people obtained the necessary financial resources to start a business from scratch. Although discussions about appropriate theory testing continued, the focus was clearly on providing a strong base of variables on which to pursue further discussion.

The initial list of items submitted by the Finance Team and other ERC teams was lengthy. As it became known how much telephone interview time was required to ask questions and receive answers, it became apparent that the total number of items in the questionnaire had to be substantially reduced. All items were reviewed for both theoretical and practical applicability and inclusion. To reduce the number of finance items, the Finance Team reviewed all items in the entire questionnaire and identified items inserted by other teams that had the same content as items that the Finance Team found essential. The items in other sections were then adopted by the Finance Team while its own identical items were deleted. This allowed the inclusion of nearly all of the necessary and desired finance items.

This chapter includes three tables that list the representative finance items in the questionnaire instruments. Table 31.1 was created from the initial telephone interview questionnaire, Table 31.2 is from the second, or follow-up, telephone interview questionnaire, and Table 31.3 is from the initial mail questionnaire. The Finance Team reduced the number of items in its list by matching items in other sections of the questionnaire. This procedure successfully retained all relevant items in the initial questionnaire.

Some Preliminary Findings

What follows are descriptive financial data from an analysis of PSED data (Stouder, 2002). The data reflect the financial decisions of a subsample of respondents; in this case it includes only those nascent entrepreneurs who created operational businesses after approximately 1 year of nascency. Overall median equity use was $10,000. Fully 96% of the sample respondents (71 of 74) used some form of equity, and 65.3% (48 of 74) used some form of debt. For those respondents who used equity, most (93.2%) make some personal equity investment. In addition, a large number of equity users (35.1%) obtain equity investment from other team members.

(Text continues on page 361)

Table 31.1 Finance Items in the PSED: First Phone Interview

Item Number[a]	Response	Question
137	Categorical: Yes/No	Have projected financial statements, such as income and cash flow statements or a break-even analysis, been developed ?
138	Continuous: Year	In what year did financial projections begin?
138a	Categorical: Month	And in what month?
139	Categorical: Yes/No	Are you now saving money to invest in this business?
140	Categorical: Finished/In Process	Have you finished saving money to invest in the new firm, or is that still in process?
141	Categorical: Intend/Finished	Do you intend to start saving money to invest in the firm, have you finished saving money to invest, or do you consider it not relevant in this case?
142	Continuous: Year	In what year did you begin savings to invest in this business?
142a	Categorical: Month	And in what month?
143	Categorical: Yes/No	Have you invested any of your own money in this business?
144	Continuous: Year	In what year did you begin investing your own money in this start-up?
144a	Categorical: Month	And in what month?
145	Categorical: Yes/No	Have financial institutions or other people been asked for funds?
146	Categorical: Completed/In Process	Is asking others or institutions for funds completed or still in process?
147	Categorical: Others/Not Relevant	Will others or financial institutions be asked for funds, or is this not relevant for this start-up?
148	Continuous: Year	In what year did seeking funds for the new business begin?
148a	Categorical: Month	And in what month?
149	Categorical: Yes/No	Has credit with a supplier been established?
150	Continuous: Year	In what year was supplier credit first established?
150a	Categorical: Month	And in what month?
160	Categorical: Yes/No/Existing Account	Has a bank account been opened exclusively for this new business?
161	Continuous: Year	In what year did you first open or begin to use a commercial bank account for the new business?
161a	Categorical: Month	And in what month?
162	Categorical: Yes/No	Has the new business received any money, income, or fees from the sale of goods or services?
162a	Continuous: Year	In what year was the first income received?
162b	Categorical: Month	And in what month?

Item Number[a]	Response	Question
163	Categorical: Yes/No	Does the monthly revenue now exceed the monthly expenses?
164	Continuous: Year	In what year did this first happen?
164a	Categorical: Month	And in what month?
165	Categorical: Yes/No	Are salaries for the managers who are also owners included in the computation of monthly expenses?
166	Continuous: Year	In what year did this first occur?
166a	Categorical: Month	And in what month?
175	Categorical: Yes/No	Has the new business paid any state unemployment insurance taxes?
176	Continuous: Year	In what year were the first unemployment taxes paid?
176a	Categorical: Month	And in what month?
177	Categorical: Yes/No	Has the new business paid any federal social security taxes (FICA payments)?
178	Continuous: Year	In what year were the first social security taxes (FICA) paid?
178a	Categorical: Month	And in what month?
179	Categorical: Yes/No	Has the new business filed a federal income tax return?
180	Continuous: Year	For which calendar year was the first federal return filed?
181	Categorical: Yes/No	To your knowledge, is the new business listed with Dun & Bradstreet, the credit rating firm?
182	Continuous: Year	In what year was it first listed with Dun & Bradstreet?
182a	Categorical: Month	And in what month?
198	Continuous: Dollar Amount	How much of your own money, in total dollars, have you put into this new start-up—either to purchase ownership or as a loan to the new business?
212	Continuous: Dollar Amount (Team)	About how much money, in total dollars, have (team owners) contributed to the new business, either to purchase ownership or as a loan to the new business?
224	Categorical: Yes/No (Team)	Has (team member) provided access to financial assistance, like equity, loans, or loan guarantees?
263	Continuous: Dollar Amount	How much in total funds, loans, and equity will the new business need before it becomes self-sustaining—that is, before monthly income is greater than all monthly expenses, salaries, supplies or parts, inventory, interest, taxes, and other expenses?
264	Continuous: Dollar Amount	How much cash will the new business need to operate for the first 30 days, regardless of the source of the funds?
265	Continuous: Dollar Amount	Businesses usually require some money before they receive financial support from the established financial community,

(Continued)

Table 31.1 (Continued)

Item Number[a]	Response	Question
		such as bank loans or purchases of ownership or equity. How much money do you think the business will need before it can expect any funds from the established financial community?
266	Categorical: Yes/No/No	Have you asked your spouse or household partner for funding for this new firm?
266a	Categorical: Yes/No/Pending	Was the answer yes or no, or is the request still pending?
268	Continuous: Dollar Amount	How much funding do you expect, in total, from your spouse or household partner?
269	Categorical: Yes/No/No	Have any of the spouses or household partners of other team members been asked to provide funding for this new firm?
269a	Categorical: Yes/No/Pending	Was the answer yes or no, or is the request still pending?
270	Continuous: Dollar Amount	How much funding do you expect, in total, from the spouses or partners of the other team members?
271	Categorical: Yes/No	Have you asked your friends and family for funding for this new firm?
271a	Categorical: Yes/No/Pending	Was the answer yes or no, or is the request still pending?
272	Continuous: Dollar Amount	How much funding do you expect, in total, from your family and friends?
273	Categorical: Yes/No	Have the family and friends of others on the start-up team been asked to provide funding for this new firm?
273a	Categorical: Yes/No/Pending	Was the answer yes or no, or is the request still pending?
274	Categorical: Yes/No/Pending	How much funding do you expect, in total, from the family and friends of others on the start-up team?
275	Categorical: Yes/No/No	Have you asked your current employer to provide funding for this new firm?
275a	Categorical: Yes/No/Pending	Was the answer yes or no, or is the request still pending?
276	Continuous: Dollar Amount	How much funding do you expect, in total, from your current employer?
277	Categorical: Yes/No/NA	Have you taken a second mortgage on your home to fund this new firm?
277a	Continuous: Dollar Amount	How much funding do you expect, in total, from a second mortgage?
278	Categorical: Yes/No	Has a bank been asked for a loan for this new firm, not including credit card loans?

Item Number[a]	Response	Question
278a	Categorical: Yes/No/Pending	Was the answer yes or no, or is the request still pending?
279	Continuous: Dollar Amount	How much funding do you expect, in total, from a bank?
280	Categorical: Yes/No	Has the Small Business Administration been asked for a loan for this new firm?
280a	Categorical: Yes/No/Pending	Was the answer yes or no, or is the request still pending?
281	Continuous: Dollar amount	How much funding do you expect, in total, from the Small Business Administration?
282	Categorical: Yes/No/No Credit Cards	Have you used credit cards to fund this new business?
282a	Continuous: Dollar Amount	How much funding do you expect in total from credit cards?
283	Categorical: Yes/No	Venture capitalists are firms or persons specializing in financing new business. Have they been asked for funding?
283a	Categorical: Yes/No/Pending	Was the answer yes or no, or is the request still pending?
284	Continuous: Dollar Amount	How much funding do you expect, in total, from a venture capitalist?
285	Categorical: Yes/No	Has a personal finance company been asked for funding for this new venture?
285a	Categorical: Yes/No/Pending	Was the answer yes or no, or is the request still pending?
286	Continuous: Dollar Amount	How much funding do you expect, in total, from a personal finance company?
287	Categorical: Yes/No	Have you asked any other source for funding for this new firm?
287a	String	What is this other source of funding?
288	Categorical: Yes/No/Pending	Was the answer yes or no, or is the request still pending?
289	Categorical: Month	How many months do you think it will take before this new firm will be able to pay back ALL the start-up costs, from all sources?

NOTE: a. Most yes/no type questions also allow for "don't know" and "refused" responses.

Only 5.4% use equity from family, friends, or relatives. We also observed that 28.3% of the sample respondents used credit cards and 23% used bank loans to start their businesses. Personal loans to the business are made by 47%, and loans from other start-up team members are used by 13.5%. Only 6.8% use loans from family, friends, or other close associates.

Based on these statistics, some comments can be made regarding start-up *equity*. First, it is very likely that at least some start-up equity will come from the

(*Text continues on page 365*)

Table 31.2 Specific Finance Items/First Follow-up Phone Interview

Item Number	Response	Question
521/522	Continuous: Dollars Amount	How much more money do you expect to contribute to the new business, either as a loan or an equity investment?[3]
594	Categorical: Yes/No	Have projected financial statements, such as income and cash flow statements or a break-even analysis, been developed?
595	Continuous: Year	In what year did financial projections begin?
595a	Categorical: Month	And in what month?
596	Categorical: Yes/No	Are you now saving money to invest in this business?
597	Categorical: Finished/ In Process	Have you finished saving money to invest in the new firm, or is that still in process?
598	Categorical: Intent/Finished/NA	Do you intend to start saving money to invest in the firm, have you finished saving money to invest, or do you consider it not relevant in this case?
599	Continuous: Year	In what year did you begin savings to invest in this business?
599a	Categorical: Month	And in what month?
600	Categorical: Yes/No	Have you invested any of your own money in this business?
601	Continuous: Year	In what year did you begin investing your own money in this start-up?
601a	Categorical: Month	And in what month?
602	Categorical: Yes/No	Have financial institutions or other people been asked for funds?
603	Categorical: Completed/ In Process	[Previous interview] you said financial institutions or other people had been asked for funds for this new business. Is asking others or institutions for funds completed or still in process?
604	Categorical: Yes/NA	Will others or financial institutions be asked for funds or is this not relevant for this start-up?
605	Continuous: Year	In what year did seeking funds for the new business begin?
605a	Categorical: Month	And in what month?
606	Categorical: Yes/No	Has credit with a supplier been established?
607	Continuous: Year	In what year was supplier credit first established?
607a	Categorical: Month	And in what month?
617	Categorical: Yes/No/Existing Account	Has a bank account been opened exclusively for this new business?
618	Continuous: Year	In what year did you first open or begin to use a commercial bank account for the new business?

Item Number	Response	Question
618a	Categorical: Month	And in what month?
619	Categorical: Yes/No	Has the new business received any money, income, or fees from the sale of goods or services?
620	Continuous: Year	In what year was the first income received?
620a	Categorical: Month	And in what month?
621	Categorical: Yes/No	Does the monthly revenue now exceed the monthly expenses?
622	Continuous: Year	In what year did this first happen?
622a	Categorical: Month	And in what month?
623	Categorical: Yes/No	Are salaries for the managers who are also owners included in the computation of monthly expenses?
624	Continuous: Year	In what year did this first occur?
624a	Categorical: Month	And in what month?
633	Categorical: Yes/No	Has the new business paid any state unemployment insurance taxes?
634	Continuous: Year	In what year were the first unemployment taxes paid?
634a	Categorical: Month	And in what month?
635	Categorical: Yes/No	Has the new business paid any federal social security taxes (FICA payments)?
636	Continuous: Year	In what year were the first social security taxes (FICA) paid?
636a	Categorical: Month	And in what month?
637	Categorical: Yes/No	Has the new business filed a federal income tax return?
638	Continuous: Year	For which calendar year was the first federal return filed?
639	Categorical: Yes/No	To your knowledge, is the new business listed with Dun & Bradstreet, the credit rating firm?
640	Continuous: Year	In what year was it first listed with Dun & Bradstreet?
640a	Categorical: Month	And in what month?
656	Continuous: Dollar Amount	How much of your own money, in total dollars, have you now put into this new start-up—either to purchase ownership or as a loan to the new business?
656a	Continuous: Dollar Amount	How much of this is considered a loan, which the new business must repay, with or without interest?
770	Continuous: Dollar Amount	Most businesses have two types of investments: (1) ownership or equity, and (2) loans or debts. Those that own equity in the

(Continued)

Table 31.2 (Continued)

Item Number	Response	Question
		business usually expect to receive a share of the profits. As of now, what is the total amount of ownership equity from all sources—that is, what is the total amount of money provided in return for a share of the profits?
770a	Continuous: Dollar Amount	The other source of money for businesses is loans or debt. This money must usually be paid back and often there is interest. Right now, what is the total amount of loans or borrowing by the business?
771	Continuous: Dollar Amount	Now, let's focus on YOUR PERSONAL contributions. How much money have you put into the business, expecting to share ownership and profits?
771a	Continuous: Dollar Amount	How much money have you loaned the business—money you expect to get back, with or without interest?
772	Continuous: Dollar Amount	Now, let's focus on OTHER START-UP TEAM MEMBERS. How much money have they PUT INTO the business, expecting to share ownership and profits?
772a	Continuous: Dollar Amount	How much money have OTHER START-UP TEAM MEMBERS LOANED the business—money they expect to get back, with or without interest?
773	Continuous: Dollar Amount	How about FAMILY MEMBERS AND RELATIVES of you OR the start-up team—how much money have they PUT INTO the business, expecting to share ownership and profits?
773a	Continuous: Dollar Amount	How much money have FAMILY MEMBERS AND RELATIVES of you OR the start-up team LOANED the business—money they expect to get back, with or without interest?
774	Continuous: Dollar Amount	How about FRIENDS AND BUSINESS ASSOCIATES of you OR the start-up team—how much money have they PUT INTO the business, expecting to share ownership and profits?
774a	Continuous: Dollar Amount	How much money have FRIENDS AND BUSINESS ASSOCIATES of you OR the start-up team LOANED the business—money they expect to get back, with or without interest?
775	Continuous: Dollar Amount	How about BANKS, FINANCIAL INSTITUTIONS, OR VENTURE CAPITALISTS—how much money have they put into the business, expecting to share ownership and profits?
775a	Continuous: Dollar Amount	How much money have BANKS, FINANCIAL INSTITUTIONS, OR VENTURE CAPITALISTS LOANED the business—money they expect to get back, with or without interest?
776	Continuous: Dollar Amount	How about PRIVATE INVESTORS—how much money have they PUT INTO the business, expecting to share ownership and profits?

Item Number	Response	Question
776a	Continuous: Dollar Amount	How much money have PRIVATE INVESTORS loaned the business—money they expect to get back, with or without interest?
777	Continuous: Dollar Amount	How about FEDERAL, STATE, OR LOCAL GOVERNMENT AGENCIES—how much money have they PUT INTO the business, expecting to share ownership and profits?
777a	Continuous: Dollar Amount	How much money have FEDERAL, STATE, OR LOCAL GOVERNMENT AGENCIES LOANED the business—money they expect to get back, with or without interest?
778	Continuous: Dollar Amount	How much money have SUPPLIERS or SUBCONTRACTORS LOANED the business—money they expect to get back, with or without interest?
779	Continuous: Dollar Amount	How much money has been borrowed on CREDIT CARDS or other forms of personal credit to the business or owners, that must be paid back?
780	Continuous: Dollar Amount	Is there any OTHER SOURCE of ownership or equity money the new firm has received? If so, how much was provided, expecting to share ownership and profits?
780a	String	What is this other source of ownership or equity money?
781	Continuous: Dollar Amount	How much money have OTHER SOURCES LOANED the business—money they expect to get back, with or without interest?
781a	String	What was this other source of loans for the business?
782	Continuous: Dollar Amount	If you and the other owners sold the business today, as a going concern, about how much would you get, after all debts were paid, including loans to the business by the owners? In other words, what is your estimate of the net worth of the business?
783	Ratio: Percentage	Right now, what percentage of the firm do you personally own?

entrepreneur or from others on the start-up team. Second, close social networks, such as family, friends, and close relations are not a common source of start-up equity. However, if and when social networks are utilized, the amount invested is likely to be high, based on the median amount ($22,000) observed in the sample.

Overall median *debt* use was $4,000 for the subsample. The median debt use for the subsample that actually used debt was $15,000, with 35.1% of those respondents reporting zero use of personal debt. Debt categories based on the survey instrument included personal loans to the start-up, other team member's loans, family and relatives' loans, friends and business associates' loans, institutional loans, private investors' loans, government loans, supplier or subcontractor loans, credit card debt, and noncategorized "other" debt.

Table 31.3 Specific Finance Items/First Mail Questionnaire

Item Number	Response	Question
A5.g	Categorical: Check all that apply [Multiple possible answers]	Which of the following led to your business idea? g. Discussions with potential or existing investors/lenders.
B1.d	Categorical: Interval: Likert: Completely disagree, Somewhat disagree, Neither agree or disagree, Somewhat agree, Completely agree	Communities vary a great deal in their entrepreneurial activity. How much do you agree or disagree with the following statements? d. Bankers and other investors go out of their way to help new firms get started.
D1.c, d, j, k	Categorical: Interval: Likert: Very low certainty, Low certainty, High certainty, Very high certainty	Considering the economic and community context for the new firm, how certain are you that the new business will be able to accomplish each of the following? c. Obtain start-up capital. d. Obtain working capital. j. Obtain a bank's help. k. Obtain a venture capitalist's help.
E1. a–i	Categorical: Check all that apply	How will the money for this new business be handled? a. No formal records b. Cash basis c. Accrual basis d. Personal checking account e. Separate business and checking account f. Owner managed accounting or bookkeeping system g. Owner managed computerized accounting system h. Use of computer software, such as Quicken i. Professionally managed (accountant or bookkeeper) accounting system
E2. a–c	Categorical: Check one box only	Who will prepare financial statements for this business? a. Owner/manager(s) b. Bookkeeper c. Accountant
E3. a–f	Categorical: Interval: Every month, Every 3 months, Every 6 months, Once a year, Never, Don't know, Not relevant Check one box for each row	Please indicate how often you expect to prepare the following statements for this new business. a. Cash statement b. Income statement c. Sales forecast d. Break-even analysis e. Balance sheet f. Cost of capital
F1. b, f, i	Categorical: Number of courses; Years of work experience	Please write in the number of courses and years of work experience you have in the following areas. b. Accounting, financial control f. Financial and capital management i. Economics
G1. g, k, n	Categorical: Interval: Likert: To no extent, To a little extent, To some extent, To a great extent, To a very great extent	To what extent are the following reasons important to you in establishing this new business? g. To give myself, my spouse, and children financial security. k. To earn a larger personal income. n. To have a chance to build great wealth or very high income.

Regarding start-up debt, almost one quarter of respondents obtained loan funds from institutional sources, such as a bank or finance company.[2] Furthermore, 47.2% made personal loans to the business.[3] However, this figure may be theoretically understated if we redefine credit card use as simply another type of personal loan to the start-up business.

The overall median total start-up funding is $20,000 ($N = 74$). This figure is substantially larger because it reflects the reduction in the number of zero use respondents in either the debt or equity category, after combining them into one category.

Funding Sources by Percent of Total Investment Dollars

It is interesting to note that about one quarter (26.86%) of total dollar funding used by the respondents in the subsample comes from the respondents' personal contributions. If we add credit cards to this total—and there is some intuitive justification for doing this—then the total is 30.44%.

Family and friends, or other close relational funding sources, are frequently mentioned in both academic and practitioner literature as providing significant amounts of funding for nascent entrepreneurs. However, in this particular sample, they constitute a very small amount (5.76%) of total funding.

Because a start-up firm has no history and no track record, it is unlikely that nascent entrepreneurs would be able to offer institutional capital suppliers enough usable information to provide them with a rational basis for funding. Yet surprisingly, institutional funding, including banks, finance companies, venture capitalists, and government sources constitute 44.19% of total start-up funding in this sample.

The data suggest that a significant source of the total funding originates from other start-up team members (18.84%). This statistic may be misleading since not all start-ups utilize start-up teams. Using data from the phone interviews (Q116, Q117, Q573, Q574), it appears that 43 of 74 (58%) nascent entrepreneurs utilized a start-up team.[4] Therefore, the proportion of total funding that comes from other team members is substantially higher for those firms that are team-based. This in turn implies that for team-based start-ups, investments and loans from other team members constitute a very high proportion of start-up funding.

Most noteworthy, Table 31.4 shows the differences between solo and team start-ups for personal equity investments and institutional debt. Note also the substantial investment from other team members (OTM equity + OTM debt = 23.40%).

Debt to Equity Ratios

We can use the underlying dollar amounts to calculate an aggregate debt to equity ratio for this sample, which is approximately D/E = 1.46. One way to restate this statistic is to say that for every $1.00 of equity start-up funding there is approximately $1.46 of debt. More generally this might suggest that neither debt nor equity is a dominant source of start-up funding, and that start-ups are not swamped with debt as is sometimes anecdotally suggested.

Table 31.4 Funding Sources: Percentage of Total Investment Dollars, Solo and Team-Based Start-ups

Variable	Source	Percentage of Total Dollar Funding Solo Start n = 31	Percentage of Total Dollar Funding Team Start n = 43	Percentage of Total Dollar Funding All n = 74
Equity	Personal	48.48	11.09	18.38
	OTM	0	17.76	14.30
	FFRelations	.74	6.37	5.26
	Inst/VC	2.96	2.33	2.45
	PvtInvest	.89	0	.17
	Total	53.07	37.55	40.56
Debt	Personal	23.15	4.93	8.48
	OTM	0	5.64	4.54
	FFRelation	.96	.39	.50
	Inst/Bk/VC	13.74	46.46	40.08
	Ccard/PersCr	9.07	2.26	3.58
	Govt	0	2.06	1.66
	Supl/Subcon	0	.72	.58
	Total	46.92	62.46	59.42
	Total Funding	99.99*	100.01*	99.88*

*Cumulative rounding errors yield ~ 100%

Another way to calculate debt to equity for the sample is to calculate the D/E ratio for each firm and then compute the median for the distribution of all firms. However, some start-up firms report using zero equity, which renders D/E calculations for those firms meaningless. If we drop out three cases in which there is zero equity and utilize this method, the median D/E is 0.85. The discrepancy between 1.46 and 0.85 suggests the presence of variance and large D/E values for some firms.

Discussion of the Results

Overall, our examination of the literature suggests that the cost of financial capital supplied by external sources will exceed the costs of capital provided by close internal sources. Furthermore, we note that the inefficiencies and information problems that plague external capital acquisition may be substantially mitigated through the use of internal and/or relational sources of funding. Therefore, we would expect nascent entrepreneurs to avoid external sources of capital and primarily utilize internal sources instead. And, in fact, this is what we have found. This wariness of external sources even extends to family and friends, as they provide a surprisingly small share of total funding. Instead, those persons close to the firm, who know the strategies, operations, and management, are the primary sources of funds. These persons are, of course, the founding team members.

The literature and results shown herein suggest the possibility of private capital market failure, driven by some degree of economic inefficiency and disorganization within private capital markets. At the same time, we must note the predicament of capital suppliers in this context, who must assess risk exposure in a highly uncertain lending situation with minimal borrower information resulting in their inability to quantify their risk so that they can balance their portfolio. Uncertainty derives mainly from the unavailability of useable information in start-up firms. In order to mitigate their risk, private capital market suppliers typically (though not always) perform a variety of costly intermediation functions such as screening prospects and writing and monitoring contracts (Berger & Udell, 1998). Therefore, it is likely that nascent entrepreneurs are paying some sort of premium for transaction cost necessary to obtain the use of external funds. We suggest here that the premium costs of external funds for new small businesses makes external funding beyond the affordable reach of most nascent entrepreneurs. This supposition is supported by the fact that almost 75% of the respondents in our research sample do not utilize any sort of external funding.

On the other hand, we reported that external funding does in fact constitute a large portion of the total dollar funding of our sample (45%). We also noted that institutional loans composed 40% of total dollar funding. This leads us to conclude that whereas most nascent entrepreneurs do not use external funding to start their businesses, those who do use fairly large amounts of it. The larger the size of funding, the less onerous the borrower's transaction costs become when measured as dollars per dollar of funded money.

We are also impressed by the high level of institutional debt funding, even at this early stage of these businesses. However, this average is undoubtedly skewed to the very large funding obtained by a few unusually attractive firms. This is likely given the large number of businesses that report zero institutional debt funding. This suggests that institutional funds are in fact available to a select group of nascent entrepreneurs.

Conclusions

Clearly, historical sources of entrepreneurial finance have not provided reliable information about the sources of funds. Much of the past research has been based on samples of questionable validity, often used to draw conclusions. Oft-cited anecdotal information and the opinions of professional writers/researchers of small businesses are largely wrong about the types of funding sources newly formed small firms use to start and operate during their first year of business. The PSED is a truly representative sample of new businesses formed in the United States during 1999. The majority of these entrepreneurs did not use money from venture capitalists nor from lending institutions—banks or finance companies—nor from family and friends. They used their own money and money from members of the founding team.

These findings are strikingly different from those found in the literature. This means that meaningful research has yet to be done to really understand the actual financing activities of entrepreneurs. For example, most of the nascent entrepreneurs before starting their businesses stated they expected to borrow start-up money from banks. They believed the myth that banks are the small business and entrepreneurs' friend. But bankers will often state that they are asset-based lenders. This means that unless a business has assets, they cannot borrow from banks. Few start-up businesses have assets to use as collateral for a bank loan, but the entrepreneurs do.

And our results show that venture capital is highly overrated as a source of entrepreneurs' funding. We have long known that of the approximately 600,000 new businesses started every year, fewer that 2,000, less than .4%, receive venture capital. Few nascent entrepreneurs of the PSED sample expected to obtain funding from venture capitalists, and their expectations were realized.

Finally, family and friends as a funding source are highly over-rated. Clearly, except in unusual cases, family and friends hesitate to invest, probably because the uncertain and risky nature of business start-ups frightens them as much as it does bankers. The real funding comes from personal assets, credit cards, and team members. These are the real struggles of entrepreneurs on the front line of creating the businesses of tomorrow.

We need more research into the PSED sample to find out the real facts of how entrepreneurs start the new businesses that will create the majority of the net new jobs in the U.S. economy over the next 10 years. We plan to continue with empirical examinations of the second and third follow-up surveys in an effort to construct a more grounded explanation of how entrepreneurs fund their new businesses.

Notes

1. It is likely that Thorne's findings are not adequately operationalized in the extant empirical literature. See Winborg and Landström's (1997) bootstrapping study.

2. Strictly speaking, due to the type of questions in the survey instrument, we cannot tell if the institutional debt source is a second mortgage, a personal loan, an SBA guaranteed loan, or something else.

3. This behavior may reflect the advice of accountants and financial advisors since personally loaned funds are typically easier to extract from the business, as opposed to equity investments.

4. Calculating actual number of team-based start-ups and subsequent funding yields ambiguous results. The answers from certain survey questions suggest 43 of 74 team-based start-ups, whereas other questions suggest 50 of 74 teams. Analysis is further hampered because only 43 are asked detailed team-related funding questions.

References

Ang, J. S. (1991). Small business uniqueness and the theory of financial management. *Journal of Small Business Finance, 1*(1), 1–13.

Ang, J. S. (1992). On the theory of finance for privately held firms. *Journal of Small Business Finance, 1*(3), 185–203.

Barton, S. L., & Matthews, C. H. (1989). Small firm financing: Implications from a strategic management perspective. *Journal of Small Business Management,* (January), 1–7.

Berger, A. N., & Udell, G. (1998). The economics of small business finance: The roles of private equity and debt markets in the financial growth cycle. *Journal of Banking & Finance, 22*(August), 613–673.

Bhide, A. (1992). Bootstrap finance: The art of start-ups. *Harvard Business Review, 70*(6), 109–117.

Chandler, G. N., & Hanks, S. H. (1998). An examination of the substitutability of founders human and financial capital in emerging business ventures. *Journal of Business Venturing, 13,* 353–369.

Churchill, N. C., & Lewis, V. L. (1983). The five stages of small business growth. *Harvard Business Review, 61*(3), 30–50.

Fluck, Z., Holtz-Eakin, D., & Rosen, H. S. (1997). *Where does the money come from? The financing of small entrepreneurial enterprises* (Working Paper). New York: New York University.

Greene, P. G., & Brown, T. E. (1997). Resource needs and the dynamic capitalism typology. *Journal of Business Venturing, 12,* 161–173.

Kirchhoff, B. A. (1994). *Entrepreneurship and dynamic capitalism.* Westport, CT: Praeger.

Levin, R., & Travis, V. (1987). Small company finance. *Harvard Business Review, 65*(6), 30–32.

Myers, S. C. (1984). The capital structure puzzle. *Journal of Finance, 39*(3), 575–592.

Ou, C. (1999, July). *Financing patterns of small firms: Findings from the 1993 National Survey of Small Business Finances.* Washington, DC: U.S. Small Business Administration, Office of Economic Research.

Stouder, M. D. (2002). *The capital structure decisions of nascent entrepreneurs.* Unpublished doctoral dissertation, Rutgers, The State University of New Jersey, Newark.

Thorne, J. R. (1989). Alternative financing for entrepreneurial ventures. *Entrepreneurship Theory and Practice,* Spring, 7–9.

Van Auken, H., & Carter, R. (1989). Capital acquisition in small firms. *Journal of Small Business Management, 27,* 1–9.

Wetzel, W. E. (1987). The informal venture capital market: Aspects of scale and market efficiency. *Journal of Business Venturing, 2,* 299–313.

Winborg, J., & Landström, H. (1997). Financial bootstrapping in small businesses: A resource-based view on small business finance. *Frontiers of entrepreneurship research.* Wellesley, MA: Babson College.

CHAPTER 32

Measures of
Financial Sophistication

Jerome Katz

Ana Cabezuelo

Consider the following contemporary observations about the financial state of Americans in general:

- They continue to amass credit card debt at record rates, over $700 billion as of August 2003 (U.S. Federal Reserve, 2003).
- They are reporting record levels of personal bankruptcy, ranging from 1.3 million filings a year in 1999 to 1.6 million in 2003 (Administrative Office of the U.S. Courts, 2003).
- They have one of the lowest savings rates in the developed world (Marquis, 2002).

Poor financial management at the individual and family level in the general population has the potential to equate to poor financial management in the pool of nascent entrepreneurs. What is likely is that there is a range of levels of financial management skills among nascent entrepreneurs, and if financial management is important to business success, then it is also likely that people with stronger financial management knowledge or skill are more likely to create businesses successfully. Operationalizing that range of financial management knowledge and skill is the concept called financial sophistication. In this effort *financial sophistication* (FS) is described as the measure of an individual's understanding of the financial elements of assets and liabilities and their interaction to create financial processes in an economic situation.

While rooted in existing measures, FS is a new measure, with its pioneering deployment in the Panel Study of Entrepreneurial Dynamics (PSED). Because of space limitations, the measure would have to be a short one, and because of the potential diversity among potential nascent entrepreneurs, measures that would be sensitive to differences in low levels of financial sophistication would be needed. With these thoughts foremost in mind, a set of questions was developed to capture the financial sophistication of nascent entrepreneurs.

The chapter starts with a theory review on what is known about financial sophistication in the general population and in small businesses. With this research foundation laid, the derivation of the FS items is given and preliminary results from the field surveys reported. The chapter concludes with a discussion about the preliminary analyses and goes on to consider analytic issues and future directions for financial sophistication research.

The original FS measure was developed at Saint Louis University by Dr. Jerome Katz, a psychologist, and Dr. Richard Green, a CPA (who is now at the College of Immaculate Conception in San Antonio, Texas), in response to concerns raised in the early meetings of the Entrepreneurship Research Consortiums (ERC). The related questions were developed by Dr. Paul Reynolds of the ERC and Babson College and Dr. Bruce Kirchhoff of the New Jersey Institute of Technology. The preliminary analyses of the FS data, research, and model development reported in this chapter have been developed by Ana Cabezuelo, a research fellow at Saint Louis University and doctoral candidate at Universidad Autónoma de Madrid, and by Dr. Katz.

The Theory Behind Financial Sophistication

As noted earlier, FS is the measure of an individual's understanding of the financial elements of assets and liabilities and their interaction to create financial processes in an economic situation. Research to date has shown that there is tremendous variation in FS within the general population and within the small business population.

In study after study of the general population, it is clear that large numbers of Americans have relatively low levels of knowledge about financial matters. For example, 9.5% have no financial accounts whatsoever (Kennickels, Starr-McCluer, & Surette, 2000). Whether looking at money saved for retirement (Attanasio, 1998; Intuit, 2001) or keeping debt to manageable levels (Kennickels et al., 2000), typically 25% to 50% or more of the respondents are facing financial hardship. Similarly, although 90.5% of households have some kind of checking account, less than half have retirement accounts, and less than one third have life insurance. Advanced accounts, such as managed asset accounts, can be found in only 3.9% of families (Kennickels et al., 2000). Because nascent entrepreneurs come from the general population, it is likely that they will show a similar range of levels of financial knowledge and financial instrument use.

The case might be made that the people who start their own businesses are more financially aware or financially sophisticated than the general population, but the support is lacking; and the small business results mirror those of the general population. For example, study after study shows that the leading cause of failure for small business start-ups comes from financial problems such as inadequate capitalization, excessive debt, and poor record keeping (Gerber, 1998; Hanks & Chandler, 1994; Lussier, 1995; McMahon, 2001; McMahon & Holmes, 1991; Monk, 2000; Rue & Ibrahim, 1998). One bright spot is that firms that undertake financial planning efforts often report enhanced rates of firm survival and financial success (Hanks & Chandler, 1994; Lussier, 1995; McMahon, 2001; McMahon & Holmes, 1991; Monk, 2000). Most often the firms undertaking such efforts are among those making use of more financial transaction instruments.

Small businesses mirror the general population in the variation in the use of financial accounts and instruments (Bitler, Robb, & Wolken, 2001; Cole & Wolken, 1995). For example, Cole and Wolken using data from the National Survey of Small Business Finances (NSSBF), found that only 40% of all firms use some kind of financial account, such as a checking account. More advanced techniques, such as cash management accounts, are only used by 2% to 6% of firms, closely paralleling the use of asset management accounts found in the household studies.

Taking these household and small business studies together, three consistencies emerge:

- Range: There is considerable range in the utilization of financial transaction and financial management instruments.
- Sequence: It appears that some instruments precede others in occurrence, implying a sequence.
- Overlap: The overall patterns for instrument use appear similar in household samples and in small business samples, suggesting that one model should work for both nascent and practicing entrepreneurs.

These findings lead to the development of an instrument for measuring financial sophistication. The first two points help operationalize the listing of instruments and offer insights on how to streamline the measure. The second idea introduces sequencing for the instrument in time and sophistication levels, whereas the third idea helps identify whether the underlying theory for FS approximates a spillover or compensatory model.

Implications of the Range and Sequence Consistencies

There is a plethora of financial transaction instruments available, but the range consistency suggests that their utilization rates are at best a near-normal distribution, though most often skewed toward the low end. This describes a distribution where a few items have high rates of use, but there are many items with low rates of use reported. Given such a distribution, it is important to develop a foundational measure that taps instruments that are likely to draw a usable response and reflect some important aspect of FS measurement.

In reviewing the literature on small and medium enterprises (SME) failure and family financial failure, what comes up repeatedly is the presence or absence of basic information on finances. Whether naïve or not, the fundamental assumption of the empirical and anecdotal efforts is that if people *knew* their financial condition, they could often avoid making mistakes. This leads to the idea of the *presence or absence of formal financial records* (QE1a) as the foundation level for FS.

The next level that makes sense appears to be the idea of individual-business differentiation. For example, the NSSBF shows that the youngest firms use personal credit cards in business far more than even slightly older firms (28.14% vs. 37.9%, Cole & Wolken, 1995). As noted above, it is likely that nascent entrepreneurs will often financially mirror their firms. In open systems theory (Katz & Kahn, 1978), this concept is called "partial inclusion" and reflects the overlap between the individual and the firm. In new SMEs, especially those without employees, the owner and the firm may appear identical. As the firm grows, it is normally expected that the owner and the firm overlap less and less (or in open systems parlance, demonstrate enhanced partial inclusion). In the corporate form of organization (which requires a higher degree of FS), one of the major problems occurs when one "pierces the corporate veil" by mixing personal and business funds. Similarly, in firms of any size, a failure to maintain taxes in escrow accounts reflects a problem of maintaining the differentiation of person and firm. Operationally, given the incidence rates for forms of transaction accounts mentioned in prior representative sample research, the best measure of individual-business differentiation would be the *presence of a business (vs. a personal) checking account* (QE1d–QE1e).

In firms characterized by the presence of formal records and the further presence of separate business accounts, the third potential level reflects a more in-depth understanding of the financial or accounting exigencies of business. There are several potential aspects of savings instrument use or credit instrument use that could be considered, but one of the most enduring aspects of sophistication in accounting, which carries over into financial projections, is the explicit consideration of time. Being able to move beyond the immediate present to consider flows of money over time represents a major element of increased sophistication. Fortunately, there is one convention in accounting and finance that is unambiguous, and considered relatively simple—it is the *choice of a cash or an accrual basis for the finances of the business* (QE1b–QE1c).

As a result, the FS measure is composed of three elements: presence of formal records, presence of a business checking account, and cash/accrual choice for accounting. The advantages of these measures are that they are relatively concrete, reflecting behavioral measures, and they are terms that at their introductory level can be understood by people with even low levels of financial information or experience. The questions composing the FS scale and its related scales are detailed in Table 32.1.

Related Scales

Although the three levels of FS should provide substantial discrimination at even the lowest levels of the FS distribution, to accommodate higher levels of FS, and variant approaches, other measures are worth considering. One supplement of interest to researchers is a set of questions about business planning in the telephone survey. The telephone survey includes questions asking if a business plan has been

Table 32.1   Financial Sophistication Items in the PSED

Method	File	Question	Item Number
Telephone questionnaire	ERCMGC21	Has a business plan been prepared?	Q111
		Has this not yet been done, or is it not relevant to this business?	Q112
		Is it in process or completed?	Q113
		Have projected financial statements, such as income and cash flow statements or a break-even analysis, been developed?	Q137
Mail questionnaire	ERCMGM21	How will the money for this new business be handled?	
		No formal records	QE1a
		Cash basis	QE1b
		Accrual basis	QE1c
		Personal checking account	QE1d
		Separate business checking account	QE1e
		Owner-managed accounting or bookkeeping system	QE1f
		Owner-managed computerized accounting system	QE1g
		Use of computer software, such as Quicken	QF1h
		Professionally managed (accountant or bookkeeper) accounting system	QE1i
		Who will prepare financial statements (Owner/manager-bookkeeper-accountant)?	QE2
		Please, indicate how often you expect to prepare the following statements for this new business.	
		Cash statement	QE3a
		Income statement	QE3b
		Sales forecast	QE3c
		Break-even analysis	QE3d
		Balance sheet	QE3e
		Cost of capital	QE3f

produced or in process and, if either is the case, whether projected financial statements, such as income and cash flow statements or a break-even analysis, have been completed. Three additional variable sets of particular interest to FS analysts are considered below: financial technology, financial delegation, and financial projection frequency.

Financial technology reflects the growing interest in the utilization of personal computers in the financial and cash management of firms. Because personal computers let the owner employ software that facilitates record keeping, accrual basis accounting systems, and projection development, it is argued that increased levels of technology use should correspond to higher levels of financial sophistication. Today, the most advanced personal computer systems and financial software involve client/server arrangements, where the owner runs software on a PC in the firm but is also networked to even more powerful systems run by the professional accountants. These systems result in both the owner and the outside accountants reviewing the data. As a result, the three levels of financial technology involve non-computerized record keeping at the lowest level, the use of a stand-alone personal computer package (e.g., QuickBooks, Peachtree, etc.) at the next level, and client/server financial system (e.g., fixed asset solutions—FAS) at the high end of this scale. These items are included in the FS item in the mail survey (QE1g–QE1h).

Financial delegation involves the choice of the nascent entrepreneur to "do it yourself" versus have others take care of the financial records of the firm. Often bookkeeping or accounting is the first service of the firm to be outsourced. This is arguably because outside of financial services industry, FS is only rarely a core competence, so it can make sense to delegate to others with more expertise. The trade-off for the nascent entrepreneur may be greater expertise in the handling of the records coupled with increased learning (and FS) by the nascent entrepreneur regarding the financial and cash situation of the firm—but possibly at the loss of a direct feel for or an appreciation of the finances of the firm. The levels of financial delegation would be record keeping by the owner as the lowest level of delegation, with a bookkeeper as the middle level, and a professional accountant as the highest level. Financial delegation is a separate item in the mail survey (QE2).

Financial projection frequency considers how often each of six projections—cash statement, income statement, sales forecast, break-even analysis, balance sheet, and cost of capital—are computed. Generally, which of these a nascent entrepreneur needs is self-determined or determined by demand characteristics from investors or banks, based on the financial support request from the nascent entrepreneur. The key issue worth considering in this area is how often are projections performed. This idea goes back to the first level in the original FS measure. In effect, having formal records is better than not having them because having information is seen as the way to avoid problems. By extension, having more recent or current information should help identify and perhaps allay problems sooner. Recognizing that entrepreneurs use the different types of financial projections with different degrees of frequency, it is important to measure projection delegation and projection frequency separately across the set of financial projection components. This leads to a set of questions asking about the frequency of six types of financial projections in the mail survey (QE3a, QE3b, QE3c, QE3d, QE3e, and QE3f).

Sampling Issues

The PSED can be bewildering in the number of groups, subgroups, and weights available to the researcher. In this section, advice is offered on how to select samples and weights to perform FS analyses.

In the PSED survey, we can discern two different groups of respondents. Persons who are involved in the creation of a new business and people who are not. This second group of people, referred to as the "comparison group," is used in the studies in which it is necessary to contrast behavior or attitude among people *with* entrepreneur profiles to behavior and attitude of people *without* entrepreneur profiles. Because the FS outcomes are related exclusively to nascent entrepreneurship, the comparison group is not used in FS analyses. Within this group, a further reduction comes from selecting only respondents who have completed the mail questionnaire because the questions related with the financial sophistication are found only in that survey (ERCMGM21). This results in a survey sample of 562 respondents, with 2 respondents who replied with Not Applicable responses, leaving an effective total of 560.

As Reynolds (2000) suggests, analyses should be based on samples reflecting respondent weights. Because of the deliberate oversampling of different subgroups (such as gender, or race) the uses of the weights allow estimates of population values and tests of statistical significance. The weights were designed so that the sum of all weights equaled the total number of respondents in the sample. Subsamples do not complete that condition. Therefore, the frequencies reported below are based on a sample of 560 respondents, such that

mailqwt*(560)/(actual sum of mail weights)

All analyses below use this adjustment for weighing.

Preliminary Analyses

The goal in building the basic measure of financial sophistication was to have a measure that served a foundational financial purpose, was widely understood, and served as a conceptual precursor to subsequent and higher levels of FS. The presence of formal records served as the key indicator, and only 2.1% of PSED respondents reported having no financial records.

Presence or Absence of Formal Financial Records

QE1a: Will the handling of the money for this new business involve?
No formal records

	%
Checked	2.1
Not checked	97.9
Total	100.0

The second level of FS came from the differentiation of personal from business checking accounts. Interestingly, approximately three times as many respondents reported having a business checking account (69.8%) than a personal one (23.1%). The difference in these rates suggests that the personal checking account question could be dropped.

Presence of a Business (vs. a Personal) Checking Account

QE1d: Will the handling of the money for this new business involve?
Personal checking account

	%
Checked	23.1
Not checked	76.9
Total	100.0

QE1e: Will the handling of the money for this new business involve?
Separate business checking account

	%
Checked	69.8
Not checked	30.2
Total	100.0

As noted earlier, the third level in the sequence was the use of a cash or accrual method for figuring the finances of the business. Cash method was reported by 30.4% of respondents, whereas an accrual basis was reported by 7.3% of respondents. Together, over 60% of respondents did not report using either technique for accounting, although the cash basis is the typical or default method. This suggests that the choice of accounting method requires a higher level of financial or accounting information than the prior questions, as would be expected.

Choice of a Cash or Accrual Basis for the Finances of the Business

QE1b: Will the handling of the money for this new business involve?
Cash basis

	%
Checked	30.4
Not checked	69.6
Total	100.0

QE1c: Will the handling of the money for this new business involve?
Accrual basis

	%
Checked	7.3
Not checked	92.7
Total	100.0

Among the related measures, 40.8% of respondents reported having an owner-managed computerized accounting system (QE1g), whereas 50.4% reported using computer software, such as Quicken (QE1h).

Most nascent entrepreneurs plan to go it alone in terms of handling their financial and accounting work, at least at first. Responding to QE2 (Who will prepare financial statements for this new business?), some 63% of respondents plan to have the owner-manager take care of the accounting, although 7.4% plan to use a bookkeeper and 29.6% report plans to use accountants.

In terms of having a business plan, 58.9% reported intention to have a plan. At the time of the mail survey, 17.4% had their business plan completed, 42.1% said their plan was in process, 22.9% said their plan was not yet done, and 17.6% said that a business plan was not relevant to their firm.

The remaining question asked for the frequency for six types of financial or accounting reports—cash statements, income statements, sales forecasts, break-even analyses, balance sheets, and cost of capital analyses. As shown in Tables 32.2 and 32.3, the modal response for each type of projection was monthly, ranging from 32.5% for sales forecasts, to 63.9% for cash statements.

Table 32.2   Types of Financial Projection, Part I

Please indicate how often you expect to prepare the following statement for this new business?

Frequency	QE3a Cash statement %	QE3b Income statement %	QE3c Sales forecast %
Never	3.0	1.1	14.5
Once a year	12.7	20.0	9.7
Every 6 months	3.7	6.3	11.4
Every 3 months	10.4	16.0	17.4
Every month	63.9	54.7	32.5
Not relevant	6.3	1.9	14.5
Total	100.0	100.0	100.0

Table 32.3   Types of Financial Projection, Part II

Please indicate how often you expect to prepare the following statement for this new business?

Frequency	QE3d Break-even analysis %	QE3e Balance sheet %	QE3f Cost of capital %
Never	9.9	3.8	13.4
Once a year	15.2	14.7	19.3
Every 6 months	12.0	5.6	5.4
Every 3 months	17.2	16.0	10.2
Every month	37.2	55.6	40.5
Not relevant	8.6	4.3	11.2
Total	100.0	100.0	100.0

Item Relation to Theory

The intent of the FS questions was to operationalize an assessment of the knowledge and behaviors nascent entrepreneurs bring to the process of organizational creation. Although there was no grand underlying theory of financial sophistication, the concept does appear to have face validity: in starting a business, having more knowledge about financial matters and procedures or instruments is often believed to be coincident with success.

The literature on financial sophistication in the general population and the small business population suggested that there was a broad range of levels of FS in both groups. This necessitated having a FS measure that starts out with a fundamental factor, in this case, keeping formal records. The default choice in QE1a was having some form of formal records, and respondents would need to check if they had no formal records. The small number of respondents checking "No Formal Records" was in keeping with the expectations from the research, where people felt they were keeping track of their money, even when the exact procedures could not be clearly specified (Intuit, 2001).

The second level of FS focuses on the individual-business distinction, and involved check-offs for the use of a personal checking account (QE1d) and/or a business checking account (QE1e). From the NSSBF (Cole & Wolken, 1995) and Kennickels et al. (2000), it was known that checking accounts were among the most common of the financial instruments in use for both the general and small business populations. The incidence rates for these two measures fell in the expected range based on prior research, although the usage rates for personal checking accounts is often higher than that for business checking accounts. One possibility is that the "business" in "business checking accounts" represents a socially desirable indicator, one that suggests the instrument's appropriateness for an emerging business and as a result generates higher levels of projected use than NSSBF results show for actual use.

The third and most sophisticated indicator of FS is the choice of a specific method of considering revenues in the business. The traditional choices, cash and accrual methods (QE1b and QE1c, respectively), were offered. Most respondents checked neither box, although all accounting is done using one approach or the other. This suggests that the terms *cash* and *accrual* themselves may involve a higher level of FS than the other terms in the model. This topping-out of the scale is consistent with expectations regarding the extreme range of FS in the population, although it is not strictly possible to interpret the nonresponse rates.

In terms of the related items, the ones included in the FS question set involved the type of accounting system in place—owner-managed manual (QE1f), owner-managed computerized (QE1g), more widely used computer-based (QE1h), or professionally managed (QE1i). Similarly, the nexus of the accounting tasks (owner-manager, bookkeeper, accountant) was checked in QE2. In both cases, the findings were sought to help understand the context for the main FS questions rather than as independent questions guided by a theory. However, additional analyses (not reproduced here) have shown that the higher levels of FS are significantly related to the use of outsiders or computer programs to perform accounting and financial activities.

The idea of FS in these preliminary results is consistent with anecdotal works by business-development specialists and empirical results from major national representative sample surveys. Thus, the FS measure for the PSED represents a reasonable first effort to model this potentially important concept. Future work will, it is hoped, further refine the measure and do a better job of showing the relation of FS to business creation.

The Future Use of Financial Sophistication Analysis

Financial sophistication is a simple idea that makes a great deal of intuitive sense. People who are better prepared to deal with the realities of finances in a new firm would seem less likely to make mistakes in cash management or financial activities. As others have reported from early PSED results, success in creating a business often hinges more on the avoidance of mistakes than on the brilliance of a product or embrace by a market. It seems obvious that people higher in FS would be more likely to know or recognize potential mistakes in accounting and financial arenas and hence be better able to minimize or avoid them.

First, the major difference may be between individuals who make no FS efforts and those who make even a small one, such as keeping formal records. There is nothing approaching a consensus about how much FS is necessary to successfully launch a firm, and anecdotal reports about microenterprises in less developed countries have suggested that small amounts of effort in FS might make a great deal of difference.

Second, FS may not be not related to education, especially at the lower FS levels. Keeping a check register, or tracking receipts, does not require more than grade school arithmetic, and these are what formal records look like in the most basic of small businesses or microenterprises. Performing accrual-based accounting, and certainly crafting a business plan with financial projections, will require more background and often the assistance of people and programs expert in these areas; but at the first two levels of FS, little formal education is needed. This may complicate correlational and linear regression-based approaches to analysis.

Third, the basic FS scale is intended as an abbreviated Rasch scale (Lord, 1980). A Rasch scale reflects an explicit hierarchy, similar to the better-known Guttman scale. Guttman scales, however, are strict in the exclusion of cases that violate the hierarchy. So, for example, a person who has no formal records but has a business checking account would be excluded. Rasch scales permit the inclusion of such cases using probability functions of the different potential sequences to handle common and exceptional cases. With this in mind, FS analysts should anticipate using all three levels in analyses and keeping all relevant cases whenever possible.

As with most other survey instruments, there are some caveats that should be kept in mind. The push for brevity in the PSED meant often one question had to "make do" where psychometrics or faculty proclivities would posit two or three questions. This is most evident in QE1 in the mail questionnaire. The question "crammed" five questions (formal records, cash/accrual, personal/business checking, computerized/manual record keeping, owner/professional accounting) into one item but did so with some expense. For example, the assumption is that people who did *not* check "No Formal Records" did in fact keep some kind of formal financial record. Analyzing the 97% of respondents who left this box unchecked, it does appear that most of them report using some other technique for formal record keeping (such as checking accounts, or the reports from QE3). Although the pattern of the data is encouraging, it is not definitive because it is always logically difficult to build a proof from the absence of response.

There is also the problem of projecting future behaviors. For many people, maintaining financial discipline and records is difficult. That is part of the reason that so many people report unexpected financial problems with their credit and checking accounts. Saying that one will pursue a disciplined financial approach in a future business is easy. Some items, such as a "Separate Business Checking Account" even telegraph what is the more businesslike type of answer. But in practice, the incidence of implementation for these items may be substantially less than the nascent entrepreneur projections would suggest; and if the FS model suggests anything, it would suggest that those least likely to implement financial controls are those with low FS levels and most in need of accounting discipline.

Ironically, the strongest supports for the question set in its current form are instrumental. The key question for FS is indeed a single checkbox question, and it does appear to work as intended. For a pioneering effort and a small space on a hotly contested survey, that is probably a better than acceptable outcome.

Conclusion

Financial sophistication (FS) represents the measure of an individual's understanding of the financial elements of assets and liabilities and their interaction to create financial processes in an economic situation. It is a new measure with its pioneering deployment in the PSED. The basis for the measure comes from research on the general population and the population of small businesses, showing that there is wide variation in the levels of financial knowledge and activity among people and firms.

This first comprehensive effort to develop a FS measure sought to build a scale that could position the majority of nascent businesses, despite the wide variation expected in financial knowledge and action. The key measures were keeping formal records, using personal and/or business checking accounts, and using a cash or accrual basis when accounting for revenue. Contextual questions on role performance and computerization were also included, as were ties to questions in other parts of the PSED related to FS.

Generally, the scale operated in the way expected based on prior research. Some variations, such as higher projected incidence rates for business checking accounts, were noted and initial explanations provided. Higher levels of FS did coincide with use of more sophisticated financial management concepts (e.g., accrual vs. cash), computerized systems, or outsourced financial work. All three instances were reasonably expected given prior research or current theorizing.

What needs to be done is to begin studies of FS in relation to start-up and survival. On one hand, higher levels of FS might result in fewer starts among the more sophisticated, as nascent entrepreneurs do a better job of evaluating prospective businesses. That said, where the early financial work suggests a viable potential business, the belief is that firms and owners with higher levels of FS are more likely to survive because of a better understanding of the cash and credit situation of the firm. Other PSED researchers, intrigued by the FS measures, have offered preliminary results suggesting the above relationships may well be true. At the other end of the spectrum, looking at how low levels of FS relate to survival, the likelihood is that, as prior research suggested, people with little expertise in financial matters are more likely to start businesses, only to see them fail. As the PSED sample matures, this idea will become testable.

Possible research extensions for the FS scale include (1) more complex psychometric models incorporating the related variables into the basic FS scale, (2) studies testing the FS items to establish norms in the larger SME population, (3) studies relating FS variables to their spillover equivalents in consumer and family finances (e.g., formal records, checking accounts, family budgets), as well as (4) studies typing FS levels to other competency-based components of the PSED. In many ways, FS research is in its own nascency and, to achieve any measure of success, will require more extensive study and utilization by entrepreneurship researchers. Overall, financial sophistication is a simple measure with strong face validity and promising preliminary results in the PSED sample. As a pioneering effort to measure FS, the current approach represents a reasonable first step.

References

Administrative Office of the U.S. Courts. (2003). *Bankruptcy cases continue to break federal court caseload records* (news release). Washington, DC: Author.

Attanasio, O. P. (1998). Cohort analysis of saving behavior by U.S. households. *Journal of Human Resources, 33*(3), 575–609.

Bitler, M., Robb, A., Wolken, J. (2001, April). Financial services used by small businesses: Evidence from the 1998 National Survey of Small Business Finances. *Federal Reserve Bulletin.* Washington, DC: Federal Reserve Board.

Cole, A., & Wolken, D. (1995, July). Financial services used by small businesses: Evidence from the 1993 National Survey of Small Business Finances. *Federal Reserve Bulletin.* Washington, DC: Federal Reserve Board.

Gerber, M. (1998). *The E-myth revisited: Why most small businesses don't work and what to do about it.* New York: HarperBusiness.

Hanks, S., & Chandler, G. (1994). Patterns of functional specialization in emerging high tech firms. *Journal of Small Business Management, 32*(2), 23–37.

Intuit. (2001, January 30). *Quicken fiscal literacy survey reveals that 55% of Americans age 65+ don't know how much they will need to retire* (news release). Mountain View, CA. Retrieved January 30, 2001, from http://www.intuit.com/about_intuit/press_releases/2001/01-30.html

Katz, D., & Kahn, R. L. (1978). *The social psychology of organizations.* New York: Wiley.

Kennickels, A., Starr-McCluer, M., & Surette, B. (2000, January). Recent changes in U.S. family finances: Results from the 1998 Survey of Consumer Finance. *Federal Reserve Bulletin.* Washington, DC: Federal Reserve Board.

Lord, F. M. (1980). *Applications of item response theory to practical testing problems.* Hillsdale, NJ: Lawrence Erlbaum.

Lussier, R. (1995). A nonfinancial business success versus failure prediction model for young firms. *Journal of Small Business Management, 33*(1), 8–20.

Marquis, M. (2002, March 29). *What's behind the low U.S. personal saving rate?* (FRBSF Economic Letter Number 2002–09). San Francisco: Federal Reserve Bank of San Francisco.

McMahon, R. (2001). Growth and performance of manufacturing SMEs: The influence of financial management characteristics. *International Small Businesses Journal, 19*(3), 10–29.

McMahon, R. G. P., & Holmes, S. (1991). Small business financial management practices in North America: A literature review. *Journal of Small Business Management, 29*(2): 19–30.

Monk, R. (2000). Why small businesses fail. *CMA Management, 74*(6), 12–14.

Reynolds, P. (2000). National Panel Study of U.S. Business Startups. In J. A. Katz (Ed.), *Databases for the study of entrepreneurship: Vol. 4 Advances in entrepreneurship, firm emergence, and growth* (pp. 153–227). Stamford, CT: JAI.

Rue, L., & Ibrahim, N. (1998). The relationship between planning sophistication and performance in small businesses. *Journal of Small Business Management, 36*(4), 24–32.

U.S. Federal Reserve Board. (2003). Consumer credit–June 2003 (Federal Reserve Statistical Release: G 19). Washington, DC: Author.

CHAPTER 33

Future Expectations for the New Business

Sherrie E. Human

Charles H. Matthews

The challenges inherent in identifying and measuring organizational outcomes are amplified when researchers focus their attention on nascent entrepreneurs. Typical business outcomes of interest to organizational scholars include financial and operational performance measures—such as sales or employee volume, market share or technological efficiencies—that are unlikely to exist at the preorganizing stage in the life of a new business. Although nascent entrepreneurs do not yet have actual business performance, such as employee and sales growth, they do have expectations of firm performance that can foreshadow their venture's actual outcomes.

Early scholars of the organizational context in general (e.g., Ajzen, 1991) and the entrepreneurial context in particular (e.g., Katz & Gartner, 1988), argued for the utility of studying phenomena before they occurred and developed conceptual frameworks for examining intentionality. In a comparative study of competing models of entrepreneurial intentions, Krueger, Reilly, and Carsrud (2000) validated that intentions have "proven the best predictor of planned behavior" (p. 411). Consequently, a growing number of researchers are examining future outcome expectations—conceptualized as growth intentions, expectations, motivations, or aspirations—in the nascent, entrepreneurial, and small firm context (Dennis & Solomon, 2001; Lau & Busenitz, 2001; Liao & Welsch, 2003; Welter, 2001; Wiklund, 2001). Further, because entrepreneurs intend or choose to start their firms, scholars argue that entrepreneurs make other fundamental choices (Shaver & Scott,

1991) such as choosing how or whether to grow the new firm (Ginn & Sexton, 1989; Kolvereid, 1992).

The literature on firm performance in smaller and newer firms also suggests that entrepreneurs' subjective perceptions of organizational performance are consistent with objective measures of performance (Dess & Robinson, 1984). Thus, examining nascent entrepreneurs' perceptions of and future expectations for the new business can provide a useful predictor of actual performance (Chandler & Hanks, 1993), a baseline upon which to compare actual performance if and when it occurs and a linkage to the large and continuously growing body of work on organizational performance.

Literature Review

Scholars examining business creation have long been interested in identifying "what . . . we mean by outcomes" (Shaver & Scott, 1991, p. 34) and in improving our constructs and measures of business outcomes (Brush & Vanderwerf, 1992). In reviewing the literature relevant for understanding the Panel Study of Entrepreneurial Dynamics (PSED) future expectations variables, we differentiate approaches that scholars have taken in conceptualizing and measuring outcomes. One long-standing approach regarding business outcomes has been a direct focus on *business growth as the primary construct of interest,* using quantitative measures such as sales and employee volume. A second approach regarding business outcomes has been to use perceptual measures such as preferences for business growth, control, or family income as *correlates or proxies for other constructs of interest,* including business type or founder type (e.g., differentiating small business vs. entrepreneurial business, or small business owner vs. entrepreneur).

Literature Using Business Outcomes as the Primary Construct of Interest

Regarding the first approach—scholars' direct interest in growth—Penrose (1959) argued that growth was a key outcome for businesses that could be explained by managerial and organizational actions and attributes. Indeed, conceptualizing and measuring organizational growth has been of interest across disciplines. Economics scholars have long been interested in examining efficiencies that affect growth over the life cycle of the firm. For instance, Evans (1987) tested alternative theories of firm growth using absolute employment numbers as a measure of firm size and change in employment numbers over 7 years as a growth rate for comparing sample firms. Evans's study confirmed earlier work in the economics literature (e.g., Jovanovic, 1982) regarding the inverse relationship between firm growth and age.

Strategy scholars' interest in planning has resulted in a stream of literature trying to predict new and small firm performance (i.e., growth) from planning activities. For instance, Bracker, Keats, and Pearson (1988) examined the impact of planning on the 5-year sales growth rate in small firms, and Robinson, Salem, Logan, and Pearce (1986) examined how planning activities of smaller retail firms related to 3 years of sales and employee growth. Although not always able to provide unequivocal evidence of the planning-performance link, these early studies provide a solid perspective worthy of continued exploration (Schwenk & Shrader, 1993).

Entrepreneurship scholars have also examined theories, concepts, and measures of growth as they relate to newer or smaller firms. Low and MacMillan (1988) discussed several theoretical approaches—strategic adaptation, population ecology, and sociocultural perspectives—on which entrepreneurship scholars could base empirical work and could identify key business outcomes of interest. For instance, they describe how the strategic adaptation perspective has examined the effect of entrepreneurs' decisions on new firm performance such as sales and/or employee growth (e.g., Roure & Maidique, 1986). They also discuss how, in contrast, the population ecology perspective has examined start-ups and exits as a function of external demographic or technological shifts (e.g., Delacroix & Carroll, 1983). Other scholars have incorporated network concepts and methodologies to examine new and small firm outcomes (e.g., Aldrich, 1999; Human & Provan, 1997).

In Brush and Vanderwerf's (1992) comparison of methods and sources of new venture performance estimates, the authors found that measures most commonly used by scholars—including owner/founder responses regarding annual sales, number of employees, growth in sales, and growth in employees—were highly reliable for research purposes. We noted that in Cooper and Gascon's (1992) review of 61 studies (published between 1960 and 1990 focusing on firm performance as the dependent variable) that 42 of those studies used one or more of the following as firm performance measures: sales or employee growth; absolute measure of sales or employees; and firm survival or firm discontinuance.

Chandler and Hanks's (1993) validation study of emerging business performance measures found that researchers' use of growth rate measures (e.g., sales growth) and business volume measures (e.g., actual sales) were rated either good or very good in terms of relevance, availability, internal consistency, interrater reliability, and external validity. In addition, the authors suggested that practicing entrepreneurs and business owners are most familiar with and frequently reference these outcome measures themselves. In Murphy, Trailer, and Hill's (1996) two-part study, the authors surveyed the entrepreneurship literature from 1987 to 1993 regarding the use of performance measures, finding that firm growth was one of eight performance dimensions used in studies—others included efficiency, profit, and size dimensions—with changes in sales and employees being the most commonly used measures for growth. The second part of their study, in which the authors examined relationships between performance variables, found insignificant or negative correlations between most performance measures. Based on these results, Murphy et al. (1996) argued that it was important for researchers to make theory-based decisions regarding which performance measures they use and to include multiple dimensions of performance when possible.

Recent reviews of the literature on organizational growth in general (Weinzimmer, Nystrom, & Freeman, 1998) and new venture growth in particular (Davidsson & Wiklund, 2000) have also argued for the importance of researchers' selecting growth measures based on theoretical rationales, highlighting the potential consequences of not doing so. For instance, Davidsson and Wiklund (2000) cited scholars who "stress that a consensus has been reached among academics that sales growth is the best growth measure" (p. 37), but also emphasized that theoretical considerations should drive future researchers' selection of particular growth measures. They illustrated their argument with four theoretical perspectives—resource-based, motivation, strategic adaptation, and configuration—suggesting that the relevant unit of analysis (e.g., individual, activity, and governance structure) for each of these perspectives would help inform researchers' decisions on using sales, employee, and/or asset measures of growth.

Finally, in addition to identifying key performance variables, scholars have also been interested in determining how long is enough time to adequately measure business performance. For both theoretical and practical reasons, the literature has included a wide range of time periods for measuring business volume and growth. Researchers have asked respondents for financial outcomes 1 year apart (e.g., Duchesneau & Gartner, 1990), as well as 3, 5, or 7 years apart (e.g., Robinson et al., 1986; Bracker et al., 1988; and Evans, 1987, respectively). Several scholars have suggested that 5 years is an adequate period over which to evaluate performance in small firms (Bettis, 1981; Bracker et al., 1988; Galbraith & Nathanson, 1978), and statistics on business survival have long cited the first 5 years after business creation as being most crucial in estimating survival and failure (Dun & Bradstreet, 1967). Well-established practitioner publications, such as *Inc* magazine, have historically used a 5-year period of sales growth for identifying fast-growing, privately held firms (Terpstra & Olson, 1993). Consequently, based on this body of literature, 5 years also seemed a useful time frame for the relevant PSED measures requested of respondents regarding future expectations for their new business.

As mentioned earlier, a second approach scholars have taken in examining business outcomes that is relevant for understanding PSED future expectations variables relates to using specific measures as categorizations or correlates for other constructs of interest. This approach is discussed in the following section.

Literature Using Business Outcomes as Categorizations or Correlates for Other Constructs

One refinement of the literature on firm growth and performance has been to categorize types of growth. Hoy, McDougall, and Dsouza's (1992) review of the literature on high performance firms noted that sales growth, as the dominant performance measure in entrepreneurship research, could also be used to distinguish high- and low-growth firms, such as whether "sales growth exceeds the average growth rate of the industries . . . or exceeds the average growth rate of the fastest-growing industries in a particular sector" (p. 347). In addition, these authors suggested that receipt of venture capital could provide a proxy measure for high-growth orientation because that particular funding source is only available to high-growth business opportunities. Monroe, Price, and Neck (1997) distinguished venture hyperperformance or "super-gazelles" from other high-growth ventures based on sales volume changes over time. Thakur (1995) and Gundry and Welsch (2001) used reported sales for different periods of time to distinguish high- and low-growth paths and ambitious and status quo firms, respectively.

A second refinement of the literature that categorizes types of growth stems from Carland, Hoy, Boulton, and Carland's (1984) highly-cited conceptual framework for distinguishing entrepreneurs from small business owners that examines respondents' preferences regarding dependence upon, as well as control of, ownership, and persistence of the new firm. For instance, Carland et al.'s classification of an entrepreneur is one who intends to grow the firm, and does not necessarily need to be in full control of the firm to achieve that growth. In contrast, the authors classify a small business owner as one who intends for the business to be his or her family's primary income, controlled primarily by the business owner. Using this conceptual framework as a foundation, it can also be stipulated that an entrepreneur might be more likely than a small business owner to accept additional outside ownership as a mechanism for growing the business. This framework has been applied by researchers to better understand differences between, for instance, those that plan and those that do not plan for their new business (Matthews & Scott, 1995) and for examining psychological profile differences among entrepreneurs, small business owners, and corporate managers (Stewart & Roth, 2001; Stewart, Watson, Carland, & Carland, 1998).

In addition to the Carland et al. (1984) classification, Birch (1987) used change in firm employment measures as a way to categorize entrepreneurs and income substitutors, and Chandler and Hanks (1993) distinguished the opportunistic from the income replacement entrepreneur by examining measures of business volume such as sales and earnings. Davidsson (1991) and Begley (1995) distinguished between entrepreneurial versus nonentrepreneurial tendencies, using sales and/ or employment growth as correlates for continued entrepreneurship. In addition, Welter (2001) argued that respondents' above average growth preferences could be correlates for economic need to contribute to household income.

Conceptual classifications for business outcome measures have also focused on constructs such as success, exit, and optimism. For instance, Duchesneau and Gartner (1990) categorized firms in an emerging industry as either successful or failed, using sales and employee volume as distinguishing characteristics for both, and using inability to contact as a further characteristic of failed businesses. Gimeno, Folta, Cooper, and Woo (1997) used a similar categorization for measuring business exits in a study of entrepreneurial human capital across firms. Regarding the optimism construct, Cooper, Woo, and Dunkelberg (1988) and Mehta and Cooper (2000) have examined respondents' perceived feasibility of business success as a measure of optimism. They found a positive relationship between respondents who perceived strong odds for the future success or persistence of their new business, classified as optimistic, and the firm performance for those respondents.

Another classification approach long used as part of practitioners' and scholars' methodologies has been to use business volume or growth measures as comparative characteristics of the sample firms or database of interest. For instance, recognized statistical databases tracking the entrepreneurial and small business contexts differentiate and categorize firm attributes by size-based measures such as sales and employee volumes (e.g., Katz, 2000; U.S. SBA, 2000).

To summarize the relevant literature for understanding the PSED future expectations variables, first entrepreneurs' future expectations for new business outcomes are viewed as valid predictors of actual business outcomes. Next, for well over a decade, the literature on new business outcomes has examined quantitative business performance and growth measures, including finer-grained performance constructs such as high and low growth. Finally, scholars have also used respondents' expectations, preferences, and actual outcomes as categorizations or correlates of other constructs of interest. The following section describes the specific variables used in the PSED to measure future expectations for the new business.

The Future Expectations Variables

Table 33.1 displays the wording of the 10 items from the telephone interview (items Q317 to Q325) that represent the Future Expectations for the New Business variables. Drawing on our discussion of the literature above, Table 33.2 illustrates how these 10 items selected for the PSED relate to constructs in the literature and to specific empirical studies. For instance, items Q317 to Q321 address important quantitative indicators of business volume and business growth—respondents' future expectations of their new business' sales and employee levels—that are well represented in the literature across disciplines and theoretical perspectives. Items Q322 to Q324, regarding respondents' preferences for future firm size as well as equity and family income positions, are well-grounded constructs for understanding how nascent entrepreneurs view their growth orientation in general and their entrepreneurial or small business orientations in particular. Item Q325, regarding likelihood of the new business operating in 5 years, is well represented in the literature on business exits, survival, or persistence, as well literature examining individual characteristics such as optimism.

Descriptive Analysis of the
Future Expectations Variables

Table 33.3 provides descriptive statistics of the 10 PSED items regarding future expectations for the new business. Due to a wide range of responses in the data for business volumes (Q317 to Q321), examination of the medians indicates respondents' three-fold growth expectations in sales, two-fold growth expectations in full-time employees, and three-fold growth expectations in part-time employees over 5 years. With two response options (i.e., a "1" or a "2") for item Q322, the mean response of 1.78 regarding respondents' overall preference for business size or growth indicates that the PSED nascent sample tends to prefer a business size they can manage themselves rather than a size that is as large as possible. This is supported by PSED respondents' expectations that they will likely retain over two thirds (mean = 70.25%) of the equity in their new business 5 years out (Q323) and will likely garner two thirds (mean = 65.36%) of their family income from their new businesses after 5 years (Q324). Overall, PSED respondents are optimistic about their new businesses persisting, estimating over 80% likelihood (mean = 81.53%) that their businesses will be operating in 5 years (Q325).

Table 33.1   The 10 Future Expectations Items in the PSED Telephone Questionnaire

Nascent Entrepreneurs: We would like to ask about your expectations regarding the future of this new firm.

Item Number	Question
Q317	First, what would you expect the total sales, revenues, or fees to be in the first full year of operation?
Q317a	And what about the fifth year? What would you expect the total sales, revenues, or fees to be in the fifth year of operation?
Q318	By the end of the first full year of operation, about how many full-time employees, not counting owners, do you expect to be working for pay at this new business? (Full-time is 35 or more hours per week)
Q319	By the end of the first full year, about how many part-time employees do you expect to be working for pay at this new firm? (Part-time is less than 35 hours per week)
Q320	By the end of the fifth year of operation, about how many full-time employees, not counting owners, do you expect to be working for pay at this new business? (Full-time is 35 or more hours per week)
Q321	By the end of the fifth year of operation, about how many part-time employees do you expect to be working for pay at this new firm? (Part-time is less than 35 hours per week)
Q322	Which of the following two statements best describes your preference for the future size of this business: 1) I want the business to be as large as possible, or 2) I want a size I can manage myself or with a few key employees.
Q323	What percentage of the firm would you personally expect to own 5 years after the firm began full operations?
Q324	On a scale of zero to one hundred, where 0 means completely unlikely and 100 means absolutely certain, what is the likelihood that this business will become the primary source of your family's income?
Q325	On a scale of zero to one hundred, what is the likelihood that this business will be operating 5 years from now, regardless of who owns and operates the firm? Zero means completely unlikely and 100 means absolutely certain.

Findings to Date

Matthews and Human (2000) used expectations of financial growth and expectations of employee growth as dependent variables predicted by individual-related attributes such as age and gender, and organization-related attributes such as business plan formalization and perception of environmental uncertainty. Initial

(Text continues on page 397)

Table 33.2   Relating Future Expectations Variables in PSED to Constructs in the Literature

Items (Brief Description)	Constructs in the Literature	Representative Empirical Literature
Q317-321 (Expected revenues and employees for the business)	Business volume and growth	Brush & Vanderwerf (1992) Sales, employees, sales growth, employment growth, net income, return on sales, and return on assets from different sources examined for research reliability. Owner/founder sources of sales, profit, and employee data found highly reliable.
Q322 (Preference for future size of the business)	Correlate for business type and/or founder type	Stewart & Roth (2001) Meta-analysis in which Carland et al. (1984) typology used to differentiate entrepreneurs (growth oriented versus income oriented) from managers.
	Correlate for growth orientation	Dennis & Solomon (2001) Respondents' answers categorized according to growth intentions, including growing the business into a large firm, developing a lifestyle business, and creating an income supplement (part-time) business.
Q323 (Expected ownership percentage of the business)	Correlate for business type and/or founder type	Stewart, Watson, Carland, & Carland (1998) Respondents' classified as either entrepreneurs or small business owners based on answers to survey using Carland et al. (1984) typology, which includes key issues of founders' independence and control of business.
	Correlate for growth orientation	Hoy, McDougall, & Dsouza (1992) Authors suggest that receipt of venture capital, which often requires substantial ownership control by VCs, is a proxy for high growth orientation.

(Continued)

Table 33.2 (Continued)

Items (Brief Description)	Constructs in the Literature	Representative Empirical Literature
Q324 (Likelihood of the business providing primary source of family income)	Correlate for business type and/or founder type	Matthews & Scott (1995) Respondents' answer to survey item based on Carland et al. (1984) typology used to categorize their firms as either entrepreneurial ventures or small businesses; authors provided validity check on categorization using 5-year period sales and earnings data.
	Correlate for growth needs	Welter (2001) Respondents who indicated above average growth intentions may reflect need to contribute to household income due to founder's lower income household situation.
Q325 (Likelihood of business remaining in operation)	Business exit, survival	Kalleberg & Leicht (1991) Authors defined company as out of business if several attempts to contact via mail or telephone were unsuccessful.
	Correlate for optimism	Cooper, Woo, & Dunkelberg (1988) Authors asked respondents "What are the odds of your business succeeding?"

Table 33.3 Descriptive Statistics: Future Expectations Variables

Unit of Analysis		Q317 Expected Firm Income: First Year	Q31[a] Expected Firm Income: Fifth Year	Q318 Expected Full-Time Jobs: First Year (Excluding Owners)	Q319 Expected Part-Time Jobs: First Year (Excluding Owners)	Q320 Expected Full-Time Jobs: Fifth Year (Excluding Owners)
N	Valid	680	663	473	469	455
	Missing	150	167	357	361	375
Mean		415,523.17	1,696,643.00	15.64	4.72	20.53
Median		31,820.00	100,000.00	2.00	1.00	5.00
Mode		10,000 [a]	100,000	0	0	0[a]
Range		45,025,000	80,000,000	5,000	350	2,000
Minimum		−25,000	0	0	0	0
Maximum		45,000,000	80,000,000	5,000	350	2,000
Standard Deviation		2685217.00	7705959.37	229.95	23.64	104.57

(Continued)

Table 33.3 (Continued)

Unit of Analysis		Q321 Expected Part-Time Job: Fifth Year (Excluding Owners)	Q322 Preference for Firm Size[b]	Q323 % Equity Expected in 5 Years	Q324 Expected Firm to be Primary Household Income	Q325 Estimated Odds Firm will be Operating in 5 Years
N	Valid	453	814	807	816	802
	Missing	377	16	23	14	28
Mean		21.59	1.78	70.25	65.36	81.53
Median		3.00	2.00	75.00	75.00	90.00
Mode		0	2	100	100	100
Range		3,000	1	100	100	100
Minimum		0	1	0	0	0
Maximum		3,000	2	100	100	100
Standard Deviation		166.30	.42	29.64	33.47	24.62

NOTES:

a. Multiple modes exist. The smallest value is shown.

b. "I want the business to be as large as possible" = 1; "I want a size I can manage myself or with a few key employees" = 2.

Descriptive statistics for Table 33.3 were run for Respondent Types 10, 11, 12 (nascent mixed gender, female oversample, and minority oversample). Due to item content (e.g., future expectations for new business), the control group data sets (Respondent Types 20 and 21) were not included.

findings suggest that for nascent or pre-start-up entrepreneurs, growth expectations do not vary with respect to individual-related attributes such as age and gender, thus providing empirical support for and linkage to studies examining post-start-up business outcomes (e.g., Kalleberg & Leicht, 1991). However, the authors found that growth expectations for nascent entrepreneurs do appear related to, and tempered by, business plan formalization and perceptions of firm operational uncertainty. In a separate analysis in which sales and employee growth expectations were distinguished by whether the nascent stage occurred for independent entrepreneurs or for corporate entrepreneurs, Matthews, Ford, and Human (2001) suggest that corporate nascents perceive less uncertainty, are more risk seeking, develop more formal business plans, and have lower growth expectations than independent nascents. Recent examination of financial and employee growth expectations as predicted by funding complexity, business plan formalization, and venture type (defined by the growth orientation correlate variable) suggests that all three variables helped explain differences in financial growth expectations but not employee growth expectations (Matthews, Ford, & Human, 2002).

References

Ajzen, I. (1991). The theory of planned behavior. *Organizational Behavior and Human Processes, 50,* 179–211.

Aldrich, H. E. (1999). *Organizations evolving.* London: Sage.

Begley, T. M. (1995). Using founder status, age of firm, and company growth rate as the basis for distinguishing entrepreneurs from managers of smaller businesses. *Journal of Business Venturing, 10,* 249–263.

Bettis, R. A. (1981). *Risks and industry effects in large diversified firms.* Paper presented at the *41st annual meeting of the Academy of Management.* San Diego, CA.

Birch, D. L. (1987). *Job creation in America.* New York: Free Press.

Bracker, J. S., Keats, B. W., & Pearson, J. N. (1988). Planning and financial performance among small firms in a growth industry. *Strategic Management Journal, 9,* 591–603.

Brush, C. G., & Vanderwerf, P. A. (1992). A comparison of methods and sources for obtaining estimates of new venture performance. *Journal of Business Venturing, 7,* 157–170.

Carland, J. W., Hoy, F., Boulton, W. R., & Carland, J. C. (1984). Differentiating entrepreneurs from small business owners: A conceptualization. *Academy of Management Review, 9*(2), 354–359.

Chandler, G. N., & Hanks, S. H. (1993). Measuring the performance of emerging businesses: A validation study. *Journal of Business Venturing, 8,* 391–408.

Cooper, A. C., & Gascon, F. J. G. (1992). Entrepreneurs, processes of founding, and new-firm performance. In D. L. Sexton & J. D. Kasarda (Eds.), *The state of the art of entrepreneurship* (pp. 301–340). Boston: PWS-Kent.

Cooper, A. C., Woo, C. Y., & Dunkelberg, W. C. (1988). Entrepreneurs' perceived chances for success. *Journal of Business Venturing, 3,* 97–108.

Davidsson, P. (1991). Continued entrepreneurship: Ability, need, and opportunity as determinants of small firm growth. *Journal of Business Venturing, 6,* 405–429.

Davidsson, P., & Wiklund, J. (2000). Conceptual and empirical challenges in the study of firm growth. In D. L. Sexton & H. Landstrom (Eds.), *The Blackwell handbook of entrepreneurship* (pp. 26–44). Oxford, UK: Blackwell.

Delacroix, J., & Carroll, G. R. (1983). Organizational findings: An ecological study of the newspaper industries of Argentina and Ireland. *Administrative Science Quarterly, 28*(June), 274–291.

Dennis, W. J., & Solomon, G. T. (2001, June). *Changes in the intention to grow over time.* Paper presented at the Babson Kauffman Entrepreneurship Research Conference, Wellesley, MA.

Dess, G. G., & Robinson, R. B., Jr. (1984). Measuring organizational performance in the absence of objective measures: The case of the privately held firm and conglomerate business unit. *Strategic Management Journal, 5,* 265–273.

Duchesneau, D. A., & Gartner, W. B. (1990). A profile of new venture success and failure in an emerging industry. *Journal of Business Venturing, 5,* 297–312.

Dun & Bradstreet. (1967). *Patterns of success in managing a business.* New York: Author.

Evans, D. S. (1987). Tests of alternative theories of firm growth. *Journal of Political Economy, 95*(4), 657–674.

Galbraith, J. R., & Nathanson, D. A. (1978). *Strategy, implementation: The role of structure and process.* St. Paul, MN: West.

Gimeno, J., Folta, T. B., Cooper, A. C., & Woo, C. Y. (1997). Survival of the fittest? Entrepreneurial human capital and the persistence of underperforming firms. *Administrative Science Quarterly, 42,* 750–783.

Ginn, C. W., & Sexton, D. L. (1989). Growth: A vocational choice and psychological preference. In R. Brockhaus, N. Churchill, J. Katz, B. Kirchhoff, K. Vesper, & W. Wetzel, Jr. (Eds.), *Frontiers of entrepreneurship research* (pp. 1–12). Wellesley, MA: Babson College.

Gundry, L. K., & Welsch, H. P. (2001). The ambitious entrepreneur: High growth strategies of women-owned enterprises. *Journal of Business Venturing, 16,* 453–470.

Hoy, F., McDougall, P. P., & Dsouza, D. E. (1992). Strategies and environments of high-growth firms. In D. L. Sexton & J. D. Kasarda (Eds.), *The state of the art of entrepreneurship* (pp. 341–357). Boston: PWS-Kent.

Human, S. E., & Provan, K. G. (1997). An emergent theory of structure and outcomes in small-firm strategic manufacturing networks. *Academy of Management Journal, 40*(2), 368–403.

Jovanovic, B. (1982, May). Selection and evolution of industry. *Econometrica, 50,* 649–670.

Kalleberg, A. L., & Leicht, K. T. (1991). Gender and organizational performance: Determinants of small business survival and success. *Academy of Management Journal, 34*(1), 136–161.

Katz, J. A. (2000). *Advances in entrepreneurship, firm growth, emergence, and growth: Databases for the study of entrepreneurship: Vol. 4.* Amsterdam, The Netherlands: JAI/Elsevier Science.

Katz, J., & Gartner, W. B. (1988). Properties of emerging organizations. *Academy of Management Review, 13*(3), 429–441.

Kolvereid, L. (1992). Growth aspirations among Norwegian entrepreneurs. *Journal of Business Venturing, 7,* 209–222.

Krueger, N. F., Jr., Norris, F., Reilly, M. D., & Carsrud, A. L. (2000). Competing models of entrepreneurial intentions. *Journal of Business Venturing, 15,* 411–432.

Lau, C. M., & Busenitz, L. W. (2001). Growth intentions of entrepreneurs in a transitional economy: The People's Republic of China. *Entrepreneurship Theory and Practice, 25*(5), 5–20.

Liao, J., & Welsch, H. (2003). Social capital and entrepreneurial growth aspiration: A comparison of technology- and non-technology-based nascent entrepreneurs. *Journal of High Technology Management Research, 14,* 149–170.

Low, M. B., & MacMillan, I. C. (1988). Entrepreneurship: Past research and future challenges. *Journal of Management, 14*(2), 139–161.

Matthews, C. H., Ford, M. W., & Human, S. E. (2001). The context of new venture initiation: Comparing growth expectations of nascent entrepreneurs and intrapreneurs. In W. Bygrave, E. Autio, C. Brush, P. Davidsson, P. Green, P. Reynolds, & H. Sapienza (Eds.), *Frontiers of entrepreneurship research* (pp. 42–52). Wellesley, MA: Babson College.

Matthews, C. H., Ford, M. W., & Human, S. E. (2002). From credit cards to venture capital: Financing complexity and planning sophistication in nascent ventures. In W. Bygrave, C. Brush, P. Davidsson, J. Fiet, P. Greene, R. Harrison, M. Lerner, G. Meyer, J. Sohl, & A. Zacharakis (Eds.), *Frontiers of entrepreneurship research.* Wellesley, MA: Babson College.

Matthews, C. H., & Human, S. E. (2000). The little engine that could: Uncertainty and growth expectations of nascent entrepreneurs. In P. Reynolds, E. Autio, C. Brush, W. Bygrave, S. Manigart, H. Sapienza, & K. Shaver (Eds.), *Frontiers of entrepreneurship research* (pp. 55–66). Wellesley, MA: Babson College.

Matthews, C., & Scott, S. G. (1995). Uncertainty and planning in small and entrepreneurial firms: An empirical assessment. *Journal of Small Business Management, 33*(4), 34–52.

Mehta, S. R., & Cooper, A. (2000). Optimism as a predictor of new firm performance. In P. D. Reynolds, E. Autio, C. G. Brush, W. D. Bygrave, S. Manigart, H. J. Sapienza, & K. G. Shaver (Eds.), *Frontiers of entrepreneurship research* (pp. 595–607). Wellesley, MA: Babson College.

Monroe, S. R., Price, C., & Neck, H. (1997). Growing "super gazelles:" An empirical study of entrepreneurial training strategies and venture hyperperformance. In P. Reynolds, W. Bygrave, N. Carter, P. Davidsson, W. Gartner, C. Mason, & P. McDougall (Eds.), *Frontiers of entrepreneurship research* (pp. 64–65). Wellesley, MA: Babson College.

Murphy, G. B., Trailer, J. W., & Hill, R. C. (1996). Measuring performance in entrepreneurship research. *Journal of Business Research, 36,* 15–23.

Penrose, E. T. (1959). *The theory of the growth of the firm.* Oxford, UK: Oxford University Press.

Robinson, R. B., Jr., Salem, M. Y., Logan, J. E., & Pearce, J. A., II. (1986). Planning activities related to independent retail firm performance. *American Journal of Small Business,* (Summer), 19–26.

Roure, J. B., & Maidique, M. A. (1986). Linking prefunding factors and high-technology venture success: An exploratory study. *Journal of Business Venturing, 1*(3), 295–306.

Schwenk, C. R., & Shrader, C. B. (1993). Effects of formal strategic planning on financial performance in small firms: A meta-analysis. *Entrepreneurship Theory and Practice, 17*(3), 53–65.

Shaver, K. G., & Scott, L. R. (1991). Person, process, choice: The psychology of new venture creation. *Entrepreneurship Theory and Practice, 16*(2), 23–45.

Stewart, W. H., Jr., & Roth, P. L. (2001). Risk propensity differences between entrepreneurs and managers: A meta-analytic review. *Journal of Applied Psychology, 86*(1), 145–153.

Stewart, W. H., Jr., Watson, W. E., Carland, J. C., & Carland, J. W. (1998). A proclivity for entrepreneurship: A comparison of entrepreneurs, small business owners, and corporate managers. *Journal of Business Venturing, 14*(2), 189–214.

Terpstra, D. E., & Olson, P. D. (1993). Entrepreneurial start-up and growth: A classification of problems. *Entrepreneurship Theory and Practice, 17*(3), 5–20.

Thakur, S. P. (1995). Size of investment, growth opportunity and human resource management typologies in entrepreneurial firms: Some observations. In W. D. Bygrave, B. J. Bird, S. Birley, N. C. Churchill, M. G. Hay, R. H. Keeley, & W. E. Wetzel, Jr. (Eds.), *Frontiers of entrepreneurship research.* Wellesley, MA: Babson College.

U.S. Small Business Administration, Office of Advocacy. (2000). *The state of small business: A report of the President, 1999–2000.* Washington, DC: Government Printing Office.

Weinzimmer, L. G., Nystrom, P. C., & Freeman, S. J. (1998). Measuring organizational growth: Issues, consequences and guidelines. *Journal of Management, 24*(2), 235–262.

Welter, F. (2001). Who wants to grow? Growth intentions and growth profiles of (nascent) entrepreneurs in Germany. In W. D. Bygrave, E. Autio, C. G. Brush, P. Davidsson, P. G. Green, P. D. Reynolds, & H. J. Sapienza (Eds.), *Frontiers of entrepreneurship research.* Wellesley, MA: Babson College.

Wiklund, J. (2001). Growth motivation and its influence on subsequent growth. In W. D. Bygrave, E. Autio, C. G. Brush, P. Davidsson, P. G. Green, P. D. Reynolds, & H. J. Sapienza (Eds.), *Frontiers of entrepreneurship research.* Wellesley, MA: Babson College.

PART IV

CHAPTER 34

Overview: The Entrepreneurial Context and Environment

Paul D. Reynolds

The central purpose of the Panel Study of Entrepreneurial Dynamics (PSED) is to answer the question, "Where do new firms come from?" or "What are the major processes that lead to the emergence of new firms?" This has led to an emphasis on the personal characteristics of those that pursue the creation of a new firm and the actual behavior initiated as a new firm is under development. However, as shown in the conceptual scheme presented in Figure 1.1 of Chapter 1, presented again here as Figure 34.1, it is assumed that the "firm birthing process" occurs within a unique entrepreneurial environment.

There is a major conceptual distinction between the context in which entrepreneurship occurs and those factors that have an immediate impact on the start-up process and those directly involved. The latter group would encompass the principals that expect to own the firm, their activities, and the assistance provided by others with an interest in seeing the firm succeed, such as friends and family members, financial investors, suppliers, employees, and perhaps the customers. The environment for this activity also has many facets. These would include both the specific economic sector in which the new firm will compete, as well as the general economic, political, and social climate of the geographic region where the new firm is being implemented.

There are, of course, a number of ways of assessing these different contextual features. One strategy is to give careful attention to existing standardized data on industry sectors and geographic regions. As the state and county are known for all

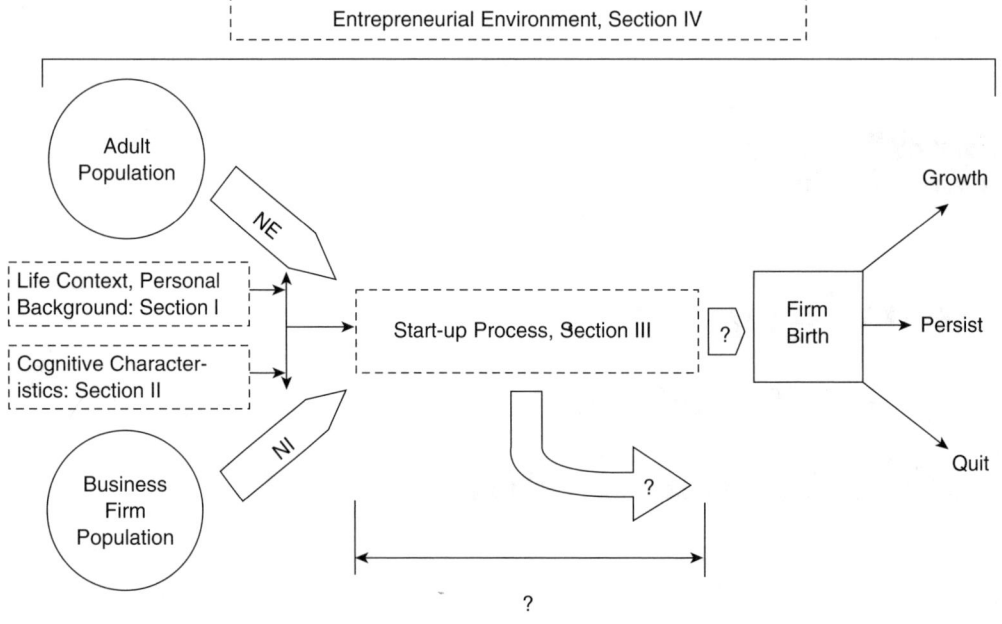

Figure 34.1   The Start-up Process and Handbook Organization

respondents who complete the screening interviews, the vast array of data describing U.S. counties can be used to characterize the context in which the start-up effort is implemented.

Another source of information would be the judgments and perceptions of the individuals themselves. Such information may be part of the interview schedules and systematically gathered from the participants in the detailed data collection. The following chapters in Part IV review four aspects of the context, or reaction to the context that were measured with special questions in the interview schedules.

Context and New Firm Births: Utilizing Standardized National Data Sets

One strategy for assessing the potential of the context to affect new firm births is to utilize existing data to determine the presence of a systematic relationship. Three elements are required: first, the definition of the unit of analysis; second, data reflecting the emergence of a new business entity; and third, data on factors that might be considered to affect variation in birth rates across the units of analysis.

This strategy has been implemented using U.S. labor market areas as the unit of analysis. These are contiguous sets of counties known to form integrated work and living zones. Cluster analysis procedures are used to identify sets of counties, based on reports of the journey to work, where individuals live or work within the same cluster. Based on 1980 U.S. census data, 382 such clusters were identified (Tolbert & Killian,

1987); with the 1990 U.S. census data the count was 394 (Tolbert & Sizer, 1996). These can be considered independent, miniature economic systems. In both assessments approximately one third include counties from two or more states, making clear that state boundaries are imprecise measures of an integrated economic region.

The measure of new business creation were counts of new entries in a business registry, either new listings in a commercial credit rating file (Reynolds, Miller, & Maki, 1995) or firms that reported the initiation of federal social security taxes for employees (Acs & Armington, 1998). The cost and sophistication of the programming required to produce such annual counts, specific to economic sector and county, is considerable but not the subject for this discussion. The result is the potential for computing firm birth rates, either the annual number of firms implemented per 100 existing firms or the annual number of firms implemented per 1,000 persons in the workforce.

Measures of the characteristics of the labor market areas involve assembling county-level data from a wide range of standardized federal sources—there are dozens of data files with thousands of variables. Three very useful sources are the most recent versions of the *County and City Data Book*, which provides over 5,000 sociodemographic and economic characteristics (U.S. Economics and Statistics Administration [1998]), the Regional Economic Information System (REIS)—which provides annual details on jobs and income by economic sector for every year following 1969 (Bureau of Economic Analysis, http://www.bea.gov), and the most recent U.S. Census data (http://www.census.gov/statab/USA98/usacount.pdf), which has detailed information about the ethnic, educational, occupation, and income distributions for the counties.

Once the data sets have been assembled with the labor market areas as the unit of analysis, attention can focus on assessing the variation in annual business birthrates (which tend to vary from 4 to 12 per 100 existing businesses). Models can then be developed to determine the relative impact of different factors on this variation in business birthrates. The results are quite consistent for the United States over time; the results based on data from 1978 to 1988 (Reynolds et al., 1995) are quite similar to those for the mid-1990s (Armington & Acs, 2002). Results were also quite similar across six advanced economies (five in Europe and the United States). Linear additive models are able to account for 45% to 84% of the variation in firm birthrates (Reynolds, Storey, & Westhead, 1994). Measures of increases in demand, urbanization, unemployment, wealth, and the presence of small firms all have a positive association with higher levels of new firm births. Detailed analysis across the United States has found increases in demand, higher proportion of well educated, mid-career adults, and greater economic diversity are major factors associated with higher firm birthrates (Reynolds et al., 1995).

PSED Data Set. The basic unit of analysis in the PSED data set is the individual (or the individual start-up effort) and not a geographically bound region, such as a county, labor market area, or state. Facilitating assessment of the impact of context on the PSED assessment of start-up activity began with tracking the location of each respondent; their state and county are included in the data sets. This could then be used to add a number of variables from the standardized federal data sets to the file.

A short list of selected variables included in the PSED data set is presented in Exhibit 34.1. Keeping in mind that the unit of analysis is the individual respondent in the screening interview, the first group of variables identifies the respondent's location—state, county, and ZIP code. The variable "STCOFIPS" is the standard 5-digit code used to identify counties in all federal data sets. The second group of variables, with "CCDB" leading in the variable name, was taken from the *County and City Data Book* files; the third group, with "REIS" leading the variable name, was taken from the Regional Economic Information System files, and the last group is transforms based on these variables. The last group of six transforms is interval and ratio measures that have been reclassified into four ordinal levels with an equal number of respondents in each group.

Exhibit 34.1   Contextual Measures, Selected, from the PSED Data Set

COSTNAME	CO NAME AND STATE ABBREV
USSTATE	US: FIPS CODES 50 STATES+WASH,DC
USCOUNTY	US: FIPS CODES EACH COUNTY
ZIP	US: POSTAL ZIP CODE
USREG9	US: 9 CENSUS REGIONS ,W/O AK,HI
USREG4	US: 4 CENSUS DIVISIONS,W/O AK,HI
STCOFIPS	STATE AND CO FIPS CODES
ITEM001	CCDB 90:Tot Land Area (SqMi)
ITEM002	CCDB 92:Tot Population
ITEM005	CCDB 90:Tot Population
ITEM006	CCDB 80:Tot Population
ITEM025X	CCDB 90:Tot Males
WHITE90	CCDB 90:TOT WHITE, ALL AGES: 1990
BLACK90	CCDB 90:TOT BLACK, ALL AGES
AMRID90	CCDB 90:TOT AMER IND, ALL AGES
ASIAN90	CCDB 90:TOT ASIAN/PACIFIC ISLD, ALL AGES
HISPA90	CCDB 90:TOT HISPANIC, ALL AGES
T212490	CCDB 90:Total 21-24 years
T253490	CCDB 90:Total 25-34 years
T354490	CCDB 90:Total 35-44 years
T455490	CCDB 90:Total 45-54 years
T556490	CCDB 90:Total 55-64 years
TOTPOP90	CCDB 90:TOTAL Population
ITEM069	CCDB 90:Tot 25-up Years
ITEM071C	CCDB 90:Tot 25-up Coll Grad or Higher
ITEM077C	CCDB 89:Tot HH w/ YrInc $50,000-74,999
ITEM078C	CCDB 89:Tot HH w/ YrInc $75,000 or more
ITEM078X	CCDB 90:Tot Households
L0102593	REIS 93:Total ALL Jobs
L0103093	REIS 93:TOTAL Personal inc ($1,000)
L2603093	REIS 93:Total proprietors
L2703093	REIS 93:Non-farm proprietors
L2803093	REIS 93:Farm proprietors

```
WHPOPPC      WHITE     % TOT POP:1990
BLPOPPC      BLACK     % TOT POP:1990
HSPOPPC      HISPANIC  % TOT POP:1990
WHSQMI       WHITES    /SQUARE MILE:1990
BLSQMI       BLACKS    /SQUARE MILE:1990
HSSQMI       HISPANICS/SQUARE MILE:1990
BLPOPPC4     BLACK % TOT POP:4 CAT:25%/50%/75%
BLPOPPC2     BLACK % TOT POP:2 CAT: 90%
HSPOPPC4     HISPA % TOT POP:4 CAT:25%/50%/75%
HSPOPPC2     HISPA & TOT POP:2 CAT: 90%
BLSQMI4      BLACK /SQ MILE:4 CAT:25%/50%/75%
BLSQMI2      BLACK /SQ MILE:2 CAT: 90%

HSSQMI4      HISPA /SQ MILE:4 CAT:25%/50%/75%
HSSQMI2      HISPA /SQ MILE:2 CAT: 90%
POPDN92      POP DENSITY:PEOPLE/SQ MILE: 1992
PCINC93      PER CAPITA TOT PERSONAL INCOME: 1993
HH75K89      PER CENT HHS W/INCOME $75K+:1989
P254490      PC POPULATION 25-44 YEARS OLD: 1990
PCOLL90      PER CENT POP 25+ WITH COLLEGE: 1990
PC8092A      ANNUAL PER CENT POP CHANGE: 80-92

POPDN924     4 CAT:POP DENSITY:PEOPLE/SQ MILE:92
PCINC934     4 CAT:PER CAPITA TOT PERSONAL INCOME:93
HH75K894     4 CAT:PER CENT HHS W/INC $75K+:89
P2544904     4 CAT:PC POPULATION 25-44 YEARS OLD:90
PCOLL904     4 CAT:PER CENT POP 25+ WITH COLLEGE:90
PC8092A4     4 CAT:ANNUAL PER CENT POP CHANGE:1980-92
```

NOTE: CCDB = County and City Data Book; REIS = Regional Economic Information System.
Some variable labels taken from the original source documents.

There are two strategies for analysis. The initial strategy might be to use geographic regions—counties, states, or perhaps multistate regions—and compare levels of entrepreneurial activity. However, even with the screening sample of over 60,000 cases, the number of respondents in most counties or even states will be so low that there would be very wide confidence intervals associated with any estimates of prevalence. There are eight states and the District of Columbia with samples of less than 500. Aggregations of states, however, may provide samples large enough to provide estimates with acceptable accuracy.

The prevalence rate of two-criterion nascent entrepreneurs for the nine U.S. census regions is presented in Figure 34.2. Both the mean and the 95% confidence intervals are presented. The wide confidence intervals, however, indicate that no region is statistically significantly different from an adjacent region. Only the extremes are clearly statistically different. There is some variation, with the rate in the Pacific Region (CA, OR, and WA) at 7%, almost twice that of West North Central (IA, KS, ND, NE, MN, MO, and SD) at 4%.

Previous studies based on the labor market area analysis would suggest that differences within these multistate regions may be as great as the differences between

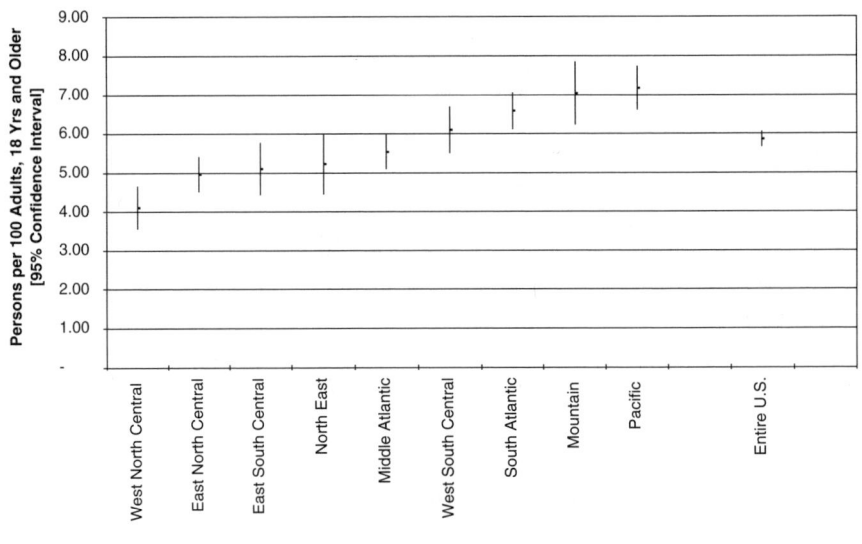

Figure 34.2   Prevalence of Two-Criteria Nascent Entrepreneurs by U.S. Region

regions. Even more unsatisfactory is that this analysis does not provide much insight into why the Pacific states would have so much higher rates of entrepreneurial activity than the states west of the Mississippi River in the Northern Great Plains. More understanding is provided if the unit of analysis is shifted to the respondent in the screening interviews.

An alternative strategy is to use the respondent as the unit of analysis and compare respondents from different contexts. One reason for creating the four-group categories for selected variables was to facilitate such an analysis. For example, one might consider respondents in different types of contexts based on two dimensions, recent population growth and population density. These two four-group categories provide 16 different types of situations. The prevalence of entrepreneurial activity can be considered for each.

Figure 34.3 presents such a joint classification scheme with the prevalence rate of the nascent entrepreneurs as the dependent variable. The results are shown as four groups of four bars each. Each group of four vertical bars represents increasing levels of recent population growth, and the steady rise from left to right makes clear this has a systematic impact on the decisions to implement a new firm.

Within each set of four bars, there is also a recurring pattern. From left to right the level of activity is generally higher among those living in counties with higher population densities—which are generally cities.

The range from low to high, from 4% among those living in low-growth counties with low population density to 7% among those living in densely populated, high-growth counties, is equivalent to that among the nine U.S. regions. But there is an added bonus: the patterns seem to provide a reasonable interpretation of why the Pacific Region would have more entrepreneurial activity than the Northern Great Plains. Citizens in the Pacific Region may be responding to the opportunities provided by a growth in demand for goods or services created by the population

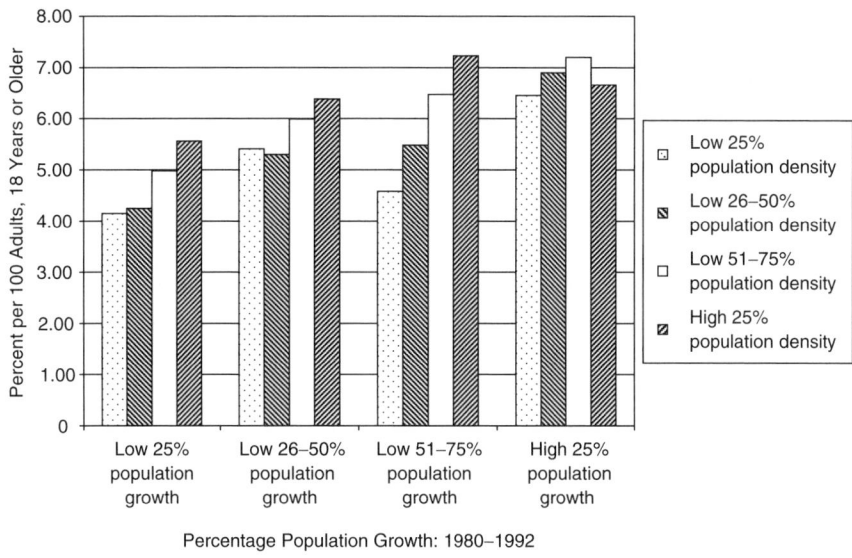

Figure 34.3   Prevalence of Two-Criteria Nascents by Population Growth and
Density; County of Residence

growth in a context where it is easy to assemble the resources—money, space, and
employees—to implement a new firm.

Context and New Firm Start-Ups:
Interview Based Perceptions and Strategies

There are, of course, many features of the context that could affect entrepreneurial
activity which are not captured in standardized national databases. One alternative
is to gather the judgment and perceptions of a representative sample of individuals
involved in business start-ups and familiar with the host economy. Four different
aspects of the perception of the context or adapting the new firm to the context
were incorporated in the PSED interview schedules.

For some time, there has been a considerable interest in determining the extent
to which a supportive "entrepreneurial climate" may be present in a community.
Substantial experience has accumulated with a multi-item scale measuring the degree
of host community support for entrepreneurship. Chapter 35, by Carter, Reynolds,
and Gartner, reports on the successful application of this measure in the PSED and
the determination that a 10-item scale might be usefully disaggregated into three
independent subscales (support groups, family and friend role models, community
models). The perception of a positive climate for entrepreneurship, however, is not
always the greatest among those actively engaged in the start-up process.

The rationale for an alternative multi-item measure of support that incorporates
judgments about both the host community and the economic sector is reviewed
in Chapter 36, by Matthews and Human. Again, the overall measure has good

reliability and can be disaggregated into three independent subscales (financial uncertainty, competitive uncertainty, and operational uncertainty).

An important feature of any start-up effort is how the new business will approach the market; success is often a function of adopting an appropriate competitive strategy. This is not a new issue and a number of different conceptual schemes for assessing competitive strategy have developed. A series of surveys of new firms has led to the development of a successful multi-item measure of competitive strategy among new businesses. Chapter 37, by Stearns and Carter, reviews the past experience and the rationale for using a multi-item measure for the PSED. The initial six dimensions were based on a 36-item battery, later reduced to 20 items, and further shortened to the 6 items for the PSED interview schedule. This was done by selecting the single item with the highest loading on each of the six major dimensions.

A major feature of the competitive strategy of many new firms is the degree of technological sophistication of their procedures, products, or services. New firms may anticipate a significant competitive advantage if they are among the first to introduce relatively new technology. One of the major measurement challenges in the study of any firm or venture, new or established, is the development of a reliable measure of technological sophistication. A review of the issues and the history of the development of the measure used in the PSED interview schedules are provided in Chapter 38 by Allen and Stearns. The PSED interviews included a reliable, valid solution to this challenging measurement issue.

Commentary

Although the major focus of the PSED initiative was the start-up process itself, the conceptual scheme recognized the impact of contextual and environmental factors. From the beginning, the project was designed to facilitate assembly of reliable measures on the county in which the respondents were located, and a small selection of these county-level variables were included in the data set. Many are known to have a statistically significant impact on the level of new firm creation; other variables could be easily added for additional analysis. Judgments about the context in which the new firm will operate and decisions regarding the strategic posture of the new business were measured as part of the PSED interview schedules; in all cases, multi-item measures with a history of successful implementation were utilized.

Further analysis will be required to determine the relative impact of the context on the successful emergence of new businesses. The opportunities to combine standardized measures of county characteristics with reliable measures of the judgments of the nascent entrepreneurs promises to facilitate a substantial contribution to understanding the interaction of environmental factors and start-up activities.

References

Acs, Z. J., & Armington, C. (1998). *Longitudinal establishment and enterprise microdata (leem) documentation* (CES 98–9). Washington, DC: U.S. Bureau of the Census Center for Economic Studies.

Armington, C., & Acs, Z. J. (2002). The determinants of regional variation in new firm formation. *Regional Studies, 36*(1), 33–45.

Bureau of Economic Analysis, Regional Economic Information System [REIS], Washington, DC: U.S. Department of Commerce.

Economics and Statistics Administration, USA Counties: (1998). Washington, DC: U.S. Department of Commerce, Census Bureau.

Reynolds, P. D. (1994). Autonomous firm dynamics and economic growth in the United States, 1986–1990. *Regional Studies 28*(4), 429–442.

Reynolds, P. D., Miller, B., & Maki, W. (1995). Explaining regional variation in business births and deaths: U.S. 1976–88. *Small Business Economics, 7,* 389–407.

Reynolds, P. D., Storey, D. J., & Westhead, P. (1994). Cross-national comparisons of the variation in new firm formation rates. *Regional Studies, 28*(4), 443–456.

Tolbert, C. M., & Killian, M. S. (1987). *Labor market areas for the United States.* (Staff report AFE870721). Agricultural and Rural Economy Division, Economic Research Service, U.S. Department of Agriculture, Washington, DC.

Tolbert, C. M., & Sizer, M. (1996). *U.S. commuting zones and labor market areas: A 1990 update.* (Staff paper AGES-9614). Washington, DC: U.S. Department of Agriculture, Economic Research Service, Rural Economy Division.

CHAPTER 35

Perceptions Of Entrepreneurial Climate

Nancy M. Carter

Paul D. Reynolds

William B. Gartner

M any stakeholders who are interested in the creation and development of new firms (e.g., policymakers, entrepreneurs, and business development providers) believe that some geographic regions have more positive entrepreneurial climates than others (Fischer & Reuber, 2003; Luthans, Stajkovic, & Ibrayeva, 2000). It has been suggested that the greater the political and social legitimacy of entrepreneurship in a particular state, region, or nation, the more likely people will be to engage in entrepreneurial activity. In turn, a higher rate of new business formation would lead to a healthier economy (Aldrich & Wiedenmayer, 1993; Baumol, 1990). In addition, some scholars have suggested that business development activities, such as providing tax incentives, enterprise zones, and new venture development and training programs, may provide a more conducive entrepreneurial climate for business start-up efforts (Isserman, 1994; Lichtenstein & Lyons, 2001; Mathur, 1999).

A number of different strategies have been used to measure entrepreneurial climate. There is a significant body of literature on the economic and demographic factors of particular states, regions, or countries that appear to influence rates of firm formation (Armington & Acs, 2002; Audretsch & Fritsch, 1994; Carlton, 1983; Davidsson, Lindmark, & Olofsson, 1994; Keeble & Walker, 1994; Reynolds, 1994). The explanatory variables from this research identify such measures as labor force growth, population density, unemployment, and taxes as factors affecting firm formation rates (Goetz & Freshwater, 2001). Other scholars have sought to study a broader range of social influences on firm formation or growth. For example, Bull and Winter (1991) found that such factors as crime, health care, climate, and recreation were negatively correlated to firm births. Gottlieb (1995) found that crime and pollution were factors that influenced firm location only in their effect on workers at their place of residence. Pennings (1982) found that factors associated with "urban quality of life" were associated with increased rates of entrepreneurial activity.

A few studies have attempted to explore whether the perceptions of entrepreneurial climate by individuals in a particular area might affect rates of firm formation. For example, Davidsson and Wiklund (1997) undertook a broad comparative survey of individuals in regions of Sweden with high and low rates of firm formation to ascertain differences in perceptions of these regions' entrepreneurial cultures. Their measures of entrepreneurial culture were divided into two broad categories: *values,* which focus on such issues as the importance of money, change, autonomy, and achievement, and *beliefs,* which focus on the value of entrepreneurship itself, such as its societal contribution, financial pay-off, risk, and personal benefit. They found that perceptions of entrepreneurial culture were correlated to the rate of business formation, but that these measures explained only a very small portion of the variation. Economic and demographic characteristics of the regions seemed to be better predictors of firm formation rates. They speculated that one of the reasons for their findings was that the measures of entrepreneurial culture were derived from an aggregation of responses from all survey respondents in each of the regions. The aggregated responses include individuals who were engaged in business formation as well as individuals who were not. Their measure of entrepreneurial culture, then, attempted to portray the overall values and beliefs of the region itself rather than the values and beliefs of individuals who were engaged in business formation activities only. It is likely that individuals who were engaged in starting new businesses perceived their environment differently than those individuals engaged in other forms of work. Differences in perceptions of the environment, overall, might therefore be a factor dependent on the number of people engaged in business formation rather than a measure of entrepreneurial climate, per se. Nascent entrepreneurs may just see their environment differently than others. Therefore, studies that aggregate responses of both nascent entrepreneurs and others might not provide an accurate picture of whether perceptions of the environment affect an individual's decision to pursue entrepreneurship.

It appears there was only one research program that sought to focus, specifically, on the environmental perceptions of individuals involved in new firm start-up. This was the Wisconsin Entrepreneurial Climate Study (Reynolds & White, 1997). Among the battery of questions asked of respondents in the

Wisconsin Study were 18 items designed to measure an individual's perception of whether the local context was a good place for entrepreneurial activity. The items were measured on a four-point scale ranging from *strongly agree* (4) *to strongly disagree* (1) such that the higher an individual's score, the more positively respondents viewed that particular dimension of their location as a place to start a new business. The results of a factor analysis (varimax rotation), weighted to be representative of the population, reduced the 18 items to one dominant dimension composed of nine items. The nine-item scale had a Cronbach's alpha (a measure of reliability) of .65. An index was constructed by computing the average score across the items. The average for all typical adults in Wisconsin was 2.48, almost exactly neutral on the scale. Wisconsin adults were seen as having neither a significantly positive nor a negative attitude about the state as a place to start a new business.

In the Wisconsin study, the entrepreneurial climate scores of individuals at various levels of involvement in the entrepreneurial process were compared. The judgments of typical adults not involved with entrepreneurial activity (those in a control group) were compared with (1) nascent entrepreneurs currently engaged in a start-up, (2) discouraged entrepreneurs who had been trying to start a business but had given up, and (3) people who had started new firms in the past 6 years (established entrepreneurs). The results indicated that the greater the involvement in the entrepreneurial process, the more negative were the judgments about the entrepreneurial climate (Reynolds & White, 1997). Nascent entrepreneurs had more positive perceptions about the climate than typical adults. Discouraged entrepreneurs were more negative than nascent entrepreneurs, and those who succeeded in putting a new business in place (entrepreneurs with established businesses) were the most negative.

Carter (1997) found that, overall, women were slightly more positive in their judgments about the entrepreneurial climate than were men but that women who had become discouraged and had given up their entrepreneurial efforts were the most negative of all. These women appeared to associate the greatest stigma to failure, were most dissatisfied that financial institutions would not help them start their businesses, and indicated they were least likely to try another entrepreneurial effort.

Since no data were available from respondents in other states, it was impossible to compare perceptions of nascent entrepreneurs in Wisconsin with those of their neighbors—Illinois, Iowa, Minnesota, or Michigan—or with those of nascent entrepreneurs in more faraway locations like California, Florida, or Texas.

Data in the Panel PSED Survey offer an opportunity to make comparisons across economic regions. The nine Wisconsin items were adapted and expanded for use in the PSED. The scale of the items was increased from four to five with; 1 = completely disagree, 2 = somewhat disagree, 3 = neither agree nor disagree, 4 = somewhat agree, 5 = completely agree. The items were included in the initial mail survey in section B1 a–j. Table 35.1 displays how the original nine Wisconsin items were adapted and expanded for use in the PSED.

Table 35.1   Comparison of Wisconsin and PSED Climate Items

Wisconsin Index Items	PSED Items
Communities vary a great deal in their entrepreneurial activity. Could you please tell us what it is like in the area where you live? AROUND HERE…	Communities vary a great deal in their entrepreneurial activity. How much do you agree or disagree with the following statements?
a. Those with successful businesses get a lot of attention and admiration	a. Those with successful businesses get a lot of attention and admiration
b. Young men are encouraged to be independent and start their own businesses	b. Young people are encouraged to be independent and start their own businesses
c. Young women are encouraged to be independent and start their own businesses	
d. State and local governments provide good support for men starting new firms	c. State and local governments provide good support for those starting new firms
e. State and local governments provide good support for women starting new firms	
f. Bankers and other investors go out of their way to help new firms get started	d. Bankers and other investors go out of their way to help new firms get started
	e. Other community groups provide good support for those starting businesses
g. There are many examples of well-respected people who made a success of themselves starting new businesses	f. There are many examples of well respected people who made a success of themselves starting new businesses
h. Among my family and friends, many of the men have started new firms	g. Many of my friends have started new firms
i. Among my family and friends, many of the women have started new firms	
	h. Many of my family and kin have started new firms
	i. The local media do a good job of covering local business news
	j. Most of the leaders in this community are people who own their own businesses

Descriptive Statistics

Of the 1,261 respondents who completed the initial phone interview in the PSED, 905 returned a completed mail questionnaire. Analyses of the responses

Table 35.2   Descriptive Statistics: Climate Perception Items

Climate Perception Items Mail Questionnaire Section B1a–j	Nascent Entrepreneurs			Comparison Group		
	N	Mean	SD	N	Mean	SD
a. Those with successful businesses get a lot of attention and admiration	552	3.89	.91	334	4.05	.90
b. Young people are encouraged to be independent and start their own businesses	552	2.75	1.19	334	2.84	1.01
c. State and local governments provide good support for those starting new firms	551	2.71	1.07	334	2.87	1.02
d. Bankers and other investors go out of their way to help new firms get started	552	2.31	1.04	333	2.45	1.02
e. Other community groups provide good support for those starting businesses	550	2.93	.98	328	3.10	.88
f. There are many examples of well respected people who made a success of themselves starting new businesses	552	4.08	.94	333	4.00	.92
g. Many of my friends have started new firms	544	2.54	1.19	331	2.44	1.19
h. Many of my family and kin have started new firms	544	2.50	1.30	330	2.52	1.24
i. The local media do a good job of covering local business news	548	2.85	1.15	333	3.27	1.11
j. Most of the leaders in this community are people who own their own businesses	552	3.38	1.03	334	3.35	1.11

to the initial phone survey revealed that six were reporting on initiatives that were already considered new businesses because they had positive cash flow for more than 90 days before the initial interview. Five of the six respondents that were judged as having new businesses returned mail questionnaires. We removed these five from our analyses of the climate items. Additionally, four respondents in the mixed gender and female oversample comparison group who completed the phone interview and 18 in the minority comparison group were found to qualify as nascent entrepreneurs. Of these 22, 18 returned mail questionnaires. We removed these 18 from our analyses leaving data on a total of 882 nascent entrepreneurs and adults in the comparison group appropriate for analyzing.

Table 35.2 displays means and standard deviations for the entrepreneurial climate perception items. The means and standard deviations are weighted by WTW1 and WTCG adjusted to reflect the attrition in the sample size from 1,261 to 882. The

Table 35.3   Factor Loadings: Climate Perception Items

Mail Questionnaire Section B1a–j	Community Support Groups	Friends & Family Models	Community Models
Sum of Square rotated loadings	2.216	1.531	1.406
Percentage of variance accounted for	22.158	15.307	14.063
d. Bankers and other investors go out of their way to help new firms get started	.776		
c. State and local governments provide good support for those starting new firms	.749		
e. Other community groups provide good support for those starting businesses	.704		
b. Young people are encouraged to be independent and start their own businesses	.520		
i. The local media do a good job of covering local business news	.482		
h. Many of my family and kin have started new firms		.844	
g. Many of my friends have started new firms		.837	
a. Those with successful businesses get a lot of attention and admiration			.777
j. Most of the leaders in this community are people who own their own businesses			.578
f. There are many examples of well respected people who made a success of themselves starting new businesses			.561

results show that, on average, the adults in the comparison group perceived the environment as slightly more positive than the nascent entrepreneurs did.

We subjected the data to a principal components factor analysis (pairwise deletion of missing values, varimax rotation). The analysis was weighted in the same way as the analysis for the descriptive statistics. Three factors were produced that accounted for 52% of the variance, and the rotation converged in 4 iterations. The factor loadings are displayed in Table 35.3.

The first factor, which we label *Community Support Groups*, involved five items. Cronbach's α reliability for the items is .68. Results from the reliability analyses are reported in Table 35.4.

The second factor involved two items depicting whether friends and family have started new ventures and it has a Cronbach α reliability of .64. We label the construct, *Friends and Family Entrepreneurial Models.* The third factor involves four items. The Cronbach α reliability is very low, .36. We label this factor, *Community*

Table 35.4   Results from Reliability Analysis of Climate Perception Items

	α If Item Deleted
Community Support Groups $\alpha = .68$	
d. Bankers and other investors go out of their way to help new firms get started	.60
c. State and local governments provide good support for those starting new firms	.60
e. Other community groups provide good support for those starting businesses	.62
b. Young people are encouraged to be independent and start their own businesses	.66
i. The local media do a good job of covering local business news	.66
Family and Friends Entrepreneurial Models $\alpha = .64$	
h. Many of my family and kin have started new firms	
g. Many of my friends have started new firms	
Community Entrepreneurial Models $\alpha = .36$	
a. Those with successful businesses get a lot of attention and admiration	.24
j. Most of the leaders in this community are people who own their own businesses	.34
f. There are many examples of well respected people who made a success of themselves starting new businesses	.25

Entrepreneurial Models. The marginal reliability of the scale is troubling. Previous research has speculated about the influence of entrepreneurial role models in influencing individuals to start businesses. Entrepreneurs in the community are presumed to provide influence. This scale would seem to be an inadequate measure for capturing this dimension of environment's influence on entrepreneurship. Researchers may want to use only the first two factors in subsequent tests of perceptions of the entrepreneurial climate of communities. And, it should be noted, that there are other items in the PSED that may be better suited to assessing the influence of community entrepreneurial role models.

Conclusions

As was suggested by Reynolds in his overview of this section of the handbook (Chapter 34), the PSED provides many opportunities for linking economic and demographic information on the location of each respondent in the data set. Researchers can therefore explore whether the "reality" of these individuals' environments is in any way correlated to their perceptions of their environment. Future research efforts using PSED data can help us better understand how the invisible hand of a social, economic, and political context affects the more visible hand of an individual's efforts to recognize and pursue opportunities through business creation.

References

Aldrich, H. E., & Wiedenmayer, G. (1993). From traits to rates: An ecological perspective on organizational foundings. In J. A. Katz & R. H. Brockhaus (Eds.), *Advances in entrepreneurship, firm emergence, and growth* (pp. 145–195). Greenwich, CT: JAI.

Armington, C., & Acs, Z. J. (2002). The determinants of regional variation in new firm formation. *Regional Studies, 36*(1), 33–45.

Audretsch, D. B., & Fritsch, M. (1994). The geography of firm births in Germany. *Regional Studies, 28*(4), 359–365.

Baumol, W. J. (1990). Entrepreneurship: Productive, unproductive, and destructive. *Journal of Political Economy, 96*(Pt. 1), 893–920.

Bull, I., & Winter, F. (1991). Community differences in business births and business growths. *Journal of Business Venturing, 6*, 29–43.

Carlton, D. (1983). The location and employment choices of new firms: An econometric model of growth with discrete and continuous endogenous variables. *Review of Economics and Statistics, 65*, 440–449.

Carter, N. M. (1997). Entrepreneurial process and outcomes: The influence of gender. In P. D. Reynolds & S. B. White (Eds.), *The entrepreneurial process* (pp. 163–178). Westport, CT: Quorum Books.

Davidsson, P., Lindmark, L., & Olofsson, C. (1994). New firm formation and regional development in Sweden. *Regional Studies, 28*(4), 395–410.

Davidsson, P., & Wiklund, J. (1997). Values, beliefs and regional variations in new firm formation rates. *Journal of Economic Psychology, 18*, 179–199.

Fischer, E., & Reuber, A. R. (2003). Support for rapid-growth firms: A comparison of the views of founders, government policy makers, and private sector resource providers. *Journal of Small Business Management, 41*(4), 346–365.

Goetz, S. J., & Freshwater, D. (2001). State-level determinants of entrepreneurship and a preliminary measure of entrepreneurial climate. *Economic Development Quarterly, 15*(1), 58–70.

Gottlieb, P. D. (1995). Residential amenities, firm location and economic development. *Urban Studies, 32*(9), 1413–1437.

Isserman, A. M. (1994). State economic development policy and practice in the U.S.: A survey article. *International Regional Science Review, 16*, 49–100.

Keeble, D., & Walker, S. (1994). New firms, small firms and dead firms: Spatial patterns and determinants in the United Kingdom. *Regional Studies, 28*(4), 411–427.

Lichtenstein, G. A., & Lyons, T. S. (2001). The entrepreneurial development system: Transforming business talent and economies. *Economic Development Quarterly, 15*(1), 3–20.

Luthans, R., Stajkovic, A. D., & Ibrayeva, E. (2000). Environmental and psychological challenges facing entrepreneurial development in transitional economies. *Journal of World Business, 35*(1), 95–110.

Mathur, V. K. (1999). Human capital-based strategy for regional economic development. *Economic Development Quarterly, 13*(3), 203–216.

Pennings, J. M. (1982). The urban quality of life and entrepreneurship. *Academy of Management Journal, 25*(1), 63–79.

Reynolds, P. D. (1994). Autonomous firm dynamics and economic growth in the United States, 1986–1990. *Regional Studies, 28*(4), 429–442.

Reynolds, P. D., & White, S. B. (1997). *The entrepreneurial process.* Westport, CT: Quorum Books.

The Economic and Community Context for Entrepreneurship:

Perceived Environmental Uncertainty

Charles H. Matthews

Sherrie E. Human

Over several decades, scholars of organization theory and strategic management have shown a remarkable interest in the study of the relationship between an organization and its context or environment. The construct of environmental uncertainty has been a primary focus of much of this inquiry (Aldrich, 1979; Downey & Slocum, 1975; Duncan, 1972, 1973; Emery & Trist, 1965; Jauch & Kraft, 1986; Miller, 1988; Pfeffer & Salancik, 1978; Smircich & Stubbard, 1985; Thompson, 1967). Scholars have developed different frameworks for describing environmental uncertainty (e.g., Aldrich, 1979; Khandwalla, 1977; Thompson, 1967), and multiple definitions of uncertainty have been offered in the literature, including lack of knowledge for decision making (Duncan, 1972; Lawrence & Lorsch, 1967; Thompson, 1967), complexity (Galbraith, 1973), unpredictability (Cyert & March, 1963), turbulence (Emery & Trist, 1965), and munificence (Dess & Beard, 1984).

Whereas much of the research on environmental uncertainty has focused on large organizations (Boulton, Lindsay, Franklin, & Rue, 1982; Duncan, 1972; Hambrick, 1983; Waldman, Ramirez, House, & Puranam, 2001), scholars have also examined how perceptions of environmental uncertainty affect small or entrepreneurial firms (Luo, 1999; Matthews & Scott, 1995; Sawyerr, McGee, & Peterson, 2001). In addition to contextual differences across studies of environmental uncertainty, scholars also differ on whether they conceive of uncertainty as an objective dimension of the external environment or as a more subjective dimension resulting from key decision makers' interpretations or perceptions of their situation (Milliken, 1987). Although we acknowledge the influence on firm performance of environmental conditions whether or not they are perceived by organizational decision makers (Osborn, Hunt, & Jauch, 1980), in this paper we follow a strong research tradition regarding organizational response to an enacted or perceived environment (Lawrence & Lorsch, 1967; Weick, 1979), and in particular, organizational response to perceptions of environmental uncertainty (Kumar & Seth, 1998; Miller, 1988; Waldman et al., 2001). We also suggest that at the emergent entrepreneurial stage, which is the focus of the Panel Study of Entrepreneurial Dynamics (PSED) (Reynolds, 2000), perceived uncertainty regarding the economic and community context or environment is of paramount concern to nascent entrepreneurs. As such, we have attempted to construct both a theoretically sound and pragmatically grounded approach to further our understanding of perceptions of environmental uncertainty in entrepreneurial nascency.

Literature Review

Milliken (1987) conceptualized three types of environmental uncertainty—state, effect, and response uncertainty—that she posited would result in different managerial responses. With *state uncertainty*, the question of the decision maker is "What is occurring or what is likely to occur in my task domain?" Thus, this type of uncertainty reflects an inability to understand or to predict the state of the environment due to information deficiencies or a lack of understanding of the interrelationships among environmental elements. According to Milliken, this is typically what researchers are referring to when they write of "environmental uncertainty" and is "the only one [of the three types she describes] that should be labeled 'perceived environmental uncertainty'" (Milliken, 1987, p. 137). With *effect uncertainty*, the question for the decision maker is "Given what is occurring in the task environment, how is this likely to affect my organization?" Thus it reflects an uncertainty over what the consequences of environmental changes will be on the organization. With *response uncertainty*, the question for the decision maker is "How should we respond to what is happening in the task environment?" Thus it reflects the decision maker's uncertainty regarding organization response options or the likely consequences of pursuing a particular option. Building on Milliken's conceptual framework, empirical evidence (Gerloff, Muir, & Bodensteiner, 1991) supports the contention that the dimensions of uncertainty should be investigated independently, as they have differential effects.

Although we believe that all three types of uncertainty are important in the nascent entrepreneurial context, we argue that it is the perceived uncertainty regarding access to key economic and community resources that is at the center of the emergent entrepreneur's mind and thus is most relevant as he or she contemplates a new venture. Thus, in the current examination of nascent entrepreneurs' economic and community context, we adopt Milliken's (1987) conceptual definition of environmental uncertainty as "state uncertainty" or the uncertainty that occurs when the nascent entrepreneur is uncertain about particular characteristics of the environment, or the context in which the potential organization is likely to operate. More specifically, we define environmental uncertainty for the PSED as the nascent entrepreneur's perception of accessibility to important resources and information relative to the economic and community context in which the new firm may operate.

This definition seems closely aligned to the activities and information gathering relevant for such early-stage entrepreneurs because much of early-stage entrepreneurship includes environmental scanning activities to determine the state of the environment or context for the emerging firm. Questions regarding how environmental conditions will affect the emerging firm (effect uncertainty) or how nascent entrepreneurs will respond to their environment (response uncertainty), although important for new venture entrepreneurs to consider, seem more relevant once the entrepreneur has a specific company to consider with respect to the environment. Thus, questions in the PSED mail survey to nascent entrepreneurs focused on emergent entrepreneurs' level of certainty regarding their ability to access key sectors of their environment, given their perceptions regarding the state of the economic and community context for their emergent business. However, for identifying the specific key sectors or sources of uncertainty on which to focus, we again were guided by the literature.

Sources of Environmental Uncertainty

The complexity and interconnectedness of the organizational environment construct make measurement and analysis of overall parameters, such as industry, difficult. Thus, a number of scholars have proposed a further differentiation of the environmental uncertainty construct by the source of the uncertainty (Duncan, 1972; Jauch, Osborn, & Glueck, 1980; Khandwalla, 1977; Tosi & Slocum, 1984). Specifying the source of uncertainty helps to more narrowly define the domain of the environment about which the manager or strategist is uncertain (Fahey & Narayanan, 1986). However, the specific sectors or sources of environmental uncertainty on which to focus vary across authors. Duncan (1972) originally specified five environmental sectors, but he included distributors as a subcategory of the customer sector, and government as a subcategory of the sociopolitical sector. Others have added the financial markets sector as an important environmental domain for entrepreneurs (e.g., Jauch et al.). More recent scholars' examination of perceived environmental uncertainty in small and entrepreneurial firms have used up to eight categories of environmental sectors, treating several, such as suppliers, as stand-alone categories rather than subcategories (Luo, 1999; Matthews & Scott, 1995). Both scholarly (Gartner, 1985) and practitioner (Timmons, 1999) examinations of existing new ventures' environments include characteristics such as financial, operational, and competitive variables (e.g., access to banks and venture capital, access to labor and suppliers, and information about competitors and new technology, respectively). Consequently, we selected variables that have been included in previous research on entrepreneurial environments (Jauch et al., 1980; Luo, 1999) and are commonly included in descriptions of entrepreneurial environments (e.g., Bygrave, 1989; Gartner, 1985). These variables, although not comprehensive, provide a full range of key environmental characteristics about which nascent entrepreneurs may or may not have certainty.

The Variables Representing
the Economic and Community Context

An 11-item measure in the PSED mail survey using a five-point Likert-type response scale was used to assess respondents' perceptions of the economic and community context for entrepreneurship or their perceptions of environmental uncertainty. Table 36.1 includes the wording for these 11 items. As discussed previously, the scale focused on state uncertainty referring to the inability of the nascent entrepreneur to understand or to predict the state of the environment due to a lack of

Table 36.1 Wording and Means for Economic and Community Context (Environmental Uncertainty) Variables in the PSED Mail Survey (Item D1)

D1: Considering the economic and community context for the new firm, how certain are you that the new business will be able to accomplish each of the following? (Circle one number in each row.)

1 = Very low certainty   4 = High certainty
2 = Low certainty   5 = Very high certainty
3 = Neither high nor low   8 = Does not apply

Item Number	Variable	Mean	Mean (weighted wtmod[a])
a.	Obtain raw materials	1.95	1.93
b.	Attract employees	2.29	2.26
c.	Obtain start-up capital	2.84	2.83
d.	Obtain working capital	2.70	2.70
e.	Deal with distributors	1.95	1.94
f.	Attract customers	1.85	1.85
g.	Compete with other firms	2.10	2.06
h.	Comply with local, state, and federal regulations	1.64	1.63
i.	Keep up with technological advances	1.84	1.80
j.	Obtain a bank's help	3.15	3.18
k.	Obtain venture capitalists' help	3.41	3.45

NOTE: wtmod = modified weighting variable. Means in Table 36.1 reflect reverse scoring for consistency with use of the term "uncertainty" in the literature (see below).

5 = Very high uncertainty   2 = Low uncertainty
4 = High uncertainty   1 = Very low uncertainty
3 = Neither high nor low   8 = Does not apply

information or uncertainty about that environment. The survey directions read, "Considering the economic and community context for the new firm, how certain are you that the new business will be able to accomplish each of the following?" The response scale was anchored by very high (5) to very low (1), including a category for does not apply (8). The items were reverse scored to be consistent with prior literature on environmental uncertainty (e.g., Matthews & Scott, 1995)

Whereas the measure was unidimensional in terms of state uncertainty, it was multidimensional in terms of the sources of uncertainty. As mentioned in the previous section, building on the extant literature (Matthews & Scott, 1995; Jauch et al., 1980; Duncan, 1972), seven a priori environmental sectors were included: customers, suppliers, distributors, competitors, government, technology, and financial markets.

An Analysis of the Variables Representing the Economic and Community Context

A principal components factor analysis with varimax rotation was conducted on the responses to the 11-item measure (Table 36.2), and three factors were extracted with eigenvalues greater than one. A scree plot suggested all three factors be retained. Four items dealing with obtaining start-up and working capital and help from a bank or venture capitalist loaded on one factor, which we termed "Financial Uncertainty." One item each on attracting customers, competing with other firms, complying with federal, state, and local regulations, and keeping pace with technological advances loaded on one factor, which we termed "Competitive Uncertainty." One item dealing with obtaining raw materials, attracting employees, and dealing with distributors loaded on one factor, which we termed "Operational Uncertainty." Cronbach's alpha for the 11-item scale is .70 and the alphas for the subscales were .77, .71, and .53, respectively, with the three factors cumulatively accounting for approximately 52% of the variance. This factor analysis was obtained by beginning with the 830 respondents that responded to both the phone and mail surveys and included the nascent mixed gender, nascent minority oversample, and nascent women oversample. Since items from both the phone and mail surveys as well as items from the oversamples were included, modification of the weighting scheme was indicated. Just prior to the running of the factor analysis, the number of cases (830) was divided by the sum (935.22) to obtain the modified weighting variable (wtmod). This adjusts for the attrition between the phone and mail survey and other adjustments to the data.

Findings to Date

Nascent entrepreneurs' perceptions of environmental uncertainty or the community context in which their emerging firm is likely to operate are an important characteristic for examination and further specification. Once these perceptions are examined and understood on their own, scholars may then empirically apply that knowledge to a number of literature streams regarding key entrepreneurial activities

Table 36.2   Factor Loadings for Perception of Environmental Uncertainty Variables and the Rotated Factor Loading Pattern[a,b] (weighted[c])

Item Number	Variable	Factors		
		Financial Uncertainty	Competitive Uncertainty	Operational Uncertainty
D1a.	Obtain raw materials			.753
D1b.	Attract employees			.529
D1e.	Deal with distributors			.579
D1c.	Obtain start-up capital	.872		
D1d.	Obtain working capital	.851		
D1j.	Obtain a bank's help	.622		
D1k.	Obtain venture capitalists' help	.460		
D1f.	Attract customers		.680	
D1g.	Compete with other firms		.761	
D1h.	Comply with local, state, and federal regulations		.622	
D1i.	Keep up technological advances		.609	
	Eigenvalue (> 1)	3.00	1.57	1.17
	Percentage of variance	27.29	14.24	10.68
	Cumulative percentage	27.29	41.53	52.21
	Cronbach's alpha (all 11 items = .70)	.77	.71	.53

NOTES:

a. Extraction method: principal component analysis. Rotation method: varimax.

b. Factor loadings of less than .30 have been suppressed for clarity.

c. Weight used is wtmod; missing variables use mean substitution.

such as planning and growth. The three factors identified here—perceptions of financial, competitive, and operational environmental uncertainty—appear to have a good conceptual fit with scholarly descriptions of what existing entrepreneurs perceive as uncertain elements of their environment. The three factors also fit conceptually with practitioner literature because much of the uncertainty that entrepreneurs attempt to minimize in preparing a business plan is targeted in the financial, operational, and competitive sections of that document.

To further explore these three aspects of nascent entrepreneurs' perceptions of their community context, Matthews and Human (2000) examined how perceptions of financial, competitive, and operational uncertainty influenced nascent entrepreneurs' future growth expectations for their emerging firms. Results indicate that only one type of perceived environmental uncertainty, operational uncertainty, aids in predicting company growth expectations. That is, it appears that nascent entrepreneurs' uncertainty over key operational resources tempers their expectations of firm growth. In addition, Matthews, Ford and Human (2001) compared growth expectations of nascent entrepreneurs and intrapreneurs—those considering starting a business independently versus within a current company setting, respectively—relative to their perceptions of financial, operational, and competitive uncertainty. Their findings suggest that although the three measures of uncertainty were not significantly correlated to measures of growth expectations, most of the correlations were negative, which is consistent with the authors' predictions that more uncertainty would temper growth expectations. Their findings further suggest that nascent intrapreneurs perceive slightly less environmental uncertainty in all three uncertainty categories than their nascent entrepreneur counterparts, raising interesting questions regarding, for instance, how or whether the corporate environment permits the intrapreneur to access more resources and structure, thus tempering perceptions of environmental uncertainty.

We believe that a framework using financial, competitive, and operational factors related to emergent entrepreneurs' perceptions of their economic and community context can contribute to both entrepreneurship scholarly work, which seeks to inform about the relationships among key variables in the entrepreneurial process, and practitioner literature, which seeks to inform and educate entrepreneurs.

References

Aldrich, H. (1979). *Organizations and their environments.* Englewood Cliffs, NJ: Prentice Hall.

Boulton, W., Lindsay, W., Franklin, S., & Rue, L. (1982). Strategic planning: Determining the impact of environmental characteristics and uncertainty. *Academy of Management Journal, 25*(3), 500–509.

Bygrave, W. D. (1989). The entrepreneurship paradigm: A philosophical look at its research methodologies. *Entrepreneurship Theory and Practice,* (Fall), 7–26.

Cyert, R., & March, J. (1963). *Behavioral theory of the firm.* Englewood Cliffs, NJ: Prentice Hall.

Dess, G. G., & Beard, D. W. (1984). Dimensions of organizational task environments. *Administrative Science Quarterly, 29,* 52–73.

Downey, H., & Slocum, J. (1975). Uncertainty: Measures, research, and sources of variation. *Academy of Management Journal, 18,* 562–578.

Duncan, R. (1972). Characteristics of organizational environments and perceived environmental uncertainty. *Administrative Science Quarterly, 17,* 313–327.

Duncan, R. (1973). Multiple decision-making structures in adapting to environmental uncertainty: The impact on organizational effectiveness. *Human Relations, 26,* 273–291.

Emery, F., & Trist, E. (1965). The causal texture of organizational environments. *Human Relations, 18,* 21–32.

Fahey, L., & Narayanan, V. (1986). *Macro-environmental analysis for strategic management.* St. Paul, MN: West.

Galbraith, J. (1973). *Designing complex organizations.* Reading, MA: Addison-Wesley.

Gartner, W. B. (1985). A conceptual framework for describing the phenomenon of new venture creation. *Academy of Management Review, 10*(4), 696–706.

Gerloff, E., Muir, N., & Bodensteiner, W. (1991). Three components of perceived environmental uncertainty: An exploratory analysis of the effects of aggregation. *Journal of Management, 17,* 749–768.

Hambrick, E. (1983). Some tests of the effectiveness and functional attributes of Miles and Snow's strategic types. *Academy of Management Journal, 26,* 5–26.

Jauch, L., & Kraft, K. (1986). Strategic management of uncertainty. *Academy of Management Review, 11*(4), 777–790.

Jauch, L., Osborn, R., & Glueck, W. (1980). Short-term financial success in large business organizations: The environment-strategy connection. *Strategic Management Journal, 1,* 49–63.

Khandwalla, P. (1977). *The design of organizations.* New York: Harcourt Brace Jovanovich.

Kumar, S., & Seth, A. (1998). The design of coordination and control mechanisms for managing joint venture-parent relationships. *Strategic Management Journal, 19,* 579–599.

Lawrence, P., & Lorsch, J. (1967). *Organization and environment.* Boston: Harvard University Press.

Luo, Y. (1999). Environment-strategy-performance relations in small businesses in China: A case of township and village enterprises in Southern China. *Journal of Small Business Management, 37*(1), 37–52.

Matthews, C., Ford, M. W., & Human, S. E. (2001). The context of new venture initiation: Comparing growth expectations of nascent entrepreneurs and intrapreneurs. In W. D. Bygrave, E. Autio, C. G. Brush, P. Davidsson, P. G. Green, P. D. Reynolds, & H. J. Sapienza (Eds.), *Frontiers of entrepreneurship research* (pp. 42–52). Wellesley, MA: Babson College.

Matthews, C., & Human, S. E. (2000). The little engine that could: Uncertainty and growth expectations of nascent entrepreneurs. In P. D. Reynolds, E. Autio, C. G. Brush, W. D. Bygrave, S. Manigart, H. J. Sapienza, & K. G. Shaver (Eds.), *Frontiers of entrepreneurship research* (pp. 55–66). Wellesley, MA: Babson College.

Matthews, C., & Scott, S. G. (1995). Uncertainty and planning in small and entrepreneurial firms: An empirical assessment. *Journal of Small Business Management, 33*(4), 34–52.

Miller, D. (1988). Relating Porter's business strategies to environment and structure: Analysis and performance implications. *Academy of Management Journal, 31*(2), 280–308.

Milliken, F. J. (1987). Three types of perceived uncertainty about the environment: State, effect, and response uncertainty. *Academy of Management Review, 12*(1), 133–143.

Osborn, R., Hunt, J., & Jauch, L. (1980). *Organization theory: An integrated approach.* New York: John Wiley.

Pfeffer, J., & Salancik, G. (1978). *The external control of organizations: A resource dependence perspective.* New York: Prentice Hall.

Reynolds, P. D. (2000). National Panel Study of U.S. business startups: Background and methods. In J. A. Katz (Ed.), *Advances in entrepreneurship research: Firm emergence and growth* (pp. 153–227). Stamford, CT: JAI.

Sawyerr, O., McGee, J., & Peterson, M. (2001, August). *Perceived uncertainty, personal networks, and firm performance: An examination of decision-makers in small high technology manufacturing firms.* Paper presented at the Academy of Management meeting, Washington, DC.

Smircich, L., & Stubbard, C. (1985). Strategic management in an enacted world. *Academy of Management Review, 10,* 724–736.

Thompson, J. (1967). *Organizations in action.* New York: McGraw-Hill.

Timmons, J. A. (1999). *New venture creation: Entrepreneurship for the 21st century.* Boston: Irwin McGraw-Hill.

Tosi, H., & Slocum, J. (1984). Contingency theory: Some suggested directions. *Journal of Management, 10,* 9–26.

Waldman, D. A., Ramirez, G. G., House, R. J., & Puranam, P. (2001). Does leadership matter? CEO leadership attributes and profitability under conditions of perceived environmental uncertainty. *Academy of Management Journal, 44*(1), 134–143.

Weick, K. E. (1979). *The social psychology of organizing.* Reading, MA: Addison-Wesley.

CHAPTER 37

Competitive Strategy

Timothy M. Stearns

Nancy M. Carter

S trategy, the firm's method of competition, has generated a volume of research as to how it is formulated and implemented. It has long been a capstone course in business schools across the United States, which underscores its significance to firm management and growth. Strategy is not merely a topic of academic study but a significant focus of actors in the corporate world who deliberate over the successes and failures that have resulted from a strategic pursuit.

For whatever reason, scholars who study and analyze strategy have been captivated by the crafting of models or typologies of strategies. Miles and Snow (1978), Porter (1980), and Mintzberg (1979) have the most recognized strategic typologies in the field. However, construction of such strategic typologies has been largely informed from knowledge acquired on corporate strategy. Only in passing do we find some effort on the part of strategic theorists to suggest that the typologies may be relevant to start-up ventures.

For the researcher interested in the early stages of venture formation, this poses a problem embedded in the rules of science. Analyzing the outcome, or end result, to explain a process falls into the teleological trap. The result predicts the past. Or in this case, the corporate strategy is an outcome of the new venture strategy which has embedded elements of corporate strategy that mature and flourish as the new venture grows and persists over time.

The questions created to measure strategy in the Panel Study of Entrepreneurial Dynamics (PSED) were validated in previous studies by Carter, Stearns, Reynolds, and Miller (1994) and Stearns, Carter, Reynolds, and Williams (1996). Both studies relied on samples of new firms under 5 years of age from Minnesota and Pennsylvania in the United States. The samples provided data points of over 2,600 new firms. Rather than impose a typology to determine the fit of strategic behaviors that conform or fail to conform to the predicted model, the authors instead used cluster analysis to identify sets of strategic activities that start-up firms were pursuing. Hence, strategies of new firms and start-ups were not deducted from analysis of corporate models. Rather, the strategies were inducted from the data analysis without presuppositions of a theoretical model.

This chapter mostly covers the themes presented in the research articles by Carter et al. (1994) and Stearns et al. (1996) and should be referenced if the reader is seeking more detail on how the strategy measures in the PSED were derived and used.

New Firm Strategy

Whether founders of new firms are constrained in their selection of strategic activities (Hannan & Freeman, 1977) or whether strategic activities are easily formulated and implemented with choice (Child, 1972), it is believed by most that the strategy of a new firm has consequences for the firm's fate. Carter et al. (1994) note that the breadth or narrowness of a new firm's strategy has consequences on resource availability. And breadth or narrowness of the strategy is likely to affect survival chances depending on environmental circumstances (Aldrich, 1979).

Other factors that can influence the outcome of the firm based on the strategy it pursues are location, industry, and the resultant interactive effects of each (Stearns et al., 1996). Location is linked to resource availability and the level of competitiveness among firms to secure those resources. Rural locations differ greatly from regional cities and large metropolitan areas and thus dictate the "bandwidth" of resources that is available to support a strategy. This is also evident by industry. New firm strategy will vary in success as determined by the conditions of the industry. Certainly the work by Porter (1980) suggests that industries vary considerably in terms of how they are structured, and this structuring will direct the method of strategy that will work best. But industries also vary by how they are situated in the value chain with mining, agriculture, and manufacturing situated upstream and distribution, retail, and services situated downstream (Stearns et al., 1996).

Traditionally, scholars have derived generic strategies for new ventures from theory and research directed at the conceptualization of corporate strategies, most commonly by the work of Porter (1980), who has articulated two distinct strategic typologies: cost leadership and differentiation. Porter suggests that this dichotomy is relevant to smaller firms that are focused on region, market segment, or product segment. However, the creation of a "focus" typology for strategy was not meant to address entrepreneurial firms in the early stage of development. Efforts to extend the Porter conceptualization into the study of entrepreneurial firms can be reviewed in the works of Miller and Toulouse (1986), Sandberg and Hofer (1987), Chaganti, Chaganti, and Mahajan (1989), Fombrun and Wally (1989), Green, Jolly, and Srivastava (1990), and Miller (1991).

Other scholars have focused on the work of Miles and Snow (1978), whose typologies of strategy included prospectors, defenders, analyzers, and reactors. With less emphasis on industry structure, Miles and Snow approached strategy as a method for negotiating environmental dynamics. Little emphasis in their writings was directed at early-stage entrepreneurial firms, and research by Rugman and Verbeke (1988) and Boeker (1989) have made an effort to extend the typologies into relevant applications for the study of new ventures.

A central focus for many scholars of entrepreneurship concerns how strategy impacts firm performance (Cooper, 1993; Chandler & Hanks, 1994; McDougall, Covin, Robinson, & Herron, 1994). But Meyer, Neck, and Meeks (2002) suggest that strategy and its relationship to firm performance is primarily in the domain of strategic management whereas the domain of entrepreneurship is more attuned to the creation of strategy. They suggest that these two perspectives can serve to build an interface and thus link the two domains via four research spaces that are differentiated by firm size (small/large) and research focus (creation/performance).

The size and scope of the data collected in the PSED offers an opportunity to examine strategy among early-stage start-up efforts. Since many of the entrepreneurs responding in the survey have yet to launch the new venture, strategy is more "intent" than "act." However, even in its formative stage, strategic intent has a powerful influence on the entrepreneur's method and process for launching the new venture. And strategic intent is informative for how the entrepreneur views entry into the market to capture opportunity. This allows the researcher to examine strategy formation at an early stage of new venture development though the strategy may evolve into a different form well beyond the nascent stage.

Rationale for Questions Asked in the PSED

Items included on the PSED for measuring intended competitive strategy derive from studies of new firms completed in three U.S. states: (1) 1986 Pennsylvania New Firm Survey sponsored by the Appalachian Regional Commission and the Pennsylvania Department of Commerce; (2) 1986–1987 Minnesota New Firm Survey sponsored by University of Minnesota, Center for Urban and Regional Affairs, City of St. Paul; Metropolitan Council of the Twin Cities Area, Minnesota Chamber of Commerce, Board of Vocational Technical Education, Minnesota Community College System, Minnesota Department of Trade and Economic Development, Minnesota Extension Service; Minnesota State Planning Agency, and the Port Authority of St. Paul (follow-up of the first two studies was conducted in 1992 sponsored by University of Minnesota and Wharton School of the University of Pennsylvania), and (3) 1992 Wisconsin Entrepreneurial Climate Study sponsored by Wisconsin Innovation Network, Inc., and the Wisconsin Housing and Economic Development Authority. Analyses of data from the Pennsylvania and Minnesota studies revealed six dimensions of strategic focus (Carter et al., 1994): price emphasis, market sensitivity, technology, product distinctiveness, site appeal, and service. Items corresponding to a seventh construct, cost containment, were added to the Wisconsin study.

The strategy focus questions were asked of the 830 respondents to the nascent entrepreneur phone interview. There was no equivalent set of questions for the comparison group. Given time limitations of the PSED phone interview, only one item was retained from the prior studies to represent each of the six strategic focus factors. However, because a number of PSED researchers were especially interested in high technology firms, two items from the prior new firm studies were retained to distinguish between product and process technology, and one new item was included, "the technical or scientific expertise of the start-up team," for a total of eight items. Each of the eight items was preceded by the interviewer asking, "Please indicate how important each of the following is for the new firm to be an effective competitor." Respondents indicated level of importance on a four-point scale: 1 = insignificant, 2 = marginal, 3 = important, 4 = critical. Table 37.1 shows the strategic focus items relative to their origin and their item number on the phone interview.

Correction for Missing Item Response and Adjustment of Weights

Of the 830 nascent entrepreneurs who completed the initial phone interview, six reported positive cash flow for more than 90 days prior to the interview. These were judged as new businesses and removed from the analysis. Another seven respondents reported that nonpersons expected to own more than 50% of the new business. We removed those cases from consideration because they were not autonomous start-ups. Additionally, a number of respondents failed to answer all eight of the strategy questions, and a number indicated that a particular item was not applicable to their situation. We assigned such responses as missing data. Consequently, the total number of respondents for the seven items varied by question from a low of 722, corresponding to the "importance of new product technology," to a high of 804, corresponding to "importance of quality product." Across the seven items, different respondents omitted different items. The result was that only 643 individuals answered all eight items. It is the responses of these individuals that are of interest here. We adjusted the weights (WTW1) to reflect the reduction in the number of cases due to missing and not applicable responses (strategy weight = 643/639.14 * WTW1).

Findings

Table 37.2 displays the weighted descriptive statistics associated with the strategy items.

We tested the validity of the model by subjecting the data to a principal components factor analysis (listwise deletion since we'd already omitted missing data, varimax rotation) with the analysis directed to produce six factors. The weighted analysis accounted for 87% of the variance, and the rotation required seven iterations to converge. Four of the six factors loaded on the theoretical dimensions as expected: price, customer service/quality, facilities and convenience, and market responsiveness. We had expected the three technology items to be associated with the technology factor. Instead, we found that two of the three, "develop new or advanced product technology," and "develop new process technology" loaded on the product distinctiveness factor. The new item that was added, "the technical or scientific expertise of the start-up team," appears to define a new factor that is negatively associated with "importance of attractive products." It may be that at this stage of firm emergence, the nascent entrepreneurs are not distinguishing the advantage of competing with process technologies that impart efficiencies and cost savings but instead are focused on the product or service they are attempting to develop and produce. Consequently, new product technology, product attractiveness, and process technology are emphasized simultaneously in order to distinguish

Table 37.1   Strategic Focus Items in the PSED

Wisconsin Entrepreneurial Climate Study	PSED Items	
Dimension and Wording	Item Number	Wording
Market Responsiveness		
Fast response to changes in markets		
Serve those missed by others	Q302b	Serving those missed by others
More effective marketing/advertising		
High Tech Products/Processes		
Develop new/advanced product technology		
Develop new/advanced process technology		
	Q302e	Developing new or advanced product technology
Utilize new/advanced product technology		
Utilize new/advanced process technology		
	Q302f	Developing new or advanced process technology
	Q302g[a]	The technical or scientific expertise of the start-up team
Product Diversity		
More contemporary attractive products	Q302d	More contemporary, attractive products
Distinctive goods/services		
Provide more product choices to customer		
Facilities and Convenience		
Superior location/customer convenience	Q302c	Superior location and customer convenience
Better, more attractive facilities		
Customer Service/Quality		
Better service		
Quality products/services	Q302a	Quality products and services
Customized product/service to clients		
Price		
Lower prices	Q302	Lower prices
Cost Containment		
Lower cost per unit		
More effective channels of distribution		
Minimize administrative and sales costs		
Worker participation in management		

NOTE: a. Item added to PSED.

Table 37.2 Descriptive Statistics: Strategic Focus Items in the PSED (*N* = 643)

Variable	Min	Max	Mean	Median	SD
Lower prices	1	4	2.56	3.00	1.03
Quality products and services	1	4	3.61	4.00	.64
Serving those missed by others	1	4	3.12	3.00	.87
Superior location and customer convenience	1	4	2.66	3.00	1.11
More contemporary, attractive products	1	4	2.55	3.00	1.06
Developing new or advanced product technology	1	4	2.48	3.00	1.10
Developing new or advanced process technology	1	4	2.51	3.00	1.05
The technical or scientific expertise of the start-up team	1	4	2.66	3.00	1.10

Table 37.3 Factor Analysis of Reasons for Strategy Focus Items: Six-Factor Solution (*N* = 643)

	Factor:	1	2	3	4	5	6
	Sum of squared rotated loadings:	1.81	1.05	1.04	1.03	1.02	1.01
	Percentage variable accounted for:	22.64	13.10	12.95	12.83	12.75	12.60
Q302 #	Cronbach's alpha:	.64					
Product Distinctiveness							
e. Developing new or advanced product technology		.84					
f. Developing new or advanced process technology		.77					
d. More contemporary, attractive products	.63		−.46				
Facilities & Convenience							
c. Superior location and customer convenience		.96					
Technology Expertise							
g. Technical or scientific expertise of the startup team			.85				
Market Responsiveness							
b. Serving those missed by others				.98			
Service/Product Quality							
a. Quality Products and service					.98		
Price							
302 Lower prices						.97	

the forthcoming product offering. The Cronbach's alpha reliability of the new scale is .64. Table 37.3 displays the results of the weighted factor analyses.

Summary and Applications to Research

The strategy measures in the PSED data provide researchers with several opportunities to understand formation of new firms. As a method of competition, the configuration of the strategy can be insightful as to how the entrepreneur intends to acquire and mobilize resources. The factor loadings provide a more robust typology that the researcher can use in the analysis and thus avoid trying to "fit" the new venture strategy into typologies that are created for corporations. For instance, how does a firm pursuing a strategy of product/service quality differ in its acquisition and distribution of resources from a firm with a strategy focused on lower prices. You may find differences in legal structure, characteristics of the team, location, perceived trends in the market and industry, and so forth.

Since the PSED is a longitudinal study, issues about the change in strategy during the formative stages of the new venture can offer insight into how strategy evolves. It is assumed by many researchers that strategy is most susceptible to change in the early years of the venture. Mintzberg (1979) suggests that strategy evolves as the firm encounters and responds to conditions in the marketplace. With less learning and more flexibility, it could be hypothesized that owners of new firms are more readily equipped to adjust their strategy while gaining feedback through information and market contact. On the other hand, the proponents of an ecological framework (Hannan & Freeman, 1977; Aldrich, 1979) contend that once a strategy has been determined, the entrepreneur reduces flexibility to change as resources configured to support the strategy are embedded in the firm.

Since each strategy has a different thrust and potentially a different organizational structure to support that thrust, one may speculate that the method for putting the firm in place may take a different path for each strategy. For instance, a firm that is attempting to pursue a strategy based on technology expertise may be more inclined to secure intellectual property protection (e.g., patents, trademarks, and copyrights) than employ other types of strategies. The firm may attempt to secure legal counsel and a semblance of research and development as well. If we assume that each strategy has differential resources to secure in order to launch the firm, then the ability to distinguish the steps and processes that the entrepreneur uses in the nascent stage of the venture should be identifiable.

The match between strategy and structure remains an important issue, not only in the entrepreneurship literature but the traditional corporate literature as well. There is potential to look at the relationship between strategy and structure and predict survival and failure of the start-up effort. Many start-up efforts are in the realm of a 1-year time frame from first efforts to launch to the actual launch of the business. The longitudinal nature of the data should provide an opportunity to study the impact of strategy and structure by association with those entrepreneurs who fail to launch the firm as well as those who fail after the firm has been launched.

References

Aldrich, H. (1979). *Organizations and environments*. Englewood Cliffs, NJ: Prentice Hall.

Boeker, W. (1989). Strategic change: The effects of founding and history. *Academy of Management Journal, 32*, 489–515.

Carter, N. M., Stearns, T. M., Reynolds, P. D., & Miller, B. (1994). New venture strategies: Theory development with an empirical base. *Strategic Management Journal, 15*, 21–41.

Chaganti, R., Chaganti, R., & Mahajan, V. (1989). Profitable small business strategies under different types of competition. *Entrepreneurship Theory and Practice, 13*, 21–35.

Chandler, G. N., & Hanks, S. H. (1994). Market attractiveness, resource-based capabilities, venture strategies, and venture performance. *Journal of Business Venturing, 9*(4), 331–349.

Child, J. (1972). Organization structure, environment, and performance: The role of strategic choice. *Sociology, 6*, 1–22.

Cooper, A. C. (1993). Challenges in predicting new firm performance. *Journal of Business Venturing, 8*(3), 241–253.

Fombrun, C., & Wally, S. (1989). Structuring small firms for rapid growth. *Journal of Business Venturing, 4*, 107–122.

Green, R., Jolly, J., & Srivastava, A. (1990). Differentiation and cost leadership strategies: A strategic continuum of alternatives. *Journal of Business Strategies, 7*, 8–17.

Hannan, M., & Freeman, J. (1977). The population ecology organization. *American Journal of Sociology, 82*, 929–964.

McDougall, P. P., Covin, J. G., Robinson, R. B., Jr., & Herron, L. (1994). The effects of industry growth and strategic breadth on new venture performance and strategy content. *Strategic Management Journal, 15*(7), 537–554.

Meyer, D., Neck, H., & Meeks, M. (2002). The entrepreneurship—strategic management interface. In M. Hitt, D. Ireland, S. Camp, & D. Sexton (Eds.), *Strategic entrepreneurship: Creating a new mindset*. New York: Blackwell.

Miles, R., & Snow, C. (1978). *Organizational strategy, structure and process*. New York: McGraw-Hill.

Miller, D. (1991). Generalists and specialists: Two business strategies and their contexts. In P. Srivastava, A. Huff, & J. Dutton (Eds.), *Advances in strategic management* (pp. 3–41). Greenwich, CT: JAI.

Miller, D., & Toulouse, J. (1986). Strategy, structure, CEO personality and performance in small firms. *American Journal of Small Business, 10*, 47–62.

Mintzberg, H. (1979). *The structuring of organizations: A synthesis of the research*. Englewood Cliffs, NJ: Prentice Hall.

Porter, M. (1980). *Competitive strategy—Techniques for analyzing industries and competitors*. New York: Free Press.

Rugman, A., & Verbeke, A. (1988). Does competitive strategy work for small business? *Journal of Small Business and Entrepreneurship, 5*(3), 45–50.

Sandberg, W., & Hofer, C. (1987). Improving new venture performance: The role of strategy, industry structure, and the entrepreneur. *Journal of Business Venturing, 2*, 5–28.

Stearns, T. M., Carter, N. M., Reynolds, P. D., & Williams, M. (1996). New firm survival: Industry, strategy, and location. *Journal of Business Venturing, 10*, 23–40.

CHAPTER 38

Technology Entrepreneurs

Kathleen Allen

Timothy Stearns

The term "high tech" has been employed rather freely to describe three completely different types of firms: (1) firms that undertake radical innovation, (2) firms that rely on incremental improvements in existing innovations, and (3) firms that use technology to facilitate their business processes. In many respects, these are three very different types of technology and very different business strategies. The U.S. Standard Industrial Classification (SIC) codes (and more recently the NAICS codes) should identify high technology firms, but they are also ambiguous, resulting in firms being classified as high tech, low tech, and no tech, all within the same industrial category (Stearns, 1994).

Even in the literature, definitions of high technology are ambiguous. In one study, a high technology industry was defined as one in which "business activities are heavily dependent upon innovation in science and technology" (Medcof, 1999). In another study, high technology was described as industries that engage in activities that have high rates of change, high levels of research and development expenditures, and innovative products. What is unsatisfactory about these definitions is that they do not acknowledge the fact that there are myriad types of technology ventures, ranging from low tech to high tech. Some research has attempted to address the issue by classifying high technology ventures as those grounded in science with technology that makes previous technology obsolete, that is, breakthrough or radical innovation (Shanklin & Ryans, 1984). More recent research defines high technology ventures as those in which R&D accounts for a substantial portion of the business' operations, in which technological innovation is on the cutting edge, and in which a large proportion of the employees have university degrees (10% or more of the employees equals a high tech firm) (Baruch, 1997). Clearly, there is no agreement in the literature on what constitutes a high technology venture.

Technology Intensity:
Defining High Technology Ventures

In an attempt to remove some of this ambiguity, we developed a measure of technology firm type that divides firm types into three categories: first mover, application or practitioner technology, and innovator technology. These categories are based principally on the seminal work of Stearns (1994). The *first mover* is a pioneering entrepreneur with a disruptive technology that creates a new paradigm and makes previous technology obsolete. Stearns's research operationalized the first-mover construct with the surrogate variable *product/service availability* (Was the product/service available 5 years ago?); that is, if the entrepreneur's technology was not available 5 years before, the entrepreneur was using a first-mover strategy to enter the market. In a *practitioner strategy*, the entrepreneur employs current technology to improve products, services, or processes. The *innovator strategy* is an incremental strategy whereby the entrepreneur modifies or improves on existing technology. These categories were deduced from a study of over 500 firms in Wisconsin that were less than 6 years of age but had at least one employee (Stearns, 1994). Eight measures were used and based on factor analytic techniques that clustered the measures into the three categories.

First-Mover Strategy

When a disruptive technology has moved from the stages of conception and development to commercialization, a first-mover strategy is often the basis for the commercialization decision. In many respects, the first-mover strategy is the most difficult because not only is the entrepreneur introducing a new technology, but because there has been no precedent for this technology, the entrepreneur must also convince early adopters of the technology's value and that the switching costs for the buyer will produce a good return on the investment. The difficulty in achieving a high acceptance rate for a disruptive technology makes the first-mover strategy more difficult to implement, which leads to higher rates of business failure. On the other hand, if the entrepreneur is successful with this strategy, supernormal profits can be the prize. First-to-market affords the entrepreneur the opportunity to set the standards for others who follow (Zahra, Nash, & Bickford, 1995). Pioneering is also a critical factor in successful niche strategies, common with entrepreneurs. First movers do not perceive their environment to be highly competitive, which is compatible with research indicating that hostile environments discourage pioneering (Zahra, 2000). By its very nature, a first-mover strategy assumes a first-to-market position and, therefore, no direct competition.

Variables significantly related to the first-mover strategy include perception of competition (negative; that is, the nascent did not perceive any competition in the environment), seeking a patent, low price (negative; that is, the first mover would not be competing on price because he holds a temporary monopoly), a new product technology, and the use of technical/scientific experts.

Practitioner Strategies

Not all technology firms are seeking to be in the forefront of invention and innovation. The practitioner technology firm enters the market with an existing technology and seeks to satisfy market demand through other competitive advantages. Practitioners see their environment as highly competitive but believe that demand exists for the product or service as they intend to offer it. Despite the highly competitive nature of the practitioner environment, competing on price does not have a significant influence on the formation of the practitioner firm. Like innovators, practitioners recognize the need for technical and scientific experts in the start-up team as well as the need to integrate product/process technology. As is true of all three strategies, intellectual property remains an important part of a practitioner strategy. Where practitioners are late entrants into a market, they may seek intellectual property protection using "spin-off" patents, trademarks, or copyrights.

Practitioner strategies pose far less risk for entrepreneurs than first-mover strategies. First-mover strategies move ideas to commercial applications; by contrast, the practitioner strategy is about making improvements in existing products or services in the market or combining existing technologies in new ways. New uses for existing products may be general to the market or specific to a specialized niche of users, and entrepreneurs who employ this strategy tend to improve a technology multiple times over its life as they respond to the changing needs of customers.

Because the investment in research and development is relatively small and the entrepreneur is leveraging the research of the first mover, the practitioner strategy tends to be a lower cost effort on the part of the entrepreneur. One of the advantages of the practitioner strategy is that the time from concept to profit is substantially shorter. On the other hand, intellectual property issues often pose a problem if the entrepreneur cannot gain access to the core technology in order to develop modifications and improvements.

Variables significantly related to the practitioner strategy include having technical/scientific experts on the team, securing a patent, employing a new process technology, superior location (negative; that is, location was not important to the practitioner strategy), expertise in the technology (negative; that is, having a specific expertise in the technology was not considered important), quality of the product (negative; presumably because the innovation is based on an existing product), and perception of competition.

Innovator Strategy

The innovator strategy is pursued by entrepreneurs who merge existing, and often unrelated, technologies to create a new technology family. Satellite radio is one such example. Innovator entrepreneurs tend to leverage experience in applied research, generally spying an opportunity while working in an industry and then leaving their employment to launch the new venture. Their years of work in the industry has given them a unique understanding of a variety of technologies such that they can make a connection between technologies that normally would not be connected. Innovator firms are also significantly associated with new product technology in addition to new process technology where operating procedures become another source of innovation. Innovator technology firms also find it necessary to keep up with the latest technological advances, which suggests that second-mover tactics are a component of this type of strategy.

It is entirely possible for a firm, over time, to employ all three strategies. For example, the entrepreneur may develop a new platform technology and employ a first-mover strategy to enter the market. Subsequently, the entrepreneur may use a practitioner strategy to develop and launch applications for the technology. In later years and with more experience in the industry, the entrepreneur may employ an innovator strategy to combine existing technologies in new ways. Our research indicates that slightly less than 6% of all nascent start-up efforts use all three strategies at the same time. This is not surprising since the first-mover strategy, the most difficult, is employed far less frequently than the other two strategies. Nearly 20% of nascent entrepreneurs in our sample employed two of the three strategies, and about 38% of the total nascent entrepreneur sample pursued one of the three strategies. It would seem from these findings that firms vary by the level of technology intensity, which may influence the manner in which the start-up is eventually built and launched.

Variables significantly related to the innovator strategy are a new product technology, securing a patent, employing a new process technology, and the need to keep up with technological advances.

One consistent factor across all levels of technology intensity is the role of intellectual property in the entrepreneur's strategy. The pursuit, acquisition, and maintenance of intellectual property are a time-consuming effort, one that can come with considerable costs. For many entrepreneurs, it may be the most expensive part of their start-up effort, depending on the technical nature of the product or service and the level of protection that is necessary to ensure future success of the firm. This cost in both funds and time can make the launch of a high technology firm more problematic than efforts by entrepreneurs who are not building companies around technology.

Although the differences between levels of technology intensity are clear, based on our research with the Panel Study of Entrepreneurial Dynamics (PSED), the differences between high tech nascent ventures and no tech ventures are even more striking.

High Tech Versus No Tech

One can also use levels of intensity to determine whether a nascent entrepreneur is high tech or no tech. In our prior research (Stearns & Allen, 2000), we defined the high technology group as consisting of those respondents who are employing two of the three categories of technology strategies. Therefore, if the nascent entrepreneur identifies his new venture strategies as innovator and first mover or innovator and practitioner, the nascent is placed in the high technology category. Similarly, those who employ only one strategy or no relevant strategy are considered low or no tech nascent entrepreneurs. A more rigorous measure would require all three categories. Although we have found that a criteria of two of the three categories implemented by the entrepreneur to qualify as high technology to be beneficial, this may conflict with a view that a first mover is by definition high technology. Hence, the researcher may want to consider whether one category in the measure of technology has more profound implications on the firm than other categories.

Research and Development

Research intensity is a good predictor of high technology ventures. *Expenditure on R&D effort relative to sales* is a good surrogate for research intensity. In general, research expenditures in high technology firms tend to outpace those of less technologically oriented ventures. R&D expenditures are also a surrogate for commitment to technological innovation (Bell & McNamara, 1991). In the case of start-up entrepreneurial firms with limited resources, R&D expenditures may be relatively small when compared to larger firms but represent, in fact, a high proportion of their total budget and signal their level of commitment to technological innovation.

Rationale for Technology Questions in the PSED

Items regarding technology of the firm were developed to measure the degree of technology intensity intended for the start-up. The term "high technology" has assumed a common reference in the media and elsewhere to companies engaged in the development, production, and distribution of computer products. This is limiting and distorts understanding of technology applications across industries. Many entrepreneurs are engaged in the development, production, and distribution of technology in markets unrelated to computers. Yet, research has made little effort to obtain clarity on the concept of high technology and how technology applied in a business model might have gradations from highly intense efforts to build a business model around technology to a business start-up that is devoid of technology as a core component of its business. Not only is it assumed that the level of intensity in the use of technology varies according to the intention of the entrepreneur, but the variation will also have different consequences for the entrepreneur and the firm.

Gradations in technological intensity can be created as a scale with four ordinal classifications: high, medium, low, and no technology. The items used to create the scale were phone interviews labeled as Q299 to Q301. Table 38.1 presents the questions asked in the phone interviews relative to the ordinal scale. The questions were replicated from an earlier study by Stearns (1994) that used multiple items to capture various dimensions believed to be important to a high technology firm: (1) Were the firm's major products or services available in the marketplace 5 years ago? (2) Is the firm making use of equipment or procedures that were not available 5 years ago? (3) Is a high level of technical or scientific expertise critical to the effective management of the firm? (4) Is awareness of state-of-the-art developments in relevant scientific or technical areas critical for the firm's future? (5) Is your firm required to constantly make major technical changes in products or processes to be

Table 38.1   Assessing Technology Intensity Items in the PSED

Item Number	Question
Q299	Were the products and services to be provided by your new business available in the marketplace 5 years ago?
	(Yes or No)
Q300	Will spending money on research and development be a major priority for this new business?
	(Yes or No)
Q301	Would you consider this new business to be high tech?
	(Yes or No)

competitive? (6) Is finding, hiring, and retaining qualified scientific and technical personnel a continuing issue for this firm? (7) Is allocating resources to research and development a major priority in budget decisions? And finally, (8) Would you consider this firm as high tech?

The items were designed to identify those firms actively engaged in process and product innovation as well as those at the cutting edge of an emerging technology. The Wisconsin study found that many of the eight items were answered in similar ways. Through factor analytic techniques, it was determined that Questions 3 (scientific expertise), 4 (awareness of state-of-the-art), 5 (constantly make changes), 6 (finding qualified personnel), and 8 (are you high tech?) would serve as a measure of high technology firms that are involved in the application of new and innovative ideas to products and services. Questions 2 (equipment not available 5 years ago) and 7 (R&D priority) suggest that the firm is active in the innovation of new products and services. Question 1 (products available 5 years ago) suggests that the firm is "first-mover" in its orientation. Based on these results and the need to economize in numbers of questions asked of each respondent for the complete PSED, one question representing each factor loading was selected to be included in the PSED questionnaire. The item that received the highest "load" value in the factor analysis was selected as the representative of that factor. In the case of the "first mover" designation, only one item represented this category, and thus the factor "load" criterion was not necessary.

The first question, Q299, was designed to measure whether the products or services offered by the new company were available 5 years ago. A negative response would imply that the firm is being positioned to be one of the first in the market with the product or service. Being a first mover can be one important element of a high technology company. First-to-market is an option in which the entrepreneur has created something novel and recognizes a commercial opportunity.

The second question, Q300, identifies the entrepreneur's expectations regarding research and development expenditures. Companies that manufacture and distribute technology products and services are usually required to continually modify and improve the product or service. It is also true of technology companies that customer responses or demands lead to alterations in the product or service in order to achieve a more useful fit with customer needs. And companies engaged in technology products or services are mindful of the need to develop additional products or services from the core technology. New product development is largely accomplished through the creation of a research and development unit or through a direct budgetary line item that will foster the ability to make these changes or modifications. Hence, an entrepreneur engaged in technology is more likely to be aware of the need to generate funds to support a sizable research and development effort within the business model. This is a key aspect of the innovator strategy of high technology.

The third question, Q301, is simple and straightforward: does the entrepreneur consider his or her company high tech? Much like researchers who have their own biases as to what constitutes high technology, entrepreneurs have biases about whether or not their start-up is high technology in nature. Self-nomination, however, is a valid tool for classification. Entrepreneurs who believe they are engaged in a high technology start-up are prone to gather information, affiliate, and market their firm as high technology. Like all measures of high technology, it is not complete but provides a unique dimension to understanding high technology. In this case, it was a strong measure of firms that are involved in a practitioner strategy.

The researcher can undertake several paths using the framework above to examine the degree of technology of the start-up company. Since each question is coded yes or no, a value of 1 for "Yes" and 0 for "No" can be assigned to each of the three items. However, Q299 will need to be reverse coded. If the respondent states "Yes" to the item, they are indicating that they are producing products or services in the market that were available 5 years or longer. As a researcher, you have options as to how you want to pursue the coding of high technology. If you want to make a nominal distinction, such as "high technology or no technology," we recommend that high technology firms be classified as having two of the three items as part of their strategy. No technology firms would have one or fewer of the three items as part of its technology strategy. A more robust way to measure technology is by a cumulative count of the technology strategy items in which a sum of 3 refers to high technology, a sum of 2 refers to medium technology, a sum of 1 refers to low technology, and a sum of 0 refers to no technology. The researcher should exercise caution in the use of this last measure. The valid number of observations in an analysis may shrink considerably if you select the "delete listwise missing cases" command. That is, the analytic software will remove all matched observations in which one of the variables has missing information, thus shrinking your sample size. When constructing the ordinal or nominal scale, be sure to assign the "Not Applicable" response as a "system missing" case. Otherwise, its assigned value of 3 in the sample set will distort the scale considerably.

Descriptive Statistics

For our analyses, we used the phone sample with the 1,261 responses. However, attrition has reduced that to just over 800 respondents. Table 38.2 displays descriptive statistics for questions about high technology strategies.

Table 38.2   Descriptive Statistics: High-Technology Measures

Variable	No. of Cases	Yes (%)	No (%)*	NA	Missing
Q299 Available 5 years ago?	806	536 (66.5)	268 (33.3)	2 (.2)	455
Q300 R&D major priority?	817	249 (30.5)	543 (66.5)	25 (3.1)	444
Q301 Business high tech?	814	288 (35.4)	508 (62.4)	18 (2.2)	447

NOTE: * "No" suggests the firm is pursuing a high-tech strategy.

The descriptive statistics in Table 38.2 report that 806 entrepreneurs interviewed responded to the question of whether the products or services were available 5 years ago. Two thirds or 66.5% stated that the products or services around which they planned to build a business were available 5 years or more ago. One third or 33.3% stated that no such products or services existed 5 years before. For this item, the response of "No" indicates that the firm is pursuing one aspect of a high technology strategy.

The item to determine if research and development expenditures were a priority for the new venture produced 817 responses. Of those responses, 249 or 30.5% stated that research and development expenditures would be a priority. Two thirds or 543 entrepreneurs responded that research and development expenditures would not be a priority for their business. Research has found that entrepreneurs seeking to create high technology companies are more likely to make research and development expenditures a priority.

When respondents were asked "Would you consider the new business high tech?" 288 or 35.4% stated they considered their businesses as high tech. The remainder, 508 or 62.4%, responded that they did not consider their business as high tech. A total of 814 respondents answered this question.

Table 38.3 displays the distribution of responses for nominal and ordinal scales of high technology by aggregating the three dimensions. The nominal measure was created using the criterion that the respondent had to answer two of the three technology questions in a way that suggested they were building a technology-based business. The tabulation was conducted by reverse coding the question about whether or not products/services were available in the market 5 years ago. Therefore, a "No" response would receive a value of 1 and a "Yes" response would receive a value of 0. For the other two questions, "Yes" received a value of 1 and "No" received a value of 0.

Classification of high technology versus no technology by nominal measure can be achieved in several ways. The respondent could have a value of 1 for the first question and a value of 1 for the second question thus meeting the criteria of an accumulated score of 2 to be considered high technology. However, this value could also be achieved by scoring a 1 on the first and third questions or by scoring a 1 on the second and third questions. We do not recommend trying to make a distinction

Table 38.3   Descriptive Statistics: High-Technology Scales: Ordinal and Nominal

Nominal Tech Measures Valid Number of Cases 763 Missing Cases 498	n	%
High Technology	217	28.5
No Technology	546	71.6
Ordinal Tech Measures		
High Technology	51	6.7
Medium Technology	166	21.8
Low Technology	282	37.0
No Technology	264	34.6

among the three questions as to which is of lesser or greater importance for gauging technology intensity of the firm because there is no theoretical or methodological justification to do so. Table 38.3 shows that 217 of the respondents indicated they are pursuing two of the three technology activities with their new venture. This represents 28.5% of the sample and can therefore be considered a high technology start-up using this classification. The majority of the sample, 546 or 71.6%, are pursuing one or none of the three activities, which leads to a "no technology" classification.

Classification by an ordinal measure is accomplished by summing the three items and using the sum to classify the intensity of technology of the firm. Using this procedure, 264 or 34.6% of the respondents scored a 0 for all three measures, producing a classification of "no technology." A sum of 1 for all three items produced a total of 282 or 37.0% of the entrepreneurs responding to the items and designated as "low technology." "Medium technology" was achieved when the summation was 2 for the three items. One hundred and sixty-six respondents or 21.8% of the sample were classified as such. Finally, only 51, or 6.7%, of the respondents indicated that they were pursuing all three technology strategies. This resulted in their efforts being classified as "high technology."

Conclusions and Implications

The PSED questions related to nascent high technology entrepreneurs can be used to address some interesting questions, particularly in the area of defining high technology ventures. Certainly, no agreement exists in the literature on the definition of a high technology venture; however, through our work with the PSED and based on prior work by Stearns (1994), we believe that we have the beginnings of a methodology for defining high tech ventures. The PSED data did not allow for as complete a distinction among the various gradations of technology as the Wisconsin study did because we were limited in the number of questions that could be asked in the technology area. Consequently, there are opportunities to compare the PSED results using nascents with other classes of entrepreneurs, like those in the Wisconsin study, on the same questions to check the robustness of the technology intensity measure.

The distribution of measures and scales for technology intensity provides useful insights into how nascent entrepreneurs view their start-up efforts in relationship to technology. For all three measures of technology intensity, about one third of the sample responds in a way to suggest they are pursuing a component of high technology. That is, they view their start-up effort as including practices of high technology. What is not clear is whether this high technology emphasis dilutes or increases in intensity as the entrepreneur moves closer to actual launch of the new venture.

We firmly believe the greatest insight can be gained in using the ordinal measure of technology intensity. The four categories ranging from high, medium, low, and no technology are robust and allows the researcher to engage in more degrees of comparison. However, we are aware that some analyses with other variables in the study may considerably reduce the total sample and thus make the scale unusable in research. An example may be if the researcher were to study technology intensity among 18 to 25-year-old females who are seeking venture capital versus those who are not. In situations similar to this example, we believe the nominal scale will yield greater potential for a valid analysis.

Theory on the environment and its effect on high technology ventures and their competitive strategies is well documented. We did not explore the environmental variables in the PSED. One interesting study might be to identify the variables in the PSED that operationalize the constructs of volatility, complexity, and hostility and correlate them to the intensity levels for the nascent high tech entrepreneurs. Other variables that we looked at in our early research with the mail questionnaire that would be good possibilities for future research include (1) the resource variables, including the use of scientists and engineers, strategic alliances, acquisition, licensing agreements, and the outright purchase of technology; (2) the intellectual property variables, such as pursuit of intellectual property and completion of a prototype; and (3) the strategic intention variables, such as overall sales growth, number of employees, and motives for entering a cooperative relationship.

Another area that we did not explore was the amount of technology that was used in the business. Technology is either the product of the business or the enabler of business processes. Our work to date has focused only on technology as the product of the business. It might be interesting to look at how nascents used technology in their businesses or projected the use of technology in their business planning.

References

Baruch, Y. (1997). High technology organization—What it is, what it isn't. *International Journal of Technology Management, 13*(2), 179–195.

Bell, C., & McNamara, J. (1991). *High-tech ventures: The guide for entrepreneurial success.* Reading, MA: Addison-Wesley.

Medcof, J. W. (1999). Identifying super-technology industries. *Research Technology Management, 42*(4), 31–36.

Shanklin, W. L., & Ryans, J. K., Jr. (1984). Organizing for high-tech marketing. *Harvard Business Review, 62*(6), 164–171.

Stearns, T. M. (1994). The role of new high-tech firms in Wisconsin. *Wisconsin's Entrepreneurial Climate Study.*

Stearns, T. M. & Allen, K. R. (2000). The foundations of high-technology start-ups: The who, where, when, and why. *Frontiers of entrepreneurship research.* Wellesley, MA: Babson College,179–192.

Zahra, S. (2000). Technology strategy and software new ventures' performance: Exploring the moderating effect of the competitive environment. *Journal of Business Venturing, 15*(2).

Zahra, S., Nash, S., & Bickford, D. (1995). Transforming technological pioneering into competitive advantage. *Academy of Management Executive, 9,* 17–31.

Conclusion

William B. Gartner

Kelly G. Shaver

Nancy M. Carter

Paul D. Reynolds

> *. . . Only in departure whole. Arrival is always partial.*
>
> —Bill Knott (2004)

W ith our combined accumulation of over 100 years of knowledge and experience in scholarly activities devoted to research on entrepreneurs and entrepreneurship, and now with our nearly 40 cumulative years involved with the Panel Study of Entrepreneurial Dynamics (PSED), we are in a position to see that where we began then is not where we thought we would end up today, or for that matter where entrepreneurship scholarship is likely to take us tomorrow. In other words, the research process is by its nature in a constant state of flux. Like the start-up businesses we seek to study, our preliminary business plan for this project bears only a family resemblance to the enterprise that has developed. Paraphrasing Albert Einstein, "If we knew what we were doing, we wouldn't call it research." The word *research,* itself, invokes an intrinsic need to "re-search," to go back and look again at what occurred. This book is both the culmination of attempts to document the theory underlying the PSED and the foundation for its further exploration. Through use of the theory provided here, or through the application of other theory using the data our theory generated, future investigators can generate new knowledge and understanding about the phenomenon. This insight recognizes that the development of the PSED as a significant milestone along the path to a better understanding of the process of business creation. But, we do not believe we have reached the end of the journey. Even if all of the empirical tests of the theory presented in this handbook were carried out, we would still have achieved only a partial exploration of all of the information that the PSED contains.

We end this book—much as we began it—with an invitation to our readers to participate in an exploration of a unique and wonderfully rich, complicated, and comprehensive data set on the process of business creation. We believe having some familiarity with the information in this handbook is critical for anyone who intends to use the PSED. Embedded in many of these chapters are critical insights about how specific questions are linked to particular theoretical ideas, and warnings about how misapplications of the use of these questions could result in erroneous findings. These chapters then, are much like "soundings" that test the depth of the waters when sailing in unknown seas. Before diving into the PSED, a reading of these chapters will help provide a sense of how deep the water really goes. There is no reason to get "stuck in the mud" on some particular topic issue when others have made significant efforts to mark the channels.

We also recognize that although the theory presented here offers ways to understand and explore aspects of the process of business creation, the accumulation of questions across all of these various theoretical perspectives provides a variety of unintended ways in which new theory about entrepreneurship and new applications of these new theories can be used to explore the PSED. It would not be facetious to suggest that there is probably a question asked in one of the surveys that would be useful for addressing other theories (your theory, perhaps) that could be used to probe the new business formation process. But, please, pay attention to prior theoretical and empirical work that has already occurred using the questions you may be interested in using.

Although the handbook is focused on theory, the foundation of the PSED could be summed up in this aphorism: "Theory without data is speculation." We believe that entrepreneurship scholarship is in need of more facts about what the phenomenon *is,* rather than more theory about what the phenomenon *might be.* The theory in the handbook provides direction for exploring the phenomenon of new business formation; yet these ideas are grounded in specific questions and specific facts resulting from these questions. The theory presented here can be tested. This is a significant advance for the entrepreneurship field. Offering an aphorism from Thomas Henry Huxley: "The great tragedy of science is the slaying of a beautiful hypothesis by an ugly fact." The PSED is an ocean of ugly facts waiting for researchers to explore so that we can discover just how beautiful some of the competing hypotheses are.

Finally, the PSED is a collaborative research project. And, it is in this original, and still current, spirit of collaboration that we ask that scholars interested in using data from the PSED seek to participate in this active community of researchers. One of the implicit aspects of work in the entrepreneurship field is a realization that our efforts are not a "zero sum game." The sharing of information about the database: insights into the nuances of particular cases, explorations of theories through factor analyses of combinations of questions, or any other work in progress toward the publication of results and findings helps benefit the entire field, as well as each scholar individually. We invite you to join us.

References

Knott, B. (2004, January 12). The answer. *The New Yorker, 79*(42), 82.

Appendix A

Data Collection

Paul D. Reynolds

Richard T. Curtin

Where Do New Businesses Come From?

The origin of new businesses is the primary focus of the Panel Study of Entrepreneurial Dynamics (PSED). The design of the research is intended to document the underlying processes and factors that lead individuals to pursue the creation of a new business firm. The optimal strategy seemed quite straightforward: Locate individuals involved in the business start-up process and determine as much as possible about their initial situation and their plans and actions to create a new business. Periodic follow-ups would provide information on the outcome of their efforts. Implementation of such a complex focus has proven difficult but feasible.

Conceptualization of the Phenomena

To facilitate discussion of the start-up process, it has been convenient to conceptualize the entrepreneurial process as occurring within a political and economic context as indicated in Figure A.1.

The process is conceptualized as having four stages with three transitions. The first transition occurs when individuals, either alone or responding to an initiative of an existing firm, elect to pursue a firm creation. These persons are classified as nascent

AUTHORS' NOTE: This appendix relies heavily on an earlier publication (Reynolds, 2000, pp. 153–228) that described the initial procedures and history of the project prepared by the first author, although all figures have been updated.

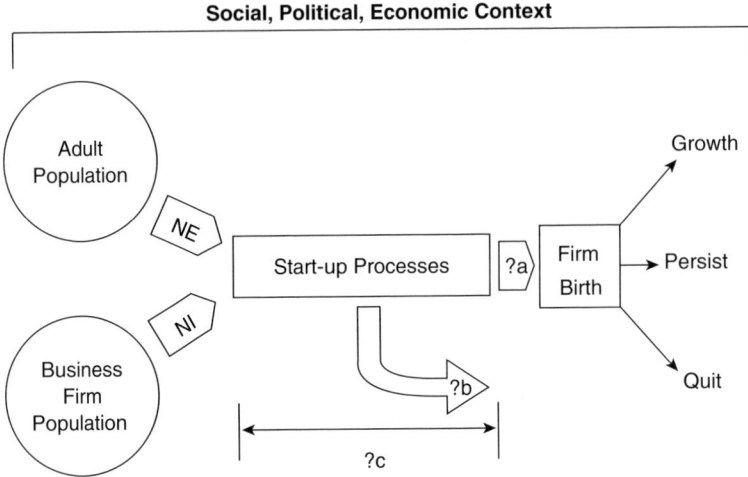

Figure A.1   Conceptualization of the Entrepreneurial Process

entrepreneurs (NE) if they represent an independent start-up effort, or, if they are sponsored by an existing business, the persons are considered nascent intrapreneurs (NI), a type of corporate entrepreneurship. Conception may be considered the beginning of this, the firm gestation process. The second transition in the life course of the firm occurs when the gestation process is complete, firm birth has occurred, and an infant firm is in place as an operating business. For many in the start-up phase, however, the next transition is to abandon the effort. The firm is, in a sense, stillborn. The third transition for infant firms is a passage into firm adolescence, a stage in which survival is considered more certain and not a constant challenge. A secondary feature of the third transition would be the nature of the growth trajectory of surviving new firms; a new firm pursing a high-growth trajectory may be considered to have a different character compared to those that are designed to persist as small firms.

Three of the critical features of the entrepreneurial process about which very little is known are represented by the question marks in Figure A.1: "?a" represents the proportion of business start-ups that complete the process with the implementation of an infant firm; "?b" represents the proportion of start-ups that never complete the process, although when they are abandoned is also a major issue about which little is known; finally, "?c" represents the features of the gestation process itself, both the length of time required to develop an infant firm and the activities that take place.

One primary objective of the research program was to provide systematic, reliable data on the basic features of the entrepreneurial or start-up process. This would include information on the nature and extent of variation in the critical aspects of the start-up process: the proportion of the adult population involved in firm conceptions, the activities that compose the start-up process, the proportion of start-ups that complete the second transition to become infant firms, and the survival and growth trajectories of the new firms.

A second objective was to provide reliable data on those factors or variables that could account for variations in these transitional events. This includes, for example, variations in the number of start-up efforts that become operating new firms or the length of time spent in the gestation phase before the efforts are completed or abandoned. Potential influences would include, but are not limited to, the following (many are discussed in detail in the chapters of this handbook):

- Economic context, including national conditions, local conditions, and conditions in the economic sector or market of the new firm
- Personal context, including work and family situations and responsibilities, as well as the presence of supportive social networks for members of the start-up team
- Personal background and relevant experience, based on early family life, educational or occupational training, or in specific economic or market sectors for members of the start-up team
- Personal predispositions, either in terms of decision-making style, risk preferences, desire for autonomy, and personal aspirations
- Sociodemographic background, such as age, gender, race, and other characteristics
- Nature and sequence of start-up activities pursued in the firm gestation process
- Nature of the markets, competition for the new firm, and the strategic focus.
- Access to and use of resources, financial and otherwise
- Access to and use of programs designed to assist start-ups and new businesses

While assessing whether or not any one of these factors might affect the start-up process was one type of research objective, most past research in entrepreneurship has emphasized one or two of the factors from this list. A second objective was to estimate the relative impact of each of these factors holding constant the impact of all other factors. Such a comparative analysis requires that data be assembled on all factors for each start-up initiative. The major challenge in the design of the project was to collect data on all of these topics from the same set of respondents involved in starting new businesses. Such a comprehensive data set was required for the research program to provide a complete description and explanation of the critical elements of the entrepreneurial process.

Based on these objectives, and the constituencies to be served by the results, the final research design should have a number of features. First, a technique must be developed to provide systematic descriptions of the start-up process from its very beginning—the beginning is assumed to occur when somebody decides to implement a new firm, before any behavior occurs. Second, the data should be based on a representative sample of business start-ups so that estimates for the entire population—of people or firms—would be possible. Third, as the creation of a new firm appears to be very complex and multifaceted—with many small factors having direct and interactive influences—it is important that all major perspectives be represented in the data collection. This is tantamount to trying to measure a wide range of potential independent variables from a variety of perspectives. Fourth, as the focus is on the process of implementing a new business, the project would need to be designed as a longitudinal or panel study.

Design History

The distinctive methodological challenge was the creation of a procedure that would capture the very beginning of the business creation process. It was necessary to identify a start-up initiative before it had been included in business registries (such as the Dun & Bradstreet credit rating files) or lists of business activity (such as the phone book Yellow Pages). The objective was to create a procedure that could be used to systematically develop a sample that would allow estimates of the total amount of activity in the population.

Although later abandoned, the initial effort to locate a random sample of nascent entrepreneurs involved an application of multiplicative sampling. Developed with Charles Palit of the University of Wisconsin Survey Research Laboratory, this application required a systematic procedure to identify the social network of a representative sample of adults (Sudman, Sirken, & Cowan, 1988; Palit & Reynolds, 1993). This involved establishing a list of each respondent's parents, siblings, adult children, coworkers, and significant other (usually a spouse) during the interview. The respondent is then asked if any of these people are currently involved in a start-up effort. If they are, the respondent is asked for details so they may be contacted for a more complete interview.

While this may appear similar to snowball sampling—in which a respondent identifies other individuals with unique characteristics—it differs in one important respect. When persons nominated by the respondent as nascent entrepreneurs are interviewed, they are asked questions that will make it possible to determine the probability they would be nominated by more than one person in the initial sample. This allows the use of the information from the procedure to adjust for potential multiple nominations and compute the probability with which nascent entrepreneurs occur in the total population.

Although the implementation of the procedure involved the creation of relatively complete and very useful descriptions of the respondent's social networks, it was abandoned for several reasons. Most important, a person nominated as a nascent entrepreneur was actually interviewed in less than 40% of the cases. There were two main problems. In 20% of the cases, the original respondents were not able to provide the full name and phone number for the nominated nascent entrepreneur—they did not have the information. In 40% of the cases, the original respondents refused to provide the full name and location information for the nominated nascent entrepreneurs. They were, after all, talking to a stranger on the phone and may not have fully believed that the interview was related to research. As a result, in only two of five cases was a network nominee called to be interviewed. A pretest effort completed in 1997 using one household member to nominate others in the same household for a nascent entrepreneur interview was also associated with very poor results; interviews were completed with very few—less than 10%—of the within-household nominees.

Several factors led to the change in procedures from multiplicative sampling to straightforward population screening. First, as discussed above, the multiplicative sampling procedure was not working well—very few of those nominated were interviewed. Second, prevalence rates of nascent entrepreneurs were four to eight times higher than the 1% to 2% initially expected. Third, it was possible to locate a commercial marketing research firm that could include two appropriate screening questions in a national survey so that the costs and benefits of identifying each nascent entrepreneur was attractive compared with other methods. The procedure amounted to asking all respondents if they were starting a business on their own or for their employer. Other questions were then used to eliminate those not considered active in a start-up, not potential owners, or not in the start-up phase itself.

The first full application of the research procedure was with the adult population of Wisconsin in 1992 and 1993 (Reynolds & White, 1993, 1997). A second application involved the purchase of time in the monthly *Survey of Consumers* completed by the University of Michigan Institute for Social Research in October and November 1993 (Curtin, 1982; Reynolds, 1997). These two studies provided similar results regarding prevalence rates (about 4% were identified as nascent entrepreneurs), demonstrated the technical feasibility of the research protocol, and indicated that costs would be high but affordable. In the first case, the initial screening was part of a special-purpose survey. In the second project, the screening was one part of a multipurpose project, in which many costs were shared with other research projects.

PSED Design

The research design for the U.S. Panel Study of Entrepreneurial Dynamics (PSED) is presented in Figure A.2. It has three components and reflects data collection from two types of respondents. The first stage involves large-scale screening to create two samples representative of the U.S. population of adults 18 years old and older, excluding residents of Alaska and Hawaii. The first sample included those involved in attempting to start a new business. These respondents are either autonomous start-ups, referred to as nascent entrepreneurs (NEs), or sponsored by an existing firm, referred to as nascent intrapreneurs (NIs). Second, a representative sample of typical adults to be used as the comparison group (CG) was identified. Both types had to meet certain criteria and be willing to participate in subsequent interviews. Once the screening procedures were completed, the second stage of data collection involved detailed phone interviews followed by self-administered questionnaires mailed to the respondents. The third stage was the follow-up phone and mail interviews completed to determine the outcome of their efforts to implement a new firm. The initial design included plans for 12- and 24-month follow-up interviews. Additional funding has allowed for 36-month follow-ups to be completed in 2003.

This design involved optimizing a number of desirable, though often incompatible, features. Among these issues were choices between the sample size versus the amount of information assembled from each respondent, the scope of information to be included in the interviews versus the desire to keep respondents involved over multiple data collection activities, which items were best suited for the phone or self-administered mail questionnaire, and the simplicity of the interview items versus the complexity of the research concepts. There is, of course, no single best solution to this optimization problem. The design of this research program was the result of both technical issues and the need to provide data for use by over 100

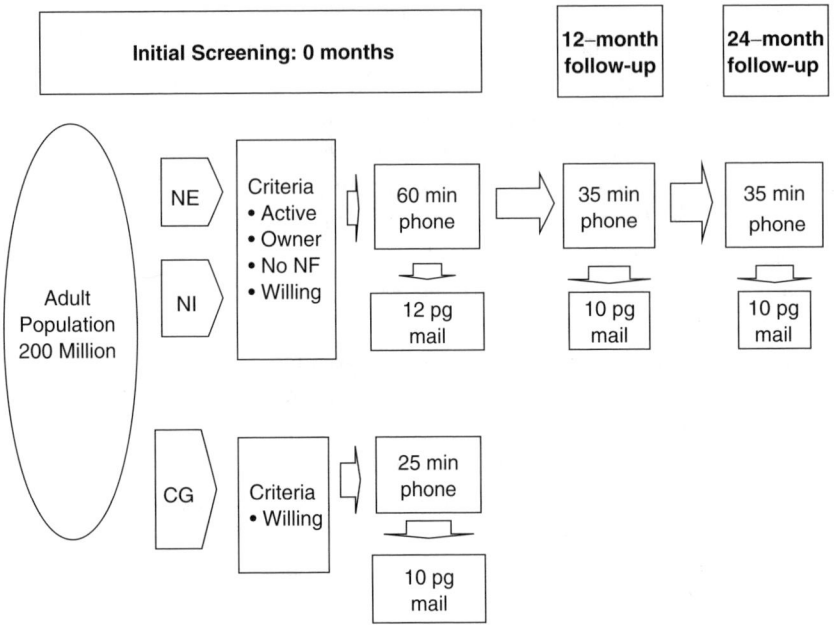

Figure A.2   PSED Research Design Overview

NOTE:

NE = Nascent Entrepreneurs; NI = Nascent Intrapreneurs; CG = Comparison Group; NF = New Firm.

scholars and researchers in the Entrepreneurship Research Consortium. A political process led to an acceptable solution for this group of scholars. Another research team might have developed another, equally appropriate, solution.

The research procedure involved the national screening, the initial round of data collection through phone and mail interviews, and the follow-up interviews. The PSED data set consists of five related samples:

- NE representative sample drawn from the original screening of the U.S. population (referred to as NE Mixed Gender)
- NE female oversample drawn from supplemental screening of the U.S. population with only females retained for sample (Carter, Brush, Aldrich, Green, & Katz, 1998)
- NE minority oversample drawn from the original screening of the U.S. population with only Blacks and Hispanics retained for sample (Greene, Carter, Reyolds, Aldrich, & Stearns, 1999)
- CG representative sample drawn from the original screening of the U.S. population of those not involved in entrepreneurship for a comparison group (referred to as CG Mixed Gender)
- CG minority oversample drawn from a screening of the U.S. population of minorities not involved in entrepreneurship for a comparison group (Greene et al., 1999)

The dates of the initial screening for each sample and the number of interviews involved at each stage of data collection are presented in Table A.1. Note that data collection for both the minority nascent entrepreneurs and minority comparison groups started 12 months after the other screening activities. So the summer 2003 period involves the third follow-up for the mixed gender and female nascent samples and the second follow-up for the minority nascent cohort. This is why no third wave follow-up data for the minority nascent entrepreneur sample will be collected.

Table A.1   Sample Selection: Cohort Size, Screening Dates, and Follow-up Samples

Sample	Initial Screening Dates	Initial Screening Sample Size	Initial Detailed Phone Sample Size	First Follow-up Phone Sample Size	Second Follow-up Phone Sample Size	Third Follow-up Phone Sample Size
NE: Mixed Gender	July 1998 to April 1999	15,118	446	342	256	Summer 2003 data
NE: Female	Sept 1998 to Dec 1998	16,143	223	159	141	Summer 2003 data
NE: Minority	July 1999 to Jan 2000	28,314	161	114	Summer 2003 data	None planned
CG: Mixed Gender	Nov 1998	2,010	223	Not applicable	Not applicable	Not applicable
CG: Minority	Nov 1999	3,037	208	Not applicable	Not applicable	Not applicable

Screening Respondents: Basic Procedure

National screening of the adult population was initiated in 1998 by a commercial market research firm [TeleNation Program, Market Facts, Inc. (now Synovate); Arlington Heights, IL] that surveyed three random samples of 1,000 adults each week in the contiguous 48 states and the District of Columbia. Random digit dial (RDD) sampling procedures avoid the problems of high percentages of households with unlisted phones to create representative samples of private households. The phone numbers themselves are randomly created. Based on TeleNation procedures, once a residential living unit was contacted, the first individual aged 18 or older that would complete the phone interview was accepted as a respondent. Quota sampling was used to ensure that half of each sample was men and the other half women. Each sample wave of 1,000 was completed in a 3-day period, with a three-call criterion (initial call and two call-backs). However, up to 2% of the respondents were called from four to nine times to complete an interview. The interviews were controlled to be less than 30 minutes long to minimize midinterview terminations.

For locating eligible nascent entrepreneurs, an equal number of samples were screened on weekdays (Monday, Tuesday, and Wednesday) and weekends (Friday, Saturday, and Sunday). The yield of eligible nascent entrepreneurs was actually about 0.5% higher for the weekend samples. Between questions about marketing issues and consumer preferences, two items were inserted to determine if a respondent might qualify as a nascent entrepreneur:

- Are you, alone or with others, now trying to start a new business?
- Are you, alone or with others, now starting a new business or new venture for your employer? An effort that is part of your job assignment?

About 88% responded "no" to both items and were not involved further. Those that answered "yes" to either (6.9% to the first or 3.6% to the second) or both (1.2%) of these items were considered candidates for the nascent entrepreneur interview if they met three criteria:

- They expect to be owners or part owners of the new firm.
- They have been active in trying to start the new firm in the past 12 months.
- The effort is still in the start-up or gestation phase and is *not* an infant firm.

The first two criteria were included as part of the initial screening interview procedure. The third criterion was incorporated in the next phase of the data collection.

Those that expected to be owners of the new firm and had been active were invited to participate in "a national study of new businesses being conducted through the University of Wisconsin" and told a cash payment would be provided. From 86% to 87% of those that met these criteria provided their first name. Their first name, along with their phone number, was then provided to the University of Wisconsin Survey Research Laboratory in Madison, Wisconsin, the unit responsible for the initial waves of the data collection.

A similar procedure was used to identify candidates for the comparison group, except that all respondents in the sample were offered a chance to participate in a "study of the work and career patterns of all Americans, including those not currently working." Again, a cash payment was mentioned as an inducement. In this case, 62% to 72% agreed to provide their first name, which was forwarded, along with their phone number, to the University of Wisconsin Survey Research Laboratory.

In addition to providing candidates for the nascent entrepreneur cohort and the comparison group, the resulting data set includes basic sociodemographic information on the respondents and their household, as well as the county and state in which the phone was located. Data on those 90% screened but not qualifying as nascent entrepreneurs were used in computing the population prevalence rates, a "screening comparison group" of about 60,000 individuals.

Completion of Nascent Screening: The Third Criteria

The first names and phone numbers of potential candidates for the nascent entrepreneur interview were relayed to the University of Wisconsin Survey

Research Laboratory. They were then assigned for a phone interview. If the respondent was involved in several start-up efforts, they were asked to focus on only the most recent start-up effort. (Up to one third reported simultaneous participation in several start-ups.) The third criterion was reflected in a series of four questions to determine the following:

■ Has the start-up had a positive monthly cash flow that covers expenses and the owner-manager salaries for more than 3 months?

If the answer was yes, the activity was considered an infant business and not a start-up effort. In these cases, the respondents were thanked for their time. As this takes less than 5 minutes on the phone, they are sent a token payment of $5 and dropped from the study. Approximately one fourth (27%) of the respondents failed to meet the selection criteria and were dropped at this stage because they were considered too far advanced in the start-up or gestation phase of the entrepreneurial process. This represented the ambiguity associated with the phrase "trying to start a new business."

Initial Detailed Interviews

Among the remaining respondents, it was not possible to locate about 7%. Another 20% of the remaining group would not or could not complete the phone interview. Hence, the cooperation rate was 80% among those that could be contacted and 71% among those that were eligible, whether or not they were contacted. The complete phone interview took an average of 60 minutes to complete. At the completion of the interview, the respondents were sent a check for $25.

A similar procedure was followed with the comparison group. For the full population comparison group, only a randomly selected subset of respondents was taken from those that volunteered during the national screening to save costs. As most nascent entrepreneurs are under 55 years of age, those over 55 were sampled at one third the rate of those under 55. For the minority comparison group, all eligible respondents were incorporated in the procedure. The comparison group phone interview took about 25 minutes to complete and respondents were also sent a check for $25.

At the completion of the phone interview, all NE and CG respondents were asked to complete a brief self-administered questionnaire for a second payment of $25. Ninety-eight percent agreed to consider completing the self-administered questionnaire. After repeated postcard reminders, mailings, and phone calls, from 53% to 71% of the nascent entrepreneurs and 76% to 83% of the comparison group respondents returned the mail questionnaire. These follow-up calls were terminated 240 days after the completion of the phone interviews when it was discovered that those that returned the mail questionnaire tended to do so within 40–50 days; 75% were received within 2 months.

The initial phone interview with the nascent entrepreneurs contained a wide range of questions, which took 60 minutes to complete. The major conceptual domains included in the nascent entrepreneur and comparison group interviews are presented in Table A.2. Full detailed interview schedules are available on the project website (http://projects.isr.umich.edu/PSED).

Table A.2   Initial Interview Topics: Nascent Entrepreneur and Comparison Group

NE Schedule	CG Schedule	Topic
		Phone Interview
X		Introductory conversation on start-up, reasons, expectations
X		Start-up activities
X		Firm registration activities
X		Nature of start-up effort: legal form, economic sector, etc.
X	X (selected)	Start-up team: composition, background, and contributions
X (start-up related)	X (career related)	Social network: scope, background, and contributions
X		Start-up funding: requirements, and expectations
X		Assessment of market, competition
X		Competitive strategy
X		Knowledge, use of assistance programs
X		Future expectations for the new firm
X	X	Personal decision-making style
X	X	Current labor force activity
X	X	Work, career experiences
X	X	Residential tenure, migration (R and parents)
X	X	Respondent birth order
X	X	Family business background
X	X	Household structure
X	X	Household income
X	X	Household net worth
X		Reaction to participation
		Mail Questionnaire
X		Opportunity recognition, information gathering assessment
X	X	Entrepreneurial climate scale
X		Start-up problems
X		Economic sector, community context assessment
X		Financial management expectations
X	X	Work, training background of respondent
X		Item inventory: Reasons for starting a new firm
X	X	Assessment of risk preferences
X	X	Personal work background details
X	X	Individual problem-solving orientation
X	X	Self-assessment inventory I: Work and start-up orientation
X	X	Self-assessment inventory II: Generalized personal domains
X	X	Time-use diaries: Recent work day and day off
X	X	Work participation history, previous 11 years

Operational Outcomes:
Respondent Cooperation and Response Rates

No survey data set is perfect, but some are more complete than others. Completeness reflects the cooperation of the respondents in terms of participation in the project as well as cooperation during the interview procedure. Because of the need to collect data over an extended period of time, a high level of respondent trust and cooperation is desirable. This seems to have occurred in this project.

The basic features of the participant processing mechanism, along with indicators of respondent cooperation, are presented in Table A.3. The first column represents the results for mixed gender and female only nascent entrepreneurs, the second for the minority nascent entrepreneurs, the third for the total population comparison group, and the fourth for the minority comparison group. The first section indicates the total counts of individuals involved at the different stages of the first round data collection process, from the thousands involved in the national screening to the hundreds completing and returning the mail questionnaire. This gives some idea of the scope of the challenge of keeping track of every individual involved, whether or not he or she is in the full data set.

The second section summarizes the level of cooperation at the different stages of the project. Potential nascent entrepreneurs were more likely to volunteer for the project than those in the comparison group, 86% to 87% versus 62% to 72%. Those in the comparison group, however, were more likely to complete all of the data collection procedure. Quite simply, the reduced cooperation from the nascent entrepreneurs probably reflected the severe time pressures on those trying to start new firms, compared to those in the comparison group.

The time and effort required to obtain completed phone interviews is indicated by the time lags between the initial screening and the phone interview, which average 41 to 62 days, with a maximum of 250 days. Further, the number of contacts required to obtain the detailed phone interviews averages seven to eight for nascent entrepreneurs and four to five for the comparison group, with a maximum of 74. Twenty-five percent of the nascent entrepreneur phone interviews required more than 9 to 10 calls, and 25% of the comparison group phone interviews required more than 5 to 7 calls. The effort required to obtain the self-administered questionnaires was reflected in the lag between completion of the phone interview and receipt of the mail questionnaire, which averaged 38 to 53 days, with a maximum of 471 days.

Reactions of the respondents were measured in several ways. Nascent entrepreneurs were asked at the end of the phone interview how the experience affected their interest in starting a new firm. As shown in Table A.3, 59% to 75% said it increased their interest, 25% to 39% said it had no effect, and 1%, 8 out of 830, indicated that it reduced their interest in starting a new firm. In fact, the positive effect may cause some problems, for some could claim that participation in the project may increase interest and, because of the content of the interview schedules, enhance the business knowledge. This may improve their chances for business success. In a sense, two "research effects" may be canceling the overall impact of the project. The *Heisenberg effect* in research refers to the impact of collecting data on a phenomenon; observations may absorb energy from the process under study.

Table A.3 Indicators of Respondent Cooperation

Respondent Cooperation Indicators	NE: Mixed Gender, Female	NE: Minority Only	CG: Total Population	CG: Minority Only
Respondent Processing				
Initial national screening: Total respondents contacted	31,261	28,314	2,010	3,037
Respondents eligible to participate in detailed interviews	1,947	1,645	2,010	509
Volunteered to participate in interviews	1,705	1,423	1,242	364
Selected to participate in detailed interviews[a]	1,163	329	275	364
Eligible to participate in detailed interviews and could be located[b]	932	232	256	305
Completed detailed phone interview	669	161	223	208
Completed detailed mail questionnaire	476	86	185	158
Respondent Participation/ Response Rates				
Agree to participate in main study during the national screening interview	87%	86%	62%	72%
Percentage eligible respondents completing phone interview	72%	69%	87%	68%
Percentage willing to complete mail questionnaire	98%	98%	98%	99%
Percentage phone completes returning mail questionnaire	71%	53%	83%	76%
Time, Effort Required to Complete Data Collection				
Days: Screening interview to phone interview completion				
Average	51	41	62	33
75 percentile	65	37	72	43
Maximum	250	225	96	61

Respondent Cooperation Indicators	NE: Mixed Gender, Female	NE: Minority Only	CG: Total Population	CG: Minority Only
Contacts initiated: To phone interview completion				
Average	8	7	5	4
75 percentile	9	10	7	5
Maximum	74	35	31	14
Days: Phone interview completed to mail questionnaire received				
Average	51	46	53	38
75 percentile	55	62	46	43
Maximum	337	157	471	146
Nascent Entrepreneur Reaction to Phone Interview				
Percentage indicating phone interview:				
Increased interest in starting a business	59.4%	75%	N/A	N/A
No effect or not sure of effect	39.4%	25%	N/A	N/A
Reduced interest in starting a business	1.2%	0%	N/A	N/A
Respondent Completion of Items				
Percent completing mail questionnaire items[c]	97%	96%	97%	96%
Completion of household financial items in phone interview:				
Household income estimate, ratio value	90%	86%	92%	84%
Household income estimate, ratio or categorical value	97%	90%	98%	99%
Household net worth estimate, ratio value	78%	76%	80%	76%
Household net worth estimate, ratio or categorical value	95%	92%	98%	97%

NOTES:

a. Cost restrictions prevented all eligible individuals from being processed for detailed phone interviews and mail questionnaires. Random procedures selected those to be approached for detailed data collection.

b. Data collection shifted from screening firm to University of Wisconsin Survey Research Laboratory.

c. Useful answers, not blank, "don't know," or "refused" were tracked for 5% of the 500 items in the interview schedule; useful answers were provided by 96% to 97% of the respondents.

The *Hawthorne effect* refers to the increase in work group productivity (or other task measures) that is known to follow if the group knows it is the subject of a research effort. Hopefully, these effects offset any impact from the project and led to a neutral impact across the respondents.

A random sample of 5% of the mail questionnaire items (19 in the nascent entrepreneur questionnaire, 16 in the comparison group questionnaire) indicates that 96% of the respondents completed the items. The mail questionnaires that were returned were almost always completely filled out.

In survey research, it is well known that the hardest information to gather are details regarding household financial status. The long-running General Social Surveys (Davis & Smith, 1996) find that 97.5% of the adult respondents will report their intent to hide a defect in a used car they wanted to sell, 99.7% would report a bankruptcy, 99.4% would report a nervous breakdown and 99.6% treatment for a mental disorder, 99.5% illegal drug use, and 98.8% would report on the number of sexual partners they had in the last 12 months; but only 91.1% will report household income. The completion rates for items regarding household income and net worth in the PSED phone interview are presented at the bottom of Table A.3. From 90% to 97% of the nascent entrepreneurs provided information on both items; 97% to 99% of the comparison group members have provided the requested information. This is to be compared to the 77.7% that provided household income in the original screener completed by Market Facts or the 76.4% to 82.8% in the 1966 National Household Education Survey (U.S. Department of Education, 1997, p. 47). In terms of respondent cooperation in survey research in the United States at the end of the twentieth century, the PSED ranks among the best.

Why were the cooperation rates and interview schedule completion rates so high? A great deal of effort, involving the interviewers themselves, was devoted to modifying and adjusting the phone procedures and wording so that the entire research staff felt comfortable with the project and the procedures. Their commitment to the project and confidence in the interview procedure was transmitted to the respondent who, in turn, reciprocated with cooperation and trust. This is, obviously, not a trivial accomplishment and reflects the sustained dedication of the University of Wisconsin Survey Research Laboratory staff.

Follow-up Data Collection

The critical dependent variable associated with the project is the tracking of the start-up initiatives to determine the outcome of these efforts.

This longitudinal study was threatened when the project was to be transferred to a new institution. In the midst of the first 12-month follow-up data collection, the University of Wisconsin made an administrative decision to close the Wisconsin Survey Research Laboratory. With financial support from the Ewing Marion Kauffman Foundation, the entire data collection mechanism, all records identifying individual respondents, and all data files were transferred to the University of Michigan's Institute for Social Research (ISR) under the supervision of Richard Curtin. Although both units focus on creating clean data and high response rates, the operational procedures are slightly different.

The timing and responsibility for these efforts is presented in Table A.4. The comparison groups are omitted as no effort was made to follow their progress after the initial interview. This information makes clear, once again, that the nascent entrepreneur minority sample was initiated 12 months following the mixed gender and female cohorts; no third follow-up is anticipated for this subsample.

Table A.4   Follow-up Data Collection: Timing and Responsibility

	NE: Mixed Gender	NE: Female	NE: Minority
Initial Data Collection			
Dates of data collection	July 1998 to April 1999	Sept. 1998 to Dec. 1998	July 1999 to Jan. 2000
Responsible agency	U. of Wis. Survey Lab.	U. of Wis. Survey Lab.	U. of Wis. Survey Lab.
First Follow-Up:			
Dates of data collection	Sept. 1999 to March 2000	Sept. 1999 to March 2000	August 2001 to Dec. 2001
Responsible agency	U. of Wis. Survey Lab.	U. of Wis. Survey Lab.	U. of Mich. Inst. for Soc. Research
Second Follow-Up:			
Dates of data collection	April 2001 to Dec. 2001	April 2001 to Dec. 2001	May 2003 to Sept. 2003
Responsible agency	U. of Mich. Inst. for Soc. Research	U. of Mich. Inst. for Soc. Research	U. of Mich. Inst. for Soc. Research
Third Follow-Up:			
Dates of data collection	May 2003 to Sept. 2003	May 2003 to Sept. 2003	None planned
Responsible agency	U. of Mich. Inst. for Soc. Research	U. of Mich. Inst. for Soc. Research	None planned

Being able to contact a willing respondent 12, 24, and 36 months after the first interview is critical for successful follow-up data collection. Several features to facilitate cooperation were included in the study. At the completion of the phone interview, each nascent entrepreneur was asked for the name and phone number of a "friend or relative that could help us locate you." In addition, a "contact postcard" was sent to all nascent entrepreneurs 6 months following their first interview. Upon receipt, the respondents were asked to confirm their present mailing address and telephone number. If these had changed, they were asked to provide the new information on the "mail-back" portion of the two-part postcard.

Follow-up Interview Schedules

The follow-up data collection included both phone and mail components. Most critical was the single item that specifies the current status of the start-up effort. Previous studies indicate that four alternatives are commonly reported (Carter, Gartner, & Reynolds, 1996; Reynolds & White, 1997, p. 68):

- Active start-up, continued efforts to implement a new firm.
- Dormant start-up, no current efforts underway, but start-up has not been abandoned.
- Abandoned start-up, not successful and no further efforts are expected.
- Going concern, the start-up has become an infant business.

A different set of questions was asked depending upon the current status of the start-up effort. All respondents, however, received the same self-administered mail questionnaire, which was a reduced form of the mail questionnaire used in the initial data collection.

The nascent entrepreneur interview completed at 12 months is complicated by the different outcomes commonly reported. Table A.5 provides an overview of the material covered for each of the four options. Those that report a dormant start-up effort or one that has been abandoned (all members of the start-up team have quit working on the start-up) had a much shorter interview that those reporting infant firms or an active start-up effort.

Two other issues complicated the follow-up interview.[1] First, a small proportion of start-up efforts changed the focus of their business. This was, however, relatively easy to accommodate in the follow-up phone interview by asking appropriate questions about any change in activity before continuing with the rest of the interview.

But there were a few cases among the half of the start-up efforts that were team initiatives in which the original respondent was no longer involved in the start-up but others on the team were still working on creating a business, sometimes with success. This occurrence reflected a major conceptual issue for the project: whether it is the study of (a) individuals trying to start firms or (b) firm start-ups, located by sampling individuals. (The average team size is slightly more than 2.) The procedure was to ask the respondent for the name and phone number of a current member of the start-up team so that information on the firm may be obtained from an active participant. While the project was generally successful in terms of getting the data on "replacement informants," a lack of funds precluded any attempt to contact these individuals. These items were eventually dropped from the third follow-up interviews in year 2003.

Follow-up Data Collection: Operational Results

The combined results for the first follow-up interviews with nascent entrepreneurs are shown in Table A.6. First round follow-ups for the mixed gender and

Table A.5   Interview Topics: Nascent Entrepreneur Follow-Up Interviews

Infant Firm	Active Start-up	Dormant Start-up	Quit Start-up	Topic
				Phone Interview
X	X	X	X	How decision made on current status of start-up
X			X	Critical events affecting decision
X	X			Start-up activities pursued since first interview
X	X			Firm registration activities
X	X			Nature of start-up effort: legal form, economic sector, etc.
X	X			Start-up team: Changes in composition, background, and contributions
X	X			Social network: Changes in scope, background, and contributions
X	X			Current employment, sales
X	X			Market, geographic concentration of customers
X	X			Future expectations for the new firm
X	X			Assessment of market, competition
X	X			Competitive strategy
X	X			Knowledge, use of assistance programs
X				Financial structure of the new firm
X				Current value (net worth) of the new firm
X				Equity value of R in the new firm, future plans
	X	X		Additional resources required for start-up
	X	X	X	Probability start-up will become infant firm
			X	Advice to others starting new firms
X	X	X	X	Current experience with other start-ups
X	X	X	X	Current labor force participation activities
X	X	X	X	Household income
X				Proportion household income from new firm
X	X	X	X	Household net worth
X				Proportion household net worth from new firm
				Mail Questionnaire
X	X	X	X	Opportunity recognition, information gathering assessment
X	X	X	X	Entrepreneurial climate scale
X	X	X	X	Economic sector, community context assessment
X	X	X	X	Self-assessment inventory I: Work and start-up orientation
X	X	X	X	Self-assessment inventory II: Generalized personal domains
X	X	X	X	Time-use diaries: Recent work day and day off

female oversample cohorts was completed by the University of Wisconsin Survey Research Laboratory, whereas the first-round follow-ups for the minority oversample cohort were completed by the University of Michigan Survey Research Center.

Table A.6   First Follow-up Outcome Summary

Outcome	Case Count	Percentage
Respondent reports an operating business	187	22.5
Respondent still active in start-up process	192	23.1
Respondent inactive in start-up process but expects to "get to it some day"	123	14.8
Respondent has quit or disengaged	113	13.6
Cannot locate or no useful information obtained	215	25.9
Total	830	100.0

It is, of course, desirable to reduce the number that cannot be located, about 26% or 215 individuals in this situation. These cases are a combination of those who could not be found to get a useful response (usually about 10%, three deaths were reported) and those that did not respond—usually by delaying the interview (by constantly rescheduling the interview appointment until the field period was terminated).

The results of the first and second follow-up efforts are combined and presented in Table A.7. The first set of columns summarizes the results of both initial follow-ups. The top section is the mixed gender and female oversamples, the middle section the minority oversample, and the bottom section combines the counts for all samples. These are unweighted raw case counts. The right columns summarize the results of the second follow-up of the mixed gender and female oversample.

The complexity of the table is due to the second follow-up effort and the phenomena itself. The University of Michigan made an effort to contact respondents not located in the initial follow-up by the University of Wisconsin. They were successful for 46 out of 168 of these cases ("no information" located in sections A:4 and B). On the other hand, they were not able to locate 62 respondents who completed the initial follow-up (section D). Further, it is of some interest that 26 of those reporting a going business in the first follow-up indicated in the second follow-up (row F) they were no longer involved, and another 5 reported that some part of a going business had been sold (section A:1). Further, no effort was made in the second follow-up to contact those 89 who reported quitting or disengagement in the first follow-up (row C).

This assessment demonstrates the complexity of the entrepreneurial process. It is clear that successful tracking of the outcomes of start-up efforts will require careful and dedicated survey research professionals. Fortunately, such individuals have been involved in the PSED.

Table A.7   First and Second Follow-up Outcome Summary

Category	Initial Follow-up Effort	Count	Second Follow-up Effort	Count	Count
	Mixed Gender and Female Samples		**Mixed Gender and Female Samples**		
A:1	Operating Business		Operating Business	105	
		110	Some Parts Sold	5	110
A:2	Active Start-up		Operating Business	45	
			Active Start-up	49	
		118	Inactive Start-up	24	118
A:3	Inactive Start-up		Operating Business	5	
			Active Start-up	12	
		46	Inactive Start-up	29	46
A:4	No Information		Operating Business	13	
			Active Start-up	7	
		27	Inactive Start-up	7	27
B	Active Start-up	17	Quit/Disengaged	17	
	Inactive Start-up	33	Quit/Disengaged	33	
	No Information	19	Quit/Disengaged	19	69
C	Quit/Disengaged	89	No Attempt to Contact	89	89
D	Operating Business	27	No Information	27	
	Active Start-up	21	No Information	21	
	Inactive Start-up	14	No Information	14	62
E	No Information	122	No Information	122	122
F	Operating Business		One Year, Firm Sold	4	
		26	One Year, Firm Discontinued	22	26
	Total Cases	669	Total Cases		669
	Minority Only				
	Operating Business	24			
	Active Start-up	36			
	Inactive Start-up	30			
	Quit/Disengaged	24			

(Continued)

Table A.7 (Continued)

Category	Initial Follow-up Effort	Count	Second Follow-up Effort	Count	Count
	No Information	47			
	Total Cases	161			
	Total Nascent Sample		**Mixed Gender and Female Samples**		
	Operating Business	187	Operating Business		173
			Going Firm Sold, Discontinued		26
	Active Start-up	192	Active Start-up		68
	Inactive Start-up	123	Inactive Start-up		60
	Quit/Disengaged	113	Quit/Disengaged		69
	No Information	215	No Information		273
	Total Cases	830	Total Cases		669

Operational Outcomes: Call-Backs and Prevalence Rates

It is quite clear, from this and other studies, that those trying to start new firms are among the busiest people in the country. Most are young adults in mid career with jobs and families, focusing on creating a new business. It would be no surprise to find they are hard to reach on the phone. The screening firm maintained a record of the number of calls required to complete an interview, and normally a potential household was dropped after three calls. However, the firm guaranteed their clients 1,000 cases per sample. When interview yields dropped, they would increase the call-backs to assure the quota of 1,000 respondents per wave; this was more cost-effective than drawing an additional sample on short notice. This operational data was provided on 53 of the samples. The prevalence rate of nascent entrepreneurs could be determined as a function of the number of calls made to complete the interview. The results are presented in Table A.8.

The results indicate that if all sample points were routinely subjected to a 10 call-back operational criteria, the nascent entrepreneur prevalence rate would be somewhat higher, perhaps by as much as 20%. Although rare for commercial market research firms, call-back standards of 20, 30, or even higher are common in academic- and policy-oriented survey research projects. This pattern suggests that all prevalence rate estimates may be conservative.

Table A.8   Calls to Complete and Nascent Entrepreneur Prevalence Rates

Calls to Complete the Interview	Percentage of the Sample	Number of Cases NE Prevalencerate	Number per 100 Respondents
One–two	89.9	47,998	6.17
Three–four	9.2	4,910	6.85
Five–ten	0.9	464	7.46
Total	100.0	53,372	6.24

NOTE: One/two versus three/ten difference is statistically significant at the 0.03 level.

On the other hand, once they start an interview, nascent entrepreneurs are hard to stop, as some talked for up to 90 minutes about their favorite subject, their new business.

Commentary

The procedures developed in this research program to locate and identify those active in the business start-up or entrepreneurial process have had very wide applications. The original panel design has been implemented in Argentina (de Rearte, Lanari, & Atucha, 1998), Canada (Menzies, Gasse, Diochon, & Garand, 2002), Greece and the Netherlands (Wolters, 2000), Norway (Alsos & Kolvereid, 1998) and Sweden (Delmar & Davidsson, 2000). In addition, this procedure has been the technical core for a large-scale, cross-national assessment of entrepreneurial activity. The Global Entrepreneurship Monitor (GEM) project has modified and extended the procedure to encompass identification of those in both the start-up process and managing new firms up to 42 months old (Reynolds, Hay, & Camp, 1999; Reynolds, Hay, Bygrave, Camp, & Autio, 2000; Reynolds, Camp, Bygrave, Autio, & Hay, 2001; Reynolds, Bygrave, Autio, Cox, & Hay, 2002). The procedure has been improved with the addition of a third screening item: respondents are asked if they are owner-managers of a going business. It was found in the PSED that a substantial proportion that considered themselves a start-up were actually operating a going business and did not qualify as nascent entrepreneurs. In a similar fashion, a substantial number of those who identified themselves as owner-managers of a going business in the GEM surveys turned out to have never paid any salaries and were clearly in the start-up phase (Reynolds & Hunt, 2001).

The use of the PSED screening procedures as part of the GEM project has led to the realization that start-up activity has reached an unprecedented global scope. As of 2002, close to half a billion adults in a world of 6 billion may be actively engaged in starting new businesses (Reynolds et al., 2002). The total amount of human effort and financial resources devoted to entrepreneurship is already enormous and is growing each day. Such an outcome was never anticipated when the initial design was being developed in Wisconsin in 1992.

Notes

1. The Swedish National Panel Study of Business Start-Ups completed a 6-month follow-up prior to the design of the 12-month follow-up for the U.S. study. The material provided by Per Davidsson and Henrick Hall, (Jönköping International Business School, Jönköping, Sweden) was very useful in developing the follow-up phone interview schedule.

References

Alsos, G. A., & Kolvereid, L. (1998). The business gestation process of novice, serial and parallel business founders. *Entrepreneurship Theory and Practice, 22*(4), 101–114.

Carter, N. M., Brush, C. G., Aldrich, H. E., Greene, P., & Katz, J. A. (1998). *The influence of founder's gender in business start-ups.* Proposal to the National Science Foundation, Grant SBR-9809841.

Carter, N. M., Gartner, W. B., & Reynolds, P. D. (1996). Exploring start-up event sequences. *Journal of Business Venturing, 11*(3), 151–166.

Curtin, R. (1982). Indicators of consumer behavior: The University of Michigan survey of consumers. *Public Opinion Quarterly 46,* 340–362.

Davis, J. A., & Smith, T. W. (1996). *General social surveys, 1972–1996: Cumulative code book* [National Data Program for the Social Sciences Series, no. 15]. Chicago: National Opinion Research Center.

Delmar, F., & Davidsson, P. (2000). Where do they come from? Prevalence and characteristics of nascent entrepreneurs. *Entrepreneurship and Regional Development, 12,* 1–23.

de Rearte, A. G., Lanari, E., & Atucha, P. A. A. J. (1998, September). El proceso de creacion de empresas; Abordaje methodologico y primeros resultados de un studio regional. Argentina: Universidad Nacional de Mar del Plata.

Greene, P. G., Carter, N. M., Reynolds, P. D., Aldrich, H. E., & Stearns, T. M. (1999). The influence of founder's race in the start-up process. [Grant SBR-9905255] Proposal to the National Science Foundation.

Menzies, T. V., Gasse, Y., Diochon, M., & Garand, D. (2002). *Nascent entrepreneurs in Canada: An empirical study.* San Juan, PR: ICSB 47th World Conference.

Palit, C., & Reynolds, P. D. (1993). *A network sampling procedure for estimating the prevalence of nascent entrepreneurs.* Proceedings of the American Statistical Association International Conference on Establishment Surveys, pp. 657–661.

Reynolds, P. D. (1997). Who starts new firms? Linear additive versus interaction based models. *Small Business Economics, 9,* 449–462.

Reynolds, P. D. (2000). National panel study of U.S. business start-ups: Background and methodology. In J. A. Katz (Ed.), *Advances in entrepreneurship, firm emergence and growth: Vol. 4* (pp. 153–228). Stamford, CT: JAI.

Reynolds, P. D., Bygrave, W. D., Autio, E., Cox, L., & Hay, M. (2002). *Global entrepreneurship monitor: 2002 executive report.* Kansas City, MO: Kauffman Center for Entrepreneurial Leadership.

Reynolds, P. D., Camp, M. S., Bygrave, W. D., Autio, E., & Hay, M. (2001). *Global entrepreneurship monitor: 2001 executive report.* Kansas City, MO: Kauffman Center for Entrepreneurial Leadership.

Reynolds, P. D., Hay, M., Bygrave, W. D., Camp, M. S., & Autio, E. (2000). *Global entrepreneurship monitor: 2000 executive report.* Kansas City, MO: Kauffman Center for Entrepreneurial Leadership.

Reynolds, P. D., Hay, M., & Camp, M. (1999). *Global entrepreneurship monitor: 1999 executive report.* Kansas City, MO: Kauffman Center for Entrepreneurial Leadership.

Reynolds, P. D., & Hunt, S. (2001). *Global entrepreneurship monitor: Data collection-operations manual: Vol. IIA Adult population surveys* [working paper]. London: London Business School.

Reynolds, P. D., & White, S. B. (1993). *Wisconsin's entrepreneurial climate study.* Milwaukee, WI: Marquette University Center for the Study of Entrepreneurship.

Reynolds, P. D., & White, S. B. (1997). *The entrepreneurial process: Economic growth, men, women, and minorities.* Westport, CT: Quorum Books.

Sudman, S., Sirken, M. G., & Cowan, C. D. (1988). Sampling rate and elusive populations. *Science, 240,* 991–996.

U.S. Department of Education, National Center for Education Statistics. (1997). *Unit and item response rates, weighting, and imputation procedures in the 1996 National Household Education Survey,* [working paper no. 97–40 by J. Montaquila & J. M. Brick. Project officer, Kathryn Chandler]. Washington, DC.

Wolters, T. (2000). Nascent entrepreneurship in the Netherlands: A glance behind the scenes of business start-ups. In P. Zevenbergen (Ed.), *Entrepreneurship in the Netherlands: Opportunities and threats to nascent entrepreneurs* (Chapter 2, pp. 3–16). Zoetermeer, NL: EIM Small Business Research and Consultancy.

Appendix B

*Data Documentation, Data
Preparation, and Weights*

Richard T. Curtin

Paul D. Reynolds

T he analysis of data from the Panel Study of Entrepreneurial Dynamics (PSED) requires a good deal of information about the design of the research. The wording of questions and how the responses were coded is just as important as how to effectively combine the answers from the different samples while preserving the confidentiality and identity of the respondents. Whereas the prior appendix focused on the sampling procedures and interview schedules, this appendix details the procedures used to collect and document the data, the development of case weights, and the procedures used to protect the confidentiality and identity of respondents.

Without a theoretical foundation, mere numbers are meaningless. Most of the descriptive and theoretical questions addressed in the PSED require multiple questions to assess. As a result, the individual questions must be interpreted within the context in which they were asked, including both preceding and subsequent questions in each sequence. Although all responses were translated into a numerical code for analysis purposes, some codes have explicit meaning—say dollars or age in years—while other coded values were assigned by convention, say "1" for a "Yes" response. Even if the coded values do not have an explicit meaning, the simple tabulation of responses will be misleading unless the responses are properly weighted to account for the differences in sample designs and nonresponse. The proper use of weighted data is critical for developing inferences regarding the population represented by the samples.

Types of Questionnaires

There were seven basic questionnaires associated with different parts of the project:

1. *Screening Questionnaire:* A short set of questions used to locate potential nascent entrepreneurs or candidates for the comparison groups

2. *Initial Nascent Entrepreneur Questionnaire:* Detailed questions asked in phone interview schedules of all eligible nascent entrepreneurs

3. *Initial Self-Administered Questionnaire:* Mail interview schedules sent to all nascent entrepreneurs that completed the phone interview and agreed to complete the questionnaire

4. *Comparison Group Questionnaire:* Initial phone interviews conducted with the comparison group respondents; a revised version of the nascent entrepreneur phone interview more appropriate for those not starting a business

5. *Comparison Group Self-Administered Questionnaire:* Mail questionnaires used with the comparison group respondents; a revised version of the nascent entrepreneur mail interview schedule more appropriate for those not starting a business

6. *Follow-up Nascent Entrepreneur Questionnaire:* Phone interview schedules used in subsequent follow-ups with the nascent entrepreneurs

7. *Follow-up Self-Administered Questionnaire:* Mail interview schedule used for all nascent entrepreneurs that completed subsequent interviews: a reduced version of the interview schedule provided to nascent entrepreneurs in the initial interviews

There are two forms of the phone interviews. The Computer Assisted Telephone Interview (CATI) schedules are relatively complicated computer programs using programming syntax. To facilitate analysis, a user-friendly form was prepared that looks like a paper and pencil interview and attempts to reflect all the features of the CATI version. The self-administered mail questionnaires are less complex and are only in one format.

Another critical document is the Codebook, which represents a compilation of the initial and follow-up data in one 450-page document. The Codebook provides a description of all variables in the data sets, the valid responses to each item, and the numeric values assigned to each response code.

These materials are much too lengthy to include in this handbook. Copies of the CATI phone interview schedules, the self-completed questionnaires, and the Codebook are available on the project Website (http://projects.isr.umich.edu/PSED) or on a CD provided by the sponsoring organizations.

Most serious researchers will produce a printed copy of the Codebook and interview schedules for reference; they fit easily in ring binders and two-sided printing is very useful for reducing the bulk. A separate binder for each facilitates simultaneous cross-referencing—reviewing the item in the interview schedule and then considering the pattern of the responses in the Codebook.

Interview Schedules

There are two types of interview schedules used in this project. The first is a phone interview during which a trained interviewer engages in a carefully constructed interaction with the respondent. These are completed with a CATI procedure during which questions appear on a computer monitor and are read to the respondent by the interviewer who then enters the responses directly into the computer. The questions asked of each respondent are adjusted based on their responses to prior questions. The computer program automatically performs consistency checks and provides immediate feedback to the interviewer in the form of clarification questions or probes (additional questions to resolve any ambiguity in the answer) so any inconsistencies can be resolved.

The second type of interview schedule is a self-completed questionnaire that was mailed to each respondent.

The screening interview is provided in Exhibit B.1 as an example of a phone interview schedule. The actual interview schedule is a sophisticated and complicated computer program. This version has been created to guide those planning to analyze the data. Most of the items are related to the personal and household situation of the respondent. Only seven questions are related to the PSED screening procedure, starting with item 1 (variable label BSTART): "Are you, alone or with others, now trying to start a new business?"

Note the important skip pattern that follows item 2 (BJOBST). This indicates that only if a respondent says "Yes" to either or both items 1 and 2 (BSTART and BJOBST) will they continue with item 3 (OWNER). If they say "No" to both questions, the program will exit the PSED section and the interviewer will be instructed to ask about the next topic of the interview. Those that stay in the section are then asked about ownership (OWNER) of the start-up and if they have been active, in the past 12 months (SUACTS). If they will not be owners or have not been active the interviewer exits the section and the respondent is not considered eligible for the detailed PSED interview. Those that qualify are given two chances to volunteer for the project (VOLUNT1, VOLUNT2) and those that agree to participate are asked to provide their first name only (NAMEVOL). All respondents, however, are asked the standard set of a dozen sociodemographic items regarding age, educational attainment, household structure, ethnic background, and so forth.

An example of one page from the self-administered questionnaire is presented in Exhibit B.2. These items were provided to all nascent entrepreneurs and all those in the comparison groups. The specific examples are concerned with preferences for different types of businesses, those with more certain payout but less risk versus those with higher risk and payouts. This is followed by items related to the previous work experiences of the respondent. Because a wide range of respondents with very diverse educational backgrounds must be able to read and interpret these items, substantial effort was devoted to making them as simple and as direct as possible.

Exhibit B.1 Example of Phone-Administered Interview Schedule: Screening (Variable labels in brackets)

[BSTART] 1. Are you, alone or with others, now trying to start a new business?

Yes...1
No 2
Don't know X
Refused...R

[BJOBST] 2. Are you, alone or with others, now trying to start a new business or new venture for your employer? An effort that is part of your job assignment?

Yes 1
No..2
Don't know...X
Refused...R

ASK QU. 3 IF "YES" TO QU. 1 OR QU. 2; OTHERWISE, EXIT INTERVIEW.

[OWNER] 3. Will you own all, part, or none of this new business?
(DO NOT READ LIST. ENTER SINGLE RESPONSE.)
All 1
Part 2
None 3   ] → **(EXIT INTERVIEW)**
Don't know X
Refused ....R

[SUACTS] 4. In the past twelve months, have you done anything to help start this new business, such as looking for equipment or a location, organizing a start-up team, working on a business plan, beginning to save money, or any other activity that would help launch a new business?

Yes 1
No...2   ] → **(EXIT INTERVIEW)**
Don't know...X
Refused ....R

[VOLUNT1] 5. A national study of those starting new businesses is being conducted through the University of Wisconsin. Those eligible will receive a cash payment. May they contact you?
Yes..1   ] → **(SKIP TO QUESTION 7)**
No 2
Don't know X
Refused..R

[VOLUNT2] 6. You need not participate, but those that have find it interesting and very useful. Can the University of Wisconsin researchers contact you and tell you what is involved? You can always turn them down.
Yes..1
No 2
Don't know X   → **(EXIT INTERVIEW)**
Refused..R

Exhibit B.2   Sample Page from Self-Administered Questionnaire

[NAMEVOL] 7. . . . May I have your first name only please?

H9. Consider two types of new businesses. Assuming you are the sole owner, which situation would you prefer? [CHECK ONE BOX ONLY]

　　1.　ALPHA - A business that would provide a good living, but with little risk of failure, and little likelihood of making you a millionaire

　　2.　BETA - A business that was much more likely to make you a millionaire but had a much higher chance of going bankrupt

H10. If you could obtain more information to make a choice between businesses ALPHA and BETA, how important would each of the following be?
[CIRCLE ONE FOR EACH ROW]

1 = Unimportant　　　　　**2 = Somewhat important**　　　　**3 = Very important**

a. The chances of going bankrupt for both ALPHA and BETA	1	2	3
b. The chances of making millions for both ALPHA and BETA	1	2	3
c. The exact amount of earnings if ALPHA and BETA were successful	1	2	3
d. The time and effort required to manage ALPHA and BETA	1	2	3
e. The opinion of family and friends about this choice	1	2	3
f. The experience of those managing businesses like ALPHA and BETA	1	2	3
g. Your feelings about the type of business activity represented by ALPHA and BETA	1	2	3

I1. Since beginning your work career, how many times have you resigned your job to take a new position . . .

　　a.　. . . with a new job lined up?　　　_____ times
　　b.　. . . without a new job lined up?　　_____ times

I2. The last time you had a job working for someone else or in an established organization, what was your job title?

_____

I3. What did you do?

_____

_____

I4. How long did you have this job? _____ years　　_____ months

I5. Following the chain of command, how many people were between you and the Chief Executive Officer? If you were the CEO, write "0."　　　　　　　　　_____ people

I6. How many people worked for this organization?　　　_____ people

Codebook Presentations

The beginning of all analysis should start with an examination of the unweighted frequency distribution of the variables under consideration. For example, the answers of 64,622 respondents approached in the screening process to the two basic items are presented in Exhibit B.3. This data is unweighted and combines the responses of all screened respondents, including those selected for the comparison groups. These questions were answered by almost all the respondents, the interviewers were instructed to get a "Yes" or "No" answer if at all possible. The few that gave "Don't know" and "Refuse" responses were recoded to "No" responses; thus all answers in the data set are either "Yes" or "No." This practice of coding "Don't know" and "refuse" as "No" was confined to the screening data set as the other databases include specific codes for these responses.

Exhibit B.3   Codebook Variable Example: Initial Screening Items

BSTART	Are you, alone or with others, now trying to start a new business?	
Frequency	Code	Response
4,465	1.	Yes
60,157	2.	No

BJOBST	Are you, alone or with others, now trying to start a new business or new venture for your employer? An effort that is part of your job assignment?	
Frequency	Code	Response
2,339	1.	Yes
62,283	2.	No

An example from the self-administered questionnaire, item QH9, as provided in the Codebook is presented in Exhibit B.4. The letter "Q" has been added to the variable label to indicate the first wave of data collection. In this case, a total of 6 respondents did not provide useful information on this item compared to 899 that were able to answer the question. Again, both nascent entrepreneurs and comparison group respondents are combined in this unweighted presentation.

To facilitate comparisons across the different waves of data collection—and consistent with the practice followed in other longitudinal studies—the answers to the same questions asked at different times are presented together. For example, respondents classified as nascent entrepreneurs were asked a number of questions about what they had done to get ready to start the business, including the question shown in Exhibit B.5, which asks about saving money to invest in the business.

Exhibit B.4   Codebook Variable Example: Mail Questionnaire Item

QH9	Consider two types of new businesses. Assuming you are the sole owner, which situation would you prefer?	
Frequency	Code	Variable
744	1.	ALPHA - A business that would provide a good living, but with little risk of failure, and little likelihood of making you a millionaire.
155	2.	BETA - A business that was much more likely to make you a millionaire but had a much higher chance of going bankrupt.
6	9.	NA (No answer)

Exhibit B.5   Codebook Variable Example: Response Categories Across Waves

Wave 1	Wave 2	Wave 3	Wave 4	Variable	
Q139	R596	S596	T596	Are you now saving money to invest in this business?	
574	37	15		1.	Yes
253	62	47		2.	No
2	0	0		8.	DK (Don't know)
1	0	0		9.	NA (Not available)

If they said "Yes" at any point, they were asked when this saving behavior began and were not asked the question in subsequent interviews. The results, taken from the most recent Codebook, indicate that 830 were asked this question in Wave 1 and 574 answered "Yes." Only those that did not say "Yes" in Wave 1 were asked this question a second time in Wave 2. Apparently 99 could be located and interviewed in Wave 2, another 37 said "Yes" and 62 said "No." Of the 62 that were contacted for the third interview, another 15 said "Yes." (The Wave 2 and Wave 3 respondents may not be the same 62, as efforts are made at each wave to locate those that could not be contacted in the previous efforts.) Such a presentation has obvious advantages for understanding the response patterns associated with each item.

Some items in the phone interview and self-administered questionnaire involve a spontaneous comment or statement from the respondent. Less than a dozen are asked of all respondents and most have been coded. These might be the type of business being created, the person's primary occupation, or perhaps the country of birth. These are reviewed by a coding team and numbers assigned to represent different responses. The Codebook provides the number/answer correspondence for these open-ended items—as well as any issues that come up in the coding. For example, the type of business activity is coded as one of over 500 Standard Industry Classifications (SIC), and respondent occupation is classified as one of over 500 U.S. Bureau of Labor Statistics Standard Occupational Codes.

A large number, however, represent comments made when a respondent considered the responses to a fixed choice item as not appropriate to their situation. In such cases, the interviewer entered a sentence or two describing their reaction. Most of these "other" responses have not been coded.

Overview of Data Sets

There are two basic PSED data sets. The first data set contains the data collected in the screening interviews to locate eligible individuals for either the nascent entrepreneur or comparison group. The second data set contains the detailed information collected in the phone and self-administered interviews with nascent entrepreneurs and the comparison groups for all waves in the panel data set.

Screening Data Set

The screening data set contains information on 64,622 individuals. These interviews consist mostly of demographic items and the items used to determine if the respondent was a nascent entrepreneur and, hence, qualified for inclusion. In addition, because the state and county of each respondent is known, a number of county characteristics have been added to each record to provide a harmonized description of the context in which the respondent made decisions either to create a new business or not to get involved. The number and source of variables for the screening data file are provided in Table B.1.

Table B.1   Source and Count of Screening File Variables

Source	Count
Specific questions asked of respondents for project	6
Transforms and recoding of PSED items	10
Sociodemographic variables asked by research firm	18
Transforms and recoding of sociodemographic items	17
Variables characterizing the county of residence	26
Transforms and recoding of county characteristics	26
Variables for operational purposes: Identification number, weights, number of calls to complete, date of interview, sample cohort, etc.	17
Total number of variables	120

The result is a single data file that has 64,622 records and 120 variables for each case. Confidential information, first name, and the phone number have been deleted to maintain anonymity. All values for all variables are numbers, some representing specific responses (Yes or No), others ratio values (population density of the county).

The two most critical variables in the data set are the unique identification number assigned to all 64,622 respondents in the screening interviews (WAVEID02) and the unique identification number assigned to all 1,261 respondents on which additional data was obtained (RESPID).

Detailed Data Set

The detailed data set is substantially more complicated, as it reflects respondents from five different samples, data collected from two different procedures (phone and mail), as well as data collected for up to four different points in time using the same questions. The result is 3,910 variables (three data collection periods through the second follow-up) on 1,261 individuals. The data set begins with the 117 variables from the screening interviews, and additional variables are added as new data sets and variable transformations are completed.

For example, it turned out that the gender of many respondents completing the initial detailed interviews was either ambiguous or incorrect. The gender appeared to have changed from the screening interview to the first detailed interview or was recorded incorrectly. As a result, considerable effort by Professor Nancy Carter was required to clarify all gender ambiguous cases—often reviewing the operational comments of the interviewer (discussed in Chapter 2). This revised gender variable is called NCGENDER. Although USGENDER is accurate and appropriate for analysis of the screening data set, NCGENDER would be the preferred indicator for the detailed data set. Similar problems developed with specification of ethnic background—the classification from the screening interview might be different from that in the initial detailed data collection. A careful review and correction of discrepancies has been completed by Professor Patricia Greene; her work is reflected in the variable PGRACE (Chapter 3).

Further complications developed with regard to the exact nature of the start-up activity. The details about the ownership of the potential new firm assembled in the initial interview indicated a substantial proportion of the ownership would be by some other entity than a natural person, for example, ownership by a different operating business or a financial institution. Careful examination of the ownership patterns (done by Professors Kelly Shaver and Paul Reynolds) led to the creation of a variable, AUTONSU, which reflects the nature and extent of major ownership patterns among the start-up efforts, as presented in Exhibit B.6. The discovery that only 721 of 830 start-ups (or 87%) will be wholly owned by natural persons is an important finding in its own right.

Exhibit B.6   Codebook Variable Example: Constructed Variable—Start-up Type

Wave 1	Wave 2	Wave 3	Wave 4		Variable
AUTONSU					AUTONOMOUS START-UP SCALE
721				1.	100% owned by natural persons, no nonperson ownership
7				2.	Less than 50% nonperson-owned: Independent start-up
52				3.	Less than 50% nonperson-owned: Franchise, multilevel marketing start-up
43				4.	Less than 50% nonperson-owned: Existing business will be partial owner
3				5.	Over 50% nonperson-owned
4				6.	100% nonperson-owned
431				9.	Comparison Group
1,261					Total

Following the initial screening interviews, detailed data was collected from respondents on four different occasions. Each occasion involved a different set (phone and self-completed mail) of interview schedules. Because many of the same items were asked of the respondents in different data collection periods, the first letter of the variable names have been adjusted to provide a guide to the data collection administration. The mixed-gender and the female oversample are represented by the initial "Q" and follow-up data collection efforts by the letters "R," "S," and "T". However, for the minority oversample, the original interview schedules were used for the initial detailed data collection ("Q"), but the first follow-up was done with the interview schedule used for the second follow-ups with the other cohorts ("S"); the second minority follow-up is completed with the third follow-up of the other two samples in which variable names begin with "T." These allocations are presented in Table B.2.

The major consequence of this is that assessments that combine follow-up data from the mixed-gender and female cohorts and the minority cohort require a reallocation of minority data in a standardized form to produce a new set of variables. For most variables this can be easily done by changing the variable labels for the minority cohort to match the other waves (rename "S503" as "R503"; rename "T503" as "S503"). The items and response frequencies should be checked before these changes are implemented to make sure the wording and response alternatives are the same for both administrations of the questions.

Table B.2   Variable Names First Letter and Follow-up Stage by Cohort

PSED Cohort	Initial Detailed Data Collection	First Follow-up	Second Follow-up	Third Follow-up
Mixed Gender	Q	R	S	T
Female Only	Q	R	S	T
Minority Oversample	Q	S	T	N/A
Mixed-Gender Comparison	Q	N/A	N/A	N/A
Minority Comparison	Q	N/A	N/A	N/A

Representative Samples and Respondent Weights

The design of the sample is based on two critical factors: the definition of the population of interest and the method by which elements in that population are selected. The definition of the population needs to be precise but could encompass nearly any collection of elements. Although this study is ultimately concerned with the population of nascent entrepreneurs, there is no comprehensive listing of such people that could be used to exhaustively define the population. Other alternative lists, such as new firms listed in commercial credit-rating registries (such as Dun & Bradstreet) were not suitable for the purposes of this project since only established firms are eligible to be included. The method selected was to define the population of all adults and then from that population precisely define the eligibility criterion for nascent entrepreneurs.

Controlled selection of population elements by probability methods is required for representative samples. Probability sampling designs require that each member of the population have a known nonzero probability of selection. An important characteristic of probability sampling is that it allows relatively few observations to generate the same results that would be obtained if interviews were conducted with the entire population. The match will not be perfect, but the accuracy of probability samples can be statistically assessed. Although members of the comparison groups were drawn in proportion to the entire population, the probability of selection for nascent entrepreneurs was the product of the overall selection probability times the probability of selection among the eligible nascent entrepreneurs.

Given a representative sample, the results drawn from the survey can be generalized to the entire population. For example, if the typical new firm is established about 12 months following the beginning of the start-up process, this finding can be generalized to the entire population of nascent firms. Importantly, a representative sample allows the calculation of standard errors of the estimates and confidence intervals. For example, assume that a representative sample of 2,000 is interviewed from a population of 200 million and that it is found that 80 individuals (4%) were nascent entrepreneurs. This would imply that the best population estimate of nascent entrepreneurs would be 4% of 200 million or 8 million in the total population. Moreover, the 95% confidence interval would be from 3.2% to 4.9% so that the population estimate would range from 6.4 million to 9.8 million nascent entrepreneurs.

In practice, no sample design is perfectly representative of the intended population. There is a wide range of potential errors in any survey. The most commonly cited are sampling errors due to the fact that not all members of the population are interviewed. With probability samples, these errors can be calculated to determine confidence intervals for any estimate, as the example above indicates.

This is not the only source of potential error. The most important of these are coverage errors due to the fact that samples do not include the entire population (such as the homeless or those without telephones). Although some of the problems of coverage errors can be avoided by simply redefining the population (for example, those living in dwellings with telephones), to an important extent there will always be some coverage bias. Good samples are designed to keep such coverage bias to a minimum, especially if the coverage errors would affect estimates of the population of interest.

Another type of error involves bias due to the question wording, the inability of respondents to articulate their answers, language, or hearing problems. Finally, some errors are due to respondent refusal to participate or the inability of the interviewers to locate the respondent. Unfortunately, there are no standard measures of the effects of these errors or any standard method to correct for any potential bias.

The sample was based on telephone ownership among households within the United States, excluding Alaska and Hawaii. Although landline phones were owned by approximately 96% of all U.S. households at the time this sample was selected, in more recent years the number of households with only cell phones has grown. All subsequent waves of interviews were conducted by contacting respondents on the phone of their choice so that the growing cell phone ownership has not had an impact on this study. Nonownership of phones is typically concentrated among lower income households, younger households, and those that recently changed residences. Those factors can be mitigated by the use of survey weights.

Most dwellings have several adult residents. If it were possible to select one adult resident at random for the interview, this would eliminate another potential bias in the sample. This is, however, relatively time consuming and expensive. A typical solution is to interview the first person 18 and older who can be reached by phone. This frequently leads to a higher number of female respondents, as women are more likely to be at home and answer the phone. This was the reason that TeleNation used gender as a control in the sample selection. Again, adjusting the weights assigned to the sample can help to mitigate this problem.

Sample Weights

Although the sampling procedures used were expected to exhibit no systematic bias, confidence that the sample represents the population increases if the sample favorably compares to a more precise description of the population provided from another credible source. Rather than simply comparing sample distributions to information contained in independent surveys, the typical procedure is to correct the sample distributions so that they match information contained in the U.S. census. Such a procedure would correct for any coverage bias as well as correct for any systematic bias due to nonresponse, panel attrition, or other reporting errors.

The four panels in Exhibit B.7 indicate how sample distributions are made identical to independent information. The example shows how a sample is made consistent with a population based on age and gender.

The first panel of Exhibit B.7, labeled "Sample," assumes the selection of 100 respondents distributed by age and gender selected from a target population of 100,000. The second panel of Exhibit B.7, labeled "Population," gives the known age and gender distribution in the target population of 100,000. The third panel of Exhibit B.7 provides the weights that transform the sample distributions into the population totals. For example, there are 5 females aged 18 to 24 in the sample but 10,000 in the population, so that each of these respondents represented 2,000 in the population. Other weight values are also the ratio of the population to the sample totals. Of course, the more important aspect of the weights is how they differ among the various population groups. For example, the largest weight difference is between the youngest and oldest respondent, indicating that the older respondents were more likely to be overrepresented and thus have the lowest weights. Alternatively, the youngest respondents were underrepresented and had the largest weights.

Although the use of the raw weights would provide a correct estimate of means and other sample statistics, it would not provide a correct estimate of the variances. Most statistical programs assume that the sum of the weights is equal to the actual cases and use that total to compute the estimates of variance and standard errors. In the example in Exhibit B.7, the sum of the raw weights equals 100,000—exactly equal to the total population. This would lead to much higher estimates of precision than justified by the size of the sample. In order to prevent this problem, it is common to normalize the weights so the average value is one, and, as a result, the sum of the weights equals the sum of the cases. For the Exhibit B.7 example, this requires dividing all weights by 1,000, to produce a sum of the weights (100) equal to the sum of the cases (100). The bottom panel of Exhibit B.7 shows the normalized weights for each cell, which average to 1.00. Examples of analysis using the weights are provided in Appendix C.

Initial Weights

In order to provide precise weights, it is important to have the same measures on both the sample respondents and on the total population. As screening samples are gathered in 3 days of phone interviewing and the data delivered to the clients within 48 hours of completing the field work, each sample is weighted in relation to the most recent Current Population Survey estimates for the United States (www.bls.census.gov.cps). This recurring U.S. census survey—done four times a year—is considered the most accurate and timely estimate of the U.S. population characteristics. In order to compute weights, the prevalence of sample cases in each of 160 cells from a four-way

Exhibit B.7   Example of Weight Calculation

Sample

Age	Female	Male	Total
18–24 Years	5	5	10
25–34 Years	10	7	17
35–44 Years	12	8	20
45–54 Years	13	8	21
55 Years and Older	20	16	36
Total	60	40	100

Population

Age	Female	Male	Total
18–24 Years	10,000	10,000	20,000
25–34 Years	10,000	10,000	20,000
35–44 Years	10,000	10,000	20,000
45–54 Years	10,000	10,000	20,000
55 Years and Older	10,000	10,000	20,000
Total	50,000	50,000	100,000

Sampling Ratios (weights)

Age	Female	Male	Total
18–24 Years	2,000.00	2,000.00	2,000.00
25–34 Years	1,000.00	1,428.57	1,176.47
35–44 Years	833.33	1,250.00	1,000.00
45–54 Years	769.23	1,250.00	952.38
55 Years and Older	500.00	625.00	555.56
Total	833.33	1,250.00	1,000.00

Weights (normalized)

Age	Female	Male	Total
18–24 Years	2.00	2.00	2.00
25–34 Years	1.00	1.43	1.18
35–44 Years	0.83	1.25	1.00
45–54 Years	0.77	1.25	0.95
55 Years and Older	0.50	0.63	0.56
Total	0.83	1.25	1.00

table is determined. The table reflects age, gender, four regions of the United States, and household income. As household income is missing for about 25% of the cases, special adjustments were made for these households.

Although this has the advantage of providing timely data for the clients, the weights that result have a wide range of values. When the original weights for the 64 PSED screening samples are combined, the range is from 0.1 to 10—some respondents were given a weight that was 100 times others. The use of a four-dimensional table with 160 cells with a sample of 1,000 would lead to an average of five to six cases per cell. Due to random and uncontrollable events, there will be samples with few or no cases in some of these cells, which lead to extreme weights.

The major disadvantage of such a spread of weights is that it can add considerable variance to the data set. Efforts to find systematic relationships between variables may be less successful because of additional variation created by the weighting scheme.

University of Michigan Revised Weights

The University of Michigan was able to recompute the weights, making several adjustments in the process. First, the entire screening data set was treated as one sample of 64,622. Second, the Current Population Survey estimates were combined for the 2-year period in which the screening took place. Third, the sample population match was based on age, gender, ethnic background, and educational attainment. Both household income and educational attainment provide estimates of socioeconomic status, but there are many fewer missing values for educational attainment (1.8% vs. 23.7%) which reduced the need to estimate weights for cases with missing values. As a major objective for the project is a more complete understanding of ethnic differences, standardizing weights on ethnic background were used to compute the revised weights. The final set of University of Michigan weights was based on age, gender, ethnic background, and educational attainment as reported in the screening interview.

Both the original and new weights have an average value of 1.00 and provide almost identical point estimates, as shown in Table B.3 for the population age distribution.

The revised weights have several major advantages:

- Range is from 0.7 to 1.7, less than a factor of 3, compared to 0.1 to 10.0, a factor of 100.
- Estimated variation contributed to estimated percentages due to weighting was reduced from 34.2% to 4.5%.

Extreme values—when there is a large range of weights—can cause problems in detailed analysis as a single case may have dramatic effects on the results. Most analysis is designed to "explain" or "account for" variation in variables and assumes that the research and measurement procedures will not be a major source of variation; if variation due to research procedures can be reduced, it facilitates analysis, for the remaining variation is due to the phenomena itself. Hence, the revised weights provide substantial advantages and all weights in the data files are based on the new weights. The original weights—based on the weights assigned by the screening firm for each sampling wave—are not included in the data sets. In all cases, the weights

Table B.3   Impact of Alternative Weights on Screening Sample Nascent
Entrepreneurs Age Distribution

Age	Original Weights	University of Michigan Weights
18–24 Years	12.62%	12.99%
25–34 Years	28.97%	28.29%
35–44 Years	30.01%	30.19%
45–54 Years	19.49%	19.80%
55 years and older	8.88%	8.73%
Total	99.97%	100.00%

Table B.4   Weights in the Data Set

Variable Label	Data Set	Description
WT_SCRN	Screening	Weight assigned to all cases
WTW1	Detailed	Weight assigned to all entrepreneurs in initial data collection
WTW2	Detailed	Weight assigned to cases providing Wave 2 data
WTW3	Detailed	Weight assigned to cases providing Wave 3 data
WTW4	Detailed	Weight assigned to cases providing Wave 4 data
WTCG	Detailed	Weight assigned to all comparison group cases in Wave 1

have been standardized so that the average value is 1.00; the sum of the cases will equal the sum of the weights.

There are five sets of revised weights in the two data sets, as presented in Table B.4.

Weights and Analysis

Weights should be used in all types of analyses. The PSED data set allows for two basic types: assessments of samples that represent the total population and comparison of the subsample of nascent entrepreneurs with a subsample of typical adults, the comparison group.

The most straightforward assessments reflecting the entire population would be analysis using the screening data set of 64 thousand cases. For example, one may wish to develop predictive equations using age, gender, household income, and educational attainment to estimate which will be associated with, and perhaps influence, those who would become active in the entrepreneurial process. Those who qualified as a start-up owner and were active in the past 12 months might be considered two-criteria nascent entrepreneurs (SUOWNACT = 1 in the screening data set). Once the variables had been assembled into a suitable file for analysis and those cases with missing values excluded, the weights should be "recentered" to an average value of one (1.000) by dividing the weight (WT_SCRN) by the average of the weights for the reduced sample. The analysis could be completed with confidence that the range of variables and scope of impact in the sample reflected the U.S. adult population.

But the variables in the screener data set are few, limited to the sociodemographic data collected for marketing purposes and some characteristics of the counties where the respondents were located. The detailed data sets allow more precise comparisons on a wide range of personal and situational attributes to determine those ways in which nascent entrepreneurs will differ from typical U.S. adults. Perhaps it would be a straightforward comparison of the household size or number of children at home for nascent entrepreneurs and typical adults, perhaps with a two-column table. In such an analysis, the sum of the weights for the nascent entrepreneurs (WTW1) should equal the number of nascent entrepreneurs included in the comparison; the sum of the weights for the comparison group (WTCG) should equal the sum of the number in the comparison group. A new variable, say WT_ANAL, equal to the two weight variables for the two subgroups should be computed. Once adjusted such that the total of all cases is equal to the sum of all weights, the patterns of difference between the subsamples will be accurately described and the statistical significance will be correctly computed.

Examples of analysis procedures using various weights are presented in Appendix C, including details of comparison group respondents considered active nascent entrepreneurs at the time of the initial data collection.

Respondent Rights and Welfare

As an observational study, there is virtually no chance that participation in the PSED data collection would lead to harm for the participants. In fact, it has been found that most nascent entrepreneurs are more interested in pursuing a start-up after completing the interview—it is assumed this is a good thing. On the other hand, a great deal of information is obtained during the interview, and the right of persons to control information about themselves is respected in two ways. Two elements are critical.

The first, an informed consent statement, is read to all participants at the beginning of the phone interview, which is as follows:

> Before we begin, I want to assure you that all of the information you give is completely confidential. None of it will be released in any way that would permit identification of you or your household. Your participation, of course, is voluntary.
>
> (OPTIONAL: To show our appreciation for your help, we'll send you $25 upon completion of this interview.)

The fact that some respondents decide not to participate suggests they are exercising their rights not to be involved. The cover page of the mail questionnaire includes the following statements:

- All information on specific firms or individuals will be kept confidential.
- The identity of firms and people involved in the survey will remain anonymous.

And supervisory control and operational procedures ensure that these promises will be honored.

The second element, and perhaps more important, is ensuring that respondents remain anonymous in the data sets. All respondents are promised anonymity and their names, addresses, and phone numbers are not provided to anyone outside the research team collecting the data. It is possible, however, that respondents with very unique profiles might be identified through comparison with public data, such as phone directories, which sometimes list occupations, and commercial credit-rating services.

This has been a realistic concern with regard to reports of personal wealth, as several respondents in low population counties reported a household net worth in excess of $10 million dollars. Since their county, occupation, and work history are included in the data set, it is possible that their specific identities could be determined. For these cases, the net worth was adjusted to equal the largest values in the continuous distribution, approximately $2.5 million.

These features are consistent with the spirit and letter of current guidelines associated with the inclusion of human participants in research (www.nihtraining. com/ohsrsite/guidelines).

Commentary

The PSED data set developed for the study of the business start-up process is not without problems. On the other hand, most of the problems have been identified and solutions developed. Perhaps the most significant problem is the complexity of the data set itself. This reflects—more than anything else—the complexity of the phenomena. Many of these complications were not anticipated when the project was designed. Some of them, and the solutions that mitigated these problems, are discussed in the different chapters of this handbook and the many analyses and papers that have been published based on the PSED data set. Now that these complications are recognized and more fully appreciated, they should lead to improved procedures in subsequent research on this topic.

Appendix C

Examples of Analysis: Work File Preparation, Comparisons, and Adjustment of Weights

Paul D. Reynolds

Richard T. Curtin

T he data sets assembled as part of the Panel Survey of Entrepreneurial Dynamics (PSED) project are complex and extensive. Analysis of such material can be a challenge, particularly for those not accustomed to large data sets based on representative samples. The complete PSED data set consists of five different samples and over 4,000 variables. The data collection procedures have been reviewed in Appendix A and the structure of the data sets in Appendix B. This appendix is designed to provide a guide to data analysis. Most critical are discussions about different subsamples may be selected from the detailed data set for different purposes and how weights should be adjusted for different options. Proper weighting will provide both accurate descriptions of the phenomena as well as appropriate inferences when statistical tests are involved.

Any analysis will involve the following steps:

1. Determine and enumerate the objective of the analysis.

2. Identify the appropriate unit of analysis and specify the aspects or characteristics relevant to the proposed analysis in terms of their conceptual features.

3. Locate the appropriate units of analysis in the data set.

4. Locate the specific variables that will provide indicators of the conceptual model.

5. Assemble a working data file based on the appropriate units of analysis which includes the variables required for the analysis and excludes the thousands of extraneous variables.

6. Using the working data file, determine those cases with complete data on the relevant variables and recenter the weights (transform the weights such that the average value is 1.00).

7. Perform the analysis and examine the relationship among variables and consider the strength of the relationship and the level of statistical significance.

8. Interpret the empirical results.

9. Proceed to the next issue.

Experienced analysts may do many of these steps simultaneously, or almost simultaneously; experienced users of the data will develop the facility to quickly determine which research questions can be approached with the existing data. The interview schedules and questionnaires provide the best information on what data is available; the Codebook provides an overview of the type of information included in the data set as well as the frequency distributions of the unweighted data.

Several practices can improve the efficiency of the analysis. Perhaps the most important is the use of batch or production processing based on explicit command or syntax files. In this mode, the analyst writes a program that will complete all the critical steps—locate and merge data files, select variables, transform variables, adjust weights, and run the analysis procedure. Although the creation of such files may take some time, they have the major advantage of providing an explicit record of all stages of the procedure and can be easily modified as the work progresses. An explicit record is critical when the analysis is to be described to others in a presentation or in a professional report or article.

The ease of modification and repeating all processing procedures is invaluable as the analysis proceeds. No one is able to get all these steps right the first time, and it is never possible to predict exactly where the problems and mistakes will occur. By having an explicit program that can be adjusted during the analysis, it becomes relatively easy, although it is never simple, to locate and correct problems, add variables, adjust transformation, and the like. The alternative, attempting cursory or immediate comparisons based on spreadsheets or temporary procedures implemented by pull-down menus, can provide "instant results" but is difficult to systematize and replicate when a series of complicated adjustments is required. They are not satisfactory for any analysis with complex data sets that require sophisticated transformations and assessments.

The second practice is very basic: *document everything*. Make sure every variable has a label, every value has a label, and the reason for any adjustment or transform or procedure is written down. This can often be done with comments inserted into the command or syntax file. With complicated assessments, the rationale for programming completed even in the last week may be lost. Documenting the reasons for all coding and transformations as they are produced is the only way to minimize lost time recreating the rationale for a given set of procedures or transforms. This is not much fun, but a necessary part of a useful, efficient data analysis that can be described to others.

The number of examples highlights a range of processes and issues associated with analysis, with a focus on adjustment of the weights. They include the following:

- Example 1: Estimate entrepreneurial activity in the total population
- Example 2: Consider the joint impact of educational attainment and ethnic background on entrepreneurial activity in the population

- Example 3: Determine the impact of household net worth on entrepreneurial activity
- Example 4: Preference for risk and entrepreneurial activity
- Example 5: Follow-up outcomes as affected by gender and ethnic background
- Example 6: Multivariate analysis with screening and detailed data sets

The first two examples utilize only the data from the screening file, the third only data from the phone interview in the initial round of data collection, the fourth uses data from the first-round phone interview and self-administered questionnaire, the fifth provides an assessment based on the initial data and the first- and second-round of follow-up interviews, and the last example reviews procedures for preparing data for multivariate analysis using both the full screener data set and the detailed data set for nascents and the comparison group.

As a set, these examples cover many of the issues that should be encountered in most types of analysis. In the interest of conserving space, details on the assembly of the working analysis file are not presented; emphasis is on the selection of respondents, proper selection of and adjustments of weights, and variable transforms. These examples of analysis are provided as demonstrations on the use of the data set. They are not presented as the definitive or final analysis of these issues. A number of these topics are receiving intensive attention by teams of scholars, and their results provide more sophisticated assessments; many are found in the previous chapters of this handbook.

Selection of Cases for Analysis

It may appear straightforward to compare nascent entrepreneurs to the comparison groups, but three issues reflecting the conceptual frameworks and data collection procedures require attention. These are related to

1. The expected ownership of the nascent firm

2. Criteria for start-up versus a new firm

3. Nascent entrepreneur included in the comparison group

Decisions on each of these issues can affect the cases chosen for the analysis and, in turn, the size of the subsample and the adjustments of the weights.

Legal Person Ownership: To determine whether the respondent qualifies as a nascent entrepreneur involved in a start-up activity, several assessments were made of the data to produce specific criteria for inclusion in the sample. Careful attention was given to the nascent firms in relation to two issues: first, reports (based on Q190) regarding outside sponsorship of the new business and, second, the extent to which those expected to own part of the new firm were considered to be nonhuman or legal persons (financial institutions, venture capital firms, other businesses, etc.). Based on this assessment, a five-category typology was developed for all respondents in the sample (AUTONSU). It is presented in Table C.1.

Table C.1   Expected Ownership of New Firm by Legal Persons [AUTONSU]

Value	AUTONSU	Nascent Entrepreneurs	Comparison Group	Total Count
1	Full independence, no corporate sponsored and no nonpersons expected to own new firm	721		721
2	Independent start-up, nonpersons own up to 50%	7		7
3	Franchise or multilevel marketing, nonpersons to own up to 50%	52		52
4	Business-sponsored, nonpersons own up to 50%	43		43
5	Nonpersons to own 51% to 100% of new firm	7		7
99	Comparison Group: Mixed-Gender and Minority		431	431
	Total Count	830	431	1,261

This was subsequently recoded into a second typology, which involved combining all start-ups in which legal persons were expected to have 1–50% of the ownership into one category, presented in Table C.2.

This distinction is quite relevant for those that conceptualize new firm creation as an individual phenomenon, one that reflects the efforts of one or more natural persons. Most efforts to explain and understand new firm creation have focused on natural persons. There is less systematic information about new business ventures implemented as collaborative efforts of natural persons and an existing business or financial institution and almost none when the new venture will be completely owned by existing legal persons.

Those who wish to focus only on natural person–created new ventures may wish to restrict analysis to only the 721 entities that will be owned by one or more natural persons (AUTONSU4 = 100). Those focusing on business sponsored start-ups may wish to restrict analysis to those 109 cases where some part of the ownership will be with legal persons (AUTONSU4 = 300). Those who wish to emphasize *any* new business creation can focus on all 830 cases.

Criteria for Start-up Versus a New Firm: One of the criteria for identifying a start-up effort that was still in the gestation period was evidence of business activity. The criterion separating start-up efforts from operating firms was the presence of positive monthly cash flow that covered all monthly expenses, including owner-manager salaries, for more than 3 months. Despite the care devoted to measuring this criterion in the interview and excluding those with new firms, subsequent analysis indicated

Table C.2   Expected Ownership of New Firm by Legal Persons [AUTONSU4]

Value	AUTONSU4	Nascent Entrepreneurs	Comparison Group	Total Count
100	Full independence, no corporate sponsored and no nonpersons expected to own new firm	721		721
200	Ownership involves business sponsorship or expectation of legal person ownership of 0% to 50% of the new firm	102		102
300	Legal persons to own 51% to 100% of the new firm	7		7
400	Comparison Group: Mixed-Gender and Minority		431	431
	Total Count	830	431	1,261

some oversights in this procedure. It was determined that six of the start-up efforts had positive monthly cash flow that covered all monthly expenses and owner-manager salaries for more than 3 months (91 days) prior to the completion of the phone interview. These cases, with their identification numbers, subsample, and reported duration of positive monthly cash flow, are provided in Table C.3. Another 19 cases were found to have positive monthly cash flow for more than 1 but less than 92 days and, therefore, met the criteria. The remaining 805 cases did not report any period of positive monthly cash flow. All six of these cases are those where natural persons are expected to own 100% of the new firm.

Table C.3   Cases With Excessive Monthly Positive Cash Flow

Identification Number	Nascent Subsample	Positive Monthly Cash Flow
RESPID	RTYPE	CFPHLAG4
328100124	10	92–183 days
328100145	10	92–183 days
328100395	11	92–183 days
328100541	10	92–183 days
337800137	12	92–183 days
328100601	10	184–275 days

Nascent Entrepreneurs in the Comparison Group Subsamples: The comparison groups were selected to be a representative sample of all adults in the United States. Some may wish to use the comparison as a representative of U.S. adults, in which case no adjustments are required. Others may wish to exclude from the comparison group those individuals who have been identified as active in entrepreneurial activity.

An assessment was completed of those individuals included in the comparison groups to determine their participation in start-ups at the time of the phone interview. For those in the original mixed-gender comparison group, this was obtained in a follow-up interview that was completed 10 to 14 months after the initial phone interview. Eighty percent (179) of the 223 in the original sample were recontacted, and 4 appeared to be actively engaged in a start-up at the time of the original phone interview. For the minority oversample comparison group, questions were included in the screening and phone interview to determine if the respondent would qualify as a nascent entrepreneur at the time of the phone interview; five appeared to so qualify. The identification numbers of these nine respondents are given in Table C.4.

Table C.4   Control Group Members Known to Qualify as Nascent Entrepreneurs at Initial Interview

Identification Number	Control Group Subsample	Reported Active as Nascent Entrepreneur or Intrapreneur	Qualified as Nascent Entrepreneur at Time of Phone Interview
RESPID	RTYPE		CGSUACT = 1
328200046	20	Yes	Yes
328100059	20	Yes	Yes
328200084	20	Yes	Yes
328200115	20	Yes	Yes
339300049	21	Yes	Yes
339300107	21	Yes	Yes
339300150	21	Yes	Yes
339300180	21	Yes	Yes
339300182	21	Yes	Yes

It was also possible to identify those in the minority comparison group who reported participation in a start-up in the initial screening interview but did not meet the criteria as a nascent entrepreneur eligible for a full entrepreneur data collection (active in start-up, expected to own part of the new firm, no positive cash flow for more than 3 months). These additional 23 cases can be identified by the start-up involvement variable (SUINVOL) that is greater than 1 and the qualified nascent entrepreneur variable (CGSUACT) that is not equal to 1.

Those doing analysis may then create three types of comparison group subsamples: one that includes all those respondents with data, for a total of 431; one that excludes those who would have qualified as nascent entrepreneurs in the initial interview, for a total of 422; or one that excludes all cases that appeared to have entrepreneurial activity of any kind during the first interview, for a total of 399 cases. The choice will depend on the purpose of the analysis.

Overview of Subsample Choices: The net result of these variations in definitions is to provide a range of options for those completing different analyses with the sample. These are outlined in Table C.5. Including all nascent entrepreneur and comparison group cases leads to the full sample of 1,261. Excluding those six cases where the nascent appeared to be reporting on a business with positive monthly cash flow for more than 3 months (91 days) reduces the nascent firm sample to 824. Excluding the seven that will be 51% or more owned by legal entities further reduces this subsample to 817 cases. If those cases in which there is any ownership by a legal entity are excluded, the nascent subsample is reduced to 716.

In a similar fashion, excluding those nine individuals who appeared to qualify as nascent entrepreneurs at the initial interview would reduce the comparison group from 431 to 422 cases; excluding individuals who reported any entrepreneurial activity at the initial interview would further reduce this group to 399. In the following examples, different subsamples will be chosen and weights adjusted for the analysis.

Developing different subsamples of cases can easily be achieved based on the variables included in the data files. Examples of how this can be achieved are provided below.

Subsample Selection—Operational Procedures: Reducing the sample by eliminating the cases that are not consistent with the conceptual framework is achieved by using syntax statements that eliminate certain types of respondents. Using the SPSS syntax, those with positive monthly cash flow of over 91 days can be deleted with the following commands. Saving the working analysis file will permanently delete these cases. It should be noted that "NE" stands for "not equal to" and instructs the program to skip cases that meet this criterion.

```
SELECT IF (CFPHLAG4 NE 91183).
SELECT IF (CFPHLAG4 NE 184275).
```

This would reduce the nascent subsample from 830 to 824 cases. Those nascent firms expecting more than 50% ownership by legal persons can be eliminated with the following command:

```
SELECT IF (AUTONSU NE 5).
```

This would reduce the nascent subsample from 824 to 817 cases. And all those nascent firms with any legal person ownership may be dropped from the file with the following syntax commands:

Table C.5 Alternative Conceptual Choices and Impact on the Sample Sizes

	Excludes New Businesses	Excludes Start-up With 1% to 50% Legal Person Ownership	Excludes Start-ups With 51% to 100% Legal Person Ownership	Total Start-up Cases	Excludes Known Nascents in Comparison Groups	Excludes Any Start-up Activity in Comparison Group	Total Comparison Group Cases	Total All Cases
A	No	No	No	830	No	No	431	1,261
B	Yes	No	No	824	No	No	431	1,255
C	Yes	No	No	824	Yes	No	422	1,246
D	Yes	No	No	824	Yes	Yes	399	1,223
E	Yes	No	Yes	817	No	No	431	1,248
F	Yes	No	Yes	817	Yes	No	422	1,239
G	Yes	No	Yes	817	Yes	Yes	399	1,216
H	Yes	Yes	Yes	715	No	No	431	1,146
I	Yes	Yes	Yes	715	Yes	No	422	1,137
J	Yes	Yes	Yes	715	Yes	Yes	399	1,114

```
SELECT IF (AUTONSU NE 2).

SELECT IF (AUTONSU NE 3).

SELECT IF (AUTONSU NE 4).
```

This would reduce the subsample further from 817 to 715 cases. If the commands are added as a set, then all specified cases are excluded.

In a similar fashion, various comparison group cases can be eliminated. All those known to be nascent entrepreneurs at the time of the first interview can be deleted with

```
SELECT IF (CGSUACT NE 1).
```

This would reduce the comparison subsample from 431 to 422 cases. Eliminating all those who reported any entrepreneurial activity in the screening interview can be accomplished by the following three commands.

```
SELECT IF ((RTYPE LT 20) OR ((RTYPE GE 20) & (SUINVOL NE 2))).

SELECT IF ((RTYPE LT 20) OR ((RTYPE GE 20) & (SUINVOL NE 3))).

SELECT IF ((RTYPE LT 20) OR ((RTYPE GE 20) & (SUINVOL NE 4))).
```

This would reduce the comparison group subsample from 422 to 399 cases.

This procedure applies only to the data file distributed at the time the handbook was being prepared. Some versions of analysis programs, such as SPSS, may require that all missing value assignments be deleted; the procedures may not allocate cases with a missing value designation leading to an undercount.

Example 1: Estimate Entrepreneurial Activity in the Total U.S. Population

One of the most important issues associated with the representative samples of nascent entrepreneurs is estimating the prevalence of the activity in the total population. In this case, the total population is all U.S. residents 18 years of age and older. Careful development of this estimate requires several steps:

1. Identify that part of the screening sample with full data on age, gender, and participation in entrepreneurial activity.

2. Adjust the weights for this part of the sample such that the average weight is 1.00.

3. Determine the average prevalence rate and standard error of the mean for each gender and age category.

4. Compute the number of individuals involved in entrepreneurial activity for each gender and age category.

5. Sum the computations across all categories to create an estimate for the entire U.S. population.

In this case, the measure of participation in start-up activity as a nascent entrepreneur is based entirely on the screening interview and consists of only two criteria: reports of active efforts to implement a new business and expectation of full or partial ownership of the new firm. This two-criterion measure of entrepreneurial activity omits the third criterion used in the selection of those for the detailed PSED data set. Specifically, the lack of monthly positive cash flow that covers all expenses including wages and salaries was assessed to select nascent entrepreneurs for the detailed data collection. This additional criterion, however, was measured at the beginning of the detailed interview and no information on this criterion is available in the screening data set.

The full screening sample of 64,622 is reduced for this analysis for two reasons. There are five different cohorts in the screening data set. The items used to identify those active in start-ups were used in four. As these items were not included in the screening of the initial comparison group sample (RTYPE = 20), these 2,010 cases are dropped from the analysis. The second factor is the absence of age data (USAGE7C) on about 3% of all cases; another 1,988 cases are dropped from the working file.

The average weights (WT_SCRN) for the 14 gender (USGENDER) and age cells can then be computed as shown in the top of Exhibit C.1. The average value for each cell is adjusted, as shown in the computation of new weights (WTAGESEX) in the center of Exhibit C.1. The results are shown at the bottom of Exhibit C.1; the average value for each cell is 1.000.

It is important to stress that this weight adjustment has been done to maximize the precision of the means and standard error of the 14 gender, age groups. If the purpose was to compare the prevalence rates using a means test or analysis of variance, it would be more appropriate to adjust the overall weight to equal one with one computation.

The next step in the procedure is to compute the mean and standard error of the mean for each of the 14 cells. The results are presented in columns 3 and 4 of Table C.6 to estimate the total number of U.S. adults involved in start-up activities. The first stage is assembling a count of the total eligible individuals, presented in Column 2 of Table C.6; data were from the U.S. Census Bureau Projections of Resident Population by Age, Sex, Race, and Hispanic Origin for 1999 (NP-D1-A). These two sets of information, U.S. population in each cell and prevalence rates and standard errors of the mean from the PSED screening sample, are used to compute the lower and upper bounds of the 95% confidence interval as well as the mean estimate, shown in columns 5 to 7 of Table C.6. The results are in terms of hundreds of thousands of individuals. As shown in the bottom row of Table C.6, the mean is about 11.9 (5.80 %) million with a 95% confidence interval from 10.6 (5.19 %) to 13.1 (6.41%) million.

Example 2: Educational Attainment, Ethnic Background, and Entrepreneurial Activity Among Men

This example uses the same two-criteria measure of entrepreneurial participation based on the screener questions but focuses on the interaction of two factors—educational attainment and ethnic identity—among men. To reduce the cohort effects associated with educational attainment among minorities (older minorities

Exhibit C.1   Example 1: Adjustment of Population Screening Weights

---

INITIAL ASSESSMENTS OF WEIGHT AVERAGE PER CELL

WEIGHT OFF.
SELECT IF (RTYPE NE 20).
SELECT IF (SYSMIS(USAGE7C) NE 1).
MEANS TABLE = WT_SCRN BY USGENDER BY USAGE7C.

Summaries of   WT_SCRN   ISR CPS BASED SCREENING WEIGHTS

Variable	Value	Label	Mean	Std Dev	Cases
For Entire Population			1.0003	.1987	60624
USGENDER	1	MALE	.9749	.1986	29903
USAGE7C	1824.00	18-24 YRS	1.0478	.0763	3739
USAGE7C	2534.00	25-34 YRS	.9450	.1721	6260
USAGE7C	3544.00	35-44 YRS	.9551	.1547	7041
USAGE7C	4554.00	45-54 YRS	.9074	.1482	5647
USAGE7C	5564.00	55-64 YRS	1.0228	.2878	3431
USAGE7C	6574.00	65-74 YRS	1.0450	.2874	2453
USAGE7C	7599.00	75 YRS AND UP	1.0481	.2901	1332
USGENDER	2	FEMALE	1.0251	.1957	30721
USAGE7C	1824.00	18-24 YRS	1.2363	.0358	3141
USAGE7C	2534.00	25-34 YRS	1.0738	.1209	5645
USAGE7C	3544.00	35-44 YRS	1.0073	.1465	6767
USAGE7C	4554.00	45-54 YRS	.9202	.1699	5843
USAGE7C	5564.00	55-64 YRS	.9893	.2496	3810
USAGE7C	6574.00	65-74 YRS	1.0146	.2413	3343
USAGE7C	7599.00	75 YRS AND UP	1.0102	.2335	2172

ADJUST THE AVERAGE WEIGHT FOR EACH CELL TO EQUAL 1.0000.

IF ((USGENDER=1)&(USAGE7C=1824)) WTAGESEX = WT_SCRN*(1.0000/1.0478).
IF ((USGENDER=1)&(USAGE7C=2534)) WTAGESEX = WT_SCRN*(1.0000/0.9450).
IF ((USGENDER=1)&(USAGE7C=3544)) WTAGESEX = WT_SCRN*(1.0000/0.9551).
IF ((USGENDER=1)&(USAGE7C=4554)) WTAGESEX = WT_SCRN*(1.0000/0.9074).
IF ((USGENDER=1)&(USAGE7C=5564)) WTAGESEX = WT_SCRN*(1.0000/1.0228).
IF ((USGENDER=1)&(USAGE7C=6574)) WTAGESEX = WT_SCRN*(1.0000/1.0450).
IF ((USGENDER=1)&(USAGE7C=7599)) WTAGESEX = WT_SCRN*(1.0000/1.0481).
*.
IF ((USGENDER=2)&(USAGE7C=1824)) WTAGESEX = WT_SCRN*(1.0000/1.2363).
IF ((USGENDER=2)&(USAGE7C=2534)) WTAGESEX = WT_SCRN*(1.0000/1.0738).
IF ((USGENDER=2)&(USAGE7C=3544)) WTAGESEX = WT_SCRN*(1.0000/1.0073).
IF ((USGENDER=2)&(USAGE7C=4554)) WTAGESEX = WT_SCRN*(1.0000/0.9202).
IF ((USGENDER=2)&(USAGE7C=5564)) WTAGESEX = WT_SCRN*(1.0000/0.9893).
IF ((USGENDER=2)&(USAGE7C=6574)) WTAGESEX = WT_SCRN*(1.0000/1.0146).
IF ((USGENDER=2)&(USAGE7C=7599)) WTAGESEX = WT_SCRN*(1.0000/1.0102).

(Continued)

Exhibit C.1 (Continued)

```
CHECKING AVERAGE WEIGHT VALUE PER CELL.

MEANS TABLE = WT_SCRN BY USGENDER BY USAGE7C.

Summaries of    WTAGESEX    WEIGHT ADJUSTED FOR GENDER, 7 AGE GROUPS
Variable       Value      Label                    Mean   Std Dev   Cases

For Entire Population                              1.0000   .1855    60624

USGENDER           1       MALE                    1.0000   .1937    29903
  USAGE7C     1824.00      18-24 YRS               1.0000   .0728     3739
  USAGE7C     2534.00      25-34 YRS               1.0000   .1821     6260
  USAGE7C     3544.00      35-44 YRS               1.0000   .1620     7041
  USAGE7C     4554.00      45-54 YRS               1.0000   .1633     5647
  USAGE7C     5564.00      55-64 YRS               1.0000   .2814     3431
  USAGE7C     6574.00      65-74 YRS               1.0000   .2750     2453
  USAGE7C     7599.00      75 YRS AND UP           1.0000   .2768     1332

USGENDER           2       FEMALE                  1.0000   .1771    30721
  USAGE7C     1824.00      18-24 YRS               1.0000   .0290     3141
  USAGE7C     2534.00      25-34 YRS               1.0000   .1126     5645
  USAGE7C     3544.00      35-44 YRS               1.0000   .1454     6767
  USAGE7C     4554.00      45-54 YRS               1.0000   .1847     5843
  USAGE7C     5564.00      55-64 YRS               1.0000   .2523     3810
  USAGE7C     6574.00      65-74 YRS               1.0000   .2379     3343
  USAGE7C     7599.00      75 YRS AND UP           1.0000   .2311     2172
```

have less education), the age is standardized at 25 to 54 years of age. Younger men are excluded, since those under 25 may not have finished all their education. The other ethnic category—composed of American Indians, a diversity of Asians, and many with complex ethnic backgrounds—is very diverse and hard to interpret and is also excluded.

Weights are computed in two ways for two different assessments. First they are computed as above, with each of 15 cells adjusted so the average weight in each cell is 1.00. This is appropriate for an assessment of the mean values and the confidence intervals associated with each ethnic, educational group. A second assessment focuses on the capacity to determine if there are statistically significant differences between the groups. A single adjustment is used to create an overall weight with an average value of 1.00. Both assessments start with identifying all the cases where full information is available on the critical variables: age, gender, educational attainment (USEDUC5), ethnic identity (USRACE4), and nascent entrepreneurship. The resulting sample has a total of 17,755 cases.

Exhibits C.2a and C.2b present the three stages of the first weight adjustment. The initial presentation shows the cell average of the initial screening weight (WT_SCRN) for all 15 cells. The second section indicates the adjustments for each individual cell. The final section indicates the results in terms of the average weights for each of the 15 cells.

Following this, the mean prevalence of participation in entrepreneurial activity and the standard error of the mean can be computed and used to compute the 95%

Table C.6   Estimates of Nascent Entrepreneurs (NEs) in the United States: 1999

	U.S. Population Counts: 1999	Prevalence of Nascents	Standard Error of the Mean	Low NE Estimate (95% CI)	High NE Estimate (95% CI)	Mean NE Estimate
	(x 1,000)	(#/100)		(x 1,000)	(x 1,000)	(x 1,000)
MEN						
18–24 Years	13,286	8.6	0.5	1,012	1,273	1,142
25–34 Years	18,847	10.8	0.4	1,888	2,183	2,035
35–44 Years	22,269	9.8	0.4	2,008	2,357	2,182
45–54 Years	17,507	8.3	0.4	1,316	1,590	1,453
55–64 Years	11,157	4.5	0.4	415	589	502
65–74 Years	8,201	1.3	0.2	74	139	107
75–99 Years	6,110	0.5	0.2	7	54	31
Total	97,377	7.6[a]		6,720	8,185	7,452
WOMEN						
18–24 Years	12,751	3.9	0.3	422	572	497
25–34 Years	19,147	6.4	0.3	1,113	1,338	1,225
35–44 Years	22,575	6.1	0.3	1,244	1,510	1,377
45–54 Years	18,310	5.4	0.3	881	1,096	989
55–64 Years	12,249	2.2	0.2	221	317	269
65–74 Years	10,028	0.4	0.1	20	60	40
75–99 Years	10,222	0.2	0.1	5	40	20
Total	105,282	4.2[a]		3,906	4,933	4,417
Total All	204,659			10,626	13,118	11,869

NOTE:

[a]Computed from the total of means estimated for each age group by gender.

Exhibit C.2a   Example 2: Weight Adjustment for 15 Ethnic, Educational Attainment Cells

```
INITIAL ASSESSMENTS OF WEIGHT AVERAGE PER CELL

WEIGHT OFF.
SELECT IF (SYSMIS(USEDUC5) NE 1).
SELECT IF (SYSMIS(USRACE4_ NE 1).
SELECT IF (USRACER LT 4).
MEANS TABLE = WT_SCRN BY USEDUC5 BY USRACE4.

Summaries of   WT_SCRN     ISR CPS BASED SCREENING WEIGHTS
By levels of   USRACE4     ETHNIC BACKGROUND: 4 CATEGORIES
               USEDUC5     EDUC ATTAINMENT: 5 CATEGORIES

Variable       Value     Label                      Mean    Std Dev    Cases

For Entire Population                                .9401    .1617    17755

USRACE4        1.00      WHITE                      .9134    .1274    14864
  USEDUC5     11.00      NO HS DEGREE              1.0780    .0452      882
  USEDUC5   1212.00      HS DEGREE                1.0751    .0439     4597
  USEDUC5   1315.00      POST HS,NO COLL DEG       .8189    .0157     3666
  USEDUC5   1616.00      COLL DEGREE               .8185    .0158     3676
  USEDUC5   1720.00      POST COLL EXPERIENCE      .8189    .0152     2043

USRACE4        2.00      BLACK                     1.1716    .2393     1700
  USEDUC5     11.00      NO HS DEGREE              1.4120    .0983      157
  USEDUC5   1212.00      HS DEGREE                1.3960    .1026      653
  USEDUC5   1315.00      POST HS,NO COLL DEG       .9677    .0978      477
  USEDUC5   1616.00      COLL DEGREE               .9639    .0987      298
  USEDUC5   1720.00      POST COLL EXPERIENCE      .9525    .1050      115

USRACE4        3.00      HISPANIC                   .9426    .1420     1191
  USEDUC5     11.00      NO HS DEGREE              1.0925    .0481      135
  USEDUC5   1212.00      HS DEGREE                1.0936    .0507      405
  USEDUC5   1315.00      POST HS,NO COLL DEG       .8166    .0163      316
  USEDUC5   1616.00      COLL DEGREE               .8181    .0177      225
  USEDUC5   1720.00      POST COLL EXPERIENCE      .8192    .0169      110

ADJUST THE AVERAGE WEIGHT FOR EACH CELL TO EQUAL 1.0000.
*.
IF ((USRACE4=1)&(USEDUC5=11))    WTEDRAC1 = WT_SCRN*(1.0000/1.0780).
IF ((USRACE4=1)&(USEDUC5=1212))  WTEDRAC1 = WT_SCRN*(1.0000/1.0751).
IF ((USRACE4=1)&(USEDUC5=1315))  WTEDRAC1 = WT_SCRN*(1.0000/0.8189).
IF ((USRACE4=1)&(USEDUC5=1616))  WTEDRAC1 = WT_SCRN*(1.0000/0.8185).
IF ((USRACE4=1)&(USEDUC5=1720))  WTEDRAC1 = WT_SCRN*(1.0000/0.8189).
*.
IF ((USRACE4=2)&(USEDUC5=11))    WTEDRAC1 = WT_SCRN*(1.0000/1.4120).
IF ((USRACE4=2)&(USEDUC5=1212))  WTEDRAC1 = WT_SCRN*(1.0000/1.3960).
IF ((USRACE4=2)&(USEDUC5=1315))  WTEDRAC1 = WT_SCRN*(1.0000/0.9677).
IF ((USRACE4=2)&(USEDUC5=1616))  WTEDRAC1 = WT_SCRN*(1.0000/0.9639).
IF ((USRACE4=2)&(USEDUC5=1720))  WTEDRAC1 = WT_SCRN*(1.0000/0.9525).
*.
IF ((USRACE4=3)&(USEDUC5=11))    WTEDRAC1 = WT_SCRN*(1.0000/1.0925).
IF ((USRACE4=3)&(USEDUC5=1212))  WTEDRAC1 = WT_SCRN*(1.0000/1.0936).
IF ((USRACE4=3)&(USEDUC5=1315))  WTEDRAC1 = WT_SCRN*(1.0000/0.8166).
IF ((USRACE4=3)&(USEDUC5=1616))  WTEDRAC1 = WT_SCRN*(1.0000/0.8181).
IF ((USRACE4=3)&(USEDUC5=1720))  WTEDRAC1 = WT_SCRN*(1.0000/0.8192).
*.
VARIABLE LABEL WTEDRAC1 'WEIGHT:25-54 YRS,MEN,NOT OTHER RACE, BY CELL'.
*.
```

Exhibit C.2b   Example 2: Weight Adjustment for 15 Ethnic, Educational Attainment Cells

```
CHECKING AVERAGE WEIGHT VALUE PER CELL.

WEIGHT OFF.
MEANS TABLE = WT_SCRN BY USEDUC5 BY USRACE4.
*.
Summaries of   WTEDRAC1    WEIGHT:25-54 YRS,MEN,NOT OTHER RACE, BY
By levels of   USRACE4     ETHNIC BACKGROUND: 4 CATEGORIES
               USEDUC5     EDUC ATTAINMENT: 5 CATEGORIES

Variable       Value     Label                    Mean   Std Dev   Cases

For Entire Population                            1.0000    .0395   17755

USRACE4         1.00     WHITE                    1.0000    .0291   14864
  USEDUC5      11.00     NO HS DEGREE             1.0000    .0419     882
  USEDUC5    1212.00     HS DEGREE               1.0000    .0408    4597
  USEDUC5    1315.00     POST HS,NO COLL DEG     1.0000    .0192    3666
  USEDUC5    1616.00     COLL DEGREE             1.0000    .0192    3676
  USEDUC5    1720.00     POST COLL EXPERIENCE    1.0000    .0186    2043

USRACE4         2.00     BLACK                   1.0000    .0896    1700
  USEDUC5      11.00     NO HS DEGREE            1.0000    .0696     157
  USEDUC5    1212.00     HS DEGREE               1.0000    .0735     653
  USEDUC5    1315.00     POST HS,NO COLL DEG     1.0000    .1011     477
  USEDUC5    1616.00     COLL DEGREE             1.0000    .1024     298
  USEDUC5    1720.00     POST COLL EXPERIENCE    1.0000    .1102     115

USRACE4         3.00     HISPANIC                1.0000    .0344    1191
  USEDUC5      11.00     NO HS DEGREE            1.0000    .0441     135
  USEDUC5    1212.00     HS DEGREE               1.0000    .0464     405
  USEDUC5    1315.00     POST HS,NO COLL DEG     1.0000    .0199     316
  USEDUC5    1616.00     COLL DEGREE             1.0000    .0216     225
  USEDUC5    1720.00     POST COLL EXPERIENCE    1.0000    .0206     110
```

confidence interval. This is displayed visually in Figure C.1. The vertical bars indicate the confidence interval. If the vertical bars for any two groups overlap, there is no statistically significant difference between the groups. This visual display facilitates comparisons among any two groups and clearly shows the lack of difference in entrepreneurial activity among White men related to educational attainment. It also makes clear the higher levels of participation among Black and Hispanic men compared to White men and the dramatic increase among Black and Hispanic men with higher levels of educational attainment. The confidence intervals also illustrate how the smaller sample sizes lead to less precise estimates for the Black and Hispanic men.

The alternative strategy is to focus on the impact of educational attainment on participation in start-ups for each ethnic group. The question of the presence of any

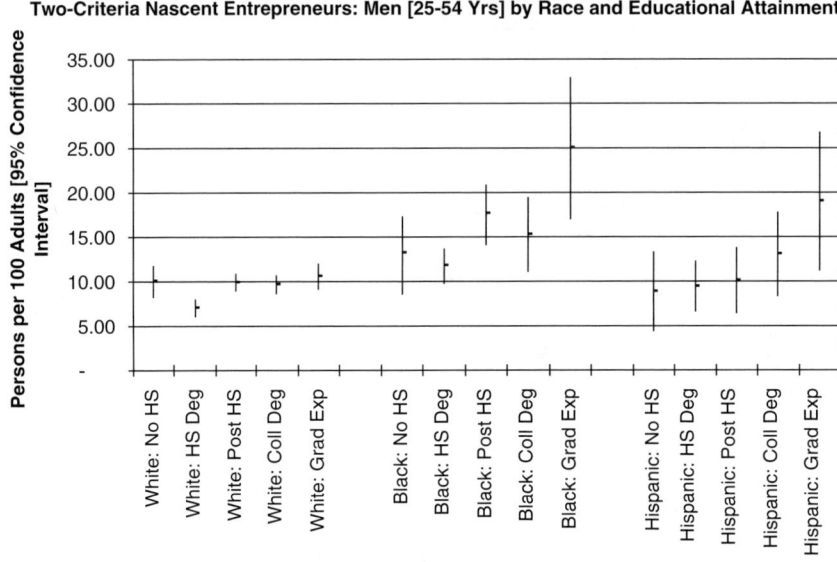

Figure C.1   Example 2: Visual Display of Means and Confidence Intervals: Entrepreneurial Activity by Ethnic Background and Educational Attainment

Exhibit C.3   Example 2: Adjustment of Weights for Full Subsample

```
WEIGHTS OFF.

DESCRIPTIVES VAR = WT_SCRN/STAT 1 10 11 12.ᵃ

Variable   Mean   Minimum   Maximum      Sum       N    Label

WT_SCRN     .94       .77      1.67   16691.22   17755   ISR CPS BASED
                                                         SCREENING WEIGHTS
*.
COMPUTE WTEDRAC2 = WT_SCRN*(17755/16691.22).
VARIABLE LABEL
 WTEDRAC2 'WEIGHT 1: MEN ADJUSTED FOR AGE, RACE, EDUC ATTAIN'.
*.
DESCRIPTIVES VAR = WTEDRAC2/STAT 1 10 11 12.ᵃ

Number of Valid Observations (Listwise) =     17755.00

Variable   Mean   Minimum   Maximum      Sum       N    Label
WTEDRAC2   1.00       .82      1.77   17755.00   17755   WEIGHT 1: MEN
                                                         ADJUSTED FOR AGE,
                                                         RACE, ED
```

NOTE: a. This produces the mean, minimum, maximum, and sum for each variable in SPSS syntax files.

impact can be determined with a cross-tabulation analysis. In this, it is preferred that variation across cells is maintained and the overall weight needs only to have an average of 1.00 for the total sample. The adjustment requires only a single correction, as shown in Exhibit C.3. In this case, a more precise adjustment is made by multiplying the original weight by the ratio of the total number of cases to the sum of the weights (17755/16691.22 = 1.064).

The resulting analysis, presented in Exhibits C.4a and C.4b, shows the three cross-tabulations, one for each ethnic group. Because of the large sample size (14,442) the educational impact among Whites is statistically significant, although the substantive impact is small. Among Blacks, the substantive impact is substantial and leads to a statistically significant difference although the sample size is rather small (2,119). Among Hispanics, the effect is less than Blacks and because the sample size is even smaller (1,194), the statistical significance is borderline, not quite at the 0.05 level. These results are consistent with the visual display provided in Figure C.1; the row values in the right columns in Exhibit C.4 are identical to the mean values for each group in Figure C.1.

Example 3: Household Net Worth and Entrepreneurial Activity

This example focuses on a single hypothesis: Does household net worth affect the tendency to participate in business start-ups? This is sometimes called the liquidity hypothesis among economists, and hypothesizes that the more funds one has personally available (liquidity), the greater the tendency to be involved in new firm creation. Data from the initial detailed phone interview provides information on household net worth for both the nascent entrepreneurs and the comparison groups. Estimates from the respondents have been aggregated into a six-level measure of household net worth (HHNETR6) for 96% of the cases. It ranges from negative net worth (5.6%) to those reporting $1 million or more in net worth (2.8%).

Several other issues need to be resolved in order to analyze this question: which of those identified as nascent entrepreneurs are to be included in the analysis and which members of the comparison group are to be excluded.

The expectation that household net worth may affect participation in business start-ups reflects assumptions about the sources of financial support. It assumes limited initial support from other businesses or banking institutions. The most appropriate test of this hypothesis would restrict analysis to nascent firms that are being started by natural persons, excluding any ownership by legal entities such as other businesses or financial institutions. In addition, the character of the subsample would be less confusing if all nascent start-up's positive monthly cash flow for over 3 months were excluded. In a similar fashion, the comparison group can be adjusted to exclude any person reporting any effort to participate in entrepreneurship. As discussed above, this is achieved with the following commands:

Exhibit C.4a Example 2: Alternative Assessments of Educational Attainment, Ethnic Background on Entrepreneurial Activity Among Men

```
WEIGHTS BY WTEDRAC2.

CROSSTABS TABLES = USEDUC5 BY SUOWNAC BY USRACE4/CELL ROW COUNT/STAT =
CHISQ.

USEDUC5  EDUC ATTAINMENT: 5 CATEGORIES  by  SUOWNACT  BUSS START-UP,
OWNER, ACTIVE LAST 12 MTH
Controlling for..
USRACE4  ETHNIC BACKGROUND: 4 CATEGORIES  Value = 1.00  WHITE
```

```
                    | SUOWNACT       Page 1 of 1
             Count  |
           Row Pct  | NO S-U A S-U ACTI
                    | CTIVITY  VITY,OWN    Row
                    |    .00 |    1.00 | Total
USEDUC5   ---------+---------+---------+
          11.00|     910 |     101 |    1011
NO HS DEGREE    |    90.0 |    10.0 |     7.0
                +---------+---------+
        1212.00|    4877 |     381 |    5257
HS DEGREE       |    92.8 |     7.2 |    36.4
                +---------+---------+
        1315.00|    2879 |     314 |    3193
POST HS,NO COLL |    90.2 |     9.8 |    22.1
                +---------+---------+
        1616.00|    2894 |     307 |    3201
COLL DEGREE     |    90.4 |     9.6 |    22.2
                +---------+---------+
        1720.00|    1591 |     188 |    1780
POST COLL EXPERI|    89.4 |    10.6 |    12.3
                +---------+---------+
         Column   13151      1292     14442
          Total    91.1       8.9     100.0
```

```
   Chi-Square          Value          DF        Significance
   ----------------    ----------     ----       ---------------

   Pearson             30.70612         4          .00000


Minimum Expected Frequency - 90.457
```

Exhibit C.4a (Continued)

```
USEDUC5   EDUC ATTAINMENT: 5 CATEGORIES  by  SUOWNACT  BUSS START-UP,
OWNER, ACTIVE LAST 12 MTH
Controlling for..
USRACE4   ETHNIC BACKGROUND: 4 CATEGORIES  Value = 2.00   BLACK
```

		SUOWNACT		Page 1 of 1
	Count			
	Row Pct	NO S-U A CTIVITY .00	S-U ACTI VITY,OWN 1.00	Row Total
USEDUC5				
NO HS DEGREE	11.00	205 87.0	31 13.0	236 11.1
HS DEGREE	1212.00	856 88.3	113 11.7	970 45.8
POST HS,NO COLL	1315.00	405 82.5	86 17.5	491 23.2
COLL DEGREE	1616.00	259 84.7	47 15.3	306 14.4
POST COLL EXPERI	1720.00	87 75.0	29 25.0	117 5.5
Column Total		1813 85.6	306 14.4	2119 100.0

Chi-Square	Value	DF	Significance
Pearson	20.69075	4	.00036

```
Minimum Expected Frequency -16.815
```

```
*.
MISING VALUES CFPHLAG4 AUTONSU4 CGSUACT CGSUNUMB ( ).
*.
SELECT IF (CFPHLAG4 NE 92183).
SELECT IF (CFPHLAG4 NE 184275).
SELECT IF (CGSUACT NE 1).
SELECT IF ((RTYPE LT 20) OR ((RTYPE GE 20) & (SUINVOL NE 2))).
SELECT IF ((RTYPE LT 20) OR ((RTYPE GE 20) & (SUINVOL NE 3))).
```

Exhibit C.4b Example 2: Alternative Assessments of Educational Attainment, Ethnic Background on
Entrepreneurial Activity Among Men

```
USEDUC5   EDUC ATTAINMENT: 5 CATEGORIES  by  SUOWNACT  BUSS START-UP,
OWNER, ACTIVE LAST 12 MTH
Controlling for..
USRACE4  ETHNIC BACKGROUND: 4 CATEGORIES  Value = 3.00   HISPANIC


                        SUOWNACT        Page 1 of 1
                Count
                Row Pct   NO S-U A S-U ACTI
                          CTIVITY  VITY,OWN   Row
                            .00  |   1.00  | Total
USEDUC5    ---------+---------+---------+
              11.00|   143   |    14   |   157
 NO HS DEGREE      |   91.0  |    9.0  |   13.1
                   +---------+---------+
            1212.00|   426   |    45   |   471
 HS DEGREE         |   90.5  |    9.5  |   39.5
                   +---------+---------+
            1315.00|   247   |    28   |   274
 POST HS,NO COLL   |   89.9  |   10.1  |   23.0
                   +---------+---------+
            1616.00|   171   |    25   |   196
 COLL DEGREE       |   87.1  |   12.9  |   16.4
                   +---------+---------+
            1720.00|    78   |    18   |    96
 POST COLL EXPERI  |   80.9  |   19.1  |    8.0
                   +---------+---------+
            Column    1064      130      1194
            Total     89.1     10.9     100.0

     Chi-Square            Value        DF        Significance
   ----------------      ----------     ----     ----------------

   Pearson                9.11725        4           .05823

Minimum Expected Frequency - 10.440
```

```
SELECT IF ((RTYPE LT 20) OR ((RTYPE GE 20) & (SUINVOL NE 4))).
SELECT IF (AUTONSU4 NE 200).
SELECT IF (AUTONSU4 NE 300).
*.
```

The resulting sample has 1,115 cases, 716 nascent entrepreneurs and 399 comparison group members. Data on household net worth (HHNETR6) is missing for 41 cases within this subsample, reducing the total number of cases to 1,074.

The next issue to confront is the assembly of a common weight for all cases. The weights were computed separately for the first round of nascent entrepreneurs

(WTW1) and the comparison group (WTCG). Creation of a new weight variable easily solves this problem.

```
IF (RTYPE LT 20) EX03CASE = 1.
IF (RTYPE GE 20) EX03CASE = 2.
*.
IF ((EX03CASE = 1)) EX03_WT = WTW1.
IF ((EX03CASE = 2)) EX03_WT = WTCG.
VARIABLE LABEL
EX03_WT 'WEIGHTS FOR NE/CG COMPARISONS: EXAMPLE 3.'
```

It turns out that almost no adjustment is required for the new weight variable for this analysis. As shown below, the sum of the weights is almost exactly equal to the number of cases without adjustment. To be consistent, however, it is adjusted so the sum of the weights equals the number of cases and the average weight is equal to 1.00.

```
*.
WEIGHT OFF.
*.
DESCRIPTIVES VAR EX03_WT/STAT 1 10 11 12. [See Note a to
Exhibit C.3].

Variable  Mean  Minimum  Maximum    Sum     N    Label
EX03_WT   1.01    .31      1.64   1079.88  1074  WEIGHTS FOR
                                               NE/CG COMPAR:
                                               EXAMPLE C.3
*.
COMPUTE EX03_WT = EX03_WT*(1074/1079.88).
DESCRIPTIVES VAR EX04_WT/STAT 1 10 11 12. [See Note a to
Exhibit 3].

Variable  Mean  Minimum  Maximum    Sum     N    Label
EX03_WT   1.00    .31      1.64   1074.00  1074  WEIGHTS FOR
                                               NE/CG COMPAR:
                                               EXAMPLE 3
```

The result of the comparison is presented in Exhibit C.5, showing the distribution of wealth among those active in start-ups with no expected business or institutional ownership with a representative sample of U.S. adults not involved in business start-ups. There is no statistically significant difference between these two groups in terms of household wealth. The bar graph presented as Figure C.2 makes the similarity of the two distributions clear.

Household net worth is highly correlated with the age of the major wage earners in a household, and since nascent entrepreneurs tend to be younger adults, a comparison that controls for age may be more appropriate. As most people involved in entrepreneurship are less than 45 years old, the comparison was done

Exhibit C.5   Example 3: Weighted Assessment of Household Wealth and Entrepreneurial
Participation

```
*.
WEIGHT BY EX03_WT.
CROSSTABS TABLE HHNETR6 BY EX03CASE/
  CELL COL/
  STAT CHISQ.
```

HHNETR6   HH NET WORTH 5 CATEG:MIN/MAX ($10,000)   by   EX03CASE   NE
AND CG   CHOSEN FOR
ANALYSIS

```
                    EX03CASE      Page 1 of 1
           Col Pct |
                   | NE W/O B CG W/O A
                   | USS OWN   NY NE   Row
                   |   1.00     2.00 |Total
HHNETR6   ---------+---------+---------+
                 0 |   6.4  |    5.6  |   66
          NEGATIVE |        |         |  6.1
                   +---------+---------+
                10 |  54.1  |   47.7  |  556
      $0 To $100K  |        |         | 51.8
                   +---------+---------+
             10025 |  13.3  |   17.3  |  158
      $100K - $250K|        |         | 14.7
                   +---------+---------+
             25050 |   5.5  |    4.6  |   56
      $250K - $500K|        |         |  5.2
                   +---------+---------+
             50100 |  17.5  |   22.4  |  208
      $500K - $1MIL|        |         | 19.3
                   +---------+---------+
            100999 |   3.2  |    2.4  |   31
      $1MIL AND UP |        |         |  2.9
                   +---------+---------+
            Column     679      395     1074
            Total      63.2     36.8   100.0
```

Chi-Square	Value	DF	Significance
Pearson	9.04309	5	.10736
Likelihood Ratio	8.97679	5	.10999
Mantel-Haenszel test for linear association	1.38016	1	.24007

Minimum Expected Frequency - 11.443

Number of Missing Observations: 0

separately for those 18 to 44 years and those 45 years and older. The results, presented in Figures C.3 and C.4, make clear that there is a statistically significant difference among the younger group: the comparison group tends to have higher household net worth than does the nascent entrepreneur group. Among those 45 and older there is no statistically significant difference.

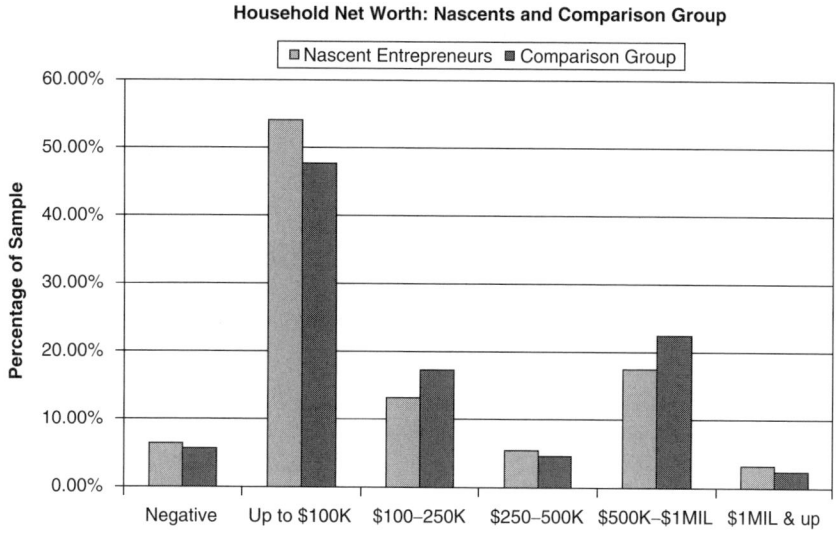

Figure C.2   Example 3: Weighted Assessment of Household Wealth and Entrepreneurial Participation

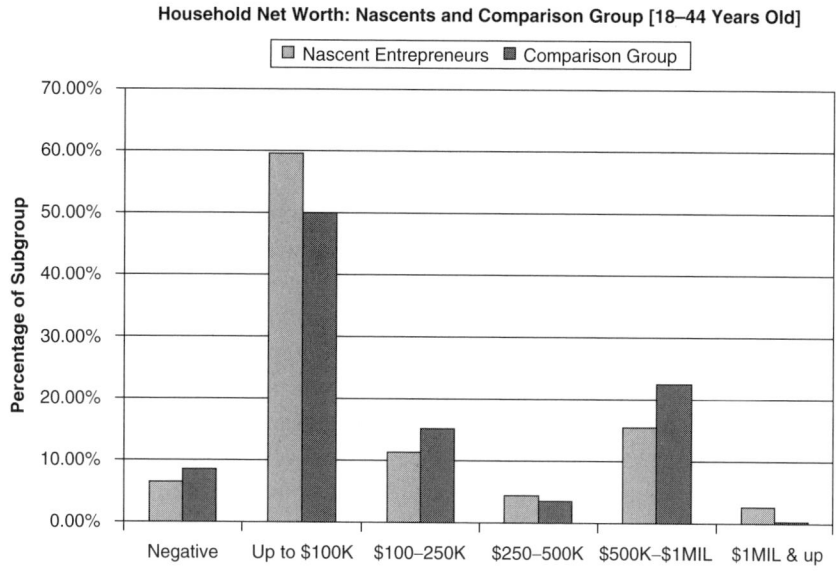

Figure C.3   Example 3: Weighted Assessment of Household Wealth and Entrepreneurial Participation (18 to 44 years old only)

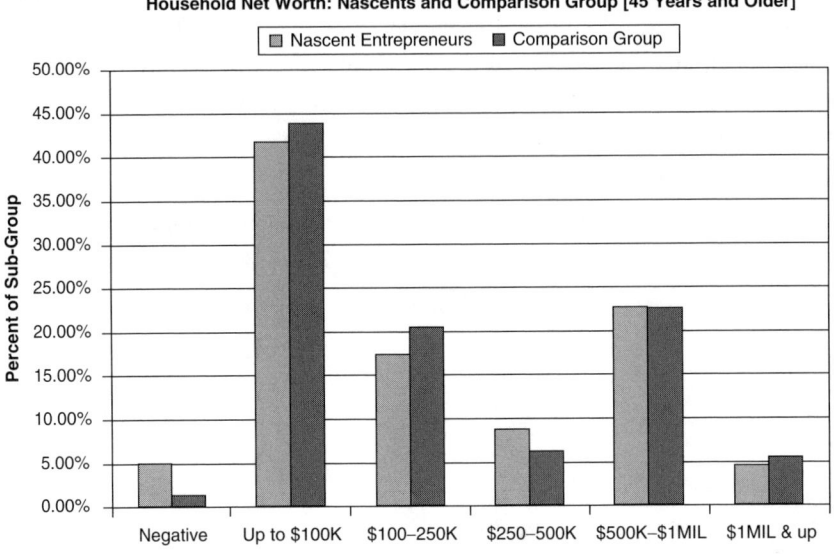

Figure C.4   Example 3: Weighted Assessment of Household Wealth and
Entrepreneurial Participation (45 years and older only)

Not only is there no explicit support for the "liquidity" hypothesis; this assessment suggests a reverse effect. Less household net worth may encourage those under 45 years old to become involved in starting a new firm. This has been an example of a basic analysis with no adjustments to control or account for any other factor except age. A more sophisticated assessment of the relative impact of household net worth and its effect on participating in a start-up in relation to 16 other factors can be found in Kim, Aldrich, and Kiester (2003).

Example 4: Preference for Risk and Entrepreneurial Activity

Perhaps no personal trait associated with starting a business gets more attention than a "preference for risk." It is widely assumed that entrepreneurs are more risk-oriented than ordinary individuals with "regular jobs." For this reason, a number of items were included in the self-completed mail questionnaire related to preferences for risk. One item, QH9 (presented in Exhibit B.2 of Appendix B) asks which of two businesses the respondent would prefer to own: Alpha, with high earnings and high risk, or Beta, with lower earnings but less risk. Following the famous assessment of the banker Rothschild, these are referred to as the "eatwell" versus "sleepwell" choices.

The analysis requires that the initial data be assembled from two sources, the initial detailed phone interviews and the self-completed mail questionnaire. Although a very high proportion (74%) of those completing the initial phone interview returned the self-completed mail questionnaire—one in four (26%) did not. Using the procedures discussed above to consolidate the weights for the initial wave as well as excluding those cases with a lack of data on the relevant variables, the total eligible case count is 793. The appropriate weights for all cases are those developed for the initial round of data collection, WTW1.

As with the previous analysis, it seems most useful to restrict this analysis to firms that will be owned only by natural persons, and it would sharpen the contrast if the analysis is restricted to those in the comparison group that are not involved in entrepreneurship in any way. Hence, the total sample was reduced using the syntax commands discussed earlier. Further, only those cases for which valid data is available for QH9 are included (values of 1 or 2); 6 cases without QH9 data are also excluded.

```
*.

WEIGHTS OFF.

MISSING VALUES CFPHLAG4 AUTONSU4 CGSUACT CGSUNUMB QH9 ( ).

SELECT IF (CFPHLAG4 NE 92183).

SELECT IF (CFPHLAG4 NE 184275).

SELECT IF (CGSUACT NE 1).

SELECT IF ((RTYPE LT 20) OR ((RTYPE GE 20) & (SUINVOL NE 2))).

SELECT IF ((RTYPE LT 20) OR ((RTYPE GE 20) & (SUINVOL NE 3))).

SELECT IF ((RTYPE LT 20) OR ((RTYPE GE 20) & (SUINVOL NE 4))).

SELECT IF (AUTONSU4 NE 200).

SELECT IF (AUTONSU4 NE 300).

*.

SELECT IF (QH9 LE 2).
```

The result is the following number of cases from the five cohorts:

```
RTYPE RESPONDENT, NATURE OF SAMPLE

Valid Cum
```

Value	Label	Value	Frequency	Percent	Percent	Percent
NE:	BOTH GENDERS	10.00	270	34.0	34.0	34.0
NE:	WOMEN OVERSAMPLE	11.00	134	16.9	16.9	50.9
NE:	MINORITY OVERSAMP	12.00	74	9.3	9.3	60.3
CG:	BOTH GENDERS	20.00	180	22.7	22.7	83.0
CG:	MINORITY OVERSAMP	21.00	135	17.0	17.0	100.0

```
———————————

Total 793 100.0 100.0
```

As with previous cases, the weights must be computed for this comparison and then standardized such that the average weight is 1.00.

```
COMPUTE EX04CASE = 9.
IF (RTYPE LT 20) EX04CASE = 1.
IF (RTYPE GE 20) EX04CASE = 2.
*.
VARIABLE LABEL
EX04CASE 'NE AND CG CHOSEN FOR ANALYSIS.'
VALUE LABEL
EX04CASE
1 'NE W/O LEG PERS OWN'
2 'CG W/O ANY NE.'
*.
IF ((EX04CASE = 1)) EX04_WT = WTW1.
IF ((EX04CASE = 2)) EX04_WT = WTCG.
*.
WEIGHT OFF.
DESCRIPTIVES VAR EX04_WT/STAT 1 10 11 12. [See Note a to
Exhibit C.3].
Variable Mean Minimum Maximum   Sum     N   Label
EX04_WT  1.02    .31     1.64   807.10 793  EXAMPLE 4 WEIGHT
*.
COMPUTE EX04_WT=EX04_WT*(793/807.12).
DESCRIPTIVES VAR EX04_WT/STAT 1 10 11 12. [See Note a to
Exhibit C.3].
Number of Valid Observations (Listwise) = 793.00
Variable Mean Minimum Maximum   Sum     N   Label
EX04_WT  1.00    .30     1.61   792.98 793  EXAMPLE 4 WEIGHT
```

Once the normalized weights are computed, the analysis can proceed.

The outcome is presented in Exhibit C.6, and it would appear that there is no statistically significant difference in a preference for a high-payoff, high-risk venture—the "eatwell" cases—when compared to a lower-payoff, lower-risk venture—the "sleepwell" cases. The overall sample of nascent entrepreneurs is very similar to the comparison group in this respect. The difference is marginally statistically significant at the 0.10 level.

The phone interview, however, contains a question about preferences for growth. Item Q322 asks if the nascent would prefer the business to "be as large as

Exhibit C.6   Example 4: Preference for Risk—Nascent Entrepreneurs and Comparison Group

```
WEIGHT BY EX04_WT.
CROSSTABS TABLES =
        QH9 BY EX04CASE
        /CELL ROW COL TOT COUNT
        /STAT=CHISQ.

QH9  Two types of new businesses-which prefer  by  EX04CASE   NE AND CG
CHOSEN FOR ANALYSIS

                       EX04CASE      Page 1 of 1
               Count
               Row Pct | NE W/O L CG W/O A
               Col Pct | EG PERS   NY NE   Row
               Tot Pct |    1.00 |    2.00 | Total
QH9          --------+---------+---------+
                   1 |    376  |    279  |  656
     ALPHA-SLEEPWELL |   57.4  |   42.6  | 82.7
                     |   80.8  |   85.4  |
                     |   47.5  |   35.2  |
                     +---------+---------+
                   2 |     89  |     48  |  137
     BETA-EATWELL    |   65.1  |   34.9  | 17.3
                     |   19.2  |   14.6  |
                     |   11.3  |    6.0  |
                     +---------+---------+
            Column       466       327     793
             Total      58.8      41.2   100.0
```

Chi-Square	Value	DF	Significance
Pearson	2.80366	1	.09405
Continuity Correction	2.49356	1	.11431
Likelihood Ratio	2.84570	1	.09162
Mantel-Haenszel test for linear association	2.80012	1	.09426

Minimum Expected Frequency - 56.562

Number of Missing Observations: 0

possible" or "a size I can manage myself or with a few key employees." For most respondents, this was answered several months before they completed the self-administered questionnaire and thus provides an assessment of their growth aspirations before their risk orientation was determined. It turns out that 464 qualifying nascent entrepreneurs answered both questions. The weight for this 464 is recomputed to equal an average of 1.00 and the impact assessed. As shown in Exhibit C.7, the result is statistically significant (at the 0.00003) level and there is substantial substantive significance. Those entrepreneurs interested in high-growth new firms are more than twice as likely (35% vs. 15%) to prefer a higher-payout, riskier venture.

The impact of this classification of nascent entrepreneurs and their comparison to the control group can be presented in graphic form, show in Figure C.5. This clearly indicates that "comfortable size" nascents are identical (not just close) to the comparison group in preference for high- versus low-risk ventures. The "growth oriented" nascent entrepreneurs are quite different from both low-growth nascents and the comparison group. For some, only those with aspirations for high growth would be considered "real" entrepreneurs. It is not possible, however, to determine which comes first—a preference for growth or a tolerance for risk; they both may be adopted at about the same time.

Exhibit C.7   Example 4: Preference for Risk and Firm Growth—Nascent Entrepreneurs

```
SELECT IF (SYSMIS(Q322) NE 1).

DESCRIPTIVES VAR EX04_WT/STAT 1 10 11 12. [See Note a to Exhibit C.3].
```

Variable	Mean	Minimum	Maximum	Sum	N	Label
EX04_WT	1.01	.49	1.46	509.06	464	EXAMPLE 4 WEIGHT

```
*.
COMPUTE EX04_WT=EX04_WT*(464/509.06).
DESCRIPTIVES VAR EX04_WT/STAT 1 10 11 12. [See Note a to Exhibit C.3].

Number of Valid Observations (Listwise) =        793.00
```

Variable	Mean	Minimum	Maximum	Sum	N	Label
EX04_WT	1.00	.45	1.33	464.00	464	EXAMPLE 4 WEIGHT

```
CROSSTABS TABLES =
        QH9 BY Q322 BY EX04CASE
        /CELL ROW COL TOT COUNT
        /STAT=CHISQ.

QH9  Two types of new businesses-which prefer  by  Q322
PREFERENCE FOR FUTURE
     FIRM SIZE
Controlling for..
EX04CASE  NE AND CG CHOSEN FOR ANALYSIS  Value = 1.00  NE W/O LEG
PERS OWN
```

```
                   Q322           Page 1 of 1
         Count
         Row Pct │ MAXIMIZE EASY TO
         Col Pct │ GROWTH      MANAGE    Row
         Tot Pct │         1 │         2 │ Total
QH9      ─────────┼─────────┼─────────┼
              1 │       58 │      316 │   374
ALPHA-SLEEPWELL │     15.5 │     84.5 │  80.7
                │     65.0 │     84.4 │
                │     12.5 │     68.2 │
                +─────────+─────────+
              2 │       31 │       58 │    89
BETA-EATWELL    │     34.9 │     65.1 │  19.3
                │     35.0 │     15.6 │
                │      6.7 │     12.6 │
                +─────────+─────────+
         Column        89        374       464
          Total      19.2       80.8     100.0
```

Chi-Square	Value	DF	Significance
Pearson	17.52826	1	.00003
Continuity Correction	16.30054	1	.00005
Likelihood Ratio	15.66833	1	.00008
Mantel-Haenszel test for linear association	17.49044	1	.00003

Minimum Expected Frequency - 17.213

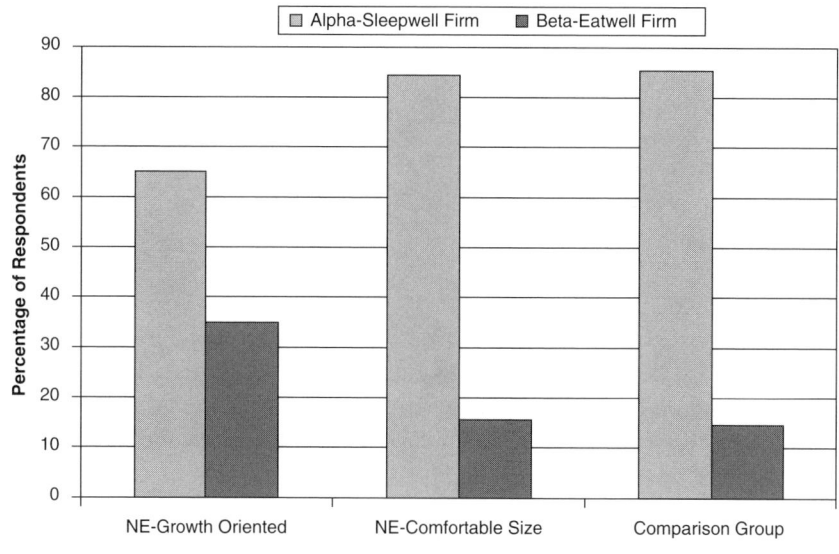

Preference for Risk: Comparison Group and Nascents by Growth Orientations

Figure C.5   Preference for Risk: Nascent Entrepreneurs by Growth Orientation and Comparison Groups

Example 5: Start-up Transitions as Affected by Gender and Ethnic Background

A primary objective of the PSED project was to determine the outcome of those who were actively involved in a business start-up. Once identified in the initial assessment as active nascent entrepreneurs, the major purpose of the follow-up data collection was to assess the current status of their efforts. All start-up efforts could be classified in one of four categories based on reports from the nascent entrepreneurs in the follow-up interviews:

- New business in place
- Active effort to complete the start-up process still underway
- No active effort to complete the start-up process, but not abandoned
- Start-up is terminated, no one is still actively trying to start the business

The first round of follow-up interviews took place 12 to 18 months after the initial interview. As an example of how analysis might proceed, the outcome information for those active in a start-up will be considered. First year outcome data is available for 74% (615 of 830) of those identified as nascent entrepreneurs and interviewed in the first follow-up after their initial interviews. This assessment will use as many of these firms as possible. Cases considered operating firms in the initial interview, with positive monthly cash flow for more than 3 months and with more than 50% of future ownership with legal persons were excluded. As before, the following commands were used to reduce the sample:

```
MISSING VALUES CFPHLAG4 AUTONSU CGSUACT CGSUNUMB ( ).

SELECT IF (CFPHLAG4 NE 92183).

SELECT IF (CFPHLAG4 NE 184275).

SELECT IF (AUTONSU NE 5).
```

In addition, none of the comparison group cases is relevant, and they are all excluded with a single command:

```
SELECT IF (RTYPE LT 20).
```

Several features of the data set need to be taken into account in completing this analysis. First are the differences in the location of the follow-up data. For the mixed-gender and female-only cohorts, the initial status is part of the second-wave data (variables starting with "R"). The first follow-up data for the minority oversample are in the third wave of data collection (variables starting with "S"). Standardizing the relationship between the initial and first follow-up data can be accomplished by creating a new set of variables associated with the outcome. This is done for the different cohorts as follows: The variable "RTYPE" distinguishes between the cohorts of nascent entrepreneurs: "10" for mixed-gender, "11" for female oversample, and "12" for the minority oversample. New variable names and value labels are also applied.

```
IF (RTYPE EQ 10) FU1_502 = R502.
IF (RTYPE EQ 10) FU1_503 = R503.
*.
IF (RTYPE EQ 11) FU1_502 = R502.
IF (RTYPE EQ 11) FU1_503 = R503.
*.
IF (RTYPE EQ 12) FU1_502 = S502.
IF (RTYPE EQ 12) FU1_503 = S503.
*.
VARIABLE LABELS
FU1_502 'CURRENT STATUS OF START-UP:1ST TRY'/
FU1_503 'CURRENT STATUS OF START-UP:2ND TRY.'
*.
VALUE LABELS FU1_502 FU1_503
1 'OPERATING BUSINESS'
2 'ACTIVE START-UP'
3 'INACTIVE START-UP'
4 'NO LONGER WORKED ON'
5 'SOMETHING ELSE.'
```

Because of the importance of the status of the start-up effort in the follow-up, the question was actually asked twice. Those who were unsure of the correct response the first time they were asked the question (R502 or S502) were asked the question a second time (R503 or S503). By asking the question twice, interviewers were almost always able to obtain a response appropriate to one of the first four categories. This means, however, that the responses to the second question must be recoded into the first to provide a single variable representing the first follow-up outcome. Those that gave a "something else" response (value 5) to the first question are adjusted to match their response to the question when it was asked the second time with the following commands:

```
IF ((FU1_502 = 5)&(FU1_503=1)) FU1_502 = 1.
IF ((FU1_502 = 5)&(FU1_503=2)) FU1_502 = 2.
IF ((FU1_502 = 5)&(FU1_503=3)) FU1_502 = 3.
IF ((FU1_502 = 5)&(FU1_503=4)) FU1_502 = 4.
```

An additional issue occurs with relation to the weights that were recalculated for each data collection wave. This can be resolved by developing a new set of weights, based on the wave in which the follow-up data is located. The programming is relatively straightforward, as follows:

```
*.

COMPUTE FU1_WT = 999.

IF (RTYPE LE 11) FU1_WT = WTW2.

IF (RTYPE EQ 12) FU1_WT = WTW3.

VARIABLE LABEL

FU1_WT 'WEIGHTS FOR FIRST FOLLOW-UP ANALYSIS.'

MISSING VALUES FU1_WT (999).

*.
```

By assigning a weight of 999 to all cases in which no relevant follow-up data is provided, and classifying this as a missing value, these cases will be automatically excluded from any analysis using FU1_WT as the weighting variable.

The remainder of the assessment is rather straightforward. The most precise measure of gender, NCGENDER (see Chapter 2), and ethnic background, PGRACE (See Chapter 3), are used for this analysis. In each analysis the sum of the weights of the relevant cases is determined and adjusted so that the average weight equals one. The following represents the correction for the gender comparison weights.

```
WEIGHT OFF.

*.

DESCRIPTIVES VAR = FU1_WT/STAT 1 10 11 12. [See Note a to
Exhibit C.3].

FU1_WT.98.38  1.84  594.94  606  WEIGHTS  FOR  FIRST  FOLLOW-UP
ANALYSIS'

COMPUTE FU1_WTS = FU1_WT*(606/594.94).

VARIABLE LABEL

FU1_WTS 'WEIGHT FOR ALL CASES WITH GENDER.'

*.

DESCRIPTIVES VAR = FU1_WTS/STAT 1 10 11 12. [See Note a to
Exhibit C.3.]

Variable Mean  Minimum Maximum   Sum    N   Label

FU1_WTS  1.00    .38     1.87   605.32 606  WEIGHT  FOR  ALL
                                            CASES  WITH  GENDER
```

The analysis related to ethnic background, in which only the White, Black, and Hispanic cases are included, required a second adjustment of the weights.

```
WEIGHT OFF.

DESCRIPTIVES VAR = FU1_WT/STAT 1 10 11 12. [See Note a to
Exhibit C.3].
```

```
Variable Mean Minimum Maximum   Sum     N   Label

FU1_WT     .98     .38     1.84   574.60 589  WEIGHTS  FOR  FIRST
                                              FOLLOW-UP ANALYSIS

*.

COMPUTE FU1_WTR = FU1_WT*(589/574.60).

VARIABLE LABEL

FU1_WTR 'WEIGHT FOR RACE:WHITE,BLACK,HISP ONLY.'

*.

DESCRIPTIVES VAR = FU1_WTR/STAT 1 10 11 12. [See Note a to
Exhibit C.3.]

Variable Mean Minimum Maximum   Sum     N   Label

FU1_WTR 1.00    .39     1.88   588.25 589  WEIGHT  FOR RACE:
                                           WHITE,BLACK,HISP
                                           ONLY
```

The analysis that was completed resulted in cross-tabulations but is easiest to present as bar graphs. The comparisons based on gender and ethnic background are presented in Figure C.6. There was no statistically significant difference related to gender, and the substantive differences are quite small: about 30% report an operating business, 30% report an active start-up effort, 20% report an inactive start-up effort, and 20% report that the start-up has been abandoned.

Differences related to ethnic background as shown in Figure C.6 are much greater and were just marginally statistically significant at the 0.05 level.

This leads to an examination of the interaction between gender and ethnic background, as shown in Figure C.7. In this case, both assessments are statistically significant at the 0.05 level, and the patterns are somewhat different for men and women.

Substantially fewer Black and Hispanic men report a going business in the first follow-up interview (18 to 22%), compared to White men (34%), and substantially more report continuing efforts in the start-up phase, active or inactive. The percentage of men who report abandoning the effort is about the same for all three groups (15% to 20%).

Among women, however, the differences are far more dramatic. Black and White women report the same proportions of going businesses, and more Black women report efforts in the start-up phase. Only 10% of Black women report that a start-up has been abandoned, the smallest proportion of any group of men or women. Hispanic women, however, are most distinctive. Exactly half report the effort has been abandoned, and only one in six (15%) reports a going business. Although there are only 14 Hispanic women, these results clearly reflect a quite different situation compared to any of the other five gender-ethnic groups. Ideally, this assessment of Hispanic women would be replicated with a larger representative sample.

Perhaps most dramatic is the contrast between the evidence of participating in the start-up process and the data on completing the process with a new firm. It was

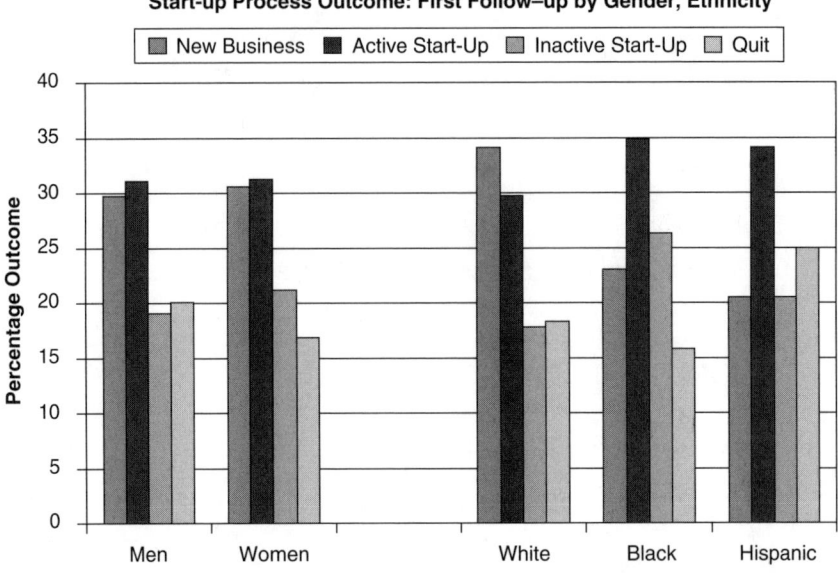

Figure C.6   Start-up Process First Follow-up Outcomes: By Gender and Ethnic
Background

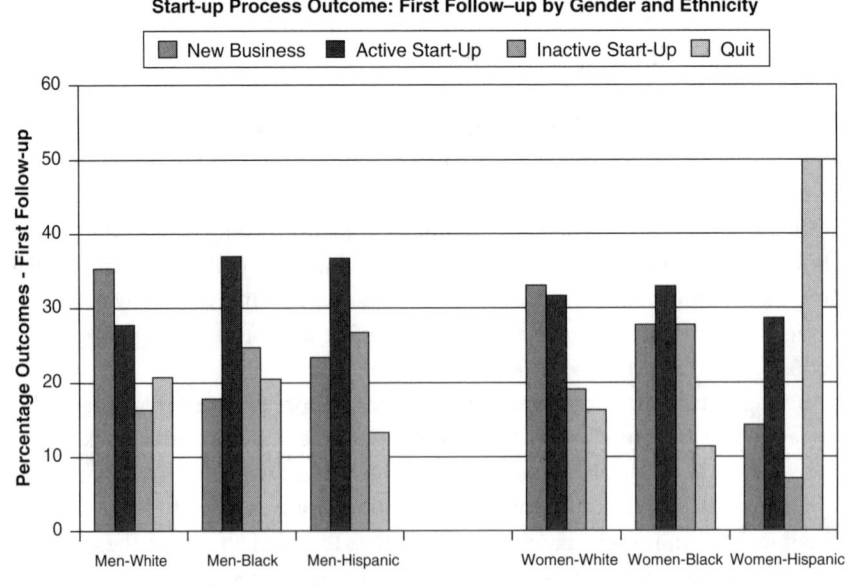

Figure C.7   Start-up Process First Follow-up Outcomes: Gender by Ethnic
Background

clear in Figure C.1 (presented in Example 2) that Black and Hispanic men are substantially more active than White men in entering the start-up process. But the evidence in Figure C.5 suggests Black and Hispanic men report less early success—although they may be simply taking longer to implement new firms than White men. More details on the extent of this "minority men effect" will be required to assess the reasons for this difference. This difference is not present when Black and White women are compared. Black women are just as successful as White women in completing the start-up with a new firm, and a very small proportion quit the start-up effort. Larger samples of Hispanic women will be required before their outcome patterns are clearly established.

A final comment is related to the nature of the procedure used to locate nascent entrepreneurs in the screening procedure. It takes months—sometimes years—to complete the start-up process. The screening procedure identifies nascent entrepreneurs at a random point in the start-up process. Measures of the time to complete the process and successful transitions from start-up to new business should be based on the point of firm conception, that date when the start-up process began. The determinations are possible with the PSED data set, but they are complex and go beyond this introductory discussion. The implementation of more precise measures of the start-up timing may affect inferences regarding the outcomes.

Example 6: Multivariate Analysis: Screening and Detail Samples

The PSED data set makes it clear that the entrepreneurial process is complex and multifaceted. The data cover a wide range of processes and factors that may affect the creation of a new business. This would lead many to consider multivariate analysis, by which the relative impact of a number of independent variables on the process might be explored. There are two options for such an analysis. The first is the most straightforward, the use of the screening data set to explore a range of factors and their relative impact on those identified as active in the start-up process. The second is to use the detailed data set for such analysis. Each strategy has advantages and disadvantages.

Screening Data Set and Multivariate Analysis. The screening data set provides two advantages. First is the large size, 64,000 cases, which allows for precise estimates of the impact of various variables. The second is the fact that it is a representative sample, which allows inferences about the entire U.S. population. This means that the average values of the independent variables as well as their dispersion (range or variation) may be considered to represent the U.S. population. So if one wanted to consider the relative impact of gender, age, and educational attainment, the procedure is relatively straightforward. These variables are identified and coded into appropriate categories, cases with missing values may be deleted, and their univariate impact can be considered.

The PSED screener, as discussed above, characterizes most respondents regarding active involvement with two criteria. First, did the respondents report that they were active in starting a new firm, and, second, did they expect full or partial ownership of the new firm? Those that satisfied these two criteria were coded as 1 for variable SUOWNACT, all others were coded zero. The only adjustment regarding the weights would require recentering weights for those cases with complete data on all variables in the analysis. Of the 64,622 cases in the PSED screener, those in the mixed-gender comparison group (RTYPE = 20), 2,010 cases, are dropped from the data set. Another 1,988 cases are dropped due to missing data on age and a further 270 due to missing data on educational attainment. (Because the screening sample was collected to have an equal number of cases on men and women, there is no missing data on gender.

Following identification of all eligible cases, the weights are "recentered" such that the average value is 1.00, using the following command syntax:

```
WEIGHTS OFF.
DESCRIPTIVES VAR = WT_SCRN/STAT 1 10 11 12. [See Note a to
Exhibit C.3.]
Variable Mean  Minimum Maximum     Sum      N    Label
WT_SCRN  1.00    .73     1.67   60374.25 60354 Screening
                                                file weights
COMPUTE WT_SCRN = WT_SCRN*(60354/60374.25).
DESCRIPTIVES VAR = WT_SCRN/STAT 1 10 11 12. [See Note a to
Exhibit C.3.]
Variable Mean  Minimum Maximum     Sum      N    Label
WT_SCRN  1.00    .73     1.67   60354.00 60354 Screening
                                                file weights
```

This, once again, produces an average weight of 1.00 and the sum of the cases equals the sum of the weights.

The univariate impact of these three variables is presented in Table C.7. Age and educational attainment have been recoded to match the values for the following discussion.

Given the discussions in previous examples and a sample size of over 60,000, it should be no surprise that the results are highly statistically significant.

As the dependent variable, participation in a business start-up is dichotomous, and all three independent variables are categorical. Logistic regression is appropriate for an initial analysis. Analysis was completed using the SPSS Windows 11.5 logistic regression procedure with forced entry of all variables. Forced entry reflects the assumption that all variables will be important and that the procedure will be used to determine relative significance, reflected in the Beta weights. The results are presented in Table C.8. All three sociodemographic variables are treated as sets of dummy variables (values of 1 or 0) compared to a base value that does not appear in the assessment: women, those 65 and older, and those with graduate educational experience.

Table C.7   Screening Sample: Univariate Impact on Two-Criteria Nascents

		Not Active (No./100)	2-Criteria Nascents (No./100)	Chi-Sq. (Pearson)	Stat. Sign.
Number of Cases		56,755	3,599		
All Cases		94.0	6.0		
Gender					
	Men	92.2	7.8		
	Women	95.7	4.3	325.51008	0.00000
Age					
	18–24 Years	93.7	6.3		
	25–44 Years	91.7	8.3		
	45–64 Years	94.6	5.4		
	65 Years and Up	99.4	0.6	736.00838	0.00000
Educational Attainment					
	Up to HS Degree	95.4	4.6		
	Post HS, no College Degree	92.7	7.3		
	College Degree	92.9	7.1		
	Some Graduate Experience	91.8	8.2	223.33424	0.00000

This makes clear that all three factors have a unique and statistically significant contribution to explaining the variation in participating in a business start-up. The overall model has a chi-square value of 1420.298 ($p < 0.000$) and has a Nagelkerke R-squared estimate of 0.064. These three variables may account for 6.4% of the variation in participation in business start-ups as a nascent entrepreneur.

Detailed Data Set and Multivariate Analysis. The major advantage of the detailed data set is the large number of variables that have been assembled for representative samples of nascent entrepreneurs and typical adults not involved in business start-ups. This reflects the decision that many factors may be of importance and worth serious consideration. Cost considerations, however, limited the number of cases that were collected for the comparison group, which is about one half the size of the nascent entrepreneur group. This is not a major concern when there are

Table C.8   Screening Sample: Logistic Regression Forced Entry Model, Three IV's

	Beta	SE (Beta)	Stat. Sign.
Constant	−5.022	0.142	0.000
Gender: Men compared to women	0.592	0.036	0.000
Age: 18–24 compared to 65 and up	2.302	0.140	0.000
Age: 18–24 compared to 65 and up	2.571	0.134	0.000
Age: 18–24 compared to 65 and up	2.123	0.136	0.000
Education: Up to HS, versus Grad Exp	−.511	0.057	0.000
Education: Up to HS, versus Grad Exp	−.108	0.061	0.076
Education: Up to HS, versus Grad Exp	−.202	0.063	0.001

direct comparisons between the two groups. A comparison of the household net worth—discussed in Example 3—illustrates such an analysis. Those identified as active in the entrepreneurial process either had about the same household net worth as those not so active or if they were under 45 years of age, typically with less household net worth.

But a different challenge arises for assessing the relative or joint impact of various independent variables. The primary complication is that the total number of cases does not provide a representative sample of the U.S. adult population. This means that the average and range of the variables for the entire sample would clearly not represent the U.S. adult population.

One solution is to adjust the weights to create a sample that has the same proportion of nascent entrepreneurs as expected among the U.S. population. Based on the analysis of the screening data as presented in Table C.7, this is 6% of the adult population. The following strategy can be adopted. Once the variables for analysis are chosen and decisions made about who is an appropriate candidate for the nascent entrepreneur and comparison groups, the nascent entrepreneurs' weights are adjusted so they are 6% of the total weighted detailed sample.

For this example, the variables chosen from the detailed sample are gender, age, educational attainment, and total years of work experience. Although the first three were gathered in the screening interview, they were obtained again in the detailed interview. The most accurate version of each (NCGENDER, EX6AGE, ITRWEDU4) were utilized, along with the phone interview item related to total years of work experience (Q340). For this assessment, only nascent entrepreneurs involved in firms in which only natural persons would be owners were retained, and all comparison group members with any indication of entrepreneurial activity were excluded (See Example 3 for the command syntax). Once all the cases with missing values on the independent variables were excluded, a total of 1,095 cases remained,

397 comparison group members and 698 active in the start-up process where only natural persons would own the new firm.

The procedure for creating, assessing, and adjusting the weights is outlined in Exhibit C.8. The first step is to create a single weight for all cases, WT_EX6. The weight is then assessed in terms of the average value for each subgroup. Use of the means procedure provides a convenient way to assess the average and sum of the weights. The weight variable WT_EX6 is then adjusted so the average value is equal to 1.00 for both the comparison and nascent subsamples. A new weight is then created so the total sample will represent the U.S. adult population, WT_EX6P. This is done by reducing the average value of the weights assigned to the nascent subsample to achieve this end. The total number of nascent cases should equal 6% of the total weighted sample, or 6/94ths of the number of comparison group cases.

The next step is to recenter the weights so that the sum of the weights equals the case count. Given that the sum of the weights is 422 and the total case count is 1,095, each weight is multiplied by 1,095/422. The procedure does not affect the proportion of nascents in the sample but corrects the sample size for statistical calculations. The last section of Exhibit C.8 shows that the proportion of nascents in the sample weighted by WT_EX6P is exactly 6%. The weighted number of nascent cases is 66, and the weighted number of comparison group cases is 1,029. It is now possible to consider the relative impact of different independent variables on variation in nascent entrepreneurs among the sample.

The impact of this adjustment on the basic patterns is presented in Table C.9, which has the same form as three of the variables presented in Table C.7, based on the full screening sample. In this case, the prevalence rate for all cases is not based on the screening data but has been adjusted to match the prevalence based on the screening data, 6 per 100 adults.

But the impact of gender, age, and educational attainment are of considerable interest. For comparison, the prevalence rates from the full screening sample in Table C.7 are provided in Table C.9 next to the population-weighted detailed sample in parentheses. The prevalence rates are very close for gender and age, with a slight difference related to educational attainment. Prevalence related to education is the highest for college degrees with the population-weighted detailed sample, and for those with graduate experience from the screening sample.

The use of corrected population weights is the only way to determine the relative impact of the wide range of variables in the detailed sample data. The focus is on identifying the relative impact of different variables on the decision to engage in starting a new business. This is done by creating alternative multivariate models and considering the overall impact of the models. For example, the same procedures discussed as the simple model with the screening data were applied to the population-weighted detailed data, again using SPSS Windows 11.5 and forced entry of all variables. The results are presented in Table C.10. Again, all three sociodemographic variables are treated as sets of dummy variables (values of 1 or 0) compared to a base value that does not appear in the assessment: women, 65 and older, and graduate educational experience. Note that although the beta weights are very similar to those reported for the full screening sample in Table C.8, none have a statistically significant contribution to the explained variance, as the standard

Exhibit C.8   Transforming Variables and Weights to Create a Population Representative Sample

```
WEIGHT OFF.
*.
EXCLUDE CASES INAPPROPRIATE FOR THE ANLAYSIS.

MISSING VALUES CFPHLAG4 AUTONSU4 CGSUACT CGSUNUMB (   ).
*.
SELECT IF (CFPHLAG4   NE 92183).
SELECT IF (CFPHLAG4   NE 184275).
SELECT IF (CGSUACT    NE 1).
SELECT IF (AUTONSU4   NE 200).
SELECT IF (AUTONSU4   NE 300).
*.
FREQ VAR RTYPE.
SELECT IF ((RTYPE LT 20) OR ((RTYPE GE 20) & (SUINVOL NE 2))).
SELECT IF ((RTYPE LT 20) OR ((RTYPE GE 20) & (SUINVOL NE 3))).
SELECT IF ((RTYPE LT 20) OR ((RTYPE GE 20) & (SUINVOL NE 4))).
*.
ESTIMATE MISSING VALUES AND RECODE INDEPENDENT VARIABLES.

MISSING VALUE ITRWAGE (   ).
IF (ITRWAGE = 9999) ITRWAGE = USAGE.
*.
COMPUTE EX6AGE   = ITRWAGE.
VARIABLE LABEL        EX6AGE    'U WIS INTER AGE: FOUR CATEGORIES'.
RECODE EX6AGE
        (18 THRU 24 = 1824)
        (25 THRU 44 = 2544)
        (45 THRU 64 = 4564)
        (65 THRU 99 = 6599)
        (ELSE = 9999).
VALUE LABELS EX6AGE
        1824 '18-24 YRS'
        2544 '25-44 YRS'
        4564 '45-64 YRS'
        6599 '65-UP YRS'
        9999 'MISSING DATA'.
*.
MISSING VALUES Q340 (   ).
*.
COMPUTE YRSWORK6 = Q340.
RECODE YRSWORK6
  (0 = 0)
  (1 THRU 5 = 105)
  (6 THRU 10 = 610)
  (11 THRU 20 = 1120)
```

```
 (21 THRU 30 = 2130)
 (31 THRU 60 = 3160).
VARIABLE LABEL
 YRSWORK6 'YEARS WORK EXP: 6 CATEGORIES'.
VALUE LABELS
 YRSWORK6
 0 'NONE'
 105 ' 1-5 YRS'
 610 ' 6-10 YRS'
 1120 '11-20 YRS'
 2130 '21-30 YRS'
 3160 '31-60 YRS'.
*.
COMPUTE NASCENT = 0.
IF    (RTYPE LT 20)    NASCENT = 1.
VARIABLE LABEL         NASCENT         'NASCENT ENT FOR HANDOOK EX 6'.
VALUE LABEL
     NASCENT
     0        'NOT INVOLVED'
     1        'ACTIVE'.
*.
EXCLUDE CASES WITH MISSING VALUES ON INDEPENDENT VARIABLES.

SELECT IF (EX6AGE NE 9999).
SELECT IF (ITRWEDU4 NE 99).
SELECT IF (Q340 NE 99).
*.

COMPUTE WEIGHTS FOR THE ANALYSIS.
*.
COMPUTE WT_EX6 = 9999.
IF (RTYPE LT 20) WT_EX6 = WTW1.
IF (RTYPE GE 20) WT_EX6 = WTCG.
VARIABLE LABEL  WT_EX6 'WEIGHT FOR HANDBOOK EXAMPLE 6'.
WEIGHT OFF.
*.
MEANS TABLE = WT_EX6 BY NASCENT/STAT ALL.

Summaries of   WT_EX6     WEIGHT FOR HANDBOOK EXAMPLE 6
By levels of   NASCENT    NASCENT ENT FOR HANDOOK EX 6

     Value   Label              Sum    Mean  Std Dev  Sum of Sq  Cases

       .00   NOT INVOLVED   403.9171  1.0174   .6406  162.4869    397
      1.00   ACTIVE         696.2707   .9975   .3565   88.6064    698
                           ------------------------------------------------
Within Groups Total        1100.1878  1.0047   .4793  251.0933   1095

*.
RE-CENTER WEIGHTS FOR BOTH NASCENT AND COMPARISON GROUPS.

IF (NASCENT = 0)    WT_EX6=WT_EX6*(397/403.9171).
```

(Continued)

Exhibit C.8 (Continued)

```
IF (NASCENT = 1)   WT_EX6=WT_EX6*(698/696.2707).
*.
MEANS TABLE = WT_EX6 BY NASCENT/STAT ALL.

Summaries of    WT_EX6    WEIGHT FOR HANDBOOK EXAMPLE 6
By levels of    NASCENT   NASCENT ENT FOR HANDOOK EX 6
```

Value	Label	Sum	Mean	Std Dev	Sum of Sq	Cases
.00	NOT INVOLVED	397.0000	1.0000	.6296	156.9694	397
1.00	ACTIVE	698.0000	1.0000	.3574	89.0471	698
Within Groups Total		1095.0000	1.0000	.4744	246.0164	1095

```
*.
```
ADJUST WEIGHTS SO NASCENTS ARE 6% OF THE TOTAL CASES.

```
COMPUTE WT_EX6P = 0.
IF (NASCENT = 0) WT_EX6P = WT_EX6*(397/397).
IF (NASCENT = 1) WT_EX6P = WT_EX6*((((0.06/0.94)*397))/698).
VARIABLE LABEL   WT_EX6P 'HANDBOOK EX 6 WEIGHT: ADJ TO POP VALUES'.
*.
```
ADJUST SUM OF WEIGHTS EQUAL TOTAL NUMBER OF CASES.

```
WEIGHTS OFF.
DESC VAR WT_EX6P/STAT 1 10 11 12. [See Note a to Exhibit C.3].
```

Variable	Mean	Minimum	Maximum	Sum	N	Label
WT_EX6P	.39	.02	1.61	422.34	1095	HANDBOOK EX 6 WEIGHT:ADJ TO POP VALUES

```
COMPUTE WT_EX6P = WT_EX6P*(1095/422.34).

DESC VAR WT_EX6P/STAT 1 10 11 12.  [See Note a to Exhibit C.3].
```

Variable	Mean	Minimum	Maximum	Sum	N	Label
WT_EX6P	1.00	.05	4.18	1095.00	1095	HANDBOOK EX 6 WEIGHT:ADJ TO POP VALUES

CHECK ON FINAL FREQUENCY OF NASCENTS WITH NEW WEIGHTS.

```
WEIGHT BY WT_EX6P.
*.
FREQ VAR NASCENT.

NASCENT    NASCENT ENT FOR HANDOOK EX 6
```

Value Label	Value	Frequency	Percent	Valid Percent	Cum Percent
NOT INVOLVED	.00	1029	94.0	94.0	94.0
ACTIVE	1.00	66	6.0	6.0	100.0
Total		1095	100.0	100.0	

Table C.9   Detailed Sample, Population Matching Weights: Univariate Impact on Three-Criteria Nascents

		Not Active (No./100)	3-Criteria Nascents (No./100)	Chi-Sq (Pearson)	Stat. Sign.
Number of Cases: Unweighted		397	698		
Number of Cases: Weighted		1,029	66		
All Cases		94.0	6.0 (6.0)		
Gender					
	Men	91.9	8.1 (7.8)		
	Women	95.9	4.1 (4.3)	7.514	0.008
Age					
	18–24 Years	94.1	5.9 (6.3)		
	25–44 Years	92.7	7.3 (8.3)		
	45–64 Years	95.1	4.9 (5.4)		
	65 Years and Up	98.3	1.7 (0.6)	4.821	0.185
Educational Attainment					
	Up to HS Degree	94.9	5.1 (4.6)		
	Post HS, No College Degree	93.9	6.1 (7.3)		
	College Degree	92.4	7.6 (7.1)		
	Some Graduate Experience	94.7	5.3 (8.2)	1.561	0.668
Work Experience					
	None	96.2	3.8		
	1–5 Years	92.5	7.5		
	6–10 Years	93.7	6.3		
	11–20 Years	93.0	7.0		
	21–30 Years	94.9	5.1		
	31–60 Years	95.6	4.4	2.382	0.794

NOTE: Numbers in parentheses based on full screening sample, taken from Table C.7.

errors of the beta weights were substantially higher. Both reflect the shift from a sample of 60,354 to 1,095.

The overall model has a chi-square value of 13.261 (7 degrees of freedom, $p < 0.058$) and has a Nagelkerke R-squared estimate of 0.034. These three variables may account for 3.4 % of the variation in participation in entrepreneurial activities.

Table C.10   Detailed Sample: Logistic Regression Forced Entry Model—Three IV's

	Beta	SE (Beta)	Stat sign
Constant	−4.499	1.011	0.000
Gender: Men compared to women	0.701	0.265	0.101
Age: 18–24 compared to 65 and up	1.281	1.026	0.213
Age: 25–44 compared to 65 and up	1.458	0.947	0.124
Age: 45–64 compared to 65 and up	1.059	0.965	0.274
Educ: Up to HS, versus Grad Exp	−.029	0.456	0.949
Educ: HS Degree, versus Grad Exp	0.107	0.399	0.788
Educ: Up to Coll Deg, versus Grad Exp	0.286	0.438	0.513

A second model that included the fourth sociodemographic variable, years of work experience, was also assessed with exactly the same procedure. In this case, the years of work experience was represented by 5 dummy variables (values of 1 or 0) compared to those with 31 to 60 years of work experience. The results are presented in Table C.11. Again, the beta weights are very similar to those for the full screen model or the three IV variable model with regards to the constant, gender, age, and educational attainment. Once again, the standard errors of the betas are quite large, and none are making a statistically significant contribution.

The enhanced overall model, however, has a chi-square value of 15.246 (12 degrees of freedom; $p < 0.228$) and has a Nagelkerke R-squared estimate of 0.038. These four variables may account for 3.8% of the variation in participation in entrepreneurial activities, an increase of 0.4% from the three variable model.

The four variable model fits about as well, or as poorly, as the three variable model, with a slight improvement in the explained variance. It would seem appropriate to assume that a modest number of years of work experience, from 1 to 20, may have an independent positive contribution to a decision to participate in a new business start-up. No experience or over 20 years of experience may reduce the tendency to participate.

Table C.11   Detailed Sample: Logistic Regression Forced Entry Model—Four IV's

	Beta	SE (Beta)	Stat sign
Constant	−4.548	1.033	0.000
Gender: Men compared to women	0.748	0.272	0.006
Age: 18–24 compared to 65 and up	1.023	1.144	0.373
Age: 25–44 compared to 65 and up	1.336	1.013	0.188
Age: 45–64 compared to 65 and up	1.091	0.982	0.268
Educ: Up to HS, versus Grad Exp	−.057	0.462	0.902
Educ: HS Degree, versus Grad Exp	0.105	0.403	0.794
Educ: Up to Coll Deg, versus Grad Exp	0.243	0.444	0.585
Years of work: None compared to 30 plus	−.127	1.154	0.912
Years of work: 1–5 compared to 30 plus	0.406	0.655	0.535
Years of work: 6–10 compared to 30 plus	0.174	0.611	0.776
Years of work: 11–20 compared to 30 plus	0.227	0.543	0.675
Years of work: 21–30 compared to 30 plus	−.149	0.521	0.774

An alternative objective is to determine whether or not a single independent variable has any statistically significant impact on the dependent variable. In that case, it is possible to simplify most independent variables to dichotomous variables and use procedures that answer only this question. Two criteria are used to assess success. Is there evidence that a given variable has any statistically significant relationship to a dependent variable? Is there an indication that the multivariable model has a statistically significant match with the data? With these objectives in mind, and using an odds-ratio measure of impact in a logit regression model, it was possible to consider a 10 variable model with 7 control variables; there was evidence that 7 had a statistically significant impact (Kim et al., 2003).

Commentary

This has been an introductory discussion of selected issues associated with analysis of the PSED data set. It has assumed some familiarity with standard data processing procedures, such as SAS or SPSS. While the initial training investment required to develop the skills to explore the start-up process in detail is not trivial, such detailed assessments can provide a greater appreciation of the diverse ways in which new firms come into being.

These examples have dealt with less than a dozen of the variables in the PSED data sets. The various chapters in the PSED handbook have dealt with hundreds of variables. There is plenty left over for everybody else. It is unlikely that the full potential of this resource will ever be exhausted.

References

Kim, P. H., Aldrich, H. E., & Kiester, L. A. (2003, August). *Does wealth matter? The impact of financial and human capital on becoming a nascent entrepreneur.* Paper presented at the American Sociological Association Annual Meetings, Atlanta, GA.

Name Index

Subject Index

Academy of Distinguished
    Entrepreneurs, 207
Achievement motivation. *See* Cognitive
    characteristics
Activity allocation, 9
Adaptor preference, 136, 173
    See also Decision-making
African American entrepreneurs, 8, 26
    education levels of, 81
    individual assets of, 30-31
    opportunities, access to, 31
    social networks of, 31
    theoretical model for, 28-29
    See also Data analysis examples;
        Minority entrepreneurs
Age variable, 6-7, 119
Anonymity, 494
Approval. *See* External validation motive
Assistance programs. *See* Business
    assistance programs
Attributional Style Questionnaire
    (ASQ), 207
Attribution theory, 136-137, 157, 205
    control over process and, 206-207
    failures/successes, response to, 207-208
    locus of causality and, 206
    person/environment influences and,
        205-206
    questionnaire items, scoring of,
        210, 211
    start-ups, rationale for, 208
    task success explanations, 206
    See also Locus of control

Babson College, xvi, xxvii, 207
Babson-Kauffman Entrepreneurship
    Research Conferences, xv, xvii
Behavioral psychology theory, 277
Bias:
    gender discrimination, 18
    paid/unpaid work, distribution of, 106

Black entrepreneurs. *See* African American
    entrepreneurs
Boot-strap financing, 53, 356
Bureau of Labor Statistics, 68, 245
Business. See Firm emergence; Growth
    expectations; Start-up activities;
    Start-up classification; Start-up
    process
Business assistance programs, 241-242,
    336, 349
    assessment of assistance, 346,
        47 (tables)
    awareness of resource options, 338-339,
        342-343
    contact statistics, 342-343,
        342-343 (tables)
    contact, time span of, 345, 345 (table)
    data collection objectives in, 340
    educational assistance, 337
    ethnic/racial minorities and, 338
    Federal programs, 337
    help provided, 345, 346 (table)
    local economic development programs
        and, 337
    nonprofit organizations and, 337
    owner-operator reports, 338
    policy issues, growth process and, 339
    previous research on, 337-339
    questionnaire items on, 340-341,
        341 (exhibit)
    start-up outcomes, 347-349, 348 (figure)
    types of programs, 343-344, 344 (table)
    See also Start-up funding

Capital. *See* Business assistance programs;
    Financial resources; Start-up funding
Career histories. *See* Work participation
    history
Career rationale, 15, 135-137, 142
    entrepreneurial careers theory, 94
    gender differences and, 145-146, 150

About the Editors

Nancy M. Carter is the Richard M. Schulze Chair in Entrepreneurship at the University of St. Thomas, Minneapolis, Minnesota; Leverhulme Visiting Professor at the London Business School; and Scholar-in-Residence at the Entrepreneurship and Small Business Research Center, Stockholm, Sweden. At St. Thomas, she directs the MBA entrepreneurship program. She serves on the International Board of Advisors, Jönköping International Business School, Sweden, and the Board of Directors of the Women's Business Research Center, Washington, D.C. She has worked professionally in advertising and marketing research and works closely with government and private sector initiatives around the world promoting female entrepreneurship. Her research interests include the emergence of organizations with a special emphasis on women- and minority-owned initiatives and the founding strategies of new businesses. Her research on women and minority entrepreneurs has been funded by awards from the National Science Foundation, the U.S. Small Business Administration, the National Business Women's Council, and the Ewing Marion Kauffman Foundation. She cofounded the Entrepreneurial Research Consortium, the organizing group for the Panel Study of Entrepreneurial Dynamics (PSED), and the Diana Project, a research consortium focusing on women and high-growth ventures in more than 20 countries. She received her PhD in business administration from the University of Nebraska, an MA in mass communications from California State University, and a BA in journalism from the University of Nebraska.

William B. Gartner is the Arthur M. Spiro Professor of Entrepreneurship at Clemson University. Prior to joining University of Southern California, he was on the faculty at Georgetown University, the University of Virginia, San Francisco State University, and the University of Southern California. He is one of the cofounders of the Entrepreneurship Research Consortium, which initiated, developed, and managed the Panel Study of Entrepreneurial Dynamics. His service to the entrepreneurship field has included two consecutive terms as Chair of the Academy of Management Entrepreneurship Division (1985, 1986), special issue editorships for the *Journal of Business Venturing* (*JBV*) and *Entrepreneurship Theory and Practice (ETP)*, and Editorial Board memberships with the *Academy of Management Review* (*AMR*), *Journal of Management* (*JOM*), *JBV*, *ETP*, and the *Journal of Small Business Management* (*JSBM*). His research has been published in *AMR, JBV, ETP, JOM,* and *JSBM;* won awards from the Academy of Management, *ETP,* and the Babson

Kauffman Entrepreneurship Research Conference; and has been funded by the Kauffman Center for Entrepreneurial Leadership, Coleman Foundation, U.S. Department of Education, Small Business Foundation of America, the *Los Angeles Times,* the Pacific Gas and Electric Company, the Corporate Design Foundation, and the National Endowment for the Arts. His research on nascent entrepreneurs explores how they find and identify opportunities, recognize and solve start-up problems, and undertake actions to successfully launch new ventures. He is also collecting and analyzing the stories entrepreneurs tell about their entrepreneurial adventures.

Paul D. Reynolds is Professor of Entrepreneurial Studies at Babson College (Wellesley, Massachusetts) and a Research Professor of Entrepreneurship at the London Business School. He served as the director of the annual Babson Kauffman Entrepreneurship Research Conference (1996–2000) and was the Coleman Foundation Chair in Entrepreneurial Studies at Marquette University (Milwaukee, Wisconsin; 1990–1995).

He was part of the team that created the Entrepreneurial Research Consortium (ERC) and has served as the Coordinating Principal Investigator through the life of the project, 1995 to 2003. He has also served as the Coordinating Principal Investigator of the Global Entrepreneurship Monitor (GEM) program since its inception in 1998. He has been the Principal Investigator on more than two dozen funded research projects.

In 2004 he was the recipient of the International Award for Entrepreneurship and Small Business Research sponsored by the Swedish Business Development Agency (NUTEK) and the Swedish Foundation for Small Business Research (SFS) in recognition of his role in developing and implementing the Panel Study of Entrepreneurial Dynamics and the Global Entrepreneurship Monitor research programs.

His educational background includes degrees in engineering (BS, University of Kansas), business (MBA, Stanford University), psychology (MA, Stanford University), and sociology (PhD, Stanford University). He has been on the faculty or staff of the University of California, Riverside; University of Minnesota; Wharton School, University of Pennsylvania; Nanyang Technical University, Singapore; INSEAD (Fontainebleau, France); and the University of Michigan Institute for Social Research. He is the author or coauthor of five conference proceedings; four books; four data sets in the University of Michigan ICPSR public archives; over 30 project reports and research monographs; over 60 peer review journal articles, chapters, or refereed conference proceeding reports; and several hundred professional conference presentations.

Kelly G. Shaver is Professor of Psychology at the College of William & Mary. From 1977 to 1979, he was Program Director for Social and Developmental Psychology in the Division of Behavioral and Neural Sciences at the National Science Foundation. He currently serves as an advisor to FamilyCareAmerica.com, is a founding director of MBATechConnect.org, and serves as a member of the international advisory board of the Entrepreneurship and Small Business Research Institute (ESBRI) in Stockholm, Sweden, where he was a Visiting Professor from 1999 to 2000.

For 5 years he was Editor of *Entrepreneurship Theory and Practice* and has served on the editorial boards of the *Journal of Personality and Social Psychology* and the

Journal of Personality. He currently serves on the editorial boards of the *Journal of Applied Social Psychology, Entrepreneurship and Regional Development,* and the *Journal of Developmental Entrepreneurship.* He is the author of seven books, coauthor or coeditor of five others, and is author or coauthor of over 140 papers and research articles on attribution processes and entrepreneurship. His paper on the motivations of nascent entrepreneurs was the winner of the Babson Kauffman Entrepreneurship Research Conference Best Paper Award for 2000, and his course on the psychology of entrepreneurship won the 2000 McGraw-Hill/Irwin Award for Innovation in Entrepreneurship Pedagogy. He is a Fellow of the American Psychological Society, a member of the Society of Experimental Social Psychology, and the current (2003–2004) Chair of the Entrepreneurship Division of the Academy of Management. His e-mail is kgshav@netscape.net; his web pages are at www.wm. edu/PSYC/shaver.html.

About the Contributors

Howard E. Aldrich is Kenan Professor of Sociology at the University of North Carolina, Chapel Hill, where he won the Carlyle Sitterson Award for Outstanding Teaching in 2002. He is chair of the Department of Sociology and Adjunct Professor of Management in the Kenan Flagler Business School. In 2000, he received two honors: the Swedish Foundation of Small Business Research named him the Entrepreneurship Researcher of the Year, and the Organization and Management Division of the Academy of Management presented him with an award for a Distinguished Career of Scholarly Achievement. His latest book, *Organizations Evolving* (Sage, 1999), won the Academy of Management George Terry Award as the best management book published in 1998 to 1999 and was cowinner of the Max Weber Award from the American Sociological Association's Section on Organizations, Occupations, and Work. He is currently engaged in three research projects: (1) the process by which entrepreneurial teams are founded, focusing on similarity and differences between team members; (2) the contribution that voluntary association membership makes to entrepreneurial success; and (3) how to design courses and classroom activities to promote active learning by students.

Kathleen R. Allen, PhD, is a Professor in the Greif Entrepreneurship Center of the Marshall School of Business at the University of Southern California and the author of *Entrepreneurship and Small Business Management* (2nd Edition), *Launching New Ventures* (3rd Edition), *Bringing New Technology to Market,* and *Growing and Managing an Entrepreneurial Business,* as well as several trade books. She is the Director of the USC Technology Commercialization Alliance, which focuses on commercializing USC's technologies, and principal investigator on a National Science Foundation grant to build a national technology commercialization network (N2TEC) that will link universities, allowing them to share knowledge and resources and to collaborate across geographic boundaries to commercialize their technologies. As an entrepreneur, she was active in commercial real estate development for 10 years, owning two businesses, is cofounder of two technology ventures, and is a director of a NYSE company.

Marne L. Arthaud-Day is a doctoral candidate in management at the Kelley School of Business at Indiana University. Her research concerns the influence of values and related social attitudes (e.g., job and life satisfaction) on strategic decision making, organizational culture, and strategic implementation. She teaches in the area of strategic management. She received her BA from Wake Forest University, M.Div. from Princeton Theological Seminary, and her MBA from the University of Texas at San Antonio.

Robert A. Baron, PhD, University of Iowa, 1968, is the Dean R. Wellington Professor of Management and Professor of Psychology at Rensselaer Polytechnic Institute. He has held faculty appointments at Purdue University, University of Minnesota, University of Texas, University of South Carolina, University of Washington, Princeton University, and Oxford University (Visiting Fellow, 1982). He served as a Program Director at the National Science Foundation (1979–1981) and was appointed as a Visiting Senior Research Fellow by the French Ministry of Research (2001–2002) at the Université des Sciences Sociales, Toulouse. He is a Fellow of both the American Psychological Association and the American Psychological Society.

He has published more than 100 articles and 35 chapters in edited volumes and he is the author or coauthor of more than 40 books in the fields of management and psychology, including *Behavior in Organizations* (8th Edition) and *Social Psychology* (10th Edition). His latest book is *Entrepreneurship: A Process Perspective*. He holds three U.S. patents and was founder, President, and CEO of Innovative Environmental Products, Inc. (1993–2000). His current research focuses primarily on social and cognitive factors in entrepreneurship.

Candida G. Brush is Associate Professor of Strategy and Policy, Director of the Council for Women's Entrepreneurship and Leadership (CWEL), and Research Director for the Entrepreneurial Management Institute at Boston University. She teaches Entrepreneurship and Strategy courses in the undergraduate, MBA, doctoral, and executive MBA programs. Her research investigates the role of resources in emerging organizations and growth strategies of women-led ventures. With four other researchers, she investigates women's access to growth capital, referred to as the Diana Project. This research is sponsored by the Kauffman Foundation and ESBRI (Swedish Research Foundation). Her most recent book is *Clearing the Hurdles: Women Building High-Growth Businesses* (2004).

Ana Cabezuelo is Associate Professor in the Business Organization Department of the Autonomous University of Madrid (Spain). She worked on the PSED as a Visiting Professor in the Department of Management, Cook School of Business, Saint Louis University. Currently she is the Project Manager of the Center of Entrepreneurship and Businesses Initiatives (C.I.A.D.E.) in Madrid. The mission of this institution is to promote the establishment of private enterprises in Madrid with special emphasis on the student community and the faculty of the niversidad Autonoma de Madrid. Her latest research, funded by Spain's State Department of Small and Medium Enterprises, identified the essential competencies to become a successful entrepreneur in the small and medium size business sector.

Richard T. Curtin is a Research Professor at the University of Michigan and the Director of the Surveys of Consumers at the Survey Research Center. His research on consumer expectations and behavior is widely utilized by businesses and financial institutions, by federal agencies responsible for monetary and fiscal policies, as well as by academic researchers. He has published more than 500 articles on trends in consumer expectations and their implications for changes in consumer spending and saving behavior and regularly consults with business firms and government officials in dozens of countries. He is a member of the American Economic Association, the National Association for Business Economics, the Association for Consumer Research, the International Association for Research in Economic Psychology, and a member of the Center for International Research on Economic Tendency Surveys. He is the Associate Editor of the *Journal of Business Cycle Measurement and Analysis.* He received his PhD in economics from the University of Michigan in 1975.

Wade M. Danis earned his PhD in strategy and international business from Indiana University's Kelley School of Business in 2000 and is presently an Assistant Professor of Management at Marquette University in Milwaukee, Wisconsin. His research and teaching focus is on strategic management, international management, and entrepreneurship. His work has appeared in the *Journal of International Business Studies,* the *Journal of World Business,* the *Journal of Developmental Entrepreneurship,* and in other journals. Prior to entering academia, he worked for many years with small business owners and entrepreneurs, first in his family's own business and later as President of the Urban Business Assistance Corporation, a New York consulting firm serving minority-owned businesses. His industry background also includes 5 years of managerial experience in the U.S. retail industry, 2 years as an in-house consultant for a major Hungarian manufacturer, and a position during 1995 as a journalist for the *Warsaw Business Journal* in Poland.

Per Davidsson is Professor of Entrepreneurship at the Jönköping International Business School (JIBS), Sweden. In addition to his professorship, he holds academic appointments in Australia, Latin America, and the United States. He researches entrepreneurship and small business from a variety of perspectives (economic, business, psychological, geographical, sociological). His numerous theoretical, empirical, and methodological contributions have appeared in a multitude of scholarly journals and books. He has served as manuscript editor for *Entrepreneurship Theory and Practice* and currently serves on the editorial review board for the *Journal of Business Venturing* and three other scholarly journals.

Amy E. Davis is a PhD candidate at the University of North Carolina at Chapel Hill, Department of Sociology. Her dissertation uses PSED data to examine the conditions under which participation in start-up teams facilitates or impedes mothers' participation in entrepreneurship. She received her MA in sociology at University of North Carolina in 2001. Her thesis examined how voluntary associations affect resource access of business owners in the Research Triangle Park area of North Carolina. She is currently working with Arne Kalleberg on a paper investigating organizations' adoption of work/family employment programs, using data from the National Organizations Study (NOS). She along with Howard E. Aldrich and Linda

Renzulli, is also studying how voluntary associations shape the social networks of entrepreneurs and nascent entrepreneurs.

William J. Dennis, Jr., is a Senior Research Fellow at the NFIB Research Foundation in Washington, D.C. and directs the foundation's activities. He has been employed since 1976 in a research capacity by the National Federation of Independent Business, the nation's largest small and independent business trade association. Prior to his affiliation with NFIB, he spent 6 years as a professional staff member in the United States House of Representatives.

His research activities focus on small business and public policy. He is a former President of the International Council for Small Business, recipient of a Special Advocacy Award for research from the United States Small Business Administration, and has served on three panels for the National Academies of Science.

Marc J. Dollinger is Professor of Business Administration in the Management Department at the Kelley School of Business, Indiana University. He received his MBA and PhD from Lehigh University (1978, 1982) in Pennsylvania and spent 5 years at the University of Kentucky before his appointment to Indiana. He is also a Visiting Professor in the International Management Department of the International University of Japan and has taught numerous times at Hong Kong University of Science and Technology.

Currently he is the Chairman of the Kelley School of Business's undergraduate program. He is also a member of the editorial board of *Entrepreneurship Theory and Practice* and a former board member of the *Academy of Management Review.* His 1990 paper, *The Evolution of Collective Strategies in Fragmented Industries,* was awarded the Best Paper Award by the *Academy of Management Review.* His textbook, *Entrepreneurship: Strategies and Resources,* was first published in 1995 and is now in its third edition.

Matthew W. Ford is Assistant Professor of Management in the College of Business at Northern Kentucky University. He holds a PhD from the University of Cincinnati. His research interests include organizational self-assessment, small firm planning, and the management and control of change. His published work includes entries in *Quality Management Journal, Business Horizons, Frontiers of Entrepreneurship, Center for Quality of Management Journal,* and *Journal of Engineering & Technology Management.*

Elizabeth J. Gatewood, PhD, is the Jack M. Gill Chair of Entrepreneurship and Director of The Johnson Center for Entrepreneurship & Innovation at Indiana University. Her work in entrepreneurial cognition received the National Foundation of Independent Business Award for best paper at the 2001 Babson Kauffman Entrepreneurship Research Conference. She is a member of the Diana project, a research study of women business owners and equity capital access, funded by the Kauffman Center for Entrepreneurial Leadership, the U.S. Small Business Administration, and the National Women's Business Council. She is a past chair of the Entrepreneurship Division of the Academy of Management. She received the 1996 Advocate Award for outstanding contributions to the field of entrepreneurship from the Academy of Management. She was named the Texas Women in Business Advocate of the Year by the U.S. Small Business Administration. She serves on the National Advisory Board for Entrepreneurship Education of the Ewing Marion Kauffman Foundation. She also serves on the Advisory Board for Spring Mill Ventures, a venture capital firm of the Village Ventures network. She holds a BS in psychology from Purdue University and an MBA in finance and PhD in business administration, with a specialty in strategy, from the University of Georgia.

Patricia G. Greene is Dean of the Undergraduate School at Babson College where she holds the President's Chair in Entrepreneurship. She earned a PhD from the University of Texas at Austin, an MBA from the University of Nevada, Las Vegas, and a BS from the Pennsylvania State University. Her research focuses on the identification, acquisition, and combination of entrepreneurial resources, particularly by women and minority entrepreneurs. She is a founding member of the Diana Project, a research group focusing on women and their business growth strategies.

Gerald E. Hills is holder of the Coleman Foundation Chair in Entrepreneurship at the University of Illinois at Chicago. His MBA and doctorate are from Indiana University. He has written and edited 17 books and written more than 75 articles in entrepreneurship and marketing journals. He has served on the editorial boards of all the leading entrepreneurship journals, including, currently, the *Journal of Business Venturing*. He is a past President of the International Council for Small Business and cofounder and first President of the United States Association for Small Business and Entrepreneurship. He served as President of the AMA Academic Council, the closest equivalent in the marketing discipline to President of the Academy of Management.

Under his leadership, UIC was ranked by *Success* Magazine number four nationally in entrepreneurship and most recently by *Entrepreneur* magazine as number two nationally. He was named a Wilford L. White Fellow of the International Council for Small Business, was named a Fulbright Scholar, and was given the Advocate Award by the Academy of Management for outstanding contributions to the field of entrepreneurship.

Sherrie E. Human is Associate Professor and an Academic Director in the Management and Entrepreneurship Department at Xavier University. She teaches courses at the undergraduate, MBA, and executive MBA levels on new venture creation, the business-planning process, and contemporary management skills. Prior to receiving her PhD in 1995 from the University of Kentucky, she founded and managed technology and technical education companies (along with a sailboat business in the Bahamas). Her research focuses on areas in which she has professional experience such as nascent entrepreneurship, new venture creation, managerial skills development, and areas that she has identified for conceptual and empirical contributions to the literature, such as interorganizational networks and entrepreneurship and ethics. Her research findings have been published in the *Academy of Management Journal, Administrative Science Quarterly, Journal of Management Education, Journal of Business Venturing, Entrepreneurship Theory and Practice, Journal of Small Business Management,* and *Journal of Small Business Strategy.*

Kevin LaMont Johnson is an Associate Instructor and PhD candidate in Strategic Management and Entrepreneurship at Indiana University, Kelley School of Business. He received his BA in engineering sciences from Dartmouth College and his MBA from Indiana University. He also served as a Senior Business Development Specialist for several years for a Fortune 500 corporation and has direct independent venture start-up experience. His research involves corporate entrepreneurship and understanding the performance of new ventures within established corporations. He teaches courses in strategic management, leadership, and entrepreneurship at the undergraduate level. He has the honor of being profiled in *Who's Who in America*® (2004).

Jerome Katz developed the financial sophistication questions of the PSED with Richard Green, PhD, CPA, of the University of the Incarnate Word, San Antonio, Texas. He participated in the PSED as a representative of the Research Institute for Small and Emerging Business. He is the Mary Louise Murray Endowed Professor of Management at the Cook School of Business, Saint Louis University. His research interests include organizational emergence, cognitive and career models of entrepreneurship, entrepreneurship education, and advanced secondary analysis approaches in entrepreneurship. His works have appeared in the *Academy of Management Review,* the *Journal of Management,* the *Journal of Business Venturing, Entrepreneurship Theory and Practice,* and the *Journal of Small Business Management.* He is Editor of Sage Publications's Entrepreneurship and Management of Growing Organizations series, as well as Senior Series Editor of Elsevier's *Advances in Entrepreneurship, Firm Emergence and Growth.*

Lisa A. Keister is Associate Professor of Sociology at The Ohio State University. She received her PhD from Cornell University in 1997 and is the recipient of the National Science Foundation's Faculty Early Development Career Award. She conducts research on wealth inequality in the United States and is the author of *Wealth in America* (2000) published by Cambridge University Press. She is currently conducting a study of wealth mobility in the United States, including an in-depth exploration of the lives of the most influential people in Columbus, OH. When she is not researching wealth ownership, She studies firm behavior during China's transition. Her second book, *Chinese Business Groups* (2000) published by Oxford University Press reported on that research.

Phillip H. Kim is a doctoral candidate in the Department of Sociology at the University of North Carolina at Chapel Hill. His research interests focus on the study of nascent entrepreneurs and new firm creation processes. Current research projects include the role of financial and human capital resources on achieving operating status and developing improved measures for understanding the new firm creation process.

Bruce A. Kirchhoff is Distinguished Professor of Entrepreneurship and Director of the Technological Entrepreneurship Program at New Jersey Institute of Technology in Newark, New Jersey. His prior credentials include service as Chief Economist for the U.S. Small Business Administration, Director of the Center for Entrepreneurship and Public Policy at Fairleigh Dickinson University, and Director of Research in

Babson College's Entrepreneurship Center. He earned his PhD in business administration from the University of Utah, where he also earned an MBA. He received a bachelor of science degree in chemical engineering from Case Institute of Technology.

Prior to receiving his PhD, he spent 7 years in sales and marketing and 3 years as area manager of international operations for Envirotech Corporation. He has served on the faculties of Chalmers Institute of Technology in Sweden; Jönköping International Business School, Sweden; Fairleigh Dickinson University; Babson College; University of Nebraska at Omaha; Purdue University; and California Polytechnic University.

Dr. Jianwen Liao is currently Assistant Professor in the Department of Management, School of Business and Management, at Northeastern Illinois University. He has served on the faculties at DePaul University; Hong Kong University of Science and Technology (HKUST), China Europe International Business School (CEIBS). His research expertise and interests are in the areas of strategic formulation and implementation, management of technological innovation, venture creation process, and entrepreneurial growth strategies. His research has been published in academic journals such as *Entrepreneurship Theory and Practice, Family Business Review, Journal of High Tech Management Research,* and *Frontier of Entrepreneurship Research.* He received his doctorate in strategic management from Southern Illinois University at Carbondale.

Tatiana S. Manolova (DBA, Boston University) is Assistant Professor of Management at Suffolk University's Sawyer School of Management. Her current research interests include competitive strategies for new and small companies, international entrepreneurship, and organizational formation and transformation in transitional economies. Recent articles were published in the *Journal of Business Venturing* (forthcoming), *Thunderbird International Business Review* (forthcoming), *International Small Business Journal,* and *Journal of Small Business Strategy.*

Charles H. Matthews, PhD, is Professor of Strategic Management and Director, U.C. Center for Entrepreneurship Education & Research, College of Business, University of Cincinnati. Dr. Matthews is an internationally recognized scholar and innovative teacher in the field of entrepreneurship. His teaching and research interests include strategic management, decision making, and leadership succession. His research has been published in the *Journal of Small Business Management, Journal of Small Business Strategy, Entrepreneurship & Regional Development, Frontiers of Entrepreneurship Research, Family Business Review,* and *Center for the Quality of Management Journal.* An award-winning teacher, he has taught over 5,000 students from freshmen to executives, from individual instruction to classes over 500. In addition to industry experience, he is the founder of the U.C. Center for Entrepreneurship (1997), which was named one of the Top 50 Entrepreneurship Programs in the United States in 2001 (*Success* magazine) and a Top Tier Program in 2003 (*Entrepreneur*).

James N. Morgan is a Research Scientist Emeritus at the Institute for Social Research and Professor of Economics Emeritus at the University of Michigan.

He codirected the Surveys of Consumer Finances, funded by the Board of Governors of the Federal Reserve System from 1949 to 1960, directed a pioneering study of income and wealth and its intergenerational aspects (Morgan, David, Cohen, and Brazer, *Income and Welfare in the United States,* 1962). From 1968 to 1986, he directed or codirected the Panel Study of Income Dynamics. He taught consumer economics and developed a binary segmentation program called SEARCH (AID). He was elected a Fellow of the American Statistical Association in 1968, a Member of the National Academy of Sciences in 1975, a Fellow of the Gerontological Society of America in 1981, and a Fellow of the American Academy of Arts and Sciences in 1984.

Janet P. Near holds the Coleman Chair of Management in the Kelley School of Business at Indiana University. Her research concerns are whistle-blowing in organizations and the relationship between work and nonwork domains of life, focusing on job and life satisfaction. She teaches in the area of organization theory and design. She received her PhD from the State University of New York at Buffalo and a BA from the University of California at Santa Cruz.

Margaret Owen is a doctoral candidate (political science/economics) at the University of Missouri–Kansas City. She currently is graduate research assistant for University Outreach and Extension's Business Research & Information Development Group (BRIDG). Previously she was a graduate research assistant with the UMKC Entrepreneurial Growth Resource Center.

Martin Ruef is Assistant Professor of Organizational Behavior and (by courtesy) of Sociology at Stanford University. He studies the social context of entrepreneurship from both a contemporary and historical perspective. He has pursued this research at several levels of analysis, including examinations of decision making on the part of individual entrepreneurs, team formation and networking among entrepreneurs, founding processes and risks for new ventures, the emergence of novel organizational forms, the "creative destruction" of existing forms, and institutional entrepreneurship leading to the creation of new organizational governance systems. He has studied entrepreneurial activity through archival research on specific fields, such as U.S. healthcare and postbellum agriculture, as well as through representative sampling of entrepreneurs operating in a variety of sectors.

Joseph C. Rode is Assistant Professor of Management in the Richard T. Farmer School of Business at Miami (Ohio) University. His research concerns the relationship between work and nonwork domains of life. He teaches in the area of organizational behavior. He received his PhD, MBA, and BA, all from Indiana University, Bloomington.

Robert P. Singh is Assistant Professor of Management and Director of the Center for Entrepreneurship and Strategy at Morgan State University in Baltimore, Maryland. He completed his PhD at the University of Illinois at Chicago (UIC) in the nationally ranked Institute for Entrepreneurial Studies, where his research focused on strategy and entrepreneurship issues in information technology start-up firms. He recently published his first book, *Entrepreneurial Opportunity*

Recognition Through Social Networks (Garland), and his research has appeared in numerous peer-reviewed journals and national/international conferences. In addition to his academic pursuits, he has founded several businesses including Blade Consulting Corporation, a management and information technology consulting firm (1994), and BouncingBaby.com, an Internet-based niche portal business (1998).

Timothy M. Stearns is the holder of the Coleman Foundation Chair in Entrepreneurial Studies and Director of the Lyles Center for Innovation and Entrepreneurship at California State University, Fresno. He received his MBA degree in management and a doctorate in management/sociology from Indiana University. He has taught and lectured on entrepreneurship, venture capital, and strategic positioning to entrepreneurs and executives in Thailand, Poland, Japan, Kazakhstan, Macau, and the People's Republic of China. He is known for his research on entrepreneurial startups and the formation of strategic networks. He has served on the board of the *Academy of Management Journal* and is a founding member of the National Network for Technology Entrepreneurship and Commercialization, a National Science Foundation-funded project that links universities to enhance and coordinate efforts to commercialize technologies (www.n2tec.org). He also serves as President of the Central Valley Business Incubator.

Michael Stouder received his doctorate from Rutgers University in New Jersey. He is a visiting Assistant Professor of Strategy and Entrepreneurship at the University of Michigan–Flint. His research interests include early-stage financing behaviors of entrepreneurs and exchange relations between entrepreneurs and resource suppliers.

Harold P. Welsch, PhD, who holds the Coleman Foundation Endowed Chair in Entrepreneurship at DePaul University, has been active in entrepreneurship development for over 20 years in his role as educator, consultant, researcher, entrepreneur, author, and editor. He is well-known for his expertise in technology commercialization, privatization of centrally planned economies, entrepreneurship career paths, formal and informal strategic planning, information seeking and decision behavior, ethnic entrepreneurship, economic development, and small business problems. His work has appeared in many journals. He was co-Editor of *Research at the Marketing/Entrepreneurship Interface* and recently published a book, *Strategic Entrepreneurial Growth* with Thompson-Southwestern.

In his position as founder of the Entrepreneurship Program and Coleman Entrepreneurship Center at DePaul University, he has served as Chairman of the Academy of Management Entrepreneurship Division, President of the International Council for Small Business (ICSB), and President of the U.S. Association for Small Business and Entrepreneurship (USASBE).